D0161628

Urban Rail in America

A REGIONAL PLAN ASSOCIATION BOOK

Urban Rail in America

An Exploration of Criteria for Fixed-Guideway Transit

BORIS S. PUSHKAREV

with JEFFREY M. ZUPAN

and ROBERT S. CUMELLA

INDIANA UNIVERSITY PRESS / *Bloomington*

All photographs not credited were supplied by the Regional Plan Association.

Manufactured in the United States of America

Library of Congress Cataloging in Publication Data

Pushkarev, Boris.
Urban rail in America.

"A Regional Plan Association book."
Includes bibliographical references and index.
1. Local transit—United States. 2. Local transit—United States—Planning. I. Zupan, Jeffrey M. II. Cumella, Robert S. III. Title.
HE4451.P87 388.4'2'0973 81-47293
ISBN 0-253-37555-X AACR2
1 2 3 4 5 85 84 83 82

Fixed guideway transit is not a universal solution nor should it be applied in all urban areas. Fixed guideway is a potential strategy, as is the bus, the ferry boat, the car pool or the van pool. In many possible applications, fixed guideway is a superior strategy. But whatever strategy is finally selected, each should be evaluated not in the narrow context of transportation alone, nor solely in the framework of accounting. It should be measured in the broader context of its contribution to the overall long-term aspirations of the urban society it is supposed to serve.

—Louis J. Gambaccini

Contents

Foreword

Policy toward rail transit—or, more broadly, fixed guideway transit—is inseparable from policy toward cities. Large downtowns can attract the ridership needed to make effective use of fixed guideway investment. There is less reason to invest in rail if there is no effort to encourage the development of downtowns, and of compact residential patterns around them. A national consensus on making such an effort has been difficult to achieve, and the controversies are reflected in conflicting attitudes toward urban rail.

Nevertheless, widely acknowledged national objectives—improved productivity of the economy, jobs for the underprivileged, equality of opportunity, energy conservation, preservation of natural areas and agricultural land—would be furthered by channeling more development into central cities. The President's 1978 Message on National Urban Policy stated: "The vitality of cities . . . is crucial to maintaining our nation's economic strength and quality of life."

In its "Policy toward Rail Transit" of the same year, the U.S. Urban Mass Transportation Administration (UMTA) wrote: "Rail transit can help in our nation's efforts to revitalize distressed cities and to prepare the way to a gradual transition to an energy-constrained future." That document proceeded to make three essential points: (1) rail transit is cost-effective in heavily traveled corridors; (2) the number of such corridors is limited; (3) site-specific alternatives analysis is needed to determine whether and what type of investment is appropriate. Judicious, cost-effective selection of possible rail routes becomes even more important under conditions of fiscal restraint that characterize the 1980s. Responding to this need, this book does three things:

(1) It explores what range of volume may in fact define a corridor traveled heavily enough to make a fixed guideway cost-effective.

(2) It offers the first rough, national assessment of the number and location of such corridors, where site-specific analysis might most profitably be focused.

(3) It provides a uniform data base and a consistent set of analytical tools to facilitate such site-specific studies. Real-world reference points of operating performance and travel demand will help the local analyst check his results for reasonableness. Models of labor and energy requirements developed here can be adapted to local conditions and used in the comparison of alternatives. The rationale for evaluating specific transit systems is readily transferable to local studies.

The book is not a replacement for such site-specific studies. It does not choose among the three types of fixed guideways investigated, nor does it compare them to other possible options. It cannot deal with precise construction costs at the local level. It merely says: Here is where fixed guideways can make sense, saving time, labor, energy and land compared to present modes of travel, if several conditions are met. The conditions are of interest in their own right, as a guide to designing new systems and improving existing ones.

Travel volume in urban corridors is obviously not the only yardstick by which to judge new guideway projects. The quality of service, environmental considerations, labor relations, fiscal arrangements, potential for traffic growth, land use controls fitting the transportation plans, supportive community attitudes, and the ability of local institutions to carry out plans, all must be considered. Still, the *starting point is whether the project is in scale with local travel needs. That is the issue in this book.*

Estimates of local travel presented here rely on an aggregate approach that is appropriate for a national study. The purpose is not to model how individual travelers make their decisions, but rather how such decisions are distributed in space, given a physical context of land use and travel facilities. By applying the same yardstick to all cities, the estimates enable consistent comparisons among cities. They are a first step toward a national model of urban travel and can, if necessary, be refined. Generally, the book—the first of its kind—is a research effort yet to be fully evaluated through review and application by professionals in transportation. It is not an endorsed UMTA methodology, nor do the findings represent an UMTA position.

Because of time and data limitations, the book does not explore the potential for commuter rail, a mode that is important in the largest cities. Express buses are referred to as a yardstick of comparison, but no measure of their potential is made. In less detail, that subject is discussed in the authors' earlier work, *Public Transportation and Land Use Policy* (Indiana University Press, 1977).

This book closes major data gaps related to the performance of public transit modes and provides historical statistics not previously available. It also points to serious remaining data gaps: (1) the lack of a national inventory of urban land use and building use and (2) the weakness of existing estimates of indirect energy consumption (for maintenance, wayside facilities, construction) by all modes of travel.

Overall, the book should clarify many issues in the national debate on what are appropriate levels of investment in urban rail, what type of payoff one can expect, and what some of the priorities for new lines might be. For the local analyst "on the firing line," it is a reference on data and methods.

Beyond that, it should interest a broader audience of students in public affairs, urban geography, and transportation engineering. Portions of it have been used by the authors as background for courses on urban transportation. A previous text with a similar title, A. Schaeffer Lang's and Richard M. Soberman's *Urban Rail Transit* (MIT Press, 1964), appeared more than a decade and a half ago, preceding rather dramatic changes in the field.

ACKNOWLEDGMENTS

This book would not have been possible without basic statistical data provided by seventeen rail operating agencies: Bay Area Rapid Transit District (BART); Chicago Transit Authority (CTA); Edmonton Transit System (ETS); Greater Cleveland Regional Transit Authority (GCRTA); Massachusetts Bay Transportation Authority (MBTA); Metropolitan Atlanta Rapid Transit Authority (MARTA); Montreal

Urban Community Transit Commission (MUCTC); New Jersey Transit Corporation (NJT); New York City Transit Authority (NYCTA); Port Authority of Allegheny County Transit (PAT); Port Authority Transit Corporation of Pennsylvania and New Jersey (PATCO); Port Authority Trans-Hudson Corporation (PATH); San Francisco Municipal Railway (MUNI); Southeastern Pennsylvania Transportation Authority (SEPTA); Staten Island Rapid Transit Operating Authority (SIRTOA); Toronto Transit Commission (TTC); Washington Metropolitan Area Transit Authority (WMATA); additional statistics were provided by American Public Transit Association (APTA) and other agencies.

An early draft of the study was circulated among several agencies and numerous professionals; their responses contributed a great deal to the final shape of the book. The respondents included Alan Altschuler, J. Edward Anderson, Paul N. Bay, J. Thomas Black, Richard J. Bouchard, Philip G. Craig, Thomas B. Deen, John A. Dyer, Stanley G. Feinsod, Louis J. Gambaccini, Neil B. Goldstein, Clark Henderson, Seymour Kashin, Robert R. Kiley, George A. Kocur, George Krambles, Damian J. Kulash, Herbert S. Levinson, Jean R. Normandeau, Jerome C. Premo, J. H. Sansom, Kenneth A. Small, Brian E. Sullivan, Richard Stanger, Edson L. Tennyson, and Vukan R. Vuchic. The draft was also extensively reviewed by U.S. Department of Transportation personnel; their numerous critical comments were considered in detail, improving both content and presentation.

Special appreciation is due to C. Kenneth Orski, who initiated the study while at the Urban Mass Transportation Administration, to Lillian C. Liburdi, who encouraged its continuation, and to Jimmy Yu, who was the UMTA official responsible for the study since its inception in 1977. About 60 percent of the project cost was funded by grants from the Urban Mass Transportation Administration (NY–06–0061), with the remainder provided by Regional Plan Association.

The final text was written by Boris S. Pushkarev, Vice President, Research and Planning, Regional Plan Association. He is also responsible for the analyses in Chapters 1 and 2 and for the historical statistics. The analyses in Chapters 3 and 4 and drafts of these chapters were prepared by Jeffrey M. Zupan, presently Director of Developmental Planning, New Jersey Transit Corporation. Robert Cumella, Senior Planner, Regional Plan Association, provided most of the research support. Research assistants included Brad Cohen, Bradford E. Gellert, Paul Glasser, Howard Mischel, and Nicholas I. Yelagin. The graphics were prepared by Jerome Pilchman.

A committee of the Regional Plan Association Board of Directors, chaired by Prof. Richard C. Wade, reviewed the findings prior to publication. Regional Plan Association, Inc., is a private, nonprofit organization engaged in urban research and policy formation. It began in 1922 as the Committee on Regional Plan of New York and Its Environs, and is located at 1040 Avenue of the Americas, New York, New York 10018.

—John P. Keith
October, 1981

SHOP
BOOKS
FLORIST
SHOES
←NORTH
SOUTH→
TERRACE RESTAURANT
N.E.

Introduction and Overview

DEFINITIONS

Public transportation using vehicles on *fixed guideways* (as opposed to free-wheeled vehicles) takes several forms. One is commuter or suburban rail, a service between a major downtown and outlying parts of an urban region, which is connected with intercity rail operations; it is treated only peripherally in this book. The emphasis herein is on rail rapid transit, light rail, and automated peoplemovers. Terrain-specialized systems (aerial tramways, inclined planes) are not treated.

Rail rapid transit, sometimes known as "heavy rail," is a system that moves *passengers in large groups* on trains over an exclusive right-of-way that may be in a subway, elevated, or grade-separated near the ground level but is usually separate from intercity railroads. It has high-level station platforms and may employ different degrees of automation.

Light rail moves *passengers in intermediate-size groups* on short trains or in single cars over a variety of rights of way: grade-separated, reserved (as in a street median), or shared with street traffic. The latter operation is traditionally known as streetcar or tramway, while one with predominantly reserved but not necessarily grade-separated right-of-way denotes "light rail" proper. Platforms are usually low-level, and operation is manual.

Automated peoplemovers, also known as automated guideway or light guideway transit (AGT), move *passengers in small groups* aboard small vehicles operating singly or in short trains over a fully grade-separated right-of-way in a fully automatic mode, with no attendants on board. Station platforms are high-level and the stations may be arranged so as to allow nonstop service on demand. In current practice, the systems are typically short (often in a shuttle or loop configuration), and the vehicles tend to be rubber-tired, though other designs are possible. Used in a downtown setting, the systems are referred to as downtown peoplemovers (DPM).

The term *rail transit* usually refers to the three rail modes, while *urban rail* refers to rapid transit and light rail alone. The term *public transit* includes both fixed guideways and buses.

THE PRESENT ROLE OF RAIL TRANSIT

Although traditional streetcars have all but left the urban scene, rapid transit and grade-separated light rail mileage world-wide has *doubled* between 1960 and 1980. Over two-fifths of the new construction was in newly urbanizing parts of the world, but an equal share was in mature urban areas with high automobile use in Europe and Canada. Nations with 84 percent of the world's automobiles today have 74 percent of the world's rapid transit mileage. The United States has lagged behind other industrial nations in urban rail construction, and New York is the only one of the world's rapid transit cities whose system shrank over the period.

This relatively poor showing is not due to a lack of patronage. Per capita, passenger-miles traveled by rapid transit in the United States are above the average of European nations. Per mile of line, traffic density on rapid transit in the United States is also above European levels, though obviously below Latin America, Asia, and the Soviet Union. Travel by rapid transit, light rail, and commuter rail combined in the United States nearly equals travel by urban buses if measured in passenger-miles.

In the early 1970s in the United States, virtually all rail transit was in six urban regions totaling 40 million residents—New York, Chicago, Philadelphia, San Francisco, Boston, and Cleveland. There, the three rail modes carried 8 percent of all travel on an annual basis, but 22 percent during the peak hour on a weekday, equaling the share carried by freeways.

The six "old" regions with rail are travel-conserving environments: their auto travel per resident is 20 to 30 percent lower than in other large urban areas. Less than a third of this difference is due to a direct replacement of auto travel with rail travel. The remainder is travel foregone—made unnecessary or discouraged by a compact arrangement of land uses. Bus travel per resident in the "old" rail regions is the same as in other large urban areas.

In the first half of the 1970s, major downtowns in the six "old" regions with rail added, on the average, somewhat more office floorspace per capita of regional population than downtowns without rail, while Washington and Atlanta—with rail systems then under construction—added nearly twice as much. Accelerated downtown development in these two cities was both a reason for and a consequence of their rail transit plans.

By 1980, the eight downtowns served by rapid transit and the two with light rail only housed nearly *one-third* of the "Fortune 500" industrial corporations in the United States, and over *two-thirds* of the 300 largest nonindustrial corporations. In addition, one out of ten of these corporations was located in downtowns with rail systems under construction or design. Despite suburbanization, the command posts of American business enterprise have a continuing stake in urban rail.

WHY BUILD NEW SYSTEMS?

The immediate purpose of a new urban rail or other fixed guideway line is to improve the movement of people in a tightly settled area, to do so in an environmentally and aesthetically attractive manner, and to provide capacity for future growth. A less direct but no less important reason is to enhance the magnetism of the city's downtown.

Rerouting the mainstream of American life back through the central cities helps to unify society, offering a place where black and white, rich and poor, young and old can mix at least in the daytime activity environment. Encouraging jobs to locate downtown makes them more accessible to the urban unemployed; it allows nonroutine white-collar activities to function in an environment where they are most productive, where spontaneous, face-to-face relations can most easily flourish. Putting new development into higher density areas reduces the need for travel and saves physical resources—primarily energy, but also water, farmland, natural open space. Energy savings result from less travel overall and more use of public transportation, from a shift in other consumer spending away from durable goods toward services, from use of larger buildings with fewer exposed surfaces, and from greater feasibility of cogeneration, district heating, cooling, and waste recycling in high density areas. Total waste emissions into the environment are reduced, even if local concentrations have to be more carefully controlled. In the long run, fiscal savings accrue to government as a result of lower costs for social services in formerly blighted areas, reuse of existing facilities, and reduced need for new infrastructure elsewhere.

FIXED GUIDEWAYS AND LAND USE

Attainment of these objectives depends on whether the concentration of land use actually occurs. That is subject to three major conditions.

First, a guideway must significantly improve the ease of existing travel. It is the travel-related benefits that cause the more accessible sites to be more desirable and ultimately translate into higher land values. When sites were accessible mostly on foot, those few that could be reached by urban rail were strikingly more desirable and buildings naturally clustered there. After the automobile had made a great many sites about equally accessible, the incentive for clustering was diminished. New rail lines, such as Boston's South Shore, Philadelphia's Lindenwold, and Washington's Metro all have been shown to influence land values and result in some reallocation of development, but their presence is only one among many, often more potent, forces in the market for land. Dramatic change—as in Toronto—requires the help of land use control.

The second condition, therefore, is a set of zoning regulations and community attitudes favorable to compact development. "Joint development" tools can further encourage clustering buildings near stations. Taxation and land use controls can discourage development at dispersed locations, where its city-building potential is dissipated. All of these are easier in a growing urban area than in a stagnant one, where there is little new development to go around. Thus, the growth prospects of an urban area are a third major condition.

A fixed guideway can do little to change the growth prospects of an urban area; it can do more as a catalyst for land use controls and urban design improvements; it can do most by providing the travel-related benefits from which the land value benefits are derived.

DEFINING FIXED GUIDEWAY CRITERIA

Because a major part of the costs of a fixed guideway is fixed, at low travel volume its cost per unit of service tends to be high, measured in passenger waiting time, labor, energy, land, or capital. As travel volume rises, all of these costs decline—and savings or benefits increase—up to a point when crowding makes further increases in travel volume unacceptable. To establish criteria indicating *at what volume of travel a fixed guideway may be justified*, six questions are asked:

(1) What is the maximum volume at which it can offer adequate space per passenger?

(2) What is the minimum volume at which it can offer adequate service frequency?

(3) What is the minimum volume at which it can attain labor savings compared to bus operations?

(4) What is the minimum volume at which it can attain energy savings compared to modes previously used?

(5) What is the minimum volume at which it can attain savings in land compared to modes previously used?

(6) What is the volume at which its construction cost becomes commensurate with recent investment decisions?

Travel-related benefits of fixed guideways are also strongly related to operating speed. To what degree the speed attainable on a fixed guideway (limited by distances between stops) can exceed the prevailing travel speed in an urban corridor is an important additional criterion for any site-specific study. At the national level, time savings can only be treated in general "if-then" terms.

Answers to all the questions on travel volume depend on what *space per passenger* in transit vehicles is assumed. For a fair comparison, the space provided by buses, rail cars, or automated peoplemovers must be brought to a common denominator. A minimum adequate space in the peak hour is taken to be 5.4 square feet or 0.5 square meters of gross vehicle floorspace per passenger, whether sitting or standing; this unit of capacity is called a passenger place. Bus-miles and car-miles operated are converted into place-miles. On existing urban rail systems in the United States, between 13 and 35 percent of the places provided are actually occupied by passengers on an annual basis, averaging 23.3 percent. This is the same as a six-passenger automobile carrying 1.4 persons.

1. Maximum Passenger-Carrying Capacity

At the standard of 5.4 square feet per passenger, and at a frequency of 30 trains an hour, existing rapid transit systems in the United States and Canada have a maximum capacity of between 20,000 and 34,000 passenger places per track per direction in the peak hour, and anticipated light rail operations, up to 16,000. These values are lower than those usually referred to in the literature because they do not assume crowded passenger conditions as a norm.

Trains on more than half the 65 rail tracks entering downtowns in the United States and Canada do in fact provide 5.4 square feet ($0.5m^2$) or more per passenger during the peak hour. Still, 21 tracks—half of them in New York City—fail to meet this standard as a matter of operating policy: they could provide more space by running more trains. Only six tracks cannot meet the standard even if maximum service were provided; five are in New York City and one in Montreal. *Building new rail lines in the United States to relieve overcrowding is only relevant in New York. The highest volumes in other cities are no more than one-third of maximum capacity.*

2. *Minimum Service Frequency*

To avoid excessive waiting time, no rapid transit or light rail operation in the United States and Canada schedules, as a rule, an interval between trains greater than 7.5 minutes (eight trains per hour) at downtown entry points during the peak hour. Taking this as a reasonable minimum service frequency and given practicable train lengths, the minimum volume per peak hour per direction becomes about 3,400 passenger places to support rapid transit and about 1,000 places to support light rail. These minimum volumes are equivalent to about 56 and 16 standard buses per direction per hour respectively. Such a level of peak-hour use at the downtown entry point translates to an *average weekday bidirectional volume* of about 15,000 passenger-miles per mile of the entire line on rapid transit, and on light rail and automated people movers to about 4,000 daily passenger-miles per mile of line. These are the lowest levels of existing service in the United States, called the *threshold of existing service* in the discussion below.

3. *Labor Savings*

Labor represents some 80 percent of the cost of operating public transportation and increasing labor output is the key to reducing this cost. A comparison of 56 transit properties in the United States and Canada shows the following averages of *labor output in passenger miles per worker per year:*

85,000 on five automated peoplemovers;
150,000 on two peoplemovers with high passenger occupancies;
150,000 on buses with mostly local service;
160,000 on light rail and streetcars;
260,000 on rapid transit overall; and
310,000 on six new rapid transit systems.

These averages of output per worker are influenced by the passenger occupancy of the vehicles, operating speed, volume of service and service frequency, and by the manning of stations and trains. A labor requirements model is developed which responds to each of these factors and assumes that the overmanning typical of some older systems is avoided.

The model shows that to attain lower labor costs per place-mile than typical urban buses (with their average 12 mph or 19 km/h operating speed), very low volumes of service on fixed guideways are sufficient. On rapid transit and light rail, they are *below* the threshold of existing service. On automated peoplemovers, they are somewhat above.

To attain lower labor costs than express buses operating at a speed equal to rapid transit or light rail (20–25 mph or 32–40 km/h), volumes on rapid transit must be one-and-one-third to twice as high as the threshold of existing service, depending on service frequency, and those on light rail twice as high even with low service frequency; fully attended stations can only be provided at about three times the threshold of existing service.

At exactly what volume in this range the labor cost of rail falls below that of express buses if their speed is equal depends on the balance between the labor needed to operate vehicles and the labor needed to maintain the right-of-way; these vary from system to system. More important than the exact difference in average costs is the difference in marginal labor requirements to provide more service when traffic growth is anticipated. If the labor cost of a given amount of service in the range indicated is set equal to 1, then that of providing double the service by articulated express buses on busway is 1.9; by light rail, 1.7; by automated peoplemover, 1.6; and by rapid transit, 1.5 to 1.4.

4. *Energy Savings*

In comparing the energy use of electric vehicles with those propelled by liquid fuels, energy losses at electric power plants and those in the refining and delivery of petroleum products must be accounted for. Compared that way in gross fuel use terms, rail cars and buses (including trolleybuses) have similar energy requirements for vehicle operation per passenger place. Buses need somewhat more energy at slow intracity speeds and less at high freeway speeds than rail cars. Both are three times more efficient than the 1972–76 automobile in urban use, at 12 miles per gallon.

The difference in energy use between the auto and public transit will shrink in the years ahead but will not be eliminated. Meanwhile, the energy cost of electricity will fall as cogeneration reduces thermal loss at power plants. This will favor electric fixed guideway vehicles and trolleybuses, but will not be enough to make the electric automobile—with its battery-related energy losses—competitive in energy consumption with vehicles that rely on a continuous electric supply.

Apart from vehicle operation, energy is required for rail vehicle maintenance, manufacture, station, and right-of-way maintenance and guideway construction. The latter two are fixed costs: as service volume increases, their magnitude per unit of service declines. Construction energy does not affect the energy cost of existing systems, and even on new systems it is not clear whether it is a net drain of energy or not. Money spent for rail transit construction typically results in less energy use than the same amount spent for consumer goods and services which would be a likely alternative expenditure.

Determining at what point a fixed guideway will actually *save* energy requires an answer to the question, "Compared to what?" Two assumptions are made about the modes previously used, one reflecting a typical mix of former auto and bus use on the line-haul trip alone, the other including a sharp increase of feeder bus use to the rail line. The circuitousness of "before" and "after" trips appears to be similar, but depends in each circumstance on the street layout and the location of the rail line. No across-the-board adjustment can be made for it. Such an adjustment is necessary, however, for auto travel foregone due to reduced auto ownership near rail stations. At medium to high service volumes, one-third or more of the energy cost of rail transit can be free—paid for by savings from reduced auto ownership.

To save energy compared to modes previously used, amortizing construction over 22 to 45 years, an above-ground rapid transit line can have a travel volume below the threshold of existing service; if in tunnel, the needed travel rises to about double that threshold.

A light rail line above ground can begin to save energy with a travel volume roughly twice the threshold of existing service above ground and roughly seven times that in a tunnel.

A peoplemover of currently prevalent rubber-tired design in a downtown application can begin to save energy at volumes 10 to 20 times above the threshold of existing service. The poor energy-saving prospects of peoplemovers in downtowns are due to the previous mode of travel used by their users (assumed to be one-third pedestrians), the lack of any reduction in auto ownership (which occurs in residential areas), and high fixed energy costs of wayside maintenance and construction even in the absence of snowmelting, which alone can exceed the energy cost of vehicle operation.

In sum, it makes sense to build rail as a medium-term (22- to 45-year) conservation measure for the full range of travel volumes currently encountered on rapid transit and for all but the lowest light rail volumes, provided that tunnels are not used for light volumes, that station and wayside energy consumption is kept in scale with that of the simpler existing systems, and that passenger occupancy is maintained not far below 23.3 percent of places provided annually. This does not consider prospective change: regenerative braking that will save energy and station air-cooling that will cost energy to improve trip quality.

5. *Land Savings*

To use the space taken up by a traffic lane on approaches to a downtown more efficiently than a freeway with some bus service, a rapid transit line requires a travel volume that is just below the threshold of existing service. For a light rail line to use space more efficiently than an arterial street lane, travel volume must be roughly at its threshold of existing service.

In addition, fixed guideways economize on land for downtown parking, which is reflected in dollars of parking costs saved.

When necessary, fixed guideways can avoid the use of land at the surface altogether by going underground at lower cost than freeways or busways, which require more ventilation and more room underground. Tunneling in lieu of elevated construction pays for itself in direct land value only at prime downtown sites—about \$5.6 million an acre (\$13.8 million a hectare) in 1977 prices. But other countries seem to feel that indirect community benefits justify much more extensive tunneling. If worldwide averages were taken as a norm, travel volumes in the light rail range in the United States would warrant placing from 10 to 35 percent of the guideway in tunnel. Travel volumes in the rapid transit range would warrant placing from 35 to 70 percent of the guideway in tunnel. With three exceptions (the major one being Washington) all urban rail systems in the United States, most notably Chicago, have far less mileage in tunnels.

6. *Construction Costs in Scale with the Travel Volume*

Half of a sample of twenty recent fixed guideway construction projects involved a capital investment of up to $1,250 per weekday passenger-mile in 1977 prices; three-quarters an investment of up to $1,800. San Francisco's BART and Washington's WMATA were near the median. Atlanta's rapid transit Phase I, the Archer Avenue subway in Queens, New York, and the Airtrans peoplemover at the Dallas–Ft. Worth Airport were near the 75th percentile.

The investment per weekday passenger-mile gives an indication of the value which public decision makers have implicitly placed on providing service by fixed guideways. At the conception of most of the twenty projects reviewed, federal funding was more limited than it later became, so that a major local commitment was usually involved.

Prorated over an amortization period of 45 to 75 years (depending on the type of construction) and assuming a 3 percent or 4 percent constant-dollar interest rate, the median investment costs 15¢ to 22¢ per passenger-mile and the 75th percentile investment 22¢ to 31¢ in 1977 prices.

Interest rates of 3 to 4 percent are current rates adjusted for the fact that lenders expect to be repaid in cheaper dollars. The interest or discount rate must be expressed in constant dollars, net of inflation, if the savings that will result from the investment are expressed in constant dollars.

Past political decisions notwithstanding: are the savings in land, energy, labor, and passenger time that fixed guideways provide commensurate with capital expenditures in the 15¢ to 31¢ per passenger-mile range?

The money values that one can place even on these four "hard" savings are somewhat arbitrary. Making *conservative assumptions,* one can show that, at the threshold volume of existing rapid transit service, an expenditure of *15¢ per passenger-mile* can be paid for about 35 percent from savings in time (reflecting trade-offs passengers now make between travel time and travel cost), 35 percent from savings in labor, 25 percent from savings in parking charges as a proxy for land savings, and 5 percent from savings in energy.

Making more *liberal assumptions* about the full economic value of energy conservation and about the proportion of auto travel diverted to a rail line, and assuming a travel volume at twice the threshold of existing service, a capital expenditure of roughly 22¢ per passenger-mile would be paid for 45 percent from reduced parking charges and 30 percent from reduced energy use, with the remaining 25 percent equally split between savings in labor and savings in time.

The important point is that between 5 and 30 percent of the investment in a rail transit line can be recouped by direct savings in energy; between 12 and 35 percent by savings in labor; and between 25 and 45 percent by savings in parking charges as a proxy for land savings, with the remainder attributable to time savings. Long-term concerns with resources, land use, and urban form are not traded in the market place. The decisions about the worth of these long-term benefits must be essentially political.

TRAVEL VOLUME THRESHOLDS

Volume thresholds for each of the fixed guideway modes can be formulated based on the foregoing, as follows:

For rapid transit above ground, the minimum existing service threshold and the level at which the "median" capital investment is justified by past expenditure decisions are identical, at about 15,000 weekday passenger-miles per line-mile. At that level, land will also be saved, labor will be saved compared to local buses, and there will be modest savings in energy.

If one-third of the rapid transit line is in tunnel, the minimum travel volume rises to 24,000 weekday passenger-miles per line-mile to justify the capital investment. Energy savings will also be attained, as will labor savings compared to buses operating at the same speed. Of course, at that volume, rapid transit above ground will save substantially more energy.

If a rapid transit line is fully in a tunnel, and assuming the 75th percentile capital investment level to reflect the community benefits of underground construction, the minimum volume becomes 29,000 weekday passenger-miles per mile of line. That volume is on the verge of attaining energy savings in a tunnel (more difficult than above ground because of fixed lighting, ventilating, and pumping costs) but will easily save labor compared to buses at the same speed.

For a very low-capital light rail line at grade but with limited grade crossings, the minimum service threshold and that of capital investment are identical, 4,000 weekday passenger-miles per line-mile. With that volume, minor labor savings compared to local buses can be realized, but there are no energy savings, and peak period use of land is just about as efficient as that of an arterial street.

For a more adequate light rail line with considerable grade separation, the capital investment criterion requires about 7,000 weekday passenger-miles per line-mile. With that volume, labor savings compared to buses at the same speed begin to be attained, land during the peak hour is used more efficiently than by a local arterial, and energy savings begin to be attained.

A light rail line with 1/5 in tunnel requires a volume of 13,500 weekday passenger-miles per mile of line, ensuring that peak period use of land is more efficient than that of a freeway lane, as well as providing savings in labor and energy.

For peoplemovers used in a downtown environment, the various criteria are more tenuous.

A low-capital peoplemover guideway with a single beam of a type still under development, carrying about 5,000 weekday passenger-miles per mile of line, allows a construction cost of roughly $6 million a mile in 1977 prices using the "median" investment level. It can begin to attain labor savings compared to downtown buses operating at a low speed; it can begin to use land more effectively than a local arterial, but it will not attain any energy savings in a downtown setting.

A heavier peoplemover guideway of the currently prevalent rubber-tired technology, with about 12,000 to 20,000 weekday passenger-miles per mile of line, allows a construction expenditure near the "median" level, attains labor savings compared to the bus at the same speed, uses land more efficiently than a local arterial during the peak hour. However, it will begin to offer energy savings only at volumes in excess of 46,000 weekday passenger-miles per line-mile, and then only if no snowmelting is required. If the guideway is in a tunnel, it can begin to provide energy savings at about five times that volume; still higher volumes would be needed to attain energy savings above ground with snowmelting.

POTENTIAL TRAVEL VOLUMES

The travel volume thresholds at which fixed guideways can begin to attain the different savings become meaningful only if one shows where such travel volumes can in fact be found.

Generally, 70 to 85 percent of all rail rapid transit trips in the United States occur between a residential corridor and a downtown. The remainder are through trips, trips stopping short of a downtown, or trips within the downtown. Trips to and from a downtown are therefore the key to rail transit feasibility, and the procedures developed in this study focus on estimating the number and length of such trips.

Trips by all modes to and from a *downtown* are firmly related to the *nonresidential floorspace* in it. For example, each 10 million square feet (0.93 million m^2) of nonresidential floorspace on the average attracts 40,000 trips a day. If one-third of these were by rail, that would be enough to support two light rail lines.

Whether or not two light rail lines could actually collect this number of passengers depends on *how population is distributed around the downtown.* If topography or other constraints have channeled half the population into one corridor one of these two lines would in fact become feasible. Ordinarily, the population is less concentrated by corridor, and a downtown of 10 million square feet would not find enough riders in any one of them to support a rail line. At least 20 million square feet—the size of Edmonton—is usually needed.

The population distribution by distance from a downtown only affects the length of trips. Downtown size and population distribution by corridor principally determine the *number* of downtown-oriented trips on a rail line.

Models to estimate per capita trip rates to a downtown, the choice of mode, and the extent of the tributary area of a rail line are but auxiliary steps to link two basic facts of urban geography—downtown size and population by corridor—to the threshold volumes that can support a rail line.

The major message of the model estimating downtown trips per capita is that they fall off steeply with distance: 5 miles away they drop to ⅓ of what they are 1 mile away, and 50 miles away they drop to $^1/_{100}$th of what they are 5 miles away.

The major message of the mode choice models is that residential density at the origin, the size of the nonresidential concentration at the destination, and the presence of rail service between them primarily determine the proportion of public transit users. They do so in the first instance by reducing auto ownership; but the mode choice of households which still own autos is again influenced by downtown size and the quality of rail and bus service.

The major message of the tributary area model is that median (not average) station access distances tend to be quite short—generally in the range of 0.5 to 2 miles. Yet even a small expansion of that distance—such as by feeder buses—can, by expanding the extent of the tributary area, have a large impact on rail patronage.

For estimating downtown peoplemover (DPM) patronage, separate procedures are developed comparing gains in time, convenience, and money for different trips within and to the downtown; on the whole, potential DPM travel becomes primarily a function of downtown floorspace, and trips to and from the downtown overwhelm the strictly internal trips.

POTENTIAL RAIL CITIES

After the decisions of the 1970s to build rapid transit in Atlanta, Baltimore, and Miami but to opt for light rail in Detroit and Pittsburgh, *there are only four cities left in the United States that are serious candidates for rapid transit. These are Los Angeles, Seattle, Honolulu, and Houston.* A more tentative candidate is Dallas–Ft. Worth; the potential of San Juan is not evaluated. The fear of a "bottomless pit" of rapid transit construction and of "little BART'S" proliferating all over the country is clearly groundless.

In Los Angeles, the Wilshire line with two westerly extensions totaling 28 miles (45 km) is shown to attract passenger volumes similar to those on the Washington Metro and to exceed the threshold for a line fully in tunnel. Additional lines of roughly 40 miles (64 km) would carry much lighter loads and would have to be mostly above ground.

In Seattle, lines one-third in tunnel appear reasonable for a distance of some 9 miles from the CBD, for a system similar in scale to the plans of the early 1960s.

In Honolulu, two 5-mile lines just about meet the threshold for a route one-third in tunnel; the threshold for a line fully above ground would be met for twice the distance.

In Houston, the threshold for a route one-third in tunnel is exceeded if increased area-wide transit orientation and reduced auto speeds are assumed. Up to four corridors of more than 10 miles each would meet the criteria in this case.

In Dallas under the same conditions, the threshold of rapid transit one-third in tunnel is barely reached in no more than two corridors.

The criteria can be compared to recent decisions in a number of cities. In Washington, the full 101-mile system under construction appears to conform to the criteria, though a somewhat shorter system would attain higher passenger use per mile of line. Atlanta and Baltimore, while generally conforming to the criteria, are flagged as high-capital-cost systems, while Miami's low-cost above-ground construction is in scale with the criteria.

Candidates for light rail are more numerous. To begin with, they include Seattle, Honolulu and Houston. Each could support light rail lines built to high standards, with 1/5 in tunnel, for distances of 9 miles and more from downtown. No judgment is made here as to whether that option is better or worse than full-scale rapid transit.

Additional candidates for high-standard light rail lines with 1/5 in tunnel are *Dallas–Ft. Worth, St. Louis, and Milwaukee.* They rank in travel volume with the two cities that are committed to light rail plans of this degree of capital intensity, namely, Detroit and Pittsburgh.

Minneapolis, Indianapolis, Louisville, Cincinnati, and possibly *Denver* exceed the threshold volume for light rail lines with considerable grade separation but no tunnels. They rank in travel volume with San Diego and Portland, which are committed to this level of capital intensity, as well as Buffalo, which is building a far more capital intensive system.

Kansas City and *Columbus* have estimated travel volumes that do not quite reach the middle threshold for considerable grade separation, but comfortably exceed the low one. Their potential travel volume is above New Orleans's, with a historic line in operation.

By contrast, Phoenix, Dayton, San Antonio, Providence, and Tampa–St. Petersburg have estimated travel volumes below the lowest light rail threshold; even doubling them would seem to provide little justification for light rail. Thus, the decision to forego a high-capital system in Denver is supported by the analysis, as is the decision not to proceed with light rail in Dayton. Still, Denver is found to be a possible candidate for low-capital light rail transit, and a more substantial light rail system is found to be possible in St. Louis, even though a local alternatives analysis decided against it for the near future.

Altogether, then, an analysis of the 29 largest urban areas in the United States (excluding the six "old" rail cities) found four candidates for rapid transit and ten candidates for light rail. This is in addition to the four cities that made rapid transit commitments and the five that made light rail commitments in the 1970s. Several additional candidates for light rail can probably be found in the next tier of 20 or so urban areas, ranking in population below the 29 studied here. These include San Jose, Sacramento, and Rochester, which have made light rail plans. Their prospects—not evaluated here—depend on their downtown floorspace, on population by corridor, and on the suitability of existing rights-of-way.

Downtown peoplemovers of current rubber-tired design, requiring heavy guideways, are limited to the largest downtowns—with more than 40 to 70 million square feet of nonresidential floorspace—if they carry internal trips only. They will be in scale with past fixed guideway investments per passenger-mile, will save some labor and land, but will not, as a rule, save any energy directly.

If their market is expanded to intercept regional trips by auto and transit, they can capture sufficient volume to be in scale with past fixed guideway investments (and attain other savings, except energy) in downtowns of much smaller size—between 20 and 30 million square feet, depending on assumptions. The applicability of past fixed-guideway investment levels to downtown peoplemovers, however, is questionable, because the benefits they produce per mile of line tend to be lower than those of line-haul, regional systems. In this light, capital-intensive peoplemover designs may not be a very attractive investment even in large and medium-size downtowns.

Lastly, if the cost (and bulk) of automated guideways were brought down sharply by use of *lightweight, single-beam designs,* the market for peoplemovers would expand to cover a large number of downtowns that have between 10 and 20 million square feet of nonresidential floorspace. At the volumes attainable in such downtowns, automated systems can produce labor savings compared to buses if the line is comparatively long, suggesting some line-haul functions and not just internal circulator functions for this technology. With single-beam designs that do not require snowmelting, that require less energy for construction and wayside facilities, and that provide service to residential corridors (where more auto trips, rather than pedestrian trips, would be diverted), peoplemovers would begin to save energy just like other fixed guideways. The search for energy and cost-efficient systems at this point seems more important than defining precisely the locations where the current generation of hardware may be appropriate.

Summarizing the potential for new rapid transit and light rail in the United

States, the possible number of new "starter lines" turns out to be quite modest. With 4 rapid transit and 10 light rail corridors totaling some 50 and 90 miles of line (80 and 145 km) respectively, its cost in 1977 dollars would be about $2.9 billion, or $2.6 billion if light rail were substituted for rapid transit in Seattle, Honolulu, and Houston.

Proceeding from "starter lines" to full networks, one can discern a total of some 14 corridors and 180 miles (290 km) of line in the four future rapid transit cities and, more conjecturally, about 250 miles (400 km) of light rail in the 10 cities, costing about $5.1 billion and $3.0 billion in 1977 dollars, respectively; the biggest single item would be the system in Los Angeles, where some 70 miles of line conform to the criteria advanced here.

Benefits from possible new rapid transit lines in existing rapid transit cities exceed those in the four "future" cities. In New York, Chicago, Philadelphia, Boston, San Francisco, and Cleveland, 16 corridors can be discerned where new lines would meet the criteria; their aggregate length is about 127 miles (204 km) and their cost some $6.7 billion in 1977 dollars.

In Washington, Atlanta, Baltimore, and Miami, approximately 10 corridors can be discerned that conform to the criteria and are not fully under construction; this would add about 55 miles (88 km) to the lines being built as of 1980, at a cost of some $1.5 billion in 1977 dollars. Light rail requirements in cities with existing or committed light rail systems are less clear but may total some 75 miles and $0.9 billion in 1977 dollars.

Altogether, potential additional rapid transit mileage in the United States conforming to the criteria presented here might total about 350 miles (563 km) in 40 corridors, which represents about a 50 percent expansion of the extant 647-mile (1,041 km) rapid transit system.

More conjecturally, potential additional light rail mileage conforming to the criteria might total about 320 miles (515 km), which represents more than a doubling of the extant 215-mile (356 km) light rail and streetcar system. Both items together would increase urban rail travel in the United States by over 40 percent of 1980 levels of use. The location of this increment in passenger-miles is schematically shown in Exhibit 0.1.

The task is of finite magnitude and would take about 30 years to accomplish at the current pace. Its cost of $17.2 billion in 1977 prices (about $22 billion at 1980 construction prices—not bid prices in 1980, which cover several years of construction and are therefore higher) is split about equally between the "future" rail cities and those with systems in existence or under construction. This refers strictly to new lines and excludes elevated removal, station reconstruction, and line rehabilitation on existing systems to bring them up to the quality of the new lines, especially in Chicago, New York, and Philadelphia.

NATIONAL POLICY IMPLICATIONS

Past answers to the question, "What cities in the United States warrant new rail transit lines?" have ranged from "None" to "Most." This book arrives at a middle position: the criteria used indicate that the 10 cities with rapid transit extant or under construction could only be joined by 4 more cities, but that the 7 cities which

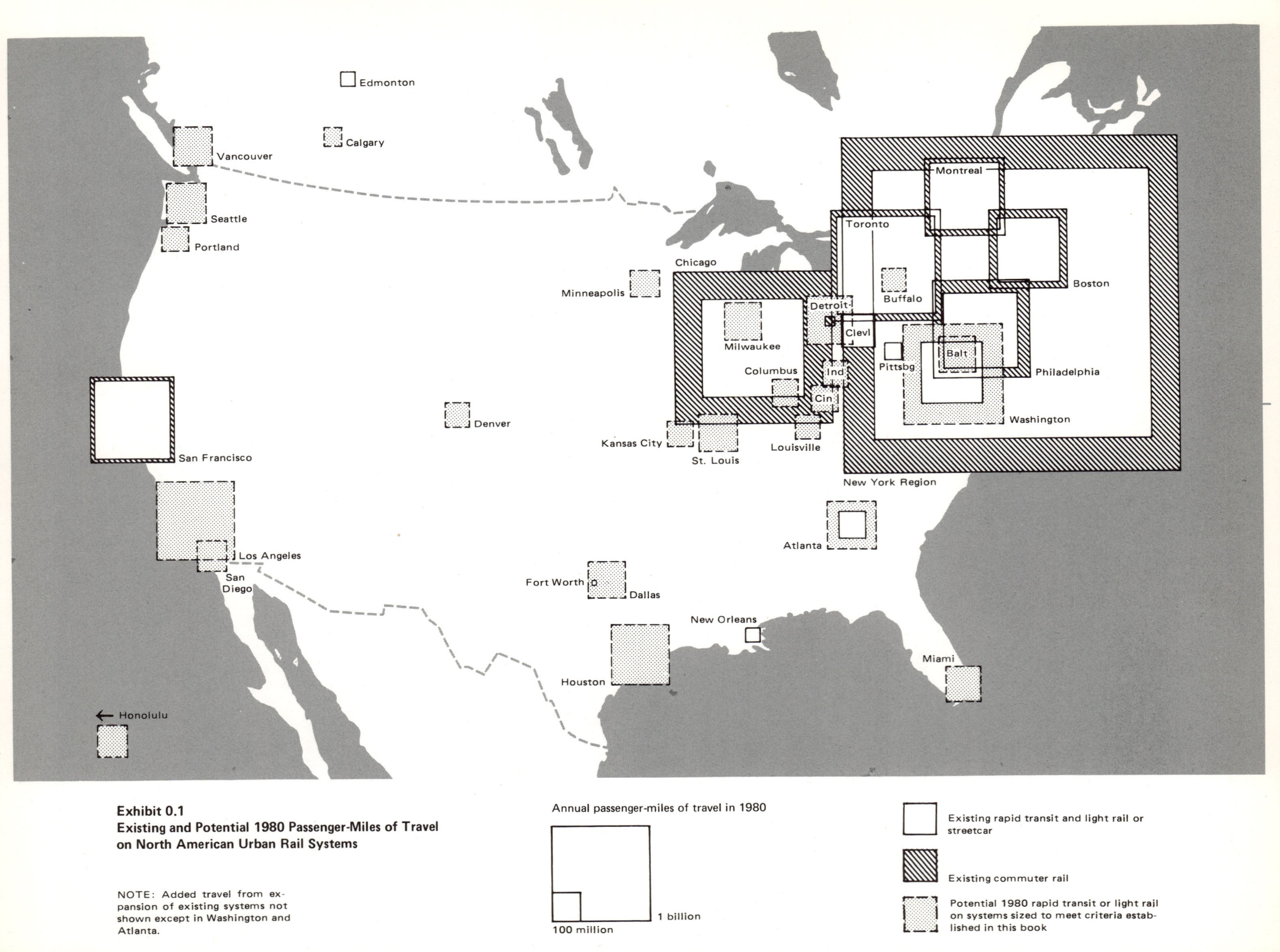

Exhibit 0.1
Existing and Potential 1980 Passenger-Miles of Travel on North American Urban Rail Systems

NOTE: Added travel from expansion of existing systems not shown except in Washington and Atlanta.

only have light rail extant or committed could be joined by at least 10 more, for a total of about 30 urban areas with some form of rail.

There has been concern that, in contrast to the Interstate Highway program, the nation's urban rail construction program is open-ended, with no defined goal or schedule. This study sketches one possibility for a finite national program: roughly a 50 percent expansion of the rapid transit system and a 150 percent expansion of the light rail system, which would require some $22 billion at 1980 costs.

Another important question is, "What will we get for the money?" This study shows that an expenditure of this magnitude, carefully related to prospective travel volumes, can be covered by "hard" savings in land, energy, labor, and passenger travel time. Contrary to some estimates, up to one-third of the capital construction expenditure can be considered an energy conservation expenditure. Indirect savings—pertaining to the investment in a more resource-conserving urban pattern—are extra.

With respect to downtown peoplemovers, the findings point to the need for light, single-beam systems that would be less costly to build, obstruct less view, and not require any snowmelting. When developed, such systems could have wide potential use, not limited to downtown circulation. In fact, an "overhead streetcar" on a single-beam two-way guideway could easily preempt most of the light rail and peoplemover market defined here, and some of the rapid transit market.

By providing complete grade-separation (and hence high speed with operation in trains) at an unusually low construction cost, the proposed manually operated "Project 21" overhead streetcar could become the first modern rapid transit system to *fully pay for its construction from savings in labor cost alone.* Based on methods presented in this study, this could be accomplished wherever travel volume in a corridor exceeds 30 to 40 buses per direction per hour, and bus operating speed is 11 mph (18 km/h) or less. About ten U.S. cities presently without rail (with downtowns the size of Honolulu, Milwaukee, Minneapolis, and larger) fit this description and added lines are possible as feeders to traditional systems. With modest subsidy, this market would be greatly widened. In an era of reduced government spending, this would open rather unexpected horizons for private investment in urban rail on a large scale. It would mean redefining our hypothetical national program to one with more mileage, substantially less investment, and a much shorter time frame.

Without dealing with bus issues directly, the study suggests that express buses—particularly of the large, articulated variety—are more of a competition for light rail than for rapid transit. The similarity of their present average operating costs over a range of volumes, however, should not obscure the fixed guideways' future advantage in terms of marginal costs to carry more riders, and in terms of electric propulsion. The latter can also lead to a widespread resurgence of trolleybuses.

Geographically, all the potential new rapid transit systems are in the West and Southwest; the potential light rail lines are mostly in the Midwest, and the extensions to existing systems are mostly in the Northeast. Urban rail—whatever technological form it takes—can therefore have a national constituency.

Finally, if quality is to reach world standards on new lines, older existing systems require investment that may exceed the new lines in scale, particularly in order to rebuild underground stations and to replace elevated lines with tunnels.

Urban Rail in America

1 Extent and Use of Rail Transit

THE FIRST WAVE OF URBAN RAIL

Historically, development of the large, contemporary city was closely tied to rail transport. After 1830, the intercity railroad freed major cities from dependence on access by water and, by expanding their hinterland, enabled them to grow to ten times their former size in a century or less. As cities outgrew the limits of walking distance that had confined them from antiquity, rail technology was called upon to help move people within cities as well.

Urban public transportation was initially provided by adapting the stagecoach to local service. A larger vehicle, the horse-drawn omnibus, was introduced in Paris in 1829 and in New York in 1831. It proliferated rapidly, but crowding and street congestion compounded the discomforts of a slow and bumpy ride on rough or nonexistent street pavements.

Putting a horse-drawn vehicle on rails offered a smoother ride, greater speed, and more output from a team of horses, which could then pull a still larger vehicle. These advantages cut the cost of transporting a passenger in half, inaugurating the nickel fare that survived in some American cities for nearly a century. The world's first horse-drawn urban street railway began operating on Fourth Avenue in New York in 1832, but such tracked *horsecars* did not begin to displace omnibuses on a large scale until 1855, when installation of sunken, rather than raised, tracks solved the problem of interference with free-wheeled street traffic. From then on, horsecar lines expanded rapidly abroad as well as in the United States, where the extent of trackage reached 6,200 miles (9,900 km)[1] by 1890, as shown in Exhibit 1.1.

Although a great improvement over the omnibus, the horsecar was still hampered by street congestion, which was especially severe in the largest cities. In Manhattan, the 5-mile (8 km) trip from the Battery to Central Park took well over an

The first urban rail vehicle—the horsecar "John Mason"—operated on Fourth Avenue in New York in 1832.

A cable car designed for San Francisco's Powell Street in 1887; the traction cable is shown below the rails in this drawing.

"Dummy" steam locomotive and cars on the Gilbert (Sixth Avenue) rapid transit elevated line in New York in 1878.

Electric streetcars in downtown Newark, N.J., prior to the advent of the automobile.

hour in the 1860s. A grade-separated or *rapid transit* system was needed to avoid congestion by travel under or above the streets. Such a system could more effectively employ mechanical rather than animal traction to further increase speed, and also to raise capacity by operating vehicles in trains.

The first rapid transit line began operating underground in London in 1863 with steam locomotives, but a similar plan for New York in 1865 did not find political acceptance. The implementation of a more attractive underground design with pneumatic propulsion, successfully tested in New York in 1870, was also blocked. Instead, rapid transit in North America took the above-ground route. After initial tests in 1867, the first elevated rapid transit line began revenue service in 1870 along Greenwich Street and Ninth Avenue in lower Manhattan. The propulsion was by means of a continuously moving cable, but after a year this was replaced by steam locomotives. In the following decades, a network of elevated lines was built in New York which reached 189 miles of track (302 km) by 1902; another, in Chicago, begun in 1892, reached 109 miles of track (174 km) by 1902.

Most smaller American cities lacked the travel volumes needed to support the cost of building elevated structures. They were seeking ways to improve the street railways, especially after animal traction proved vulnerable to the Great Epizootic of 1872, which killed horses by the tens of thousands. Steam locomotives in street service were unwieldy, and frightened animals. An interim solution was propulsion by cable from stationary steam engines. Abandoned on the New York elevated, this system was perfected in San Francisco, whose steep hills made horse traction particularly difficult. *Cable car* service there began in 1873 and was an instant success, since the cars could negotiate 20 percent grades without slowing their unheard-of 9.5-mile-per-hour (15.2 km/hr.) pace. Eventually, San Francisco built 112 miles (179 km) of cable car track and by 1890 there were 376 additional miles (600 km) in other American cities, notably New York, Chicago, and St. Louis.

In the late 1890s, both horsecars and cable cars were rapidly displaced by the *electric streetcar* or tramway. Horsecars ceased operating by 1923. The last surviving cable cars ended service in Seattle in the 1930s and would have ended service in San Francisco two decades later had it not been for the municipal ordinance of 1955 which assured "in perpetuity" operation of the last 10.5 miles (17 km) of track. Electric propulsion was far superior to its antecedents in cost, performance, and amenity. It was experimented with for half a century, but its practical application had to await commercial electric power and reliable means to collect that power in motion.

Much of the development work was done in Germany, where revenue service on the Lichterfelde line near Berlin began in 1881. Experimental lines in several North American cities followed between 1884 and 1887. The one in Richmond, Va., installed in 1888, is widely credited with having perfected the technology for reliable commercial service. It triggered the phenomenal expansion for electric streetcar lines throughout North America and the world. Including interurban lines, streetcars in the United States had 44,000 miles (70,000 km) of track at their peak in 1917. With an average of 1.36 tracks per mile of line, the length of their right-of-way was three-quarters that of today's interstate freeways.

Electric traction also had a decisive influence on rapid transit. In 1897, a six-car multiple-unit electric train began operating on the South Side Elevated in Chicago, and between 1898 and 1903 the New York elevateds were electrified. Objections to underground transit because of the hazards of smoke and steam became moot, and subway construction in New York finally began in 1900. By that time, electric subways were already operating in London, Budapest, Glasgow, Boston, and Paris. With electrification, rapid transit track-miles in the United States more than quadrupled between 1902 and 1937. Over nine-tenths of this mileage was in New York and Chicago; Philadelphia and Boston accounted for the remainder.

The effect of electric railways on the pattern of national urban settlement was pervasive.[2] The period from 1880 to 1920 was important in the formation of American cities. Population in cities over 10,000 people grew from 11 million to nearly 45 million, or almost one-half of the national total. Urban rail ridership increased from 0.6 billion to 15.5 billion trips annually. The development pattern of urban cores and of the nearby suburbs was shaped during that period. It was a pattern of moderately high densities compactly arranged within walking distance of the streetcar lines. The population of these areas grew and then declined in subsequent years, but perhaps one-quarter of the nation still resides in urban and suburban cores whose spatial organization was shaped by the streetcar. Its grid covered not only the old eastern cities, but the young western cities as well. Los Angeles, for example, had two streetcar systems (a standard-gauge and a narrow-gauge one) which at their peak totalled over 1,500 miles (2,400 km) of track, some of which was in use until 1963.

The nation's streetcar system, which took less than thirty years to build, was torn down over the next sixty years. Immediately after World War I, lightly used lines began to be cut back, though ridership increased until 1923. Operating costs were rising, but the income of streetcar companies was controlled by franchise agreements which often mandated the nickel fare. The short-lived appearance of jitneys further hurt electric railway revenues just as they were needed for capital replacement between 1910 and 1920. *Jitneys* were private motor cars that served passengers for a fee. Their routes, while flexible, generally paralleled streetcar lines. As the 1920s progressed, rapidly rising auto ownership began to reduce demand for all forms of public transportation. Not only did the auto deprive the streetcar of riders, but streetcar service began to deteriorate due to rising auto congestion. Because of conflicts at intersections, this was even true of systems that had private rights-of-way. While rising costs of replacing and maintaining trackage had to be covered from passenger revenues, dramatic improvements to street pavement for free-wheeled vehicles were made from public funds. Between 1904 and 1940, paved mileage in the United States increased from 9 to 47 percent of the total street and road mileage.

Under these conditions the *motor bus*, which appeared on the American scene in New York in 1907, began to look more and more attractive to transit operators. It was easier to maneuver in heavy auto traffic. More importantly, it had to make only a nominal contribution to the costs of right-of-way, which it shared with a multitude of other free-wheeled vehicles and with the public at large. "Motor bus routes involve no construction costs [!] and may be extended or contracted as circumstances dictate with little or no sacrifice of financial investment. Street railway track, however, requires heavy expenditure . . ." the American Transit Association explained.[3] Under the strained conditions of the 1930s, as transit ridership was falling, streetcar track was rapidly reduced. Its discontinuance was temporarily halted during World War II, but by 1946 only one-third of the 1917 mileage, owned by 120 companies,

Exhibit 1.1
Total System Extent of Urban Rail in the United States, 1855-1985

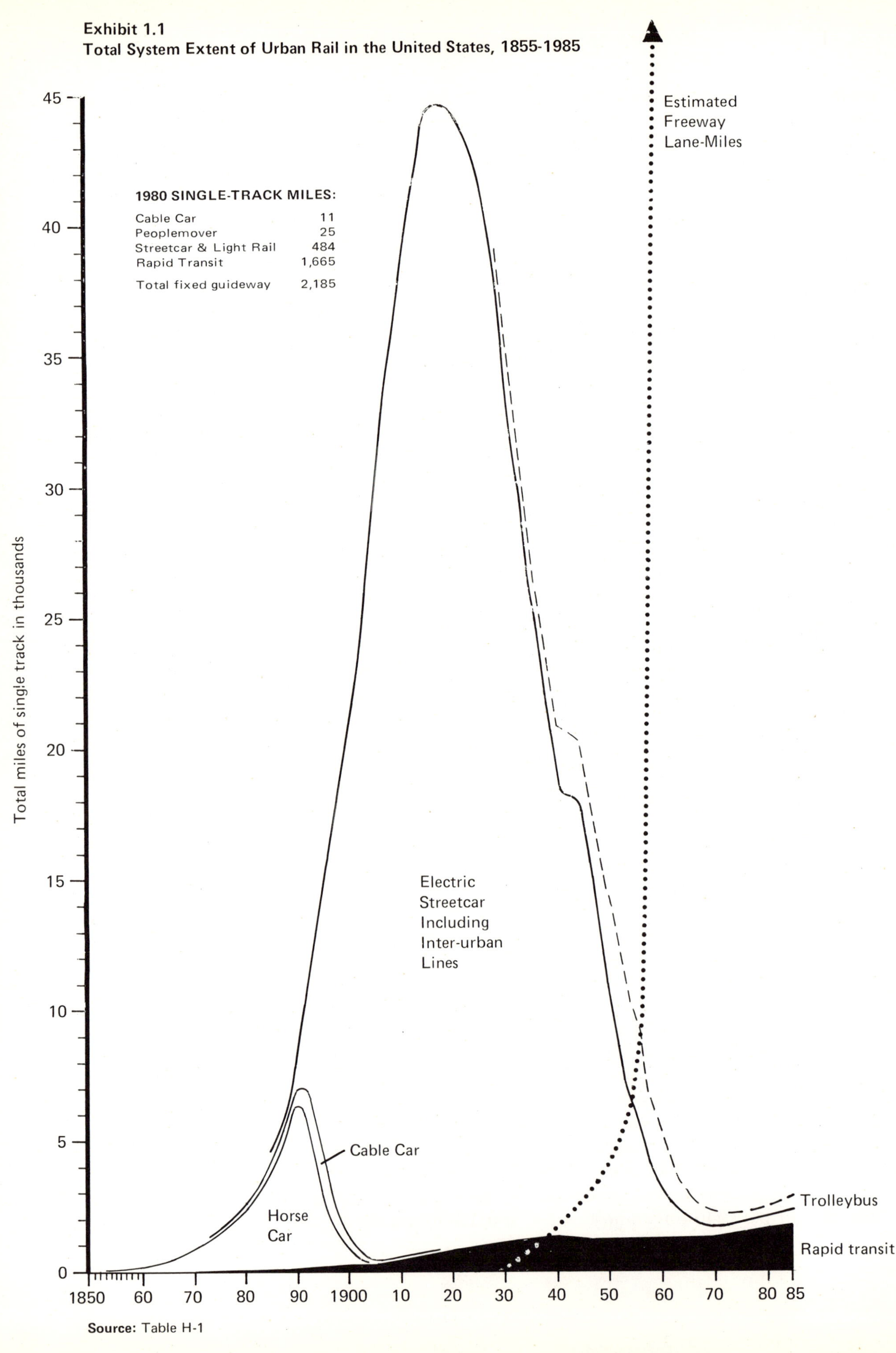

Source: Table H-1

remained. Most of that was gone by the time urban freeway construction began on a nationwide scale in the mid-1950s. Before 1950, over half of the nation's few freeways were confined to the New York urban region, and were not directly competing with intraurban rail.

In an effort to preserve the advantages of electric traction while avoiding the capital costs of replacing track, the trackless trolley or *trolleybus* was in relatively wide use for a time. Introduced in continuous service in 1923 in Philadelphia and in 1928 in Salt Lake City, the trolleybus peaked in 1952 at 3,700 miles (5,980 km) of dual overhead wire but then declined in step with the streetcars, as Exhibit 1.1 shows.

Still, the streetcar operators did not give up without a struggle. In a bold attempt to regain passengers by superior speed and comfort, the Electric Railway Presidents' Conference Committee (ERPCC) developed an advanced streetcar design—the PCC car—that did attract added ridership on the routes where it was used. The design, manufactured in the United States from 1936 to 1952 and still unsurpassed in many respects, was widely emulated in Eastern Europe and other parts of the world.[4]

Also, the switchover from electric streetcars to buses was not all preordained. High-pressure tactics to accelerate conversion, practiced by the National City Lines holding company, have been widely discussed,[5] as has been the reluctance of public agencies to assume those right-of-way costs that were otherwise in the public domain. None other than the Automobile Club of Southern California suggested incorporating streetcar rights-of-way in freeways in the 1940s but the state's Department of Public Works showed little interest. Citizen action in favor of preserving streetcar lines was widespread, but such action lacked the bite it acquired in later years. Though civic battles in many cities—Baltimore, Camden, Minneapolis, Milwaukee, and Washington—were lost, the preservation of electric street railways in the seven United States cities where they did survive (Boston, Cleveland, New Orleans, Newark, Philadelphia, Pittsburgh, and San Francisco) was in large part due to community action. In Canada, only Toronto preserved its streetcar lines. Public ownership was, in most cases, the necessary institutional ingredient. The physical characteristic that most surviving systems had in common was that significant portions of their mileage were on reserved or on fully grade-separated rights-of-way (see Table H-3). This ensured speed and reasonable adherence to schedules. During the period 1955–1969, it is notable that three of these lines—in San Francisco, Cleveland, and Newark—lost no ridership. Rapid transit ridership dropped only 5 percent, while surface lines in general (both streetcar and bus) sustained as much as a 40 percent loss.

The historic pattern of public transit ridership in the United States—both rail and bus—is shown in Exhibit 1.2. The pattern is not as smooth as that of system extent, shown earlier, because ridership responds to short-term conditions; it was powerfully affected by both the Depression of the 1930s and reduced gasoline availability during World War II. Only by the mid-1950s did these effects wear off. Removing the influence of such traumatic events, one can see a long-term trend of seven decades of transit ridership growth until 1926–27, then a forty-five-year decline until 1972, with renewed growth since that date.

To explain this pattern, three sources of transit ridership should be identified. The first is *growth in economic activity* in compact urban environments, which are

Exhibit 1.2
Total Passenger Trips on Urban Transit in the United States by Mode, 1855-1980

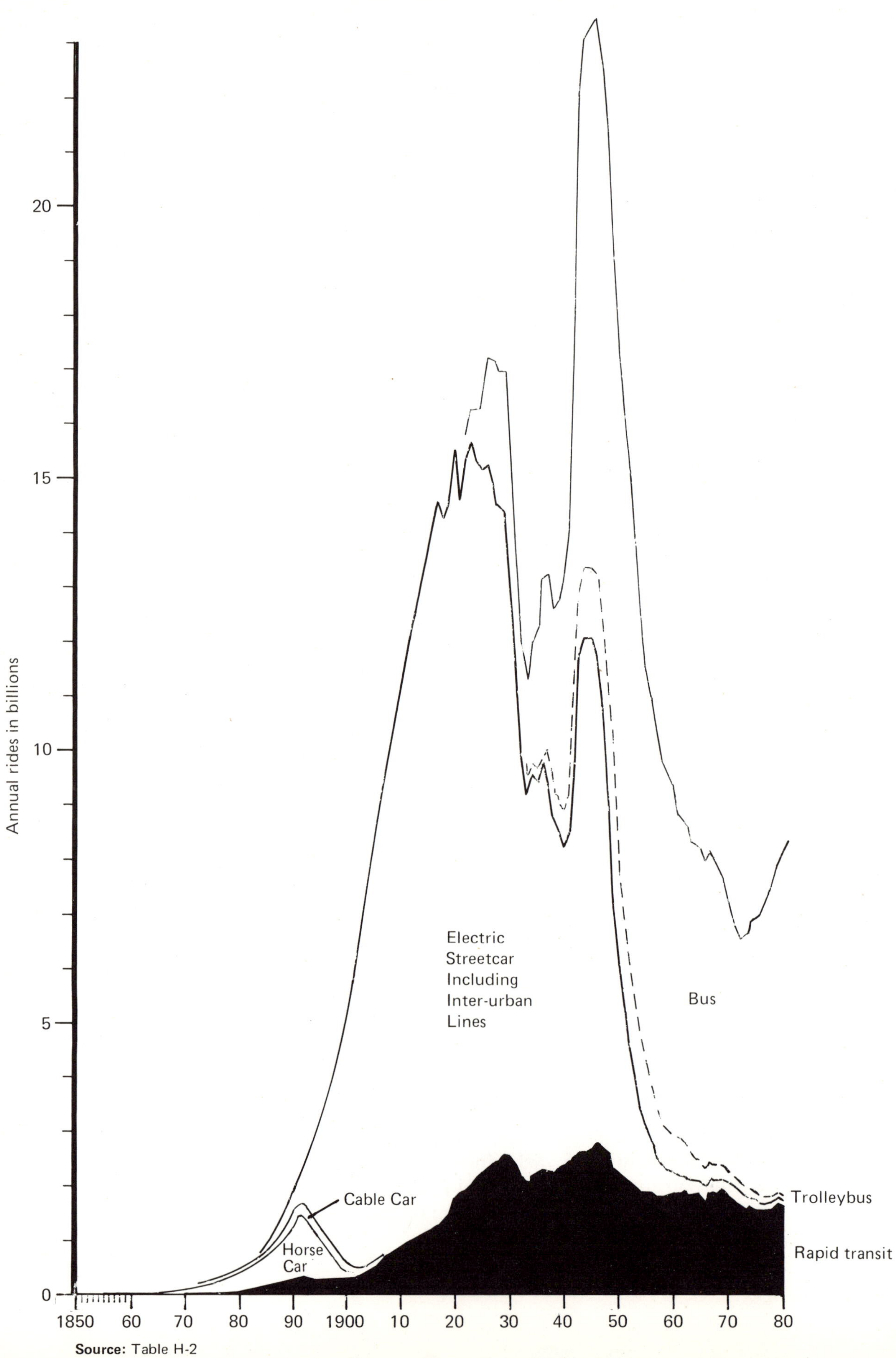

Source: Table H-2

inhospitable to the automobile. The second is *improvement of transit service*. The third is *restraints on the competing mode*—the automobile. The first seven decades of ridership growth were indeed characterized by expansion of economic activity in compact urban environments. Except for the last fifteen years of that period, the auto was not competing. The forty-five years of decline were characterized by a nearly three-fold increase in auto ownership per capita and a sharp reduction in vehicle-miles of transit service; typically, the substitution of buses for streetcars in and of itself meant declining service. When rail lines were discontinued, buses inherited only a part of their ridership, unless the service was seriously dilapidated. While suppressed auto use in 1942–46 created a temporary ridership peak, after the war the growth of economic activity shifted from urban to auto-oriented environments, depriving transit of new patronage.

The post-1972 resurgence in ridership is more complex, having begun in the face of continuing urban dispersal and rising auto ownership. Initially, it was triggered by improved bus service. With infusion of public subsidy, bus-miles traveled began to expand for the first time in twenty years, and fares began to decline (in constant dollars) for the first time in twenty-five years. Yet, even as bus improvements led an increase in bus patronage, rapid transit patronage declined. Most of this decline was due to a traumatic drop in economic activity between 1969 and 1977 in the Central Business District of Manhattan,[6] where over 55 percent of the nation's rapid transit trips originate or terminate. Sharp ridership declines were registered for similar reasons in Philadelphia and Cleveland, while those in Chicago and Boston, with healthier economies, were small. With the resurgence of Manhattan after 1977 national rapid transit ridership also turned upwards, helped by new systems in Washington, San Francisco, and Atlanta. Finally, the gasoline shortages of 1974 and 1979 and rising fuel prices in their wake—the first restraints on auto use since World War II—strongly contributed to the upswing of both bus and rapid transit use. Because buses operate in auto territory more than rapid transit systems do, their response to auto restraints is naturally more volatile.

Service increases in excess of ridership growth—such as those which triggered the rise in bus use of the early 1970s—cannot continue indefinitely. Restraints on automobile use and modest trends toward urban reconcentration could promise further growth in public transit demand, but fare increases will dampen it. Projecting this growth even for the near term is not as simple as projecting the growth in the extent of urban rail systems, where committed construction enables one to see the upswing in mileage through 1985, as shown in Exhibit 1.1.

Both the system extent and the ridership graphs display patterns typical of the logistic growth curve, with its four stages: (1) conception and development, (2) takeoff and rapid growth, (3) maturity and subsequent decline, and (4) tailing out, or the "nostalgia" stage. Yet, the curves also show that not every mode of transport is necessarily on its way to extinction after decline has set in. Some do experience a "second youth" and the beginning of a new life. Such a second life may be the result of qualitative changes within the system, or of external circumstances favorable to new growth, or both, and must be distinguished from temporary fluctuations.

Exhibit 1.3 lists the beginning dates of each of the transport systems discussed, their peak dates, which were followed by decline, and, where applicable, the bottoming out dates, after which renewed growth began.

Exhibit 1.3
Chronological Benchmarks in the Development of Rail and Other Urban Transit in the United States

Transit System	Prototype operation	Beginning of reliable service, with subsequent growth	Peak system extent, with subsequent decline	Peak ridership, with subsequent decline	End of service, if any	System extent bottoms out, with subsequent growth	Ridership bottoms out, with subsequent growth	Trough system extent as a percent of peak	Trough ridership as a percent of peak	
Omnibus	1827	1831	1860	1860	1908	–	–	–	–	
Horsecar	1832	1855	1890	1890	1923	–	–	–	–	Rail Systems
Rapid Transit	1867	1870	1937	1946 (1929)*	–	1954	1977	92%	57%	Rail Systems
Cable car	1873	1873	1894	1894	(1955)**	–	–	–	–	Rail Systems
Electric streetcar (incl. Light Rail)	1884	1888	1917	1923	–	1975	1977	1%	0.9%	Rail Systems
Automated Peoplemover	1966	1971	–	–	–	–	–	–	–	Rail Systems
Trolley bus	1910	1923	1952	1949	–	1978	1978	9%	4%	
Motor bus	1907	1920	***	1948	–	–	1972	–	42%	
Total transit (excluding commuter rail and ferries)	1827	1831	n.a.	1946 (1926)*	–	n.a.	1972	n.a.	28%	

n.a.--not applicable.
* Peak year excluding World War II.
** Since 1955, remaining cable car lines in San Francisco have been preserved for historical and tourist reasons.
*** Motor bus route-miles of service have been continually expanding and have not reached a distinct peak.

The beginning dates are somewhat subjective (it is debatable which of several experiments should be called the "prototype operation," and exactly what can be considered the "beginning of reliable service"), but the two points of inflection—the peak and the trough—are quite firm, whether one deals with system extent or with ridership. Exhibit 1.3 indicates that of the urban rail—or, more broadly, urban fixed guideway—modes discussed, only the horsecar is firmly extinct, and the cable car is semiextinct, consigned to a "moving museum" role since 1955. Rapid transit, the oldest of the active modes, and declining somewhat for a time, has displayed significant growth in system extent since 1954 and appears to have bottomed out in ridership in 1977. Besides, its ridership decline compared to the peak was the smallest among the modes considered (the ninth column in Exhibit 1.3).

The streetcar may almost disappear as a mode operating in mixed traffic, though some surface street mileage was recently rebuilt in San Francisco, Toronto, Detroit, and Philadelphia. More importantly, mileage on predominantly reserved or fully grade-separated right-of-way—representing "Light Rail" in the narrow sense of the term—is committed to increase in the 1980s. Trolleybus mileage has bottomed out as Seattle, one of the five remaining United States trolleybus cities, nearly doubled the extent of its system in 1980. In Canada, with four trolleybus cities, conversions from diesel to trolleybuses have been made in the 1970s on two routes, one in Toronto and the other in Edmonton. Ridership on light rail and trolleybuses has not yet fully responded to the improvements, but the bottoming-out dates appear to be 1977 and 1978, respectively.

The exhibit also lists a new mode, the automated peoplemover, or small vehicle Automated Guideway Transit (AGT). With a prototype tested in South Park in Pittsburgh in 1966, revenue-type operation began since 1971 at airports, and in an urban setting in Morgantown in 1975 (various amusement park or exhibition operations are not considered here). As of 1980 the five urban-type peoplemovers in the United States accounted for over 1 percent of the total fixed guideway track miles, and a somewhat smaller share of ridership.

The automated peoplemover was consciously designed in response to the woes of both conventional fixed guideways and free-wheeled buses in an auto-dominated setting: routes too widely spaced, infrequent service when vehicles are relatively large, slow operating speed with stops to pick up passengers. Remedying these disadvantages with ordinary public transit quickly translates into sharply rising labor costs. By cutting labor costs with automatic operation (tested on the Times Square Shuttle of the New York subway in 1962, but terminated after a disastrous fire) small vehicles traveling on fully grade-separated guideways could attain a frequent service even at low travel volumes. Accepting low volumes, a closely meshed network could be built, bringing service close to the doorstep. An additional refinement would be station-to-station service on demand in family-sized vehicles bypassing intermediate stops, leading to "personal rapid transit" (PRT). While this concept still awaits much development work, the present generation of automated peoplemovers faces a more immediate hurdle: bulky grade-separated guideway designs require large capital investment and are not energy-efficient. At low volumes the capital cost per passenger is high. To attain a "takeoff" stage on the growth curve, the automated peoplemovers of the 1980s await a truly light guideway design, much as the horsecars of the 1840s awaited the design of a rail that was flush with the pavement.

The cycles of growth, decline, and resurgence of fixed guideways make it tempting to surmise that growth curves related to free-wheeled vehicles will also level off and enter a period of decline at some point in the future. In fact, some auto-related indicators in the United States have been showing signs of maturity for some time—the number of gas stations peaked in 1972; constant-dollar expenditures on highway construction peaked in 1966 and have shrunk in half since. Motor vehicle production appears to have reached a plateau and the seemingly inexorable growth in vehicle-miles traveled showed the first interruption since World War II in 1974, and a second, more prolonged one, in 1979–80. Speculating on what form the decline of auto-related systems might take is, however, not the point of this book.

Rather, its purpose is to explore the potential for three fixed guideway modes: primarily *rapid transit* and *light rail*, secondarily *peoplemovers*. Because of the technological uncertainties attached to the last, it is explored mostly in the limited area of downtown applications. Commuter railroads—which generally share track with intercity railroads and have not been discussed so far—are referred to only peripherally, where necessary to round out the total picture of urban rail. The remainder of this chapter focuses in more detail on the turnaround in rail transit both nationally and worldwide, scales the role it plays in America today, and then discusses both the rationale for new systems and the criteria that might be used to make decisions regarding new routes.

BEGINNING THE SECOND WAVE

The first American rapid transit cities paid dearly for their decision to follow the low-capital elevated route. Unsightly and noisy, the structures were a blight on surrounding areas. Elevated construction of the traditional type ceased for the most part in the early 1920s and removal of elevated lines became a key plank in the platform of urban betterment. New subways were planned with that goal in mind.

In New York, the opening of 59 miles (94 km) of subway line between 1930 and 1940 permitted demolition of elevated lines on a large scale; in the four decades between 1937 and 1977, 62 miles (100 km) of line were removed. In Chicago, 18 miles (29.1 km) of elevated structure were removed in the same period, and only partly compensated by that city's first passenger subways in 1943 and 1951. In Boston, 4.8 miles (7.7 km), and in Philadelphia, 3.6 miles (5.8 km) were removed. In the four cities taken together, 43 percent of the elevated mileage standing in 1937 was gone by 1977. New construction did not keep up with the demolitions for some time, so that the total length of rapid transit lines in the United States shrank between 1937 and 1954. Public attention was focused on ridership declines from the war-induced peak and on the accommodation of auto users. For the most part ambitious rail plans of the 1920s were forgotten. New plans for rail transit were modest.

As Herbert S. Levinson and F. Houston Wynn put it in 1961 in a seminal study[7] sponsored by the Automobile Manufacturers Association, "In most cities, future rapid transit will take the form of express bus operations on freeways. In cities where the attractiveness . . . of the central business district will encourage high-density development within select corridors, some new rail rapid transit may be desirable. Similarly, where existing rights-of-way can be incorporated into transit systems, it may be economical to consider rail transit."

That last precept—use of existing rights-of-way—was a starting point for the gradual rise of a new wave of rapid transit expansion. As is evident from Exhibit 1.4, most new rapid transit lines built since the 1950s in the regions of Chicago, Boston, and Philadelphia were of the "open" type, which avoided both the environmental damage of old-style elevated lines and the high cost of tunnels.* Boston opened such a low-cost extension of its Blue line in 1952, and converted a railroad to grade-separated streetcar service in 1959. In Cleveland, the first new rapid transit system in the United States in half a century opened in 1955 on a railroad right-of-way. Chicago followed with three major rapid transit lines in freeway medians in 1958, 1969, and 1970, and converted an abandoned interurban line near Skokie to light-density rapid transit in 1964. The Lindenwold line in the New Jersey suburbs of Philadelphia in 1969 followed an old railroad, as did Boston's South Shore extension in 1971. Several of these extensions were aimed at capturing the suburban clientele that was leaving the city as a place of residence and, without convenient transit, might also have left it as a place of work.

New York, which converted an abandoned railroad stretch in the Bronx to rapid transit in 1941, followed with the conversion of the Rockaway line in 1956, but that addition did not balance the closing of two rapid transit branches on Staten Island and the continued demolition of elevated lines. Minor subway additions notwithstanding, the New York Region's rapid transit system continued to shrink until 1978—the only one in the world to do so.

Inexpensive as available rights-of-way may be, they rarely go where most people want to go: railroads typically traverse industrial areas, and freeways usually avoid areas of intense residential and commercial activity. The Cleveland system, for example, was handicapped from the start by lack of downtown distribution. A voter-approved downtown subway in Cleveland never materialized in the 1950s because of opposition from the County Engineer; but in the rapidly expanding economy of the 1960s, major investment in city-building exemplified by underground construction no longer seemed out of order in other urban areas. There was a desire to rectify the imbalance between "private opulence and public squalor" and a rising consciousness of environmental values.

The massive urban freeway construction of the 1950s and 1960s engendered opposition and led to a "freeway revolt" in 1959 in San Francisco, then in other cities. As freeway plans were scaled down, it became possible to speak of rapid transit as a substitute for new freeways, not merely an adjunct to them. At the same time, the huge freeway expenditures whetted the appetite of transit advocates. If location and design standards for a freeway can be set first, and whatever money required to implement them will be forthcoming, why should transit lines be tailored to meager available funds? Why not aim first for what is right?

Doing what was "right" for rapid transit at that time meant four things: (1) providing direct service to clusters of intense urban activity in an environmentally acceptable manner, basically underground; (2) making sure that underground access is not a deterrent to riders, but is convenient and inviting; (3) getting away from the tradition of "sardine cans on wheels" and providing rolling stock that is

*The system extent in Exhibit 1.4, in contrast to the preceding three exhibits, is shown in line-miles rather than track-miles, to display more adequately the systems outside the New York Region. The average number of tracks per line of rapid transit today is about 3.5 in the New York Region, and about 2.4 outside. The track-miles, throughout the study, include yards and sidings.

Exhibit 1.4
Line-miles of Rapid Transit by Urban Area, 1867-1980

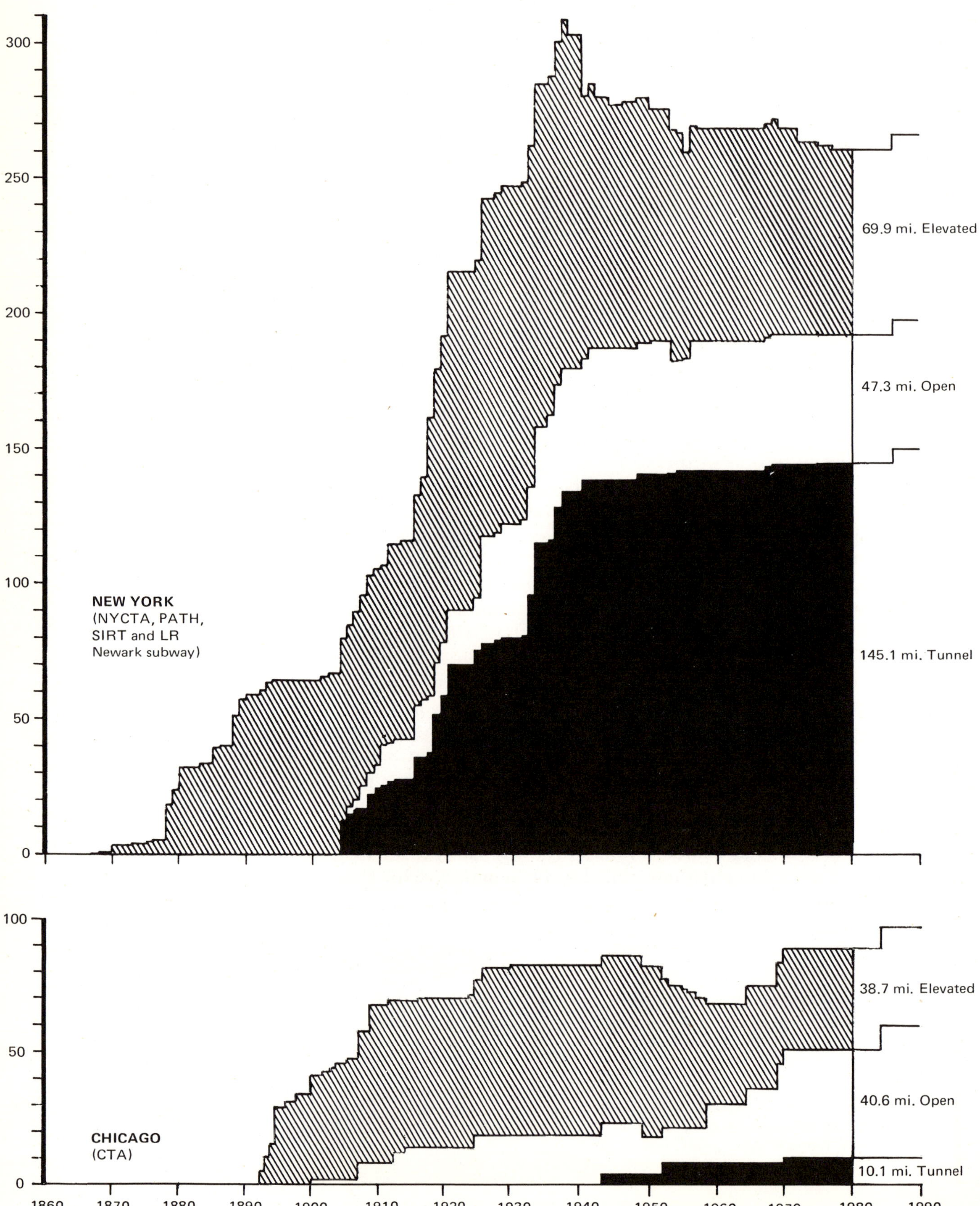

Exhibit 1.4 (cont'd.)
Line-miles of Rapid Transit by Urban Area, 1867-1980

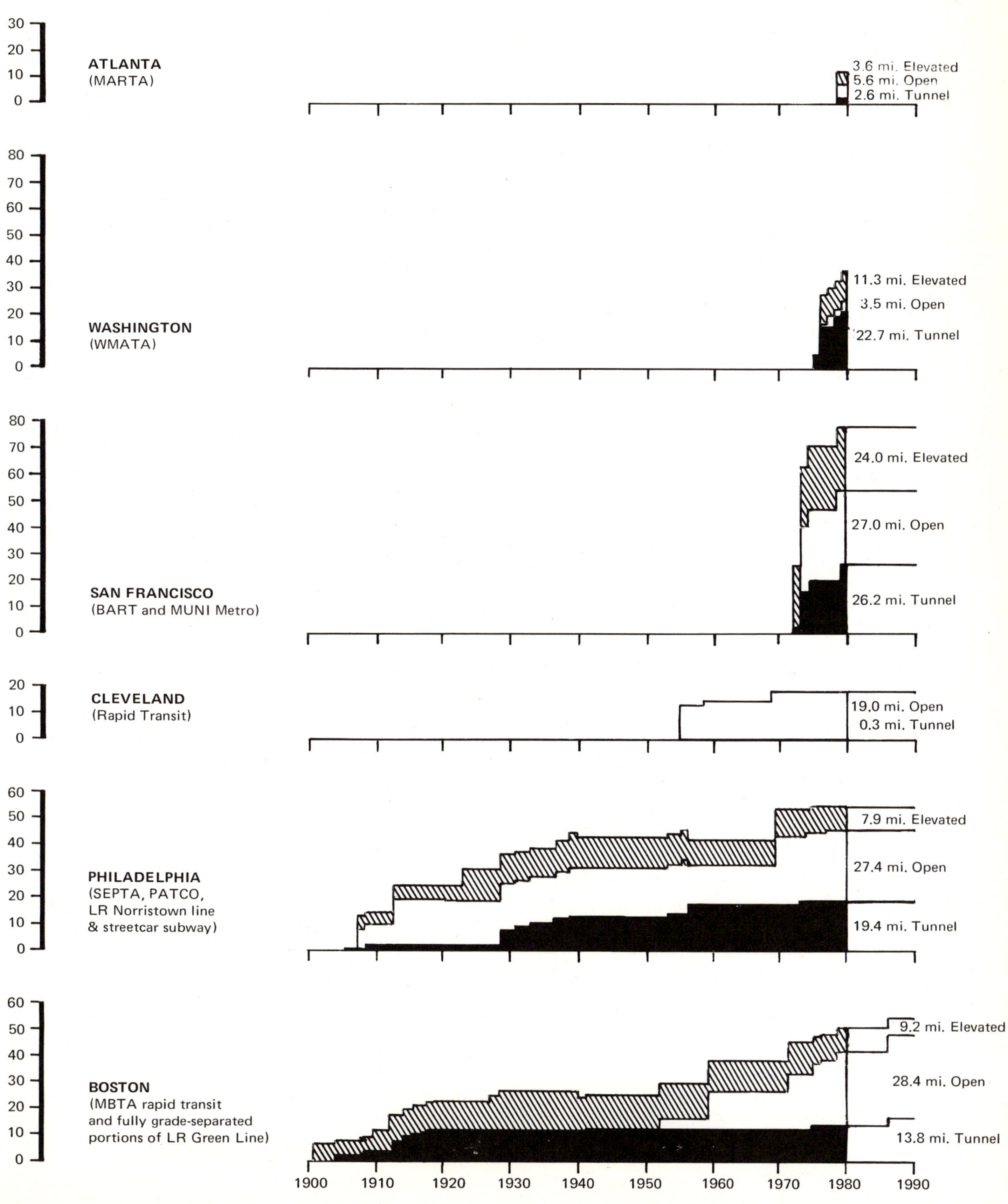

spacious, quiet, and climate-controlled; (4) providing a roadbed that allows quiet operation, high speed, and increased labor productivity. To compete seriously with the automobile, rapid transit had to shed the negative attributes which it had inherited from an earlier era through years of parsimony and retrenchment. The overhead monorail was considered as one approach to the problem, but Seattle's 1962 experiment showed that this technology did not offer any shortcuts to major investment in improving traditional rail.

Toronto's new subway, opened in 1954, was of the conventional type. Montreal was the first city to seek dramatic innovation in the four areas outlined; in 1961 it decided to build a rapid transit system superior in amenity to any other then in existence. In 1962, the San Francisco Bay Area Rapid Transit system (BART)—five times as large—was approved by the voters to compete with the auto for downtown access on a regional scale. Opened in 1966, the Montreal system, fully in a subway, made a lasting contribution with its spacious and inviting multilevel pedestrian areas, but its rubber-tired rolling stock remains controversial. San Francisco's BART, opened in 1972–74, likewise created a progression of significant urban spaces in the far-flung centers of activity which it tied together. It introduced elevated structures acceptable in low-density areas, and has a multitude of engineering accomplishments to its credit. Yet BART reached beyond its grasp in vehicle design and automatic train operation and the unreliability of these systems plagued it for a decade, delaying the attainment of full-scale service. Simpler automated systems, such as the Lindenwold line, functioned without serious problems. Quiet and air-conditioned rolling stock gradually became the rule for new car orders on existing systems, and automatic train operation the rule on new systems.

The expansionary political and economic climate of the 1960s raised sights with respect to system extent as well. In 1969, Washington embarked on the construction of a 101-mile (162 km) system, compared to 34 miles (55 km) envisioned in 1958. Atlanta voters in 1971 approved a 53-mile (85 km) system, compared to 16 miles (25 km) envisioned in 1961. Seattle stepped up its plans from 20 to 46 miles (32 to 74 km), Los Angeles from 22 to 201 miles (35 to 323 km), and even St. Louis in 1971 advanced a proposal for an 86-mile (138 km) system, 67 miles of which (108 km) would be in subway! Altogether, 25 out of 60 urban areas with populations over 400,000 in the United States had plans for building urban rail in 1972.[8] Collectively, their ambitious goals would have more than tripled the then existing rail system to over 2,200 miles (3,540 km) of line by 1990. Typically, these plans lacked systematic yardsticks for evaluation, and reflected exaggerated demographic and economic forecasts that characterized 1960s planning in general.

Changing conditions led to a reevaluation of transit planning in the mid-1970s. In the face of renewed employment decline in major downtowns, earlier ridership forecasts appeared unrealistic. In the face of budgetary constraints, the expenditure of $42 billion in constant 1971 dollars for the 25 systems planned was not likely. At a time when a schedule for reducing the energy requirements of the automobile was embedded in law, the rising energy requirements of rail transit for high acceleration, high speed, air-conditioning, and other amenities came to be questioned. In academic circles, blanket arguments against rail transit and for reliance on buses and more efficient automobile use erupted with new vigor.[9] The Federal policy response was more cautious: it required a more thorough evaluation of alternatives as a prerequisite to Federal funding; it limited Federal commitments to "operable

A rich variety of spacious and inviting underground pedestrian spaces: a lasting legacy of the Montreal subway, opened in 1966.

segments" of new lines rather than to entire regionwide systems, and urged consideration of light rail—that is, partially, rather than fully, grade-separated rail lines—as an alternative to rapid transit for cities with moderate passenger volumes and comparatively short trips.[10]

These changing perspectives notwithstanding, the extent of rapid transit in the United States did increase significantly over three decades, as Exhibit 1.5 indicates. From 1954 to 1980, Chicago, Boston, and Philadelphia gained 42 miles (68 km) of rapid transit line, though this was moderated by a net loss of 7 miles (11 km) in New York. The new systems of Cleveland, San Francisco, Washington, and Atlanta added 139 miles (224 km) of rapid transit line. Taken together, the four "old" rapid transit regions just about returned to their peak system extent of 1937, while the four "new" regions added a one-third increment. In addition, in 1980, 17 miles (27 km) of new line were under construction in three of the "old" rail regions, while in Washington, Atlanta, Baltimore, and Miami, 68 miles (109 km) were being built.

Partially grade-separated light rail lines were under construction in San Diego and Buffalo, and under design in Pittsburgh, Portland, and Detroit. This form of rail transit originated in the United States in the form of streetcar subways in Boston in 1897, Philadelphia in 1905, Rochester in 1927 (abandoned in 1956), and Newark in 1935; but, in the rush to eliminate streetcars, it was forgotten. In the mid-1950s, it was resurrected in Stuttgart, Cologne, and other cities in Europe that had to contend with the identical problem of freeing streetcars from street congestion. This produced a variety of partially grade-separated systems, sometimes called pre-Metro* or semi-Metro. When the time came to build the Market Street subway for BART in San Francisco, it was recognized that a second tunnel level (initially considered for rapid transit) would greatly benefit surviving streetcar operations into downtown. Due to problems with rolling stock, the opening of this line was delayed for nearly a decade. Meanwhile, Edmonton in Canada opened a new 4.5-mile (7.2 km) light rail line with a short downtown subway in 1978, and Calgary followed with an 8.3-mile (13.4 km) line that entered downtown on a surface mall in 1981. Exclusive busways did not achieve the widespread application envisaged in earlier years, but one was built near Washington, one in Los Angeles, and two in Pittsburgh, for a total length of about 34 miles (55 km). The first now operates as a feeder to Washington's rail rapid transit system.

In countries outside the United States, the reduction in rapid transit mileage caused by the removal of elevated lines did not occur. Only the construction pace slackened between 1940 and 1960. Yet, the "second youth" of rapid transit was even more remarkable. Compared with a 38 percent increase in rapid transit mileage in the United States between 1960 and 1980, the increase in the rest of the world was 127 percent. In 1960, only 26 cities in the world had rapid transit, and the bulk of the mileage was in 12 cities that had started operations prior to World War I. By 1980, the number of world cities with full-scale rapid transit increased to 60. A dozen additional cities built downtown subways for light rail. The pace at which new rapid transit lines were opened to traffic increased from about 9 miles (15 km) a year worldwide from 1940–1960 to 50 miles (80 km) a year from 1960–

*An early "pre-Metro" system was the Brighton, Culver, West End, and Sea Beach lines in Brooklyn, which progressed from steam excursion railroads, to "light rail" and mixed "light rail" and rapid transit service, to full rapid transit service between 1890 and 1915.

Exhibit 1.5
Total Miles of Line of Grade-Separated Rail Transit in the United States, 1870-1980

RAPID TRANSIT: Length of line or first track, as of year end (miles)

		1880	1900	1920	1940	1960	1970	1975	1980	Under Constr.
New York	(1867)	32.2	64.6	216.1	277.0	265.0	265.4	258.9	258.0	+ 6.4
Chicago	(1892)		41.4	71.1	82.4	67.5	89.4	89.4	89.4	+ 7.6
Boston	(1901)			16.1	19.5	24.3	24.3	32.9	36.7	+ 3.2
Philadelphia	(1907)			7.0	24.9	26.5	37.4	38.6	38.6	
Cleveland *	(1955)					15.2	19.3	19.3	19.3	
San Francisco	(1972)							71.0	71.0	
Washington	(1976)								37.2	+27.0
Atlanta	(1979)								11.8	+11.6
Baltimore	(1983)									+ 8.5
Miami	(1984)									+20.5
Subtotal		**32.2**	**106.0**	**310.3**	**403.8**	**398.5**	**435.8**	**510.1**	**562.0**	**84.8**

LIGHT RAIL: Portions of line with fully grade-separated right-of-way, as of year end (miles)

		1880	1900	1920	1940	1960	1970	1975	1980	Under Constr.
Boston	(1897)		1.5	5.7	4.5	14.7	14.7	14.7	14.7	
Philadelphia	(1905)			18.0	18.5	16.1	16.1	16.1	16.1	
Cleveland	(1920)			4.5	6.0	3.5	3.5	3.5	3.5	
Rochester	(1927-56)				10.0					
Newark	(1935)				4.3	4.3	4.3	4.3	4.3	
San Francisco	(1980)								6.2	
Buffalo	(future 1.2 miles at grade, 6.4 miles total)									+ 5.2
San Diego	(1981) 15.9 miles has no fully grade-separated right-of-way									
TOTAL, grade separated **		**32.2**	**107.5**	**338.5**	**447.0**	**437.1**	**474.4**	**548.7**	**606.8**	**90.0**

* The Cleveland RT system shares 2.5 miles of line with Light Rail.

** In addition, there are 1.2 miles of grade-separated Light Rail in Fort Worth; reserved right-of-way Light Rail lines totalled 53.1 miles in 1980, and street-running lines, 100.5 miles; see Table H-3.

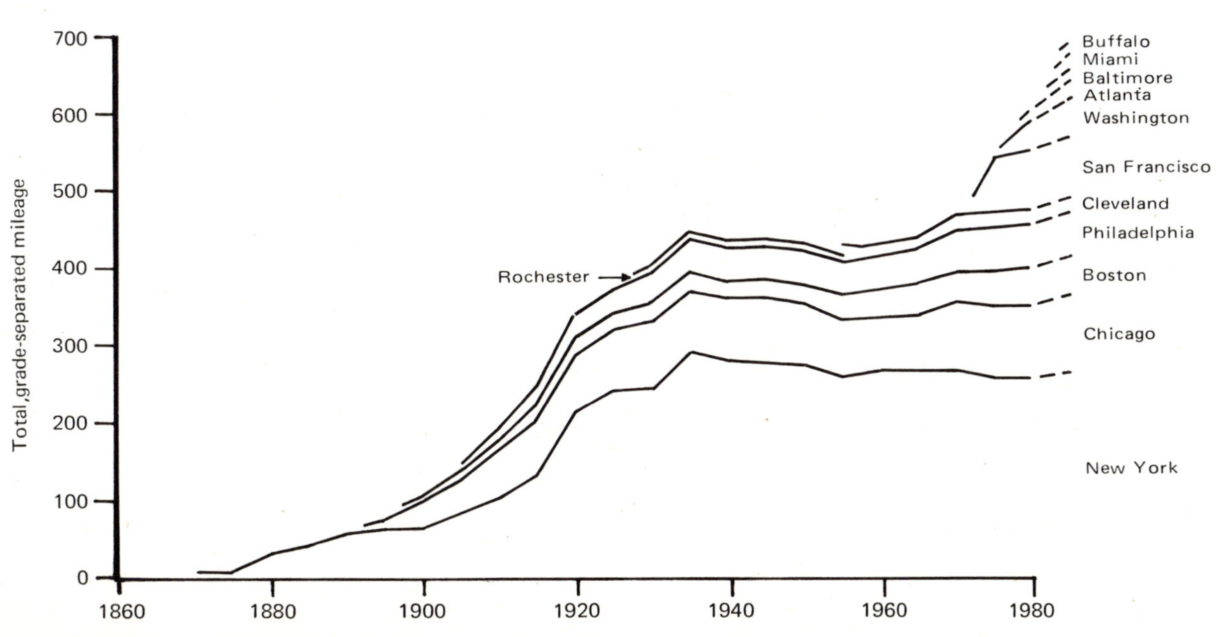

Exhibit 1.6
Miles of Line of Grade-Separated Rail Transit in the World, 1860-1980

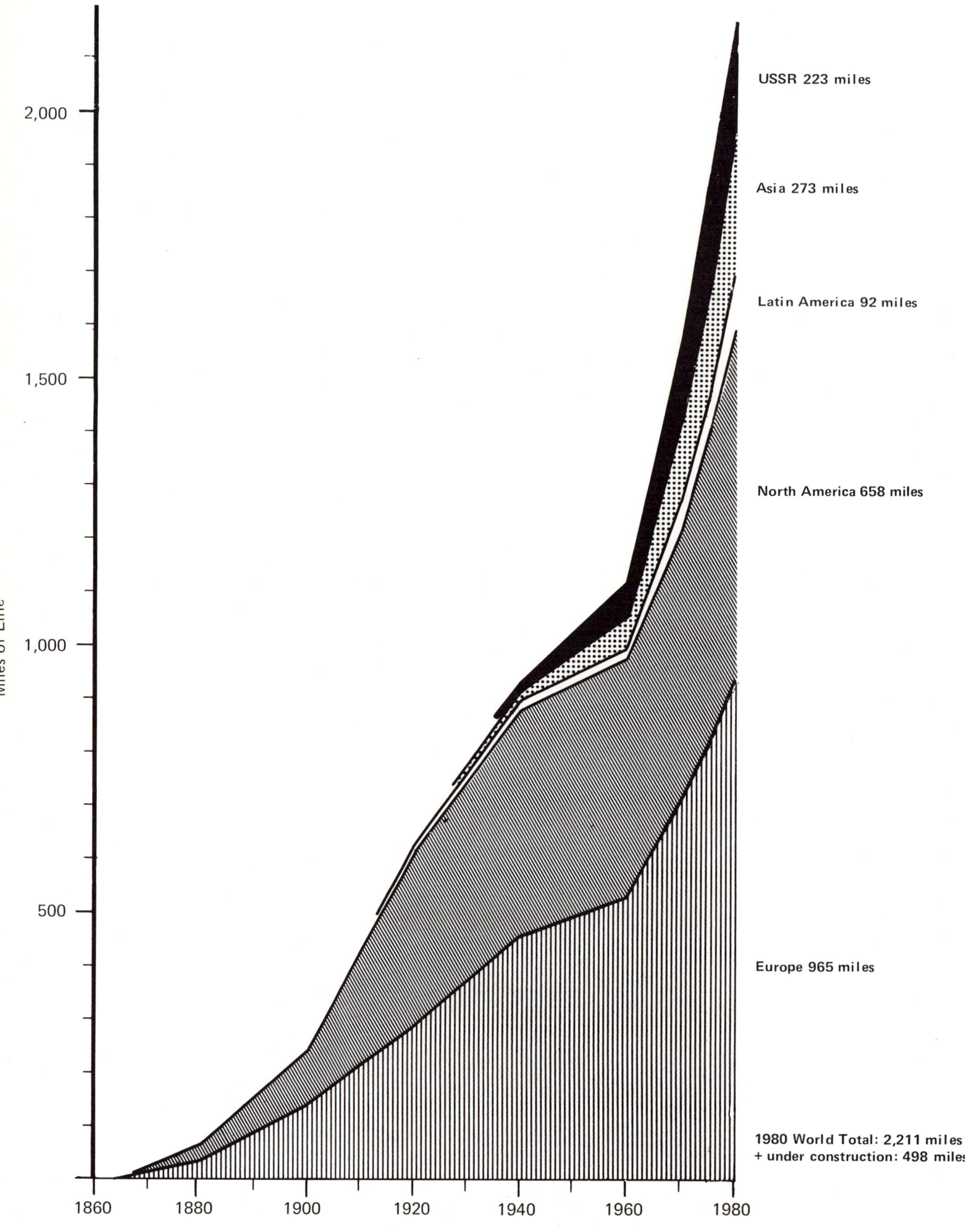

Source: Table A-2

1975 to 70 miles (113 km) in 1976–77. By 1980, an estimated 2,210 miles (3,557 km) of grade-separated rail transit were in existence in the world, compared to 1,120 miles (1,804 km) in 1960. This upswing is shown graphically in Exhibit 1.6, with detailed data in Table A-2.

To be sure, the worldwide resurgence after 1960 was in part due to new urbanization in Asia, Latin America, and the Soviet Union. Yet these parts of the world account for little more than one-fifth of mileage built from 1960 to 1980. A nearly equal amount was built in Canada and Western Europe. The United States accounts for less than one-sixth of the new construction.

In the developed countries, which are no longer experiencing the precipitous urbanization typical of Asia, Latin America, or the USSR, it was the difficulty of handling masses of automobiles in cities that gave the impetus to the new age of rail transit. Thus, 74 percent of the existing world rail rapid transit mileage is located in Europe and North America, which own 84 percent of the world's passenger automobiles. The growing share of rail transit in Asia and Latin America has been expanding pretty much in step with their growing share of private autos. Only the Soviet Union has expanded its share of the world's rapid transit faster than its share of automobiles.

RAIL TRANSIT USE IN THE UNITED STATES

The benefits that rail transit offers arise from its use by people. It is therefore appropriate to review the present use patterns or urban rail in the United States in the aggregate, compare them to those in other countries, and then focus on ridership on particular systems and lines. The historical transit use data displayed earlier in Exhibit 1.2—the only ones available for the long time span shown—have several shortcomings. They contain inconsistencies in accounting for transfer trips; they omit trips by commuter rail (usually listed in intercity railroad statistics); and they take no account of trip length.

The use of transportation systems is better measured in passenger-miles (or passenger-kilometers) of travel, i.e., the number of trips multiplied by their length. The average trip length in the United States in the late 1970s was 21.7 miles (34.9 km) by commuter rail, 6.9 miles (11.1 km) by rapid transit, 3.1 miles (5.0 km) by streetcar and light rail and an estimated 3.5 miles (5.6 km) by urban bus. This includes as separate trips those taken by separate modes, but excludes intramode transfers (e.g., a bus-to-bus transfer is counted as one bus trip).

Public transit travel in the United States in passenger-miles by mode, with a breakdown for the major urban regions, is shown for selected years in Exhibit 1.7. The bars show that *in 1971* (the year of a comprehensive national survey), *the rail modes accounted for more than half of all urban travel by public transit* (not counting taxicabs). Buses accounted for somewhat less than half. In later years, this relationship was reversed, mostly because job losses caused a sharp drop in rapid transit travel in New York City, as discussed earlier. Commuter rail ridership, oriented to higher-paying, more stable jobs, was level and then grew. Bus ridership grew nationwide due to service expansion and reduced fares.

Because of the allocation formula of the 1974 Mass Transportation Assistance Act, which favored cities with low transit use, the Federal contribution to operating

Exhibit 1.7
Urban Mass Transit Travel in the United States, 1971-1979

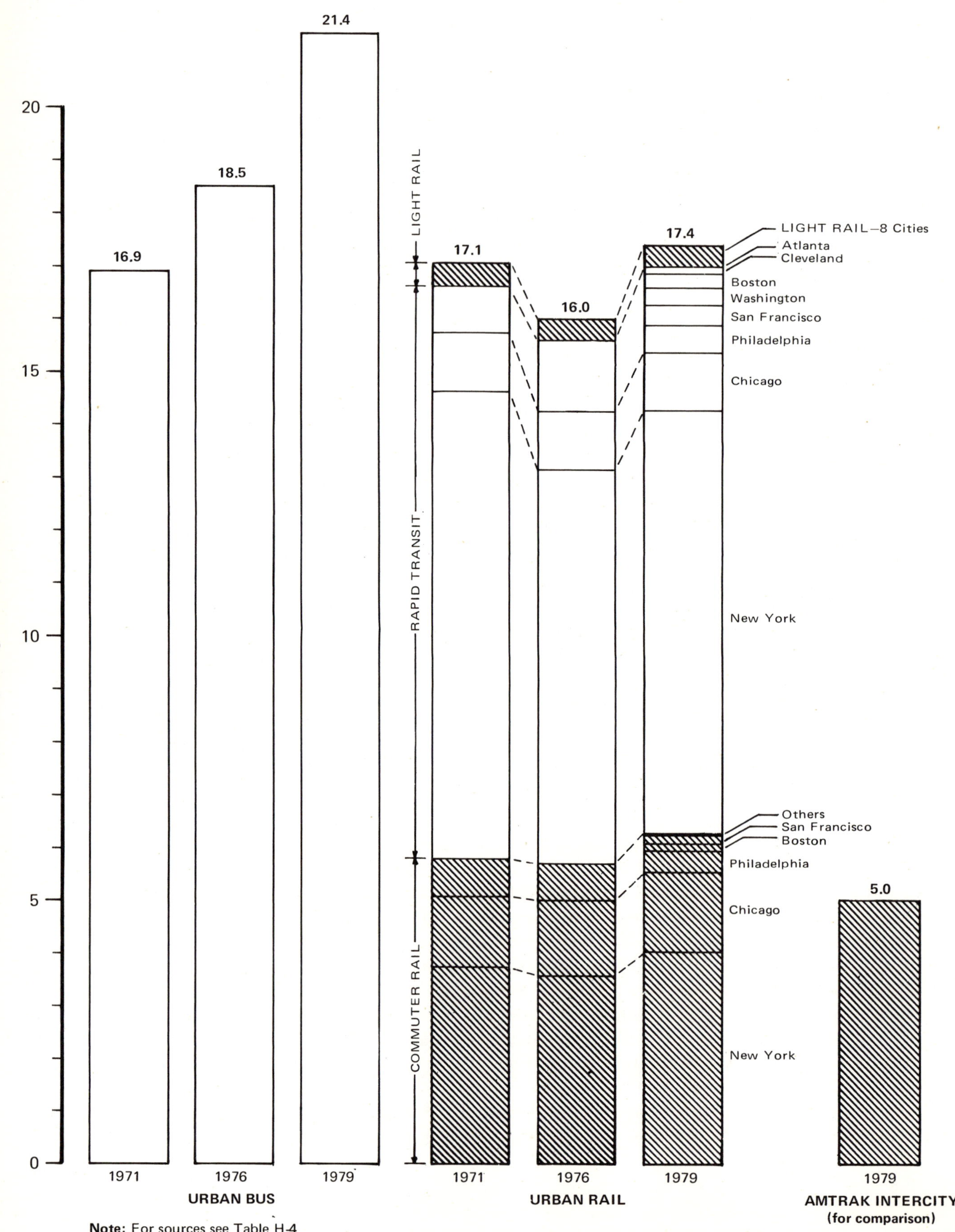

Note: For sources see Table H-4

subsidies for buses was about double that for urban rail. In 1976, the federal operating subsidy averaged about 1.7¢ per passenger-mile on urban buses compared to about 0.9¢ and 0.8¢ on rapid transit and commuter rail,[11] respectively (this is in contrast to Amtrak intercity rail riders, who received ten times more or 8.0¢ per passenger-mile). Of course, rail transit received the bulk of federal capital funds, but many of the funded projects are not yet in service.

In 1978, total urban rail travel increased for the first time in eight years as a result of an economic upswing in central cities, and in 1979 a further increase was registered in the wake of gasoline shortages, which had a more lasting effect than those of 1974. Oriented toward suburban auto territory, commuter railroads registered the largest increases among the fixed guideway modes, followed by rapid transit and streetcar lines: total urban rail travel in the United States returned to the 1971 level of some 17 billion passenger-miles (27 billion pkm) annually in 1979.

In 1971, prior to the opening of new systems, virtually all (99.5 percent) of the nations's travel by urban rail took place in six urban areas, namely New York-Northeastern New Jersey, Chicago, Philadelphia, San Francisco, Boston, and Cleveland. These traditional "rail regions" contained 40.7 million residents—one-quarter of the nation's urban population. In Exhibit 1.8, rail, bus, and auto travel per resident in 1971 is shown for the six "rail regions" and for 235 remaining urban areas, arranged into three groups by population size.[12] Several important messages emerge from the chart.

(1) *Urban rail travel is highly concentrated in time and space. In six "rail regions" in 1971, it accounted for 8 percent of all travel on an annual basis but for 22 percent of weekday peak hour travel.* In fact, peak hour rail travel in the six regions taken together is roughly the same as peak hour travel on freeways. The combined usage of freeways in the regions of New York, Chicago, Philadelphia, San Francisco, Boston, and Cleveland would have to double during the peak hour to carry the passenger-miles that rail does.

(2) *Urban rail travel generally does not displace bus travel: per capita passenger-miles of travel by bus in the six "rail regions" are the same or slightly higher than in other urban areas.* In other words, rail travel occurs predominantly at the expense of auto travel. This observation, apparent from cross-sectional data in Exhibit 1.8, tends to be supported by time-series data as well. The opening of BART added over 20 percent to the number of daily trips by mass transit in the San Francisco Bay Area between 1972 and 1975; yet, while some 44 percent of the BART patrons came from buses, total non-BART trips by mass transit (mostly by bus) also increased during this period.[13] Bus feeder trips to and from the new rail system and a general increase in transit orientation more than compensated for the bus trips replaced by rail. Similarly, the introduction of rail rapid transit in Washington in 1976 did not reduce the number of bus trips; they numbered 122.8 million in 1975, and 137.4 million in 1979, even as rail trips increased from nothing to 69.2 million. Before and after data on a passenger-mile basis are not available for San Francisco; in Washington bus passenger miles do seem to have dropped about 18 percent over the period. Still, for every two bus passenger-miles diverted to rail, roughly one passenger-mile was newly attracted to buses.

(3) *Total mass transit travel per resident in the "rail regions" is four to five times higher than in bus-only regions.* While this total is heavily weighted by New York, each of the rail regions taken separately displays an above-average level of

Exhibit 1.8

The Role of Rail in U.S. Cities, 1971

(Commuter Rail, Rapid Transit and Light Rail)

Per capita travel by all modes (height of bars)
Total volume of travel by all modes (area of bars)

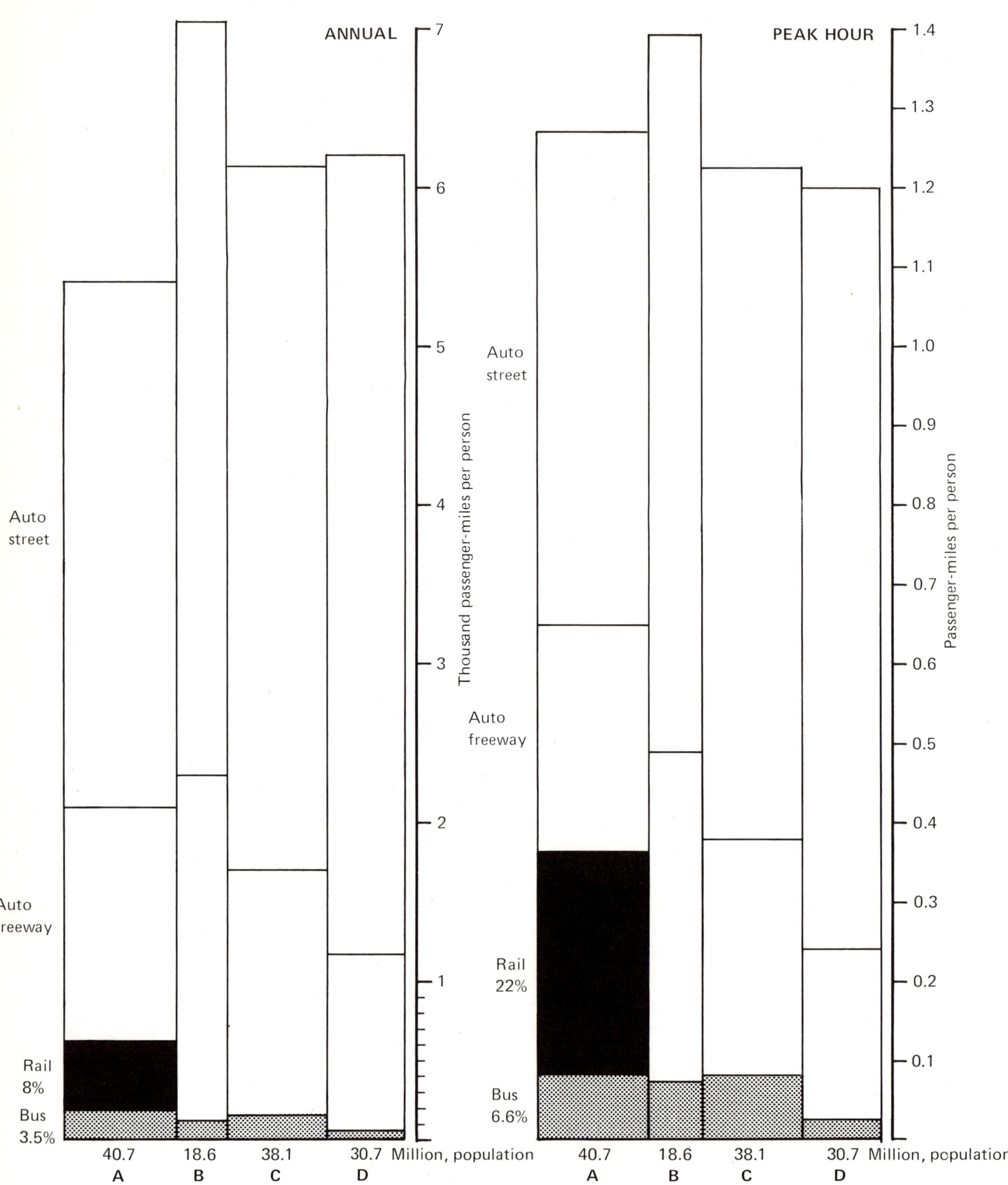

A — 6 Urban areas over 2 million with major rail systems
B — 4 Urban areas over 2 million without major rail systems
C — 42 Urban areas with 0.5 to 2 million
D — 189 Urban areas with 0.05 to 0.5 million

Source: Table A-3, based on U.S. DOT 1974 National Transportation Report.

public transit use, measured in trips or in passenger-miles. Even small rail systems, such as the one in Cleveland, provide an increment of transit travel that rises above the general level of bus use.

(4) *The reduction of auto travel in the six "rail regions" is much greater than that attributable to the direct replacement of auto travel by rail travel.* On the average, auto travel per capita in the six major urban areas with rail was 30 percent lower than in four urban areas of comparable population size that had no rail in the early 1970s. (The four were Los Angeles, Detroit, Washington, and St. Louis, and are represented by the second bar in Exhibit 1.8.) Auto travel per capita in "rail regions" was also 20 percent lower than in 42 urban areas with populations in the 0.5 to 2.0 million range served by bus (the third bar in Exhibit 1.8). Direct replacement of auto travel with rail travel would only suggest a 6 to 7 percent reduction in each case. The remainder can be attributed to lower auto ownership and less travel per auto in the "rail regions."

This below-average auto ownership and use is not related to income; in fact, the median income in the "rail regions" is slightly higher than in the regions without rail. Their freeway supply is also similar, with about 70 miles (some 110 km) of freeway per million residents in each of the two groups in 1972.

The principal reason for the suppression of both auto ownership and auto use is high density of development, especially in and near large downtowns, which are simultaneously made possible and stimulated by rail access. To a lesser degree, this effect can also be observed in Baltimore and Pittsburgh, which did not have major rail systems in the early 1970s, but which did, historically, develop above average densities in the core.

Density acts as a barrier to auto use by reducing speeds and increasing the costs of owning and operating an auto. In addition, auto ownership in urban cores is more sensitive to income than that in suburban areas, where auto ownership is more necessary even among low-income households.

Not only are fewer autos owned in higher-density areas, but those that are owned are driven less. A recent study suggests that autos owned by lower-income households in urban core areas are driven about 25 percent less than those in suburban and about 20 percent less than those in rural areas. Those owned by middle- and upper-income households are driven about 20 percent less in urban areas than in suburban ones, and 30 to 45 percent less in urban areas than in rural ones.[14]

Lastly, higher density is associated with more transit service. Auto ownership does respond, to some degree, to the level of bus service provided.[15] This effect is even more pronounced in the case of rail service. Auto ownership (adjusted for income and urban density) tends to be lower in the vicinity of rail stations (both rapid transit and commuter) than in surrounding territory, as shown subsequently in Exhibit 3.22. Therefore, the auto travel saved by rail is not just that actually shifted to rail, but also all the other travel that would have been made by the autos which would have been owned were it not for rail.

The overall reduction in auto use, associated directly and indirectly with the presence of rail on the nationwide scale, is portrayed in Exhibit 1.9. In addition to the direct diversion of the equivalent of 11.6 billion vehicle-miles (18.7 billion vkm) of auto travel to rail annually, the six rail regions effected an indirect saving of four times as much auto travel (47.1 billion vehicle-miles or 75.7 billion vkm) in the early 1970s. This is more than all the annual auto travel in the Los Angeles region.

Exhibit 1.9
The Effect of the "Rail Regions" on the Reduction of Auto Travel

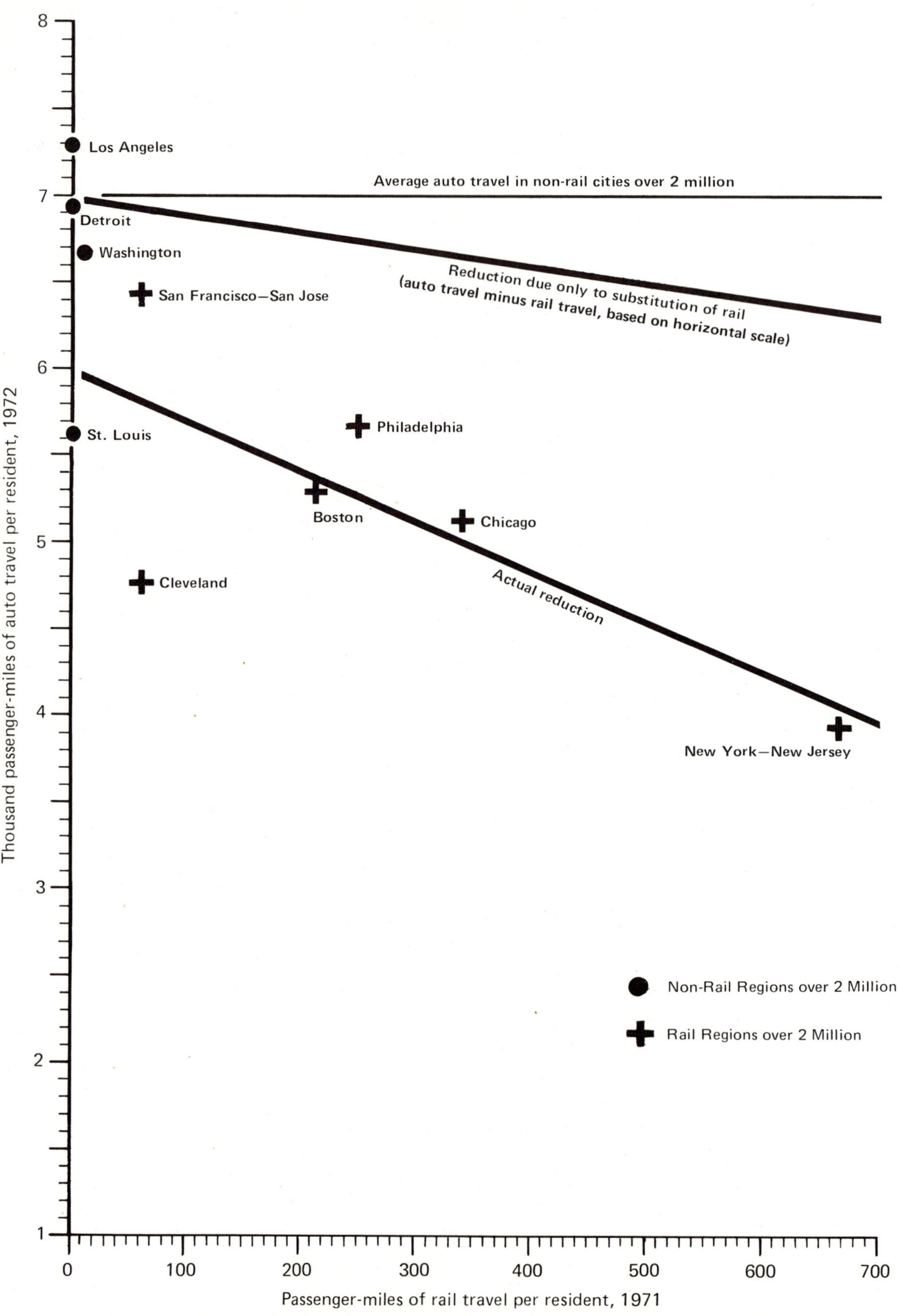

Source: 1974 U.S. DOT National Transportation Report Urban Data Supplement

Obviously, though, this synergistic effect of rail transit and compact land use cannot be expected to develop immediately after new rail systems are put in operation.

(5) *The nation's six major rail regions do represent travel-conserving environments. As a result of their reduced auto use, their total travel per resident is lower than in any other urban size group.* While the journey to work does tend to get shortened with smaller city size—typically associated with lower density—the saving in work travel in the smaller cities is negated by an increase in discretionary travel. This confirms a general rule—the lower the density of settlement, the more travel per person.

The surfeit of travel in low-density areas should not be equated with greater mobility. Equal amounts of mobility—defined as access to desired destinations—require considerably different amounts of travel in different settings. It is precisely the lack of desired destinations nearby that causes much of the extra travel in low-density areas. The low perceived cost of travel is another factor.

The exceptionally high volume of auto travel in the United States—a consequence and a cause of low-density settlement—makes the urban rail *share* of all nationwide travel low. Since urban mass transit travel by all modes is only about 4 percent as large as urban auto travel, and about 2 percent as large as total auto travel, the share of urban rail is 2 percent and 1 percent, respectively.

On a per capita basis, however, the United States is more comparable to other countries in urban rail transportation. Excluding commuter and light rail, for which world data are not readily available, the 10.3 billion passenger-miles (16.5 billion pkm) of rapid transit travel in the nation represented over one-sixth of the world total in 1975. Per capita of national population, passenger-miles traveled by rapid transit in the United States were below Japan, the Soviet Union, and Canada, but above the average level of 14 European nations with rapid transit.

Throughout the world, rapid transit is a highly specialized mode, serving strategic concentrations of population and economic activity. Its benefits, and those of other fixed guideway systems, must therefore be evaluated in the context of the immediate environments they serve. The "importance" of rail transit cannot be equated with its "share" of national travel.

PASSENGER LOADS ON SYSTEMS AND LINES

The patterns of rapid transit use in different parts of the world are portrayed in Exhibit 1.10. System extent is shown horizontally, and annual traffic density, or load per mile of line, vertically. The area of the rectangle represents the passenger-miles (or passenger-kilometers) carried by each system as of 1975.

In the newly urbanizing parts of the world, systems tend to be short, reflecting primarily a shortage of capital funds. Conversely, loads per line are very high. In the Soviet Union, with its extremely crowded urban conditions and low auto ownership, loads average 90 million passenger-miles of travel (PMT) per mile of line (90 million pkm/km) annually. Next comes Latin America, with short systems that are very heavily used (nearly 70 million PMT/mile or pkm/km), in part due to the additional midday siesta peak. Asia follows, represented mostly by Japan and South Korea (60 million PMT/mile or pkm/km). Heavy use of commuter rail for urban travel in Japan results in a short average trip by rapid transit: in Tokyo, as an exam-

Exhibit 1.10
World Rapid Transit Use by Urban Area, 1975
(Excludes Commuter Rail and Light Rail)

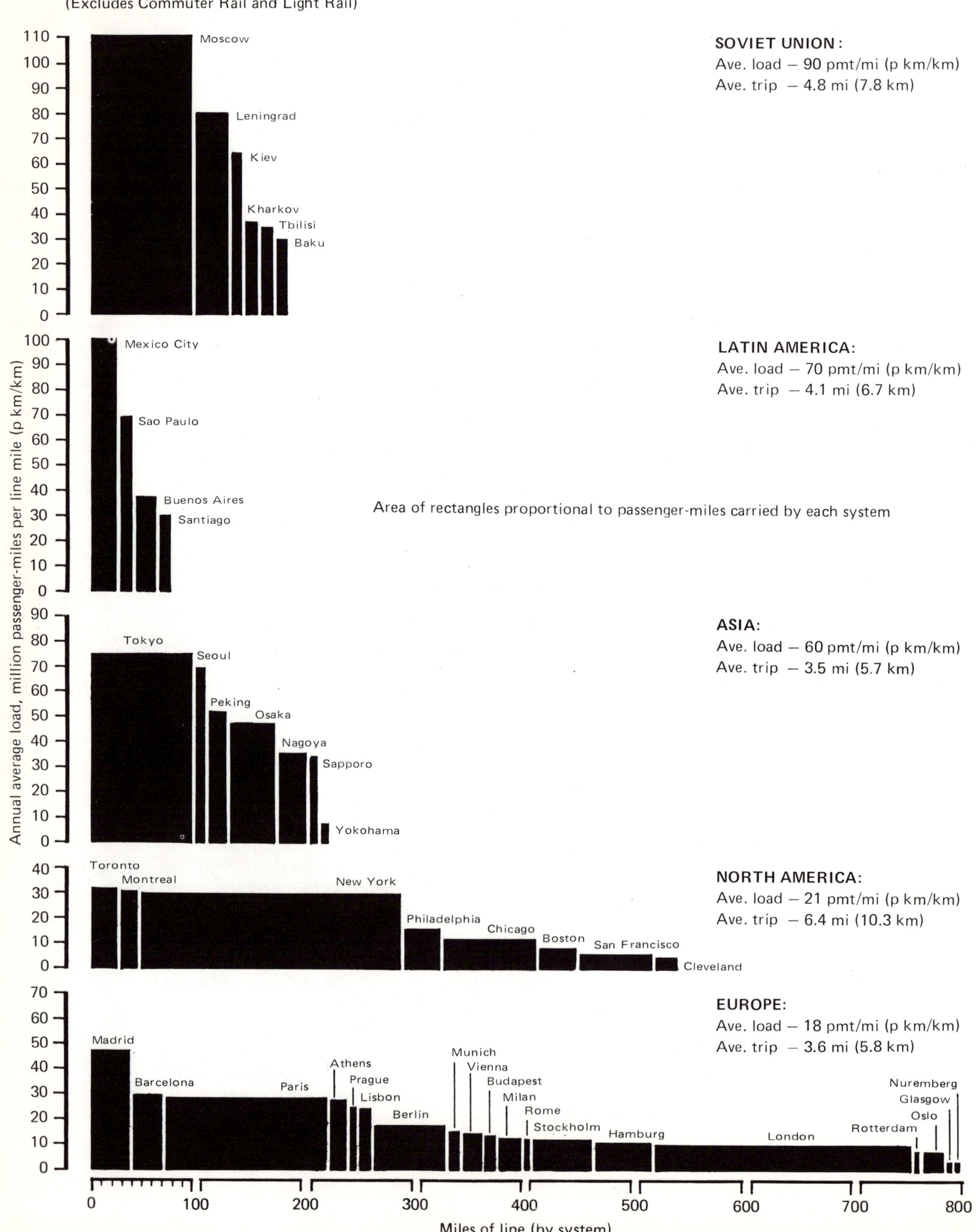

ple, two-thirds of the urban rail trips are carried by railroads and only one-third by rapid transit.

The pattern is different in countries with older urbanization. Their system extent corresponds more closely to the geographic extent of their urban areas. Other than London and Paris, the cities of Europe and Canada cover relatively small areas. Hence rapid transit systems are short—half the systems in Europe are shorter than 16 miles (about 26 km). The two Canadian systems averaged 20 miles (32 km) in 1975. This is reflected in a short average trip length—under 3.7 miles (6.0 km) in Europe and Canada. By contrast, the United States has more large cities, which, in addition, are spread out. Accordingly, even excluding New York, rapid transit networks averaged 50 miles (80 km) in extent, and carried trips that were twice as long as those in Canada and Europe.

The greater trip length in the United States compensates for fewer riders per line, so that on balance the load per line is 20 million PMT/mile (pkm/km), compared to 18 million in Europe. *Moderate loads per mile are not a uniquely American phenomenon: they are generally characteristic of affluent societies with older urbanization.* They make it possible to provide comfortable levels of service: annual volumes of more than about 25 to 35 million PMT/line mile tend to be indicative of peak hour overcrowding.

Individual cities follow the national patterns. Rapidly growing cities in countries with moderate incomes have extremely high average loads per line—in the range of 45 to 110 million PMT/line mile (pkm/km) annually. Foremost among them is Moscow, followed by Mexico City, Leningrad, Tokyo, Sao Paulo, Seoul, Kiev, Madrid, and Osaka. New York was also in that category—in 1930. By 1976, the New York Region was down from 53 to 30 million PMT/line mile (pkm/km), a level similar to that of Toronto, Montreal, Barcelona, and Paris. This is about the maximum attained today in countries with high incomes and older urbanization.

The great majority of European rapid transit systems, including both large networks such as those of London, Berlin, Hamburg, or Stockholm, and medium-sized ones such as Milan, Munich, Vienna, or Oslo, carry between 4 million and 18 million PMT/line mile (pkm/km). American systems serving Philadelphia, Chicago, Boston, San Francisco (BART), Washington (not shown in the 1975 chart), and Cleveland fall in the same range. Passenger volumes on rapid transit lines in the United States outside New York are low by world standards, but they are not low by the standards of the developed countries of Europe, where current auto ownership rates are comparable to those of the United States in the 1950s and 1960s.

Loads on light rail are plausibly lower than on rapid transit. The nationwide average for the surviving streetcar lines in the United States (half of which have a reserved or a grade-separated right-of-way) was 2.5 million PMT/mile (pkm/km) in 1976, which happened to be similar to the nationwide average for commuter rail. Comparable foreign light rail and commuter rail statistics are not readily available. The five automated peoplemovers in the United States, referred to earlier, averaged about 1.8 million PMT per mile of two-track equivalent guideway.

The average annual load per mile, discussed above, conceals peaking patterns (both weekly and daily) and the spatial distribution of travel among lines on a system. The weekday peak hour one-directional load at the maximum load point (which usually occurs at the edge of downtowns) is a more specific figure for planning purposes. In Exhibit 1.11, the one-directional peak hour loads are displayed for 62 tracks entering 13 North American downtowns in 1976–1980.

Exhibit 1.11
Weekday 8-9 A. M. Passenger Entries into North American Downtowns by Track, 1976

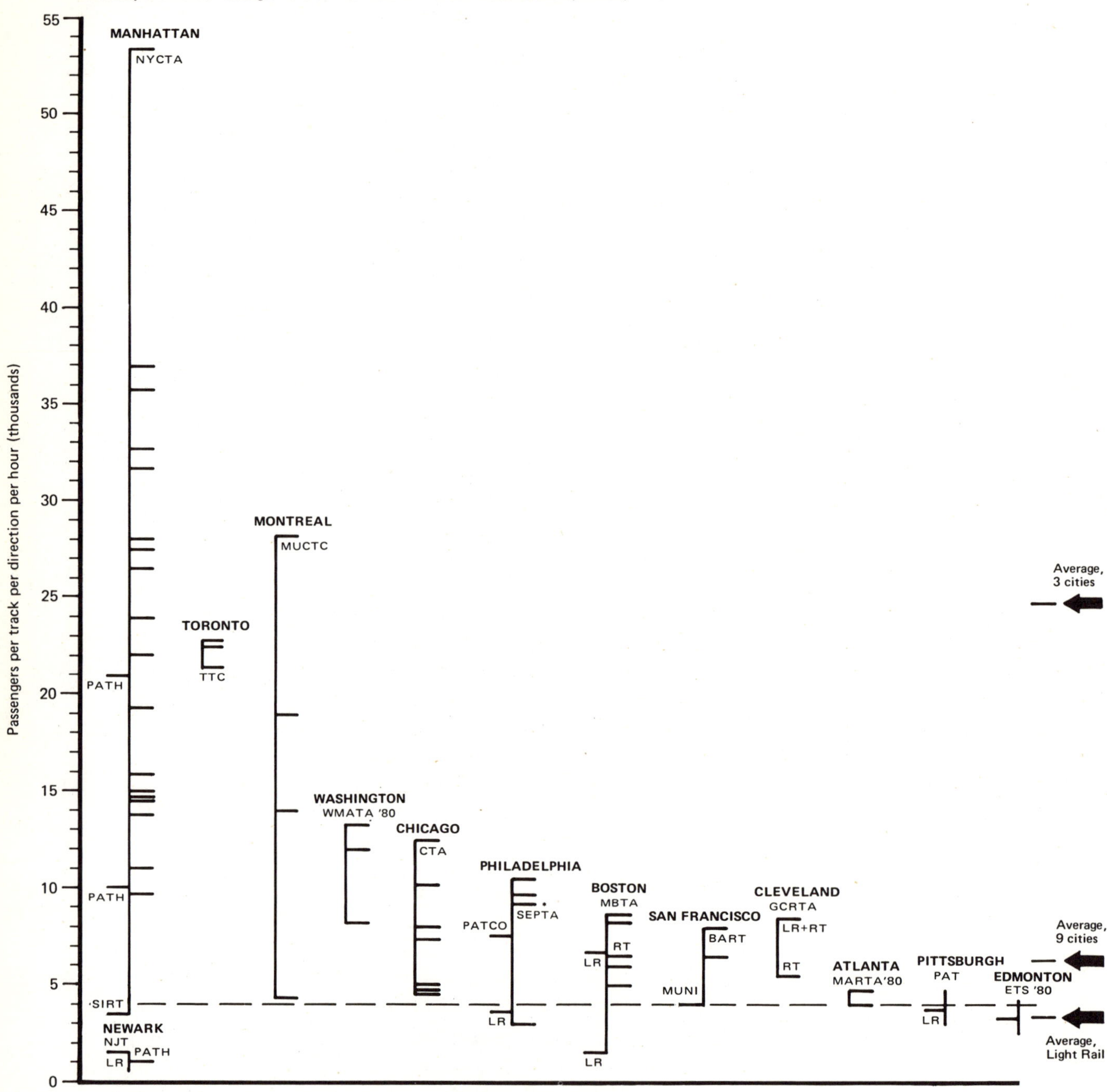

* 2 inbound tracks each, not shown separately.

Source: Table A-4

LR—Light Rail

RT—Rapid Transit

Not surprisingly, systems with high annual loads—New York, Toronto, and Montreal—also have high peak period volumes. The 28 rapid transit tracks entering these three downtowns in 1976 averaged 21,500 persons per track in the peak hour, in contrast to 6,500 per track on the 24 tracks entering the downtowns of Chicago, Philadelphia, Boston, San Francisco, and Newark. Three tracks into downtown Washington averaged an estimated 11,000 peak hour entrants in 1980. The six light rail tracks entering Philadelphia, Boston, San Francisco, Pittsburgh, and Newark on grade-separated facilities (or about to be relocated to grade-separated facilities) averaged 3,400 inbound passengers in the peak hour. This compares to roughly a 4,000 average on the rapid transit tracks into downtown Atlanta and over 2,000 on the Edmonton light rail track in 1980.

Rail advocates have not tired of pointing out that a single rapid transit track can carry over 40,000 passengers per direction per hour. Indeed, the one most heavily used track in New York, with 53,000 inbound peak hour passengers through the 53rd Street tunnel, does carry as many people as are carried to downtown Chicago by all its rapid transit tracks. Under conditions of extreme congestion, passenger flows may exceed 70,000 per track per peak hour per direction as in Moscow or Tokyo. Yet, in the United States outside New York, the maximum need, represented by Chicago and Washington, is for about 13,000 passengers per track per peak hour per direction.

The huge possible capacities of rapid transit have often created the impression that rapid transit is not justified unless capacities of this magnitude are in fact attained. Prior to the institution of short headways (intervals between trains) in 1980, BART was criticized for the allegedly low level of use on its Trans-Bay tube—8,000 passengers per track per peak hour per direction. This flow—respectable compared to other U.S. downtowns outside New York—fell far short of potential demand because of long headways necessitated by train control problems, and because of lack of service integration with buses. In 1981, the peak directional volume was 12,500 passengers per hour.

In fact, even downtown entry volumes of 4,000 to 6,000 passengers per track per peak hour are not trivial. Assuming stable flow conditions (1,700 automobiles per lane per hour) and an occupancy of 1.4 persons per auto in weekday rush hour traffic, one track carrying such passenger volumes does a job equivalent to two to three lanes of freeway.

The level of about 4,000 passengers per peak hour at downtown entry points is one at which tradeoffs between standard rapid transit and light rail occur, as seen in Exhibit 1.11. Volumes lower than 4,000 passengers per direction per peak hour at downtown entries, and down to 1,500, are (with four exceptions) carried by light rail. Heavier volumes (with three exceptions) are carried by rapid transit. Present levels of rail use are not necessarily a norm for the development of new systems. Yet, if planning is to remain realistic, these levels must be recognized.

IMPACT ON URBAN DEVELOPMENT

The travel volume on a rail line is, among other things, an indicator of the amount of access it provides, and hence of the amount of urban development it supports. The amount of development on any site, while affected by its topography

Exhibit 1.12
The Effect of Access on Urban Development

ILLUSTRATIVE DISTRIBUTIONS OF A POPULATION OF 1.5 MILLION OVER 121 SQUARE MILES OF LAND.

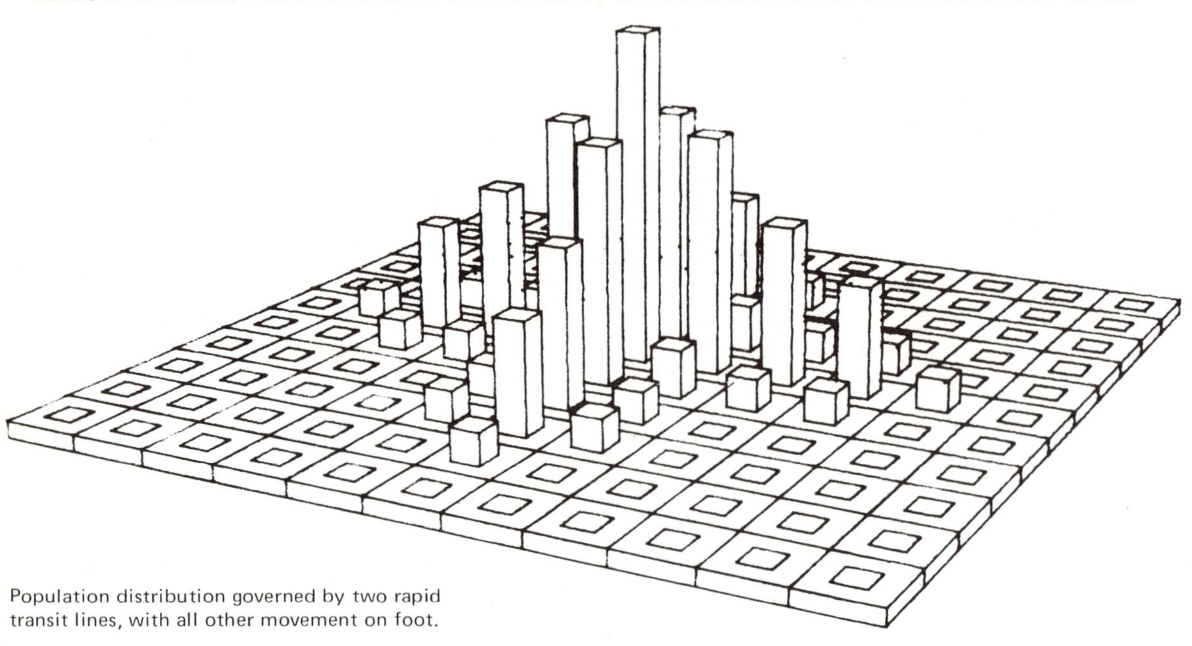

Population distribution governed by two rapid transit lines, with all other movement on foot.

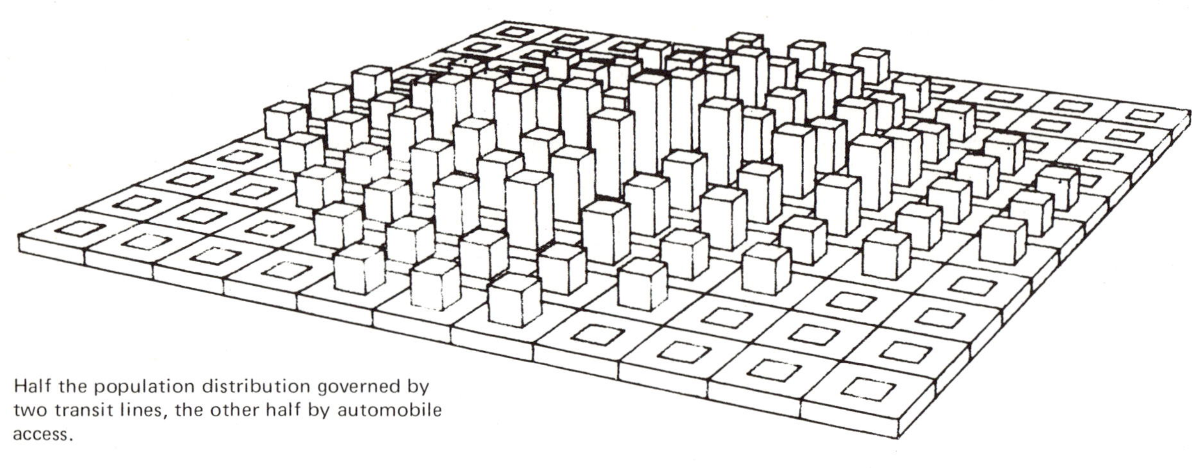

Half the population distribution governed by two transit lines, the other half by automobile access.

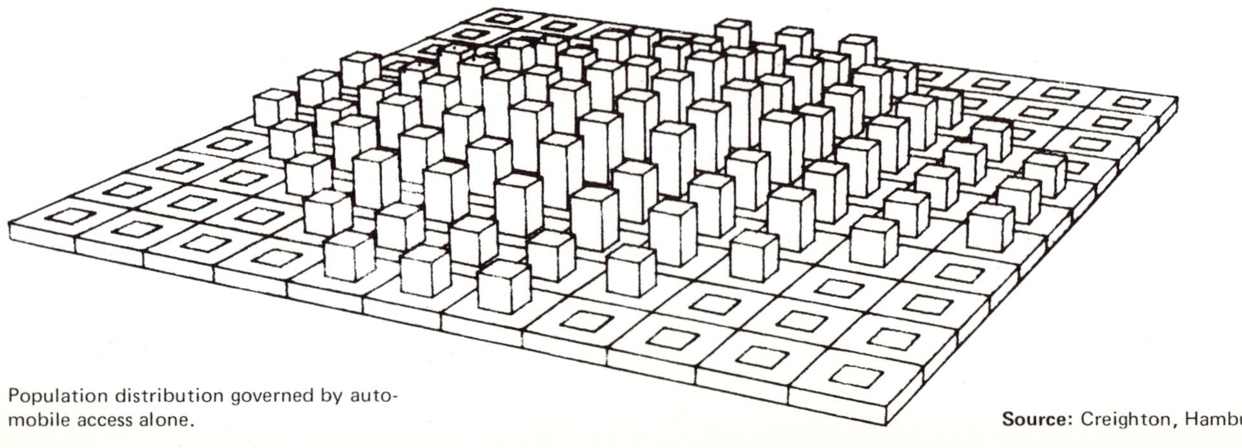

Population distribution governed by automobile access alone.

Source: Creighton, Hamburg Inc.

and other qualities, tends toward an equilibrium with the *accessibility* of the site.[16] Accessibility reflects the ease of reaching each of all the other sites in an urban area from the site in question, and the distribution of development among them. The ease of reaching them is measured by the time, money, and discomfort which movement along the transportation network requires, and by people's propensity to incur such expenditures for each increment of distance. At a greater level of detail, the question "accessibility to what" assumes importance. Thus, accessibility to blue-collar workers has little relevance for the location of an office building. Because they provide concentrated access, and because they can avoid detracting from the sites they serve, fixed guideways are logically suited to compact patterns of land development.

One must, however, bear in mind that the access advantage that any transportation improvement creates is a relative one, measured in comparison with surrounding sites. In the nineteenth century, when all sites were basically accessible on foot, those few that could be reached with much greater ease by streetcar had a significant access advantage indeed, and building floorspace naturally clustered there. When the automobile allowed travel with greater ease than the streetcar over a much wider area, a great many sites became about equally accessible, and the incentive for clustering was drastically diminished.

These theoretical considerations are illustrated in Exhibit 1.12, which shows computer drawings derived from a mathematical model of land use-travel mode relationships.[17] All three drawings show a hypothetical population of 1.5 million distributed over an area of 121 square miles. In the top drawing, the area is traversed at right angles by two rail lines which serve 13 square miles with one station each. They allow travel at 25 mph for a fare of 10¢. The remaining 108 square miles are only accessible on foot, at 3 mph and no cost in money. The extreme degree to which population would be clustered in the accessible square miles under these conditions is apparent.

In the middle drawing, a network of arterials is introduced which allows auto access to all square miles at 20 mph and 2¢ a mile. Half the population is permitted to distribute itself along the transit spines, the other half in auto territory. As a result, peak densities are greatly diminished. In the bottom drawing, only the auto network governs the population distribution. The density gradient becomes very flat, but some clustering toward the core, where the accessibility is still greater than on the periphery, is retained. This would only disappear if speeds on the arterial grid were increased to some unrealistic level—say 100 mph—so that no square mile would have any access advantage over another.

The drawings approximate actual stages in the history of large cities. It has been shown that central city densities reflect the mode of intraurban travel prevailing at the time they were built.[18] Big walk-only cities required very high densities; these were lowered when streetcars opened large land areas for development.[19] In the period from 1920 to 1970, "secular increases in automobile ownership have had an enormous impact on land use patterns. Together with increases in the urban highway system, higher levels of automobile ownership have resulted in substantial reductions in the density of incremental development. Bus and rail systems have played a much smaller role." Nevertheless, "a greater rail system has indeed encouraged higher residential densities, and some calculations suggest that rail has had a substantial impact. How bus systems affect densities is more problematical. Increased bus networks might have encouraged lower density rather than higher."[20]

Today, the question is, what happens if a new mode, such as a modern rapid transit line, or a downtown peoplemover, is introduced into a basically auto-dominant setting? Here, too, theory suggests some answers. "If a new mode is added to the system, it will attract trips from its neighboring modes but will also increase the total trips generated. However, the closer it is in speed and cost to some other mode, the less the increment of trip generation."[21] In other words, induced trips are created in proportion to the relative advantage that the new mode holds over competing modes. To the extent that induced trips are created, the access potential, and hence the development potential, of an entire region is increased. More importantly, of course, the intraregional pattern of access is reallocated with the shift from preexisting modes to the new one. Once again the magnitude of this shift depends on the magnitude of the *relative* advantage the mode offers in terms of time, cost, and comfort.

Empirical studies of these relationships are hindered by the difficulty of fine-tuning the measures of accessibility, and by the difficulty of isolating the effect of transportation improvements from numerous other factors that influence change in urban development. Studies of the impact of belt freeways indicate that shifts in accessibility which these facilities caused did result in a faster population shift to the suburbs, greater declines in downtown retail sales, and faster growth of peripheral shopping centers than was the case in cities without them. These studies also suggest, though not conclusively, that the total growth rate in the regions with the added access was higher.[22]

Nevertheless, there is a widespread perception that additions to the transportation system within a region have no measurable effect on its aggregate economic activity. This divergence between theory and empirical findings is probably due to the fact that the increases in total regional accessibility resulting from intraregional transportation improvements are, in the aggregate, quite small. If one assumes that the increase in total accessibility is proportional to induced traffic, then the case of BART is instructive. In 1974, 15.5 percent of its riders responded that they "did not make the trip before" and could thus be considered induced. Since BART carries about 2 percent of all regional trips, the induced component adds at most 0.3 percent to total trips in the region and, by inference, to regional accessibility. Still, such an increment can be significant if it is narrowed to a particular market segment (i.e., trips to educational institutions, office buildings, or restaurants), or confined to a specific place, such as downtown. For example, an increase in economic activity in the Atlanta region as a whole after its rapid transit system opened may be hard to trace statistically, but particular headquarter relocations into its downtown from other cities (such as Georgia-Pacific) can still be a tangible result of the new access.

In sum, while total regional accessibility may be modestly enhanced, the main effect of a new fixed guideway is to reallocate existing accessibility, thereby altering the spatial distribution of urban property values and of new development. This effect, too, is only a product of transportation-related advantages, such as savings in time, money, and discomfort. It is the localized travel advantages in comparison with preexisting modes, perceived as savings by travelers, that tend to be capitalized (probably not fully, but with some consumer surplus remaining) in increased property values in the affected area. Such property value increases are not an extra benefit of transit, as is sometimes supposed, and may be accompanied by relative property value declines elsewhere. They are, however, an index of how much the transit improvement is worth in the marketplace. Moreover, the resulting intensification of land use can lead to second-order benefits, such as reduced expenditures for streets, sewers, water lines, electricity, gas and telephone connections, and related savings in government expenses in other parts of an urban area.

Empirical studies of the impact of transportation improvements on land value vary widely in quality. One of the more rigorous studies (which contains an analysis of the voluminous literature)[23] indicates that land values in Washington do indeed rise with proximity to Metrorail stations, and are also influenced by the opening date of stations. However, factors unrelated to rail transit—those having to do with population composition and the character of the sites—have a much larger impact on property values than transit access. Several studies of the Lindenwold line show a substantial increase in property values—up to a $3,000 difference in sales price per single family house for each dollar of travel savings per day.[24]

Increased land values are reflected in intensified development. At the suburban end of the line, intensified residential development has been documented on the Lindenwold line and on the South Shore extension in Boston.[25] The effect of BART on residential development has been much more limited. To what extent suburban rail extensions may reallocate residential development *away* from central cities is a question that has not been answered conclusively. Offsetting forces are at work which may make this effect negligible.[26]

The most pronounced impact of new rapid transit lines could be expected in downtown areas, where the improvement in access is concentrated, and amplified by nonlinear agglomeration effects. In Toronto, the increment of growth along the original Yonge Street subway, compared to growth in the rest of the city, was enough to produce more than $5 million in annual property taxes, compared to about $4 million in annual carrying charges for the bonds issued for construction. In Washington, ongoing or committed private development in various ways related to Metrorail has been put at about $3 billion since 1976.[27] Figures of this nature abound, but it is virtually impossible to prove to what degree such development is in fact related to the transit improvement, how much of it would have occurred anyway, and how much of it would have occurred elsewhere.

Recent growth in downtown office floorspace in twenty-five major American cities is shown in Exhibit 1.13, and related to the presence of rapid transit. Despite the heavy concentration of office growth in Southern and Western cities in general, the nine cities with rapid transit in existence or under construction in 1975 do average roughly a 17 percent greater per capita increment of downtown office floorspace than the remaining cities.[28] Excluding Newark, N.J., from among the rail cities raises the difference to 30 percent. Among the twelve fastest-growing downtowns, half had rapid transit in existence or under construction. Undoubtedly, the relationship is circular to some extent; downtown office growth can encourage rapid transit construction (as in Washington and Atlanta) as much as the presence of rapid transit may encourage office growth (as in Boston, New York, Chicago, and San Francisco). Also, in the absence of badly needed regionwide floorspace inventories it is impossible to tell whether the growth shown in Exhibit 1.13 was focused on the downtown, or whether it was merely a reflection of regionwide office expansion.

An overview of fixed guideway land use impacts has shown that they vary widely from city to city depending on a variety of supporting factors.[29] Principally, there must be exogenous demand for development: if no new construction takes

Exhibit 1.13

1970-75 Increase in Downtown Office Floorspace, Square Feet Per Capita of 1972 Urbanized Area Population

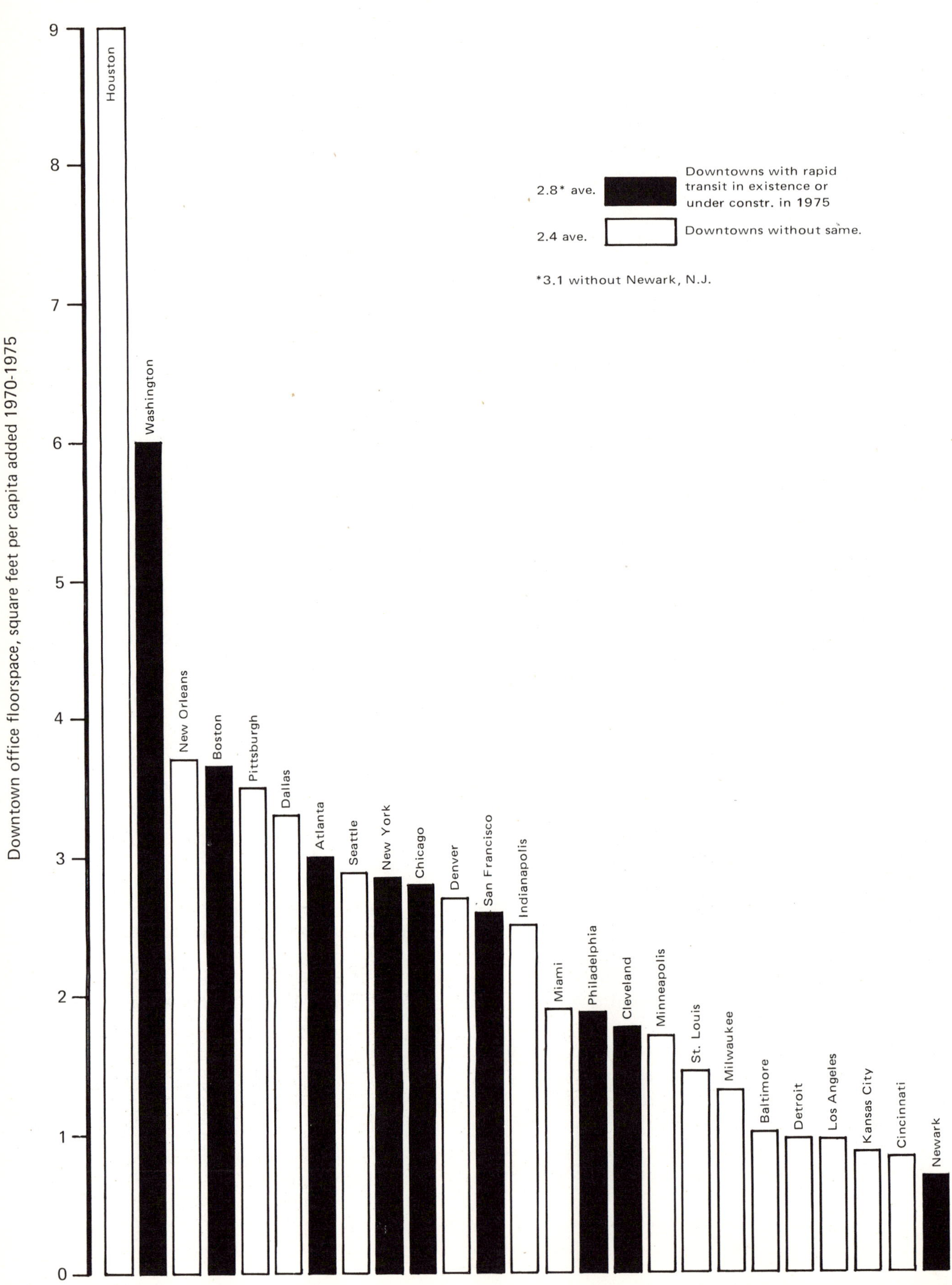

place, changed accessibility cannot redistribute building floorspace. Furthermore, there must be favorable conditions in the market for land—the sites that are made more accessible must possess additional qualities which make them attractive to developers, including ease of assembly and favorable neighborhood conditions. Lastly, public policies must be favorable to development, rather than frustrating it through rezoning for lower densities, as has occurred around several BART stations.

Overall, the land use impacts of fixed guideway investment cannot be viewed as deterministic in the same way as time savings, which definitely will occur if fast service is provided. They will occur to a greater or lesser degree, depending on the overall economic climate and on supporting public action.

Because the access advantage alone that a new rapid transit line offers in an auto-dominant setting is often insufficient to trigger large-scale changes in land use, attention has increasingly focused on the concept of *joint development*, which involves a deliberate effort to place large-scale projects adjacent to transit facilities. Close public-private coordination of financing, design, and construction may be further aided by deals related to such things as air rights, zoning incentives, land assembly, provision of added public facilities, lease agreements, and shared responsibilities for operation.[30] Generally, even in urban areas with a slow rate of growth there is some demand for high-rise condominiums, retail malls, office buildings, and other high-intensity forms of land use. If left to locate randomly at the fringes of an urban area, their city-building, transit-supporting, and resource-conserving potential is dissipated. "Joint development" seeks to provide incentives for location, so that their synergistic relationship with high-capacity public transit is reestablished.

Because of the huge passenger-carrying capacity of rapid transit, the potential development a line can support is very large. For example, it has been shown that *one peak hour subway train* can serve up to 1 million square feet (93,000m^2) of office floorspace at the downtown end, and the equivalent of 4,000 to 6,000 housing units at the residential end.[31] Conversely, the clustering of development can have a strong impact on transit patronage. Merely clustering, say, 2,000 apartments within walking distance of a rapid transit station at a moderate distance from a moderate size downtown and at an existing density of 15 dwellings per acre, instead of spreading them evenly across a square mile, can add nearly a carload of riders a day to the transit system.[32] As automobile access is restrained by fuel availability, and as more effective land use management tools come into use, one can expect that opportunities such as these will be increasingly utilized. Also, as new perceptions about the effects of energy costs arise in the real estate community, they will increasingly be reflected in development.[33]

OBJECTIVES OF BUILDING NEW LINES

Rail originated as a substitute for pavement. Urban rail systems proliferated because they eased the switch from animal to mechanical traction at a time when easily portable sources of power were lacking, and because they permitted train operation. Fixed guideway transit survived and is growing again primarily to the extent that it is grade-separated and thus avoids surface traffic. These lessons from the past help put in perspective the reasons for building new lines.

In a world with millions of miles of smooth pavement, the fourfold advantage in tractive resistance that rail offers compared to good pavement is a relatively minor consideration in passenger transport.* Vehicle weight per passenger place is much more important for energy use, and in this respect downsized automobiles are getting closer to fixed guideway vehicles: a "mini-compact" Honda Civic weighs about as much per passenger place as the BART car (some 185 kg); a "subcompact" VW Rabbit as much as some of the automated peoplemover vehicles (210 kg) and a Dodge Omni as much as the DuWag light rail vehicle (245 kg). An old urban bus is still the lightest (150 kg per place); new buses are heavier.

Rising costs of easily portable petroleum fuels may make some forms of fixed or semi-fixed guideways (such as trolleybus wires) more attractive again on heavily used routes, where the density of vehicles per mile of route is such that the sum of the savings on each vehicle outweighs the higher per-mile cost of the route. However, new forms of portable power (such as flywheels and stored hydrogen) are under development and may enter the picture.

Compared to free-wheeled vehicles, fixed guideways are distinguished by a simplicity of guidance that makes it easy to operate multivehicle trains and thereby to achieve very high passenger capacity economically. However, in the "post-industrial" urban setting the demand for high-volume facilities is limited; moderate volumes can be served by single vehicles, especially large ones, such as the articulated or the double deck bus.

This leaves grade separation—or "limited-access transit," by analogy with limited access highways—a major reason for fixed guideway construction. A separate right-of-way, necessary for reliable high-speed service, is the key to transit performance in competition with the automobile. Such a right-of-way is also the major item of capital cost, regardless of whether rail cars, buses, or automated cabins operate on it. In practice, the decision often swings toward rail cars in preference to buses simply if there is a community requirement for downtown operation in tunnels. Bus tunnels require costly ventilation facilities, larger station areas for the same capacity, and cannot adequately control noise.

In theory, the choice among different types of hardware is more complex, involving a variety of tradeoffs with respect to cost and quality of service. Such a comparative evaluation can be carried out only in a site-specific setting. The questions to be answered here are more general: if fully or partially grade-separated rail facilities are to be provided, where do they make sense? Where do they fulfill their avowed objectives in comparison with preexisting conditions? To what degree do they fulfill their objectives in different settings? Answering these questions will delineate a domain in which fixed guideways are worthy of consideration as an element in the total transportation picture, without specifying what combination of modes is "best."

Overall, *the objective of fixed guideways is to improve the movement of people in tightly settled urban areas, and to do so in an environmentally and esthetically attractive manner. This includes providing better quality of access by public transportation to support existing downtown activities and offering greater public transportation capacity to enable future downtown growth.*

*The tractive resistance of steel wheels on steel rails is about 2.5 kg/ton compared to 10 kg/ton for rubber wheels on concrete. This difference, however, is much more important for freight transport, where power to weight ratios are lower, and railroads operate with much lower acceleration and flatter grades than trucks.

More specifically, the objective is to attain a variety of *benefits*, some of which are directly transportation-related, while others are indirect, related to changes in land use. In an illustrative manner, the former are grouped in Exhibit 1.14 under the major headings of (1) increasing public transit ridership by reducing user costs, (2) providing travel benefits to nonusers, (3) reducing unit operating costs, (4) saving energy and improving the environment, and (5) enabling urban reconstruction. These are followed by a listing of objectives that may be fulfilled indirectly, as a result of urban reconstruction toward more compact form.

1. A primary transportation-related objective is to *increase public transit ridership by reducing user costs.* The users typically include (a) former users of transit, predominantly bus; (b) former users of autos and for-hire vehicles such as taxicabs; (c) induced riders. The former group benefits mostly from *reduced travel time* and *improved service.* For the second group, good service is essential to minimize losses in travel time but *reduced monetary costs* tend to be the major net benefits. These include out-of-pocket costs of operating and parking an automobile, of renting a car or hiring a cab, and reduced fixed costs of owning an auto insofar as auto ownership is reduced. The third group, the induced riders, did not find it worthwhile to make trips from their present origins to their destinations before the transportation improvement was made; following economic theory, the average benefit of the trip to them is assumed at half the value of the riders diverted from other modes.[34] In the long run, a fourth group may appear, riders generated by new development.

Free from the impediments of surface traffic, a reserved guideway can offer gains in *travel time, reliability* (reduced variation of travel time), and *ride quality.* By concentrating the travel stream, it can offer *greater off-peak service frequency* than is offered by an individual bus route. Off-peak service increases peak-period travel as well, by offering greater choice in the timing of return trips. These advantages tend to be such that people are willing to travel much longer distances to reach a rapid transit or commuter rail line than a bus line. Median walking distances to rail stations are typically two to three times longer than to bus stops, and trips by mechanical feeder modes are even longer, despite the fact that the negative value which people attach to access time is high.

There is some evidence that fixed guideways *attract more patronage than one would expect on the basis of time and money savings alone;* thus, on trans-Hudson trips in New Jersey, corridors with rail service divert a much larger share of total traffic from autos than corridors served by express buses alone.[35] Aside from ride quality and space per passenger, social acceptability, simplicity of orientation, and better connectivity among different parts of an urban area probably contribute to greater passenger attraction. The very image of a permanent physical presence seems to play a role: past market surveys distinguished "tangible" facilities, rail and trolley bus, from "intangible" facilities, which were assumed to inspire less patron confidence.

A high-quality, all-day service is able to *serve multiple markets*, in contrast to such single-market services as express buses or vanpools; this broadens mobility for the young, the old, and other transportation-disadvantaged. The high capacity of fixed guideways enables them to *handle surge loads* at sports stadiums and other special events with relative ease.

2. A secondary objective is to offer *transportation benefits to nonusers.* These are usually taken to mean reduced congestion costs to truckers and motorists re-

Exhibit 1.14
Illustrative Summary of Fixed Guideway Objectives

Measurable in $$	Difficult to measure in $$
I. Direct transportation-related objectives	
1. Increasing public transit ridership by reducing user costs	
a. Time savings to former transit users b. Time savings to former auto users c. Reduced out-of-pocket money costs to former auto users (mostly parking fees minus transit fare) d. Reduced cost of using taxis and other for-hire vehicles e. Reduced costs of auto ownership other than above due to fewer autos owned f. Savings to induced travellers (at ½ the value to diverted travellers)	g. Greater reliability h. Improved ride quality (less jerk and vibration) i. Improved space standards (if applicable) j. Permanent physical presence and improved orientation k. Ability to serve multiple markets, hence greater mobility for young, old, and other transportation disadvantaged l. Improved area-wide connectivity m. Reduced accidents and fatalities not included in insurance component of operating costs
2. Providing travel benefits to non-users	
a. Time savings to autos and trucks if congestion reduced b. Operating cost savings, ditto	c. Greater flexibility in choosing time and routing of trips d. Option value to non-users
3. Reducing unit operating costs of transit	
a. Labor savings compared to pre-existing services b. Other operating cost reductions	c. Improved utilization of intersecting bus lines
4. Saving energy and improving the environment	
a. Energy savings from direct replacement of auto trips (minus dissavings from replacement of bus trips, if any) b. Energy savings from overall reduction in travel and autos no longer owned	c. Shift to non-petroleum energy sources d. Reduced air pollution e. Reduced noise f. Reduced visual obstruction, if tunnel
5. Enabling urban reconstruction	
a. Reduced land requirements for transportation and parking (to the extent not covered under 1c) b. Increased accessibility in selected corridors	c. Reserve transportation capacity for future growth and auto disincentives d. Amenity benefits of urban design, pedestrian space and community improvements incidental to guideway
II. Indirect objectives of urban reconstruction	
1. Economic objectives	**2. Social equity objectives**
3. Resource conservation objectives	**4. Long-term fiscal objectives**
	5. Cultural objectives

maining on highways. In fact, such benefits are often obscured by pent-up highway demand, which tends to quickly fill the available highway capacity. The true magnitude of the nonuser benefits becomes apparent in a negative way, in the congestion that develops when a transit strike or some other breakdown interrupts rail service. In the normal course of events, the benefits that highway users realize appear not so much in the form of time savings as in the form of changes in the timing (more peak hour concentration) and in the routing of trips. In addition, a fixed guideway has an *option value* to nonusers, being present in case it is needed, such as during a fuel emergency.

3. Compared to a system using largely existing streets and freeways, a fixed guideway may offer several *operating advantages*. High speed allows the vehicle to produce more miles of service per hour, thus using labor and equipment more productively. Grade separation increases the reliability of service and makes automated operation possible. The larger tributary area makes it possible to trade coverage for greater density of service; the latter facilitates vehicle operation in trains, further reducing labor requirements. To the extent that intersecting bus lines become feeders to the guideway with its greater passenger attraction, their utilization may be improved. All of this tends to translate into lower unit operating costs for the transit agency; its total operating costs of course are likely to rise, simply because the combined rail-bus system will serve more passengers.

4. *Energy conservation and environmental objectives* can obviously be pursued in a variety of ways that are more direct than building fixed guideways. Smaller automobiles and restraints on auto use are the most salient examples. The point to be made here is that a shift in travel toward rapid transit or light rail can result in still further savings, whose magnitude will depend on how much auto travel is diverted and how much the fixed guideway is used. In particular, significant savings can result from autos no longer owned because of the presence of the fixed guideway. Besides, a shift in travel toward electrically propelled modes may shift energy consumption from petroleum to local sources.

With respect to the quality of the environment, electrically propelled systems attain the objectives of removing the source of pollution from the passenger, of eliminating odor, reducing noise and vibration, and permitting service in tunnels without costly ventilation. The extent to which total emissions into the environment are reduced depends on the magnitude of auto diversion to the fixed guideway, as well as on the energy sources used and the pollution control devices installed at electric power plants.

5. Last but not least, fixed guideway construction pursues a number of *urban design objectives*, notably reducing existing and prospective land requirements for transportation (such as urban freeways and downtown parking), protecting surrounding development from the negative effects of transportation by means of tunnels and other forms of grade separation, and offering the opportunity to build a variety of pedestrian-oriented urban spaces, including grade-separated passageways, sunken plazas, multi-level concourses, traffic-free squares, and malls. By providing a large margin of reserve capacity, fixed guideways are an *enabling investment* for future restraints on auto use and for urban reconstruction. The fact that the investment is not "flexible," but permanent, is part of the objective of obtaining long-term land use commitments.

As indicated earlier, urban reconstruction cannot be viewed as an automatic response to the provision of fixed guideway transit: it may or may not occur depending on a variety of exogenous forces. Still, its objectives are worth recalling briefly.

1. *Economic objectives.* Business can be drawn into the central cities with an expanded labor market opened by radial guideway lines, and the volume of transactions within the Central Business District can be increased by improved internal circulation; business productivity may be enhanced by encouraging economies of agglomeration.

2. *Social equity objectives.* The increased economic activity downtown, close to areas of concentrated underemployment, can provide additional job opportunities for the underprivileged; their number will depend on the skill composition of the new downtown employment. An active downtown with close ties to suburban areas will tend to relieve segregation by race, class, and age at least within the daytime activity environment, and possibly in some nearby residential areas as well. Increased center city activity may also encourage a pluralism of lifestyles, making the alternative to an auto-oriented way of life more attractive.

3. *Resource conservation objectives.* Compact urban environments can save energy in five ways: (a) by shifting more travel to public transportation and to movement on foot; (b) by reducing the total amount of travel; (c) by reducing energy requirements in buildings due to fewer exposed surfaces; (d) by shifting consumption patterns of residents from energy-intensive goods to less energy-intensive services; (e) by offering opportunities for more efficient methods of energy supply (cogeneration, district heating) and resource recovery. Other resource savings resulting from center city as opposed to fringe development include water, farmland, natural open space, as well as a variety of metals and other materials required to satisfy suburban consumption patterns, oriented toward durable goods.

4. *Fiscal objectives.* In the long run, savings to government and to public utilities may accrue as a result of increased central city activity, reflected in lower costs for social services in formerly blighted areas, reduced parking subsidies, and reduced costs for infrastructure elsewhere in an urban region.

5. *Cultural objectives.* Electronic aids and the value of seclusion notwithstanding, cultural activities strongly depend on face-to-face contact and continue to require the support of compact urban environments. To the extent that the consumption of physical resources is constrained, the consumption of basically unlimited cultural resources is bound to grow in importance.

In the reality of political life, the process of fixed guideway construction itself may be viewed as a major objective, since it infuses money and jobs into a local economy for a period. This, however, is not a benefit in the strict economic sense of the term if, without the project, the money would have been spent to create other jobs. Only insofar as otherwise unemployed resources are put to work is the true economic cost of the project lower than the contract price.

EVALUATING THE ATTAINMENT OF OBJECTIVES

To what degree a fixed guideway in a specific urban corridor can actually attain these objectives depends on a variety of factors. Thus the magnitude of time savings to users will depend on the speeds prevailing on existing streets and freeways, guideway layout, and local travel patterns. The attainment of labor economies will

Opportunities for urban reconstruction—indeed, for a new, three-dimensional order of urban pedestrian space—opened by subways are illustrated by these sunken plazas in San Francisco (above, Powell Street) and New York (below, Citicorp at 53rd Street).

be influenced by the ability to reach appropriate agreements with labor unions. The attainment of environmental objectives will be affected by the physical characteristics of the system itself (e.g., its noise abatement features), and of the power plant that feeds it (e.g., the degree of emission control). Dependability of the system will reflect the mechanical reliability of its rolling stock—a problem that unexpectedly surfaced in the space age. Provision of pedestrian amenities will be affected by agreements with abutting real estate developers and imaginative design, and the growth potential of a central city will depend on its role in the national economy.

One can think of *criteria for investment* in new lines related to each of these factors; for example, preference might be given to cities that have stable labor relations, choose reliable rolling stock, have clean power plants, firm land use controls that encourage concentrated development, no plans for freeway expansion, and a potential for economic growth. This would improve the likelihood that the various objectives are, in fact, attained; but this does not answer the question whether the investment is justified to begin with, whether it is in scale with local travel needs.

One might try to apply traditional benefit-cost analysis, assigning monetary values to each separate benefit item, as has in fact been done. Typically, the results have been erratic.[36] This is not surprising; Exhibit 1.14 reveals that half of the thirty benefit items listed are difficult to measure in dollars; monetary values assigned to them will of necessity be arbitrary. Moreover, even items that seem easily quantified are not that easily translated into money terms.

One example is the cost of time, the dominant component of any "user benefit" calculation. The monetary values people place on saving time vary over a broad range depending not only on trip purpose, time of day, the travel environment, and the income of the user, but also on the external yardsticks against which the value of time is measured, such as auto costs and transit fares. A fare increase will create the impression of an increase in the value of time that is almost (though not quite) as high. For simplicity of measurement, qualitative aspects of a trip are usually lumped in with its time savings; in reality, the time savings may not deserve the prominence they receive in "user benefit" calculations. More direct yardsticks, such as increases in ridership as a result of travel improvements, can be a better indicator of "user benefits."

Another example is accident costs. Basically, their monetary value is included in auto and transit operating costs, where it appears as liability insurance. Such insurance is a small item in the rapid transit operating budget (typically less than 2 percent, or 0.2¢ per passenger-mile in 1977 prices), but it looms large in the cost of owning and operating an auto in an urban area; per passenger-mile, the difference in accident cost measured this way is about tenfold. A similar advantage of both rapid transit and bus compared to the urban auto can be seen in *vehicle occupant fatalities* per billion passenger-miles: these numbered 0.7 for rapid transit and urban bus in 1975, compared to 6.4 for urban autos in the United States (the occupant fatality rate for autos on rural roads was 18.6). However, if one looks at *total fatalities* on a system—including pedestrians, bicyclists, motorcyclists as well as, in the case of rail transit, persons falling between cars, employees, trespassers, murder victims and probable suicides—the safety advantage of the transit modes shrinks. The total fatality rate becomes 5.3 for rapid transit and 5.7 for urban buses, compared to 12.6 for urban autos.[37] The fact that transit operates in a dense and complex human environment takes its toll. The difference is even less if only daytime fatalities are compared. Depending on the index one chooses one can argue that transit is twice as safe, or that it is ten times as safe as auto; "intermodal safety comparisons are surprisingly difficult to make."[38]

Attempting to develop any value such as the "full cost" of a mode or its "total benefit" can easily obscure, rather than illuminate, analysis because of the multiplicity of hidden assumptions that have to be made. Instead, the evaluation approach chosen here is first of all discrete, dealing with a few selected objectives one at a time. Second, the approach seeks to stay away from monetary measures as long as possible, focusing instead on physical quantities, such as space, time, labor, energy, and land. One can always attach to these quantities any desirable set of prices, if one wishes. Third, the approach concentrates on the easily measurable transportation-related objectives. This is not to deny the importance of land use impacts, which have been sufficiently emphasized. Rather, it is to recognize that these impacts are not easily predictable; when they do occur, they are related to improved *access*, meaning the provision of transportation-related benefits.

The one factor that is both an indicator of transportation-related benefits and reasonably predictable is *travel volume*. Whether a fixed guideway can in fact attain the enumerated objectives, and to what degree, depends in large measure on its travel volume. Because a major part of the costs of a fixed guideway is fixed, at low travel volume, its cost per unit of service tends to be high measured in labor, energy, land, capital, or passenger waiting time. As travel volume increases, all of these costs decrease. At some point, as volume rises, the unit costs of fixed guideway service become lower than those of the preexisting mix of free-wheeled vehicle modes. Those costs tend to rise with rising demand, mainly due to congestion. At that point, the fixed guideway mode starts fulfilling its objectives.

The task then is to portray the functions that relate each of the various resource costs of fixed guideway service to travel volume. Once that is done, one can pick any number of benchmarks along these functions as criteria or warrants. Based on this reasoning, five volume-related criteria for the deployment of fixed guideways are suggested:

1. *Possibility of attaining adequate passenger space and service frequency;*
2. *Possibility of attaining labor savings compared to bus operations;*
3. *Possibility of saving energy compared to modes previously used;*
4. *Possibility of attaining land savings compared to modes previously used;*
5. *Level of investment per unit of service provided.*

Because the first four ways of scaling the traffic volume at which construction of a fixed guideway may be justified are only partial reflections of the objectives illustrated in Exhibit 1.14, the fifth criterion is meant to be a more inclusive measure of cost-effectiveness. The issue of travel time savings—possibly overrated in the past, but still very important—is not dealt with directly. This is so because the simplified procedures used for estimating potential travel volumes at an aggregate level for numerous urban areas bypass the step of simulating travel networks along which travel times can be measured. The influence of differences in speed between the preexisting system and new lines on potential demand is treated exogenously in the concluding chapter. The decisive influence of speed on operating performance is highlighted earlier.

Lastly, one might reiterate that the basis for comparisons is the *status quo*. No

attempt is made to project future development, or changes in the availability of travel modes, such as may result from reduced supply of gasoline. Comparison of alternative systems is not attempted, except by way of illustration, or when one of the modes analyzed, such as light rail, may meet certain criteria in one city, whereas another one, such as rapid transit, may not. No comparisons are attempted where both meet the criteria.

Still, the methodology developed here is designed to be of use in comparative studies of alternatives at specific sites.[39] Such studies need cost-volume functions such as are provided here for rapid transit and light rail and, in a more sketchy manner, for automated peoplemovers. They need a common data base, and comparisons with the performance of existing systems, which this study provides. Other studies will have to develop comparable functions for other modes, such as commuter rail, express bus on grade separated guideway, or high-frequency bus service on existing streets and freeways, expedited by auto restraints. Only after such studies are done will one be able to say conclusively whether, for example, a bus-only system can be designed that will attain the same passenger attraction, the same reduction in auto ownership, and the same support for a downtown as a combined fixed guideway and bus system, but at a lower cost in the range of volumes that are suggested here for fixed guideway transit. All one can say at this point is that bus-only systems seem indicated for those cities where fixed guideway systems fail to meet the criteria developed here. Clearly, there is a band of cities where either approach is workable.[40] Neither delineating this band nor deciding which is preferable when both are workable is within the scope of this book.

With this background in mind, Chapter 2 is devoted to showing how the selected costs of waiting time, labor, energy, land, and capital vary with travel volume; it concludes by presenting a set of threshold criteria for each of these. In Chapter 3, potential travel volumes in urban corridors are estimated first as a function of total population, its density distribution, the geographic shape of the urban area, and downtown size. Then the share of corridor traffic that might be attracted to a fixed guideway is estimated. Lastly, Chapter 4 assigns the potential travel volumes to hypothetical routes, scales them against the criteria presented in Chapter 2, and concludes with a discussion of the overall potential for fixed guideways in 29 of the largest cities in the United States.

EXIT
L

2 Operating Performance

PASSENGER SPACE AND SERVICE FREQUENCY

A "desirable" range of passenger volumes on a fixed guideway has an upper and a lower limit based on service quality alone. Very high volumes may mean insufficient *space per passenger* and result in overcrowding. Very low volumes may mean insufficient *service frequency* and result in excessive waiting time. To develop volume-related criteria for new guideways, these service-related limits first need to be explored.

Passenger space standards are best defined by the type of behavior that a given amount of space allows. Unencumbered, reclining seating for every passenger—offered by two-and-two seats in a railroad car—requires about 11 square feet (1.0 m^2) per passenger including aisle space and non-passenger compartments. Justified for long trips, this amount of room is comparable to that of a large auto or a first-class seat in an airplane, but is more spacious than necessary for short urban transit trips.

For a tighter, but still comfortable, seat (such as three-and-two seating in a railroad car or a coach seat in an airplane) a net space of close to 5.0 square feet (0.46 m^2) is required. This is also the minimum that standees select voluntarily, for example when they wait in a group for a traffic light: they do not touch each other and circulation through the group is possible.[1] With typical vehicle designs shown in Table A-5, such net interior area represents about 5.4 square feet (0.5 m^2) of gross vehicle area measured by outside dimensions.

To visualize the level of comfort such a space standard allows, one may note that many transit vehicles, ranging from the small IRT cars to the large R-46 cars in New York and from the Edmonton light rail to the Dallas–Ft. Worth Airtrans peoplemover cars, give seats to about half the riders if filled at the rate of 5.4 square

(Photo credit: San Francisco Municipal Railway)

feet (0.5 m^2) of gross floor area per person. With tighter seat configurations, 65 to 80 percent can be seated.* On a transit bus with 49 seats, this amount of room allows 12 standees, a desirable comfort level for local trips.[2] *In all subsequent discussion, 5.4 square feet (0.5 m^2) of gross vehicle floor area is treated as a basic unit of comfortable capacity, a passenger "place," and vehicle output is measured in identical "place-miles"* (vehicle-miles multiplied by places per vehicle).

The lower limit of gross floor area necessary either for a seat or for standing with some freedom of action (such as the ability to read a newspaper) is around 3.75 square feet (0.35 m^2). Sitting passengers unavoidably touch each other and standing room is tight, but this standard has been used to calculate a "normal design load" by several agencies.[3] With sparse seating, about one-third, and with dense seating, up to half the passengers can be seated.

Pressed together with no ability to move, standees can occupy as little as 2.15 square feet (0.2 m^2) of gross vehicle floor area per person—the least amount of space that is occasionally accepted by North American passengers for a brief ride in an elevator where little internal circulation is necessary when stops are approached.** This is roughly the figure used by transit agencies to calculate "maximum practical" peak hour capacity or "crush" load. Encountered on overloaded systems from Moscow to Sao Paulo, and before 1960 in New York as well,[4] this has been characterized as "level of service F," a completely unacceptable degree of congestion.[5] Four service levels are suggested here: "ample" (1 m^2/passenger), "adequate" (0.5 m^2/passenger), "tolerable with difficulty" (0.35 m^2/passenger), and "totally intolerable" (0.2 m^2/passenger).

All of these values are averages and as such, are rarely encountered in real life. In reality, passenger volumes are unequally distributed within the peak hour (the peak 20-minute average is considerably higher than the peak hourly average), and passengers are unequally distributed among cars on a train (the middle cars tend to be more heavily loaded than the end cars). As a result, even a seemingly adequate standard of 5.4 sq. ft. (0.5 m^2) of gross floorspace per person on the average between 8:00A.M. and 9:00A.M. will offer substantially less room to some passengers during some part of the peak hour.

Empirically, more than half of the rail tracks entering North American downtowns do in fact meet this standard. Trains on 38 out of the 65 entryways did provide a space of more than 5.4 sq.ft. (0.5 m^2) per passenger between 8 and 9 A.M. in 1976–80. This is shown graphically in Exhibit 2.1, based on Table A-4. With one minor exception, every rapid transit or light rail track entering the downtowns of Chicago, Philadelphia, Washington, San Francisco, Newark, Atlanta, and Edmonton met this standard. In New York, however, only four of the 18 NYCTA tracks entering the Manhattan Central Business District conformed to this standard; of the two PATH tracks, one conformed while the other nearly did.

Of the 27 tracks which provided less than 5.4 square feet (0.5 m^2) per

*A single standard of gross floor area may not compare particular vehicles with dissimilar seating and non-passenger compartment arrangements accurately. In these cases, a separate analysis of interior sitting and standing space is called for. In the aggregate, however, the refinement is minor and is not used in this book due to the large variety of interior vehicle layouts.

**With passengers hanging over its sides, the San Francisco cable car is reputed to have occasionally attained space allocations as low as 1.6 sq. ft. (0.15 m^2) per passenger.

Exhibit 2.1
Space per Passenger Related to Peak Hour Flow

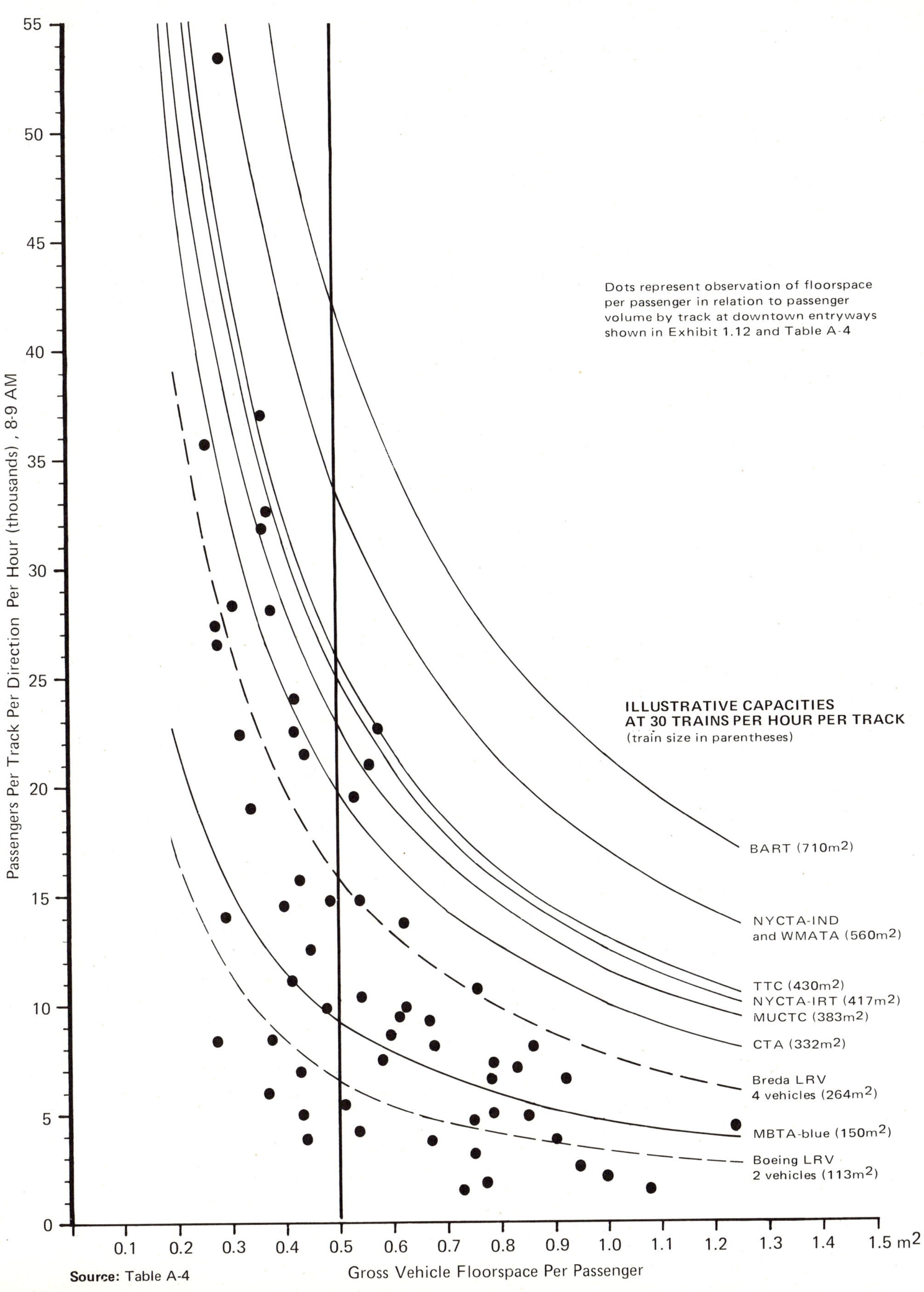

Source: Table A-4

passenger, 15 were in New York City; most of the remaining 12 were in Toronto, Montreal, and Boston, with Cleveland and Pittsburgh also represented. The "rock-bottom" standard of 3.75 square feet (0.35 m^2) was not met by 5 tracks in New York, 2 in Montreal, and 1 in Boston.

The lines experiencing crowding are distributed over the full range of passenger volumes; quite a few lightly traveled lines are nevertheless crowded. Only six tracks are incapable of providing 5.4 square feet (0.5 m^2) of gross vehicle floorspace per passenger with present-day loads even if maximum service were offered. In New York, these are the 53rd Street Queens IND, the Flushing line IRT, the Lexington Avenue IRT express and local, and the Broadway IRT express. In Montreal, it is the Rue Berri subway. Construction of the 63rd Street tunnel and of the defered Second Avenue subway in New York has been aimed at relieving the former five; in Montreal, what amounts to an additional north-south line is to be provided as a part of an expanded commuter rail network.

The low space allocations on the remaining 21 lines do not reflect physical limitations but rather a policy aimed merely at reducing operating costs. A more generous policy, practiced by the majority of the operators, if applied in New York, Montreal, Boston, and Cleveland, would result in 92 percent instead of 58 percent of the downtown rail corridors providing floorspace per passenger with or close to the 5.4 square foot (0.5 m^2) standard.

In sum, under current conditions, *most of the overcrowded lines in the United States and Canada can be relieved by offering more service on existing lines. Relieving overcrowding as a justification for new rail transit lines is principally applicable to construction that has at some point been committed in New York and Montreal.*

The physical capacity to carry passengers varies among transit lines. Frequently misunderstood, this subject requires elaboration. Once the policy determination of what passenger space to provide is made, capacity depends on three factors: (1) car width, (2) train (i.e., platform) length, and (3) minimum headway or interval between trains.

Rapid transit cars come in a bewildering array of dimensions (few systems outside the Soviet block have the same car), but they may be classified as either "narrow," meaning about 8 feet 10 inches or 2.5 to 2.8 m in width (such as the IRT and PATH in New York, the Market Street line in Philadelphia, as well as Montreal, Chicago, and Boston) or "wide" meaning about 10 feet or 3.05 to 3.2 m in width, (such as the IND and SIRT in New York, the Broad St. line and PATCO in Philadelphia, as well as Toronto, Cleveland, BART, Washington, and Atlanta).* Light rail vehicles in North America tend to be about the same as "narrow" rapid transit cars; peoplemover vehicles are still narrower, about 7 ft. (2.1 m).

The maximum length of the train into which the cars are coupled is set by the length of the station platforms. Dimensions range from about 230 feet (70 m) on one line in Boston to 700 feet (213 m) on BART. Still longer platforms are used by some commuter railroads, but such lengths become impractical for urban transit. How-

*The majority of foreign systems, including those of the USSR, have "narrow" cars; Madrid, some Berlin lines, and the original 1896 Budapest line have cars as narrow as 7.5 feet (2.3 m). "Wide" cars are to be found in Amsterdam, Munich, Oslo, the shallow lines in London, the Paris Regional System (RER), Rome, Seoul, Rio de Janeiro, and Sao Paulo, among others.

ever, on rapid transit lines with short platforms, the lengthening of platforms is an attractive option for increasing capacity. The maximum train lengths used on the different systems are listed in Table A-5, and the resulting typical floor areas of rapid transit trains are displayed in Exhibit 2.1.

Light rail cars are traditionally run singly or in trains up to three cars, as in Boston. For the Presidents' Conference Committee (PCC) cars (which also come in different sizes) this results in a maximum train area of some 1,323 square feet (123 m^2), slightly larger than the size shown in Exhibit 2.1 for a train of two new articulated light rail vehicles. If four somewhat larger vehicles are operated together, like the new ones in Cleveland, the light rail train floor area is about doubled.

Among currently used peoplemover vehicles, both the Dallas–Ft. Worth airport Airtrans car and Westinghouse (Seattle and Tampa airports) car have entraining capability, while the Boeing Morgantown vehicle runs singly; thus, peoplemover "train" size may vary from some 100 square feet (9.3 m^2) to 700 square feet (65 m^2) or more.

The curves in Exhibit 2.1 show how capacity varies with train size and space allocation per passenger. The headway is assumed to be two minutes in all cases, meaning the operation of 30 trains an hour. The intersection of the thin curves with the heavy vertical line denoting an allocation of 5.4 square feet (0.5 m^2) per person displays the rail track capacity for this comfort standard under the various assumptions of train size. Excluding BART (designed for more space per passenger) and the MBTA (limited to short trains until a platform-lengthening program is completed), the present *range of comfortable rapid transit capacity is from 20,000 to 34,000 persons per direction per hour on North American systems, if the 5.4 square foot (0.5 m^2)per passenger standard is used.* The *light rail* operation with articulated two-car trains shows *6,800 persons per direction per hour; this can be raised to 15,900 if trains of four somewhat larger cars are assumed.*

The high end of the rapid transit capacity range represents "wide" cars and long trains, as in Washington and on the New York IND-BMT. The low end represents "narrow" cars and medium-length trains, as in Chicago. Montreal and Toronto display intermediate combinations of car width and train length. Beyond the rather obvious point of physical train size, an important message of Exhibit 2.1 is the degree to which any "capacity" figure is subject to assumptions about comfort standards. *Reducing the space standard to 3.75 square feet (0.35 m^2) per passenger raises the range of rapid transit capacity to between 29,000 and 48,000 persons per direction per hour, and the capacity of the illustrative light rail lines to between 10,000 and 23,000.* Undesirable for day-to-day operation, capacities in this range are important for handling surge loads, such as during sports events, and emergencies. On the other hand, if 100 percent seating at the ample standard of 11 square feet (1.0 m^2) per person is assumed, even the BART capacity shrinks to 21,600 persons per direction per hour with a two-minute headway.

Maximum service frequency, treated as a constant so far, is itself an important variable, affecting both the quantity of vehicle floor area offered per hour and the passengers' waiting time. The maximum reliable service frequency (or the minimum headway) depends primarily on: (1) the type of *signaling* used to ensure safe stopping distances between trains, (2) the *complexity of the route* (whether there is merging with other routes), and (3) the *station delay* caused by passengers boarding and alighting. Insufficient door width on the cars or insufficient room on platforms and stairways can increase station delay and reduce the maximum service frequency.

On rapid transit lines with conventional block signals, 30 trains during the peak hour, or a 2-minute headway, is widely considered to be a limit of reliable performance. On the more heavily used lines of the New York subway, this was the typical peak period schedule until the service cutbacks of 1972–1977. However, the actual number of trains operated between 8:00 and 9:00A.M. on routes where trains merged often fell somewhat short of 30, even when up to 32 were scheduled. On the other hand, simple routes without merging, such as the Flushing line, have routinely operated 33 trains per peak hour for years.[6] Moscow, with a similarly simple layout, operates up to 40 trains an hour. The highest frequency in North America—38 trains in the peak hour—has been attained since 1967 on the PATH World Trade Center line, which feeds into a multitrack terminal.

On many streetcar-type routes, service frequencies are higher than on rapid transit: slow operating speed allows cars to follow each other closely with or without signal control. Thus, Pittsburgh ran 51, San Franscisco 68, and Philadelphia 73 individual streetcars per track per hour at downtown entry points as of 1976. Boston, which operated two- and three-car streetcar trains, ran 36 of them during the peak hour through the Central Subway, while Cleveland mixed 20 streetcar trains with 9 rapid transit trains on the same track.

In earlier years, high-frequency streetcar operations were common. The Newark subway operated 60 single cars per hour into downtown in the 1940s, and on Philadelphia's Market Street subway between 1956 and 1962 as many as 124 (one car every 29 seconds) were operated at a speed of 12.5 mph (20 km/m) with block signaling. In Pittsburgh, 23.5-second headways were attained by PCC cars in the 1940s. Such frequencies were predicated both on relatively low speed, which allows a short braking distance, and on single-car operation. Difficulties in loading second and third cars on a train make multicar operation at such frequencies impracticable. As new light rail systems are designed for train operation and for substantially faster speeds, their maximum service frequency is likely to drop closer to that of rapid transit. This issue is being faced by the San Francisco MUNI operation through the new Market Street tunnel, where 90-second minimum headways make it necessary to couple single cars into trains to maintain necessary capacity.

The technology of *automated "peoplemover"* systems is still under development, one of the goals being the attainment of very short, 3-second headways. Currently, the Morgantown vehicle can attain 15-second headways with off-line stations, i.e., with no passenger boarding delay, and Airtrans at the Dallas–Ft. Worth airport achieves 18-second headways. With these headways, reached during short periods of maximum demand, the theoretical *hourly capacity of* Morgantown could be *4,600 passenger places,* and that of Airtrans, with two-car trains, *11,880 places.*

Actual operating frequencies on most North American rapid transit lines fall far short of the attainable maxima either because of operating policy or because greater frequency is in fact unnecessary to attain a reasonable comfort standard. As Exhibit 2.2 shows, in 1976 only 5 rapid transit lines (3 in New York, 1 in Toronto, and 1 in Chicago) operated near or below a 2-minute headway during the peak hour (however, 5 out of 7 streetcar-type lines did so). For the rest of the lines, peak hour headways tended to be in the range between 2.5 and 7.5 minutes. Typically, headways greater than 4 minutes occur on rapid transit lines with passenger volumes below 10,000 persons per direction in the peak hour.

The service frequencies and passenger volumes portrayed in Exhibit 2.2 are recorded at downtown entry points. Because many of the lines branch before entering downtown, not all passengers can avail themselves of the frequency shown. In New York, many peak hour headways shown as being between 2.5 and 3.5 minutes are in the 5-to-7 minute range for those passengers who can only use one of two routes operated on a given track.

The curves in Exhibit 2.2, drawn analogously to those in Exhibit 2.1, show how capacity varies with service frequency, given a fixed space standard. Because long trains are cheaper to operate per passenger place than short ones, the operator seeks to increase headways if the facility for long trains exists.

From the viewpoint of the passenger this can result in an onerous increase in waiting time. The longest headways shown imply a rather low valuation of passenger waiting time—on the order of 1.5 to 3.5¢ per minute in 1977 prices. This is roughly the range of incremental cost needed to reduce headways from 10 to 6 minutes divided by the passenger-minutes saved, as can be deduced from Exhibit 2.10 later in this chapter. In the 6-to-3-minute range, the cost of reducing headways rises steeply, and can easily exceed the value of passenger time saved, which may average around 5¢ a minute on transit in 1977 prices.[7]

Formal calculations seeking to "optimize" service frequency so as to keep the sum of the costs to the operator and to the passenger at a minimum should, however, be done with caution. Applying externally derived values of time can easily exaggerate the frequency needed, and most of the added cost may not be "collectible" from the passenger even in terms of added patronage. Since both cost functions vary from system to system, no general "optimizing" approach is attempted here. Rather, Exhibit 2.2 simply shows that *peak hour headways longer than 6 minutes are deemed by the operators to be unacceptable to the passenger in more than 90 percent of the cases, and those longer than 7.5 minutes, in all cases.**

The average waiting time (half the headway or 3.75 minutes) may not appear overly long, but in operating practice there tends to be a link between peak period headway and off-peak, or "base period," headway. The latter is typically 2 to 3 times the former, though no fixed ratio need apply. Thus, a 7.5-minute headway during the peak may translate into a 15-to-20-minute headway in midday or evening hours. This is not an attractive service for spontaneous, walk-in traffic. It is supportable mostly on commuter railroads, where travel distances are long and passengers are inured to watching the schedule and catching a specific train.[8]

In sum, if a train of three large rapid transit cars (with 140 passenger places each) were a minimum economical unit for peak hour service, and a 7.5-minute peak period headway were the maximum acceptable to the passenger, then a *peak hour one-directional flow of some 3,360 passenger places* (the equivalent of 55 buses) would be the minimum to *support a rapid transit operation based on service frequency alone.* If a light rail vehicle with 122 passenger places (such as the Edmonton car) were to be operated on a similar schedule, the *minimum peak hour flow to support light rail—based on frequency alone*—would be *about 1,000 passenger places* (the equivalent of 16 buses). These figures are in scale with the minimum passenger flows actually encountered on rail systems. The minimum

*An exception not shown on the chart was the startup operation in Atlanta, with 10-minute peak hour headways in 1979–81.

Exhibit 2.2
Schedule Frequency Related to Peak Hour Flow

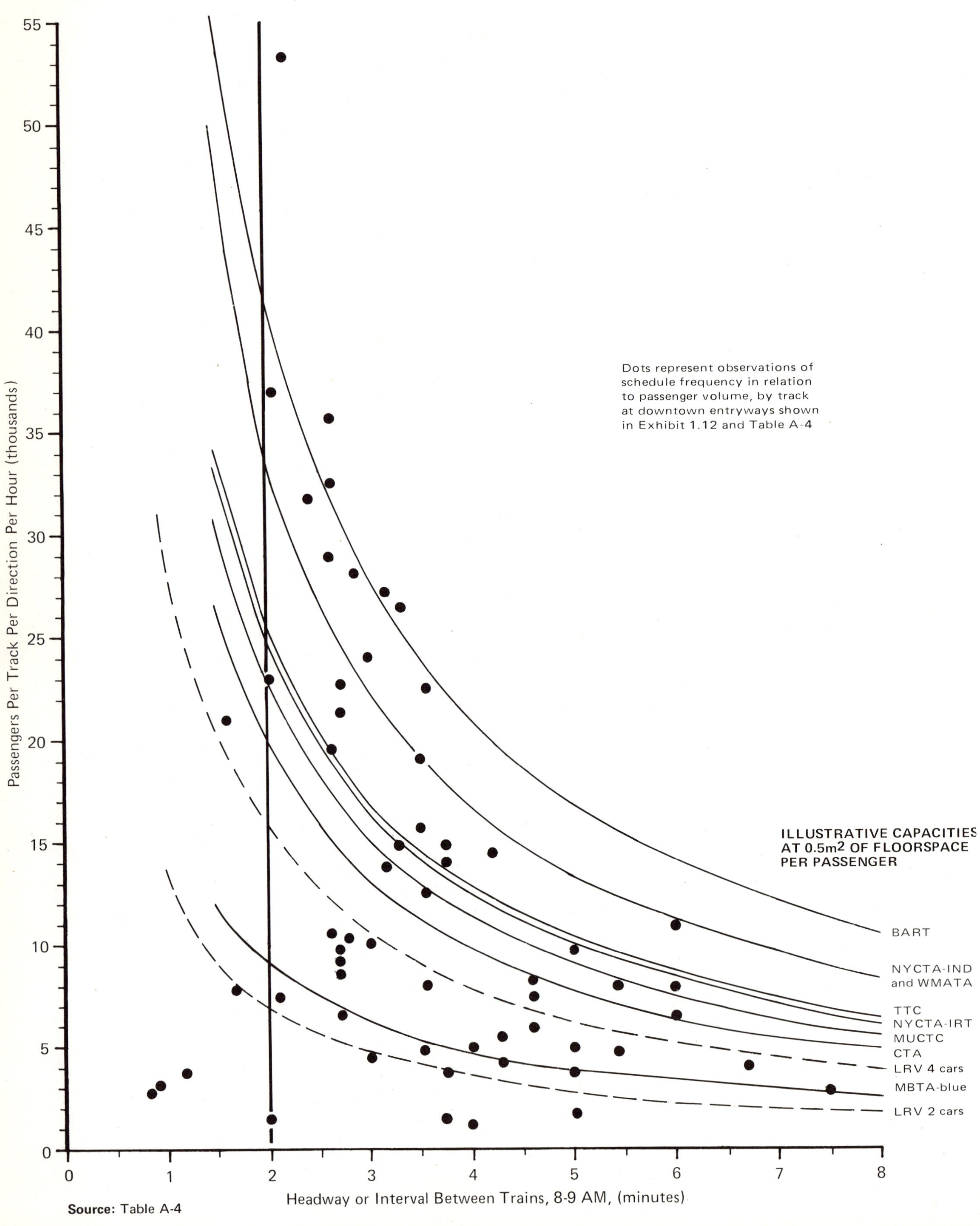

Source: Table A-4

flows are about one-tenth of the maxima attainable with a comfortable space allocation per passenger.

OPERATING SPEED

Vehicle speed is of decisive importance in transit operations. Unlike increasing space and service frequency, which necessitate higher costs to the operator to satisfy passenger convenience, increased speed reduces costs both to the passenger and to the operator. For the passenger, travel time is reduced; for the operator, fewer vehicles and fewer employees are needed as vehicles turn around faster.

Travel of individually moving units (whether buses, automobiles, bicycles, equestrians, or pedestrians) is subject to the law of declining speed with rising volume of flow. This results from individual efforts to adjust speed to available stopping distances to avoid collisions. Fixed guideways are subject to this law only with respect to minimum train spacing on different types of systems. Surely, high-speed operations need much longer intervals between trains than slow ones, so as to maintain safe stopping distances; but up to a point, greater train length can more than compensate for the longer intervals, so that both speed and passenger flow can increase. *Exclusive of boarding delay, fixed guideway speeds are basically independent of the volume of flow.* This independence is illustrated in Exhibit 2.3.

The volume of service is shown along the horizontal axis of the exhibit by system (not by particular downtown entries, as previously) and is expressed as the number of passenger places (gross vehicle floorspace divided by 5.4 square feet or 0.5 m^2) passing a point along an average line (not the maximum load point) in a year in both directions. One million annual place-miles per mile of line by this definition equals on the average about 185 places per line in one direction during the peak hour on a weekday, the equivalent of 3 buses.* As for the definition of speed in Exhibit 2.3, it is expressed as gross average operating speed, meaning annual vehicle-miles divided by annual vehicle-hours, including layover time at terminals.

None of the fixed guideway modes show any decline in operating speed with rising volume of service. The arrangement of their domains tends to show an opposite pattern. Rapid transit serves the highest volumes at high speeds. Light rail serves intermediate volumes at intermediate speeds. Commuter rail serves intermediate volumes at the highest speeds. Existing peoplemovers serve volumes that overlap the upper bus range, the entire light rail and the lower rapid transit range. Their speeds are the slowest. This reflects a very short trip length on existing systems, as well as speed limits to ensure protection against rear-end collision with short headways, particularly if loss of adhesion occurs on a wet concrete guideway.

By contrast, local bus speeds show a decline with rising volume of service. This

*Because of different weekly and daily peaking patterns, an annual average of one million place-miles per line-mile may actually represent anywhere from 2 to 4 bus-equivalents crossing the maximum load point in the peak hour, if service along a line is even. If service drops off toward outlying points due to branching of lines or short-turning of trains, the equivalent of an annual average of one million place-miles per line-mile may be as high as 10 buses crossing the maximum load point per direction per hour.

Exhibit 2.3
Operating Speed Related to Service Volume

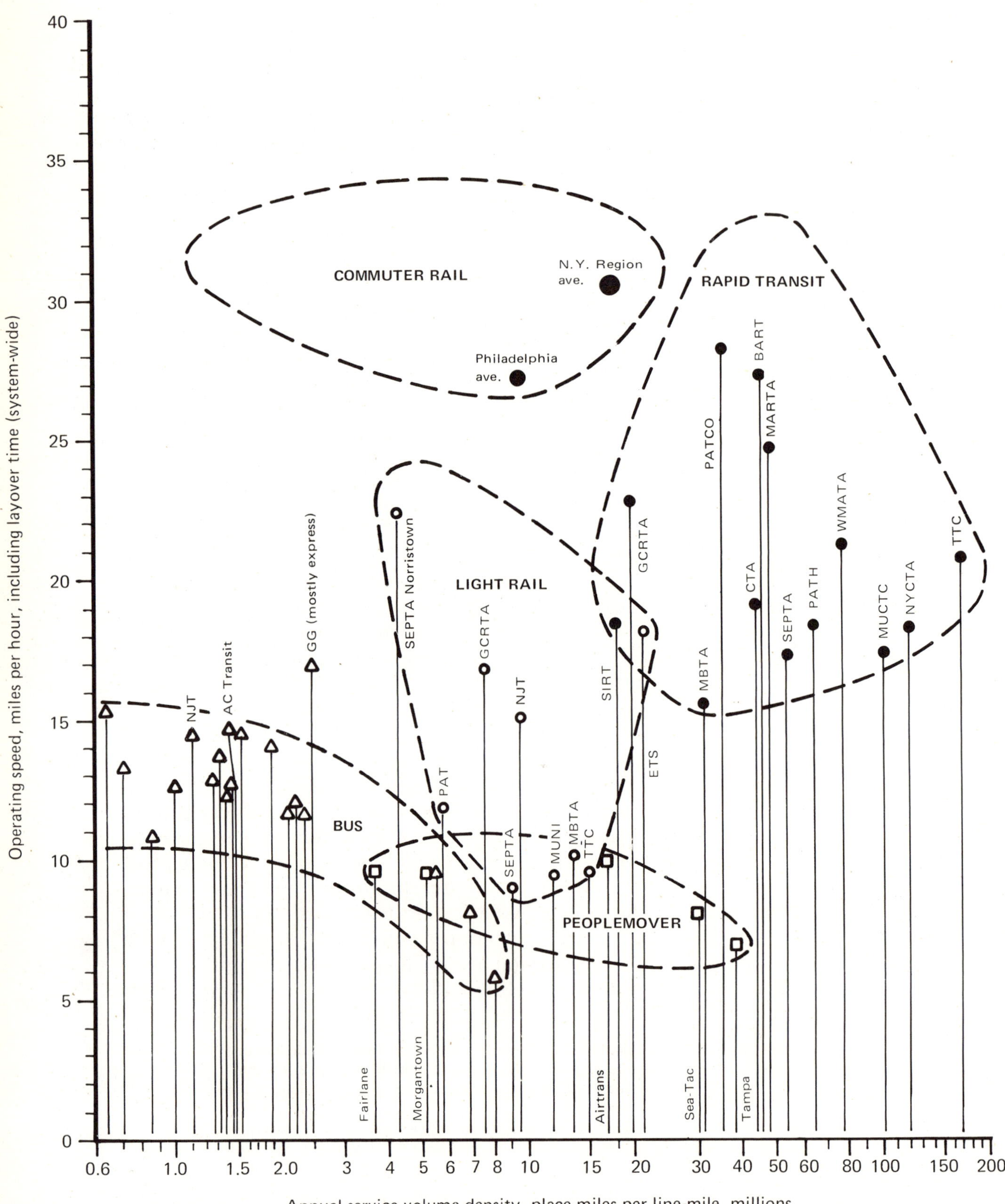

Source: Table A-6

is so because higher service volumes are associated with higher urban densities, which reduce the prevailing speed of street traffic. The relationship between local bus speed and the density of development is, in fact, a close one.[9] The 20 bus systems shown (selected because speed and volume data were readily available, see Table A-6, Part III) offer predominantly local service, but include express operations.[10] Systems with significant shares of express service are singled out in the Exhibit (Alameda–Contra Costa=AC; Golden Gate=GG; New Jersey Transit=NJT). Separate data for express operations are not readily available. Nor are exclusive busways included in the Exhibit; they represent for the most part only the nonstop portion of a group of services, and thus are not comparable to the systemwide data displayed. Altogether, bus systems are shown to serve the lower domain of volumes, between 0.6 and 8.4 million place-miles per line-mile, at average speeds that range from 15.3 mph (24.6 km/h) in Phoenix, Arizona to 5.6 mph (8.9 km/h) in Manhattan and the Bronx.

Because new fixed guideways are typically inserted into an environment where bus systems operate, this bus speed range is a useful yardstick against which to measure fixed guideway performance. Systemwide rapid transit speeds, between 15.6 and 35 mph (25 and 56 km/h), are roughly twice as fast as bus speeds. Systemwide streetcar and light rail speeds, between 9 and 22 mph (14 and 35 km/h), are moderately faster. On particular lines the advantages may differ. Similarly, the low speed of peoplemovers in airport and downtown applications (7 to 10 mph or 11 to 16 km/h) must be compared to bus speed in heavy traffic, which in the core of any major city is in the 5 to 10 mph (8 to 16 km/h) range.

Two principal avenues for increasing speed are *reducing conflicts with surface traffic by means of grade separation* and *reducing the number of stops*. Rapid transit is by definition fully grade-separated; light rail and streetcar systems vary in their degree of grade separation.

The SEPTA Norristown line, at 22 mph (35 km/h) by far the fastest, is fully grade-separated. Of the three next fastest lines, which average some 17 mph (27 km/h), GCRTA Shaker Heights is grade-separated for nearly half its length (with the remainder in reserved street medians), but the grade-separated portion carries about two-thirds of the car-miles operated. The ETS Edmonton line in 1980 had close to one-quarter of its length in tunnel, with the remainder on reserved right-of-way with protected street crossings. The NJT Newark line is grade-separated except for one street crossing.

The next group, averaging just over 10 mph (17 km/h), includes the PAT South Hills lines in Pittsburgh and the original subway-surface operations of the MBTA in Boston and SEPTA in Philadelphia. The former runs mostly on private right-of-way with grade crossings, but enters downtown on surface streets. The latter two enter downtown in tunnels and run mostly (as in Boston), or to a small extent (as in Philadelphia), in reserved street medians outside, with the remainder on surface streets.

The last group, averaging about 9 mph (15 km/h) consists of traditional surface street operations with some reserved mileage in Toronto and in San Francisco prior to 1980. By converting downtown operations from surface to tunnel, San Francisco nearly tripled its operating speed along Market Street to 20 mph (32 km/h), thereby raising the systemwide speed nearly 50 percent. Statistics of fully grade-separated, reserved, and surface street mileage for all United States systems are listed in Table H-3 in the Appendix.

Exhibit 2.4
Operating Speed Related to Station Spacing

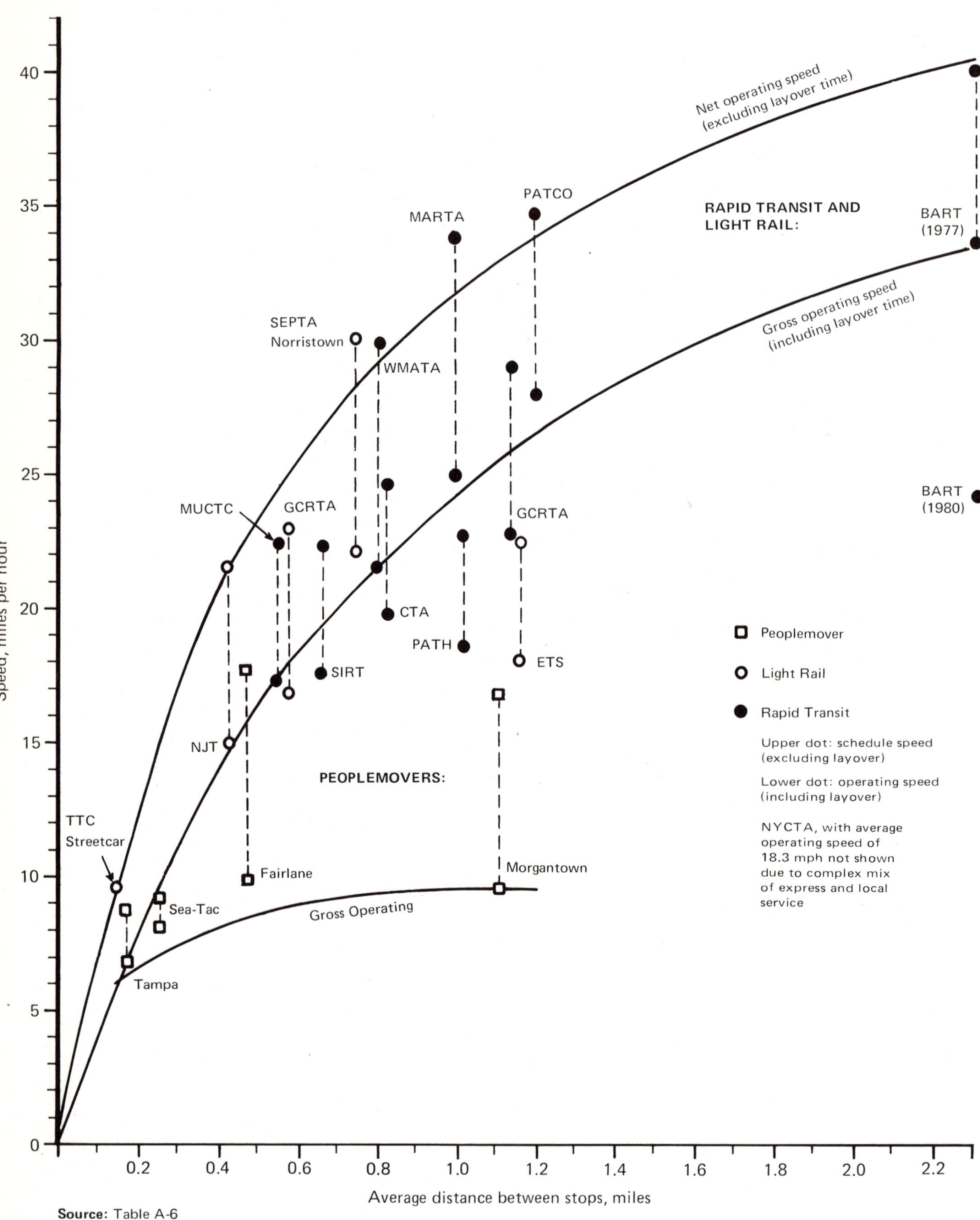

Source: Table A-6

On partially grade-separated lines there are numerous impediments to speed, including the volume of conflicting traffic, its pattern of turning movements, the frequency of at-grade crossings, the lack of signal preemption to give rail vehicles priority, and passenger boarding delay resulting from rudimentary station arrangements.[11] As these types of delay are reduced by increased grade-separation, speed becomes principally a function of station spacing. The relationship between speed and the average distance between stops for systems most of which are grade-separated is displayed in Exhibit 2.4.

The definition of speed in this exhibit is refined to include both gross average operating speed, including layover time at terminals,* and net average operating or schedule speed, which is based on running time as perceived by the passenger and excludes layover time. The gross definition is relevant for calculations of operating cost. The distance between stops is that encountered by an average car on the system and not the physical distance (total line miles divided by the number of inter-station links). Because of the complexity of some operations (notably the New York City Transit Authority), the more accurate definition of distance between stops is not available for some systems and these are not included in the chart.

The approximate limit of current rail technology, taking into account passenger comfort criteria with respect to acceleration, is represented by the two curves relating average speed to distance between stops. The lower, or gross average operating speed, curve shows that to exceed the upper bus range of 15 mph (24 km/h), the station spacing must be greater than 0.45 miles (0.7 km); but it takes a 1.6-mile (2.6-km) spacing to double the gross speed to 30 mph (48.3 km/h). The net speed experienced by the passenger at this point averages 38 mph (61 km/h).

To what extent actual operations match the curves shown depends in large measure on rolling stock performance, i.e., the ability to sustain fast acceleration and to reach a maximum speed appropriate for a given station spacing. Both are related to a vehicle's power-to-weight ratio. Among the top performers, the Washington (WMATA) and Atlanta (MARTA) rapid transit cars are equipped with about 20 hp per metric ton of empty vehicle weight; the Lindenwold line (PATCO) and the Norristown light rail line cars with about 17 hp per metric ton. The Norristown line reaches its rather exceptional net operating speed of 30 mph (48 km/h) at 0.74 miles (1.2 km) between scheduled stops because of signs which enable cars to pass stations at full speed if no passengers are boarding or alighting.

High-performance rolling stock includes the PCC car, last manufactured in 1952, and the BART car, produced in 1972; both are equipped with about 23 hp per metric ton. Among the properties shown in Exhibit 2.4, PCC cars operated on the Toronto street system, the Newark and Shaker Heights lines. The speed on the last is curtailed by sections of nonexclusive right-of-way. The speed of BART (cut back substantially between 1975 and 1980) is depressed by problems with automatic train control.

The lower-than-possible operating speed of the other systems is explained by lower car performance and other factors. For example, Staten Island and Cleveland rapid transit, with noticeably lower positions on the chart, use cars averaging 11.6 to

*Some softness in the gross operating speed data should be recognized, since the definition of "vehicle hours" depends in part on work rules defined in union agreements.

roughly 10 hp per ton, which is typical of older transit systems. The Edmonton cars have sluggish acceleration (58 seconds from 0 to 50 mph, compared to as little as 25 seconds on the new Breda Cleveland cars not shown in Exhibit 2.4) and are restricted by signal delays. The SIRT cars are not operated at "full throttle" due to power supply restrictions, while tight curves and other geometry constraints limit the speed of the CTA in Chicago and of PATH in New Jersey and New York.

Also included in Exhibit 2.4 are available data on peoplemovers. These have operating speeds similar to rail at short station spacings, but fall behind at longer distances between stops especially if cars idle waiting for passengers in a demand-responsive mode, such as in Morgantown. Automated peoplemover speed has much less of an effect on labor cost than that of manned systems, but it still affects the number of vehicles needed.

LABOR REQUIREMENTS

In addition to improving service, reducing unit operating costs is an important rationale for new fixed guideway systems. To determine the magnitude of the possible savings, the labor output of different transit systems is examined in terms of place-miles and, following a discussion of vehicle occupancy, in passenger-miles. The labor requirement (the inverse of labor output) is then assessed in relation to place-miles (thus equalizing for vehicle size compared to the more customary car-miles or bus-miles) and place-hours (thus equalizing for speed). The latter measure enables one to observe the changes in labor requirements related to service density. Based on the relationships uncovered, a *labor requirements model* is developed which is sensitive to operating speed, service density, service frequency, train manning, and station manning assumptions. This model makes it possible to compare the labor cost of different transit modes under different conditions, suggesting thresholds at which fixed guideways have lower labor requirements than various types of bus operation.

Labor represents about 80 percent of current expenses (excluding capital charges) for all public transportation in the United States, a figure that applies to fixed guideway systems as well.[12] Expressed in money terms, however, the cost of labor varies by geographic area and rises over time due to inflation. Accounting practices also vary: several multimodal agencies do not disaggregate costs by mode. All these problems are avoided if one simply deals with the number of employees (or man years) needed to perform different transit tasks. The differences in cost per worker for five major tasks examined here are generally within 15 percent of the average cost per worker[13] and do not have a decisive effect on total labor expenditures. Hence, the *number of workers is used as the basic measure of labor expense;* it can be always converted into money terms to fit the prices of any particular time and place.

The systems examined include all 13 rapid transit operations in the United States and Canada as of 1980, 9 out of 14 light rail operations,* 5 out of 14 peo-

*Omitted are: the SEPTA Media-Sharon Hill line, because of insufficient data; the SEPTA City streetcars (other than the 5 subway-surface routes), because of erratic operation as a result of equipment shortages during the study period; the small downtown operations in Ft. Worth and Detroit; and the St. Charles line in New Orleans, which operates historic equipment, unlikely to be replicated.

plemovers,* and about two dozen bus systems in larger cities for which pertinent data are available.

For fixed guideways the analysis is based on data supplied directly by the operating agencies, presented in Tables A-4, A-6, and A-7. Some data, particularly on bus systems and on vehicle dimensions (Table A-5), derive from published American Public Transit Association (APTA) sources. Occasionally, the data had gaps (e.g., either passengers or some categories of workers were not allocated by mode). In these cases, estimates were necessary, indicated by the letter (e) in the tables. Throughout the book, *employment figures exclude police* (a community, rather than a transit, function) *and employees concerned with construction* (a capital budget expenditure which includes "de-bugging" on new systems). While questions about some figures remain and strict comparability of the employee classification cannot be claimed, a comprehensive data base of employment and operating statistics of this type has never been assembled before for the fixed guideway systems in North America.

The data can legitimately be used to derive overall relationships which show how much labor is required under different conditions. They should not, however, be used to compare individual systems. Each system tends to have idiosyncrasies related to route configuration, patronage, equipment type, the regulatory framework, and labor relations which can make such comparisons invalid. And even the overall relationships cannot account for many important *qualities* of service, such as clean stations, clean cars, or on-time performance, which also require labor.[14]

Labor output in place-miles per worker on different systems provides a good overview of the fixed guideway modes in comparison with buses—the principal alternative. Place-miles are what transit workers produce; the measure is reliable, based on annual car-miles (a firmly established statistic) and car size. Admittedly, it can be spurious on occasion: running full-length trains in the evening, for example, will produce place-miles per worker but will be of no value if the places are empty. Therefore, place-miles utilized, meaning passenger-miles, require equal attention.

The output per employee on rapid transit exceeds that of bus systems by a wide margin, as Exhibit 2.5 demonstrates. It will be shown shortly *that this is primarily a function of speed and secondarily of vehicle operation in trains. Most of the rapid transit systems shown produce between 1 and 2 million place-miles of service per worker per year; the bus range—with predominantly local service—is below 1 million, and down to 0.5 million.* Pairing off rapid transit with bus systems operating in the same territory produces a similar relationship: the output of place-miles per worker on the Toronto and Washington subways is 2.5 times that of TTC and WMATA buses; that on BART and PATCO, more than twice that of the AC Transit and NJT buses respectively; that on rapid transit in New York, Cleveland, Montreal, and Chicago exceeds that of buses in the respective areas by 2.0 to 1.4 times. One rapid transit operation that apparently falls below the bus in output per employee is the MBTA in Boston, where "work rules and state crew laws tend to defeat much of the inherent advantage of rapid transit."[15]

The labor output on North American rapid transit compares favorably with that in other countries, where relatively few systems (among them Stockholm, Moscow,

*Omitted are 8 systems in amusement parks and intramural system at the Houston airport.

Mexico City) equal the output of 1.1 million place-miles per worker typical of New York; some systems fall just below that level (Lenigrad, Oslo), but many fall substantially below (London, Milan, Osaka, Kiev, Buenos Aries). Comparable labor figures for foreign light rail systems are not available; indications are that German streetcar and light rail systems exceed local buses in output per worker by a considerable margin.

Compared to rapid transit, the labor output of existing streetcars and light rail in North America shows much less of an advantage over the bus. Most place-miles per employee are produced by the NJT Newark subway, followed by the ETS Edmonton light rail line, the SEPTA Norristown line, the San Francisco MUNI streetcars, and the GCRTA Shaker Heights lines. The first has about the same output per employee as NJT buses (which include many express runs), while the other four do somewhat better than buses operated by the respective agencies. The remaining four systems do worse than their respective buses in large part because of their slow speed. Moreover, the traditional streetcar-type systems do not or cannot avail themselves of the advantages of train operation. Two of the systems that do operate trains still use one worker per car, negating possible labor savings. Only the new Edmonton system operates one-man trains, but some of this labor saving is negated by fully manned stations, to which one-third of all employees are assigned.

The low output per worker on some of the traditional systems makes it understandable why so many streetcar lines lost out in competition with buses. One can draw useful lessons from the experience of the older lines, but they should not be confused with light rail as envisaged for new systems. Among the basic differences between past and future lines are:

(1) *higher speeds* due to separation from traffic and coordination with traffic signals;

(2) *larger vehicles operated in trains whenever possible;*

(3) *self-service fare collection* to permit one-man train operation with

(4) *simple stations* in a street environment;

(5) *a close coordination with feeder buses* to enlarge the tributary area of a high-capacity line and to use each mode in a setting to which it is suited best.

These differences are taken into account in the labor requirements model presented later in this chapter.

Employment data for automated peoplemovers are much less reliable than those for the conventional systems. Maintenance work done by outside contractors has to be translated into staff position equivalents. There is the difficulty of allocating the time of general airport staff who devote some of their effort to tending the airport peoplemover. If it were an independent operation, many of these part-time responsibilities would require full-time positions. In part because of these accounting difficulties, the labor output of the five systems investigated varies over an extremely broad range.

The two simple and short (less than one mile of two-track equivalent guideway) shuttle-loop systems at Seattle–Tacoma and Tampa airports, with high volumes of service, have the highest output, 1.1 to 1.6 million place-miles per employee annually, comparable to rapid transit. The much larger (6.4 miles of two-track equivalent) Dallas Airtrans system produces about 0.7 million place-miles per employee annually, comparable to the San Francisco MUNI and Cleveland Shaker Heights light rail operations, to which it is similar in volume of service per line-mile. Not

Exhibit 2.5
Labor Output of Transit Operations

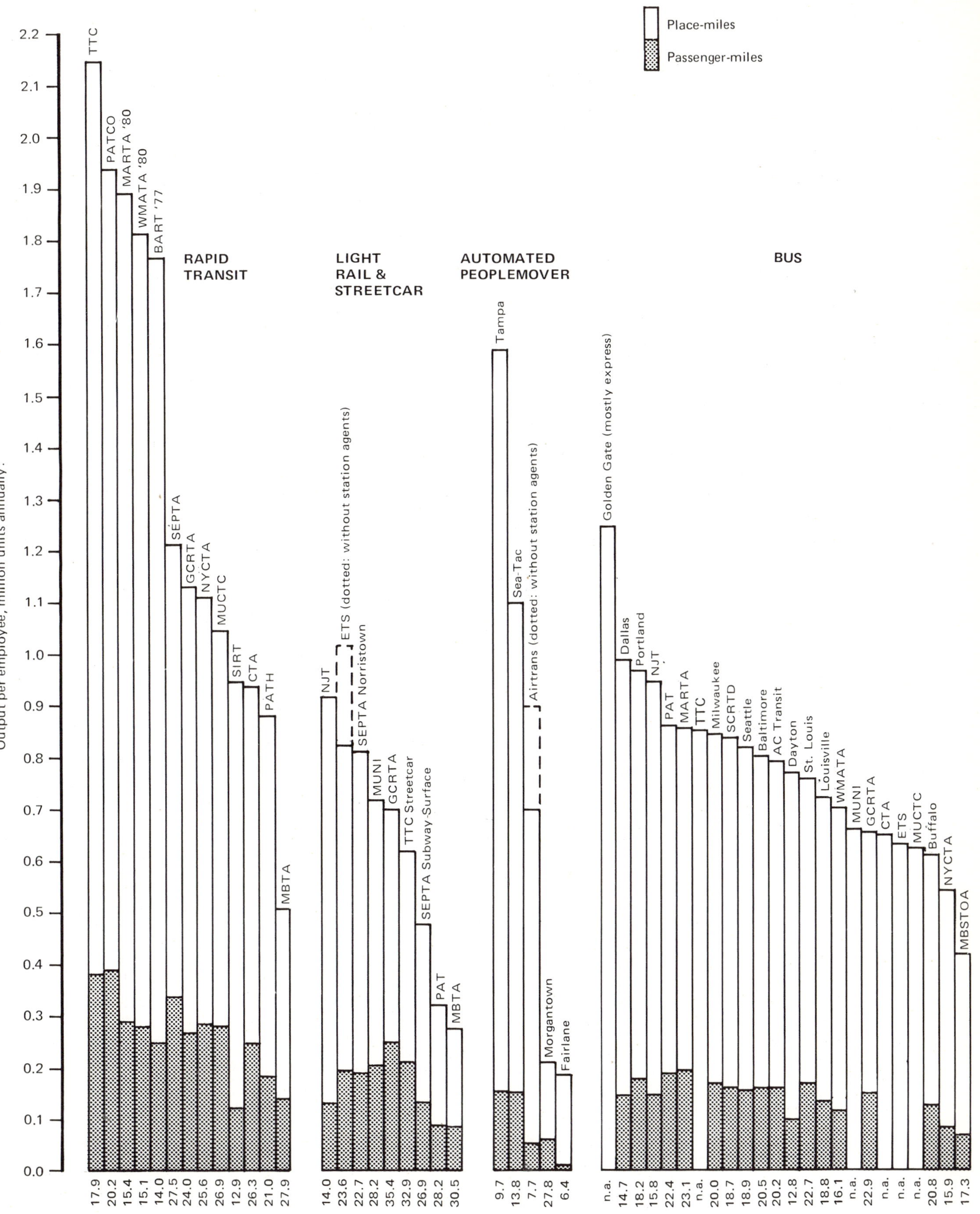

counting Airtrans station attendants as employees raises its output to 0.9 million place-miles per worker. Morgantown in 1977 produced 0.2 million place-miles per employee, similar to the most labor-intensive streetcars. Lastly, the small "ACT"shuttle at the Fairlane shopping center in Dearborn, Michigan, with about 0.18 million place-miles per employee and the lightest volume of service, appears to be similar in labor output to the historic cable cars in San Francisco.

Because of the unreliability of peoplemover employment data, it is worth cross-checking these findings with operating and maintenance costs in dollars developed in the course of recent Automated Guideway Transit assessment studies.[16] In 1976 dollars, the operating and maintenance cost of the three airport systems ranged from 1.88¢ to 2.85¢ per place-mile, but that of Morgantown and Fairlane was 12.3¢ and 21¢ respectively. These magnitudes are roughly in scale with the labor output reported here. It will be recalled from Exhibit 2.3 that the service volumes (place-miles per line-mile) on the three airport peoplemovers are about six times those on the other two systems, suggesting a link between service volume and labor output. For comparison, 1976 bus operating and maintenance costs were in the 2¢ to 5¢ per place-mile range. This supports the finding of Exhibit 2.5, that the more productive automated peoplemovers do in fact exceed the bus in output per worker, being similar in this regard to rapid transit, wheras those with light volumes of service fall far behind.

To conclude the discussion of output per worker, a caveat is in order. Long rail transit lines inherently tend to have higher output in place-miles per worker than short ones. This is so because their vehicle requirements—and as a result, many labor requirements as well—are set by the peak hour capacity needed at the maximum load point on the downtown edge. Once that requirement is satisfied, running trains for a somewhat longer distance out from downtown and clocking additional place-miles may require only modest additional labor.

If one measures *output in places delivered to downtown during the peak hour per worker*, instead of in place-miles produced annually per worker, the shorter systems among those shown in Exhibit 2.5 move up significantly in rank. PATH moves up in rank from 13 to 4, Edmonton from 14 to 8, and MBTA rapid transit from 18 to 12. All three have average round-trip runs of 9 to 11 miles (14 to 18 km) per downtown entry. By contrast, systems with long round trip runs, notably the NYCTA (27.7 miles or 44.5 km) and BART (52.5 miles or 84.5 km) move down in rank, the former from 8 to 18, and the latter from 4 to 16. If one wishes to focus on downtown access irrespective of trip length, one can measure worker output in peak hour passenger places delivered.

Measured either way, output per worker fluctuates over time. Because of fixed costs, it rises when service is expanded (as on the new systems), and falls when service is reduced. On the NYCTA, for example, annual place-miles produced per employee dropped from 1.29 million in 1970 (when it was second in output per worker only to PATCO) to 1.02 million in 1979 because a 26 percent cutback in service could not be matched by proportionate reductions in labor. Even so, cutbacks in car maintenance staff caused severe deterioration of the rolling stock and of service reliability, conditions that are not reflected in place-miles per worker. Since the data for Exhibit 2.5 were prepared, a similar 20 percent cutback in service occurred on the SEPTA city subways in Philadelphia. This points out once again that data presented for purposes of aggregate analysis should not be used to judge particular properties.

The passenger occupancy of transit vehicles obviously affects the labor cost of the end product, namely the passenger-miles traveled. The range of observed occupancy values is listed at the bottom of Exhibit 2.5. The percent places occupied, or load factor, is expressed as the ratio of annual passenger-miles traveled to annual place-miles of service offered, with places defined at 5.4 sq. ft. (0.5 m^2) of gross vehicle floorspace.

The unweighted average annual occupancy of the 13 rapid transit systems, at 21 percent (24 people per car), is only slightly higher than that of buses, presumed to be 19 percent (11.5 people per bus).[17] However, the difference between the highest and the lowest rapid transit figure is more than twofold and deserves elaboration. The average percent places occupied reflects several operating features: (a) space per passenger provided during the weekday peak hour at downtown entry points, (b) the distribution of passenger trips along the lines, i.e., the extent to which the "tail ends" near outlying terminals are utilized, (c) the provision of cars in relation to available passengers during off-peak weekday hours, and (d) on weekends. The pertinent statistics are listed in Tables A-4 and A-7.

Average annual passenger occupancies of 26 to 28 percent were attained in 1976 by rapid transit in New York, Montreal, Boston, Philadelphia, and Chicago. In the first two of these cities, they meant severe overloads (133 percent of places occupied) at the downtown cordon in the peak hour, and in the third a minor overload. Chicago and Philadelphia managed to avoid overloads because the peaking of their passenger traffic—at least during the 8:00A.M. to 9:00A.M. period—appears to be less pronounced. They also have a more even distribution of passengers along the length of lines than New York, where the tail ends of long and slow lines in Brooklyn and the Bronx are lightly used. Montreal, Boston, and Philadelphia attain very high loadings at outer terminals, which serve as collector points for buses or streetcars.

Average annual passenger occupancies of 18 to 24 percent were attained between 1976 and 1978 by Toronto, PATCO in New Jersey and Philadelphia, PATH in New Jersey and New York, the Edmonton and the Cleveland lines. Of these, only Toronto and Cleveland experienced minor peak hour overloads, despite the fact that passenger demand on the suburban commuter-oriented PATCO and PATH lines is very sharply peaked. The average annual occupancies of PATH and Edmonton are enhanced by high utilization at terminals, which serve as transfer points from commuter rail and buses, respectively; the Cleveland line has an exceptionally high utilization rate in off-peak hours, attained by running many one-car trains, in contrast to a four-car average during the peak hour. The use of outer terminals is relatively low in Toronto, on PATCO, and in Cleveland.

Lastly, Staten Island Rapid Transit, which maintains an adequate space standard in the peak hour, had at 13 percent the lowest annual passenger occupancy of any system. Three factors combine to explain this: the lowest off-peak weekday occupancy (because trains cannot be cut to one car, as in Cleveland), the lowest weekend occupancy (a weekend service three-quarters that of the weekday is maintained as a matter of policy even as demand falls to one-fifth), and the lowest outer terminal utilization (0.7 percent of places occupied at the distant Tottenville station on an average weekday).

In the early stage of their operations, new systems—BART, WMATA, and MARTA—also had occupancies around 15 percent. These cannot be considered typical of mature operations except for BART, which was *designed* for a very generous space standard with 100 percent seating, akin to a commuter railroad. If evaluated in terms of *seat-miles*, rather than place-miles, its 1980 load factor becomes about 30 rather than 15 percent.

Light rail occupancies appear to be high, averaging about 27 percent (20 people per typical PCC car). Peak hour overloads are frequent, even though the peaks in intracity travel are relatively flat. Incomplete cordon count and lacking station count data make it difficult to explain the patterns in detail or to verify the occupancy figures.

Occupancy data on automated peoplemovers are very poor, extensive federally funded assessment studies notwithstanding. Most of the figures are rough management or consultant estimates; only Airtrans and Morgantown actually count their passengers. The airport operations appear to have occupancies in the 8 to 14 percent range, while Morgantown boasts 28 percent, a reflection of a partially demand responsive operation and multiple peaks throughout the day, as students move between classes on a university campus.

In sum, because of strong directional imbalances during peak periods, and because of the dropoff in traffic toward the end of lines, most urban systems cannot hope to attain occupancies on the order of 50 percent, such as are realized by intercity buses on a seat-mile basis, without very severe peak hour overcrowding. Still, *average annual occupancies of some 25 percent or more can be attained without peak hour overloads* (i.e., no less than 5.4 sq. ft. per passenger during weekday peaks) *if two conditions are met:* (a) *train length is cut back during off-peak and weekend hours to reflect demand*, and (b) *the lines are not extended so far as to result in low use at outer terminals.*

To what extent cutbacks in train length between peak hours can actually result in labor savings is a question for which there is no certain answer; much depends on whether cars are designed for easy uncoupling and on the location of facilities to store them. It is only the energy savings from shorter off-peak train length that are certain. Lastly, occupancy factors also change over time, just as worker productivity does. By 1979, the New York subway occupancy was up to 31 percent, compared with 25.6 percent shown here for 1976, due to rising patronage and higher peak overloads.

Labor output in passenger-miles on existing systems, shown by the shaded bars at the bottom of Exhibit 2.5, can be summarized after this discussion of passenger occupancy in terms of the following *averages per worker per year*:

85,000 passenger-miles per worker on five automated peoplemovers;

150,000 passenger-miles on two airport peoplemovers with highest occupancies;

150,000 passenger-miles on buses;

160,000 passenger-miles on light rail and streetcars;

260,000 passenger-miles on rapid transit overall;

310,000 passenger-miles on six new rapid transit systems.

All of these averages are unweighted, to avoid giving undue prominence to New York. It is clear that low occupancies, characteristic of startup operations on several new systems, do not prevent new rapid transit systems as a group from having twice the output per worker of buses on a passenger-mile basis.

Labor requirement per place-mile is the reciprocal of labor output in place-miles per employee, and is a value that can be directly translated into labor cost in dollars. To determine the factors that influence this value, it is first necessary to see how it varies with operating speed. This is shown in Exhibit 2.6, which relates the labor required to produce a million place-miles of service annually to operating speed. Viewed this way, the labor requirements of buses and to some extent of rapid transit and light rail fall into a narrow band, which can be defined by constant cost per place-hour (cost per place-mile multiplied by operating speed in miles per hour).

For example, the labor cost of NYCTA buses is 1.852 employees per million place-miles, while that of NYCTA rapid transit is 0.902, a twofold difference. Multiplied by the respective operating speeds, however (8.08 and 18.33 mph), their labor cost per million *place-hours* becomes similar—15.0 versus 16.5 employees. The numerical data for all the other systems are given in Table A-6.

All 29 bus systems for which data are assembled fall in the cost range between 13 and 19 employees per million place-hours; 6 out of 13 rapid transit systems are roughly in this band, as are 4 out of 9 light rail systems; 3 rapid transit systems fall below. However, only one automated peoplemover is in this band; the others are either far above or far below. This huge dispersion, with very small differences in peoplemover operating speed, indicates that other factors (including service volume and route length) explain the variation in labor requirements among these systems. For conventional systems, a different conclusion is in order.

More than *half* of the difference in labor requirements per place-mile among bus systems is due to differences in operating speed. Differences in labor requirements among rail systems shrink by *two-fifths* when equalized for speed. The effect of speed on labor costs is pervasive, and not limited to the ability to get an extra run out of a peak hour train as is sometimes believed.

The labor requirement per place-hour removes most of the effect of speed and enables one to observe the impact of *service volume* on labor cost. The range of labor requirements per million place-hours is wide—from more than 35 workers on two old rail systems with lighter volumes and single-car operation to fewer than 13 workers on three new systems with medium to high service volumes which operate trains. The pattern is erratic and not easily interpreted in the aggregate. Exhibit 2.7 disaggregates the labor requirement by 5 major functions and plots each against service volume.

Starting at the bottom, the employee requirement in *administration* does not change perceptibly with the volume of service per mile of line. Some of the variation from system to system is simply due to differences in worker classification. The *average requirement across all volumes is about 2.4 administrative workers per million place-hours of service, similar to the bus average of* 2.3.

Next, *vehicle maintenance* requirements also fail to show any change with rising volume of service. However, vehicle maintenance requirements, even when calculated per place-hour, still have a tendency to rise with operating speed because of greater vehicle use per hour at higher speeds. This relationship is portrayed subsequently in Exhibit 2.8a. Excluding the exceptionally high maintenance needs of the Boston and Pittsburgh streetcars, the average labor requirement rises from about 3.1 vehicle maintenance workers per million place-hours annually at an operating speed of 9 mph (14.5 km/h) to about 4.4 at 30 mph (48 km/h). *At an average bus speed of 12.5 mph (20 km/h) the rail vehicle maintenance requirement of 3.3 workers per million place-hours is identical to that of the bus*. Theoretically,

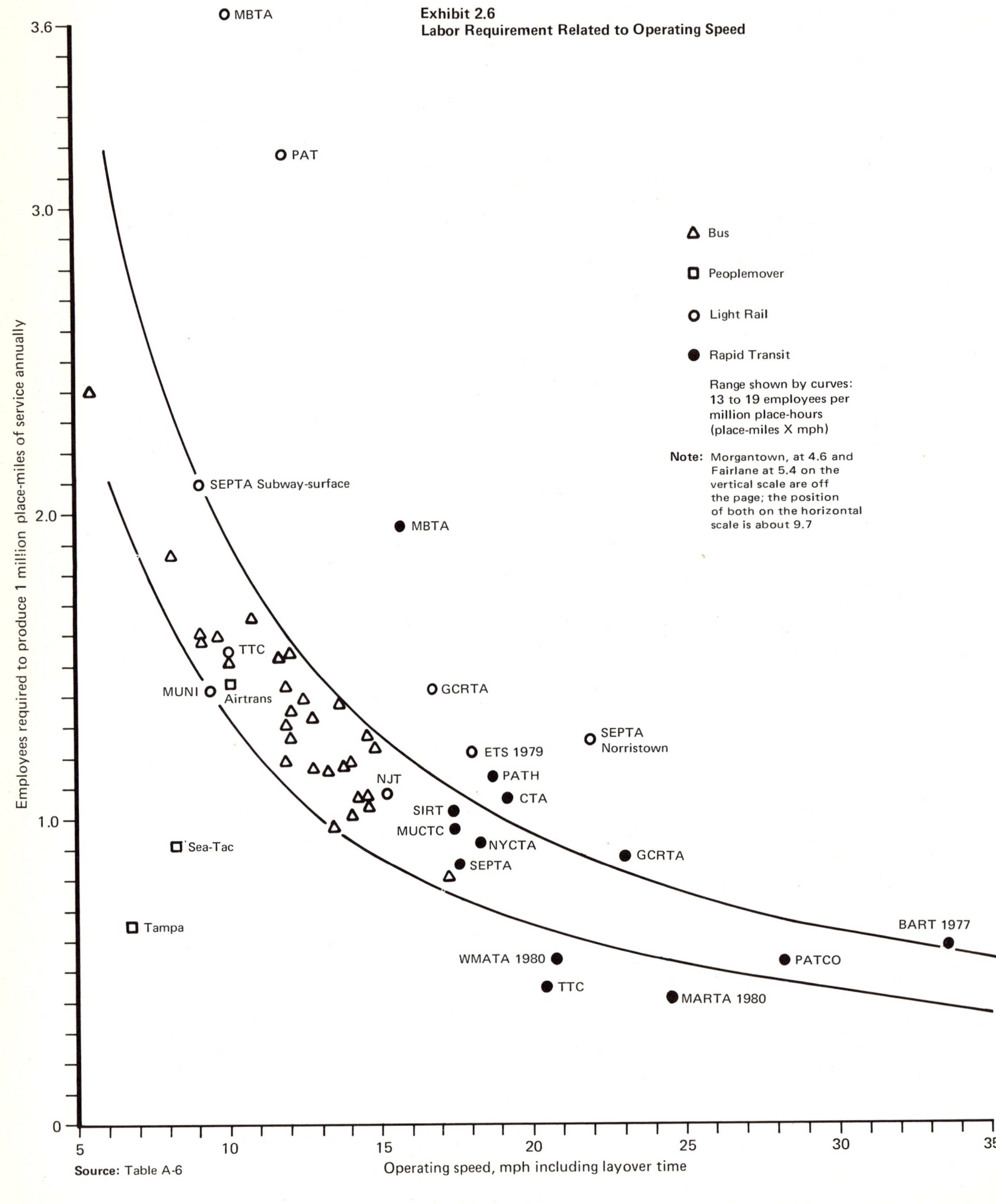

Exhibit 2.6
Labor Requirement Related to Operating Speed
Employees required to produce 1 million place-miles of service annually
Operating speed, mph including layover time
3.6
3.0
2.0
1.0
0
5
10
15
20
25
30
35
Bus
Peoplemover
Light Rail
Rapid Transit
Range shown by curves: 13 to 19 employees per million place-hours (place-miles X mph)
Note: Morgantown, at 4.6 and Fairlane at 5.4 on the vertical scale are off the page; the position of both on the horizontal scale is about 9.7
MBTA
PAT
SEPTA Subway-surface
MBTA
TTC
MUNI
Airtrans
GCRTA
SEPTA Norristown
ETS 1979
PATH
NJT
CTA
SIRT
MUCTC
NYCTA
GCRTA
SEPTA
Sea-Tac
Tampa
BART 1977
WMATA 1980
PATCO
TTC
MARTA 1980

Source: Table A-6

one would expect electrically propelled rail vehicles to be less costly to maintain than buses. Also, one would expect rail vehicles equipped with automatic train operation (ATO) to have above-average maintenance requirements. The data reported by the transit agencies fail to show any such patterns if vehicle size and operating speed are properly taken into account, as in Exhibit 2.8a.

Returning to the top of Exhibit 2.7, one can see that the labor requirement for *rail vehicle operation* does indeed decline rather consistently with service volume, from about 10 to 13 workers per million place-hours at the lowest volume to 1.5 at the highest. This compares to about 10.4 vehicle operating employees per million place-hours on buses. Workers engaged in vehicle operation are defined here to include motormen or drivers and conductors as well as dispatchers and similar stationary personnel.

The savings in operating labor at higher volumes of service are in part offset by two categories of workers who nominally do not exist on bus systems, namely those engaged in *maintenance of way, power, and signals* and those in *station maintenance and fare collection.* On newer systems in the upper range of service volume per line-mile, the requirement for maintenance-of-way personnel averages about 3.4 per million place-hours. Some older systems, particularly those with multitrack layouts (New York, Philadelphia), require substantially more. In the lower range of service volume, the need for a fairly constant minimum number of employees per mile of line causes the requirement per place-hour to rise hyperbolically with declining volume. The station requirement increases from zero on the more lightly traveled surface streetcar lines to some 2.5 on more heavily used rapid transit systems; it can be substantially higher if moderate volumes are served by fully manned stations.

For rail systems to have lower labor requirements than buses at an equal speed (fewer workers per place-hour), *the economies attained by train operation must exceed the added cost of stations and right-of-way maintenance.* This is not possible at very low volumes of service, where operating savings are small and the fixed costs of right-of-way maintenance are large. It is possible at moderate volumes, if close attention is paid to maintenance-of-way labor, station labor, and train operation.

Most automated peoplemovers are not included in Exhibit 2.7 because the observations are so widely scattered and no labor classification comparable to rail is available. Discussion must necessarily focus on Airtrans, which provides such classification. The tradeoff between unmanned vehicles and the high cost of maintaining them at Airtrans works out modestly in favor of automation. Conventional rail vehicles with its service volume and speed require some 6 workers per million place-hours for operation, and about 3 for maintenance; Airtrans requires nearly 7 for maintenance but only 1 for operation. Way and power and station labor requirements per million place-hours at Airtrans are similar to conventional rail. Administrative requirements are low, being in part carried by the airport agency. Even raising them to the transit industry average, the total labor requirement of Airtrans becomes 15.6 (instead of the actual 14.4) workers per place-hour, just below the 16 worker per million place-hours average of buses.

Design of fixed guideway operations. The discussion so far has indicated the extent to which *higher speed*, *higher service volume*, and *automation* can reduce the labor cost of fixed guideway operations under conditions that are pretty much

Exhibit 2.7
Labor Requirement Related to the Volume of Service, by Function

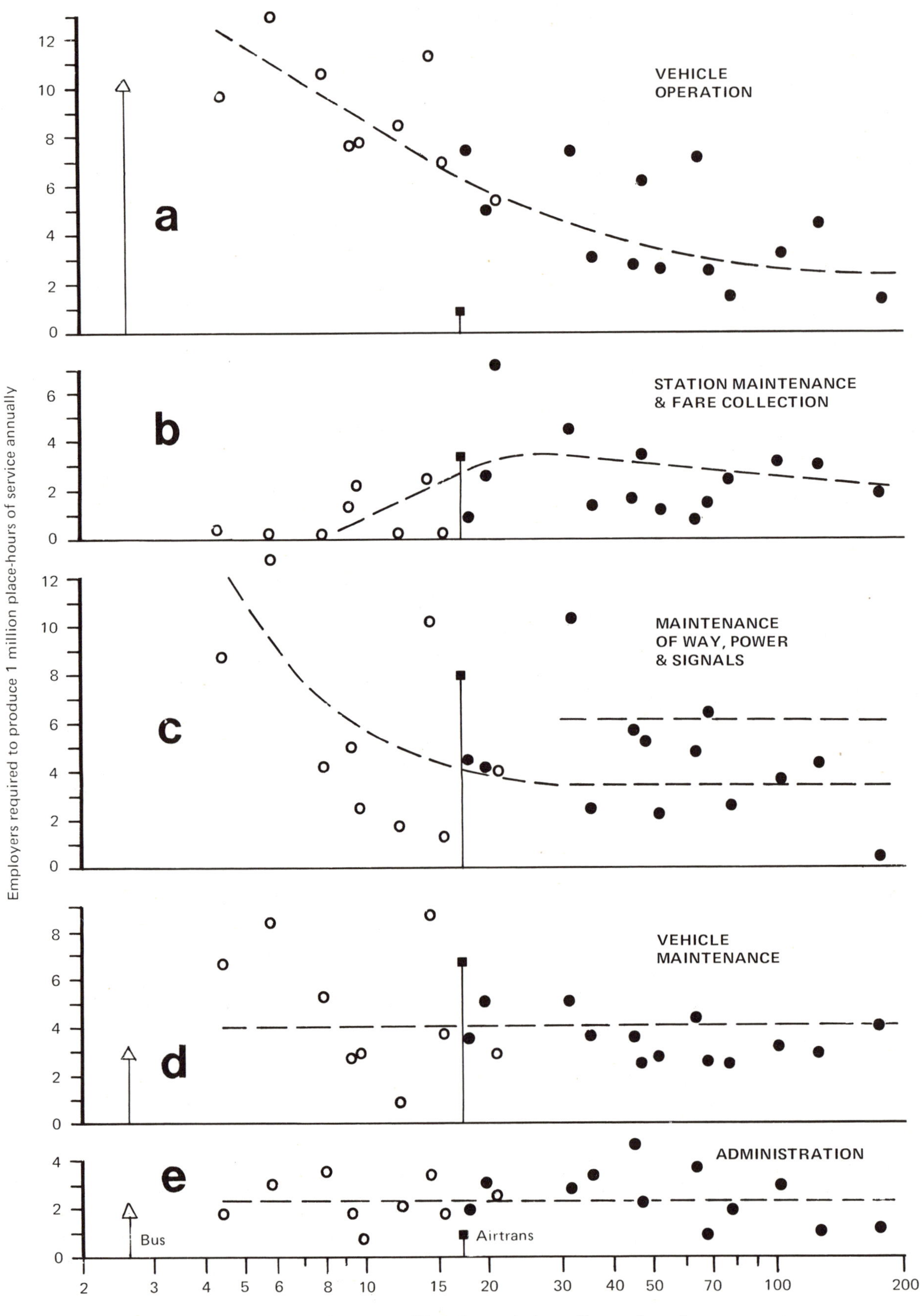

average, including a variety of physical and institutional constraints that can be avoided on new systems. Two questions are appropriate: How far can labor requirements be reduced under the *best existing, rather than average,* conditions? What is the lower volume threshold of fixed guideway operation at which labor savings compared to buses can be attained?

To construct *a model of labor requirements on future systems* approaching the best existing, rather than average, practice, two assumptions are made at the outset. One, following Exhibit 2.7, is that the number of employees needed for *administration* is constant across all operating conditions, and equals the present bus and rail average of 2.3 per place-hour. While some properties may be administratively top-heavy, there are others whose management capabilities would be enhanced by more administrative personnel.

The second assumption is that *vehicle maintenance* needs are also set at present average levels per place-hour, which vary in relation to speed as depicted in Exhibit 2.8a. Variation in vehicle maintenance requirements from system to system suggests that economies in this category are possible. However, the trend for vehicles to have air-conditioning, more sophisticated electrical equipment, finer passenger appointments, and a more complex structure (such as an articulation joint on large light rail cars) will tend to push maintenance costs up, even when well-publicized bugs in the recent generation of equipment are removed. For small, fully automated vehicles with no operator on board, the maintenance requirement is assumed at twice that of conventional vehicles at comparable speed. This is significantly below Morgantown, slightly below Airtrans, but substantially above the other two airport peoplemovers. The labor requirement per place-hour—not per place-mile, per vehicle, or otherwise—is chosen for these two categories because it has the least variation around the mean value.

With these two types of labor set essentially at present levels (which, except for peoplemover car maintenance, are applicable to buses as well), the remaining categories of right-of-way maintenance, stations, and train operation require closer attention.

The labor needs for *maintaining way, power, and signals* are best related directly to the length of a line, adjusted for the number of tracks. Newer rapid transit systems average about 2.3 track-miles per line-mile, and the number of employees per mile shown in Exhibit 2.8b is standardized for this trackage; the light rail figures are not adjusted. Three outlying observations aside, the number of employees per mile of light rail or streetcar line is in the range of 1.6 to 5.1; the Airtrans peoplemover is also in that range. Older systems and the complex Montreal rubber-tired-and-steel-wheel guideway aside, the number of employees per mile of rapid transit line ranges from 3.3 on PATCO and 4.9 on TTC to 7.9 on BART and 10.3 on WMATA. There is some tendency for the maintenance of way, power, and signals employees to increase with increasing service volume. In deference to this, the selected function ("assumed" lower range in Exhibit 2.8b) is taken to rise between a volume of 10 million and a volume of 50 million place-miles per line-mile as shown. At lower and higher volumes the labor requirement for maintenance of way, power, and signals is assumed to be constant per mile of line. This overstates the requirement of systems such as MARTA and TTC by over 50 percent, and may understate the requirement of systems in the lowest volume range, but seems to fit the important intermediate range reasonably well. For light rail, the maintenance-of-

Exhibit 2.8
Employee Ratios for Maintenance of Vehicles and Right-of-Way

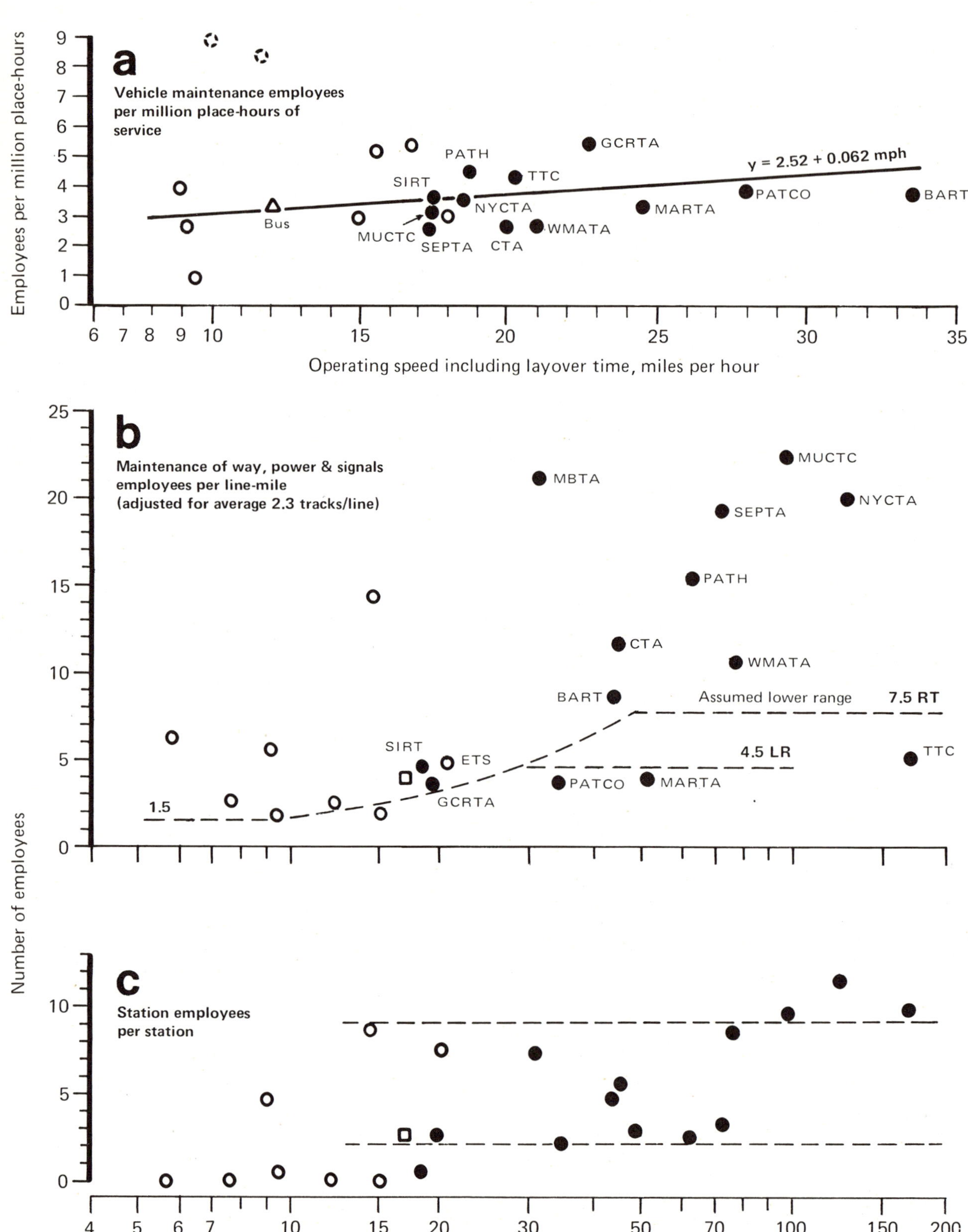

way requirement may be set at a constant 4.5 workers per mile above 30 million place-miles per line-mile.

The labor needs of *station maintenance and fare collection* are best related to the number of stations. The chart in Exhibit 2.9c indicates that there are mainly three kinds of fixed guideway operation: (a) streetcar-type, which have no station employees at all; (b) those with unattended enclosed stations, which require upkeep of platforms and of fare collection equipment; (c) those with fully attended stations, which have a passenger service agent present at most times, and which typically also require more upkeep. At least 2.0 employees per station are required for the second type of operation, and at least 9.0 for the third type. Depending on how frequently stations of each type are spaced (a function of operating speed), the station labor requirement becomes a fixed cost per mile of line, so that the station cost per place-mile declines with traffic density, but the cost per place-hour increases with speed. Unless carefully controlled, this fixed station labor requirement can negate economies of train operation at moderate to low volumes of service.

The labor requirement for *vehicle operation* on conventional systems is primarily a function of train size. The dashed line in Exhibit 2.9 shows the theoretical peak hour train size at each volume of service, *if* one assumes that the headway stays at 7.5 minutes (8 trains per hour) and if average peaking conditions prevail. Above-average peaking of service could conceivably increase the train size at each level of annual volume by 20 percent or more, but reducing the minimum peak hour headway to a more convenient 6 minutes would reduce it by 20 percent. The curve is closely approached by six existing operations.

If the vehicle operator requirement were directly proportional to the number of individual operating units (buses or trains), train operation at the assumed frequency would indeed result in very dramatic reductions in manpower. At a volume of 5 million place-miles per line-mile (950 places per direction per peak hour or the lower threshold of existing light rail operations), 8 trains would replace 16 regular (61-place) or 10 articulated (93-place) buses, for a 50 or a 20 percent saving, respectively. At a volume of 20 million place-miles per line-mile (the threshold of existing rapid transit operations), the respective savings in operating labor would be 87 or 80 percent.

Why are savings of this magnitude not evident on existing systems? First of all, most of the existing streetcar lines do not operate trains; their vehicle size, only marginally larger than a bus, does not begin to compensate for the extra cost of right-of-way maintenance. Second, of the three light rail systems that do operate trains, two require an operator on each car, negating possible savings. Rapid transit systems other than those with ATO, as a rule, operate trains with two crew members on board. Third, the hours of operation for a train are inherently longer than for a bus, requiring more backup workers for other shifts. There is less of a difference between rail cars and buses in terms of hours operated per vehicle, but rail cars dropped from a train during off-peak hours result in no saving in operating labor, while buses not operating off-peak do result in fewer employees needed per peak hour bus. Thus a typical requirement per bus in use during the peak hour that may clock no more than 3,000 hours a year is about two bus drivers; a train which averages 3,600 hours of annual operation (Table A-7) would require closer to three motormen for that reason alone. In addition, rail systems require more off-vehicle operating personnel for dispatching, control, and operation of yards, which easily

Exhibit 2.9
Train Size Related to Service Volume

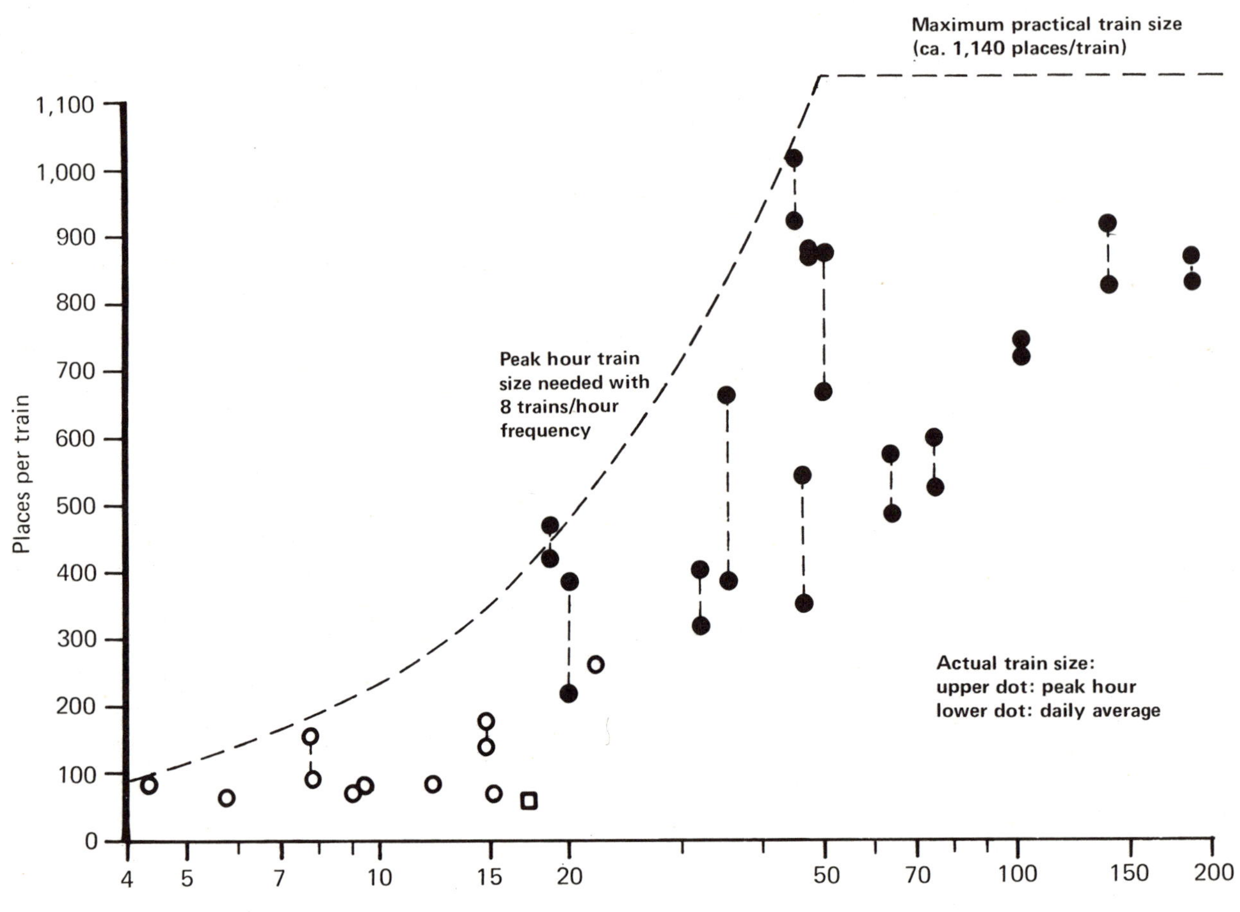

adds 20 to 30 percent to the motormen and conductors. Also, work rules and crew assignment practices on rapid transit tend to require more workers than would be needed on a bus or on a streetcar. The New York City Transit Authority requires 5.2 motormen* alone per peak hour train in use. In part, this is a consequence of long runs per train. It is difficult to fit these into the working day of a crew, considering breaks for lunch and the time the crew needs to get to the train. With a smaller system, Toronto requires only half as many. To ensure observance of its close 1.5-minute headway, PATH places special car inspectors at key locations during peak periods. These are not needed on systems with less stringent schedules.

In practice, the number of vehicle operating employees (not just motormen) per train varies over a broad range, even if crew size is the same (line 25 in Table A-6). A reasonable minimum with one-man crews is 4.5 operating personnel per peak hour train in use, similar to PATCO, WMATA, and Edmonton. With curtailed evening and weekend service, and with a simple operation requiring few off-train operating workers, this figure may drop to 3.0.

The number of trains that have to be in use during the peak hour to operate a given schedule—such as the 8 train per hour frequency assumed in Exhibit 2.9—will depend on how fast a train can turn around. For example, for a one-mile run at 16 mph (or two miles round-trip) one train can return 8 times, providing the necessary frequency. Therefore, 4.5 operating employees per line-mile are needed to carry any volume up to about 60 million place-miles per line-mile, at which point an assumed constraint on train length (10 cars @142 places) precludes further reductions in operating cost (for the lower labor requirement of 3.0 employees per peak hour train, appropriate for simple light rail operations, a similar train size constraint is assumed at 3 cars @113 places). At a higher speed, fewer trains, and at a lower speed, more trains per mile will be needed.

On fully automated systems, vehicle operator requirements represent, within limits, a fixed figure. Only 8 to 12 people at the central console operate in shifts systems as varied as Seattle–Tacoma, Airtrans, and Morgantown, which differ sevenfold in the number of place-miles produced. In this case, increasing the speed will not reduce the operating personnel needs, and the relationship to volume per line-mile will depend on the length of the route. The shorter systems, and the ones with lighter volumes, will tend to be penalized. Assuming 10 employees per central operating console, the operating labor requirement for a one-mile system with the traffic density of Fairlane (4 million place-miles per line-mile) will be 2.5 workers per million place-miles, two and a half times greater than a bus at comparable speed. For a five-mile system with the traffic density of the Tampa airport peoplemover (40 million place-miles per line-mile), the labor requirement will be only 0.05 workers per million place-miles, or 5 percent of what it costs in manpower to operate a bus. Of course, for a comparative assessment, all the other categories of labor must be added to that of vehicle operation.

Illustrative calculations of labor requirements for rapid transit, light rail, and automated peoplemovers, based on these detailed assumptions, are presented in Exhibit 2.10. They are shown for arbitrarily selected levels of service volume, and for a range of service frequencies (or route lengths, in the case of peoplemovers).

*Of these, 26 percent are yard motormen, solely concerned with train movements in yards.

Exhibit 2.10

Illustrative Calculations of Labor Requirements for Rapid Transit, Light Rail, Bus on Busway, and Automated Peoplemover

Given: **a) Rapid transit line** 9 miles long with 5,700 peak-hour passengers in one direction at maximum load point on a weekday; 25 mph gross operating speed including layover (32 mph net speed); cars of 71m^2 gross floor area or 142 places each; unattended stations, no short-turning of trains, 1 passenger for 1 place in peak hour at maximum load point.

Assume: Typical peaking at about 11.8% of all-day service in 1 direction during peak hour, 310 weekday equivalents in a year.

Therefore: 5,700: 0.118 = 48,400 (rounded) places per direction per day x 2 directions x 9 miles x 310 days = **270 million annual place-miles; 10.8 million annual place-hours; 30 million place-miles/line-mile**

and: 5,700: 142 places/car = 40 (rounded) cars needed crossing cordon in 1 direction during peak hour.

Assuming the following headways:	10 min.	7.5 min.	6 min.	4 min.	3 min.
This requires a frequency of:	6 trains @ 7 cars	8 trains @ 5 cars	10 trains @ 4 cars	15 trains @ 3 cars	20 trains @ 2 cars
18-mile round-trip of 25 mph requires 0.72 hours, meaning actual train sets needed for peak-hour operation exclusive of spares and rounded up (30-35 cars needed; this variation ignored in calculations below):	5 trains	6 trains	8 trains	11 trains	15 trains
Operating workers needed @ 4.5 assumed in text per peak-hour train set in use (rounded up):	23	27	36	50	68
Vehicle maintenance workers needed at 25 mph @ 4.2/million place-hours (Exhibit 2.9a):	45	45	45	45	45
Maintenance-of-way workers needed @ 4.5/mile at 30 million place-miles/line-mile (Exhibit 2.9b):	41	41	41	41	41
Station workers needed for 10 unattended stations at 25 mph @ 2 per station (Exhibit 2.9c):	20	20	20	20	20
Administrative workers needed @ 2.3/million place-hours (Exhibit 2.8e):	25	25	25	25	25
TOTAL WORKERS NEEDED:	**154**	**158**	**167**	**181**	**199**
per million place-miles:	0.570	0.585	0.619	0.670	0.737
per million place-hours:	14.25	14.63	15.46	16.75	18.43
Estimated dollar cost per place-mile in 1977 prices assuming $20,700 per worker per year and labor cost as 80% of operating and maintenance cost:	1.47¢	1.51¢	1.60¢	1.73¢	1.90¢
Estimated dollar cost per passenger-mile in 1977 prices assuming 23% average occupancy:	6.4¢	6.6¢	7.0¢	7.5¢	8.3¢

Exhibit 2.10 (cont'd.)

Illustrative Calculations of Labor Requirements for Rapid Transit, Light Rail, Bus on Busway, and Automated Peoplemover

Given: **b) Light rail line** 9 miles long with 2,800 peak-hour passengers in one direction at maximum load point on a weekday; 20 mph gross operating speed including layover (27 mph net speed); cars of $70m^2$ gross floor area or 140 places each; curbside-type stops with self-service fare collection; no short-turning of trains, 1 passenger for 1 place in peak hour at maximum load point.

Assume: Typical peaking at about 11.8% of all-day service in 1 direction during peak hour, 310 weekday equivalents in a year.

Therefore: 2,800: 0.118 = 23,730 places per direction per day x 2 directions x 9 miles x 310 days = **132.4 million annual place-miles; 6.6 million annual place-hours; 14.7 million place-miles/line-mile.**

and: 2,800: 140 places/car = 20 cars needed crossing cordon in 1 direction during peak hour.

Assuming the following headways:	12 min.	7.5 min.	6 min.	3 min.
This requires a frequency of :	5 trains @ 4 cars	8 trains @ 2.5 cars	10 trains @ 2 cars	20 trains @ 1 car
18-mile round-trip at 20 mph requires 0.9 hours, meaning actual train sets needed for peak-hour operation exclusive of spares and rounded up:	5 trains @ 4 cars	8 trains @ 2.5 cars	9 trains @ 2 cars	18 trains @ 1 car
Operating workers needed @ 3.0 assumed in text per peak-hour train set in use:	15	24	27	54
Vehicle maintenance workers needed @ 3.8/million place-hours (Exhibit 2.9a):	25	25	25	25
Maintenance-of-way workers needed @ 2.2/mile at 14.7 million place-miles/line-mile (Exhibit 2.9b:	20	20	20	20
Administrative workers needed @ 2.3/million place-hours (Exhibit 2.8c):	15	15	15	15
TOTAL WORKERS NEEDED:	**75**	**84**	**87**	**114**
per million place-miles:	0.566	0.634	0.657	0.861
per million place-hours:	11.32	12.69	13.14	17.22
Estimated dollar cost per place-mile in 1977 prices assuming $20,700 per worker per year and labor cost at 80% of total operating and maintenance cost:	1.46¢	1.64¢	1.70¢	2.22¢
Estimated dollar cost per passenter-mile in 1977 prices assuming 23% average occupancy:	6.4¢	7.1¢	7.4¢	9.6¢

Exhibit 2.10 (cont'd.)
Illustrative Calculations of Labor Requirements for Rapid Transit, Light Rail, Bus on Busway, and Automated Peoplemover

c) Express bus on exclusive busway comparison for identical conditions.

2,800 peak-hour places per direction at maximum load point : 63 places/standard bus = 45 buses crossing cordon, or:		1.33 min headway
2,800 : 93 places/ articulated large bus = 30 buses crossing cordon, or:	2 min. headway	
18-mile round-trip at 20 mph requires 0.9 hours, meaning actual buses needed for peak-hour operation exclusive of spares and rounded up:	27 buses	41 buses
Operating workers needed @ 2 per peak-hour bus in use (incl. dispatchers & supervisors):	54	82
Vehicle maintenance workers needed @ 3.8/million place-hours (same as above):	25	25
Maintenance-of-way workers needed assumed @ 0.75/mile:	7	7
Administrative workers needed @ 2.3/million place-hours (same as above):	15	15
TOTAL WORKERS NEEDED:	**101**	**129**
per million place-miles:	0.763	0.974
per million place-hours:	15.25	19.48
Estimated dollar cost in 1977 prices assuming $20,700 per worker per year and labor cost at 80% of total operating and maintenance cost:	1.97¢	2.52¢
Estimated dollar cost per passenger-mile in 1977 prices assuming 23% average occupancy:	8.6¢	11.0¢

Given: **d) Automated peoplemover** 1 mile, 3 miles, and 5 miles long with a service density of 15 million annual place-miles per line-mile, gross operating speed of 10 mph and partially attended stations a'la Airtrans. Annual total 15, 45 and 75 million place-miles; 1.5, 4.5 and 7.5 million place-hours, respectively.

	1 mile	3 miles	5 miles
Operating workers needed @ 10 per central console:	10	10	10
Vehicle maintenance workers at twice the rate of Exhibit 2.9a or 6 worker/million place-hours at 10 mph:	9	27	45
Maintenance-of-way workers @ 2/station with ½ mile spacing:	6	14	22
Administrative workers @ 2.3/million place-hours (Exhibit 2.8c):	3	11	17
TOTAL WORKERS NEEDED:	**31**	**69**	**106**
per million place-miles:	2.06	1.53	1.41
per million place-hours:	20.6	15.3	14.1

Repeated for each level of service volume, these calculations result in the curves shown in Exhibit 2.11, which indicate how labor cost in workers needed per million place-miles varies with service volume, if operating speed, service frequency, and the type of stations are specified, and if conditions approaching the best existing practice, rather than average practice, are assumed for operating and wayside personnel.

From Exhibit 2.11 one can draw the following conclusions:

(1) *For fixed guideways to attain lower labor costs per place-mile than prevailing bus operations, extremely low volumes of service are sufficient.*

(a) At 4 million place-miles per line-mile (equivalent to 13 buses per direction in the peak hour of the lowest light rail volume encountered in practice), a lean *light rail line* operating at least 8 trains an hour at 20 mph (32 km/h) may begin to offer labor economies compared to buses at the typical areawide operating speed of 12.5 mph (20 km/h).

(b) At 6 million place-miles per line-mile—one-third of the lowest volume encountered in practice—a *rapid transit line* with unmanned stations operating 8 trains an hour at 25 mph (40 km/h) may begin to offer labor economies compared to buses at the typical areawide operating speed of 12.5 mph (20 km/h). This threshold moves up to 18 million place-miles per line-mile (56 bus equivalents) if the service frequency is doubled to 16 trains an hour and if, in addition, the stations are fully attended.

(c) At 10 million place-miles per line-mile (31 peak hour bus equivalents) an *automated peoplemover* 1 mile long operating at 10 mph (16 km/h) may begin to offer labor economies compared to buses at the typical downtown speed of 6 mph (10 km/h). This threshold can be reduced if the peoplemover is longer.

(2) *For fixed guideways to attain lower labor costs than buses at an equal speed, substantially higher volumes of service are required.*

(a) At about 8 million place-miles per line-mile (26 peak-hour bus equivalents) a *light rail* line operating at least 8 trains per hour at 20 mph (32 km/h) may begin to offer labor economies compared to a mix of local and express buses at an equal speed.

(b) At about 23 million place-miles per line-mile (72 peak-hour bus equivalents and just above the threshold of existing service) a *rapid transit* line operating at least 8 trains per hour at 25 mph (32 km/h) may begin to offer labor economies compared to a mix of express and local buses at an equal speed. This threshold moves up to 35 million place-miles per line-mile (109 peak hour bus equivalents) if the service frequency is doubled to 16 trains an hour; and to about 70 million place-miles per line-mile (218 peak hour bus equivalents) if in addition the stations are fully attended.

(c) At about 23 million place-miles per line-mile (72 peak hour bus equivalents) an *automated peoplemover* one mile long operating at 10 mph (16 km/h) may begin to offer labor economies compared to buses operating at the same speed. This threshold can be reduced to 14 million place-miles per line-mile (44 peak hour bus equivalents) if the peoplemover is about three miles (4.8 km) long. It can be reduced further, to about 7 million place-miles per line-mile, if, in addition, its stations are completely unattended.

It is clear that the degree of station attendance has a significant influence on the labor cost of all fixed guideway systems. If the object is to attain labor economies

Exhibit 2.11
Illustrative Comparisons of Minimum Fixed Guideway Labor Costs

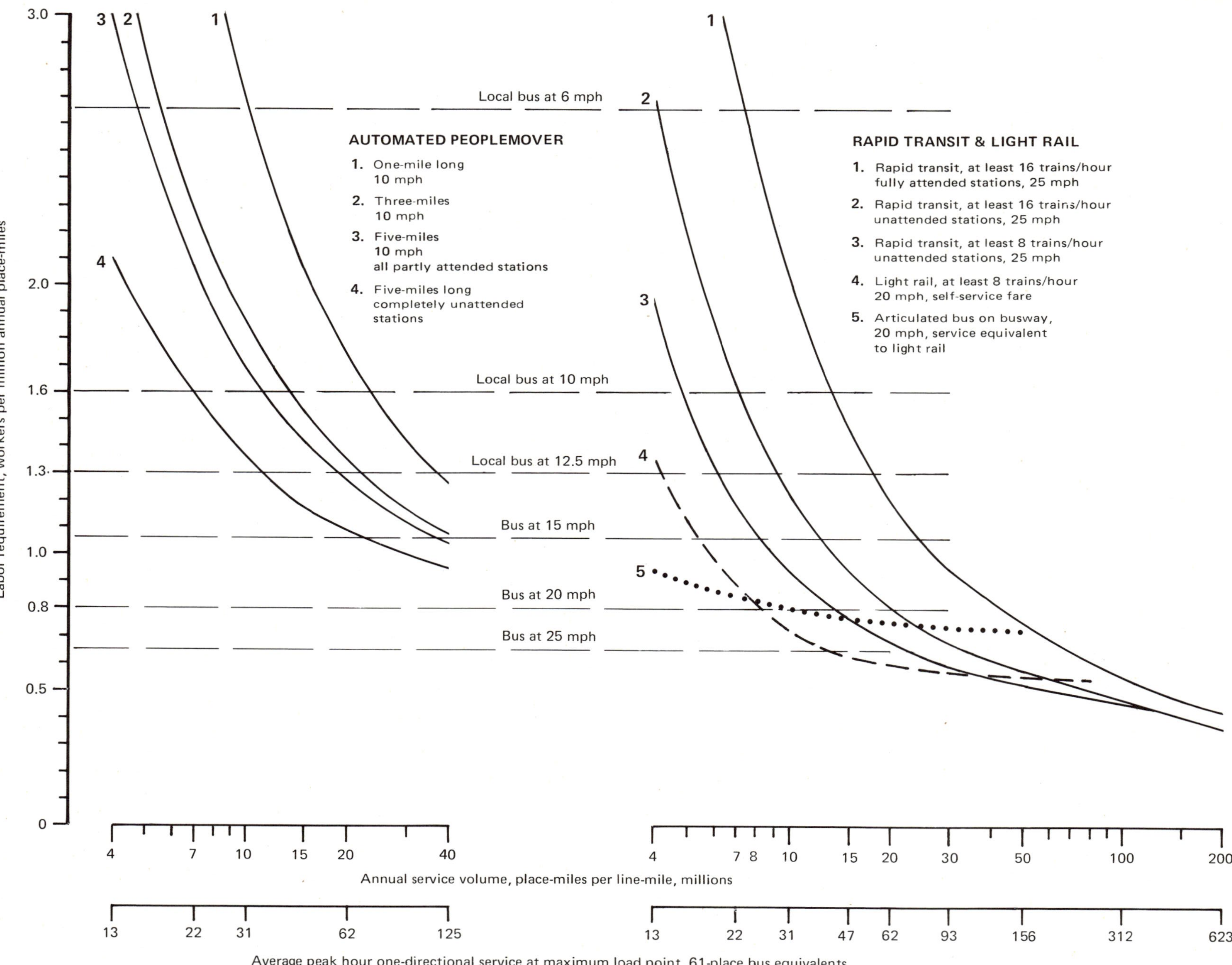

compared to the bus at the same speed, fully attended stations on rapid transit can only be provided in the high-volume range of 70 million or more place-miles per line-mile annually, comparable to WMATA. For lower volumes, high-level platforms with either automatic or self-service fare collection are appropriate. Yet even the cost of unattended enclosed high-level platform stations begins to be a burden at traffic densities below about 23 million place-miles per line-mile, at which point sidewalk-level platforms with basically no station expense become appropriate in the pure light rail mode. Of course, boarding delays associated with low-level platforms and the limited grade-separation restrict the operating speed in this case to at most 20 mph (32 km/h), as in the illustrative operation shown in Exhibit 2.10 and 2.11.

A note on express bus operations. As a yardstick of comparison, Exhibit 2.11 uses bus labor costs at speeds of 6, 10, 12.5, 15, 20, and 25 mph, derived by dividing the average systemwide bus requirement of 16 workers per million annual place-hours by the respective operating speed. However, systemwide operating speeds above 15 mph (24 km/h) do not occur in practice. Such speeds imply a strong presence of express services. An operating speed of 25 mph (40 km/h) is about the limit of urban express runs, since it represents a schedule speed of about 35 mph, which is rarely reached on an entire route.

It is by no means clear that the systemwide labor requirement per place hour which holds true in the 6 to 15 mph range also continues in the express range, because of numerous idiosyncrasies of the express operations. For example, they often have extensive deadhead mileage (up to 60 percent of daily vehicle-hours) and a low utilization of bus driver time, unless part-time workers are employed or split shifts are common. Because of the part-time nature of the services, the driver requirement per peak hour bus in use may often appear to be very low, but the resulting service is in no way equivalent to fixed guideway service with reasonable off-peak and weekend frequency.

While empirical analysis of express bus operations is beyond the scope of this book, the data presented so far make it possible to synthesize the labor requirements of an express bus operation on busway that would provide service pretty much equivalent to a fixed guideway. It is recognized that a bus on busway may not attain the same speed with the same number of stops as, let us say, light rail throughout the day because of vehicle performance and station boarding delay, but instead may provide greater service frequency. Usually, the tendency in designing express bus operations is the opposite, namely to reduce the number of stops to maximize speed, sacrificing some travel between intermediate points. The exact magnitude of these tradeoffs can be determined only in a site-specific analysis of alternatives when exact origins, destinations, and the potential time savings between them are known. For a generic comparison, it is assumed that an express bus service with large, articulated vehicles can attain the same 20 mph operating speed (27 mph schedule speed) as light rail with stops every 0.7 miles. This illustrative service is depicted in Exhibit 2.10c and marked by the dotted curve in Exhibit 2.11.

A basic premise of the labor requirements model used here is that vehicle maintenance and administrative costs of buses and fixed guideways on a place-hour basis are the same. This leaves only the vehicle operator and the maintenance-of-way requirements to be compared, since station labor on express buses (except in the case of operations into bus terminals, off-vehicle fare collection on high-density routes, or upkeep of bus shelters) can be largely ignored.

If 20-hour service comparable to a fixed guideway is to be provided, with half the weekday service on weekends and holidays, as is assumed here for the rail systems (310 weekday service equivalents in a year), then a ratio of 1.5 vehicle operating personnel per bus in peak hour service or less, typical of many local bus systems, is not sufficient. Including dispatchers and line supervisors, at least 2 workers per bus are needed, compared to an assumed 3 operating workers per peak hour light rail train in use and 4.5 per peak hour rapid transit train in use.

If the operation is to be on an exclusive busway, maintenance-of-way personnel are also needed. One way to estimate this requirement is by comparison with freeways which carry heavy vehicles. The New Jersey Turnpike and the New York State Thruway employ an average of 0.52 maintenance-of-way workers per lane-mile, suggesting 1.04 per two-lane mile of busway. An alternate estimate by Louis T. Klauder and Associates[18] is about 0.65 per two-lane mile. An intermediate value of 0.75 is used in Exhibit 2.10c. It is lower than that on light rail because no electrical systems are involved. The earlier replacement need of highway-type pavement is ignored, being basically a capital expense.

Adding these labor needs for an illustrative service with 2,800 passengers per hour per direction at the maximum load point (14.7 million place-miles per line-mile, same as on the light rail line shown in Exhibits 2.10 and 2.11) results in a requirement for 19.5 workers per million place-hours with standard 63-place buses, and 15.3 workers per million place-hours with articulated 93-place buses. This is more than the 16 and 12.6 workers per million place-hours that one would expect by simply extrapolating from standard buses in local service, and more than is shown for light rail with 6- to 12-minute frequencies in Exhibit 2.10b.

As a result, Exhibit 2.11 suggests that an express bus operation with large, articulated vehicles on an exclusive busway attains lower labor costs than a light rail line with equivalent service only at volumes below 8 million place-miles per line-mile (about 25 regular bus equivalents per peak direction per hour), a volume at which the provision of any exclusive guideway—bus or rail—begins to be touch-and-go.

The example is presented to illustrate the issues involved, not to "prove" that light rail is necessarily more labor efficient than articulated bus on busway at volumes above 8 million place-miles per line-mile. The issues revolve around the *operating labor requirement per peak hour moving unit* (bus or train) *in service, and guideway maintenance requirements. Their relative magnitudes determine where the break-even point between bus-on-busway and light rail occurs.* Unfortunately, data for precisely these two functions show large variability from system to system in the rail case, and are based on indirect evidence in the bus case. Because the express bus and rail labor cost curves intersect at small angles, a modest vertical shift in total labor requirements results in a large shift in the "break-even" service volume on the logarithmic horizontal scale. For example, if the light rail labor requirement for maintenance-of-way were 3.0 rather than 1.5 workers per mile of line, articulated bus-on-busway would be more labor efficient at volumes up to 13 rather than 8 million place-miles per line-mile. Both the nature of the data and the nature of the relationship are such that arguments concerning the labor-saving merits of articulated buses versus light rail vehicles cannot be easily settled.

More important than the exact break-even point in bus-to-rail comparisons is the *marginal labor required for providing more capacity.* A moot issue in years of transit ridership decline, this becomes important when transit ridership is growing. If one sets the labor cost of providing the equivalent of 15 million annual place-miles of service per mile of line by any mode equal to one, then the cost of doubling and quadrupling this amount of service by each of the modes is as shown below based on the labor requirements model presented.

	Articulated bus on busway	*Light rail at equal speed*	*Automated people-mover*	*Rapid transit @8 trains/hour*	*Rapid transit @16 trains/hour*
Labor cost of providing 15 million place-miles per mile of line annually	1.0	1.0	1.0	1.0	1.0
Labor cost of doubling service volume	1.9	1.7	1.6	1.5	1.4
Labor cost of quadrupling service volume	3.8	3.0	2.8	2.5	2.1

It is clear that in the range of service volumes shown—from 2,850 to 11,400 places per peak hour per direction at the maximum load point (the equivalent of 47 to 187 standard buses per hour)—the fixed guideway modes show very dramatic returns to scale. If traffic growth is anticipated, the marginal labor cost of providing more service cannot be overlooked in comparing alternatives.

ENERGY REQUIREMENTS

From the energy viewpoint, the key feature of urban fixed guideways is that they rely on electric propulsion. The differences between it and liquid fuel propulsion, which is typical of most free-wheeled vehicles, concern both the quality of the environment and the quantity of the primary energy resources consumed. Environmental side effects are mentioned here only briefly, because they depend in large part on the means of electric power generation. The focus is on the ability of rail systems to attain savings in primary energy resources compared to the modes previously used. For that purpose, what amounts to an energy requirements model is developed, which first focuses on the difference between gross resource input and net energy requirements. It then deals with energy requirements for vehicle operation, vehicle maintenance, vehicle manufacture, wayside facilities and stations, and guideway construction. The latter two categories represent fixed expenditures which cause total energy requirements to vary with travel volume. To calculate actual energy savings, both indirect effects of travel diversion to rail, and prospective changes in the energy efficiency of different modes are dealt with in conclusion.

Electricity vs. liquid fuels: environmental side-effects. Electric propulsion has the obvious advantage of removing the source of air pollution from the passenger and, under favorable conditions, also reducing the total emissions into the atmosphere. The latter will depend on the fuel used and the control devices installed at local power plants. With the national average mix of fuels used to generate electricity and no stack controls, carbon monoxide and hydrocarbon emissions are cut about 90 percent compared to diesel propulsion. Nitrogen oxides are moderately reduced. Sulfur oxide and particulate emissions are greatly increased, though power-plant particulates may be less toxic than diesel particulates. The net effect is to increase total emissions, measured in grams per place-mile, by about 20 percent compared to diesel bus; however, if stack controls removing only *half* the sulfur oxides and particulates are in operation, electric propulsion results in about 30 percent less total emissions than diesel.[19] Greater efficiencies of stack controls or power plants less dependent on fossil fuels than the national average will provide greater gains.

Important both for passenger comfort and the well-being of pedestrians, electric propulsion is odorless and quiet. It eliminates the vibration characteristic of reciprocating internal combustion engines, thereby prolonging vehicle life. It sharply cuts the need for guideway ventilation if the system operates in a tunnel, and therefore usually remains the only feasible choice when underground operation is envisaged. Last but not least, close to one-quarter of the nation's electrical energy already comes from solar (hydropower) and nuclear sources rather than from burning petroleum or other fossil fuels.

Electricity vs. liquid fuels: requirements for vehicle operation. With respect to the total amount of energy consumed, the energy system associated with the diesel engine, used on most buses, is often credited to be more economical than present-day electrical systems. This premise requires investigation.

To begin with, the difference between *net and gross energy consumption for operating the vehicles* must be established. Net energy is that delivered to the vehicle, whether in the form of electricity, diesel oil, or gasoline. Gross energy is the amount of primary energy sources (coal, crude oil, or their equivalent in other energy forms) that must be extracted to make the eventual delivery to the vehicle. From the viewpoint of the national economy, it is the gross cost in resources that matters. Between extraction and final delivery, numerous steps involve energy losses, as shown below.

	Electricity		Transport fuels
Gross use, energy units	*1,000*		*1,000*
−1.5% used in delivery	985	−17.3% used in delivery and lost in refining and distribution[21]	
−67.1% heat loss at powerplants	324		
−8.0% loss in transmission	298AC		
−2.5% loss in conversion[20]			
Net available for vehicle operation	*290 DC*		*827*
Gross as a multiple of net	3.45		1.21

Only 29.0 percent of the energy originally contained in the coal extracted at a mine, for example, reaches the electric transit vehicle, whereas 82.7 percent of the energy in the crude oil extracted reaches the internal combustion-powered vehicle.

For this reason, the heat content of the energy used by electric and diesel vehicles, 3,413 Btu per kilowatt hour and 136,000 Btu per gallon diesel oil, must be multiplied by 3.45 and 1.21, respectively, to bring both measures to the common denominator of gross energy input needed for vehicle operation.* It is on this basis that the comparison between liquid fuel and electric vehicles in Exhibit 2.12 is made. As in the rest of this chapter, energy use for vehicle operation is given per place-mile, rather than per vehicle-mile, to take account of different vehicle sizes; it is then related to average operating speed.

The gross energy requirements for vehicle operation on most of the eight *rapid-transit* systems for which comparable data are available (and on the electrified territory of the Long Island Rail Road, with rolling stock similar to rapid transit) are tightly clustered around the average value of 0.057 kwh or *670 Btu per place-mile* (150 cal. per place-km). This value is nearly independent of speed: the energy needed for frequent acceleration on the slower systems roughly balances that needed to attain high speed on the faster systems. The two outlying observations in the high-speed range, PATCO (highest energy use) and BART (lowest energy use), are explained by differences in weight and in the electrical system.** Both of these cars, and the LIRR cars, have air-conditioning, which many of those in the lower speed range do not.

Buses, if measured in terms of gross energy use for vehicle operation per place-mile, are not necessarily more energy efficient than rapid transit. The intersection of the two curves in Exhibit 2.12 shows that in the speed range where most urban buses operate—around 12 mph (19.3 km/h)—they use the same gross energy as electric rapid transit, about 670 Btu per place-mile (105 cal per place-km). This figure (which at 0.25 gallons per vehicle-mile also represents the national average for 1976***) may rise to 800 Btu (126 cal/km) in downtowns where speeds are slow and decline to 415 Btu (65 cal/km) at intercity freeway speeds, where buses need less energy to operate than rapid transit.

Light rail energy statistics are sparse.[22] It is often difficult to separate the electricity used by different types of vehicles operated by a multimodal agency supplied from a common network. The handbook figure of 4.6 kwh per vehicle-mile for a typical PCC car[23] translates into *about 785 Btu per place-mile* (123 cal per place-km) by the accounting used here. This, however, reflects a driving cycle with some 10 stops per mile (6 per km). The NJT Newark line, with 2.3 stops per mile,. reports its use of electricity at 4.2 kwh per vehicle-mile, the same as rapid transit on a place-mile basis. Energy use figures listed in Table A-6 for other streetcar and light rail systems include shop power and wayside facilities and do not show the consumption for vehicle operation separately. The electricity use of the Boeing light rail vehicle is reported to be about 26 percent higher than that of the PCC car.[24] By contrast the new Edmonton system uses 3.82 kwh per vehicle-mile or 370 Btu

*The 0.29 energy efficiency of the electrical system may not be applicable in areas where marginal additions to electrical capacity can be provided from hydro power.

**BART has chopper controls and is designed for regenerative braking, but the latter is not fully effective with low service frequency, when the third rail lacks receptivity for the regenerated power.

***Nationally fuel use per bus-mile has not been static, but has increased from 0.240 gallons in 1970 to 0.264 gallons in 1978; advanced-design buses use close to 0.300 gallons per bus-mile.

Exhibit 2.12
Gross Energy Requirement for Vehicle Operation

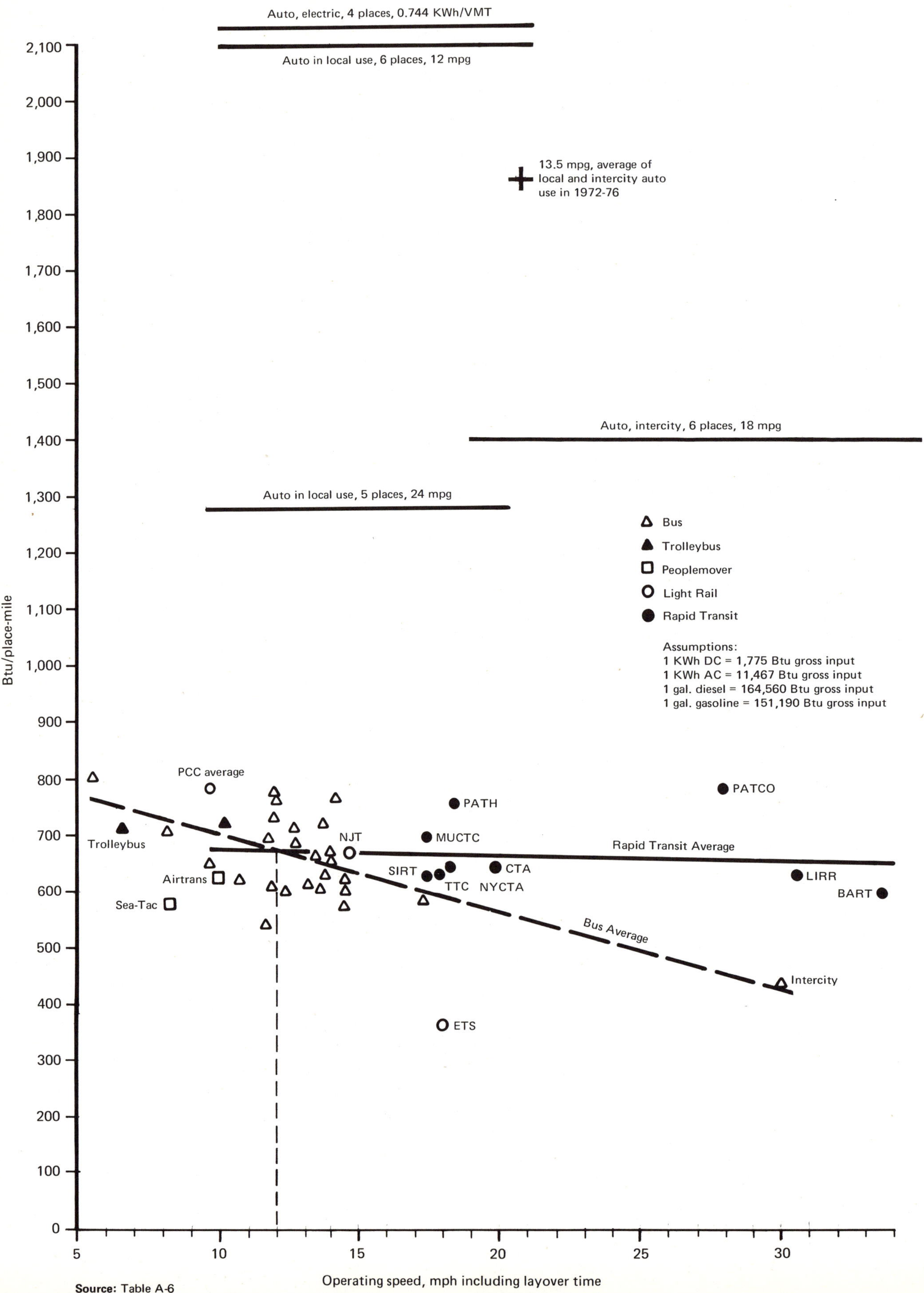

Source: Table A-6

per place-mile (58 cal/km). Because its German DuWag car is used on new systems in Calgary and San Diego, this value is adopted for Exhibit 3.13. However, the performance of the car is sluggish, and for an operating speed of 20 mph it requires close to a 1-mile station spacing, not the 0.7 mile used elsewhere in this study.

For small vehicle, driverless *peoplemover systems,* the Airtrans and Sea-Tac data on electricity use for vehicle operation appear to be fairly representative, averaging 580 Btu of gross use per place-mile (91 cal per place-km). This is similar to the energy use of another rubber-tired vehicle propelled by electricity, namely the trolleybus, which uses about 700 Btu per place-mile (110 cal/km). Two trolleybus observations* are included in Exhibit 2.12. The inherent energy disadvantage of rubber-tired vehicles compared to those with steel wheels is not apparent from the exhibit, because differences in vehicle weight per passenger place play a larger role than the difference in rolling resistance.

The overall pattern is that *both fixed guideway and free-wheeled mass transit vehicles have similar energy requirements for vehicle operation, regardless of diesel or electric propulsion.* The greater efficiency of the electrical motor compared to the diesel engine is offset by greater losses in conversion from the primary energy source. Thus, both bus and rail requirements are about one-third those of the old-style auto in local urban use.[25] Obviously, if recalculated per passenger-mile, these levels will vary depending on how many of the passenger places are in fact occupied.

A 23.3 percent occupancy, average for the urban rail systems reviewed here (but optimistic for the bus, which averages 19 percent), corresponds to 1.4 persons per auto with six passenger places. Such an occupancy is not atypical for *urban weekday use*[26] and for that case the relationships shown remain valid with respect to energy required per passenger-mile as well as per place-mile.

Unquestionably, the short-term prospect is for the energy gap between the auto and the mass transit modes to narrow. Yet, even if energy consumption per mile for *all* autos were cut in half compared to 1972–1976 levels shown in Exhibit 2.12, in local urban driving the auto would still use 45 percent more energy than existing rail transit if 1.4 persons per car and 23.3 percent transit occupancy are assumed. For the auto to become competitive with rail at that point its occupancy would have to increase to 2.0, or transit occupancy would have to drop to 16 percent.

For the long term, further reductions in auto energy use per mile—say, to one-third the 1972–76 level—will be more difficult to attain and offset to some extent by changing relationships between gross and net energy use. With more cogeneration to reduce thermal loss at power plants, the energy cost of electricity will decline. Meanwhile, if synthetic fuels are substituted for petroleum, the energy cost of liquid fuels will rise. Oil extracted from the Athabasca sands delivers but 70 percent of the original energy to the consumer. The conversion efficiency for oil from shale is expected to be around 60 percent, and that for advanced coal liquification methods 65 to 55 percent. Coal liquification processes developed in Germany by

*In New York City in 1954–57, trolleybuses averaging 6.64 mph used 3.64 kwh per vehicle-mile; in Dayton, Ohio, in 1975 trolleybuses averaging 10.09 mph used 3.63 kwh per vehicle-mile. Each had about 60 passenger places. Interestingly, with a diesel fuel cost of $1.00 per gallon, electricity for trolleybuses becomes less expensive if it costs less than 7.2¢ per kwh.

1929 have a conversion efficiency of 45 to 37 percent, not much better than electricity generation.

The convergence in efficiency rates between electricity and liquified fuels will tend to favor fixed or semi-fixed guideway vehicles that rely on continuous or at least frequent electric supply—be they rail vehicles, trolleybuses, or flywheel buses—at the expense of vehicles which rely on liquid fuels. Regenerative braking with or without flywheels (which have shown energy savings on the order of 20 percent)[27] also seems to be more suitable for electric vehicles.

The prospect of an electric automobile relying on battery-stored, rather than continuous, supply of electricity promises no more competition to the fixed guideway modes than an efficient internal combustion auto. This is so because electric autos incur energy losses during battery charge and in the battery itself; these total 40 to 48 percent at present. Also, the weight of the battery leads to unproductive energy expenditures in driving. Current models average about 0.185 kwh per seat-mile (0.115 kwh per place-km, measured at the wall outlet) for vehicles with 4 passenger places.[28] This performance is indicated at the top of Exhibit 2.12 and is very similar to the 1972–1976 internal combustion auto in urban use, prior to the advent of federal standards. The best performance currently hoped for, with improved batteries and regenerative braking, is 0.1 kwh per seat-mile for a 4-seat auto. On Exhibit 2.12, this would appear in a position similar to the internal combustion auto in urban use at 24 miles per gallon, still significantly above the mass transit modes.

Energy requirements for other than vehicle operation are poorly documented, but cannot be overlooked. On rail lines, the energy consumed by maintenance yards, wayside equipment, and stations may add up to 40 percent or more to the energy for vehicle operation. Vehicle manufacture and guideway construction require additional energy. For a sense of scale, the indirect consumption by all transportation in the United States, estimated from input-output data, adds about 40 percent to the gross fuel used for operating vehicles, or 70 percent to the net fuel used.[29] For the private auto at nationwide average fuel efficiency, the increment to gross fuel used for operation is composed of about 20 percent for repair, service, and sales, 11 percent for manufacture, and 9 percent for roadway construction and resurfacing. Bus energy requirements for maintenance alone have been estimated to add anywhere from 2 to 20 percent to the gross fuel use.[30]

On fixed guideways, *maintenance energy and wayside energy* must be viewed separately. The energy used for vehicle *maintenance* depends on fleet size and, related to fleet output, has been estimated at 0.003 kwh per place-mile.[31] By contrast, *wayside and station* energy is mostly a fixed cost that declines per place-mile as traffic density per line of mile increases. It varies with the spacing of stations, the type of construction (aboveground or underground), and the type of ventilation (with or without costly air-cooling). Wayside and station energy requirements for three systems—CTA, NYCTA, and the new PATCO line—appear to be similar, averaging 130,000 kwh annually per mile of above-ground line and 900,000 kwh* per mile of underground line. These values are arrived at by assuming that differences

*This is mostly AC current, and hence convertible into Btu at 11,467 rather than 11,775 Btu per kwh. With 8,760 hours in a year, the tunnel figure represents about 100 kw per mile.

among the three systems are due to different mileages of tunnel. BART is about 36 percent higher, while PATH is 38 percent lower. The former two values are used to calculate total energy costs in Exhibit 2.13. The extra cost of air-cooling can be estimated, based only on the PATH World Trade Center Station, at 2.14 kw per 1,000 cubic feet (28.3 m^3) including track areas, and depends on the hours of the cooling season.

Comparable maintenance, wayside, and station energy data for *light rail* may be inferred by subtracting the "handbook" value of PCC car electric consumption from "total power purchased" by four systems that operated such cars in 1976 and are listed in Table A-6. This excess of total power purchased over power assumed to be used for vehicle operation averages about 36 percent. It includes power for vehicle maintenance, shops and yards, wayside facilities including station lighting, and in some cases also converter losses substantially in excess of the 2.5 percent used earlier because of obsolete equipment. Assuming that vehicle maintenance requirements remain the same as for rapid transit at 0.003 kwh per place-mile, and making an allowance for the extra losses, one concludes that wayside, yard, and station-related power needs may average some 230,000 kwh annually per mile of line or, given the proportion of lines above ground and underground, perhaps *two-thirds* the level of rapid transit. On the other hand, Edmonton's requirements for wayside and station energy, averaging about 1 million kwh per mile of line (22 percent of which is in tunnel), are about *three times* what one would expect on the basis of average rapid transit requirements.[32] Two elaborate downtown subway stations are responsible for most of this use. Clearly, without closer engineering investigation, light rail wayside and station energy costs cannot be estimated with certainty. For purposes of Exhibit 2.13, the same figures as for rapid transit are used.

The excess of electric power purchased over power used to operate *peoplemovers* is 80 percent or more, exclusive of snowmelting. Subtracting the small vehicle maintenance requirement (assumed at twice the rate of rail vehicles) and prorating over the length of guideway equivalent to two lanes or tracks, one is left with an annual wayside and station energy consumption of 680,000 kwh/mile on Airtrans and 900,000 kwh/mile on the underground Sea-Tac system. These figures are used in Exhibit 2.13 to calculate above-ground and below-ground peoplemover requirements.

The current generation of rubber-tired peoplemover vehicles which use concrete guideways and apply power through the wheels may incur a very large additional wayside energy expense for snow removal. The Morgantown line was built to melt snow by piping a liquid heated by natural gas through the guideway; Fairlane uses electrical resistance heating. Airtrans was not equipped to melt snow and even the modest snowfall in the Dallas–Ft. Worth area put it fully or partially out of service for 142 hours in the winter of 1976–77. That same winter the Morgantown heating system operated for 350 hours on a total of 80 days, and the previous winter, for 558 hours on 41 days.[33] The 1976–77 Morgantown heating requirement at 10.4 billion Btu (2.62 billion cal.) of gas per year per single-lane mile of guideway was about 1.6 times that of all other operating and wayside energy. The Fairlane heating requirement, at 1.3 million kwh (14.9 billion Btu) per year per single-lane mile of guideway for an unspecified number of hours the same year, was about 2.2 times that of all other operating and wayside energy. For the next season, Fairlane adopted a policy of operating at half speed when snowfall is light, and shutting down the system to clean it mechanically when snowfall is heavy. Other systems, serving less discretionary traffic, may find it difficult to accept this degree of unreliability.

For Exhibit 2.13, a heating period of 250 hours per year is selected to reflect middle-latitude United States cities with about 25 inches (64 cm) of annual snowfall, and the thermally more efficient gas heating system is assumed, for an annual requirement of 15 billion Btu per two-lane mile (2.35 billion cal per two-lane km).

Obviously, there are ways of avoiding the guideway heating requirement altogether. One is to build rubber-tired systems only in snow-free climates, such as Miami or Los Angeles. Another is to accept more or less severe service interruptions, as on Airtrans and, later, Fairlane. A third is to place the guideway entirely underground, as Sea-Tac (and the Montreal rapid transit system) have done. As will become apparent from Exhibit 2.15, underground operation can be more energy efficient than snowmelting, the higher energy cost of underground construction and operation notwithstanding. A fourth and *seemingly most promising way is to abandon rubber-on-concrete propulsion and support systems* and use weather-protected rail with traction from a linear motor as the Cabintaxi system does, or an adaptation of the conventional steel-wheel-on-steel-rail technology, as the overhead streetcar on a two-in-one guideway known as "Project 21" proposes to do.[34]

The energy needed to *manufacture* and periodically replace vehicles is a small fraction of total transportation energy, but it does vary among modes according to the longevity of the different equipment. Studies using different methods agree that it takes about 80,000 Btu (20,160 cal) to manufacture 1 kilogram of an automobile.[35] While a similar figure is used for buses, estimates for rail cars vary as much as sixfold, some being much lower, some much higher per unit of weight. This is in part due to differences in materials, e.g., steel vs. aluminum. Here it is assumed for simplicity that rail cars and peoplemover vehicles have the same energy cost per unit of weight as autos and buses. On that basis, using unit weights from Table A-5, annual miles per vehicle from Table A-6, and typical replacement cycles (35 years for rail cars, 20 years for peoplemover vehicles, 12.5 years for buses, and 10 years or 100,000 miles for the auto), manufacturing energy costs per place-mile are estimated in the fourth column of Exhibit 2.13. Rapid transit by this reckoning has the lowest requirement, about 2 percent of its gross vehicle operating energy, and the bus averages about 5 percent. It is clear that even doubling or tripling the rail vehicle manufacturing energy consumption will not make any major comparative difference.

Lastly, there is the fixed energy cost of *building a guideway*, and of replacing its parts as they wear out. Estimates of the energy used for construction are either derived from input-output analysis or from engineering inventories of materials and processes used in construction. The first method is subject to error because it may be difficult to identify mass transit projects in aggregate economic statistics. Also, differing inflation rates for different inputs and changes in technology toward greater or lesser energy intensity make it difficult to convert historic input-output data to present-day dollars. The second method lacks any control totals and fails to account for indirect effects. As a result, past estimates of the energy needed per dollar of construction expenditure for rail transit have varied as much as tenfold.[36]

Fortunately, two recent studies have resolved some of the differences and narrowed this range greatly, to between 62,447 and 71,000 Btu per 1967 dollar, when total national energy use stood at 74,260 Btu per dollar of Gross Domestic Product[37] (GDP). By 1977, GDP cost 40,800 Btu per dollar, and the energy content of a fixed guideway construction dollar shrank to between 26,000 and 34,000 Btu, depending on which of the several indices of inflation in the construction industry one uses to adjust the 1967 figures and ignoring as unknown the impact of technological change. The average of the two latter values, 30,000 Btu in 1977 prices, is the figure used to calculate guideway construction expenditures in the fifth column of Exhibit 2.13.

As an aside, it is worth noting that this construction energy per dollar is lower than the average energy cost of all goods and services in the Gross National Product. One might argue that investing money in transit construction rather than spending it on the average basket of goods and services in and of itself represents an energy saving. On the other hand, the Btu per dollar value for rail transit construction is not much below the highway construction value, contrary to earlier estimates.

The one-time energy expenditure for construction must be converted to an annual cost based on the useful life of the various facilities. The major difference between highway and fixed guideway construction is in longevity. Highway pavements and structures do begin to fall apart after 20 years or earlier, even if terrain modification lasts indefinitely. By contrast, track and wayside mechanical and electrical equipment has at least the same life as rolling stock—35 years. Elevated structures and stations may require basic rehabilitation after 75 years.* Tunnels may last indefinitely, but to avoid statistical distortion, their amortization period here is limited to 100 years. These lifetimes, weighted according to the share of total construction cost that the particular component of construction represents (see Exhibit 2.17), average out to the lifetimes listed in the fifth column of Exhibit 2.13. The indicated cost per mile of line in 1977 dollars, multiplied by 30,000 Btu, is prorated over this lifetime and divided into place-miles per line-mile for each of the fixed guideway systems.

Determining the energy cost of pavement construction and replacement for buses is difficult because of well-known problems with singling out the costs occasioned by any one particular vehicle class. The massive American Association of State Highway Officials (AASHO) Road Test of the early 1960s[38] has shown that, irrespective of pavement strength, most pavement deterioration is caused by the heaviest vehicles, even if they represent a small fraction of total traffic, because pavement damage rises with the *fourth power* of axle-load applications. The axle-load of a bus being roughly 10 times that of an auto, it would cause 10,000 times the damage per vehicle-mile, or about 1,000 times the damage per place-mile. Yet the roadway construction and replacement cost per auto place-mile, estimated from input-output data at 160 Btu, consists mostly of rural and suburban highways on which few if any buses operate. The repavement cost of urban streets and freeways which are used by buses is not known, though the damage to them is quite visible,

*Rubber-tired peoplemover structures exposed to the elements are assumed to require much earlier replacement of the wearing surface. If the concrete is sufficiently coarse to maintain traction as the surface wears, water penetration begins to cause corrosion of the reinforcing bars and spalling.

Exhibit 2.13
Illustrative Gross Total Energy Requirements, Btu per place-mile*
(See text for explanation of assumptions)

Mode			Vehicle operation	Maintenance + wayside	Veh. manuf.		Guideway construction	TOTAL	Snowmelting	TOTAL with Snowmelting
			Energy requirements per place-mile							
(1)			(2)	(3)	(4)		(5)	(6)		
Urban auto	**@ 12mpg**									
(1,600 Kg, 6 places)			2,100	375 + 206	215		160	**2,870**		
Urban auto	**@ 24 mpg**									
(1,100 Kg, 5 places			1,260	375 + 206	175		160	**1,990**		
Local bus	@ 6 mph		760	68? + 206	33		320?	**1,201**		
	@ 12 mph		670	68? + 206	33		320?	**1,111**		
	@ 18 mph		590	68? + 206	33		320?	**1,031**		
Rapid Transit	10		670a	34 + 149	13	**$18 mill.**	819	**1,685**		
(1/3 grade, 1/3	20	million	670a	34 + 75	13	mile	410	**1,202**		
cut & fill, 1/3	30	pl.-mi.	670a	34 + 50	13	66 yrs.	273	**1,040**		
elevated)	50	line-mi.	670a	34 + 30	13		164	**911**		
	100		670a	34 + 15	13		82	**814**		
	200		670a	34 + 8	13		41	**766**		
RT underground	20		670a	34 + 516	13	**$52 mill.**	867	**2,100**		
	30		670a	34 + 344	13	mile	578	**1,639**		
	50		670a	34 + 206	13	90 yrs.	347	**1,270**		
	100		670a	34 + 103	13		173	**993**		
	200		670a	34 + 52	13		87	**856**		
Light Rail	5		370	34 + 298	24	**$ 9 mill.**	1,200	**1,926**		
(2/3 grade, 1/3	10		370	34 + 149	24	mile	600	**1,177**		
cut & fill)	15		370	34 + 99	24	45 yrs.	400	**927**		
	20		370	34 + 75	24		300	**803**		
	30		370	34 + 50	24		200	**678**		
	50		370	34 + 30	24		120	**578**		
LR underground	10		370	34 + 1,032	24	**$50 mill.**	1,667	**3,127**		
	15		370	34 + 688	24	mile	1,111	**2,227**		
	20		370	34 + 516	24	90 yrs.	833	**1,777**		
	30		370	34 + 344	24		555	**1,327**		
	50		370	34 + 206	24		333	**967**		
Peoplemover	5		580	68 + 1,560	19	**$15 mill.**	2,000	**4,227**	3,000	**7,227**
(3/4 elevated,	10		580	68 + 780	19	mile	1,000	**2,447**	1,500	**3,947**
1/4 grade)	15		580	68 + 520	19	45 yrs.	666	**1,853**	1,000	**2,853**
	20		580	68 + 390	19		500	**1,557**	750	**2,307**
	30		580	68 + 260	19		333	**1,260**	500	**1,760**
	50		580	68 + 156	19		200	**1,023**	300	**1,323**
PM underground	10		580	68 + 1,032	19	**$37 mill.**	1,233	**2,932**		
	15		580	68 + 688	19	mile	822	**2,177**		
	20		580	68 + 516	19	90 yrs.	617	**1,800**		
	30		580	68 + 344	19		411	**1,422**		
	50		580	68 + 206	19		245	**1,118**		

* One place = 5.38 sq. ft. or 0.5 m^2 of vehicle area: multiply x 0.157 for Cal. place-Km).
a: Subtract 130 for regenerative braking.
b: Street lighting.
c: Snow melting where required; varies depending on weather conditions. 250 annual heating hours assumed.
?: Indicates large uncertainty about the accuracy of underlying data.

Exhibit 2.14
Illustrative Gross Total Energy Savings, Btu per place-mile

				Gross total energy requirement per place-mile with amoritization period cut in half	Energy saving compared to former mode 58% bus, 42% auto	Energy saving compared to former mode 29% bus, 71% auto	Energy saved through reduced auto ownership near stations with 24 mph urban auto*	Total savings per place-mile Sum columns 2 + 4 (low)	Sum columns 3 + 4 (high)
				(1)	(2)	(3)	(4)		
					(1,545 Btu/pl.-mi. over 33 yrs.)	(1,845 Btu/pl.-mi.)			
Rapid Transit (1/3 grade, 1/3 cut & fill, 1/3 elevated)	10	million pl.-mi./line-mi.		2,504	− 959	− 659	+ 360	− 599	− 299
	20			1,612	+ 67	+ 233	+ 360	+ 427	+ 660
	30			1,313	+ 232	+ 532	+ 360	+ 592	+ 892
	50			1,075	+ 470	+ 770	+ 360	+ 830	+ 1,130
	100			896	+ 649	+ 949	+ 360	+ 1,009	+ 1,309
	200			807	+ 738	+ 1,038	+ 360	+ 1,098	+ 1,398
					(1,484 Btu/pl.-mi. over 45 yrs.)	(1,742 Btu/pl.-mi.)			
RT underground	20			2,967	− 1,483	− 1,225	+ 360	− 1,123	− 865
	30			2,217	− 733	− 475	+ 360	− 373	− 115
	50			1,617	− 133	+ 125	+ 360	+ 227	+ 484
	100			1,166	+ 318	+ 576	+ 360	+ 678	+ 936
	200			943	+ 541	+ 799	+ 360	+ 901	+ 1,159
					(1,644 Btu/pl.-mi. over 22 yrs.)	(2,012 Btu/pl.-mi.)			
Light Rail (2/3 grade, 1/3 cut & fill)	5			3,126	− 1,482	− 1,114	+ 216	− 1,266	− 898
	10			1,777	− 133	+ 235	+ 216	+ 53	+ 451
	15			1,327	+ 317	+ 685	+ 216	+ 533	+ 901
	20			1,103	+ 541	+ 909	+ 216	+ 757	+ 1,125
	30			878	+ 766	+ 1,134	+ 216	+ 982	+ 1,350
	50			698	+ 946	+ 1,314	+ 216	+ 1,162	+ 1,530
					(1,484 Btu/pl.-mi. over 45 yrs.)	(1,742 Btu/pl.-mi.)			
LR underground	10			4,794	− 3,310	− 3,052	+ 216	− 3,094	− 2,836
	15			3,338	− 1,854	− 1,596	+ 216	− 1,638	− 1,380
	20			2,610	− 1,126	− 868	+ 216	− 910	− 652
	30			1,882	− 398	− 140	+ 216	− 182	+ 76
	50			1,300	+ 184	+ 442	+ 216	+ 400	+ 658
			With Snowmelting	Without Snowmelting	33% walk, 33% auto, 33% bus with snowmelting	33% walk, 33% auto, 33% bus without snowmelting			
					(1,163 Btu/pl.-mi. over 22 yrs.)	(1,163 Btu/pl.-mi.)			
Peoplemover (3/4 elevated, 1/4 grade)	5		9,227	6,227	− 8,064	− 5,064	none	− 8,064	− 5,064
	10		4,947	3,447	− 3,784	− 2,284	none	− 3,784	− 2,284
	15		3,519	2,519	− 2,356	− 1,356	none	− 2,356	− 1,356
	20		2,807	2,057	− 1,644	− 894	none	− 1,644	− 894
	30		2,093	1,593	− 930	− 430	none	− 930	− 430
	50		1,523	1,223	− 360	− 60	none	− 360	− 60
						(1,037 Btu/pl.-mi. over 45 yrs.)			
Peoplemover underground	10			4,165		− 3,128	none		− 3,128
	15			2,999		− 1,962	none		− 1,962
	20			2,417		− 1,380	none		− 1,380
	30			1,833		− 796	none		− 796
	50			1,363		− 326	none		− 326

* See text; assumes 5 autos saved per million place-miles by rapid transit, 3 by light rail, and 7,250 miles of annual use foregone in excess of that diverted to rail.

Exhibit 2.15
Illustrative Gross Total Energy Requirements Related to Service Density

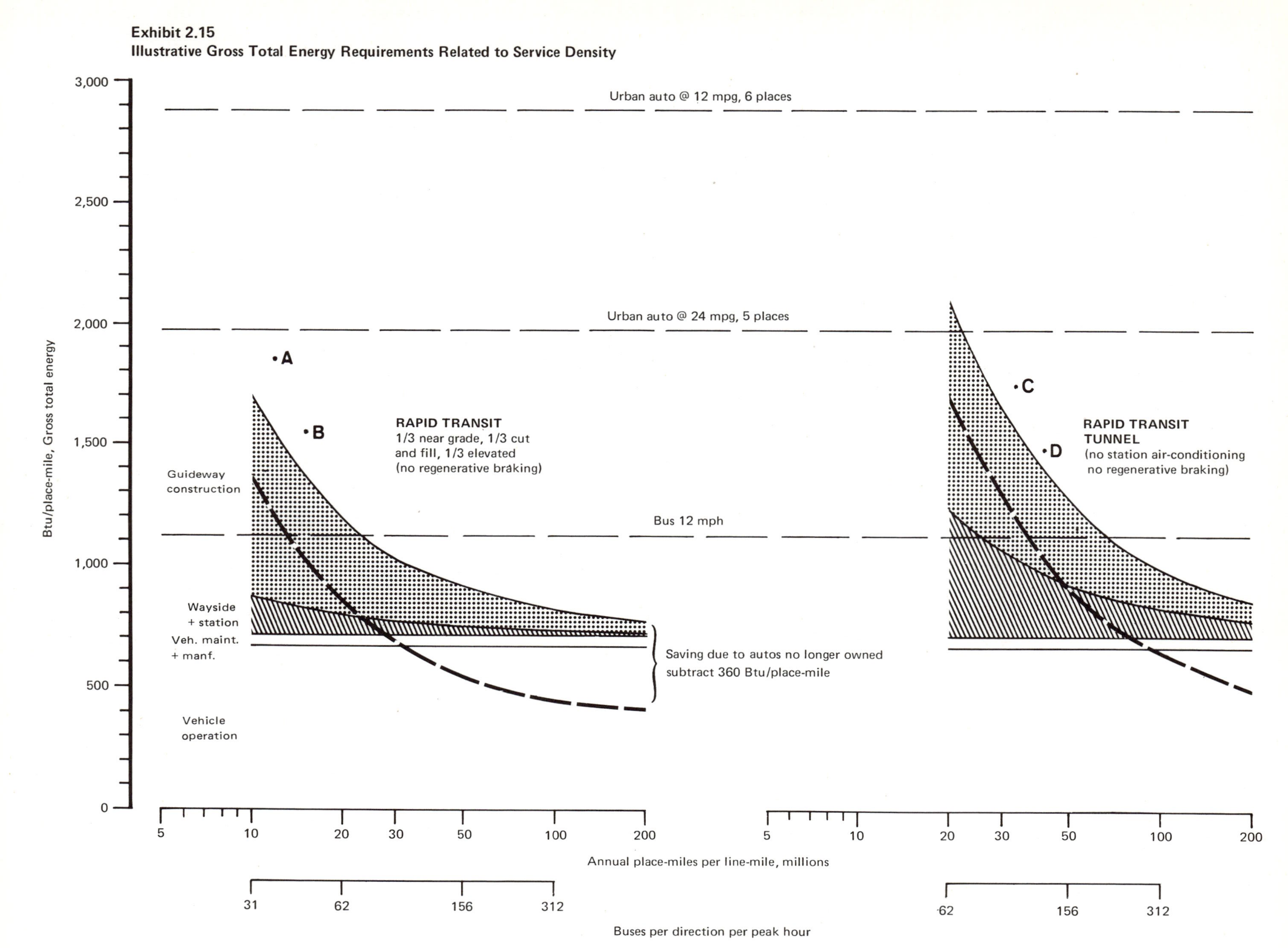

Exhibit 2.15 (cont'd.)
Illustrative Gross Total Energy Requirements Related to Service Density

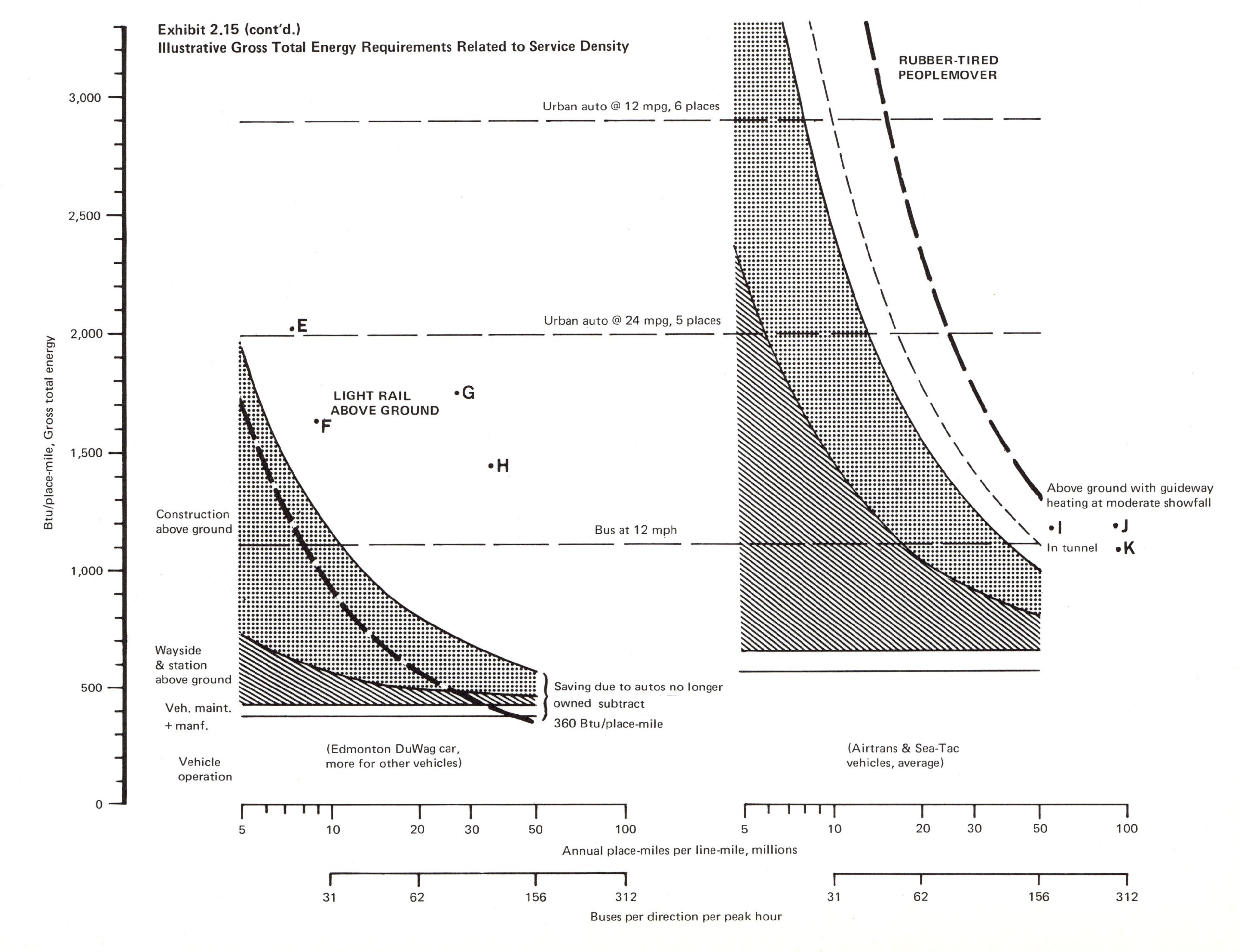

especially at bus stops (where special concrete pads are often provided) and on curves (where lateral displacement of asphalt occurs). Therefore, it does not seem unreasonable to assume that buses require twice the roadway construction energy of autos per place-mile. An alternative scaling exercise is to look at the energy cost of building a bus-only facility, such as the El Monte busway in Los Angeles was intended to be. Its current volume of buses would have to continue to use it for 63 years without repavement for the construction energy per place-mile to come down to twice that of the auto, or 320 Btu. Most likely this figure, assumed for buses in general, is not excessive.

Estimates of the total gross energy cost of autos, buses, and fixed guideway vehicles, consisting of vehicle operation, maintenance, wayside and station requirements, vehicle manufacture, and guideway construction are summarized for different levels of volume per line-mile in column 5 of Exhibit 2.13 and shown graphically in Exhibit 2.15. Clearly, the total energy requirement of a mode is not a fixed number but a variable, strongly dependent on traffic volume in the case of fixed guideways and influenced by speed in the case of buses. Additional factors, such as regenerative braking on rapid transit, air-conditioning of enclosed stations, and the presence or absence of snowmelting equipment on rubber-tired peoplemovers, can strongly affect the final total. The following conclusions can be drawn from Exhibit 2.15.

1. *For rail systems to attain lower total energy costs per place-mile than a 5-place auto in urban use at 24 mpg—a performance unlikely to be attained fleet-wide until the late 1990s—very low volumes of service are sufficient:* about 5 million place-miles per line-mile for light rail, 8 million place-miles per line-mile for rapid transit above ground, and 22 million place-miles per line-mile on rapid transit in a tunnel.

2. *Rail systems can attain lower total energy costs than buses operating at an average urban speed of 12 mph (19 km/h) at medium to high service volumes:* 11 million place-miles per line-mile on light rail, 23 million place-miles per line-mile on above-ground rapid transit, and 70 million place-miles per line-mile in a tunnel. Regenerative braking or gravity-assisted profiles in tunnels (dipping between stations) can significantly reduce these thresholds, while station air-conditioning will raise them.

3. *Rubber-tired peoplemovers at low volumes exceed the present urban auto in total energy consumption per place-mile.* For them to attain lower total energy costs than the future auto in urban use at 24 mpg, service volumes above 13 million place-miles per line-mile are needed without snowmelting, and above 24 million place-miles per line-mile with snowmelting in moderate climates. Without snowmelting, they attain lower total energy costs than buses at 12 mph (19.3 km/h) only above 40 million place-miles per line-mile.

To convert the total energy costs per place-mile into total costs per *passenger-mile,* the values in the sixth column of Exhibit 2.13 must be multiplied by 4.3—the inverse of the average 23.3 percent occupancy ratio. This yields, for example, 12,340 Btu per passenger-mile for the old-style auto in urban use, 8,560 Btu for the assumed future auto, 4,780 Btu for the bus at average urban speed, 4,430 Btu for rapid transit that is one-third underground and carries 50 million place-miles per line-mile, 3,450 Btu for light rail at 20 million place-miles per line-mile with a frugal car, and so on.

The basic similarity of average occupancies per passenger place among urban autos in weekday use, rail systems, buses, and the only automated peoplemover that operates partly in a downtown setting (Morgantown) makes it possible to bypass this step in calculating energy savings from new fixed guideways. This introduces, at most, a small bias in favor of the bus, and possibly some bias against the future auto.* Only if there is reason to expect different occupancies must the conversion to passenger-miles be made. Thus the BART occupancy of 15 percent results in a total energy use of 6,800 Btu per passenger-mile under the assumptions used here, not the 4,430 just mentioned. Actual BART use is higher largely because station, wayside, and maintenance energy are above the averages assumed here.

Calculation of energy saving attained by new fixed guideways requires two types of additional information: one, knowledge of the former travel mode of the new fixed guideway users; two, consideration of any external effects that occur beyond the portion of the trip that is replaced by the new facility. Such effects involve changes in the mode of travel for the remainder of the trip, changes in door-to-door trip length, and changes in auto ownership.

The mix of modes that a fixed guideway replaces has a strong bearing on how much energy it saves; it is basically the diversion from automobiles that results in savings. Travel surveys on the PATCO Lindenwold line, on BART, and on MBTA South Shore extension show similar distributions of passengers by former mode, averaging 44 percent diverted from buses, 36 percent diverted from autos, 5 percent diverted from other modes, and 15 percent newly induced.[39]

The travel estimates for future systems presented later in Chapter 4 exclude induced travel. For consistency, it should therefore be excluded from the calculation of energy savings as well. Grouping the few former users of "other modes" with bus riders, the former mode that rail replaces can be taken as 58 percent bus and 42 percent auto.** On downtown peoplemovers, roughly one-third of the travelers are likely to be former pedestrians, with the rest evenly split between auto and bus. A weighted average energy consumption of the "former mode" for downtown peoplemovers is therefore significantly lower than for line-haul rail systems. Subtracting the energy consumption of a fixed guideway from that of the modes formerly used by its patrons, one can arrive at a value of the energy saving, as shown in column 2 of Exhibit 2.14.

The saving thus calculated relates only to that portion of the trip which is replaced by the fixed guideway. On the *access* portion of the trip, several changes are likely to take place. Many auto drivers who switch to rail will continue to use the auto for the access portion of their trip, causing little if any additional gain or loss. Others may choose to have a family member make a special trip to drop them off, thus doubling the energy consumption for the access portion of the trip, but

*With 5, rather than 6, places per auto, a 23.3 percent occupancy means fewer than 1.2 occupants per auto. This figure may not be unrealistic for the future in light of declining household size and more autos per household. After all, it is members of a household rather than unrelated carpoolers that account for a vast majority of the non-driver auto occupants.

**The mode that would be used "without Metrorail" was reported by a 1979 WMATA passenger survey as follows: 54.4 percent bus, 23.4 percent auto driver, 8.3 percent taxi passenger, 4.3 percent auto passenger, 2.3 percent walk, 2.2 other, and 5.1 percent "would not have made this trip," a measure of induced travel.

perhaps saving energy overall by owning fewer autos. A third group will choose buses for the access trip, while a fourth group, living in close proximity to a new station, will walk. Because access modes at particular stations vary from 90 percent driving to 90 percent walking, it is difficult to make a generalized estimate of the algebraic sum of these energy losses and gains directly.

However, evidence referred to in Chapter 1 shows that the introduction of a fixed guideway is followed by the attraction of new riders to buses, for access trips and otherwise. Per capita bus use in the older rail cities being no lower than in the non-rail cities, the implication is that bus travel diverted to rail is fully compensated for by additional bus travel attracted by the combined bus-rail system and that, in effect, 100 percent of the rail travel occurs at the expense of the auto. On new systems, this effect is not quite as strong. Washington data for 1979—after 3 years of rail operation—suggest that for every two bus passenger-miles diverted to rail, roughly one new bus passenger-mile was generated, which in large measure represents access trips. Thus, at least half the bus travel diverted to rail may be compensated for by new bus travel which takes place largely at the expense of the auto. The equivalent former mode of rail users then is no longer 58 percent bus and 42 percent auto, but 29 percent bus and 71 percent auto. This is shown in column 3 of Exhibit 2.14.

The issue of whether a combined auto-and-rail or bus-and-rail trip is more circuitous than a straight auto or bus trip has been raised. The circuitousness was measured for a sample of census tracts served by the PATCO Lindenwold line; auto-and-rail and auto-only trips were found to be virtually the same, 1.236 and 1.242 times longer, respectively, than the air-line distance.[40] This is plausible, since both rail access and freeway access usually require some deviation from the shortest path; in fact, freeway routing, which seeks to bypass densely developed areas, is often more circuitous. By cutting a street grid on a diagonal, as in Edmonton, a rail line may offer savings in distance compared to bus routes as well. On the other hand, if feeder routes are laid out perpendicularly to a rail line, the distance will be longer than a diagonal by 18 percent if the access trip is one-fifth of the line-haul trip, as on BART. More typically access trips are shorter, and they rarely are perpendicular: they tend to be slanted in the direction of travel, as in Atlanta, and a true diagonal is rarely available as an alternative. In Chicago, public transit trips in general have been found to be 1.09 times longer than the airline distance, compared to 1.20 times for auto trips.[41] In sum, any gains or losses in before-and-after travel distance strongly depend on site-specific route layout; for a generic analysis, they can be ignored.

What cannot be ignored is the suppression of auto ownership in the immediate vicinity of rail stations which occurs even at stations that rely predominantly on auto access for the longer trips. This is shown in Exhibit 3.22 and discussed in more detail in Chapter 3. Normalizing for residential density, income, and household size, this reduction can be related to service volume in million annual place-miles.*

*Solving the equations in Exhibit 3.22 with appropriate factors for household size, income, and residential density as of 1970 yields an estimate that *all of these factors aside,* the New York City rapid transit system saved about 175,000 autos and the Long Island Railroad about 21,000. Divided by 35,000 million and 6,700 million annual place-miles of service, respectively, this yields a saving of 5 autos per million place-miles for rapid transit and 3 autos per million place-miles for commuter rail. In the

The energy saving resulting from auto travel foregone (other than diverted to the fixed guideway) because of autos not owned in the immediate vicinity of stations compared to the remaining urban territory is shown in column 4 of Exhibit 2.14 and indicated by the heavy dashed lines in Exhibit 2.15. Its magnitude is such that *at service volumes in excess of 50 million place-miles per line-mile one-third or more of the energy cost of rail transit may be free—paid for by savings from reduced auto ownership.*

In calculating energy savings, the time period over which they occur must be considered. Based on the longevity of different types of construction, the fixed energy investment as shown in Exhibit 2.13 is amortized over periods that vary from 45 to 90 years. In light of the urgent nature of energy problems, policy makers are unlikely to be interested in energy savings 90 years from now. To illustrate the degree to which fixed guideways can—or cannot—save energy in a time frame of more immediate interest, one can cut the amortization period of fixed energy investment in half, to between 22 and 45 years. In effect, this doubles the construction energy in column 5 of Exhibit 2.13. The correspondingly greater total energy requirement is shown in column 1 of Exhibit 2.14.

Reducing the period over which costs are amortized also enables one to deal with more predictable measures of savings. The assumed energy cost of travel by the former mode must be tailored to the period over which savings are to occur. For a short time frame, the energy costs associated with a 12 mpg urban auto and a 4 mpg bus would be appropriate. For a medium time frame, one can make a reasonable estimate of when 24 mpg in urban use can be attained fleet-wide. For a very long time frame, future auto energy use becomes speculative.

Given the miles-per-gallon shortfall in over-the-road driving compared to test-stand results, the actual reduction in fuel use per vehicle-mile attained by new 1985 autos is likely to be 30 percent, rather than the mandated 50 percent of the 1972–1976 level. If improvements in fuel economy continue at the same pace, an actual over-the-road reduction of 50 percent will not be reached by new cars until 1992. Allowing 10 years for fleet turnover, one cannot expect a *fleet-wide* average 24 mpg in urban driving much before 2002. This indicates an average fuel economy of 16.6 mpg in urban driving over the intervening 22-year period. If one assumes, rather optimistically, that this is raised to 33 mpg in urban driving (meaning 50 mpg in highway driving) over the following 11 years, the annual average fuel economy over the entire 33-year period becomes 20.5 mpg. Assuming no further improvement, it becomes 23.8 mpg over a 45-year period. These values are used to determine total auto energy per place-mile in columns 2 and 3 of Exhibit 2.14. For buses, a constant value of 4 mpg is used for all periods, even though this understates the actual consumption during the 1980s and probably beyond. The prospective convergence in production efficiency between electricity and liquid fuels discussed earlier would make these projections even less favorable to vehicles propelled by liquid fuels. Hence, the estimated fixed guideway energy savings are conservative. For autos no longer owned as a result of the existence of a fixed guideway, the energy saving is

absence of other data, the latter, more conservative figure is applied to light rail, while the former is applied to rapid transit. Verification of these rates for new rail transit systems will be possible when 1980 Census auto ownership data by census tract and related land area and demographic statistics become available.

calculated on the basis of a 24 mpg fuel efficiency in urban driving irrespective of the amortization period.

The calculations made on this basis and shown in Exhibit 2.14 result in the following *volume-related thresholds above which fixed guideways begin to save energy, compared to the modes previously used, over the next 22 to 45 years:*

> *12 to 15 million place-miles per line-mile for above-ground rapid transit* (points A and B in Exhibit 2.15) depending on whether the effect of increased bus service is included or excluded.
>
> *33 to 40 million place-miles per line-mile for rapid transit in tunnel* (points C and D) depending on whether the effect of increased bus service is included or excluded.
>
> *7 to 9 million place-miles per line-mile for above-ground light rail* (points E and F) depending on whether the effect of increased bus service is included or excluded; the volume for light rail underground is about 27 to 35 million place-miles per line-mile (points G and H).
>
> *55 to 90 million place-miles per line-mile for downtown peoplemovers above-ground* depending on whether snowmelting equipment is not needed or needed (points I and J); the volume for downtown peoplemovers underground is about 80 million place-miles per line-mile (point K).

The surprisingly high service volume—not attainable with present capacity—that needs to be reached by a downtown peoplemover for it to save energy compared to previous modes even in the absence of snowmelting is explained primarily by three factors: (1) The source of patronage; if no pedestrians were diverted, and the former mode of downtown peoplemover users were the same as on line-haul rail transit, the volume needed to attain energy savings with a foreshortened amortization period would be reduced from 55 to about 27 million place-miles per line-mile. (2) The lack of an auto ownership reduction factor; if the peoplemover operated through residential areas where nearby residents had the option of station access on foot, by bus, or by "kiss-and-ride," thus reducing auto ownership by the same amount as assumed for light rail, the volume needed to attain energy savings would be reduced further to about 22 million place-miles per line-mile. (3) The high fixed wayside energy costs; these result from rather elaborate stations (often enclosed, with air-cooling and other amenities) and the generally capital-intensive character of automated rubber-tired vehicle guideways as they now exist. If wayside energy costs were the same as on above-ground rapid transit, the volume needed by a peoplemover to attain energy savings would be reduced to roughly 18 million place-miles per line-mile, quite similar to rapid transit. Further significant reductions—close to the range of light rail—could be attained by employing a less capital-intensive guideway. In sum, automated guideways operating in a different setting, not confined to a downtown and using a much lighter guideway design, do have the potential of attaining energy savings.

By contrast, energy savings of rapid transit and light rail are quite manifest, given the parameters used in this study. *It makes sense to build rail transit even as a medium-term (22-to-45-year) energy conservation measure for nearly the full range of service volumes currently encountered on rapid transit, and for all but the lowest volumes currently encountered on light rail provided that the vehicle occupancy does not fall much below 23 percent of the places offered, provided that tunnel routing is used sparingly on the more lightly used lines, and provided that wayside and station energy costs are kept similar to those of the simpler systems, such as* CTA, NYCTA, *or* PATCO.

Diversion of auto travel and of slow bus trips (12 mph or less) to existing rail transit lines can offer greater energy savings, because the sunk energy cost of building them need not be included in the calculation.

These findings contradict some recent studies.[42] While they vary in method, several of them share one or more of the following: (1) Failure to fully account for the energy cost of highway fuel production and distribution. (2) An understatement of bus fuel use at slow urban speeds and of indirect bus energy requirements for maintenance of vehicles and streets. (3) An overstatement of indirect rail energy requirements, all too often patterned after BART simply because it has the best data. Methodological errors in this area include translating transit workers' wages into Btu's as an "indirect energy cost" of rail. The energy cost of a piece of final demand (such as place-miles offered) is built up from streams of interindustry purchases. One cannot add workers' wages to this, since the energy purchased for them is but a different slice of final demand. What matters is marginal energy expenditure or saving to produce the piece of final demand. These are not affected if transit workers were to be fired by a transit agency, for they would still need to consume Btu's in their private lives. (4) Exaggeration of the energy used for access trips to a rail line. Thus, one study assigns a false 30 percent penalty to combined auto-and-rail trips on the assumption that they are that much more circuitous than auto trips. (5) Failure to account for reduced auto ownership as a result of rail transit, a factor that strongly contributes to energy savings calculated here.

In defense of the earlier studies and of the alternative calculations presented here, one should stress that methods of transportation energy accounting are not well developed and the data base is incomplete, necessitating many assumptions. For example, more detailed and up-to-date input-output data may well cause some downward revision of the auto energy estimates made here. This, however, is unlikely to change the overall tenor of the results, especially in an environment where rising passenger volumes are making fixed-guideway travel more energy-efficient overall.

LAND REQUIREMENTS

The ability of fixed guideways to use land much more intensively than surface streets or freeways when traffic volumes are high is evident from the discussion of capacities earlier in this chapter. It is this space-saving feature that makes fixed guideways especially compatible with compact, pedestrian-oriented downtown environments. However, where transit demand is low, the question can be raised: would not a given right-of-way be more fully used if it were to allow mixed traffic, instead of being reserved for a fixed guideway?

The *minimum clear traveled way width* required by a two-track fixed guideway is generally similar to that required by two highway lanes, and comprises about 24 feet (7.3m) for rapid transit with standard "wide" cars, about 22 feet (6.7m) for light rail, and 18 to 22.5 feet (5.5 to 6.9m) for existing peoplemovers. Depending on location, a buffer space (such as catwalks in a tunnel) of between 4 and 12 feet (1.2 to 3.7m) or more may have to be added to that,[43] while significantly wider shoulders and lateral setbacks are needed on a highway. A fixed guideway requires a minimum of two tracks (except at the lightest volumes) while a minimum of four are required for a freeway.

The tradeoff between devoting land to a highway as against a fixed guideway during the peak hour may be considered in two typical situations: a freeway leading to downtown and a downtown surface arterial. A freeway operating at the upper limit of so-called service level D—approaching unstable flow—during portions of the peak hour is likely to carry, in the course of the entire peak hour, the equivalent of some 1,700 passenger cars. With 1.4 persons per car, this equals 2,400 persons per lane per direction. Assuming that a fixed guideway provides as many passenger places per direction per peak hour, its service volume will be about 13 million place-miles per line-mile annually. A fixed guideway with a lower service volume can be said to use land during the peak hour less efficiently than an auto-only freeway at the entry point to a downtown.

If 20 percent of the peak hour freeway travelers are bus passengers—as is often the case in medium-sized downtowns without rail—the volume per lane rises to 3,000 persons per hour, and only a fixed guideway with a service volume above *16 million place-miles per line-mile* will use land more efficiently than a freeway.

A downtown arterial (exclusive of curb lanes, which can be counted as shoulders) will, under average intersection conditions, have a maximum hourly throughput on the order of 450 to 550 passenger car equivalents per 11-foot lane. With the same occupancy, this represents 630 to 770 persons per lane per hour. Therefore, a lane preempted by a fixed guideway, such as light rail or a peoplemover, will have an equal passenger-carrying capacity in the peak hour if its service volume is 3 to 4 million annual place-miles per line-mile. With, say, 40 percent of the arterial travelers in buses, the equivalent fixed guideway volume rises to *approximately 6 million annual place-miles per line-mile.* A reserved or exclusive guideway with a lower service volume than that will use land during the peak hour less efficiently than an urban arterial with modest bus traffic.

Obviously, one can increase the bus traffic component of a freeway lane or a local arterial over an extremely broad range, all the way to making them into exclusive bus facilities. At that point, with some 500 buses or 30,500 places per lane per direction in the peak hour, the exclusive freeway lane can match the maximum comfortable capacity of a rapid transit track, though in a very different, nonstop service pattern. With on-line stops, the capacity of an exclusive lane drops much below light rail, to approximately 6,000 places per direction per hour.[44] Nevertheless, land consumption is not a decisive consideration in choosing between exclusive rail and exclusive bus facilities. What matters is the difference in land consumption between either of them and typical preexisting conditions, namely auto roadways with a small bus component near downtown entry points during the peak hour.

If the requirement were for an exclusive facility to use land more efficiently than a predominantly auto roadway on a 24-hour average annual basis, and not just during the daily peak, the minimum volumes at which fixed guideways begin to save land would have to be at least tripled, compared to the values shown earlier. This is due to the differences in peaking between auto and transit. Such a requirement appears unnecessarily stringent. During off-peak hours there is plenty of unused travel space throughout an urban area, and its allocation between roadways and fixed guideways is of little consequence.*

In addition to land required for movement, land required for parking is an important consideration, especially in high-density areas where space is at a premium. In the larger central business districts, land used for off-street parking can easily add 30 to 50 percent to the land in street rights-of-way. For every automobile destined to a downtown, some 0.3 to 0.5 parking spaces are required in medium-sized to large downtowns.[45] Unlike savings in land used for the traveled way, which are difficult to capture in money terms because street and highway travelers pay no rent for the land they use, savings in the land for parking are in large measure translated into dollars for travelers who switch from auto to transit. Daily parking rates in the core of downtown ranged from about $2.50 in Central Business Districts of 30 million square feet (2.8 million m^2) to about $4.00 in those of 100 million square feet (9.3 million m^2) in 1977 prices.[46] If the traveler is not subsidized to avoid parking charges when traveling by auto, avoiding charges of this magnitude is a significant incentive for choosing transit when it provides relatively comparable service.

Lastly, a major advantage of fixed guideways is that, when necessary, they can avoid the use of surface space altogether by entering high-density parts of urban areas by means of tunnels which can be built with much greater ease than underground freeways and busways. The latter require a wider gross section for the same travel volume and incur additional ventilation costs. One need only compare the cost of building rail subways with that of such environmentally responsive highway designs as the Inner Leg freeway in Washington, Interstate 95 along the Delaware in downtown Philadelphia, or the Fort Henry tunnel in Baltimore. The latter cost around $600 million a mile in 1980 bid prices. The proposed Westway in Manhattan and the undergrounding of the Central Artery in Boston would incur similar costs.

Many examples, ranging from the Berkeley bond issue to the tearing down of the Third Avenue elevated in Manhattan, can be marshaled to show that the value placed by the community on undergrounding is very high. In the first case, Berkeley residents taxed themselves to put a prospective elevated BART structure through their city underground; in the second case, the "tax" is being paid not only in reduced access but also in extreme crowding on a parallel subway for the duration of at least 40 years. Nevertheless, the wisdom of the decision has not been questioned, and not just in the light of the building boom that completely transformed Third Avenue in two decades after the elevated was removed.

*By way of illustration, the land used by pavement or tracks per unit of passenger travel on an *annual average day* basis can be estimated for the 31-county New York Region from 1970 land use and travel data as follows: light rail—0.68 acres per 1,000 passenger-miles; auto—0.64 acres; commuter rail—0.40 acres; bus—0.05 acres; rapid transit—0.05 acres (1 acre = 0.4 ha). Moderate service volumes and low use on weekends and at night explain the relatively high commuter and light rail use of land, while the fact that buses predominantly follow arterial streets which in addition carry heavy volumes of auto traffic reduces their use of land even after account is taken of their slow speed. For this calculation, it is assumed that pavement accounts for 60 percent of the total land area in public rights-of-way. Rail property beyond main passenger carrying tracks is similarly ignored.

In principle the cost of tunneling is not a pure transportation investment. It is in large part a city-building investment which cannot be fully accounted for in transportation benefit-cost terms, much as an urban park may not withstand benefit-cost analysis in recreation terms alone. Creation of a "second street level" underground with related architectural and urban design improvements aboveground, such as downtown pedestrianization in Munich and lesser-scale changes of the cityscape in Hamburg, Frankfurt, Vienna, Sao Paulo, and other cities, reach far beyond the issue of delivering x number of people downtown at y cost. The pedestrian malls, underground concourses, and sunken plazas made possible by the tunnels have both an urban design and a real estate value in their own right.

Still, in line with the basic approach of this book which seeks to relate the scale of improvements to their prospective use, it is not unreasonable to link the appropriateness of tunnels to the volume of passengers who use them. Exhibit 2.16 relates existing passenger volumes (passenger-miles per line-mile or passenger-kilometers per line-kilometer) on rail systems both in the United States and abroad to the proportion of the guideway that is located underground. There is a clear link between the two—the higher the volume, the more tunneling. This largely reflects the higher density of urban development along the more heavily used lines, which warrants more protection from the nuisance of elevated structures.

It is also clear that, compared with other countries' systems, and adjusted for traffic volume, rapid transit systems in the United States use tunnels most sparingly, reflecting perhaps a sense of values bent toward the "disposable city," rather than urban permanence. New York, Boston, and particularly Chicago show a dramatically lower percent of tunnel routing than is customary in the rest of the world, including Canada. The Washington rapid transit system, with partial operation in 1980 shown, is above average because its outlying, aboveground portions will be the last to open. For special reasons some of the American light rail lines, notably the Newark subway and the San Francisco MUNI railway (including the new Market Street tunnel), display above-average proportions of tunnel routing.

In the traffic volume range where most prospective new United States rapid transit systems are likely to fall (5 to 10 million passenger-miles per line-mile, or 20 to 50 million place-miles per line-mile), at least one-third of the routing could be expected in tunnels by current world standards; for light rail systems (in the 2 to 5 million passenger-miles, or 10 to 20 million place-miles per line-mile range), the proportion would be at least one-fifth. A peak hour one-directional flow of 8,000 passengers has been suggested as the lower limit of tunnel feasibility by one recent study;[47] this figure, of course, may drop if cost of the tunnel section is spread over an entire line.

An alternative way to look at tunneling feasibility is in terms of prevailing land values. If the added cost of tunneling compared with that of elevated construction is about $24.4 million per mile in 1977 prices, as will be shown shortly, and if a mile of fixed guideway structure preempts at least 4.4 acres (assuming a 36-foot right-of-way), then land values in excess of $5.6 million an acre ($129 per square foot or $13.8 million per hectare in 1977 prices) would seem to make tunnels worth considering. While land values as high as $300 to $1,000 a square foot are not difficult to find in Midtown Manhattan, in medium-sized downtowns such values are in the $100 to $450 range at prime locations.

Exhibit 2.16
Fixed Guideway Passenger Volumes Related to Percent Guideway in Tunnel

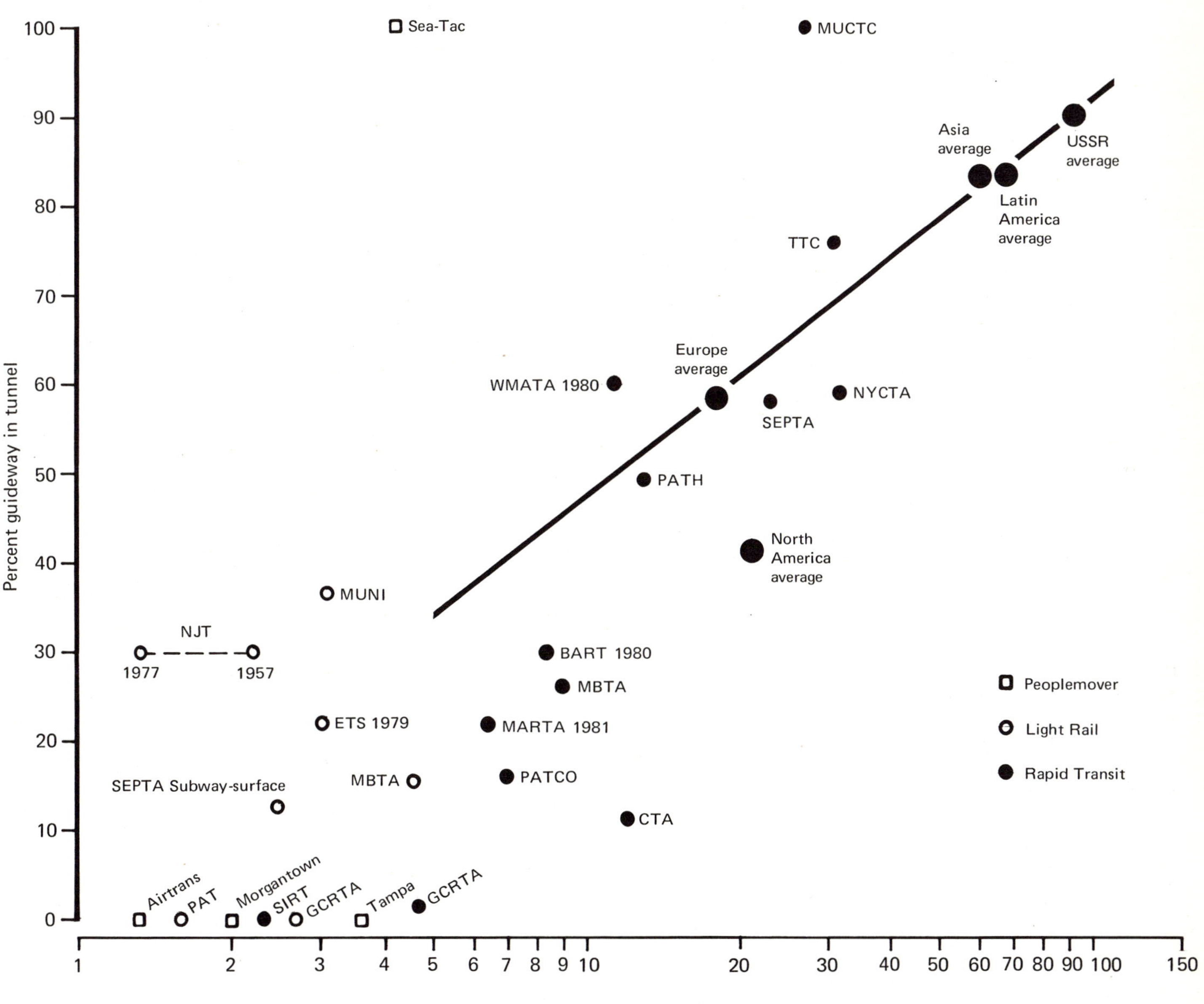

Source: Tables A-1 and A-6

Exhibit 2.17
Summary of Capital Costs of Construction

A. AVERAGES BY TYPE OF CONSTRUCTION

Millions of constant 1977 $$ per mile of two-track equivalent guideway

RAPID TRANSIT	Structure	Track & Electrical Work	Stations	Total
At grade	3.2	4.2	2.9 (1/mi)	**10.3**
Cut or fill	8.8	4.2	3.9 (1/mi)	**16.9**
Elevated	20.3	4.3	3.2 (1/mi)	**27.8**
Underground	40.2	4.3	7.7 (1.5/mi)	**52.2**
LIGHT RAIL				
At grade	2.00	2.90	0.06 (2/mi)	**4.96**
Cut or fill	8.84	3.00	4.78 (2/mi)	**16.62**
Elevated	20.29	3.10	4.35 (2/mi)	**27.74**
Underground	40.23	3.21	6.90 (2/mi)	**50.34**

All costs are averages of high and low observations; they exclude shops, yards, and land acquisition.
Source: Thomas K. Dyer, Inc.; converted from 1974 constant $$ by ENR cost index 1.28.

B. AVERAGES BY PROJECT	Passenger use, weekday PMT/mile of two-track equivalent guideway	Construction cost, million 1977 $$ per mile of two-track equivalent guideway	Construction cost, 1977 constant $ per weekday PMT
1. CTA Dan Ryan (freeway median)	74,037	10.0*	135
2. LIRR Merrick-Bellmore (suburban elevated)	30,000	9.8	327
3. NYCTA Second Avenue (subway)	150,000e	56.0**	373
4. CTA - Milwaukee (freeway median & subway)	43,262	22.9*	529
5. Caltrans El Monte Busway (near grade)	13,000	8.0	615
6. MBTA South Shore (near grade)	25,462	16.5	648
7. NYCTA 63d St. (tunnel incl. LIRR)	190,000e	143.0	752
8. TTC Yonge St. Extension (subway & cut)	68,474	58.6	855
9. Light Rail Edmonton (77% grade, 23% tunnel)	16,300	15.3	939
10. BART (36% grade, 37% elevated, 31% tunnel)	28,745	36.2	1,259
11. WMATA (cost reflects Phase II, 90% tunnel)	42,170	54.6	1,295
12. CTS - Airport extension (near grade)	7,662	10.4	1,357
13. Peoplemover Tampa (elevated)	12,087	18.4	1,523
14. MBTA Haymarket North (tunnel & grade)	21,164	35.5	1,677
15. MARTA Phase I (20% grade, 45% elevated, 35% tunnel)	27,168	49.7****	1,829
16. Peoplemover - Airtrans (80% grade, 20% elevated)	4,483	8.2	1,829
17. NYCTA Archer Avenue (subway)	40,000	73.5	1,837
18. Peoplemover - Sea-Tac (subway)	14,093	37.4	2,654
19. Peoplemover - Morgantown (elevated)	6,607	20.4	3,088
20. SEPTA Snyder-Pattison (subway)	8,000***	48.1	6,016

* Excludes interstate highway expenditures in preparing right-of-way.
** No stations included in sections built.
*** Excludes heavy weekend use.
**** Includes construction attributable to northern leg not yet in use in 1980

Source: Contract cost data from respective agencies—unless furnished in constant dollars—were adjusted to mid-year of construction period by ENR cost index, then converted to 1977 dollars; cost data for peoplemovers based on N.D. Lea & Associates, *Summary of Capital and O&M Cost Experience of AGT Systems,* 1978. Passenger use data from Tables A-6 to A-8. BART use based on 1980 level of 160,700 weekday passengers.

All construction costs actual, not estimated; all PMT data actual, except for NYCTA where estimated present use levels are shown, if lines were operational and connected to feeders as intended.

CONSTRUCTION COSTS

The economies of time, labor, energy, and land that fixed guideways attain are purchased at the price of capital investment. Exaggerated by extraneous factors, such as the general inflation rate in the construction industry, the capital cost of fixed guideways is highly visible.

The level of capital construction costs per mile of fixed guideway in 1977 prices, broken down by three components of construction and four types of structure, is presented in the top part of Exhibit 2.17. The data are based on a detailed examination of actual construction contract documents of both light and heavy rail in 14 cities in America and Europe, undertaken by an engineering firm for the Urban Mass Transportation Administration.[48] The original data appear as ranges of high and low values; they have been aggregated for purposes of this study.

Obviously, any aggregate averages of this type have to be treated with caution; they cannot reflect the large variation in site-specific construction conditions, including geology and groundwater, the method of construction, the amount of utility relocation, the need to underpin buildings, local labor relations, and the prospect for administrative or other construction delays, which increases bid prices as contractors try to anticipate expenditures in future, inflated dollars. Nevertheless, the averages presented show good agreement with actual expenditures.

In the second column, the lower part of Exhibit 2.17 shows comparable costs per mile for 20 specific projects, including rapid transit, one commuter rail structure, one light rail line, four of the five peoplemovers previously discussed, and one busway. Taking into account the predominant structure type, their costs closely follow the pattern established in the top part of the exhibit, though there are deviations, usually for a good reason.

Facilities which are predominantly near grade—be it Chicago's Dan Ryan rapid transit line in a freeway median, the Cleveland Airport rapid transit extension, or the El Monte busway in Los Angeles, cost around $10 million for a two-track mile in 1977 prices. Very simple at-grade light rail structures can be built for less: the mostly single-track San Diego line cost under $2 million a mile in 1980 prices, exclusive of land acquisition and purchase of rolling stock.

Full subways, be they on Yonge Street in Toronto or Broad Street in Philadelphia, cost $50 to $60 million for a two-track mile in 1977 prices, but special conditions, as on 63rd Street in Manhattan (complex deep-level excavation and underwater tubes), can nearly triple this cost. In Montreal, on the other hand, small-cross-section subways cost about $48 million a mile in 1980 prices (not shown in the Exhibit).

Generally, cities with recent underground construction—New York, Washington, Baltimore, Boston, and San Francisco—are characterized by difficult subsurface geology. Conditions much more favorable to tunnel excavation by high-speed boring machines (firm soil or soft sandstone and shale above the water table) prevail in a number of cities where rail transit has been under consideration—Los Angeles, Detroit, Denver, Houston, Dallas, Seattle—and their tunnel costs could therefore be comparatively low.[49]

Different mixes of at-grade, elevated, and tunnel construction for BART, MBTA, and Edmonton projects in the lower part of Exhibit 2.17 produce values intermediate between the roughly $10 million of near-grade and the $50 million of tunnel construction per two-track mile. It should be emphasized that these values cannot be compared with recent bid prices, which may appear much higher (i.e., $180 million a mile for a tunnel in Boston in 1979) without adjusting not only for inflation between 1977 and the bid date, but also for future inflation over the duration of the construction period, which is always built into the bid price.

To shed light on differences between light rail and rapid transit construction costs, the two are shown separately in the top part of Exhibit 2.17. The cost of structures for the two modes is almost identical; trackwork for light rail is less expensive, and stations are still less expensive, but that saving is partly offset by more frequent station spacing; overall, *by structure type,* light rail construction is shown to be only 7 percent less costly than rapid transit construction. Clearly, if light rail is to attain major construction cost economies compared to rapid transit, these must come from a *different mix of structures,* such as more at grade and less elevated and tunnel routing; but such savings tend to be reflected in lower performance and lower benefits.

Also of interest is the *cost of peoplemover structures:* it averages about 30 percent less than that of the respective rapid transit structures, because of smaller cross-section and lighter axle loads. Airtrans, 80 percent at grade with the airport built around it, has by far the lowest cost, at $8 million a mile of two-track equivalent. Sea-Tac, completely in a subway, cost $37.4 million a mile in constant 1977 prices, in scale with other subways, given its smaller cross-section. Morgantown, mostly on elevated structure, cost $20 million a mile, roughly 30 percent less than a rapid transit elevated would cost, while easier construction conditions at Tampa Airport brought its elevated structure in for $18 million per mile of two-track equivalent. Adjusted for inflation, and for structure type and width, the seemingly bewildering array of fixed guideway construction costs in fact makes very simple sense.

From the viewpoint of the transit operator, a rather crucial capital expenditure is the purchase of *rolling stock.* On rapid transit systems, the cost of purchasing the first generation of rolling stock may add between 8 percent (in the case of BART) and 18 percent (CTS Airport extension) to the cost of construction. On Edmonton's light rail, the addition was 13 percent, while on the five peoplemovers discussed here the cost of rolling stock added an average of 20 percent to the cost of construction.

However, if the object is to seek thresholds at which fixed guideways may be more effectively deployed than free-wheeled vehicle systems, the cost of rolling stock is not a major consideration, because it is not fixed, but rather proportional to the volume of service. Any transit system requires vehicles; calculated per place-mile or per place-year of service and amortized over their life span, the differences in capital cost between buses and rail cars are not decisive; only peoplemover vehicles stand out as having a higher capital cost per place-mile because of the automation expense. Thus, the discussion here is limited to fixed capital investment.

Capital costs related to passenger use. To assess the effectiveness of capital expenditures for fixed guideway construction, the simplest approach is to see how these expenditures relate to the use of the facility. In the first column, the bottom part of Exhibit 2.17 lists average weekday volumes for 20 projects, expressed in passenger-miles per two-track line mile, while the third column shows the ratio of construction cost per mile to passenger-miles per mile. This varies from $135 to $6,016 per weekday passenger-mile, with a *median value of about $1,250.*

The low-cost Chicago lines, with respectable passenger volumes, show up among the biggest bargains; the two Manhattan lines, despite high construction costs, also show low costs per passenger-mile, in scale with the El Monte Busway in Los Angeles. BART and WMATA are close to the median value, while Edmonton's light rail line is lower. All peoplemovers are in the upper range of the cost-per-passenger-mile scale. Also in the upper range are fairly high-cost rapid transit projects with moderate passenger volumes, like MARTA's first phase, MBTA's Haymarket North, and NYCTA's Archer Avenue subway. SEPTA's cost per weekday passenger-mile for the Snyder-Pattison extension of the Broad Street line creates a false impression because its major function is to provide weekend access to a cluster of sports stadiums.

Despite such idiosyncrasies, the investment per passenger-mile does provide an indication of the value which public decision-makers have implicitly placed on providing service by fixed guideways. At the time of conception of most of the projects listed federal participation in funding was more limited than it later became, so that most of them involved a substantial local commitment. *As an aid in evaluating future projects, it is reasonable to relate them to these past levels of commitment. One such investment yardstick could be the median value of past expenditures per daily passenger-mile, or $1,250 in 1977 prices.* This yardstick is very stringent, for by definition half the projects listed would not qualify. *A more liberal yardstick would be the 75th percentile value, or about $1,800 per weekday passenger-mile in 1977 prices.*

It has been suggested that these values, showing the "revealed preference" of decision-makers, may be strongly influenced by the degree to which specific projects did in fact receive federal funds. Data on the source of funds are not available in sufficient detail to test this. Offhand, a strong relationship of this type does not stand out from Exhibit 2.17. A number of other variables, such as the absolute size of the project, and anticipated rather than actual ridership levels, have played a role in the local decisions.

To interpret a value such as $1,250 in construction cost per passenger-mile carried on an average weekday, this capital expenditure must be annualized over the lifetime of the facility. This requires choosing both an appropriate lifetime and an appropriate discount or interest rate. As pointed out in connection with amortizing energy expenditures, some elements of fixed guideways do have to be replaced periodically, while others have a virtually indefinite lifetime. It is appropriate to treat each of these categories of capital stock separately in any detailed analysis. For illustration, weighted lifetimes of 45 and 75 years are used below. The former period can represent the weighted lifetime of a light rail facility with no tunnels, the latter the weighted lifetime of a rapid transit facility with nearly half its length in tunnel.

In choosing a proper discount rate, it is most important to distinguish between the true long-term opportunity cost of capital and the lenders' anticipation of future inflation. One can use the current gross interest rate (which includes both) to compare capital costs with operating costs on an equal footing, but then future operating costs—or future savings—must be also expressed in future, inflated dollars. To avoid assumptions about future inflation, it is simpler to express operating costs or savings in constant dollars and use a discount or interest rate that also reflects constant prices, net of inflation.

Following Office of Management and Budget guidelines, a 10 percent discount rate has been widely used in evaluating public capital expenditures. Inflation having averaged 6.7 percent annually over the decade of the 1970s (measured by the implicit price deflator of GNP), this corresponds to a net, or real-dollar discount rate of 3.1 percent.* This is in scale with the 3 percent that is widely considered to be the historic, long-term cost of capital.

One can include a risk factor—essentially, insurance against the eventuality that the investment will be abandoned prematurely—and use a 4 percent or higher discount rate. On the other hand, it has been argued that the risk factor in public investment can be disregarded because it is spread over so many risk-takers, namely taxpayers.[50] For purposes of illustration, both rates are used here. The $1,250 median construction expenditure per weekday passenger-mile, with a rail transit average of 280 weekday passenger equivalents in a year, prorated over a 45-year life of a facility becomes about 22¢ with a 4 percent discount rate and 18¢ with a 3 percent discount rate; if a 75-year lifetime is assumed, the two values drop to 18¢ and 15¢ per passenger-mile respectively. The 75th percentile capital expenditure of $1,800 in 1977 dollars similarly becomes equivalent to anywhere from 22¢ to 31¢ per passenger-mile.

What kind of savings can cover this kind of an investment? Recognizing all the difficulties, emphasized in Chapter 1, of conducting a bona-fide "benefit-cost" analysis, it is still instructive to compare—very roughly—the labor, energy, and land savings discussed so far with the capital expenditure. This is done, using an aboveground rapid transit line for illustration, in Exhibit 2.18.

The savings in labor—compared to the labor needed to carry the same passenger volume by bus—can easily be translated into dollars by using the 1977 average transit labor cost of $20,700 annually per worker. The magnitude of these savings will vary mainly depending on what share of the rail travel comes from buses. In the left part of the Exhibit, it is assumed that bus was the former mode of 58 percent of the rail travel. In the right part, which assumes significant expansion of bus feeder services, the net former bus share drops to 29 percent.

Conversely, energy savings, based on Exhibit 2.14, are calculated on the left side on the assumption that 42 percent of the travel is diverted from autos; on the right side, 71 percent. Because the energy savings represent gross input into the economy, an appropriate price is not the retail price of diesel fuel, but rather the world price of crude oil, taken to be $30 per barrel (5,800,000 Btu). It has been argued that the marginal social cost of imported petroleum is, in fact, much higher. As a yardstick for evaluating conservation measures, the Harvard Business School Energy Project has suggested a value of $80 per barrel.[51] This value is used for illustration on the right side of Exhibit 2.18.

Savings in land are harder to define in monetary terms because systematic data on urban land values are virtually nonexistent, and public land in streets and other transportation facilities pays no rent. In downtowns, however, parking charges are a

*The "real" interest rate is given by the formula $(1+r)$: $(1+p)$, where r is the nominal or gross annual interest rate and p the annual rate of inflation; both are expressed as fractions of 1. For small values of r and p, this is nearly equivalent to $r - p$.

Exhibit 2.18

Illustrative Comparison of Capital Investment Levels with Selected Savings Expressed in Monetary Terms

Capital amortization assumptions

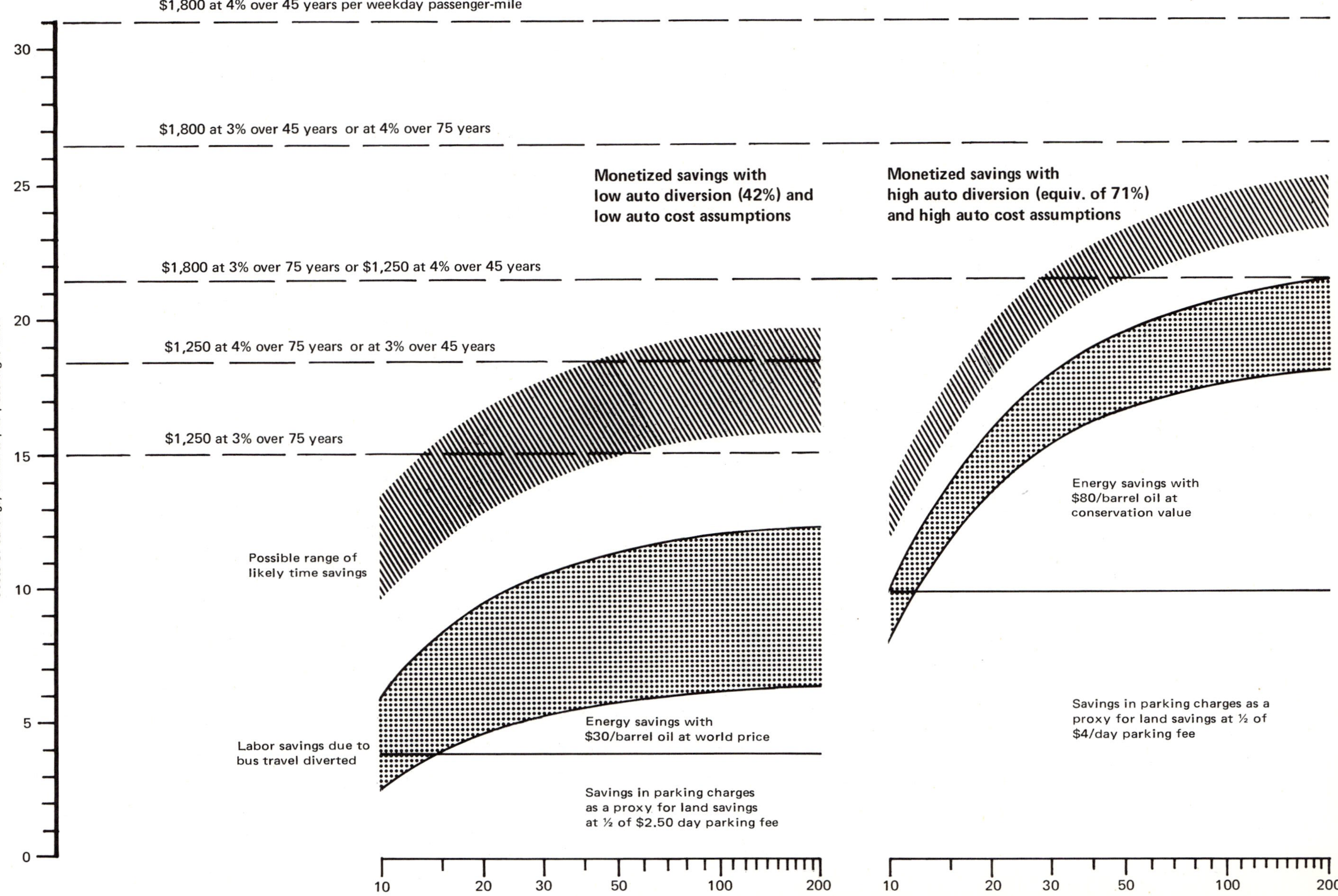

reasonable reflection of prevailing land rents even though they include labor costs and other items. Daily parking rates in the core of downtowns vary from about $2.50 at a downtown size of 30 million square feet (2.8 million m^2) to about $4 at a downtown size approaching 100 million square feet (9.3 million m^2) in 1977 prices, as shown subsequently in Exhibit 3.16. The lower of these two values is used on the left side of the Exhibit, and the higher one on the right side, assuming that each auto trip diverted to rail would have carried 1.4 passengers over a 5-mile distance inbound and outbound. Not every auto user would have paid such a parking fee in full; to reflect parking turnover the figure is cut in half.

The point of this very rough scaling exercise is to show that hard monetary savings on the order of 10 to 12 cents per passenger-mile in 1977 prices are not difficult for a rapid transit line to develop if its service volume is in the 20 to 70 million place-miles per line-mile range, and if conservative assumptions about auto diversion are made. With more liberal assumptions about auto diversion, and placing a higher value on auto-related savings, the monetary value of the total labor, energy, and land savings can rise to 16 to 22 cents per passenger-mile in the same range of service volume. Likely time savings (realized primarily by former bus users and prorated over all travelers) might add 4 to 8 cents to the left side of the Exhibit and 2 to 4 cents to the right side in 1977 prices.

The commensurate levels of capital investment will vary, depending on the discount rate and amortization period used, as seen in Exhibit 2.18. On the whole, the median investment of $1,250 per daily passenger-mile is more in scale with the conservative assumptions on the left, and the 75th percentile value of $1,800 per daily passenger-mile more in scale with the liberal assumptions on the right. In the former case, energy savings represent about one-eighth, in the second case, about one-third, of the total savings shown. This is of interest for deciding what share of rail transit investment can reasonably be funded from energy conservation budgets. The labor savings in the high bus diversion case are on the order of 5 to 6 cents per passenger mile, indicating that they alone are sufficient to offset a capital investment of at most $500 per weekday passenger-mile, if amortized at 3 percent over 75 years.

Needless to say, the three "hard" savings shown and the approximate indication of time savings are but a part of the long list of fixed guideway benefits presented earlier in Exhibit 1.14. No attempt is made here to place a monetary value on all the other items. It is deemed sufficient that there be proof of quantifiable savings recouping a stated *portion* of the investment; the worth of other benefits can then more easily be left to judgment.

A significant point in Exhibit 2.18 is the variation in savings per passenger-mile with rising volume of service. The saving in parking charges is constant, being a function of downtown size, the percentage of rail travel diverted from autos, and trip length. The time saving is also independent of volume. High-speed lines can attain large savings even at low volume. Labor and energy savings, by contrast, increase from negative values at very low volumes rather rapidly through the middle range, and then more slowly at high service volumes. At a point just after the labor-saving or energy-saving threshold is crossed, the absolute magnitude of these savings is small. Therefore, an absolute criterion, such as the capital investment allowable per passenger-mile, should ideally vary with volume. It seems more appropriate to use a higher investment yardstick for high-volume facilities and a lower investment yardstick for low-volume facilities.

Based on typical construction cost figures shown earlier in Exhibit 2.17, one can relate various assumed combinations of structure type to the passenger volumes or service volumes needed to support them as follows:

	Construction cost in 1977 $$, millions/mile	*Weekday passenger-miles per line-mile*	*Annual place-miles per line-mile, millions*
RAPID TRANSIT, assuming $1,250 per weekday passenger-mile investment criterion:			
⅓ grade, ⅓ cut & fill, ⅓ elevated	18	14,400	18
⅓ tunnel, rest as above	30	24,000	29
All tunnel	52	41,600	50
RAPID TRANSIT, assuming $1,800 per weekday passenger-mile investment criterion:			
⅓ tunnel, rest as shown	30	16,700	20
All tunnel	52	28,900	35
LIGHT RAIL, assuming $1,250 per weekday passenger-mile investment criterion:			
At grade, minimum construction	5	4,000	5
⅔ grade, ⅓ cut & fill	9	7,200	9
⅕ tunnel, rest as above	17	13,600	16
All tunnel	50	40,000	48
PEOPLEMOVER			
¾ elevated, ¼ at grade	15	12,000	14
All tunnel	37	29,600	35

Obviously, in any site-specific situation, combinations of structure types different from those shown will be encountered. It is an easy matter to recalculate the appropriate minimum passenger volumes accordingly. For this study, the combinations shown are retained as illustrative of fairly typical conditions.

SUMMARIZING THE THRESHOLD CRITERIA

A summary of the volume thresholds at which fixed guideways become worthy of consideration, based on the criteria of providing minimum service frequency, attaining labor savings, attaining energy savings, attaining land savings in downtowns, and keeping the investment per passenger-mile around the median value of recent projects, is presented in Exhibit 2.19.

RT 1: For *aboveground rapid transit,* the minimum service and capital investment criteria are identical, at about 18 million place-miles per line-mile annually, or 15,000 weekday passenger-miles per mile. Meeting these criteria also ensures meeting the land-savings criterion, attaining savings in labor compared to local buses and modest savings in energy.

RT 2: If *one-third of the rapid transit line is in tunnel,* the capital investment criterion becomes critical, and the minimum service volume rises to 29 million place-miles per line-mile or 24,000 weekday passenger-miles per mile. With that volume, the higher requirements for energy saving will also be satisfied, and labor savings will be attained compared to buses operating at the same speed as rapid transit.

Exhibit 2.19
Minimum Volume Thresholds at Which Guideways Become Worthy of Consideration

CRITERION	RAPID TRANSIT	LIGHT RAIL	PEOPLEMOVER
	Service volume, annual place-miles per line-mile		
1. Minimum service frequency in scale with existing lines	**18 million**	**5 million**	**4 million**
2. Possibility of attaining labor savings compared to indicated bus operation	**9 million** at 25 mph, 16 trains/hr compared to urban bus at 12 mph	**4 million** at 20 mph, 8 trains/hr compared to urban bus at 12 mph	**6 million** at 10 mph, 3-mile line compared to urban bus at 6 mph
	23 million at 25 mph, 8 trains/hr compared urban bus at same speed	**8 million** at 20 mph, 8 trains/hr compared urban bus at same speed	**10 million** at 10 mph, 1-mile line compared to bus at 6 mph
3. Possibility of attaining energy savings within 22 to 45 years compared to modes previously used	**12-15 million** if above ground **20-25 million** if 1/3 tunnel **33-40 million** if in tunnel	**7-9 million** if above ground **11-14 million** if 1/5 tunnel **27-35 million** if in tunnel	**55 million** above ground, no snow melting **90 million** with snow melting **80 million** in tunnel
4. Peak-period use of land at least as efficient as an auto roadway with modest bus use	**16 million** compared to freeway	**16 million** compared to freeway **6 million** compared to arterial	**6 million** compared to arterial
5. Limitation of investment per passenger-mile to median of current practice ($1,250/weekday PMT in 1977 prices) assuming load factors indicated below	**18 million** if above ground (1/3 grade, 1/3 cut and fill, 1/3 elevated) **29 million** if 1/3 in tunnel, remainder as above	**5 million** (if minimum construction) **9 million** if above ground (2/3 grade, 1/3 cut and fill) **16 million** if 1/5 in tunnel, remainder as above	**14 million** if above ground (3/4 elevated, 1/4 at grade) **35 million** if all tunnel
At $1,800/weekday PMT	**35 million** all tunnel		

CONVERSION FROM ANNUAL PLACE-MILES PER LINE-MILE TO WEEKDAY PEAK, WEEKDAY AVERAGE AND ANNUAL AVERAGE PASSENGER-MILES
(assumes 100% peak hour, peak direction occupancy and 23.3% average annual occupancy)

(1) Annual place-miles of service per line-mile, millions	(2) Annual PMT/line mile average over entire line millions 23.3 percent of (1)	(3) Weekday PMT/line mile average in both directions (2): 280	(4) Weekday persons per direction per hour at maximum load point one person = one place (2) x 0.5 x 0.26 x 1.754*
5	1.17	4,170	950
10	**2.33**	**8,339**	**1,900**
15	**3.50**	**12,509**	**2,850**
20	**4.67**	**16,678**	**3,800**
30	7.00	25,017	5,700
50	11.67	41,695	9,500
100	23.35	83,391	19,000
150	35.02	125,086	28,500

* Based on Table A-7. Assumes passenger trip length as 57% of car trip length.

If the *high capital* expenditure of $1,800 per weekday passenger-mile is admissible, for the same type of construction, the minimum volume falls to 21 million place-miles per line-mile annually or 17,140 passenger-miles per mile daily. At this level, energy savings are questionable and buses are more labor efficient at the same speed. This is not advanced as one of the threshold criteria.

RT 3: If a *rapid transit line is fully in tunnel,* one may consider the high-capital expenditure of $1,800 per weekday passenger-mile, to reflect the land-use benefit of tunneling. The minimum volume then becomes 29,000 weekday passenger-miles or 35 million annual place-miles per line mile. This will be on the verge of attaining energy savings (more difficult with a tunnel) but well within the range of labor savings compared to buses at the same speed.

LR 1: For a very *low-capital light rail line near grade,* the minimum service and capital investment criteria are identical, at 5 million annual place-miles per line-mile, or 4,000 weekday passenger-miles per mile. With that volume, minor labor savings compared to existing buses can be realized, but there will be *no* energy savings, and peak period use of land will be *no* more efficent than that of an existing arterial street.

LR 2: For a more adequate *light rail line with considerable grade-separation,* the capital investment criterion becomes critical, requiring a minimum volume of 9 million annual place-miles per line-mile, or 7,200 weekday passenger-miles per mile. With that volume, labor savings compared to buses at the same speed begin to be attained, land during the peak is used more efficiently than by a local arterial, and energy savings begin to be attained.

LR 3: For a *light rail line with 1/5 of the route in tunnel,* the capital investment criterion again governs, requiring a minimum volume of 16 million annual place-miles per line-mile, or 13,600 weekday passenger-miles per mile of line. That volume will also ensure peak period use of land more efficient than that of a freeway lane, as well as savings in labor and energy.

The six threshold levels outlined—termed RT 1, RT 2, RT 3, LR 1, LR 2, and LR 3, are used in Chapter 4 for comparison with estimated volumes of travel.

For *peoplemovers* of the prevailing rubber-tired technology used in a downtown environment for internal circulation, the various criteria do not fall into a neat progression. At 6 million place-miles per line-mile annually, or about 5,000 daily passenger-miles per mile, labor savings begin to be attained compared to a local bus at downtown speeds if the peoplemover is about 3 miles long and land begins to be used more intensively than by a local arterial. However, the capital-intensive structure, assuming 3/4 elevated routing, requires a volume of 14 million place-miles per line-mile annually, or 12,000 daily passenger-miles per mile, to satisfy the capital investment criterion. Energy savings, even without snowmelting, cannot be attained with volumes less than 55 million place-miles per line-mile, or 45,300 weekday passenger-miles per mile. Ranges related to these values are used in Chapter 4.

With the accounting system used here, four measures—annual place-miles per line-mile, annual passenger-miles per line-mile, weekday passenger-miles per line-mile, and weekday persons per direction per hour at maximum load point—can be used interchangeably; the conversion factors are given in the bottom part of Exhibit 2.19. This, however, assumes that for any one system, the average relationships shown are maintained. If this is not the case, appropriate adjustments must be made.

Second Avenue subway construction 1975–76. *(NYCTA)*

To facilitate comparison with passenger volume estimates in Chapter 4, which are developed on a weekday basis, the threshold criteria applied there are expressed in weekday passenger-miles per mile of line. This still maintains the two assumptions that these passenger-miles are carried by vehicle places which are 23.3 percent occupied, on an annual average basis, and that there are 280 weekday equivalents in a year. As indicated earlier, actual passenger occupancies on rail systems vary between about 15 and 35 percent, and may require adjustment in specific cases. The daily to annual travel relationship is more stable, and varies only from 297 weekday equivalents in New York to 256 on systems that are closed on weekends.

With minimum volume thresholds that are likely to ensure the attainment of the several fixed guideway objectives thus established, one can proceed to look for the travel corridors where such travel volumes can be found.

Lewisdale
M
metro

3 Travel Demand

THE EFFECT OF POPULATION DISTRIBUTION

The purpose of this chapter is to prepare an estimate of the travel volumes that could be attracted by fixed guideways in American urban areas currently without them. To this end, previously developed travel demand models[1] are validated and adjusted. These consist of a trip attraction model, which estimates total travel between a residential and a nonresidential area, and a mode choice model, which estimates the share of total trips that will be made by particular transit modes. Central to each of these models is the pattern of residential location in an urban area and the amount of nonresidential activity in its downtown.

The geographic population patterns of American cities are examined first. Three characteristics are pertinent: the total population of an urban area, its ring or radial distribution indicative of the density gradient, and its sectoral or circumferential distribution, usually a result of topographic constraints.

The total population of an urban area has often been used as an index of rail transit feasibility in the past. It is a very rough index, because total population distributed over an unspecified land area does not determine—except in a very broad range—how many people are likely to live near a potential rail line in a specific travel corridor and how many of these will in fact find the line useful for their daily trips. Of further interest is the length of the anticipated trips, since it also affects the future travel volume—passenger-miles (and hence place-miles) per mile of line. In the discussion that follows, relationships between the total population of an urban area and its radial and circumferential distributions are examined to pinpoint the population of particular travel corridors.

The radial population distribution is shown for each of 34 large urban areas in the United States in Exhibit 3.1, which depicts the accumulated percent of total

(Photo credit: Washington Metropolitan Area Transit Authority)

Exhibit 3.1

Radial Population Distribution, 1970
34 Urban Areas

Urban Area	1970 Population (000's) Urbanized Area	SMSA	SMSA Population at 20 Miles (000's)	Percent of SMSA Population within Given Mileage from Center 2	4	6	8	10	12	14	16	18	20
Urbanized Area Population over 5,000,000													
New York	16,207	11,572	12,129	3	12	28	43	56	71	83	91	98	104
Los Angeles	8,351	7,041	6,164	2	8	17	27	37	50	61	71	79	88
Chicago	6,715	6,978	5,075	1	8	19	31	43	52	59	65	68	73
Urbanized Area Population 2,000,000 to 5,000,000													
Philadelphia	4,021	4,822	4,038	6	20	32	45	56	63	69	76	80	84
Detroit	3,971	4,204	3,592	2	9	19	31	43	55	67	75	81	86
San Francisco	2,988	3,108	2,282	14	25	32	37	48	63	74	83	91	98
Boston	2,653	2,754	2,850	5	22	39	52	65	74	81	89	95	103
Washington	2,481	2,862	2,676	5	18	34	53	67	76	84	88	91	93
Dallas-Ft. Worth	2,015	2,318	1,478	2	12	21	33	40	48	56	57	61	64
Urbanized Area Population 1,500,000 to 2,000,000													
Cleveland	1,960	2,064	1,930	3	15	29	49	65	74	83	87	90	93
St. Louis	1,883	2,363	2,066	2	15	27	41	52	63	73	78	82	87
Pittsburgh	1,846	2,401	1,887	5	18	32	44	52	59	64	69	74	78
Minneapolis-St. Paul	1,704	1,814	1,724	4	17	35	51	67	78	84	90	92	95
Houston	1,678	1,985	1,671	4	18	38	46	72	78	81	82	82	84
Baltimore	1,580	2,071	1,857	12	27	47	61	71	77	80	84	87	90
Urbanized Area Population 1,000,000 to 1,500,000													
Milwaukee	1,252	1,404	1,310	8	30	51	66	76	80	83	87	91	93
Seattle	1,238	1,425	1,307	4	15	29	42	55	63	74	82	88	92
Miami	1,220	1,268	1,427	7	24	38	56	71	83	91	101	109	112
San Diego	1,198	1,353	1,107	4	18	36	50	65	73	77	79	81	82
Atlanta	1,173	1,390	1,342	7	21	36	50	61	71	80	87	93	97
Cincinnati	1,111	1,385	1,314	9	24	38	56	67	77	84	85	90	95
Kansas City	1,102	1,256	1,173	3	18	34	50	67	78	85	88	90	93
Buffalo	1,087	1,349	1,221	10	25	44	59	67	76	77	82	89	91
Denver	1,047	1,230	1,105	9	27	48	69	81	85	87	88	88	90
Urbanized Area Population under 1,000,000													
New Orleans	962	1,046	1,000	18	46	68	78	88	92	92	94	95	96
Tampa-St. Petersburg	864	1,013	733	7	18	28	36	39	43	43	48	57	72
Phoenix	863	968	919	7	21	39	56	71	79	84	89	93	95
Portland	825	1,007	949	11	30	46	63	74	83	86	89	92	94
Indianapolis	820	1,111	941	7	27	46	63	69	74	78	82	83	85
Providence	795	914	1,157	13	34	51	61	70	81	91	105	121	126
Columbus	790	916	894	8	35	58	74	83	89	91	94	97	98
San Antonio	773	864	834	11	40	65	81	90	91	93	96	97	97
Louisville	739	827	959	17	34	55	71	84	94	97	100	103	104
Dayton	686	850	878	12	33	49	61	72	77	84	91	96	103

Note: Urban areas with existing or committed fixed guideway systems shown in bold type.
Source: *Urban Data Book,* U.S. Department of Transportation

Exhibit 3.2
Population-Distance Profiles
New York, Los Angeles, Chicago, Philadelphia

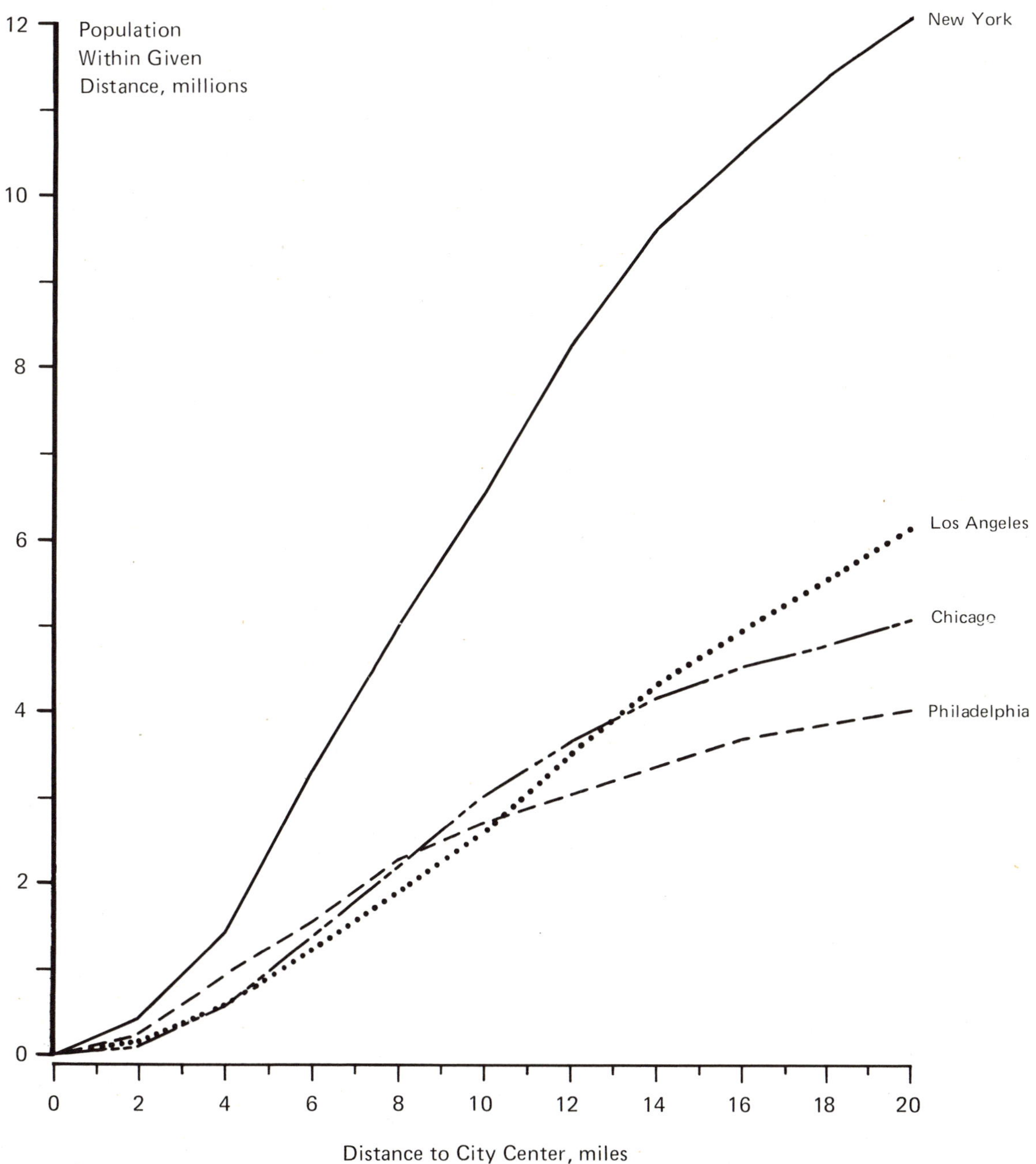

Exhibit 3.3
Population-Distance Profiles
Detroit, San Francisco, Boston, Washington, Baltimore

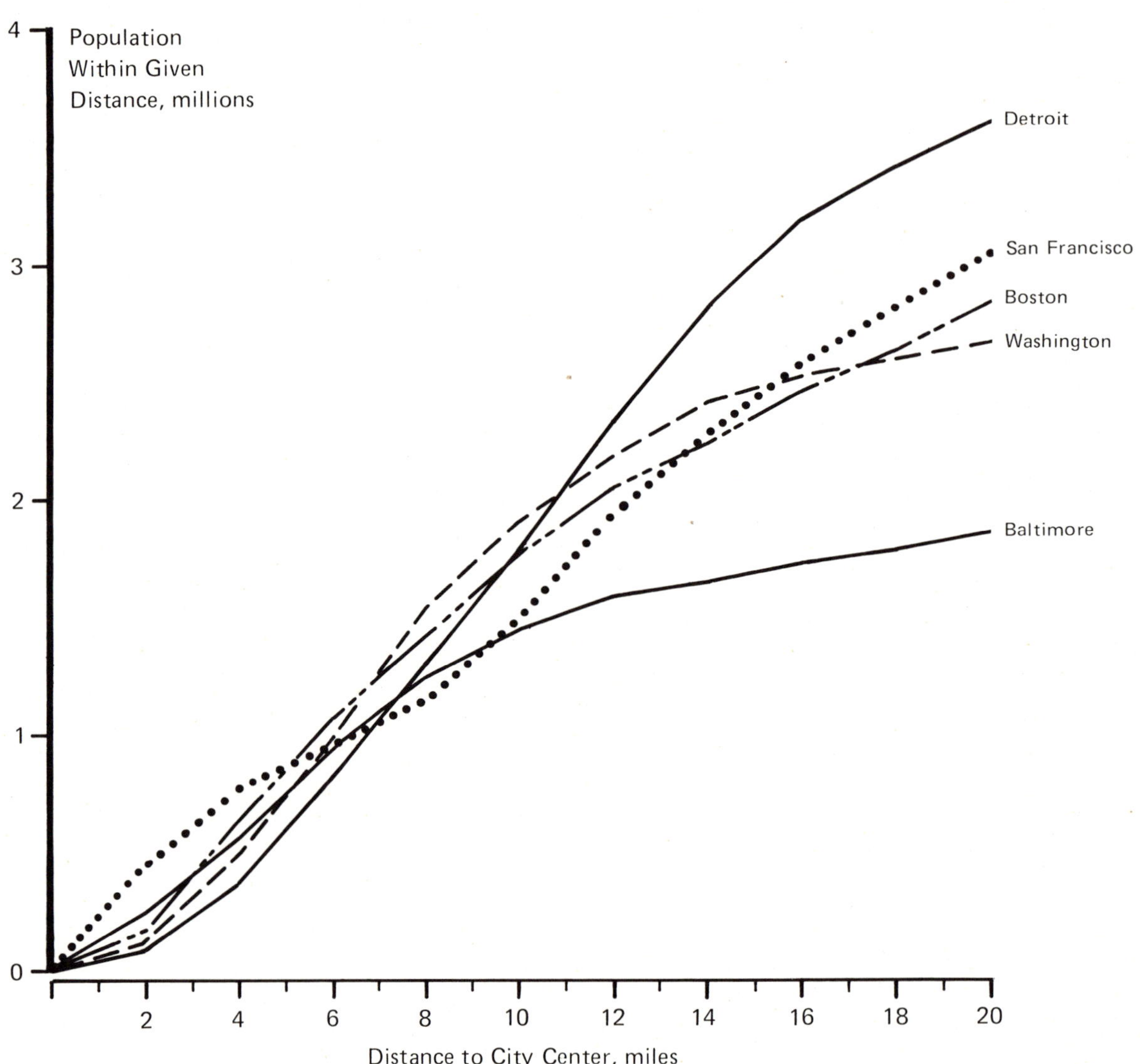

Exhibit 3.4
Population-Distance Profiles
St. Louis, Cleveland, Pittsburgh, Minneapolis-St. Paul, Houston, Milwaukee, New Orleans

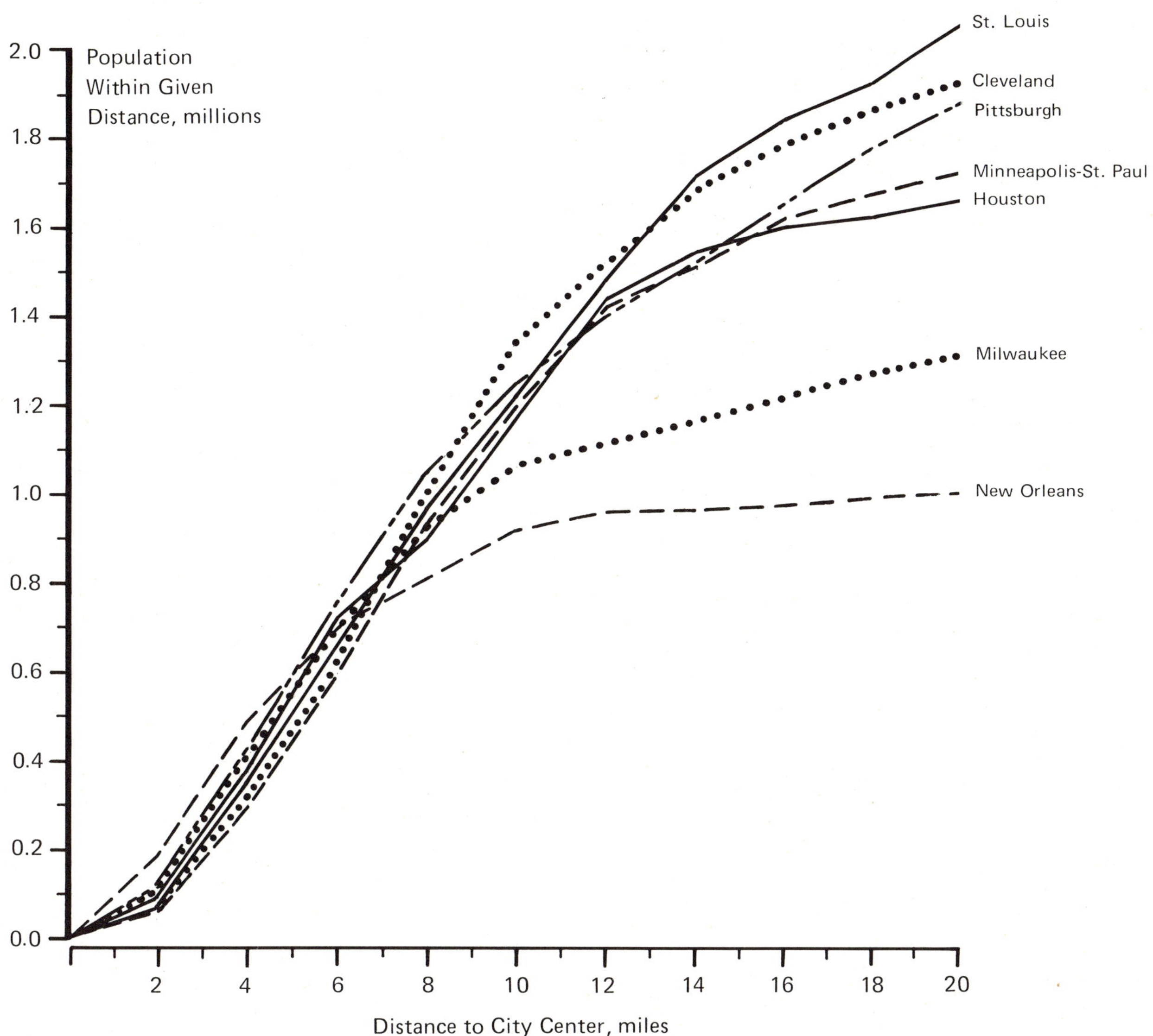

Exhibit 3.5
Population-Distance Profiles
Dallas-Ft. Worth, Miami, Atlanta, Cincinnati, Seattle, Buffalo, Kansas City, San Diego, Denver

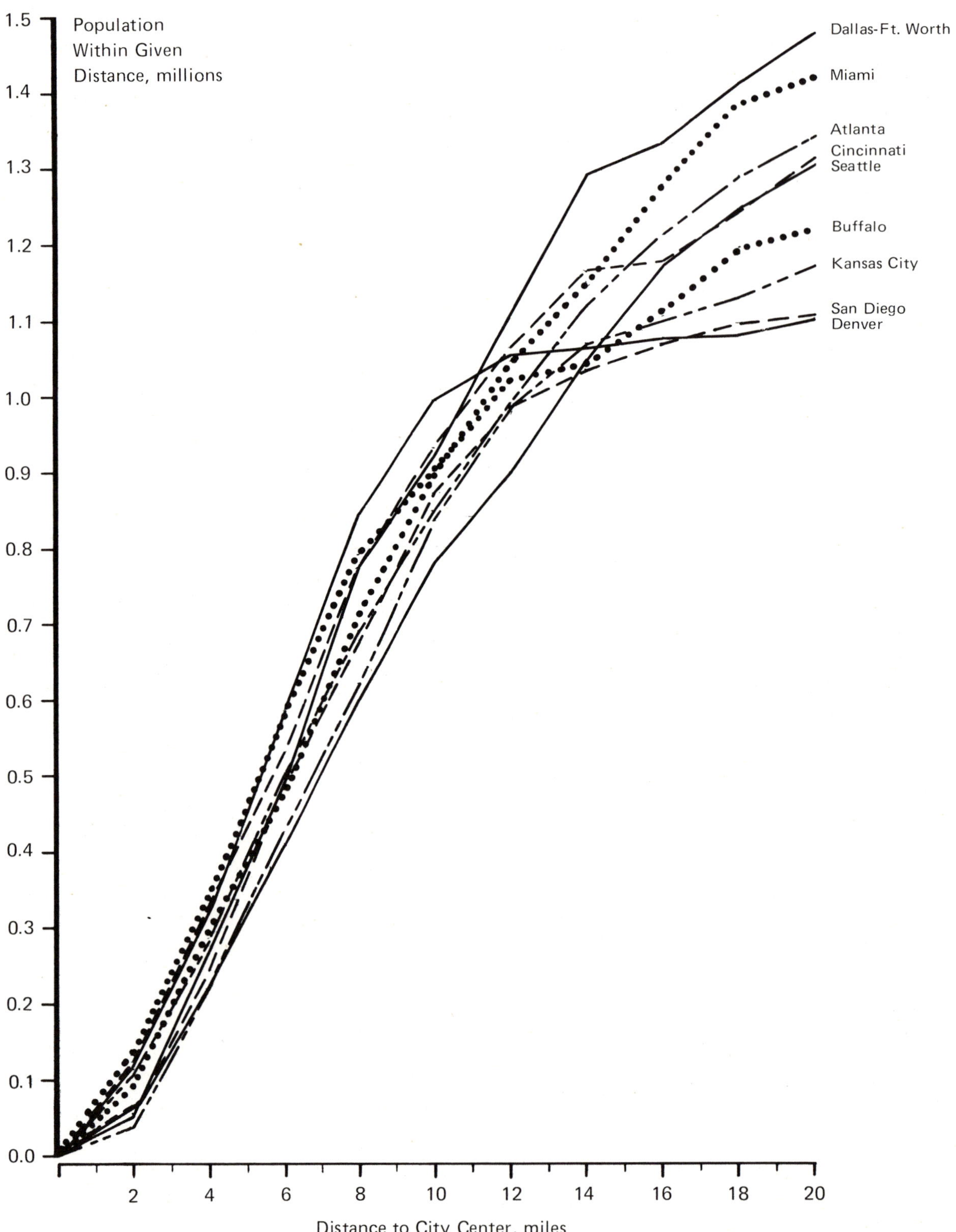

Exhibit 3.6
Population-Distance Profiles
Providence, Portland, Indianapolis, Phoenix, Columbus, Dayton, Louisville, San Antonio

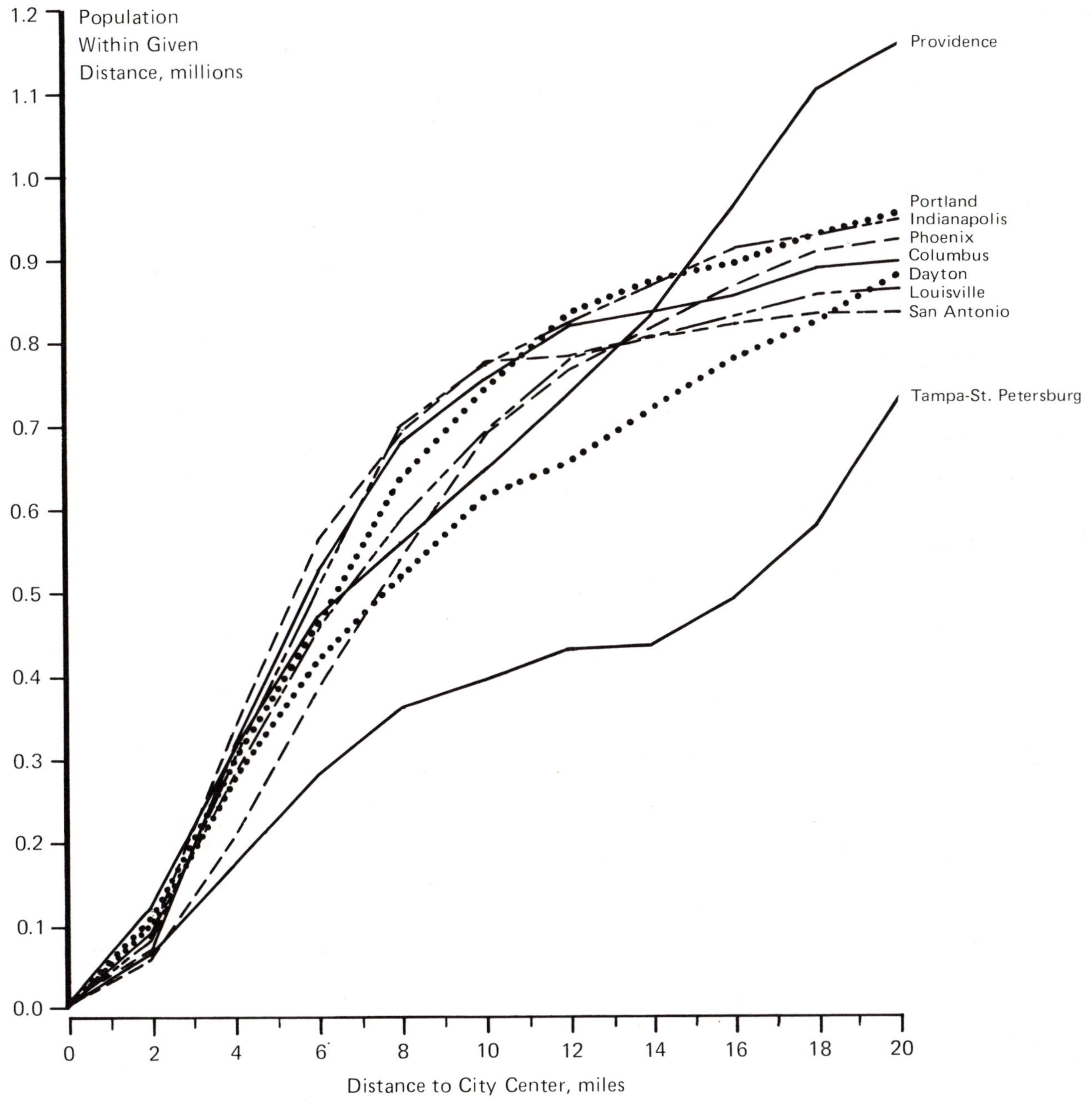

Exhibit 3.7
Radial Distances to Reach a Given Population in 34 Urban Areas

	Distance (miles) to Reach Given Population						
	Population (millions)						
Urban Area	**0.50**	**0.75**	**1.0**	**1.5**	**2.0**	**3.0**	**4.0**
New York	2.2	2.8	3.3	4.1	4.6	5.7	6.9
Los Angeles	3.8	4.6	5.4	6.9	8.3	10.9	13.6
Chicago	3.9	4.6	5.3	6.5	7.7	10.4	13.7
Philadelphia	2.6	3.4	4.2	6.0	7.5	12.0	20.0
Detroit	4.6	5.8	6.9	9.0	10.9	15.6	--
San Francisco	3.4	6.2	9.2	12.5	16.6	--	--
Boston	3.5	4.5	5.7	8.4	11.8	--	--
Washington	3.8	4.9	5.8	8.0	10.8	--	--
Dallas-Ft. Worth	6.2	8.6	10.9	--	--	--	--
Cleveland	5.3	6.6	8.0	11.8	--	--	--
St. Louis	5.2	6.7	8.2	12.1	19.2	--	--
Pittsburgh	4.3	5.9	7.9	13.4	--	--	--
Minneapolis-St. Paul	5.2	6.8	8.5	13.0	--	--	--
Houston	5.3	7.0	8.8	13.2	--	--	--
Baltimore	3.6	4.9	6.2	10.7	19.2	--	--
Milwaukee	4.5	6.3	9.2	--	--	--	--
Seattle	7.0	9.7	13.5	--	--	--	--
Miami	6.1	8.3	11.9	--	--	--	--
San Diego	6.2	8.7	12.5	--	--	--	--
Atlanta	6.0	8.7	12.2	--	--	--	--
Cincinnati	5.6	7.8	11.2	--	--	--	--
Kansas City	6.8	9.3	12.4	--	--	--	--
Buffalo	5.4	7.8	11.7	--	--	--	--
Denver	5.4	7.3	10.3	--	--	--	--
New Orleans	4.1	6.9	20.0	--	--	--	--
Tampa-St. Petersburg	16.5	--	--	--	--	--	--
Phoenix	7.5	11.6	--	--	--	--	--
Portland	6.4	10.1	--	--	--	--	--
Indianapolis	5.9	9.2	--	--	--	--	--
Providence	6.9	12.6	16.6	--	--	--	--
Columbus	5.7	9.8	--	--	--	--	--
San Antonio	5.5	9.1	--	--	--	--	--
Louisville	6.7	11.6	--	--	--	--	--
Dayton	7.6	15.4	--	--	--	--	--

Notes: Dash indicates that the population is not reached in 20 miles.
Urban areas with existing or committed fixed guideway systems shown in bold type.

Exhibit 3.8
Accumulated Radial Population

Urban Area	Accumulated Population at Given Mileage from Center, 000's									
	2	4	6	8	10	12	14	16	18	20
1. Los Angeles	117	576	1,203	1,929	2,622	3,507	4,309	4,969	5,536	6,163
2. Washington	137	509	987	1,523	1,910	2,186	2,407	2,526	2,608	2,675
3. Detroit	83	361	814	1,299	1,787	2,323	2,831	3,169	3,423	3,594
4. Baltimore	243	567	914	1,272	1,474	1,593	1,657	1,735	1,792	1,861
5. Pittsburgh	120	425	766	1,049	1,242	1,407	1,530	1,657	1,785	1,887
6. St. Louis	58	347	638	970	1,226	1,478	1,714	1,842	1,928	2,066
7. Minneapolis-St. Paul	65	305	639	934	1,210	1,414	1,529	1,629	1,677	1,724
8. Houston	87	357	749	910	1,185	1,433	1,547	1,614	1,629	1,671
9. Milwaukee	118	416	721	930	1,065	1,117	1,169	1,212	1,277	1,310
10. Denver	113	333	588	846	997	1,051	1,066	1,077	1,084	1,105
11. Cincinnati	126	332	533	778	933	1,067	1,165	1,180	1,242	1,315
12. New Orleans	190	483	713	813	921	963	967	982	998	1,001
13. Dallas-Ft. Worth	50	270	498	776	920	1,108	1,292	1,332	1,413	1,478
14. Buffalo	134	344	589	794	902	1,022	1,040	1,112	1,198	1,222
15. Miami	92	298	486	714	897	1,047	1,150	1,280	1,387	1,421
16. San Diego	58	247	484	679	873	986	1,038	1,070	1,095	1,107
17. Atlanta	103	286	506	693	850	991	1,119	1,214	1,292	1,343
18. Kansas City	39	220	429	623	838	984	1,072	1,105	1,130	1,174
19. Seattle	54	220	411	602	782	900	1,049	1,174	1,248	1,307
20. San Antonio	91	343	564	697	779	784	805	826	835	835
21. Indianapolis	80	303	506	696	771	823	868	909	923	941
22. Portland	114	307	465	635	743	832	871	898	927	949
23. Columbus	69	318	529	677	761	817	833	858	887	894
24. Phoenix	67	204	380	539	691	767	808	861	905	919
25. Louisville	95	282	455	591	694	780	805	830	854	859
26. Providence	120	315	470	561	639	737	836	964	1,105	1,156
27. Dayton	106	280	419	520	613	652	713	775	819	879
28. Tampa-St. Petersburg	72	180	285	368	397	431	433	490	581	735

Note: Urban areas with existing or committed fixed guideway systems shown in bold type.
Source: *Urban Data Book,* U.S. Department of Transportation

population up to 20 miles (32 km) from the city center. These distributions are based on 1970 Census Standard Metropolitan Statistical Area (SMSA) data reported in the *USDOT Urban Data Book.*[2] Cities with major rail transit systems in existence or under construction in 1980 are shown in bold type.

Generally, metropolitan areas of 2 to 10 million average some 90 percent of their population within a radius of 20 miles (32 km); an exception is the two-centered area of Dallas–Ft. Worth. Though one has to go a similar distance—an average of 17 miles from the center (27 km)—to reach 90 percent of the population in metropolitan areas on the order of 1 million, a much smaller absolute population will be reached. It is clear that a rail line of similar length will have fewer potential riders living nearby in the smaller cities.

Therefore, while population-distance profiles given in percent are of interest, more relevant for estimating travel is the absolute number of people found within a given distance from the city center. This is shown in Exhibits 3.2 through 3.6, which are grouped to compare urban areas of similar total population.

The first in the series, Exhibit 3.2, includes New York, Los Angeles, Chicago, and Philadelphia. While New York stands out with 9 million people living within 13 miles (21 km) of its center, the Los Angeles and Chicago profiles resemble each other quite closely, a fact not readily apparent from Exhibit 3.1. Each has 4 million people within 13 miles (21 km) of its center. Philadelphia, with a considerably smaller total population than Los Angeles or Chicago, has more residents within an 8-mile (13-km) radius—about 2.4 million.

In the next group of urban areas with 2 to 4 million residents in Exhibit 3.3, Boston and Washington show very similar distributions, reaching about 2 million residents at a distance of 11 miles (18 km); Detroit reaches the same point more gradually. Baltimore, with a much smaller total population, has nevertheless about as many residents within 6 miles (10 km) as San Francisco, Boston, Washington, or Detroit. San Francisco has more residents than the others within 5 miles (8 km), but at longer distances its profile becomes erratic due to the voids resulting from topography.

In Exhibit 3.4, all seven urban areas in the 1 to 2 million population group have similar profiles close to the center, with roughly 0.9 million residents living within 8 miles (13 km). Farther out, New Orleans and Milwaukee have few additional residents. The profiles of Pittsburgh, Minneapolis–St. Paul, and Houston stay close together up to 15 miles (24 km), at which distance each reaches almost 1.6 million. The larger urban areas of St. Louis and Cleveland contain about 1.75 million residents at that distance.

In Exhibit 3.5, Dallas–Ft. Worth, Miami, Atlanta, Cincinnati, Buffalo, Kansas City, San Diego, and Denver all have between 0.9 and 1.0 million residents within 11 miles (18 km) of their centers; at greater distances, there is considerable divergence. The Seattle curve falls below the others between about 4 and 14 miles (6 and 23 km) because of topographic voids.

Lastly, in Exhibit 3.6, Providence, Portland, Indianapolis, Phoenix, Columbus, Louisville, and San Antonio all appear with 0.7 to 0.8 million residents within 11 miles (18 km) of their centers. Their population distribution curves stay fairly close together at longer distances as well, except for the metropolitan area of Providence, which contains several smaller cities beyond the 11-mile (18-km) radius. By contrast, Dayton and Tampa–St. Petersburg have only 0.6 and 0.4 million residents, respectively, at that distance.

It is useful to express the curves of Exhibits 3.2 through 3.6 in terms of the distance required to reach a given number of people living around an urban area's center. These distances represent a rough measure of how long a radial transit system should be to reach a given number of potential users and are shown in Exhibit 3.7 for each of the 34 urban areas graphed.

It can be seen, for example, that a population of 0.75 million is reached within 11 miles (18 km) or less by *all areas except* Tampa–St. Petersburg, Dayton, Louisville, Providence, and Phoenix. By contrast, double that population, or 1.5 million, is reached within 11 miles or less by New York, Philadelphia, Chicago, Los Angeles, Washington, Boston, Detroit, and Baltimore, in that order. Somewhat longer distances are required to reach 1.5 million in Cleveland, St. Louis, San Francisco, Minneapolis–St. Paul, Houston, and Pittsburgh. Lastly, a population of 3 million is reached within 11 miles (18 km) or less by New York, Chicago, and Los Angeles; somewhat longer distances are required in Philadelphia and Detroit. Among urban areas that did not have rail transit in being or under construction as of 1980, Los Angeles and, to a lesser extent, Detroit rank high in terms of population concentration.

This suggests a sequencing of urban areas by radial population characteristics. The absolute levels of population within the first few miles out from the center assume considerable importance for such an exercise, while population levels near the area's edge are less important. This is so because the total number of trips to downtown is heavily influenced by the close-in population which tends to make the largest number of such trips per capita.

Accordingly, Exhibit 3.8 shows the accumulated urban area population by two-mile rings in sequence by the population within the 10-mile (16-km) mark. Omitted are the six traditional "rail regions" discussed earlier in Chapter 1. Exhibit 3.8 indicates that Los Angeles has about 50 percent more people living within 10 miles (16 km) of its center than Washington or Detroit. Baltimore and Pittsburgh follow, each with some rail transit in existence or under construction. These are followed by St. Louis, Minneapolis–St. Paul, Houston, and Milwaukee, all with more than 1 million people within 10 miles (16 km). In addition, four areas have as many or more people at 10 miles than Buffalo, Miami, San Diego, and Atlanta, all with rail systems under construction. The four are Denver, Cincinnati, New Orleans, and Dallas–Ft. Worth.

The circumferential population distribution can significantly alter the radial figures when it comes to particular travel corridors. It makes a great difference whether, for example, the 1 million residents living within a 10-mile radius of an urban center occupy the full circle around the center, or only half, the other half having some feature that makes it largely uninhabited such as a body of water, or mountains or desert.

Ideally, both radial and circumferential population distributions are built up from small-area census tract statistics. Such an integrated mapping of the population topography of all of the nation's major urban areas was beyond the resources of this study. Instead, most circumferential distributions are derived from secondary sources, primarily area transportation studies of United States and Canadian cities.[3] Consequently, the 20 urban areas for which circumferential distributions are shown are not chosen systematically, but according to data availability. Additional areas could have been included if the transportation reports had made a habit of reporting basic data in sufficient detail for further analysis. Still, a wide spectrum of urban sizes is represented, ranging from Honolulu to the New York–Northeastern New Jersey urbanized area. Two inconsistencies occur in these data sources: the year of the population data varies over a 13-year period, and outer boundaries of the urban area are based on varying definitions; some go only to the central city limits, while others extend into exurbia. However, the basic distribution by sector in any one area does not change greatly over time (shifts in the radial distribution are quite another matter), nor do these distributions change much, as a separate analysis has shown, if the urban area boundaries are extended or cut back.

Accumulated population distributions are developed by dividing each urban area into as many sectors as convenient with the data at hand, ranking each sector by gross population density and then accumulating the percent of the population and the percent of the area in each successively lower density sector. Sectors with little or no population because of bodies of water, mountains, or deserts, are included. This is done to show that in urban areas with such features, population is indeed concentrated over a narrower sweep of the compass.

Exhibit 3.9 displays the accumulated population distributions separately for four groups of urban areas, varying in size from at least 2½ million people down to some 800,000 or fewer. The curves are constructed so that the more evenly distributed an area's population is, the closer the curve is to a 45-degree line. In the unlikely event of a completely even distribution over a featureless plain, 20 percent of the population would be in 20 percent of the circumferential area, 40 percent in 40 percent, and so forth. For populations concentrated in a few corridors, the curve would begin more steeply, approaching the 100th percentile within a small proportion of the circumferential area.

The curves indeed show distinct differences in the manner in which urban populations reach the 100th percentile. In the first group, the lakefront cities of Chicago and Toronto contain 100 percent of their population within 50 percent of their area, or a 180-degree sweep of the compass. Similarly, the coastal cities of New York and Boston reach their 100th percentile at roughly two-thirds and three-quarters of their respective areas. Only Salt Lake City and Honolulu, among the urban areas plotted, both in the fourth set of curves, show a similar feature. Other urban areas, notably Montreal and Denver, likewise have relatively concave curves by virtue of topographic constraints.

Distinctions among urban areas can also be made by examining the percent of circumferential area required to include 50 percent of the population. New York, Chicago, Salt Lake City, and Honolulu reach that in less than 20 percent of their respective areas; Toronto, Montreal, and Denver reach it in about one-quarter of their areas, and the remaining cities require 30 percent or more of their areas. The various indicators of circumferential population distribution are listed in tabular form in Exhibit 3.10.

For transit planning, the curves can indicate how many people are contained in a given wedge. For example, if 12.5 percent of an area that is a pie-shaped sector of 45 degrees is thought of as a potential transit corridor, then the population within that area becomes an indicator of potential ridership. Exhibit 3.10 shows this population in percentage and absolute terms with 1970 urbanized area population as the base. Salt Lake City, New York, Chicago, and Honolulu—all strongly affected by topography—stand out above all others with 40 percent or more of their population within one 45-degree sector. Toronto and Montreal, each with 29 percent of their

Exhibit 3.9
Circumferential Population Distributions in Twenty Urban Areas

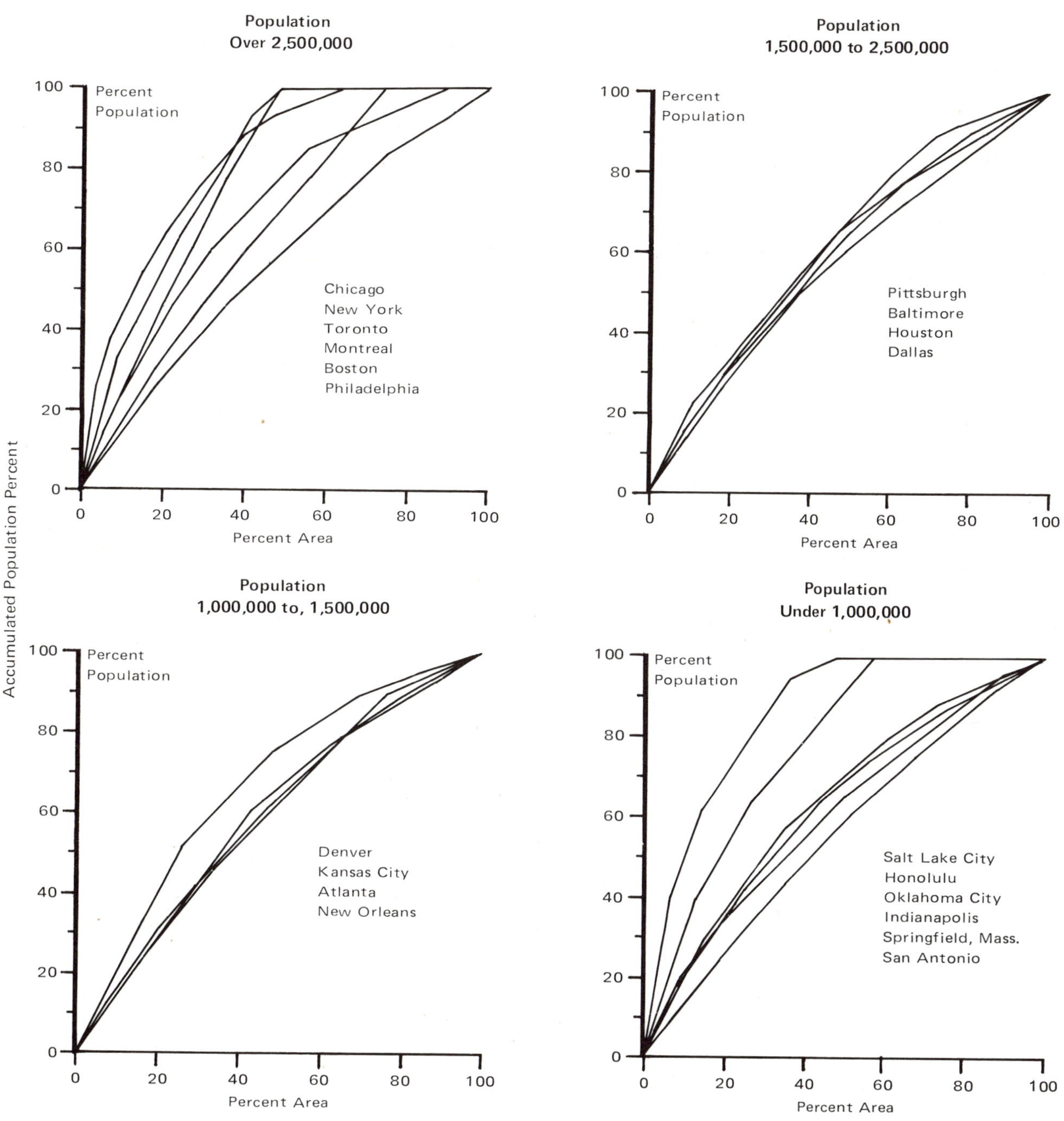

Note - Urban areas listed in order of curves as shown from left to right

Exhibit 3.10
Numerical Indicators of Circumferential Population Distribution

Urban Area	Urbanized Area Population, 1970 (000's)	Population used in Exhibit 3.8 (000's)	Percent of circumferential area containing 50 percent of population	Percent of circumferential area containing 20 percent of population	Population within 12.5 percent of circumferential area	
					%	Number (000's)
New York	16,207	17,380	13	3	49	7,941
Chicago	6,715	5,116	17	5	40	2,686
Philadelphia	4,021	3,927	40	14	18	724
Montreal	2,743	2,758	25	7	29	795
Boston	2,653	2,924	33	12	21	557
Toronto	2,628	2,105	22	8	29	762
Dallas	2,015	1,185	38	14	18	363
Pittsburgh	1,846	1,492	33	10	25	462
Houston	1,678	1,187	37	12	21	352
Baltimore	1,580	1,608	35	12	21	332
Atlanta	1,173	687	38	13	18	246
Kansas City	1,102	853	38	14	19	231
Denver	1,047	817	25	10	25	262
New Orleans	962	789	35	13	19	183
Indianapolis	820	740	32	10	24	197
San Antonio	773	668	41	16	16	124
Oklahoma City	627	569	30	10	24	150
Springfield, Mass.	566	512	35	10	24	136
Salt Lake City	516	390	10	3	57	294
Honolulu	446	448	18	6	40	178

Sources: U.S. Bureau of Census, various local reports and Exhibit 3.8.

Exhibit 3.11
Circumfrential Population Distributions
Four Generalized Curves

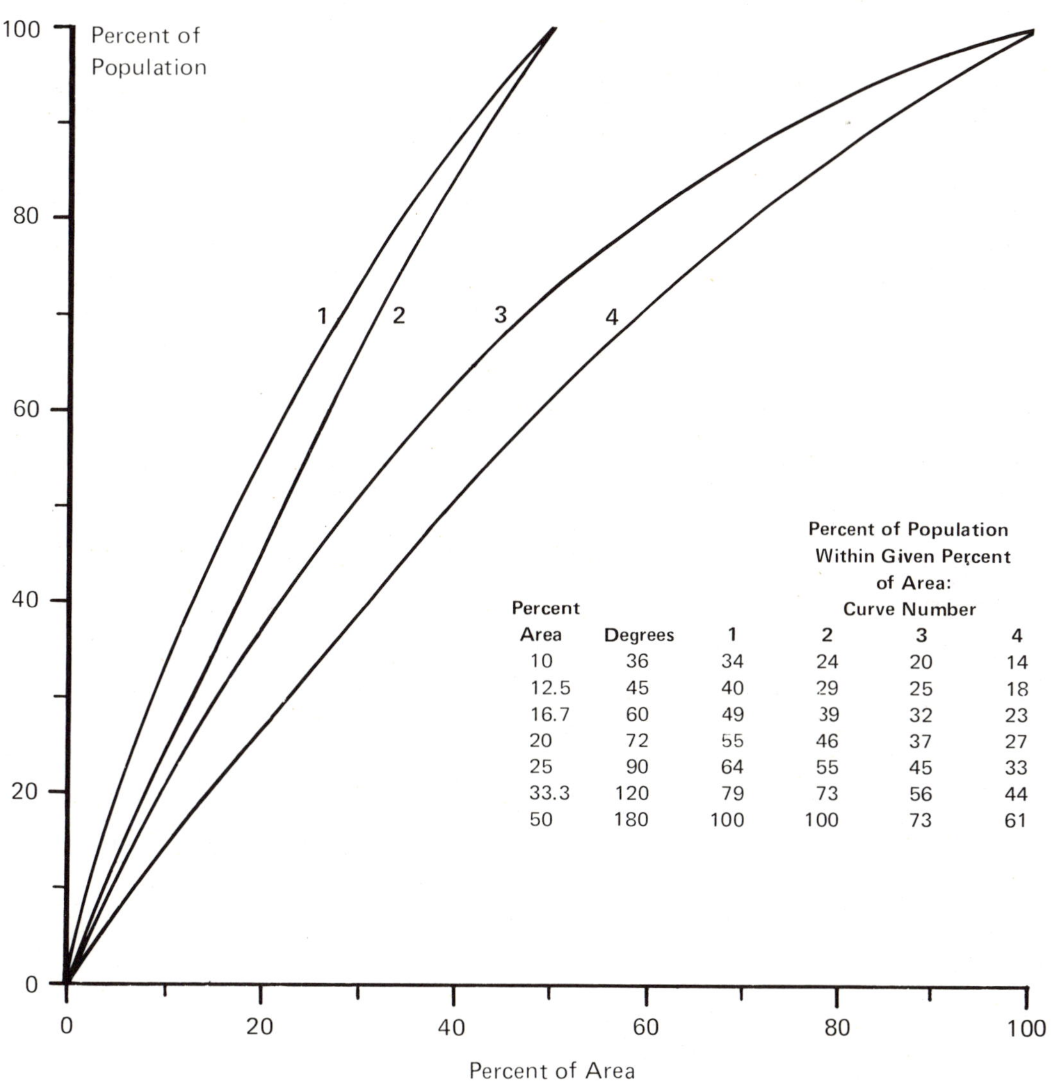

Percent Area	Degrees	Percent of Population Within Given Percent of Area: Curve Number 1	2	3	4
10	36	34	24	20	14
12.5	45	40	29	25	18
16.7	60	49	39	32	23
20	72	55	46	37	27
25	90	64	55	45	33
33.3	120	79	73	56	44
50	180	100	100	73	61

population within such a sector, are next, followed by Denver, Pittsburgh, Indianapolis, Oklahoma City, and Springfield, Massachusetts, each with about one-quarter of their population contained in a 45-degree sector. The remaining urbanized areas fall in the 18 to 21-percent range, with San Antonio at 16 percent.

Interestingly, Chicago's densely populated lakefront corridor contains a higher proportion of that city's population within 45 degrees than does Toronto's, though both cities are confined by water to one-half the sweep of the compass. Boston, with a 90-degree wedge occupied by Massachusetts Bay, contains a lower proportion of its population in the densest 45-degree corridor than Indianapolis or Oklahoma City and no higher than Houston, with no such water constraints. In the last column in Exhibit 3.10, the total population living within the densest 45-degree sector is shown. This combines a measure of the total population and of the sectoral distribution in an urban area.

While each urban area has a unique circumferential population distribution, it remains possible to generalize. Four typical configurations are advanced in Exhibit 3.11: (1) half of the area completely constrained by water or topography and the other half characterized by a relatively high corridor concentration, e.g., Chicago; (2) half the area similarly constrained but the remaining half characterized by a relatively even corridor distribution, e.g., Toronto; (3) development within 360 degrees but relatively high corridor concentration which may be a result of topographic features, e.g., Denver, Pittsburgh; and (4) development within the full 360 degrees with moderately concentrated corridors. Also shown is the percent of population that would be found in one-tenth, one-eighth, one-sixth, one-fifth, one-fourth, one-third, and one-half of the full 360-degree sweep of the compass.

From the four generalized curves it is possible to estimate how much denser the densest sector will be than the average sector. For example, a sector of 45 degrees will have about 3.2 times the average density for curve type one, 2.3 times for curve type two, 2.0 times for curve type three, and 1.4 times for curve type four. As the sector gets narrower, the ratio will tend to increase, since it is equal to the slope of the curve at any particular point. By assuming the appropriate curve for each urban area among the four shown in Exhibit 3.11, and using the incremental population in each ring in Exhibit 3.8, the density in the maximum density corridor can be estimated. The choice of the appropriate curve in each urban area is made with the assistance of available density maps, including dot maps in the *Urban Data Book*. Where circumferential population distributions are readily available, the density multiplier is calculated directly.

In Exhibit 3.12 the average gross population densities in the densest corridor are shown, based on the estimated density multiplier or on the actual one, when available. Of the 10 urban areas with actual data available, eight are estimated remarkably well by assigning one of the four circumferential distribution curve types. The two exceptions are Baltimore and Houston; these occur because Baltimore Harbor places the Baltimore distribution somewhere between a type two and type four curve, and because the southern corridor in Houston is surprisingly denser than the average.

The maximum density figures by ring and sector in Exhibit 3.12 are also checked against actual data when available. The comparisons between actual and synthesized data are usually quite close. Small modifications are necessary, at some distances for Detroit, Los Angeles, Washington, Seattle, and Minneapolis–St. Paul,

Exhibit 3.12
Gross Population Densities by Distance from Center by Corridor

	Circumferential	Density Multiplier		Density in Maximum Density Corridor, Population per square mile, 000's At Given Mileage Increment										Data
	Curve Type	Estimated	Actual	0-2	2-4	4-6	6-8	8-10	10-12	12-14	14-16	16-18	18-20	Quality
1. Detroit	1	3.2		35*	28*	22*	15*	12*	8	7*	5*	4*	3	B
2. Baltimore	4	1.4	1.80	41	35	20	8.8	5.1	2.7	0.8	1.7	1.2	1.0	A
3. Los Angeles	--	--	n.c.	15.3	28	20*	16.2	13.8	10*	9*	9*	8.9	8.9	B
4. Miami	1	3.2		27.5	18.1	11.5	11.6	8.3	6.3	4.0	4.8	3.8	1.2	C
5. Washington	4	1.4		30*	14*	13.1	8	6.2	4.3	3.2	1.5	1.2	1.0	A
6. St. Louis	3	2.0		18	20	15	10.6	7.4	6.7	5.8	3.1	2.2	2.9	C
7. Seattle	3	2.0		22*	18*	16	8	5.1	3.0	3.8	3.1	1.7	1.2	B
8. Minneapolis-St. Paul	3	2.0		25*	13.8	12.8	9.4	7.8	5.4	2.8	2.4	1.2	1.0	B
9. Pittsburgh	3	2.0	1.83	20.6	20.0	14.0	8.7	5.0	4.0	3.0	2.9	2.9	2.2	B
10. Buffalo	2	2.3		28.8	13.9	10.8	11.1	3.5	3.6	0.6	2.0	2.2	0.4	C
11. Milwaukee	2	2.3		25.4	16.7	13.4	7.7	4.5	1.6	1.6	1.6	1.4	1.0	C
12. Honolulu	--	--	n.c.	18.2	20.5	10.1	3.0	1.5	n.c.	n.c.	n.c.	n.c.	n.c.	A
13. Cincinnati	3	2.0		23.5	7.0	7.7	7.8	4.3	3.4	3.4	0.4	1.4	1.4	C
14. Houston	4	1.4	1.96	16.1	14	8	5.0	7.0	6.5	2.0	0.4	0.3	0.7	B
15. New Orleans	4	1.4	1.48	26.0	12.4	5.9	2.4	2.2	0.9	0.0	0.2	0.2	0.0	B
16. San Diego	2	2.3		12.4	12.4	10.4	7.1	6.2	3.4	1.4	0.9	0.7	0.3	C
17. Indianapolis	3	2.0	1.97	14.7	12.6	7.6	6.0	2.1	1.3	0.6	0.5	0.2	0.2	B
18. Columbus	3	2.0		12.9	14.2	8.0	4.8	2.4	1.3	0.2	0.3	0.3	0.1	C
19. Louisville	3	2.0		17.7	10.8	6.6	4.3	2.9	2.3	0.6	0.7	0.5	0.0	C
20. Providence	2	2.3		22.4	5.4	5.8	2.8	2.2	2.5	1.2	1.5	1.6	0.5	C
21. Denver	3	2.0	2.06	12.9	10	8.5	4.5	1.4	0.9	0.4	0.2	0.2	0.4	B
22. Atlanta	4	1.4	1.46	14.0	7.7	6.1	4.3	3.2	2.7	2.2	1.5	1.2	0.7	A
23. Dallas-Ft. Worth	4	1.4	1.54	7.1	9.7	6.8	6.9	3.2	3.9	3.2	0.7	1.2	1.0	B
24. Portland	3	2.0		7.3	11.0	6.0	5.5	3.0	2.3	1.0	0.8	0.7	0.2	C
25. Tampa	2	2.3		15.5	7.1	4.7	3.0	1.0	1.0	0.0	1.3	2.4	3.6	C
26. Kansas City	4	1.4	1.53	5.5	7.9	6.6	4.8	4.6	2.8	1.6	0.5	0.5	0.5	B
27. San Antonio	4	1.4	1.26	10.7	9.1	5.5	2.5	1.4	0.2	0.2	0.2	0.1	0.0	B
28. Dayton	4	1.4		13.7	6.8	3.5	2.2	1.8	0.4	0.7	0.7	0.5	0.6	C
29. Phoenix	4	1.4		8.8	5.5	4.7	3.5	3.0	1.4	0.5	0.6	0.5	0.1	C

Notes: Urban areas with existing or committed fixed guideway systems shown in bold type.
Asterisk indicates estimates based on actual population density data.
Final Los Angeles calculations in Chapter IV based on actual data in Wilshire corridor. Honolulu also based on actual data.
n.c.—not calculated.

Source: Regional Plan Association

shown by asterisks in Exhibit 3.12. In Atlanta, average densities in the maximum density corridor check remarkably well with actual population density data, and no changes are necessary. Honolulu, by virtue of its unique corridor concentration, is included in Exhibit 3.12. Its gross population densities are calculated directly.

To suggest the quality of the population data, each urban area is assigned a grade in Exhibit 3.12, A if maximum density is based on direct population statistics, B if the actual density multiplier is available, or if density data are obtained from generalized population density maps, and C if the data are synthesized with no direct crosschecks.

The urban areas are listed in sequence according to the sector density within the first five rings. Of interest is the shift in sequence compared to Exhibit 3.8. Urban areas with heavy population concentrations in a few corridors, such as Detroit, Cleveland, Miami, Seattle, and Buffalo move upward, while those with populations more evenly distributed, such as Los Angeles, Washington, Atlanta, Dallas–Ft. Worth, and Kansas City move downward. The figures in Exhibit 3.12 represent the final population estimates that are used to arrive at travel volumes in Chapter 4.

THE EFFECT OF NONRESIDENTIAL ACTIVITY

Estimating downtown activity. The amount of travel to and from a downtown or another cluster of nonresidential activity depends on the amount and type of activity found there. The scale of activity can be estimated most readily with two measures: employment and floorspace. Most central cities have collected such data from time to time, but rarely on a regular basis, and there are many difficulties in their use, stemming largely from the lack of any central collection mechanism to assure uniformity for all cities.

The major inconsistency is in defining the areal extent of the downtown, or Central Business District (CBD) itself. Some CBD's are defined very narrowly to include only a few blocks of the most intensive use; others encompass a number of square miles, including a substantial area in residential or manufacturing use. U.S. Census definitions, though uniform, are based on retail activity alone and are usually far too restricted. For urban areas of about 1 million residents, it is generally desirable to include a land area of at least one square mile (2.59 km^2) within the CBD, unless topographic constraints or the contiguous pattern of nonresidential development dictate otherwise. Conversely, land areas of several square miles in medium-sized cities are likely to overstate the true CBD size and exaggerate its attraction for trips by public transporation, as will be shown later.

There are definitional problems with respect to employment and floorspace as well. Employment may mean the number of jobs held in the CBD, the number of job-holders (somewhat lower because some workers hold more than one job), or the number of workers working in the CBD on an average weekday, deducting for vacations and other absences. Employment data are inflated if all employees of an establishment with a CBD address are counted, irrespective of whether they actually work in the CBD.

Floorspace data likewise suffer from inconsistencies. In some cases, residential floorspace is included, in others only office and retail floorspace is counted, but not other nonresidential uses, such as manufacturing and warehousing. The mix of the types of floorspace is important because different types of floorspace generate trips at varying rates. For example, retail generates up to 10 times more trips per unit than office floorspace, but trips to office buildings have substantially sharper peaks. Manufacturing and warehousing floorspace, by contrast, generates less than one-quarter of the person-trips of offices.

Office floorspace as a percent of total nonresidential floorspace rises with CBD size, while the relative amount of retail floorspace declines. In medium to large CBD's, office floorspace tends to be 40 percent or more of total floorspace. Retail floorspace declines from about 20 percent in small CBD's to 10 percent in large ones.

Even when local sources do specify floorspace by type of use, its definition is not always clear. Some floorspace data may be based on the outside or gross dimensions of buildings, other data only on the net or inside rentable area, some 15 percent smaller. Floorspace data may also overestimate activity if vacancy rates are high. Still, despite the difficulties of measurement, the number of employees or the amount of floorspace is a key determinant of travel to a CBD.

For purposes of this book, floorspace is defined in gross terms (measured from outside dimensions of buildings), and downtown activity is measured by *nonresidential floorspace,* which excludes private residences but includes commercial uses such as hotels, as well as retail, office, government, institutional, manufacturing and ancillary building uses.

While strict adherence to this definition cannot be verified, a recent estimate of nonresidential floorspace in the Central Business Districts of major urban areas of the United States is presented in Exhibit 3.13. These data vary in reliability, ranging from recent block by block inventories performed by local planning agencies to rough approximations. Indicated is the method used to make the estimate, with a letter to suggest its reliability or quality. "A" is reserved for data based on inventories of floorspace; "B" is used for data expanded to include a larger area definition of the CBD, or data inferred from two corroborating pieces of evidence (such as employment and past inventory figures); "C" is used if only office floorspace measures are available, and total nonresidential floorspace is estimated on the assumption that offices comprise 43 percent of it, or as in the case of the Buffalo CBD, only trip destinations are known and these are converted to floorspace; lastly, "D" denotes a rough approximation based on population of the central city. Of the 29 urban areas, 14 receive an "A" rating and four a "B" rating.

Methods of expansion and conversion used when current CBD activity data are incomplete are based on historical relationships displayed in Exhibits 3.14 and 3.15. The first of these shows the internal distribution of activity within Central Business Districts of 10 selected cities. Of general interest for downtown planning purposes, the exhibit can be used to estimate the floorspace within one square mile if only the floorspace within half a square mile is known. It shows that on the average, the 20 percent of CBD area with the densest development is likely to contain about 50 percent of CBD activity; 50 percent of CBD area is likely to contain about 80 percent of CBD activity. As with population distributions within an urban area, the internal distributions of CBD activity vary from city to city. Among the cities shown, Houston has the most concentrated and Milwaukee the least concentrated distribution. The activity distributions in the other cities are not very far apart, though both large and small downtowns are included.

Exhibit 3.15 contains three graphs with display relationships among measures

Exhibit 3.13
Estimated Central Business District Nonresidential Floorspace

Urban Area	Nonresidential Floorspace (msf)	Area (sq. miles)	Year	Source	Quality
1. **Washington**	89	1.71	1973	Local inventory	A
2. Los Angeles	79	3.5	1975	Local inventory	A
3. Dallas	61	1.37	1975	Local inventory	A
4. Houston	61	1.51	1975	Local inventory	A
5. Detroit	51	1.10	1975	Expanded from 22 msf office floorspace	C
6. **Atlanta**	45	2.22	1975	Local inventory	A
7. St. Louis	41	1.31	1975	Local inventory	A
8. Baltimore	40	0.8	1975	Expanded from 30 mst in 0.3 sq. mi. using Exhibit 3.14	B
9. **Pittsburgh**	39	0.5	1967	Converted from 99,000 employees using Exhibit 3.15 consistent with 32 msf in 1962	B
10. Seattle	36	0.69	1975	Expanded from 31 msf in 0.3 sq. mi. using Exhibit 3.14	B
11. Milwaukee	35	1.4	1972	Local inventory	A
12. Indianapolis	31	4.5	1975	Local inventory	A
13. Kansas City	30	0.78	1977	Local inventory	A
14. Minneapolis	30	0.86	1975	Expanded from 13 msf office floorspace	C
15. Cincinnati	30	n.a.	1975	Expanded from 13 msf office floorspace	C
16. **Miami**	30	1.0	1975	Based on partial local data expanded to include total non-residential and CBD of 1.0 sq. miles	C
17. Denver	27	0.84	1975	Local inventory	A
18. Portland	27	1.03	1970	Converted from 60,000 jobs using Exhibit 3.15	C
19. **Buffalo**	27	1.0	1962	Converted from 110,000 trip destinations using Exhibit 3.15	C
20. Louisville	26	1.1	1975	Local inventory	A
21. Columbus	26	3.19	1972	Local inventory	A
22. New Orleans	26	n.a.	1975	Expanded from 8.2 msf net office floorspace and assuming gross floorspace is 15 percent greater than net	C
23. Honolulu	25	0.5	1970	Converted from 52,400 CBD jobs using Exhibit 3.15 and expanded from 23 msf in 0.22 sq. mi. using Exhibit 3.14	C
24. **San Diego**	23	2.06	1975	Local inventory	A
25. Dayton	16	0.6	1974	Local inventory	A
26. Phoenix	16	n.a.	1975	Expanded from 7 msf office floorspace	C
27. San Antonio	15	n.a.	--	Estimated	D
28. Providence	12	1.0	1977	Expanded from 9.6 msf in 0.55 sq. mi. using Exhibit 3.14	D
29. Tampa	10	n.a.	--	Estimated	B

Note: Urban areas with existing or committed fixed guideway systems shown in bold type.
msf = million square feet (92,900m^2)

Exhibit 3.14
Central Business Districts Activity Distribution

CBD	Area (sq.miles)	Activities	Percent of Activities in 50 Percent of Area
Houston	1.21	138,110 jobs	93
Norfolk	1.03	24,816 jobs	90
Portland	1.03	59,990 jobs	83
Philadelphia	2.40	396,585 trip dest.	82
Los Angeles	1.86	60.0 msf floorspace	81
Boston	3.35	290,626 jobs	78
Pittsburgh	0.48	98,739 jobs	76
Chicago	1.08	296,500 jobs	74
Memphis	0.28	9.0 msf floorspace	73
Milwaukee	1.4	35.2 msf floorspace	64

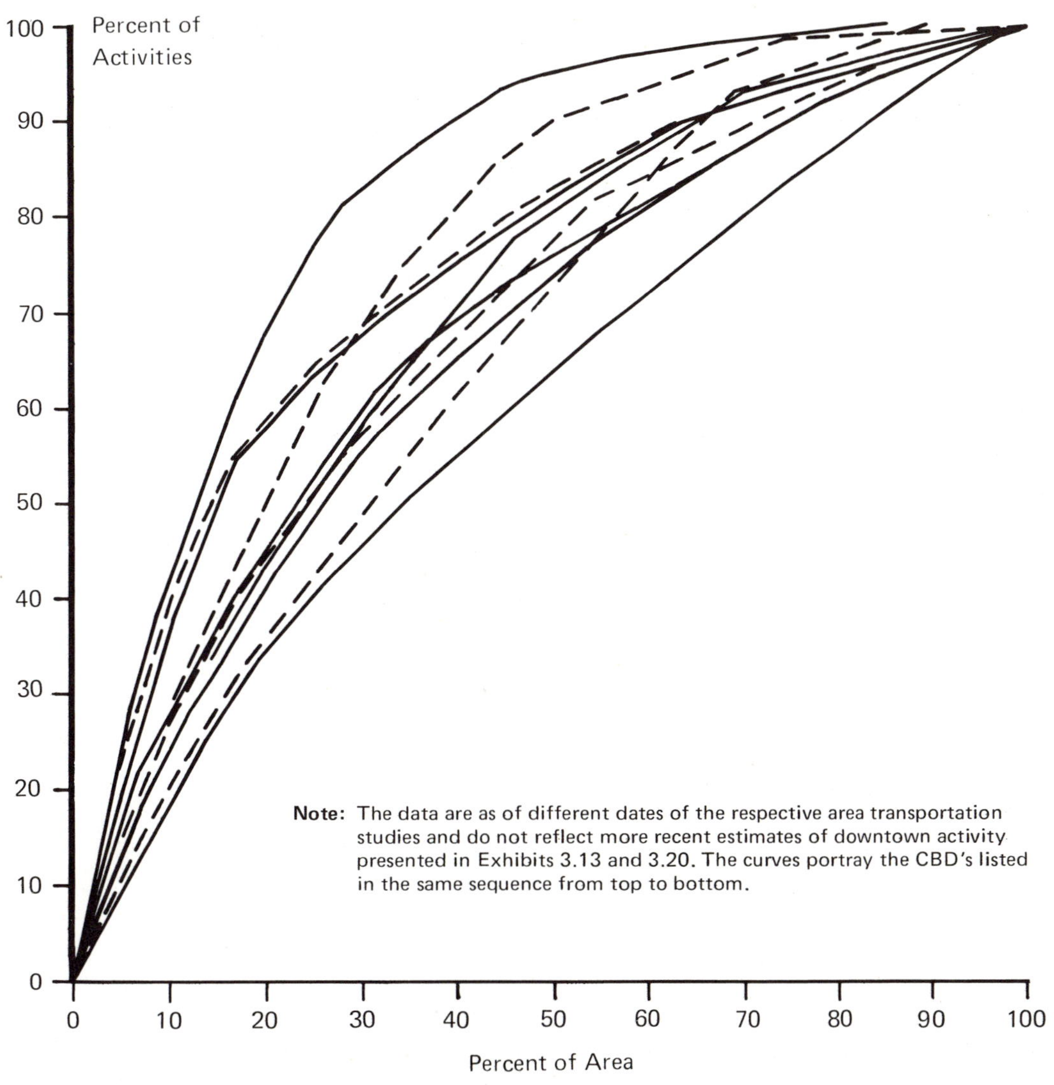

Percent of Activities
100
90
80
70
60
50
40
30
20
10
0
0
10
20
30
40
50
60
70
80
90
100
Percent of Area
Note: The data are as of different dates of the respective area transportation studies and do not reflect more recent estimates of downtown activity presented in Exhibits 3.13 and 3.20. The curves portray the CBD's listed in the same sequence from top to bottom.

Exhibit 3.15
Historical Activity and Trip Data for Selected Central Business Districts

CBD	Area (Square Miles)	Year	Employment (000's)	Floor Space (Msf.)	Trip Destinations (000's)
Los Angeles	0.6	1960	130	42	158
Chicago	1.1	1956	300	92	466
Philadelphia	2.2	1960	225	124	389
Detroit	1.1	1953	114	50	253
San Francisco	2.2	1965	282	88	423
Boston	1.4	1963	246	90	400
Washington	4.5	1955	315	n.a.	442
Cleveland	1.0	1963	117	47	123
St. Louis	0.8	1957	119	39	125
Pittsburgh	0.5	1958	84	32	154
Minneapolis	0.9	1958	90	n.a.	188
Houston	0.9	1960	120	n.a.	113
Baltimore	0.8	1962	85	33	130
Dallas	1.5	1964	135	31	164
Milwaukee	0.9	1972	91	31	134
Seattle	0.6	1970	60	37	145
Miami	0.9	1965	28	12	49
Atlanta	0.6	1961	75	30	94
Cincinnati	0.5	1965	n.a.	35	113
Kansas City	0.9	1957	65	n.a.	107
Buffalo	0.9	1962	48	28	104
Denver	0.5	1959	50	24	105
New Orleans	1.5	1960	60	n.a.	129
Phoenix	0.7	1957	21	n.a.	65
Indianapolis	n.a.	1964	85	30	150
Nashville	0.6	1959	34	n.a.	64

CBD	Area (Square Miles)	Year	Floor Space (Msf.)	Trip Ends (000's)			%
				Total	Transit	Auto	Transit
Atlanta	2.9	1961	40	284.5	65.5	219.0	23.0
Baltimore	0.5	1962	30	216.8	86.7	130.1	40.0
Boston	2.3	1963	100	700.6	373.1	327.6	53.0
Cleveland	n.a.	1976	47	400	150	250	37.5
Columbus	3.2	1972	25	162.8	28.7	134.1	17.6
Dallas	1.5	1964	31	292.3	46.0	246.3	15.7
Denver	0.5	1959	24	203.4	39.2	164.2	19.3
Detroit	1.2	1953	50	472.2	202.6	269.8	42.9
Houston	0.7	1960	35	269.6	53.4	216.2	19.8
Indianapolis	3.6	1964	23	268.6	36.2	232.4	13.5
Kansas City	0.5	1957	25	227.4	60.1	267.4	26.4
Montreal	4.3	1974	90	678.8	368.0	310.9	54.2
Oklahoma City	0.9	1965	n.a.	149.5	9.5	140.0	6.4
Philadelphia	1.9	1960	124	699.1	422.9	276.2	60.5
Salt Lake City	1.0	1960	n.a.	197.5	16.6	180.9	8.4
San Antonio	0.9	1969	n.a.	127.2	18.7	108.5	14.7
Springfield, Mass.	1.1	1965	n.a.	101.8	14.4	87.4	14.1

Source: Origin-destination studies, see footnote 3.
n.a.—Not available.

Exhibit 3.15 (cont'd.)

Relationships among CBD Employment, Floorspace, and Trip Destinations

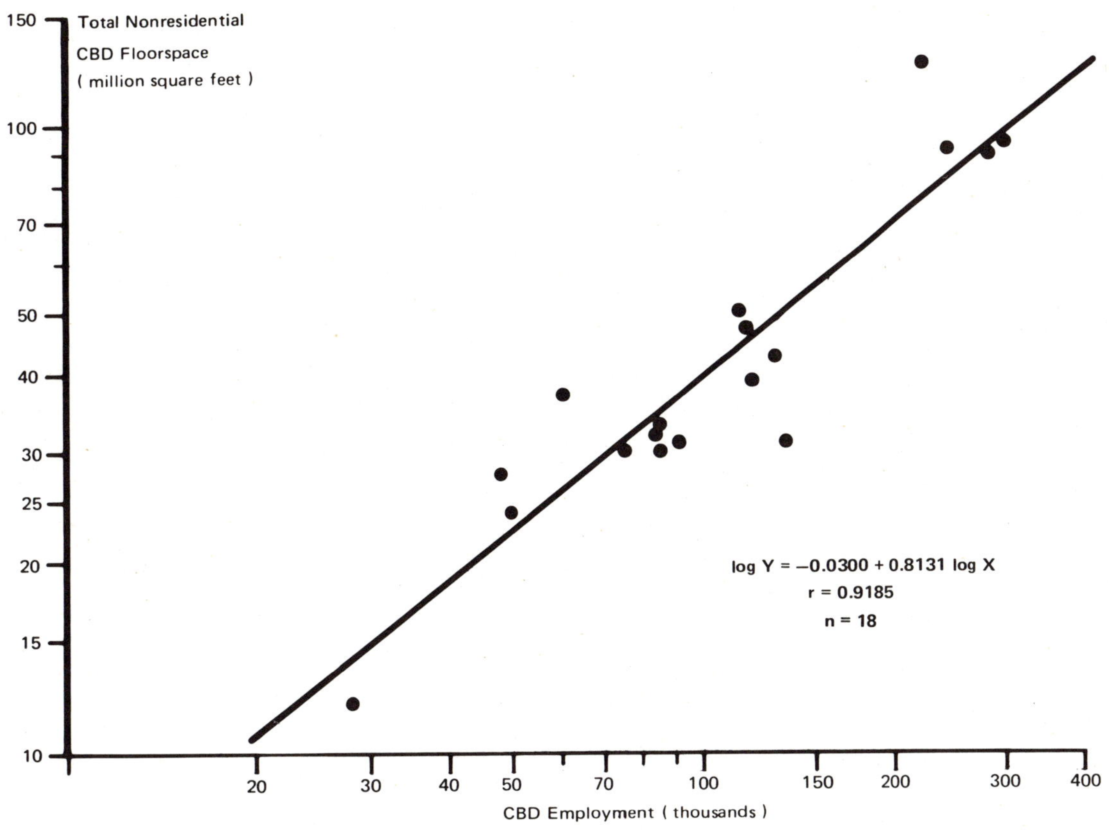

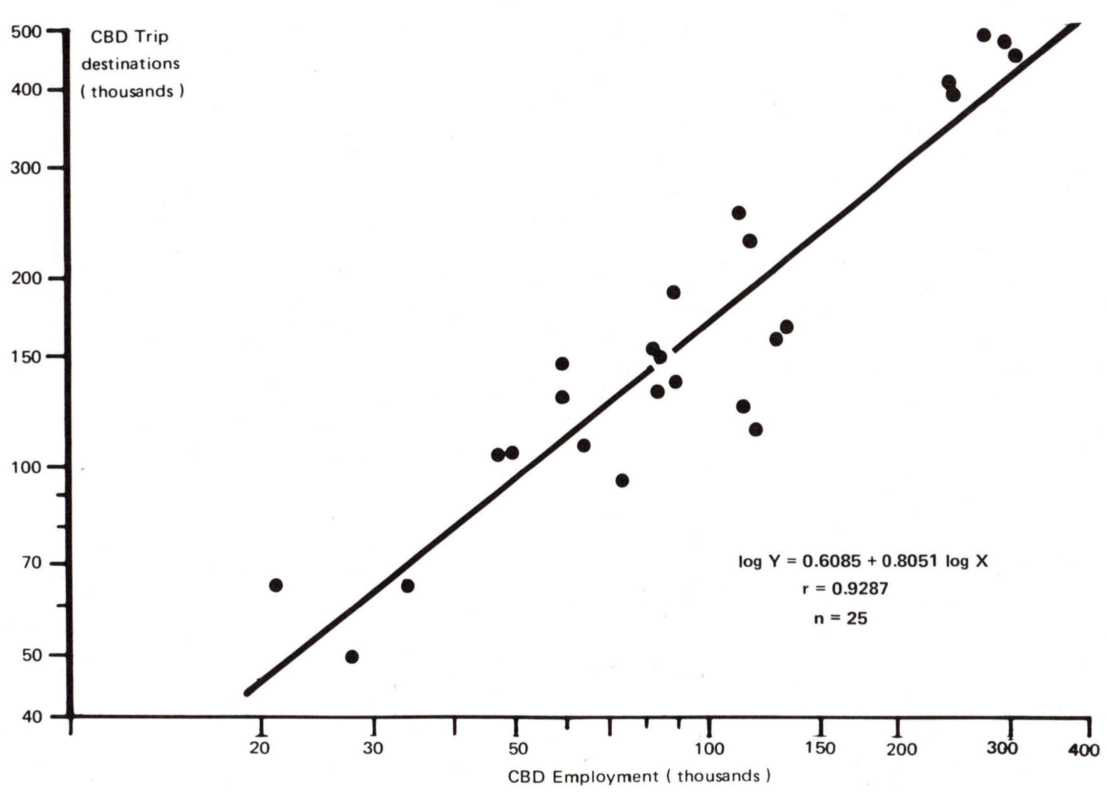

Exhibit 3.15 (cont'd.)
Relationships among CBD Employment, Floorspace, and Trip Destinations

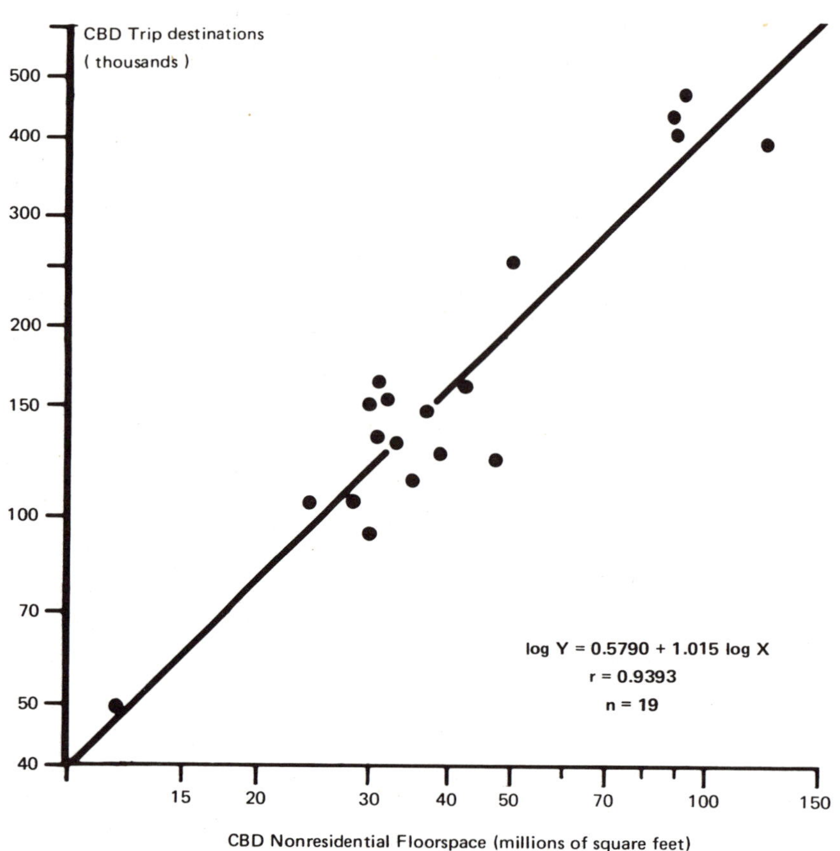

Exhibit 3.16
Parking Rates and CBD Floorspace

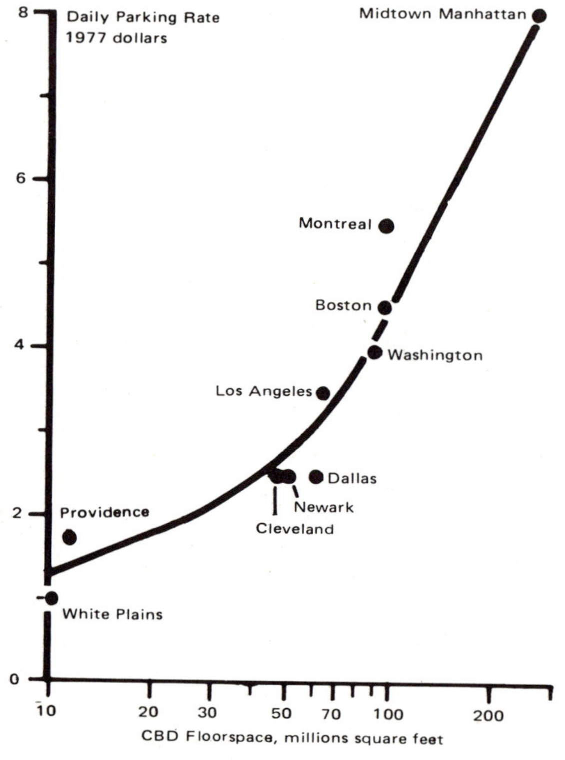

of CBD activity; the underlying data are also tabulated. The first graph shows the aggregate relationship between CBD employment and CBD floorspace. It can be used to estimate floorspace, if only employment is known, or vice versa. The regression equation in Exhibit 3.15a can be transformed (by taking the antilog of both sides) to read as follows: CBD jobs = 0.934 $(\text{floorspace})^{0.8131}$

The equation's exponent of less than unity indicates that a given percent increase in employment is associated with a somewhat smaller percent increase in nonresidential floorspace, suggesting that floorspace per employee tends to decline with increasing CBD size; some 450 square feet (41.8 m^2) per employee is generally found in CBD'S with 50,000 jobs, (22.5 million square feet) declining to about 350 square feet (32.5 m^2) per employee in CBD'S of 200,000 jobs (70 million square feet).

The other two graphs can be used to estimate total one-way CBD trip destinations (including both auto and transit) from either CBD employment or nonresidential floorspace and vice versa, if needed. The floorspace relationship has a slightly higher correlation coefficient, but both relationships are strong, allowing one to use either floorspace or employment as an estimator of a downtown's trip attraction. Floorspace is preferred here as a measure of attraction mostly because it provides a common denominator for activites that may have few employees, and because it can be measured with greater accuracy at the local scale. The regression equation in Exhibit 3.15c can be transformed to read as follows: CBD total trip destinations = 3.78 $(\text{floorspace})^{1.015}$

The near unity value of the slope of the line (the floorspace exponent) suggests that CBD trip destinations increase at about the same rate as CBD floorspace; CBD's of 20 million square feet (1.86 million m^2) attract, on the average, about 80,000 daily trip destinations, 40 million square feet (3.72 million m^2) about 160,000 trips, and so on. This relationship provides a valuable estimate of total travel into a CBD, which is used in subsequent analysis.

Lastly, Exhibit 3.16 portrays, for reference, the relationship between CBD floorspace and daily parking charges in the downtown core. This is a significant measure of auto disincentives and an indicator of land value, which is referred to earlier in Chapter 2.

TOTAL TRAVEL TO A DOWNTOWN

Knowing how many potential travelers reside in the highest density corridor of each urban area, and how much floorspace there is in each downtown to attract them, it is possible to estimate how many trips over what distance will take place between the two. The estimating procedure is based on the proposition that the trips originating in a residential area and destined for a nonresidential area are directly proportional to the residential population, directly proportional to the amount of activities in the nonresidential area, and inversely proportional to the separation between them. They are also affected by the size and nearness of competing attractions. This is more than a little reminiscent of the traditional gravity model, which is calibrated by matching actual and model generated distributions of some measure of travel distance. This model,[4] calibrated with travel data for 24 downtowns ranging in size from 4 million to 267 million square feet (0.37 to 24.81

million m²) of floorspace in the Tri-State New York–New Jersey–Connecticut Region, is essentially a simplified gravity model. It avoids the task of simulating travel networks and instead uses airline distance as the measure of separation between trip ends.

The core of the model is a *decay function* which shows how the probability that a person will make a trip to a chunk of nonresidential floorspace declines with an increase in distance from that chunk and with decline in its size. Two equations showing this decline are presented here. One, at the top of Exhibit 3.17, is used to estimate daily work trips per worker as a function of downtown size and distance from downtown. The other, at the top of Exhibit 3.18, is used to estimate daily nonwork trips per resident as a function of downtown size and the distance from it. Downtown size, (F) in both cases, is expressed in million square feet of nonresidential floorspace, and the distance (D) in miles. Converting the work trips per worker into work trips per capita by means of a suitable labor force participation rate (such as 0.4) and adding them to the nonwork trips per capita yields total daily one-way trips per capita from a given distance to a downtown.

Because the form of the two equations that portray the decay function is rather unwieldy, they are most easily solved by using the nomographs reproduced here as Exhibits 3.17 and 3.18. The Y-scale on the nomograph shows that trip rates do indeed decline very rapidly with distance; for example, within 1 mile of a downtown of 30 million square feet the probability of a resident worker going to work in that downtown may be 0.36; at a distance of 5 miles, it would be 0.11, and at a distance of 50 miles, 0.001.*

To adjust this CBD trip attraction model for use outside the Tri-State Region where it was calibrated, the model is applied to nine urban areas for which actual CBD-bound trips and population data are readily available on a small-area basis and where a reasonable estimate of CBD floorspace for the relevant year can be made. The model's initial ability to estimate the total number of trips to these CBD's is somewhat mixed, as shown in Exhibit 3.19. Of the nine urban areas, only three (Boston, Dallas, and Houston) are estimated within 4 to 9 percent of their actual CBD trips; five are estimated within 11 to 35 percent. One, Philadelphia, is overestimated by 75 percent. This spotty showing cannot be explained by CBD size or total trip ends. Two reasons for it are indicated. First, the orientation of a particular urbanized area toward the CBD may be weak or strong with competing nonresidential activities outside the CBD attracting a relatively large (or small) share of the area's trip ends. This is essentially the M factor in Exhibits 3.17 and 3.18, which measures the dampening effect of competing nearby nonresidential floorspace, Manhattan in the case of the Tri-State Region. Second, a systematic bias may exist in the model's distance variable.

To examine this, the relative amounts of over- or underprediction of CBD-bound trips for each two-mile ring in each of the nine urban areas are calculated, revealing that the model tends to overpredict trips close to the CBD and underpredict the

*The nomographs are used by first connecting the point on the D-scale for which the trip rate per capita is being sought (say, 5 miles from a downtown) to the top of the M-scale (assuming that the downtown in question is beyond the influence of Manhattan). Then the intersection of that line with the vertical pivot line is connected to the appropriate floorspace on the F-scale (say, 30 million square feet). The result is read off the Y-scale (0.11 trips per worker).

Exhibit 3.17
Trip Attraction Model Nomograph, Work Trips

Daily work trips per worker = $10^{-27.6}$ (log $F^{-2.775}$ x $D^{0.488}$)

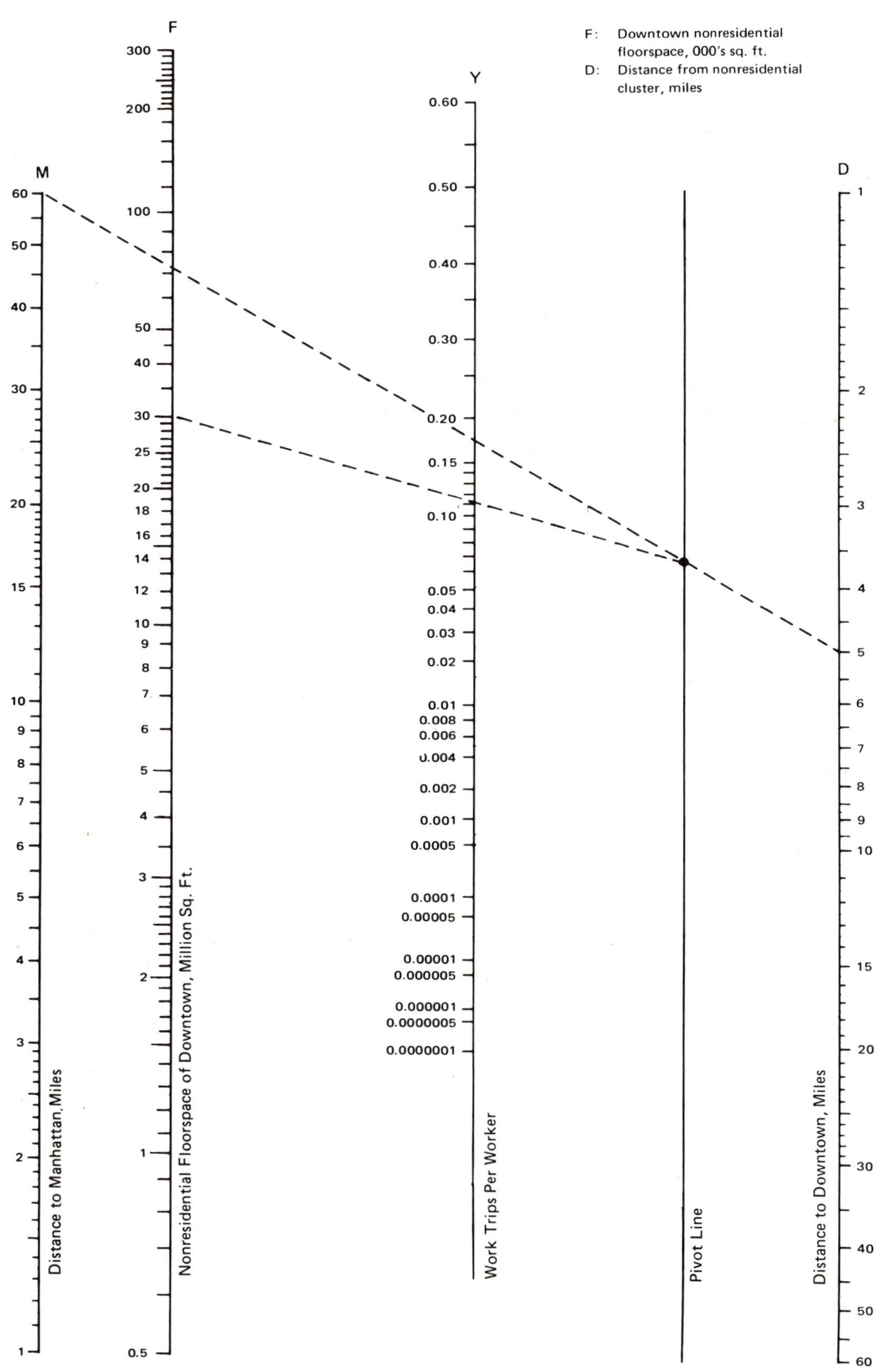

Source: Exhibit 7.8, *Public Transportation & Land Use Policy.*

Exhibit 3.18
Trip Attraction Model Nomograph, Non-Work Trips

Daily Non-work Trips per Capita = $10^{-5.21}$ (log $F^{-1.562}$ x $D^{0.538}$)

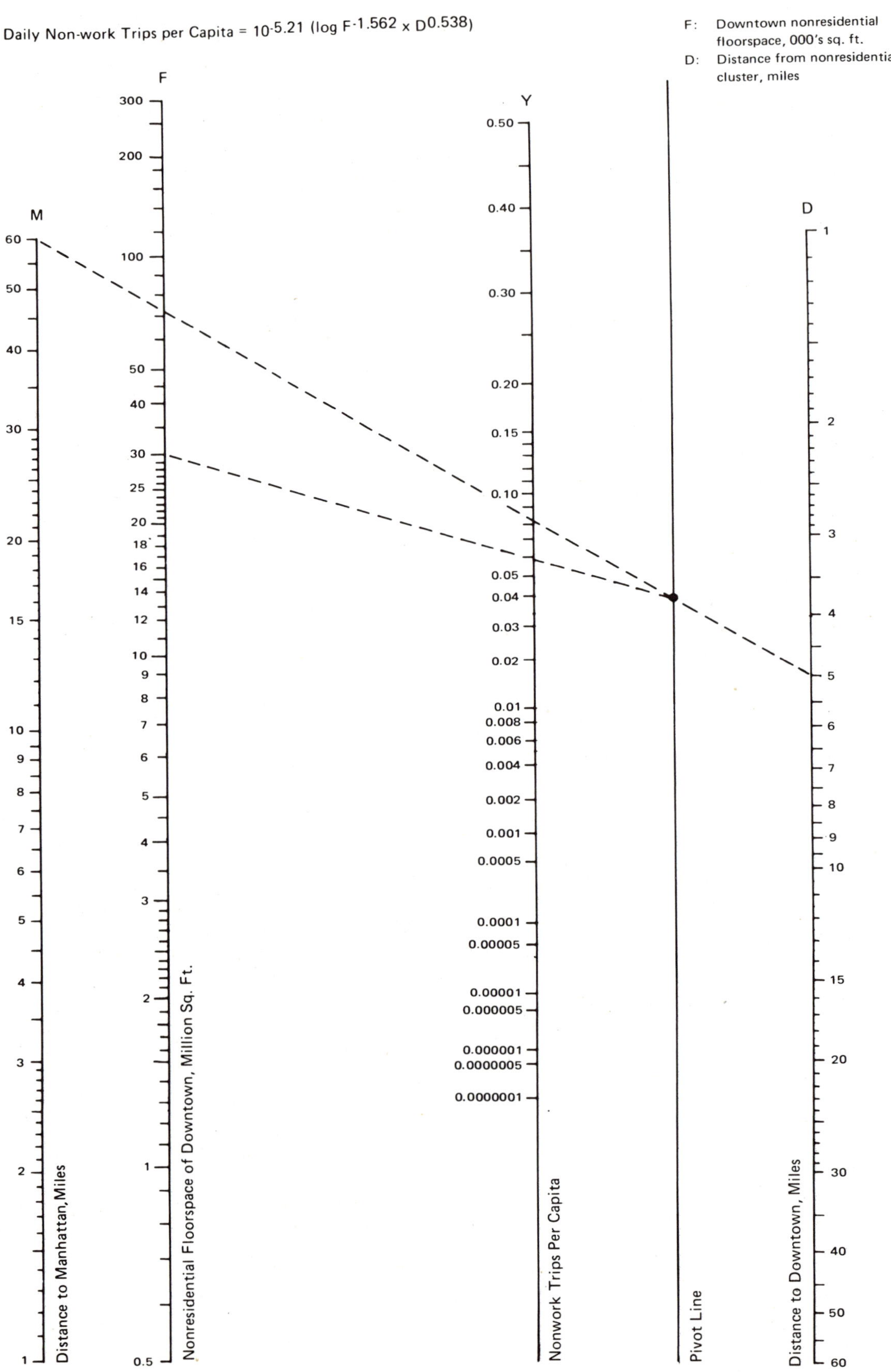

Source: Exhibit 7.9, *Public Transportation & Land Use Policy*

more distant trips. This is part of the reason why areas with a relatively tightly clustered population around the core, such as Philadelphia and Pittsburgh, are overpredicted. By plotting the ratio of actual to estimated trips for each ring as a function of distance, the original model is modified. The plots reveal that the four older, more tightly settled, urbanized areas, Boston, Montreal, Philadelphia, and Pittsburgh, each with a rapid transit system (or, in the case of Pittsburgh, light rail) require a different modifying curve than the other five urban areas. For the four older areas: Y = 0.0374 D + 0.613; for the five newer areas: Y = 0.0633 D + 0.637, where Y = modifying factor and D = distance from the center of the urban area. Trips originating from a residential zone as determined from Exhibits 3.17 and 3.18 are multiplied by this factor. Exhibit 3.19 shows the estimated CBD-bound trips using this modification.

Four of the nine urban areas, including three of the four most poorly estimated ones, show substantial improvement, but three areas are more poorly predicted with the modification. Still, the overall root-mean-square error of the ratio of estimated to actual trips is reduced from 0.30 to 0.19. More important is the removal of the systematic bias by distance. No longer are trips from close in consistently overpredicted and trips from farther out consistently underpredicted. Of the 81 two-mile-wide concentric rings in the nine urban areas, almost 70 percent are estimated more closely with the modified model. The distance modifications make the trip attraction model representative of a wide spectrum of urban areas, and not primarily the Tri-State Region around New York.

Next considered is the effect of competing opportunities. To this end the number of trips that the modified trip attraction model sends to the CBD is compared with the number of trips that the CBD would receive based on its floorspace alone, as indicated by Exhibit 3.15c earlier. The ratio of the latter to the former trip estimate, called here the CBD orientation factor, is shown in the fourth column of Exhibit 3.20.* If the CBD trip attraction model sends more trips to the CBD than the amount of floorspace would accept, then these trips are in fact going elsewhere to competing attractors in non-CBD locations, and the urban area can be said to have a low CBD orientation. Examples of such urban areas, with the CBD orientation factor substantially less than unity, are Los Angeles, Detroit, San Antonio, and Providence, all known to have relatively small downtowns compared with the urban area population. Conversely, if the CBD trip attraction model does not send enough trips to the CBD to match the actual floorspace there, then floorspace must be located in that CBD which would be located elsewhere in a more decentralized urban area. Examples of such areas, with the CBD orientation factor substantially greater than unity, are Dallas, Houston, Atlanta, Seattle, and Honolulu. The average of the CBD orientation factors in Exhibit 3.20 is 1.06, suggesting that, in the absence of the control total in column (a), the modified model in column (b) would be sending roughly 6 percent too few trips to the downtowns, on the average. The floorspace data and the orientation factors shown in Exhibit 3.20 represent final figures used to calculate the travel volumes in Chapter 4.

*Calculations in this Exhibit are based on aggregate population data by distance as shown in Exhibit 3.8 (except for Honolulu, calculated directly from the United States Census). CBD floorspace data are based on Exhibit 3.13, modified somewhat to reflect recent tendencies toward CBD growth or decline.

Exhibit 3.19

Comparisons of Estimated and Actual CBD Trip Ends, Nine Urbanized Areas

Urbanized Area	CBD Trip Destinations (000's)			Ratios	
	Actual	Unmodified Estimate	Modified Estimate	Unmodified to Actual	Modified to Actual
Boston	350	320	269	0.91	0.77
Philadelphia	350	612	491	1.75	1.40
Montreal	329	445	348	1.35	1.06
Dallas—Ft. Worth	146	152	148	1.04	1.01
Pittsburgh	137	183	138	1.33	1.01
Houston	135	140	132	1.04	0.48
Indianapolis	134	96	85	0.72	0.63
Kansas City	114	101	89	0.85	0.78
Denver	112	128	107	1.14	0.95

Exhibit 3.20

Central Business District Orientation

Urban Area	Nonresidential Floorspace (msf)	Estimated Trip Destinations (000's) Based on Downtown Floorspace Only (a)	Based on Modified Trip Attraction Model (b)	CBD Orientation Factor (Ratio of a:b)
1. Washington	100	402	368	1.09
2. Los Angeles	80	321	556	0.58
3. Dallas	70	280	157*	1.78
4. Houston	70	280	201*	1.39
5. Atlanta	50	200	140	1.43
6. Detroit	50	200	290	0.69
7. Seattle	40	158	112	1.41
8. Pittsburgh	40	158	138*	1.15
9. St. Louis	40	158	174	0.91
10. Baltimore	40	158	182	0.87
11. Denver	35	138	127*	1.09
12. Milwaukee	35	138	150	0.92
13. Indianapolis	31	122	152*	0.80
14. Portland	30	118	95	1.24
15. Kansas City	30	118	113*	1.04
16. Miami	30	118	115	1.03
17. Cincinnati	30	118	120	0.98
18. Minneapolis	30	118	135	0.87
19. Buffalo	27	106	122	0.84
20. Louisville	26	102	85	1.20
21. Columbus	26	102	101	1.01
22. New Orleans	26	102	128	0.80
23. Honolulu	25	98	50	1.96
24. San Diego	25	98	91	1.08
25. Phoenix	20	79	64	1.23
26. Dayton	16	63	68	0.93
27. San Antonio	15	59	75	0.79
28. Providence	12	47	61	0.77
29. Tampa	10	40	44	0.91

Notes: Urban areas with existing or committed fixed guideway systems shown in bold type.
Asterisks indicate distance modifications based on empirical data, not modifying equation discussed in text.

One last point about CBD orientation: some corridors within the same urban area may generate more CBD-bound trips than others, even with a similar population distribution. This may occur if a large proportion of CBD workers reside in a particular corridor because of its white-collar orientation or other socioeconomic characteristics. Other corridors may produce fewer CBD-bound trips than expected because of the pull of another nonresidential concentration of activity nearby. The nine areas shown in Exhibit 3.19 were used to test the degree to which some corridors were over- or underpredicted as compared with the overall urbanized area under- or overprediction. Results indicate that the probability of a corridor being underpredicted or overpredicted by one-third or more is about 1 in 10. About 60 percent of the corridors were estimated within 20 percent of their actual values. The model tended to do relatively better in the more important highest volume corridors.

In sum, a model from previous work has been validated, with two significant modifications, to allow an estimate of the number of daily trips that will be made to a CBD from a radial corridor, given the number of people residing at each distance along the radial line, the nonresidential floorspace in the CBD, and the CBD orientation of the particular urban area. Determining the share of those trips that will use a fixed guideway is the next task.

THE CHOICE OF RAIL TRANSIT

The share of total travel attracted to transit has been a major subject of transportation research for many years. Most models of so-called modal split emphasize the relative time and cost of travel by auto and transit, auto availability, and socioeconomic characteristics of the travelers. Recent emphasis has been on understanding behavior at the micro-level using highly disaggregated models. Less attention has been paid to how the physical context of development density or the presence of a fixed guideway affects behavior.

The mode choice model developed in the predecessor study[5] shares a number of features with earlier models, but emphasizes the relationship between mode choice and land use. It also deals explicitly with differences between bus transit, rail rapid transit, and commuter rail. In keeping with the network-independent structure of the trip attraction model treated above, it does not deal directly with network-related variables, such as relative travel time or cost, though these can be applied exogenously. Instead, it uses aggregate, area-related characteristics of density, auto ownership, and transit service.

Central to the structure of the mode choice model—portrayed schematically in Exhibit 3.21—is the proposition that transit use is closely associated with the number of autos available to a household. Hence its starting point is an estimate of automobile ownership in a particular residential area. Variables that are used to determine the average number of autos per household are median income, number of persons of driving age, net residential density, and proximity to rail transit, shown in the boxes on the left. To account for the latter variable, three distinct auto ownership equations are developed: for residential areas with rapid transit (at least half the census tract within 2,000 feet or 610 m of a rapid transit station), for resi-

Exhibit 3.21
Structure of Mode Choice Model

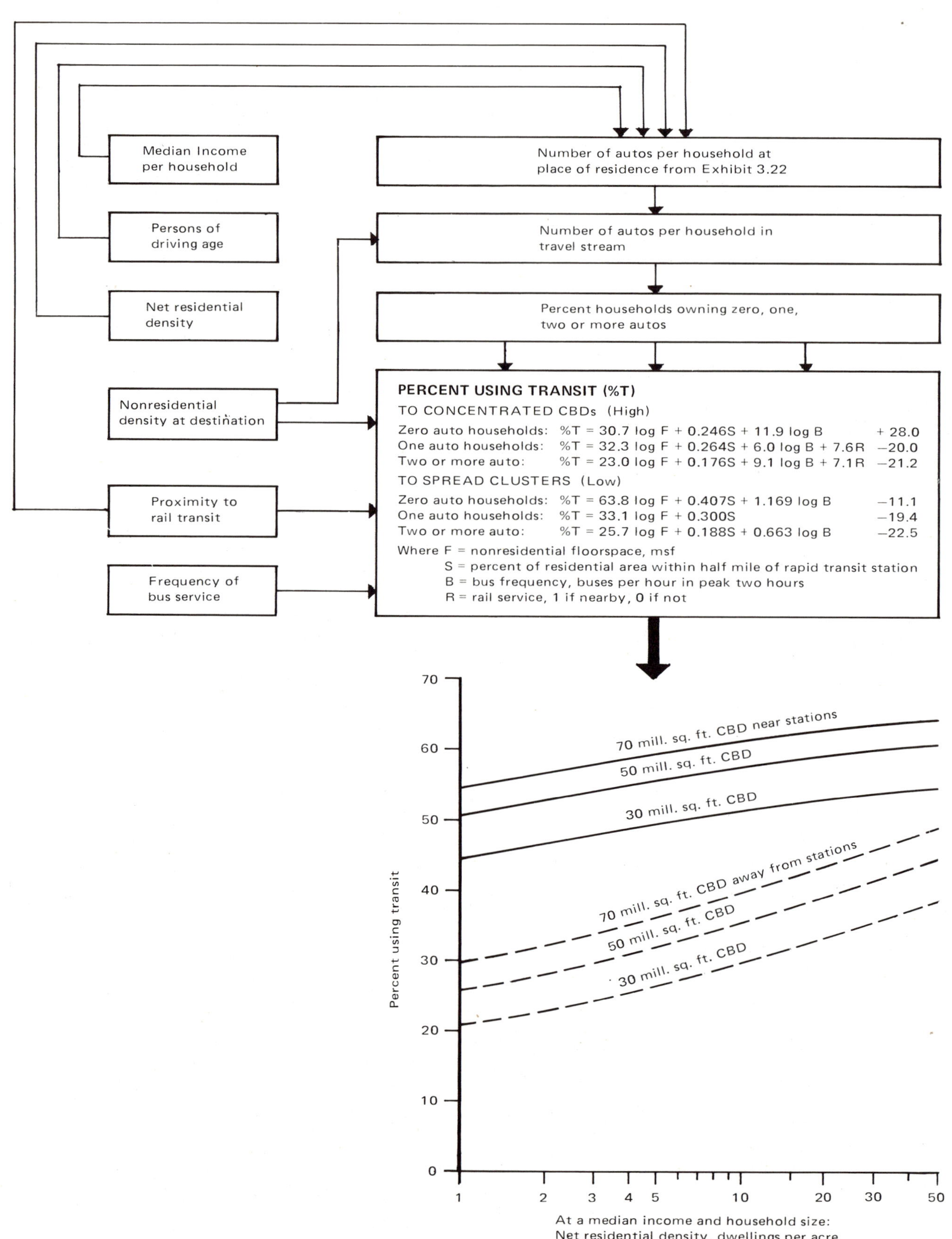

Median Income per household
Persons of driving age
Net residential density
Nonresidential density at destination
Proximity to rail transit
Frequency of bus service
Number of autos per household at place of residence from Exhibit 3.22
Number of autos per household in travel stream
Percent households owning zero, one, two or more autos
PERCENT USING TRANSIT (%T)
TO CONCENTRATED CBDs (High)
Zero auto households: %T = 30.7 log F + 0.246S + 11.9 log B + 28.0
One auto households: %T = 32.3 log F + 0.264S + 6.0 log B + 7.6R –20.0
Two or more auto: %T = 23.0 log F + 0.176S + 9.1 log B + 7.1R –21.2
TO SPREAD CLUSTERS (Low)
Zero auto households: %T = 63.8 log F + 0.407S + 1.169 log B –11.1
One auto households: %T = 33.1 log F + 0.300S –19.4
Two or more auto: %T = 25.7 log F + 0.188S + 0.663 log B –22.5
Where F = nonresidential floorspace, msf
S = percent of residential area within half mile of rapid transit station
B = bus frequency, buses per hour in peak two hours
R = rail service, 1 if nearby, 0 if not
70 mill. sq. ft. CBD near stations
50 mill. sq. ft. CBD
30 mill. sq. ft. CBD
70 mill. sq. ft. CBD away from stations
50 mill. sq. ft. CBD
30 mill. sq. ft. CBD
Percent using transit
0
10
20
30
40
50
60
70
1
2
3
4
5
10
20
30
50
At a median income and household size:
Net residential density, dwellings per acre

dential areas with commuter rail (at least one-fifth of the census tract within that distance of a railroad station), and for residential areas with neither of these, relying on bus service in varying degrees. For reference, these relationships are reproduced here as Exhibit 3.22. It should be emphasized that they do not portray just New York City conditions. In particular, the 541 census tracts with commuter rail service (out of a total 4,223 investigated in the Tri-State Region) include low-density, auto-oriented areas on Long Island, in Connecticut, and in New Jersey, where most access to stations is by auto. Even there, auto ownership is dampened near railroad stations, especially in high-income areas. The dampening impact of rapid transit—compared to areas of equal density and income without such service—is, predictably, much stronger.

For particular households in a residential area, the auto ownership rate is further affected by the nonresidential density at their habitual destinations. A household with two wage earners working at suburban locations is likely to own more automobiles than a household with one or both working downtown. The model introduces an appropriate adjustment for that. The adjusted ownership rate in a particular travel stream is then translated into *proportions* of households owning zero, one, and two or more automobiles. A separate mode choice equation is calibrated for each of these three groups, based on travel to 56 different nonresidential concentrations in the Tri-State area. Three-quarters of these are outside New York City.

Independent variables that determine the percent of trips taken by transit by each of the three auto ownership groups are nonresidential floorspace at the destination, proximity to rapid transit, bus service frequency, and presence or absence of commuter rail. Separate equations are calibrated for traditional central business districts and for spread clusters of nonresidential activity. These equations are shown in Exhibit 3.21.

The output of the model is a set of graphs, presented in detail in the original study,[6] which makes it possible to relate percent of trips taken by transit to the net residential density in dwellings per acre at the origin end, the size of a downtown in million square feet of nonresidential floorspace at the destination end, and the type of transit service provided, whether bus with a specified service frequency, rapid transit within or outside a specified distance from stations, or commuter rail.* It is further possible to take into account an area's income and household size at the residential end and make a distinction at the nonresidential end between a traditional downtown and a looser, more auto accessible "spread nonresidential cluster."

As evident from Exhibit 3.21, both downtown size and proximity to rail transit enter the model twice: once as determinants of auto ownership, and a second time as determinants of the choice of mode by particular auto ownership groups. It is therefore not surprising that both exert a very strong influence on the choice of mode. By depressing auto ownership in the first instance, they give greater weight to the "zero-car household" and "one-car household" mode choice equations which strongly respond to downtown floorspace and rail service in the second instance. Net residential density has a much weaker influence on modal choice, especially if

*Because of the small size of the Newark light rail operation, included in the study area, separate estimates for light rail were not made; it was included with rapid transit.

Exhibit 3.22
Auto Ownership Model

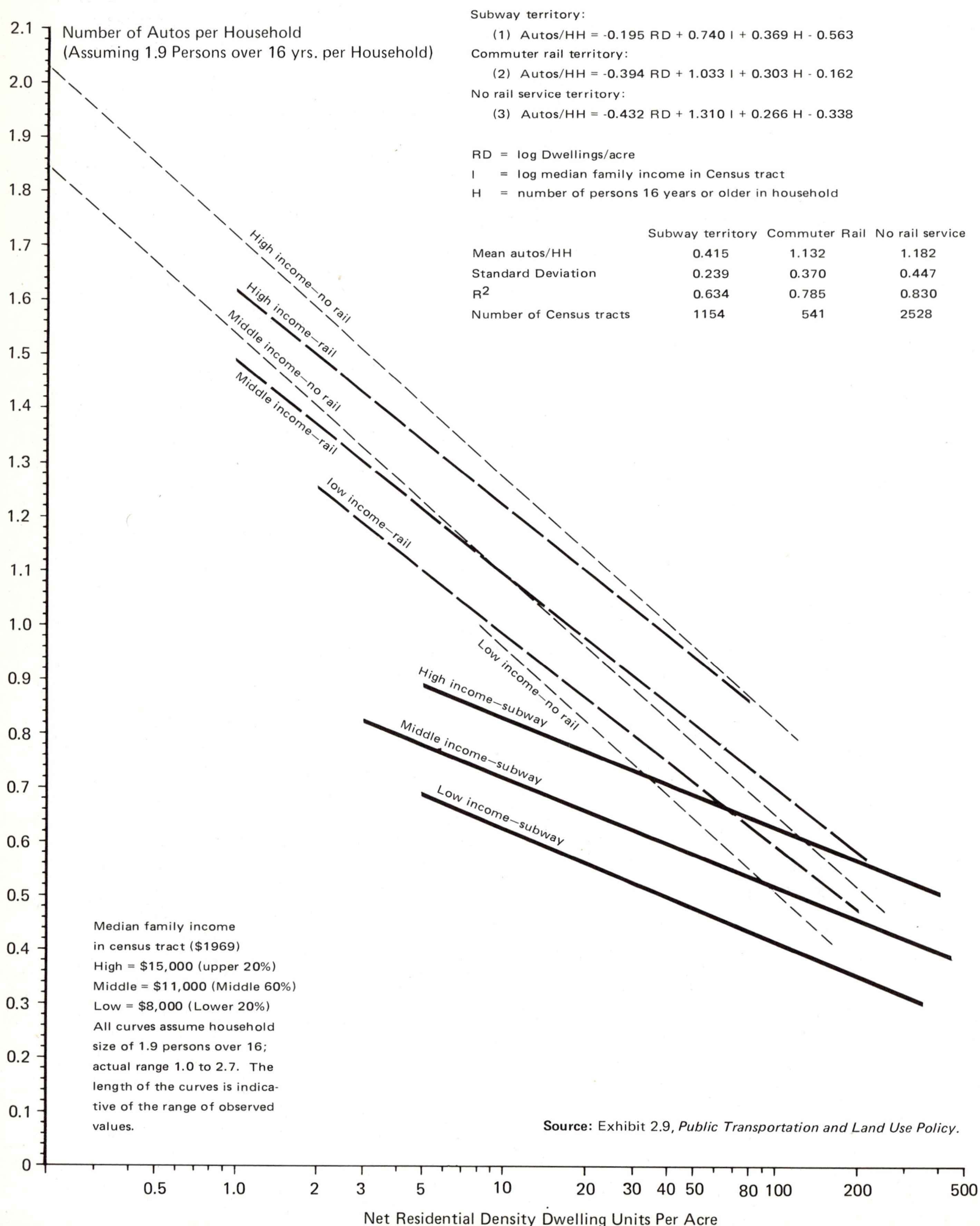
Number of Autos per Household
(Assuming 1.9 Persons over 16 yrs. per Household)
Subway territory:
(1) Autos/HH = -0.195 RD + 0.740 I + 0.369 H - 0.563
Commuter rail territory:
(2) Autos/HH = -0.394 RD + 1.033 I + 0.303 H - 0.162
No rail service territory:
(3) Autos/HH = -0.432 RD + 1.310 I + 0.266 H - 0.338
RD = log Dwellings/acre
I = log median family income in Census tract
H = number of persons 16 years or older in household
Subway territory Commuter Rail No rail service
Mean autos/HH 0.415 1.132 1.182
Standard Deviation 0.239 0.370 0.447
R2 0.634 0.785 0.830
Number of Census tracts 1154 541 2528
High income—no rail
High income—rail
Middle income—no rail
Middle income—rail
low income—rail
Low income—no rail
High income—subway
Middle income—subway
Low income—subway
Median family income
in census tract ($1969)
High = $15,000 (upper 20%)
Middle = $11,000 (Middle 60%)
Low = $8,000 (Lower 20%)
All curves assume household
size of 1.9 persons over 16;
actual range 1.0 to 2.7. The
length of the curves is indicative of the range of observed
values.
Source: Exhibit 2.9, Public Transportation and Land Use Policy.
2.1
2.0
1.9
1.8
1.7
1.6
1.5
1.4
1.3
1.2
1.1
1.0
0.9
0.8
0.7
0.6
0.5
0.4
0.3
0.2
0.1
0
0.5
1.0
2
3
5
10
20
30
40
50
80
100
200
500
Net Residential Density Dwelling Units Per Acre

rail transit is provided. Without rail service, net residential density has more impact because it serves, in part, as a proxy for the quality of bus service. The suppressing effect of bus service quality on auto ownership has been shown by others but is not captured by the model due to its collinearity with residential density.

It is worth noting that the model shows the preference for rapid transit over bus to be strongest among one-car households. The impact on attracting transit ridership from a zero-car household is about the same if 50 percent of a residential area is within 2,000 feet (610 m or an 8-minute walk) of a rapid transit station, or if the downtown bus frequency is 12 buses an hour. By contrast, according to the model, there is *no* realistic bus frequency sufficiently high to make a one-car household find bus as attractive as rapid transit within that access distance. With two-or-more-car households, the overall attractiveness of transit is cut nearly in half, and distinctions between rail and bus are harder to interpret.

To test the reasonableness of the mode choice model for areas outside the Tri-State New York–New Jersey–Connecticut Region, two calculations are made. One is to take the lowest density and the highest density residential zones in each of 14 urban areas and to estimate the proportions of trips by transit from them to the respective Central Business Districts. The CBD floorspace for this comparison is estimated for the year in which available travel surveys were made. The resulting percentages of transit use, shown in the third and fourth columns of Exhibit 3.23, bracket the actual percentage of transit use, shown in the last column, reasonably well in 11 out of the 14 urban areas, though Pittsburgh falls near the top and Denver and Houston near the bottom of the range. Only Dallas, Columbus, and Indianapolis fall outside. If applied on a detailed zone by zone basis, the model would undoubtedly overpredict their share of transit.

To explore the reason for this discrepancy, the laborious second calculation is made, applying the model zone by zone in two urban areas where sufficient local detail was available, namely Baltimore and Dallas. In Baltimore, the detailed calculation estimates the choice of transit precisely at 40 percent. In Dallas, the estimate is a 36 percent transit share compared to an actual 15.7. Given the dependence of the model on auto ownership rates, the hypothesis is tested that Dallas households living at similar densities and with similar incomes own more autos than those in the Tri-State New York Region. This hypothesis is proven wrong. Autos per household at the time of the survey in Dallas were no higher than those in non-rail territories of the New York Region for similar densities and incomes. This suggests that characteristics of the transportation system to the CBD, namely a low level of bus service and a high level of auto accessibility (i.e., parking supply), are responsible for the discrepancy.

The second version of the mode choice model, pertaining to "spread clusters" of nonresidential activity with a low transit use (as opposed to Central Business Districts), was calibrated on areas with such characteristics. This version is applied on a zone-by-zone basis to Dallas, yielding a closer estimate of 22 percent transit. If applied to the lowest and the highest density residential zones in Columbus, Denver, Houston, and Indianapolis, the "spread cluster" model also yields closer estimates; they are shown in parentheses in Exhibit 3.23.

The fact that the "spread cluster" model seems to fit the downtowns of Columbus and Indianapolis better than the CBD model is not surprising, in light of the overbounded local definition of the two CBD's (3.1 and 4.5 square miles, or 8.0 and

Exhibit 3.23
Aggregate Mode Choice Comparisons for Central Business District Trips

			Estimated Percent Transit to CBD			
	Survey Year	Estimated CBD Floorspace	From Low Density Residential Areas	From High Density Residential Areas	From All Residential Areas	Actual Percent Transit to CBD From All Residential Areas
Atlanta	1961	30	19	40	n.c.	23.0
Baltimore	1962	30	22	47	40	40.0
Boston	1963	80	36	67	n.c.	53.5
Columbus	1972	25	19	35	n.c.	17.6
			(12)	(27)		
Dallas	1964	50	25	45	36	15.7
			(14)	(30)	(22)	
Denver	1959	20	17	33	n.c.	19.2
			(11)	(26)		
Detroit	1953	50	30	55	n.c.	42.9
Houston	1960	35	20	38	n.c.	19.8
			(13)	(28)		
Indianapolis	1964	25	19	35	n.c.	13.5
			(12)	(27)		
Kansas City	1957	20	17	33	n.c.	25.0
Montreal	1974	80	28	67	n.c.	54.2
Philadelphia	1960	100	40	69	n.c.	60.5
Pittsburgh	1958	35	30	52	n.c.	50.9
San Antonio	1969	10	11	26	n.c.	15.1

Note: Estimates in parentheses made with "spread cluster" mode choice model.
n.c. — not calculated, mostly due to insufficient small-area data.

11.7 km², respectively). The other overestimated downtowns are not overbounded, and the level of transit use in an urban area is advanced as a criterion of which of the two mode choice models to apply. This can be measured by annual total transit trips per capita, what used to be known as the "riding habit." This index is shown in Exhibit 3.24 for 1972 and, where available, for 1976. Urban areas are ranked from the highest trips per capita to the lowest, based mostly on the 1976 trip data and on 1972 urbanized area population from sources indicated in the Exhibit.

Honolulu and New Orleans stand at the top in terms of transit trips per thousand residents (though New York's ratio, not shown, is 139). A sizable group of urban areas follows, ranging from Baltimore's 69.5 to San Diego's 31.8 trips per thousand residents (Chicago, Philadelphia, and Boston, all not shown, are in the 80s; San Francisco is in the 50s). The next 12 urban areas range progressively downward from St. Louis's 29.7 to Dayton's 14.6. Tampa–St. Petersburg and Phoenix stand alone at the botton with fewer than 10 annual transit trips per thousand residents.

The urban areas for which there is some evidence that the spread cluster mode choice model might be more suitable, namely Houston, Denver, and Dallas–Ft. Worth, fall in the lower half of the distribution, as do Columbus and Indianapolis; all have annual transit trip rates in the 30 to 16 range. This might suggest that all urban areas with similar ratios would be candidates for a "low transit orientation" designation. However, this would ignore the clear indication from Exhibit 3.21 that the ratio of trips per capita can change markedly in a few years. Atlanta Honolulu, Los Angeles, Washington, Portland, San Diego, and Cincinnati have all scored impressive gains in the four-year period. It would be presumptuous, then, to burden those urban areas in the lower group, Dayton up through St. Louis, with a mode choice equation that estimates fewer transit trips. Besides, two downtowns for which the "high transit orientation" model yields accurate estimates—at least for conditions as of the 1950s when travel inventories were made—namely, Detroit and Kansas City, now fall in this lower range. For these 12 urban areas, then, it would be best not to prejudge which of these two mode choice models is most suitable. Only Tampa–St. Petersburg and Phoenix have sufficiently low transit trips per capita to give assurance that the "low transit orientation" model is best suited for them. At the upper end of the scale, all urban areas from Honolulu through San Diego would appear to be sufficiently transit-oriented to warrant the concentrated CBD mode choice model. Accordingly, we have indicated the model or models to be used to estimate mode choice for each urban area by an "H" (high) or "L" (low) in Exhibit 3.23.

Because the models do not include the travel time differences for transit and auto, they are insensitive to the speed of service provided, and do not account for differences in transit ridership that might result from such system variations as station spacing or comparative highway speeds. These adjustments can be made using prevailing relationships between travel time differences and mode choice. For medium-sized cities the percent of travel by transit among auto owners declines by about 1.35 percentage points for each additional minute by which the transit trip is longer compared to the auto trip. Using this relationship and accounting for known differences in travel time, it is possible to adjust the mode choice results for various assumed auto speeds or transit station spacing.

Exhibit 3.24
Annual Transit Trips per Capita

Urban Area	1972 Urbanized Area Population, 000's	Annual Transit Trips, 000,000's		Annual Transit Trips per thousand Population		Concentrated (C) or Spread (S) Model
		1972	1976	1972	1976	
1. Honolulu	446	24	62	53.8	139.3	C
2. New Orleans	962	117	91	121.6	94.0	C
3. Baltimore	1,827	118	127	64.6	69.5	C
4. Atlanta	1,305	44	78	33.7	59.7	C
5. Milwaukee	1,217	58	69	47.6	56.3	C
6. Pittsburgh	1,994	104	105	52.6	52.7	C
7. Miami	1,300	59	63	45.4	48.5	C
8. Washington	2,840	96	128	33.8	45.0	C
9. Minneapolis-St. Paul	1,814	57	80	31.4	44.3	C
10. Portland	907	17	35	18.7	38.1	C
11. Los Angeles	9,501	208	347	21.9	36.5	C
12. Buffalo	1,130	58	41	51.3	36.2	C
13. San Antonio	682	21	24	30.8	35.6	C
14. Seattle	1,328	34	44	25.6	33.1	C
15. San Diego	1,256	16	40	12.7	31.8	C
16. St. Louis	2,135	59	63	27.6	29.7	S/C
17. Denver	1,099	28	33	25.5	29.6	S/C
18. Dallas-Ft. Worth	1,330	32	38	24.1	28.5	S/C
19. Houston	1,331	29	37	21.8	27.8	S/C
20. Cincinnati	1,299	22	34	16.9	26.2	S/C
21. Detroit	4,116	140	88	34.0	21.4	S/C
22. Indianapolis	850	18		21.2	n.a.	S/C
23. Providence	882	19	17	21.5	18.8	S/C
24. Louisville	801	18	14	22.5	17.8	S/C
25. Columbus	860	15	14	17.4	16.5	S/C
26. Kansas City	1,161	19		16.4	n.a.	S/C
27. Dayton	700	10	10	14.3	14.6	S/C
28. Tampa-St. Petersburg	1,123	10		8.1	n.a.	S
29. Phoenix	978	4	8	4.1	8.0	S

Notes: Sequence based on 1976 data if available.
1976 Transit Trips per thousand population based on 1972 population.
Urban area with existing or committed fixed guideway systems shown in bold type.

Source: *1974 National Transportation Report-Urban Data Supplement,* U.S. Department of Transportation, May 1976 and *APTA Transit Operating Report for 1976.* November, 1978.

The application of the mode choice models requires one piece of bookkeeping. Because population distributions in the maximum corridor are measured in population per square mile, and the mode choice model requires net densities measured in dwellings per net residential acre, a conversion is required. In Exhibit 3.25, curves are presented to permit this conversion based on small area data for five urban areas where both measures of density were available. The essential point is that above about 5,000 people per square mile, corresponding to about 7 dwellings per net acre, there is a common curve. Below that point the curves diverge with first Dallas–Ft. Worth, then Indianapolis, and then Baltimore peeling off. Philadelphia and New York remain coincident. This occurs because at the higher densities all urban areas are fully urbanized or "filled in," and the gross versus net relationship is a constant one. At low gross densities, young urban areas are less likely to be fully developed; attaining a given gross density will require a higher net density for a young area than for a mature one. By using the curves in Exhibit 3.25, gross density as found in Exhibit 3.12 can be converted to net densities and the mode choice model can be applied.

EXTENT OF TRIBUTARY AREA

To use the trip attraction and mode choice relationships the area over which they are to be applied needs to be defined. This is best accomplished by examining the *median* access distance to stations. Since, by definition, half the riders will have trip ends within that distance, the task becomes one of defining that median distance, calculating the area it circumscribes, determining the trips made to and from that area, and doubling these trips to account for those coming from an undefined area beyond.

The median access distance or trip length and the full tributary area beyond it are influenced by many factors. The longer the line-haul portion of the trip, the larger the tributary area. Potential riders are willing to travel a greater distance with a perpendicular component to the radial route as the access portion of their trip becomes a smaller portion of the total trip. Similarly, the tributary area is enlarged around the terminal station, drawing travelers from beyond the end of the line, as the access portion of their trip is in the direction they wish to travel. The availability of parking will expand the area, attracting riders from beyond walking distance, especially if no residency restrictions are placed on parking spaces. The quality of the service will expand the area, as riders will travel farther to reap the benefits of speedier service. For example, people walk longer distances to rail lines than to local buses. The route and station configuration can also influence the tributary area. If stations are closely spaced or if competing radial routes exist, areas served by the system will overlap, thereby shortening the access trip length to stations. Finally, residential densities also play a role; stations in higher-density areas tend to have a higher proportion of riders arriving on foot. Also, access speeds by bus and auto decline as density increases, reducing the access trip length.

A generalized quantification of the interplay of these factors has never been accomplished, in part because the variables are highly site-specific, and in part because many of the factors are closely correlated with one another. For example, station distance from the CBD and residential density tend to be highly correlated, blurring distinctions between the two.

Exhibit 3.25
Relationship between Gross and Net Densities, Five Urban Areas

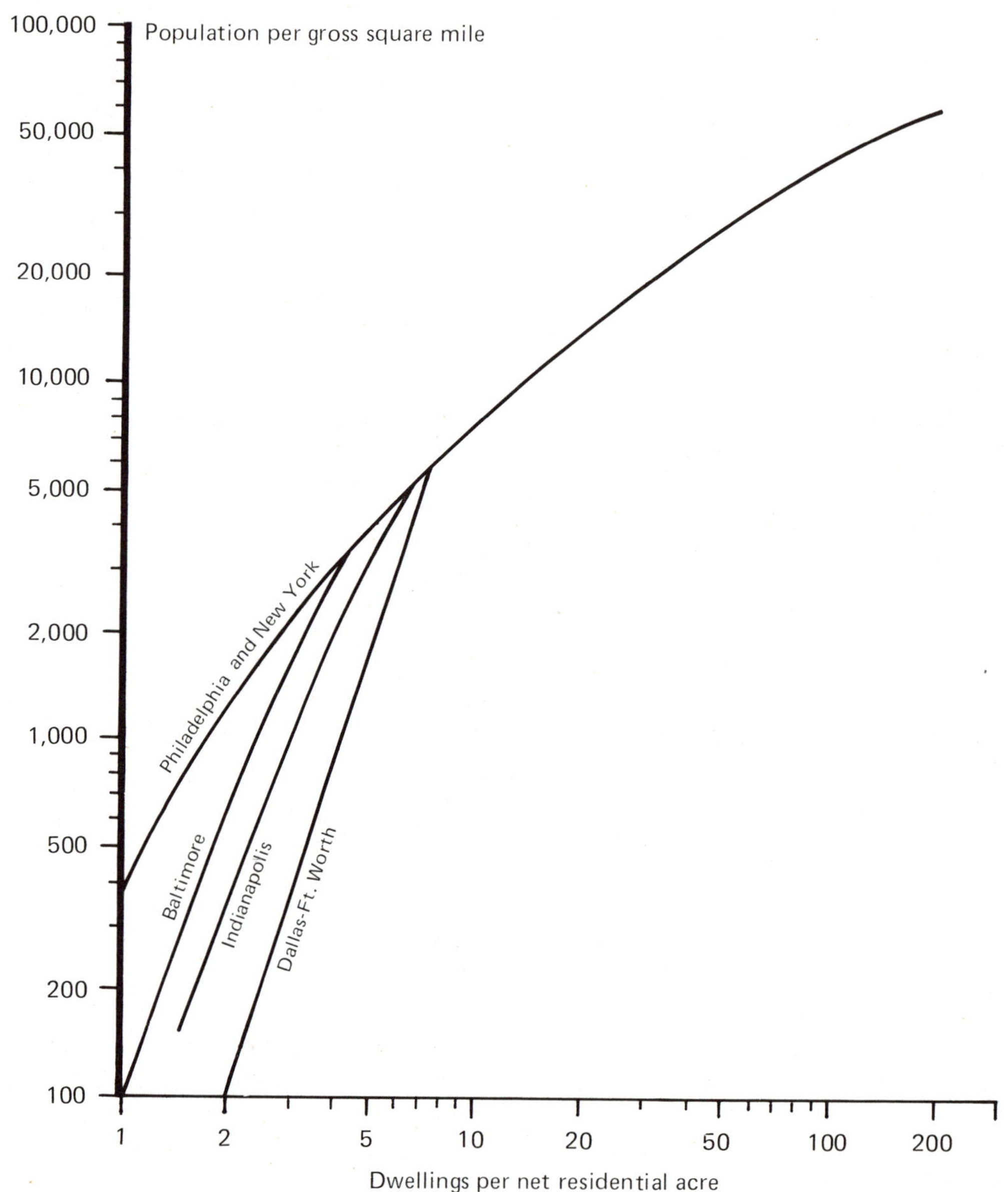

In Exhibit 3.26, the distance of each station from the CBD terminal is plotted on the horizontal axis and the median access trip length is plotted on the vertical axis for 66 commuter rail stations in New Jersey based on a consistent set of data gathered by the Port Authority of New York and New Jersey. Comparable data from other urban areas, unfortunately, could not be obtained. The data set at hand has two shortcomings: all stations are 10 or more miles from the CBD and buses as an access mode are negligible. The Exhibit shows that at a 10 to 15-mile distance (16 to 24 km) from the CBD median access trips by most modes are less than 1.0 mile (1.6 km). Beyond 10 miles, median access trip length increases by about one half mile for every ten additional miles out along the radial rail line. Those stations with substantial park and ride facilities (letter P) and terminal stations (letter T) have significantly higher median access distances. The straight line of best fit for the non-park and ride stations is the lower heavy line; the upper heavy line shows the straight line of best fit for the park and ride stations. For the former group the median access trip length is in the range of 11 to 6 percent of the radial distance; for the latter group it is 25 to 12 percent.

The variation of median access trip length by access mode in relation to line haul distance is also shown in Exhibit 3.26. For the auto driver, park and ride stations have median access trip lengths ranging from about 2.5 miles (4 km) at 10 miles (16 km) from the CBD to over 5.0 miles (8 km) at 40 miles (64 km) out. Stations without extensive park and ride facilities attract drivers from distances that are only three-fifths as long. Auto passenger access trips do not vary by type of stations. They are shorter than the auto driver trips. This reflects the desire to economize on travel when the time of two individuals is involved one of whom derives no transportation benefit and usually must make a "dead-head" return trip. The median access trip on foot, also shown for both types of stations combined, varies only slightly with distance from the CBD averaging between 0.5 and 0.6 miles (0.8 to 1.0 km).*

The mix of access modes is reflected in the overall median access trip length. Typically, at stations with median access trip lengths of one mile (1.6 km), 40 to 50 percent of the access trips are on foot while 35 percent are auto drivers, the remainder being auto passengers. At double that access trip length, 20 percent are on foot while half are auto drivers. Obviously, these relationships will differ if, as on new rapid transit systems in Washington and Atlanta, a large proportion of access trips is made by bus.

At a distance of 6 to 10 miles (10 to 16 km) from the center of Washington, the access modes to residentially oriented WMATA stations with parking are roughly 30 percent bus, 32 percent auto driver, 15 percent auto passenger, 21 percent walk, and 2 percent other modes. Assuming that the median access trip lengths by these modes are as shown in Exhibit 3.26, then the *median* access trip by bus would have to be about 1.9 miles (3 km) long for the aggregate median access trip to fit the 1.57 miles (2.53 km) predicted by the "park-and-ride" station equation at that distance from downtown. This is shorter than the auto driver trip and is not implausible,

*This appears to be quite long; New York City median walking distances to subway stops are about 0.35 miles (0.6 km) when there are no competing stops nearby; median access distances by bus in outer Queens are about 2.6 miles (4.2 km). These figures are based on spot-checks. Comprehensive data from the 1979 origin-destination survey of the New York City subway system were not available when this book went to press.

Exhibit 3.26

Median Access Distance as Function of Line Haul Distance to CBD for 66 Commuter Rail Stations in New Jersey

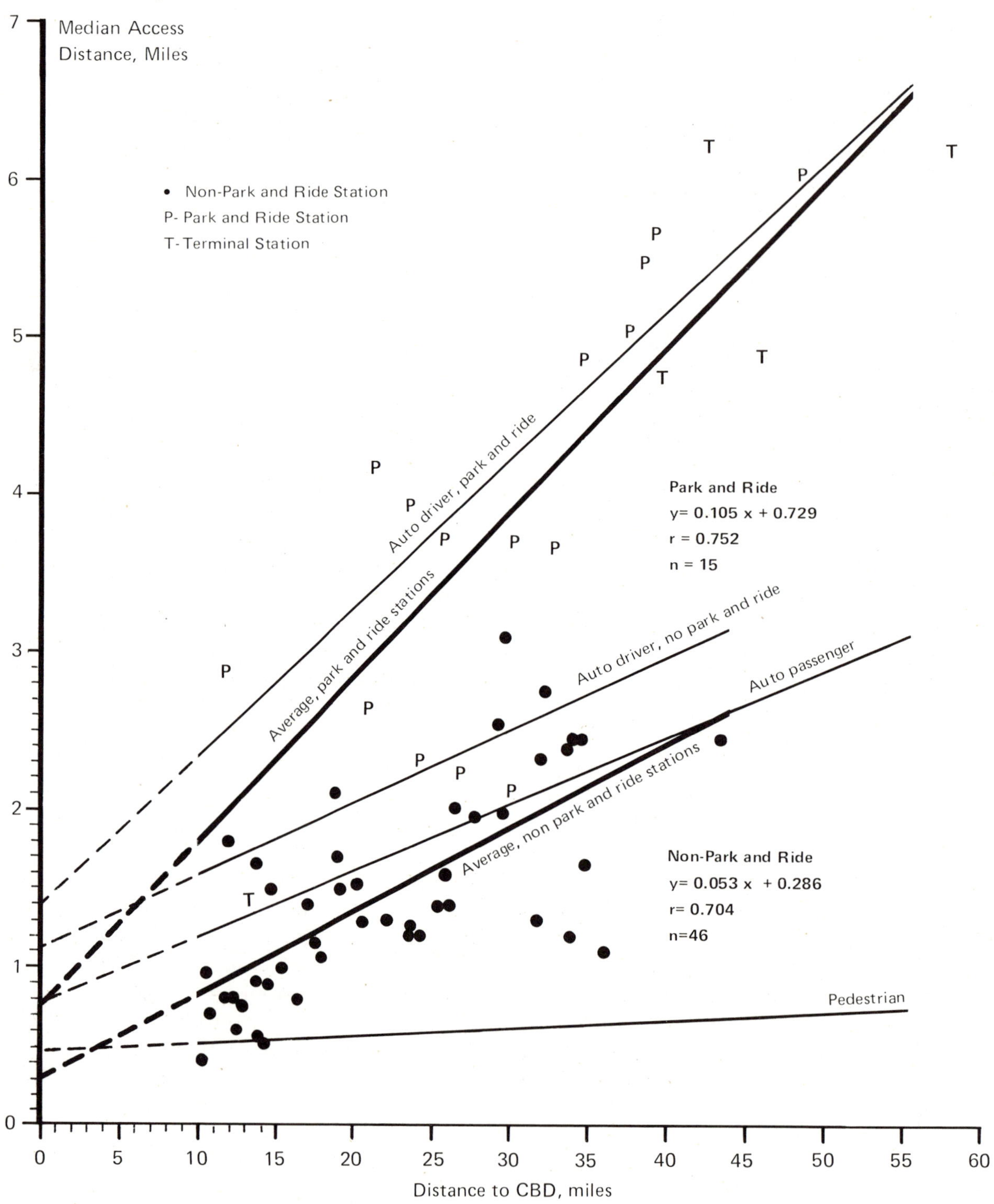

given that the *mean* bus trip for all purposes in Washington is 3.3 miles (5.3 km). The evidence, while circumstantial, suggests that the New Jersey relationships shown in Exhibit 3.26 are *not out of scale* with those in the Washington area, at least. In the absence of other access trip length distribution data, these relationships are used in Chapter 4 to define the tributary areas of stations.

TRAVEL WITHIN DOWNTOWNS

Procedures for estimating fixed guideway travel demand presented so far in this chapter are tailored to a predominantly residential corridor leading to a downtown. While small-vehicle automated guideway or peoplemover technology might also serve such a corridor, the current intent of peoplemover systems is to serve either travel internal to the CBD or travel that arrives at its edge by some other mode, and then transfers. Hence, estimating travel demand for *downtown* peoplemovers (DPM) calls for procedures distinct from those presented so far.

Such procedures were developed concurrently with this book for a separate publication. Only a summary of the planning implications that emerge from the demand analysis[7] is presented here along with some quantitative results. The reader is referred to the detailed discussion in the manual *DPM: Planning for Downtown Peoplemovers.*[8]

In contrast to rapid transit and light rail, there is little experience for evaluating downtown peoplemover demand. Consequently, a parametric technique is used, i.e., an "if-then" approach, assuming values of important parameters and variables. These variables fall into four categories. First are the characteristics of the CBD: the amount of CBD activities measured by nonresidential floorspace or by employment, the distribution of CBD activities (either spread or concentrated), and the land area. Second are the characteristics of the DPM: number of stations, station spacing, loop or shuttle configuration. Third are the DPM operating characteristics: operating speed, headways, and fares. Fourth is the configuration of other transportation facilities' line-haul transit delivery system to the DPM, location and capacity of fringe park and ride lots, and the highway network configuration.

Three traditional methodological steps are used: trip generation, trip distribution, and mode choice. The *trip generation* procedure yields total CBD trip volumes in five categories, each with potential for diversion to peoplemovers. They are (a) regional (one end inside, one end outside the CBD) CBD transit trips, (b) regional CBD auto trips, (c) internal (both ends inside CBD) CBD walk trips, (d) internal CBD transit trips, and (e) internal CBD auto trips. Regional CBD trips by transit and auto are estimated by simple regression techniques relating CBD floorspace and CBD employment to CBD trip ends. These relationships were illustrated earlier in Exhibit 3.15. Internal CBD trip ends are estimated by first using prevailing trip end rates per unit of floorspace by type (office, retail, other) to estimate *all* trips with at least one end in the CBD. Internal trips are then derived by subtracting the regional CBD trip ends from the total trip ends. Internal trips are further subdivided, splitting out walk trips based on available walk trip rates by floorspace type, and transit from auto on the basis of existing data in 10 CBD's.

The *distribution of trips* to zones around DPM stations that might serve those trips is made with the aid of Exhibit 3.14. By assuming that trips occur in proportion to the activities within 2000 feet (610 m) of a DPM station, trips are assigned to pairs of DPM stations, with the distribution depending on whether the CBD has its activities relatively spread or concentrated. The distribution also depends on the particular DPM system configuration: closer station spacing will translate into fewer potential trips assigned to any one station.

The *mode choice*, or diversion rate, is treated next. Estimates of DPM trips diverted from other modes are calculated separately for each of the five trip categories. All estimates are developed first in terms of percentages and then applied to the aggregate trip volumes. Each diversion calculation requires a comparison of the non-DPM (auto, transit, or walk) trip with that of a DPM trip for the same DPM station pair. If the DPM alternative is "cheaper" in terms of travel time, money cost, and convenience all trips are assigned to it. If the non-DPM alternative is "cheaper" no trips are assigned to the DPM.

To estimate the diversion rates for *regional transit trips*, assumptions must be made as to where the transit passengers are delivered. If the line-haul system is arranged to deliver passengers to DPM stations at the fringe of the CBD, a large proportion of the riders will find themselves with only the choice of a long walk to their CBD trip end. This transit delivery arrangement may be achieved more easily if the transit mode is local bus which can be rerouted to feed the DPM system, obviating the slow CBD portion of the trip. The line-haul system might also deliver passengers more centrally to the CBD, more likely for a rapid transit line, which will tend to dampen this element of DPM demand. In either case, the inclusive cost to the traveler of using the DPM can be calculated for any station spacing and number of stations configuration if DPM operating speed (to calculate in-vehicle time), DPM headway (to calculate waiting time), and DPM fare are assumed along with a cost of ascending and descending to and from the DPM station. The non-DPM, or walk, alternative for the regional transit traveler is merely the cost of the walk. Because the cost of access to the DPM has not been calculated, the amount by which the non-DPM alternative exceeds the cost of the DPM alternative can be thought of as the break-even cost of access. This cost is converted to break-even distance assuming a value of walking time, and the percent of activities within that distance is assumed to equal the percent of trips diverted.

The method to determine *regional auto trips* to a DPM is similar to that for transit trip diversion—with two important distinctions. First, the cost of parking in the CBD must be included. To account for its impact, empirical data shown partly in Exhibit 3.16 are used. The second distinction involves the availability of sufficient fringe parking and highway capacity to accept those auto drivers prepared to transfer to the DPM.

The diversion of *internal walk trips* is calculated in much the same manner as other trips; the cost to the traveler of using the DPM is compared with the cost of not using it. An added consideration is the difference in walk trip length by amount of CBD activity.

To estimate the diversion of *internal transit trips* to the DPM, it is necessary to assume operating characteristics of the existing transit system, usually buses, and compare them to those of the DPM.

The calculation of the diversion of *internal auto trips* is somewhat more complex. Three subgroups of internal auto users must be considered. First are the auto users reimbursed for their parking costs, assumed to be 20 percent of the total auto users—and not divertible to the DPM. Second is the group who did not take the opportunity, for whatever reason, to divert to the DPM for the line-haul trip to the CBD. These people, while not impervious to eventual DPM diversion inside the CBD, are at least more resistant to using the new system because they have their autos in the CBD. They are assigned values of walking time that reflect a greater reluctance to divert than the third group—those who left their autos behind at the fringe station and are assumed to behave like internal transit travelers.

The procedures above were used to estimate demand for a variety of CBD characteristics (floorspace, land area, spread or concentrated activity distribution), DPM characteristics (station spacing, number of stations, fare, headways, and speed), and transportation layouts (fringe park and ride, rerouting of existing bus system). The numerical results will not be detailed here, for they depend on the assumptions used. The realism of the assumptions for any particular downtown cannot be tested except in a site-specific setting. To give the reader a sense of scale, one hypothetical example is shown.

Assume a CBD of 0.8 square miles (2 km²) with 35 million square feet (3.25 million m²) of nonresidential floorspace and a relatively spread activity distribution, a downtown not dissimilar to Miami, Milwaukee, or Minneapolis.

Assume a DPM line just under a mile in length with 5 stations and 2-minute headways operating at a net or scheduled speed of 10 mph (16 km/h) and no fare.

The diversion of *internal CBD trips* can then be estimated as follows:

10,000 weekday trips diverted from walking
1,000 weekday trips diverted from intra-CBD bus travel
1,000 weekday trips diverted from intra-CBD auto travel.

12,000 weekday intra-CBD trips diverted to DPM

The diversion of *regional trips to the CBD* can be estimated as:

10,000 weekday bus trips *if* 20 percent of all bus passengers are funneled to transfers with the DPM
15,600 weekday auto person-trips assuming two fringe parking lots of 3,500 spaces each (28 acres or 11 ha)
25,600 weekday regional CBD trips diverted to DPM
37,600 total weekday trips diverted to DPM

It is evident that even with modest assumptions about the share of trips originating or destined outside the CBD and diverted to the DPM, these external or regional trips overwhelm the internal trips and comprise over two-thirds of the total DPM travel.

For comparison, it might be noted that one system that performs the *function* of a downtown peoplemover at present—the 1.2 mile (1.9 km) long streetcar subway line in Fort Worth—carried 5,600 weekday passengers in 1980, virtually all regional auto users switching to or from the line at an outlying 25-acre (10 ha) parking lot, accommodating about 3,000 cars. The privately owned line charges no fare. Another *functionally* similar system of the same length but different technology is the Seattle monorail, which connects the retail core of the Seattle CBD to outlying exhibition grounds. It carries 9,500 weekday passengers, few of whom are outlying parkers, and charges a standard transit fare. The two downtowns have about 10 and 40 million square feet (0.93 and 3.7 million m²) of nonresidential floorspace respectively.

Proposed interchange of the regional rapid transit line (upper level), and the downtown peoplemover (DPM, lower level), in Miami. The patronage of the peoplemover will consist in large part of transfers from the rapid transit line.

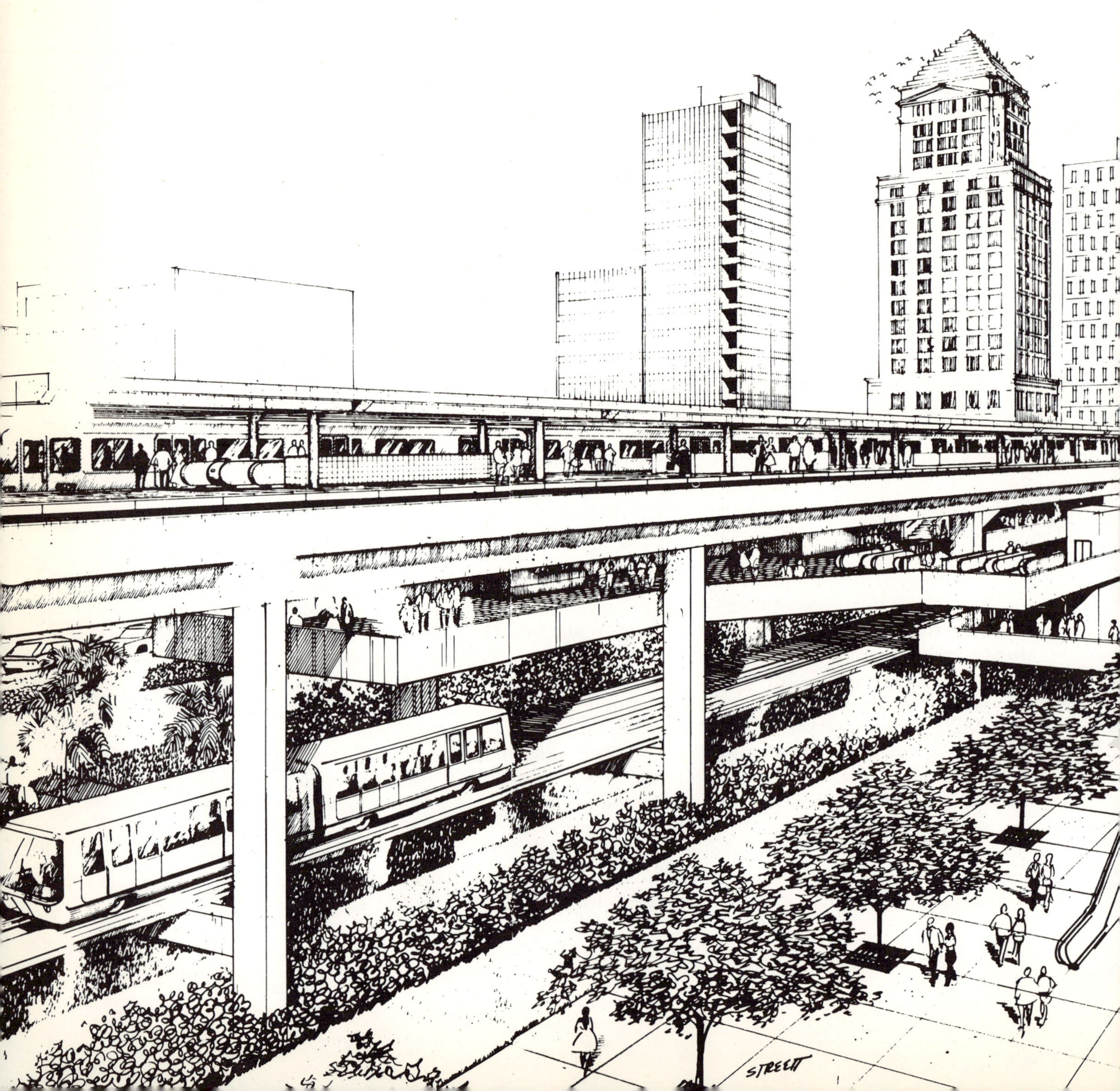

New trips *induced* by a downtown peoplemover must also be considered, because increased downtown activity resulting from induced travel is—following the logic outlined in Chapter 1—one rationale for building such systems. Another one is to permit more compact CBD development, as the Fort Worth line does. Data on induced travel are weak. Three observations can be referred to. Passenger surveys at the Dupont Circle station of the Washington Metro indicate that 12.8 percent of the passengers were induced in 1976, when the initial five-station segment of the subway acted much like a downtown peoplemover. In Milwaukee, 8.2 percent, and in Los Angeles, 16.5 percent of passengers on CBD shuttle buses claimed they would not make the trip if the service did not exist. The Los Angeles survey preceded the introduction of the service. A conservative judgment would be that not much over 10 percent of DPM travel is likely to be induced.

Exact numerical values aside, a number of planning conclusions can be drawn from this analysis.

1. For *regional auto trips,* often the largest potential market, the following should be noted:

a. Provision of fringe parking—particularly if linked to parking restraints in the core of the CBD—is the greatest lever for increasing DPM travel at the expense of auto travel. Physical limits to the size of fringe parking facilities are likely to be the key factor restraining diversion of regional auto trips.

b. Diversion of regional auto trips is directly related to total floorspace and floorspace density of the CBD because the cost of parking near the core of the CBD depends on them. In small CBD's, parking costs are usually sufficiently low that there is little incentive to avoid them.

c. A CBD with a large land area will require a longer DPM system to attain the same diversion of auto trips as a CBD with a smaller land area, given the same total floorspace.

d. Diversion of auto travel changes little with changes in operating characteristics, such as speed and frequency of service. In larger CBD's, the saving in parking charges is sufficient to outweigh small differences in travel time; in small CBD's, these differences cannot be sufficient to encourage a change of mode, unless parking supply in the CBD core is restricted.

2. For *regional transit trips,* often the second-largest DPM market, the following observations hold:

a. Forced diversion from buses is an effective way to build up DPM travel volumes. Yet, in practice, it is difficult to intercept all bus passengers, because they arrive from different directions. Nor is it necessarily desirable, because many of them would have to travel in an indirect way, and all would incur transfer costs. Still, the number of bus passengers who will transfer to the DPM depends primarily on the way in which the bus system is modified to create the necessity for such transfers. If the existing line-haul system, whether bus or rail, is left, little diversion can be expected.

b. The potential for diversion from buses increases with total floorspace and floorspace density in a CBD because both suppress auto travel and tend to make bus service more frequent.

c. Increasing the route length tends to increase diversion proportionately; more stations for the same route length produce only marginally more diversion. Station spacings on the order of 1,200 feet (366 m) appear desirable for the diversion of transit passengers.

d. A hypothetical increase in schedule speed from 10 to 20 mph (16 to 32 km/h) diverts few additional transit passengers because the time saving on the short section of the total trip made on the DPM is small. More frequent service has a similarly limited effect. Doubling frequency, such as reducing headway from two minutes to one minute, shaves only 30 seconds of waiting time for the average passenger, a small portion of the inclusive "cost" of the DPM trip. Even an increase in headway to 4 minutes reduces the diversion of regional transit passengers only moderately.

e. By contrast, the imposition of a fare can have a sizable effect on diversion to DPM. The percent reduction in ridership for a 25¢ fare is greater for the smaller systems. This conforms to the general pattern of greater passenger responsiveness to fares in smaller cities. The magnitude of the difference between a paid and a free system is in scale with the experience of internal CBD bus systems, which suggests that ridership for these short trips doubles when fares are eliminated.[9]

3. For *internal walk trips* the following findings are of interest:

a. A DPM can rarely attract more than one-third of all walk trips in a downtown, because most of these trips are very short. Two-thirds of all CBD walk trips are shorter than 600 to 1,400 feet (182 to 427 m), depending on downtown size. The potential for diversion increases with increasing total floorspace, because walk trips tend to be longer in larger downtowns.

b. Compact CBD's tend to have higher pedestrian diversion rates for the same system configuration than spread ones. Up to one-third more pedestrians can be diverted in a compact CBD because more of them will find their origin or destination close to a DPM station. This, of course, is dependent on the placement of the stations.

c. Diversion rates for pedestrian trips generally increase at least in direct proportion to the number of DPM stations. For pedestrians, maximum diversion occurs with a substantially shorter average distance between stations than needed for the diversion of transit passengers.

d. Service characteristics of speed and headway affect the diversion of pedestrian trips more than they do the diversion of transit and auto trips.

e. The imposition of a fare causes a dramatic drop in the diversion of pedestrians. A 10¢ fare (in 1977 prices) cuts diversion nearly in half, and a 25¢ fare reduces it by two-thirds or more.

4. For *internal transit trips,* unlike some of the other trip categories, the diversion to a DPM is very sensitive to the operating policies assumed, because the competition in this case, the local bus, has directly comparable features. Small changes can easily tip the scales toward one mode or the other. That is not the case for diversion of regional auto trips where the cost of central CBD parking and the availability of fringe parking at a DPM station weigh more heavily than changes in DPM operation. Nor is it the case for walking trips, where the trip distance largely determines diversion rates.

5. For *internal auto trips,* the major point is that the vast majority of diverted auto trips comprise those who left their autos at the fringe, becoming "captive" transit riders for their internal trips. This diversion, then, depends heavily on the number of park and ride spaces and their location at the CBD fringe.

It is clear from this summary that estimating potential travel volumes on an internal CBD circulation system is a complex matter, because competition in a variety of very diverse travel "markets" is involved. Yet, throughout the analysis, the *total amount of floorspace* in a downtown remains the overriding consideration, and the best estimator of potential trips in the aggregate. Furthermore, the strictly internal market remains rather weak until large downtown size is reached. With the external market dominant at all downtown sizes, the tradeoff between building a downtown-only system or a system oriented toward regional trips that also doubles as a downtown distributor becomes a serious policy issue.

4 Fixed Guideway Potential

GUIDEWAYS IN AN URBAN CORRIDOR

With the means to estimate fixed guideway travel in hand, it becomes possible to see where travel volumes in the range defined by the criteria presented in Chapter 2 can, in fact, be found. Rapid transit and light rail lines are examined for radial corridors using population distribution and CBD floorspace data for 29 urban areas as developed in Chapter 3. Peoplemovers are examined for generalized downtown settings.

One result of the procedures in Chapter 3 is an estimate of *daily passengers* traveling to a CBD from the densest corridor in an urban area, shown in Exhibits 4.9 and 4.10 at the end of this chapter. This gives an indication of the *passenger load at the maximum point*. That load will vary depending on the length of the route; a longer route will attract more passengers. Extending the route beyond some point, however, will tend to lower the *average load* over the entire line expressed in *passenger-miles per line-mile*. This measure, displayed graphically in Exhibits 4.5 and 4.6, makes possible to estimate what route length in a corridor will attain the volume necessary to meet the criteria.

Some of the criteria advanced in Chapter 2, such as those pertaining to capital investment, were originally derived in terms of weekday passenger volumes. Others, notably those pertaining to labor and energy requirements, had to be derived in terms of annual service volumes. For convenience in dealing with passenger data, all are converted here into *weekday passenger volumes*, using the factors in Exhibit 2.19. The key assumptions are that passengers occupy 23.3 percent of the places provided on an annual basis and that there are 280 weekday passenger equivalents in a year (i.e., Saturday, Sunday, and holiday traffic averages 22 percent of the weekday). No assumptions are made about the magnitude of the

(Photo credit: Metropolitan Atlanta Rapid Transit Authority)

daily peak hour volume which averages 26 percent of the daily one-directional load at the maximum load point on existing systems. Rather, the implication is that whatever the daily peaking factor, service can be fitted to it and to the average trip length calculated here such that one-directional weekday peak hour occupancy at the maximum load point does not exceed 100 percent and average annual occupancy is held to about 23.3 percent. Following the discussion of passenger occupancies in Chapter 2, this is realistic.

The steps used to calculate average weekday passenger volume on a radial line are summarized in Exhibit 4.1. The method depends on an estimate of the number of passengers boarding at each distance interval from the CBD. For this purpose, a prototypical line must be laid out. Nine such prototypical layouts tested are shown in Exhibit 4.2. For rapid transit, route lengths of 5.5, 9, and 15 miles (8.8, 14.5, and 24 km) are examined with 7, 9, and 12 stations respectively, of which 2 are located in the CBD. For light rail, route lengths of 4, 6, and 9 miles (6.4, 9.6, and 14.5 km) are examined with 9, 12, and 16 stations respectively, 3 of which are in the CBD. The resulting station spacings allow average operating speeds of about 25 mph (40 km/h) for rapid transit and about 18 mph (29 km/h) for light rail. In both cases, there is some variation depending on line length.

The stations are surrounded by tributary areas within the median station access distance, which increases with distance from the CBD.The diamond shape of these areas, reflecting a rectilinear street grid, is divided into two parts: the "rail territory" within one-half mile of a station and the "non-rail territory" beyond one-half mile. The choice of mode of travelers from these two territories differs. In addition, stations which predominantly depend on mechanical access modes (including buses) and have a large tributary area are distinguished from those which mostly depend on walking and have a smaller tributary area. The access distance in the former case is assumed to follow the "park and ride stations" relationship in Exhibit 3.26 and in the latter, the "no park and ride" relationship.

Within 4 miles (6.4 km) of the CBD, all rapid transit and light rail stations are assumed to have only the smaller tributary area, to reflect the fact that for short travel distances a change of mode is rarely in the passenger's interest. At longer distances, the time loss and inconvenience of a change in modes are more likely to be offset by a faster line-haul trip by rail. This distance assumption is conservative. Edmonton, for example, diverts all local bus trips to light rail stations that are as close as 2 to 3 miles (3.2 to 4.8 km) to the CBD. This economizes on operating costs but has elicited complaints from riders residing near the CBD, whose trips on occasion take more time.[1]

Beyond 4 miles, all rapid transit stations are assumed to have the larger tributary area, reflecting considerable reliance on feeder modes. For light rail, two assumptions are used. The first is that only the terminal station has the enlarged tributary area. The second is that all stations beyond 4 miles have it. This results in six, rather than three, light rail configurations being examined.

The median distances to stations thus established, the land area within the median distance is calculated separately for the "rail" and "non-rail" territories, excluding any overlap between stations. Multiplied by the population density at the appropriate distance from the CBD shown in Exhibit 3.12, this yields the population residing within the median access distance. Per capita trip rates from the modified trip attraction model are applied to this population, using the appropriate distance from the CBD and CBD floorspace.

Exhibit 4.1
Flow Chart for Calculation of Daily Travel Volume on a Rail Line in a Corridor to a Central Business District

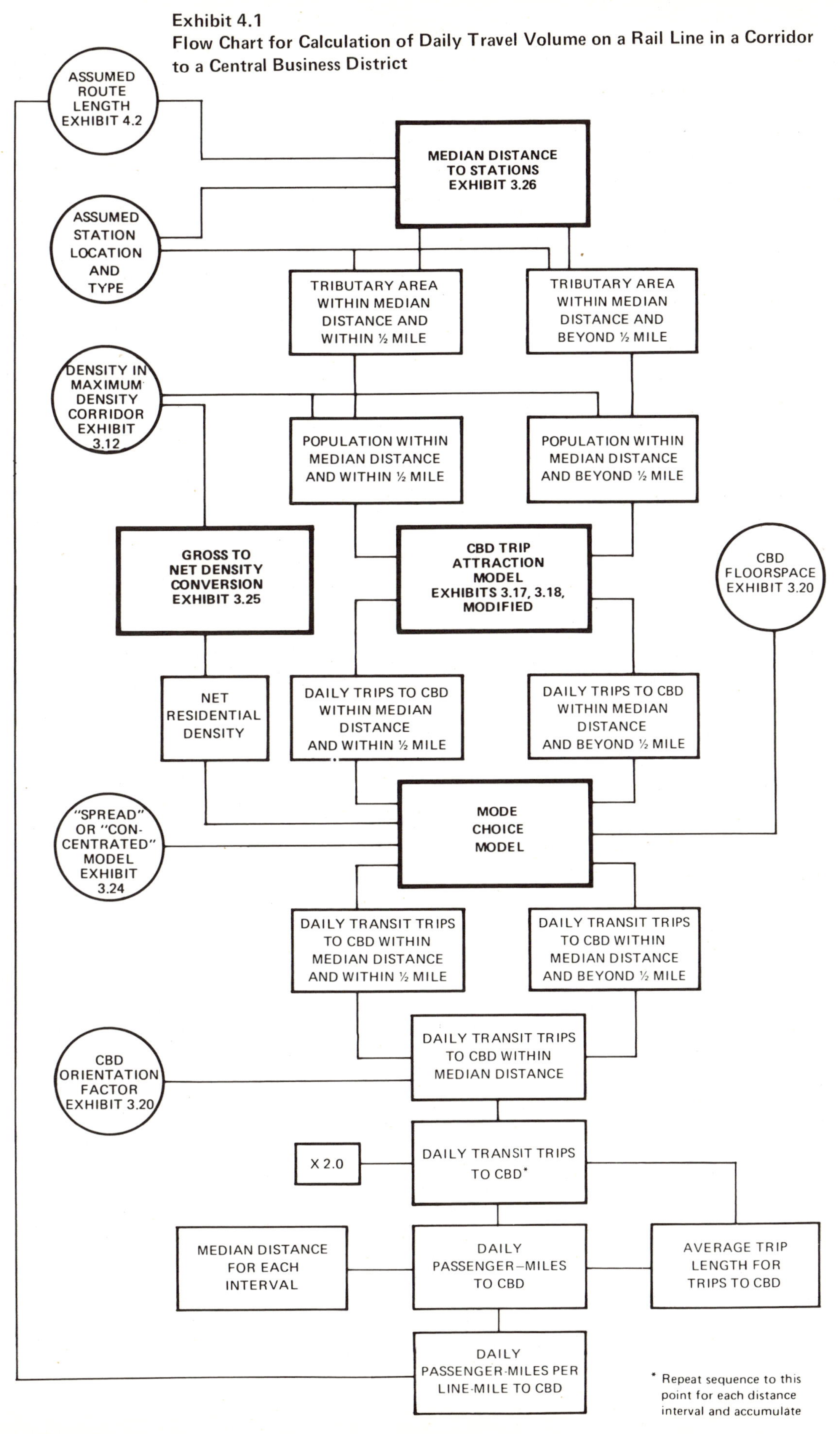

* Repeat sequence to this point for each distance interval and accumulate

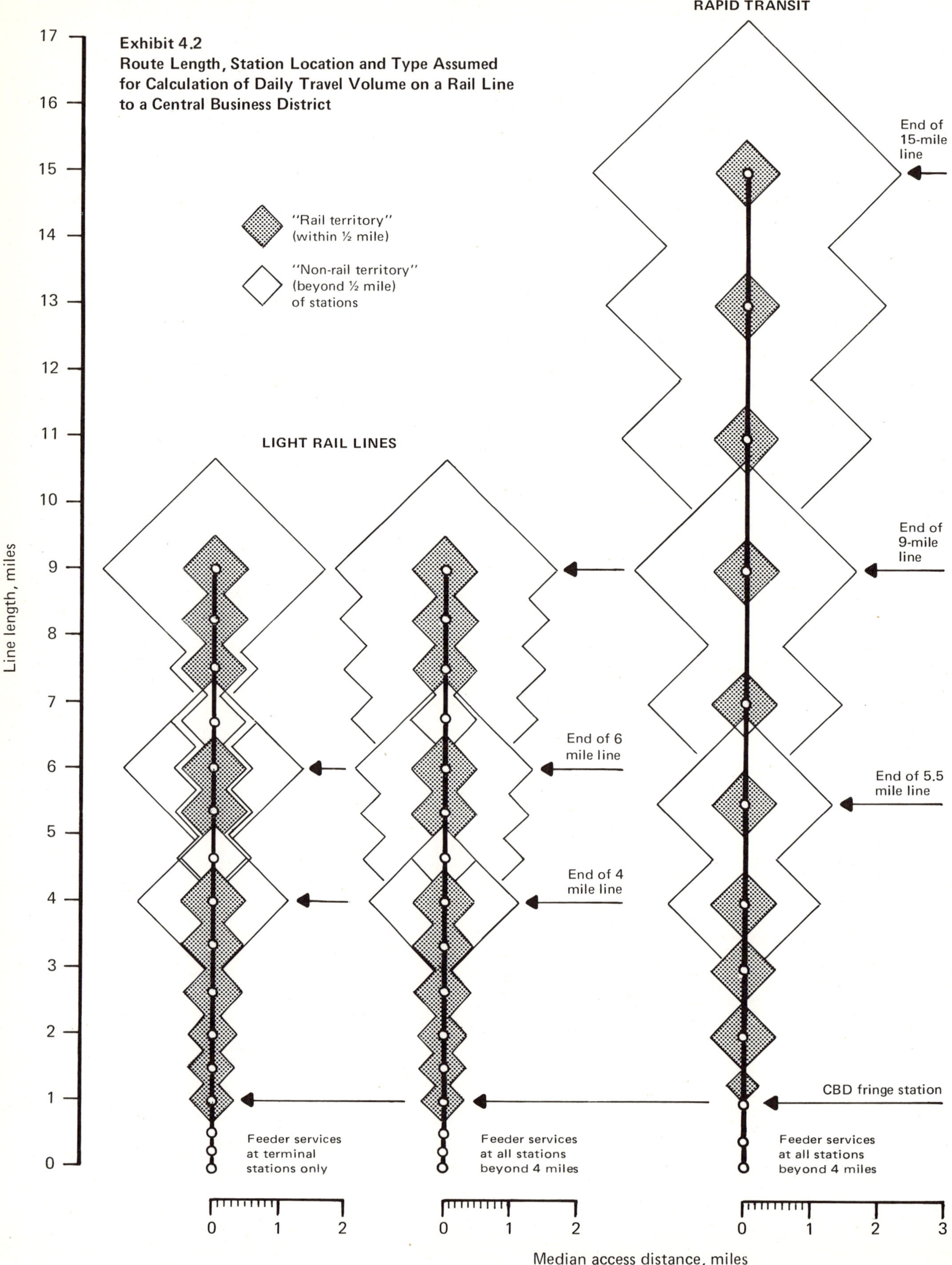
Exhibit 4.2
Route Length, Station Location and Type Assumed for Calculation of Daily Travel Volume on a Rail Line to a Central Business District
RAPID TRANSIT
LIGHT RAIL LINES
"Rail territory" (within ½ mile)
"Non-rail territory" (beyond ½ mile) of stations
End of 15-mile line
End of 9-mile line
End of 6 mile line
End of 5.5 mile line
End of 4 mile line
CBD fringe station
Feeder services at terminal stations only
Feeder services at all stations beyond 4 miles
Feeder services at all stations beyond 4 miles
Line length, miles
0
1
2
3
4
5
6
7
8
9
10
11
12
13
14
15
16
17
0
1
2
0
1
2
0
1
2
3
Median access distance, miles

The share of these CBD-bound trips that will use the rail line is determined using the mode choice models. Within one-half mile of the transit station the mode choice reflects the auto ownership levels in "rapid transit" territory. Beyond one-half mile the mode choice reflects the higher auto ownership levels of "non-rail" territory. The diversion rates for auto-owning households in the two territories also differ. Furthermore, a decision is made as to whether the mode choice model to be used reflects the "high" or "low" transit use set of equations; that designation is shown in Exhibit 3.24. For some urban areas both are tested. For light rail, the impact of the variable in the mode choice equations called "rail presence" is somewhat arbitrarily cut in half. Once again, this tends to make the estimate conservative.

The trips from the two "territories" around a station are then combined, multiplied by the CBD orientation factor (Exhibit 3.20) and multiplied by 2.0 to include the half of all rail trips excluded so far because the analysis was confined to the tributary area within the median access distance, which by definition is where only half the trips come from. With daily one-way CBD-bound trips from each distance interval known, daily passenger-miles are obtained by summing the passenger-miles originating at each interval. Dividing by the length of the line and multiplying by 2.0 to account for both directions, one obtains daily passenger-miles per line-mile.

In a refinement of the mode choice model, the rail transit trips estimated are adjusted to reflect speeds on the competing highway network. The higher of the two mode choice estimates in each case assumes auto speeds that are about 5 mph (8 km/h) below average levels. In this calculation, differences in both auto and rail speeds by trip distance are taken into account.

Limitations of the travel estimates must be recognized at this point. The per capita trip rates supplied by the trip attraction model refer only to trips from residential origins to nonresidential destinations. They exclude residence-to-residence trips and trips from nonresidential origins to nonresidential destinations. Purely residential trips are not a significant component of weekday rail travel, but nonresidence-to-nonresidence trips can be significant. A related and more pertinent breakdown is by geography. *The trips estimated so far are only those from a residential area to a CBD and back*. On an urban rail system, *three additional types* of trips are made:

(1) Trips originating in a residential area and stopping *short* of the CBD. These can be appreciable if nonresidential floorspace is located along a line outside the CBD, such as in Rosslyn and Crystal City on Washington's Blue line, or in Decatur on Atlanta's East line.

(2) Trips originating in a residential area and traveling *through* the CBD in those cases when the rail line serves more than the one corridor discussed so far.

(3) Trips originating and terminating *within* the CBD. Such trips with nonresidential floorspace at both ends can extend to neighboring nonresidential clusters as well.

It should also be clear that the models only estimate the diversion of existing trips and take no account of new trips induced by the travel advantages of a new facility.

Lastly, the basis of the travel estimates are 1970 population data and floorspace estimates of the late 1970s. Neither changes in the intervening period nor future growth are taken into account, further contributing to the conservative character of the estimates. To the extent that future auto travel restraints will find expression in reduced auto ownership levels, the mode choice model can reflect them. However, if gasoline prices or shortages change the mode choice of auto-owning households, exogenous corrections will have to be introduced.

Projections of future travel are not the intent of this study and are not considered any further. With or without corrections, the models can be applied to any projected population distribution and any projected magnitude of downtown floorspace.

Nor is induced travel further considered as such, largely because of the difficulties of measurement. Travel survey respondents who report "not making the trip before," typically 15 percent or more, are not necessarily induced riders; some are simply people who had no need for that particular trip previously, or who newly moved into that area. Survey respondents who report that they "would not make the trip" *if* the facility did not exist are less numerous, only 5 percent in the case of the Washington Metro. How reliable the answers to such a hypothetical question are is difficult to say. To avoid tenuous assumptions, no adjustment for induced travel is made here. Taking account of trips other than those between a residential corridor and a downtown is necessary, however, and for that purpose the estimates must first be compared to actual travel data.

Validating the travel estimates. After the estimates were made in 1978, actual travel data became available for two of the cities, namely Washington and Atlanta,[2] and the relevant comparisons are shown in Exhibit 4.3. The models fit the Washington area remarkably well, estimating existing *average corridor* trips to the CBD and average trip length almost exactly, particularly if an interpolation is made to reflect the actual, rather than assumed, line length. With service in existence as of September 1979, however, it is not possible to compare the estimates to actual trips originating in the densest corridor which the models are meant to measure. These, most likely, would be understated by 10 to 15 percent or more.

In Atlanta, the average corridor trips to the CBD are estimated closely for a point in time immediately after inauguration of full first phase service, but fall considerably short of actual traffic half a year later. The reason is a large understatement of trips at the two outer terminals, which in fact account for half of all station boardings outside the CBD of Atlanta. With exceptionally heavy reliance on feeder buses, the tributary area of the terminal stations is much larger than assumed. In effect, Atlanta, with 5.9-mile average radial lines, has what amounts to 9-mile radial lines. Estimates made on that basis reflect both passenger trips and average trip length much more closely, especially if one subtracts those passengers who continued to the CBD by bus until their bus routes were short-turned at rail stations. Still, the understatement would be greater if travel data from the densest corridor (not in service in 1980) were available.

Based on the Washington and Atlanta experience one can conclude that the travel estimates presented are conservative and may represent, for practical purposes, close to the *average, rather than the densest corridor in a city*. To repeat, they only represent trips between a residential corridor and a Central Business District. Estimates of traffic density in passenger-miles per line-mile remain incomplete without considering the other types of trips.

An accurate estimate of trips and passenger-miles originating in a residential

Exhibit 4.3
Comparison of Actual and Estimated Travel to Two Central Business Districts

	Radial line length (miles)		Rail trip length (miles)		CBD rail trip destinations per corridor	
	Actual	**Assumed**	**Actual**	**Estimated**	**Actual**	**Estimated**
Washington, Sept. 1979						
Average, 3 corridors	10.3	9.0 (10.3)	4.89	4.58 (4.83 int.)	32,646	31,600 (32,800 int.) (100.5%)
Atlanta, Jan. 1980						
Average, 2 corridors	5.9	5.5	4.2(e)	3.58	9,450	10,000
Atlanta, June 1980						
Average, 2 corridors	5.9	(5.9)	4.2(e)	(3.71 int.)	14,380	(10,000 int.)
Without short-turning of bus routes		(5.9)		(3.71 int.)	12,040	(10,300 int.)
Assuming 9-mile line		9.0		4.66		12,500 (85.5 to 103%)

(int.) = interpolated between the lower and the next higher line length assumptions.
(e) = estimated; origin-destination data for Atlanta not available; CBD destinations based on CBD station counts.

Exhibit 4.4
Origin-Destination Patterns of Rapid Transit Trips on Selected Systems

		Trips from residential corridor to CBD and back	Trips from residential corridor short of CBD and back	Trips from residential corridor through CBD and back	Trips internal to the CBD
		(as percent of total station boardings)			
Washington WMATA	(1979)	73.9	6.4	5.5	14.2 (5.2)
San Francisco BART	(1977)	70.2 (74.4)	10.5 (6.5)	7.6 (12.9)	11.7 (6.2)*
Toronto TTC	(1975)	53.8	24.0	12.7	9.5
Atlanta MARTA	(1980)	75.4	23.1 (both columns combined)		1.5
Cleveland GCRTA	(1976)	69.6	30.4 (both columns combined)		none
Philadelphia PATCO	(1976)	87.2	12.8	negligible	negligible
New York SIRT	(1976)	74.7	25.3	none	none
Edmonton ETS	(1979)	95.1	4.9	none	negligible

* CBD on BART includes both Oakland and San Francisco downtowns; trips between them are counted here as internal.
Figures in parentheses indicate percent of passenger-miles, where available.

corridor but stopping *short* of the CBD, going *through* the CBD, and *internal* to the CBD can only be made with site-specific origin-destination data. An overview of such data from existing systems can give a general impression of the magnitude of this travel. This is shown in Exhibit 4.4, which indicates that *these types of trips can easily add one-third to the trips with one end in the CBD.* Much depends on the layout of the rail system and on the structure of the urban area.

If the rail system consists of only one radial line to the CBD, the addition of trips stopping short of the CBD is likely to expand trips by a factor anywhere from 1.05 to 1.45, compared to trips with one end in the CBD only. The increment of passenger-miles traveled will be smaller, because the added trips are necessarily shorter. The proportion of the added trips depends on the length of the line, the presence of intervening nonresidential land use, and the habit of making short non-CBD trips by transit, which is clearly high in Toronto and low in Washington.

If the rail system consists of at least two radial lines, the addition of trips passing through the CBD will expand the trips to and from the CBD by an additional 1.07 to 1.24 times, based on the data in Exhibit 4.4. This range largely depends on the length of the line and the nonresidential opportunities that lie beyond the CBD. The increment in passenger-miles traveled will be greater than that, because the trips will necessarily be longer.

Lastly, the internal CBD trips depend on the areal extent of the downtown, the number of stations in it, and downtown floorspace. While such trips can contribute noticeably to the social usefulness of a rail system and to its revenues, they do not add much to the passenger-miles traveled, because the trips are short. In Washington in 1979, the 14.2 percent of all rail transit trips that was internal to the CBD translated into only 5.2 percent of rail passenger-miles.

In sum, with one radial rail line in a corridor, the passenger-miles traveled to and from the CBD can be raised some 3 to 15 percent to account for trips stopping short of the CBD. This adjustment is not made in the analysis that follows. For a rail line passing through the CBD, another 10 to 20 percent can be added for through trips. This adjustment is discussed, where appropriate. With these considerations in mind, one can turn to comparing the estimated travel to and from the CBD with threshold criteria for rapid transit and light rail.

RAPID TRANSIT

To compare potential rail travel to the threshold criteria presented in Chapter 2, rapid transit corridors are examined in 16 cities, and light rail corridors in 24 cities. Only one line extending in one direction from the CBD is tested in most cases, consistent with recent practice of starting "operable segments" rather than entire rail systems. The feasibility of additional lines is discussed later. The urban areas selected for *rapid transit* analysis are mostly those with more than 30 million square feet of downtown floorspace, plus Honolulu, which has been considering rapid transit. The results are presented in Exhibit 4.5 graphically and in Exhibit 4.9 in tabular form. In the graphs, route length is plotted against the estimated daily downtown travel in passenger-miles per line-mile for each urban area. At least two travel estimates are given in each case, one representing lower, one higher auto speeds on the competing highway network. If there is some question whether in a particular urban area the "high transit use" or the "low transit use" mode choice model is appropriate, both results are shown; the model used is indicated by the letters "H" or "L". The more likely set of curves is shown with heavy lines. The quality of the underlying population and floorspace data is indicated by letters A through D, following Exhibits 3.12 and 3.13 earlier.

The curves are drawn based on travel volume estimates for each of the three line lengths tested and allow one to interpolate probable usage for intermediate line lengths. The slopes of the curves reflect patterns of population distribution. Urban areas with a tight settlement pattern around a downtown tend to exhibit a downward slope, because extending a route adds relatively few additional passengers; Baltimore and Honolulu are typical examples. Urban areas with a more even settlement pattern have curves close to the horizontal, as for example Detroit, where a 5-mile (8 km) and a 15-mile (24 km) line attract virtually the same average passenger volume per line-mile.

Drawn horizontally across the graphs in Exhibit 4.5 are dashed lines representing the rapid transit threshold volumes defined earlier in Chapter 2. To recapitulate briefly, these are:

RT-1: *Rapid transit above ground* with 15,000 daily passenger-miles or 18 million annual place-miles per line-mile is in scale with prevailing minimum service frequency, allows a construction expenditure of about $18 million a mile in 1977 prices at the median investment level, saves land compared to freeways, saves labor compared to local buses, and can attain modest savings in energy.

RT-2: *Rapid transit up to one-third in tunnel* with 24,000 daily passenger-miles or 29 million annual place-miles per line-mile offers more than minimum service frequency, allows a construction expenditure of about $30 million a mile in 1977 prices at the median investment level, saves land compared to freeways, can save labor compared to express buses on busways, and attain savings in energy.

Relaxing the median investment level of $1,250 per weekday passenger-mile in 1977 prices to the 75th percentile level of $1,800 lowers the volume necessary for this type of construction to about 17,000 daily passenger-miles or 20 million annual place-miles per line-mile; however, both labor savings compared to express buses and energy savings become problematic. This modified middle threshold is not shown in the charts but is referred to in the text on two occasions.

RT-3: *Rapid transit fully in tunnel* with 29,000 daily passenger-miles or 35 million annual place-miles per line-mile offers good service frequency, allows a construction expenditure of $52 million a mile in 1977 prices with the relaxed 75th percentile investment level (assuming some non-transportation benefits of tunnels), can save labor compared to express buses on busways, and can begin to attain energy savings under some conditions.

The 16 urban areas examined fall into a somewhat loose continuum with respect to reaching these rapid transit threshold volumes.

Washington stands out, exceeding the upper, all-tunnel rapid transit criterion for line lengths of 10 to 15 miles (16 to 24 km, depending on competing auto speeds), even though tunnels for only about half the route length are actually planned. However, the line length which maximizes passenger volume per line-mile might be in the 7 to 10 mile (11 to 16 km) range, shorter than the 14.4-mile (23.2 km) average planned. It is generally recognized that maximizing passenger use per line-mile was not among the goals of planning Washington's outer suburban

Exhibit 4.5
Rapid Transit Travel to the CBD by Corridor Compared to Threshold Levels
16 Urban Areas

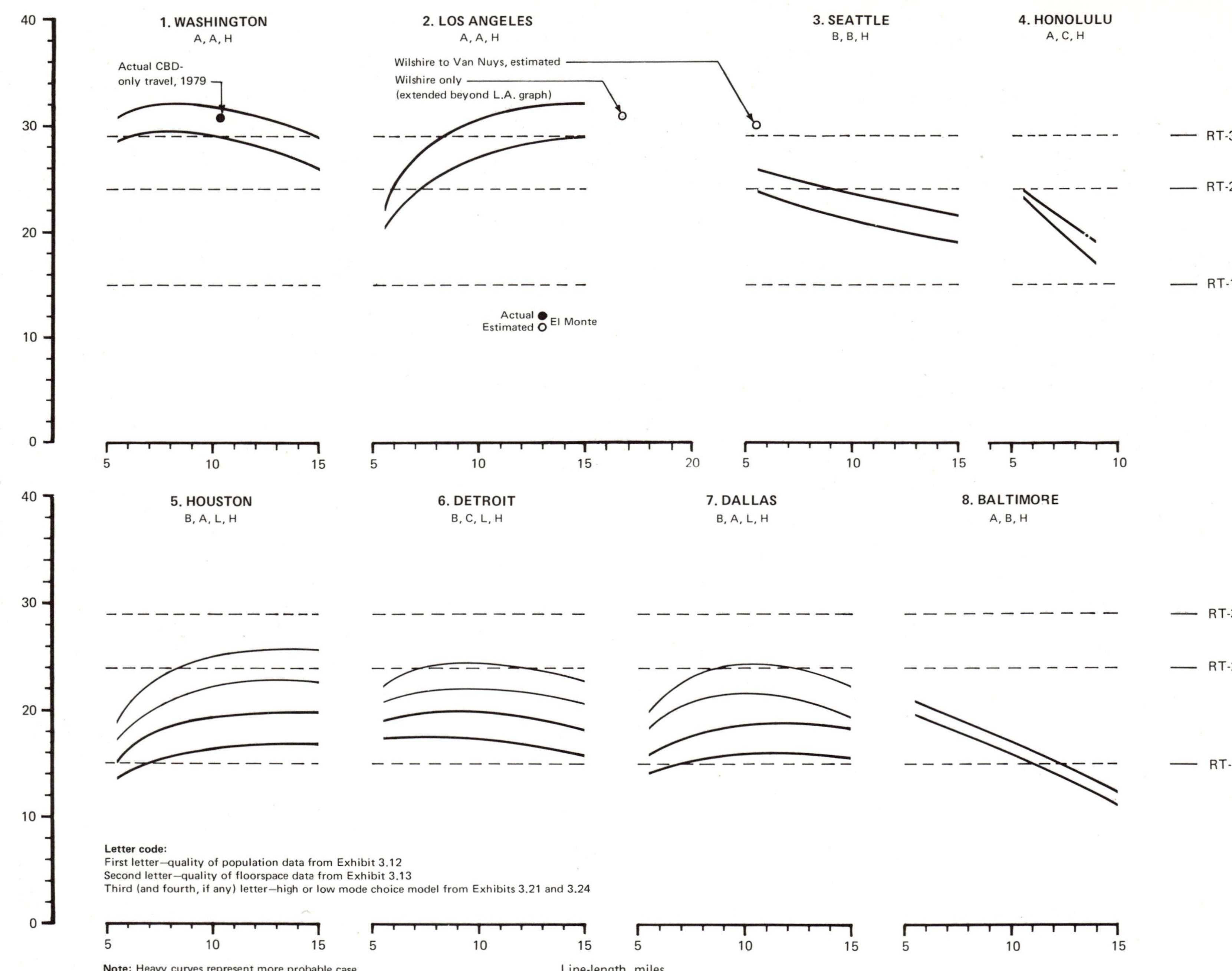

Letter code:
First letter—quality of population data from Exhibit 3.12
Second letter—quality of floorspace data from Exhibit 3.13
Third (and fourth, if any) letter—high or low mode choice model from Exhibits 3.21 and 3.24

Note: Heavy curves represent more probable case

Exhibit 4.5 (cont'd.)
Rapid Transit Travel to the CBD by Corridor Compared to Threshold Levels
16 Urban Areas

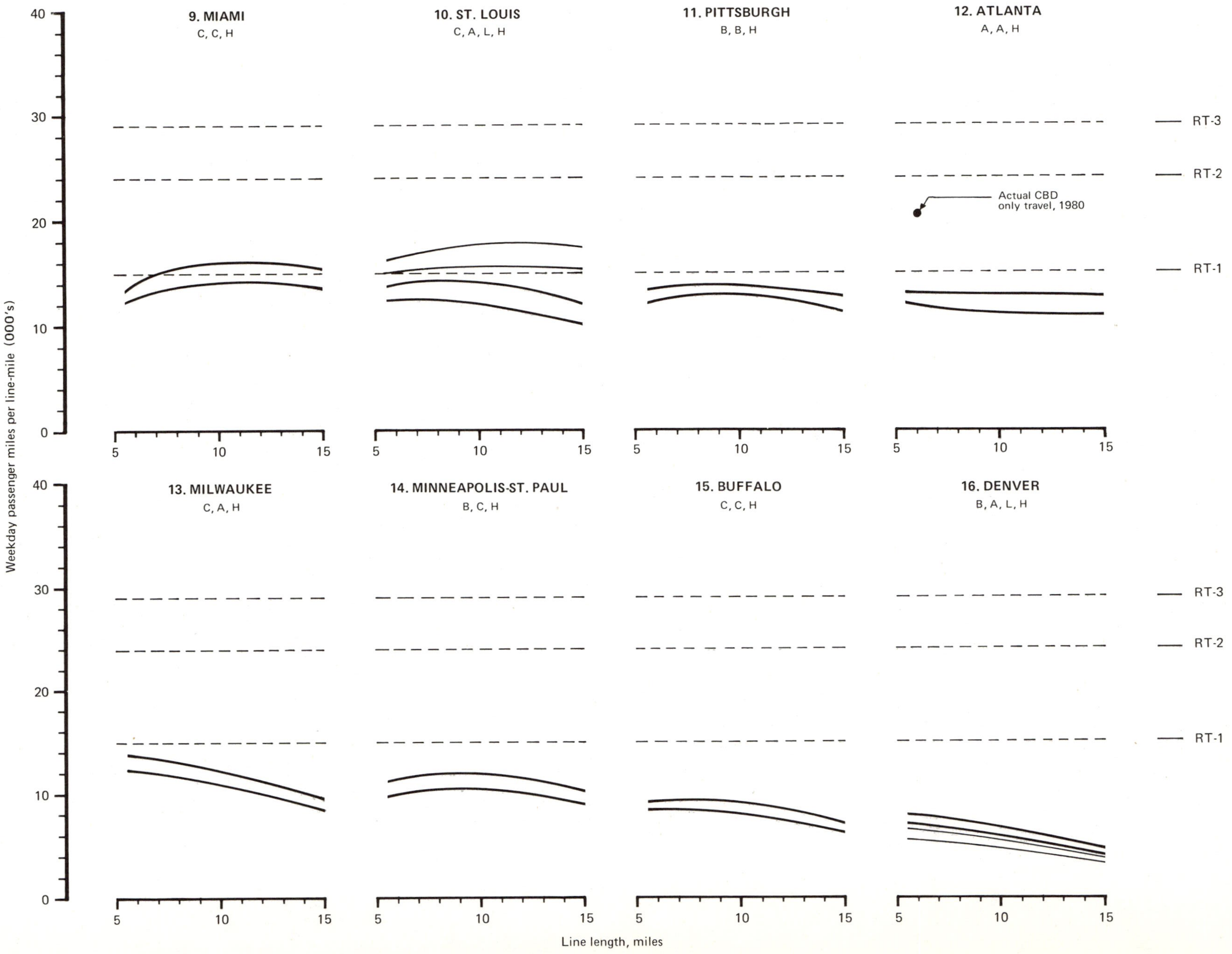

extensions. Considerations of not disturbing existing communities with terminal stations and of providing for future growth dominated. Because population distribution among corridors in Washington is relatively even, the estimates shown should be fairly representative of a number of corridors and not only the densest corridor; comparisons with actual ridership given earlier indicate that such is indeed the case. Overall, the full seven-leg 101-mile (163 km) system under construction appears to be in scale with the criteria advanced here. Additional proposed above-ground extensions would have to attain about half the passenger volume attained on the one-third of the system in operation in 1979 to meet the low, above-ground rapid transit threshold.

Los Angeles exceeds the upper, all-tunnel criterion for a line over 15 miles (24 km) long in the densest corridor. The likely passenger volume there is similar to Washington's, and it is for the densest corridor along Wilshire Boulevard that an 18-mile (29 km) rapid transit line, mostly in tunnel, is under design. Separate exploratory calculations suggest that westerly extensions to this line in a tunnel to Westwood and in a rail right-of-way to Van Nuys would add enough travel to keep a 28-mile system above the upper rapid transit threshold, at 30,000 passenger-miles per line-mile. However, estimated travel on the El Monte busway converted to rail would be only about 12,000 passenger-miles per line-mile, not quite meeting the low above ground threshold volume. A southerly Harbor Freeway route would have a volume between these two values, as seen in Exhibit 4.9. Because the non-CBD component of trips stopping short and traveling through downtown should be particularly high in Los Angeles, where a string of nonresidential clusters with at least one-third as much floorspace as the CBD itself extends from Westwood to downtown along the Wilshire corridor, both the El Monte route and the Harbor Freeway route appear reasonable given this additional traffic. The former would be strictly above ground with minimal construction costs, while the latter could justify some tunneling in downtown Los Angeles and Long Beach. A northerly route to Pasadena was tested but fell about 50 percent short of the volume needed for an above-ground rapid transit line. It would be suitable for light rail.

Seattle follows Los Angeles as a candidate for rapid transit. Its highest corridor volume never reaches the high all-tunnel threshold, but lines one-third in tunnel appear reasonable for a distance of 5 to 9 miles (8 to 15 km) from the CBD, basically in a north-south direction. This is similar in scale to the original 20-mile (32 km) Seattle plan of 1967. A separate consideration in Seattle is an easterly leg across Lake Washington, where transit use would be enhanced if highway bridge capacity across the lake were constrained. No volume estimate is attempted for this strictly site-specific condition which strongly affects any rail transit plans for Seattle.

Honolulu comes next, with a 5-mile (8 km) line just about meeting the middle threshold of rapid transit one-third in tunnel, and a 10-mile (11 km) line exceeding the lower, fully above-ground criterion. Because of topography, only two such lines radiating from the downtown are at issue, with a total length in scale with extant proposals for a 14- to 23-mile system.

The urban areas of *Houston*, *Detroit*, and *Dallas* follow. All three are characterized by relatively low levels of current transit use. Therefore, alternative calculations of potential travel volume assuming both low and high transit use levels are made. The lower estimate of daily rapid transit travel exceeds only the low above-ground rapid transit criterion for lines 6 to 15 miles (10 to 16 km) in length in all three cases. If the estimate is raised to allow for greater transit orientation in the future, Houston exceeds the middle criterion for a line one-third in tunnel under the assumption of reduced auto speeds; the other two cities barely reach it. Houston and Detroit have relatively even travel distributions by corridor as shown by local origin-destination studies; these indicate that possibly four lines would meet the criteria in Houston, and three in Detroit. In Dallas, the distribution is more skewed, and the feasibility of more than one, or at most two spokes from the CBD is not indicated.

Baltimore and Miami come next, both with rapid transit under construction. Both exceed the low, above-ground rapid transit threshold for line lengths of 13 to 15 miles (21 to 24 km). Miami, in fact, is building two legs of 10 miles (16 km) each, fully above ground. Baltimore's 13-mile (21 km) Northwest line also matches the length indicated by the criteria, but one-third of it is in tunnel. The middle rapid transit criterion with the capital investment requirement relaxed to allow the 75th percentile construction expenditure would match Baltimore's Northwest line more closely.

Pittsburgh and *Atlanta* follow, with estimated travel volumes not quite reaching the low, above-ground rapid transit criterion. Pittsburgh after two decades of controversy settled on a combination of light rail with a short downtown tunnel, to be discussed shortly, and two exclusive busways, while Atlanta built a rapid transit system. Atlanta's actual volume on the East-West line in 1980, including only CBD-oriented trips, was not 13,000 as indicated in the charts, but an estimated 20,500 daily passenger-miles per line-mile. This still does not meet the middle rapid transit criterion for a rapid transit line one-third in tunnel, which is what Atlanta's Phase I system provides. It comfortably meets the modified middle criterion, which allows higher capital expenditure. In this respect, Atlanta's position is similar to that of the relatively high-cost Baltimore system. As explained earlier, the excess of the actual over the estimated downtown travel volume comes from not considering usually heavy bus diversion to rail at terminal stations and from a resulting underestimate of average trip length. The option of heavy bus diversion to terminal stations is available (if often to a lesser degree) to many urban areas and could enhance their prospects for rapid transit compared to the levels shown here.

St. Louis either follows or precedes Pittsburgh and Atlanta, depending on which of the four travel estimates calculated for it one chooses. Assuming low auto speeds and low region-wide transit use, the above-ground rapid transit threshold is almost met for a line of some 9 miles (15 km); at higher competing auto speeds, that threshold is never reached. Assuming high region-wide transit use, the low, above-ground rapid transit threshold is exceeded for any of the line lengths investigated; the suitability of only an above-ground line for downtown St. Louis can obviously be questioned. A local alternatives analysis decided on a bus-only system for the St. Louis area for the next 10 to 15 years.[3]

Lastly, *Milwaukee*, *Minneapolis*, *Buffalo*, and *Denver* do not reach the travel volume postulated for even an above-ground rapid transit line under any assumptions of line length, auto speed, or transit use and do not appear to be likely candidates for rapid transit. Attainment of bus diversion to terminal stations on the scale of Atlanta is unlikely because their prospective travel volumes drop off more sharply with distance from the CBD. If one assumes that the travel volume estimates could be raised 40 percent with large-scale bus diversions to rail terminals, only

Milwaukee and Minneapolis begin to exceed the threshold for an above-ground rapid transit line; any tunneling downtown would have to be on a small scale or require relaxing the capital investment criterion.

LIGHT RAIL

The 24 urban areas selected for *light rail* analysis are all those discussed previously in Chapter 3 with the exception of Washington, Los Angeles, Baltimore, Miami, and Atlanta, which are committed to rapid transit. The data are presented in Exhibits 4.6 and 4.10 analogously to that for rapid transit, with the exception that two distinct sets of assumptions are made concerning access to stations: with and without feeder modes, as shown in Exhibit 4.2. The median access distance for feeder modes to light rail is the same as to rapid transit, and may equally understate the maximum possible diversion of bus trips. Still, the difference in relying primarily on pedestrian access compared to predominant access by feeder modes illustrates the importance of a restructured bus system and of park and ride facilities.

Drawn horizontally across the graphs in Exhibit 4.6 are dashed lines representing the light rail threshold volumes defined earlier in Chapter 2 as follows:

LR 1: *A very low-capital light rail line near grade* with 4,000 weekday passenger-miles or 5 million annual place-miles per line-mile is in scale with prevailing minimum service frequency, allows a construction expenditure of $5 million a mile in 1977 prices, offers minor labor savings compared to local buses, but offers no energy savings and no savings in land compared to a local arterial street. Its major justification would have to be in terms of travel speed and convenience.

LR 2: *A light rail line with considerable grade-separation but no tunnels* with 7,200 weekday passenger-miles or 9 million annual place-miles per line-mile allows a construction expenditure of $9 million a mile in 1977 prices, begins to offer labor savings compared to buses operating at the same speed, uses land during the peak period more efficiently than a local arterial, and begins to offer energy savings.

LR 3: *A light rail line with 1/5 of the route in tunnel* with 13,600 weekday passenger-miles or 16 million annual place-miles per line-mile allows a construction expenditure of $17 million a mile in 1977 prices, offers labor savings compared to buses operating at the same speed, energy savings compared to modes previously used, and uses land during the peak period more efficiently than a freeway lane.

The 24 urban areas examined fall into four distinct groups with respect to reaching these light rail threshold volumes.

Seattle, Detroit, Honolulu, Houston, Dallas, St. Louis, Pittsburgh, and *Milwaukee,* roughly in that order, exceed the high threshhold volume necessary to support a light rail line built to high standards with 1/5 in tunnel for distances of 9 miles (14.5 km) and usually more; only in Milwaukee is a somewhat shorter line indicated. However, only in Seattle, Detroit, Honolulu, Houston, and possibly Dallas can such lines be supported predominantly by walk-in traffic and still meet this criterion, usually for a shorter line distance. In the other cities, a greater level of integration with feeder systems must be assumed. Among these cities, only Detroit and Pittsburgh were committed to light rail in 1980; both projects do include tunnels.

Minneapolis–St. Paul, Buffalo, San Diego, Indianapolis, Portland, Louisville,

Exhibit 4.6
Light Rail Travel to the CBD by Corridor Compared to Threshold Levels
24 Urban Areas

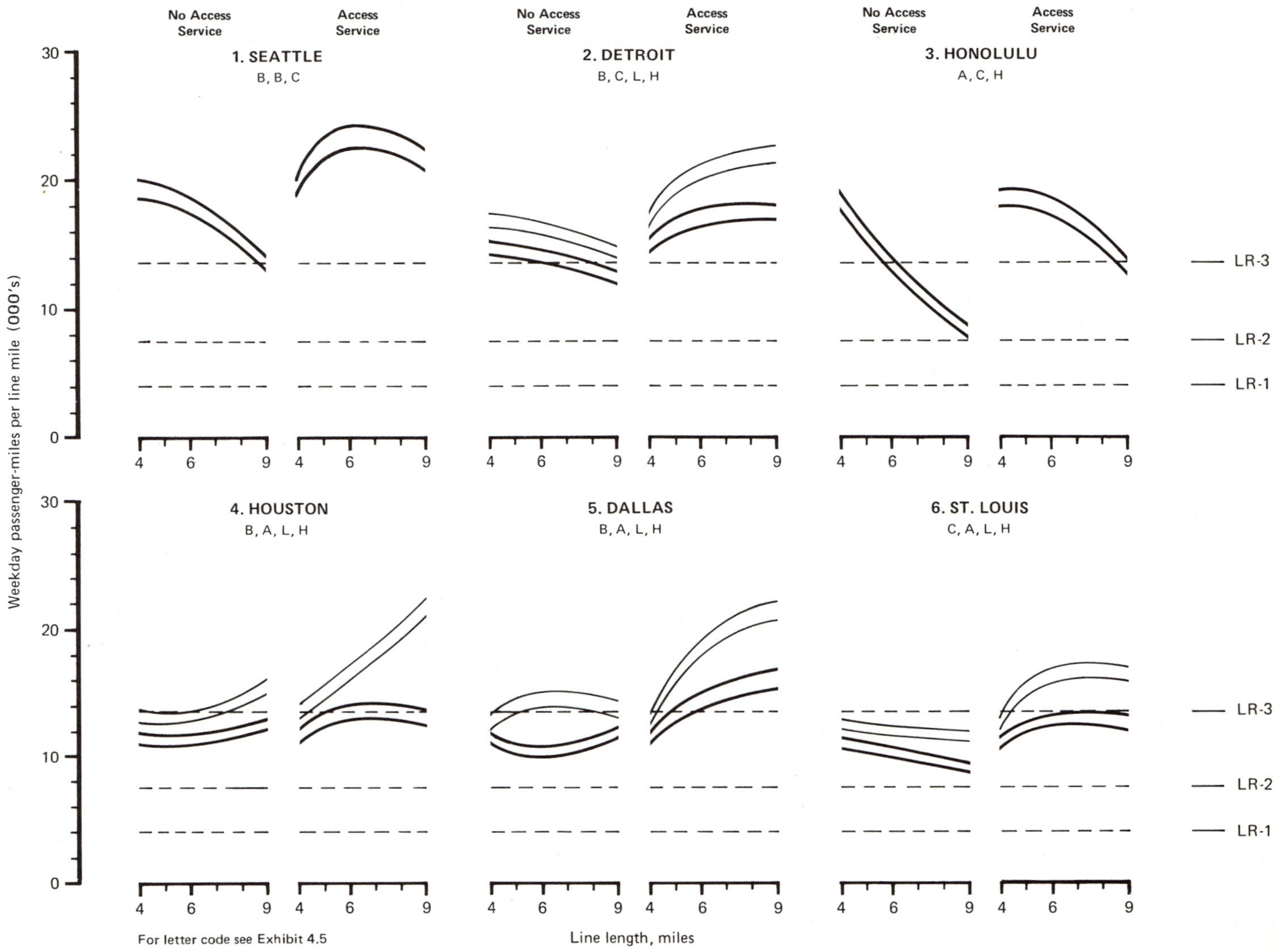

No Access Service | Access Service

1. SEATTLE
B, B, C

2. DETROIT
B, C, L, H

3. HONOLULU
A, C, H

4. HOUSTON
B, A, L, H

5. DALLAS
B, A, L, H

6. ST. LOUIS
C, A, L, H

Weekday passenger-miles per line mile (000's)

0 10 20 30

LR-3
LR-2
LR-1

4 6 9

Line length, miles

For letter code see Exhibit 4.5

Note: Heavy curves represent more probable case

Exhibit 4.6 (cont'd.)
Light Rail Travel to the CBD by Corridor Compared to Threshold Levels
24 Urban Areas

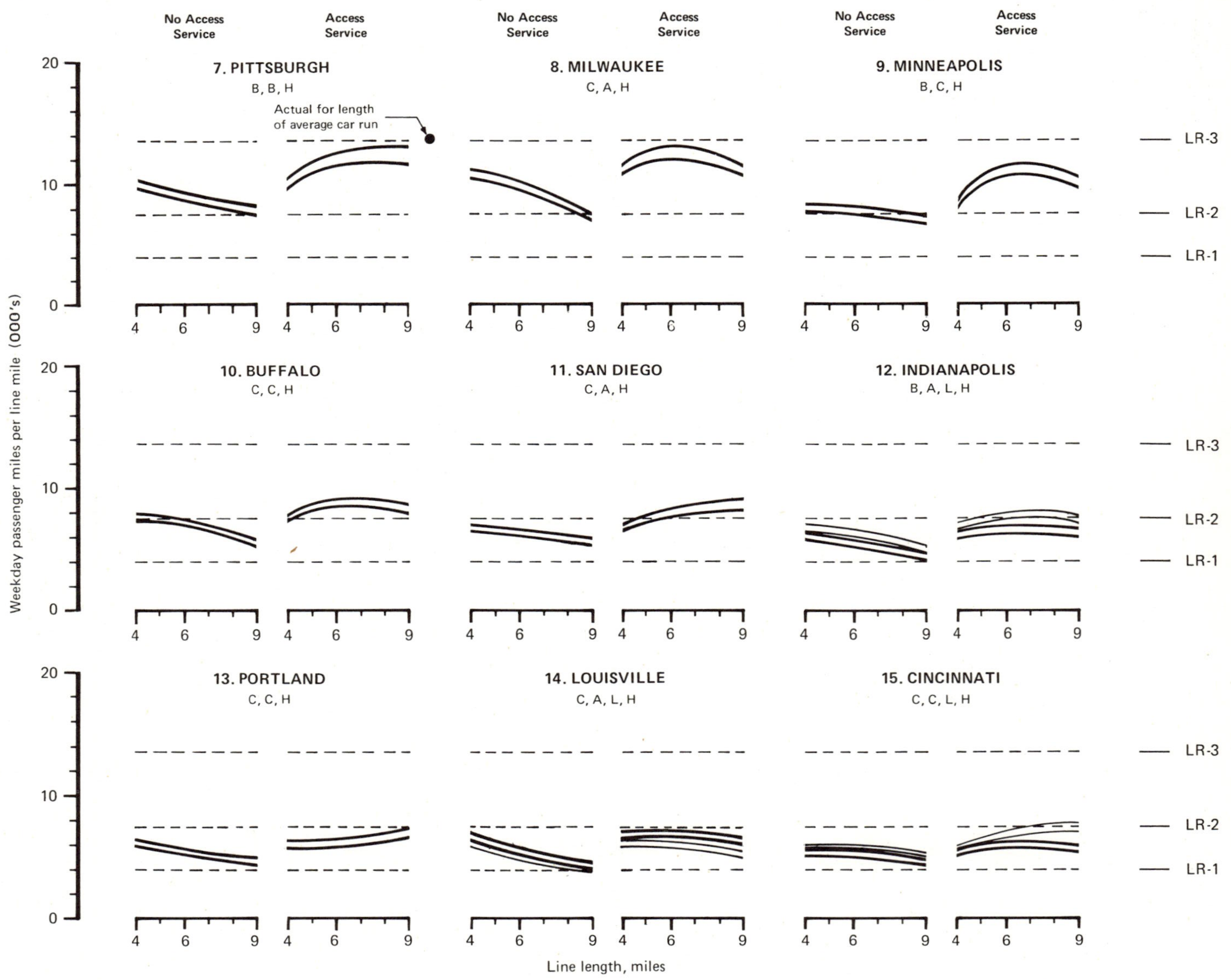

No Access Service
Access Service
No Access Service
Access Service
No Access Service
Access Service
7. PITTSBURGH
B, B, H
Actual for length of average car run
8. MILWAUKEE
C, A, H
9. MINNEAPOLIS
B, C, H
10. BUFFALO
C, C, H
11. SAN DIEGO
C, A, H
12. INDIANAPOLIS
B, A, L, H
13. PORTLAND
C, C, H
14. LOUISVILLE
C, A, L, H
15. CINCINNATI
C, C, L, H
LR-3
LR-2
LR-1
20
10
0
4
6
9
Weekday passenger miles per line mile (000's)
Line length, miles

Exhibit 4.6 (cont'd.)
Light Rail Travel to the CBD by Corridor to Threshold Levels
24 Urban Areas

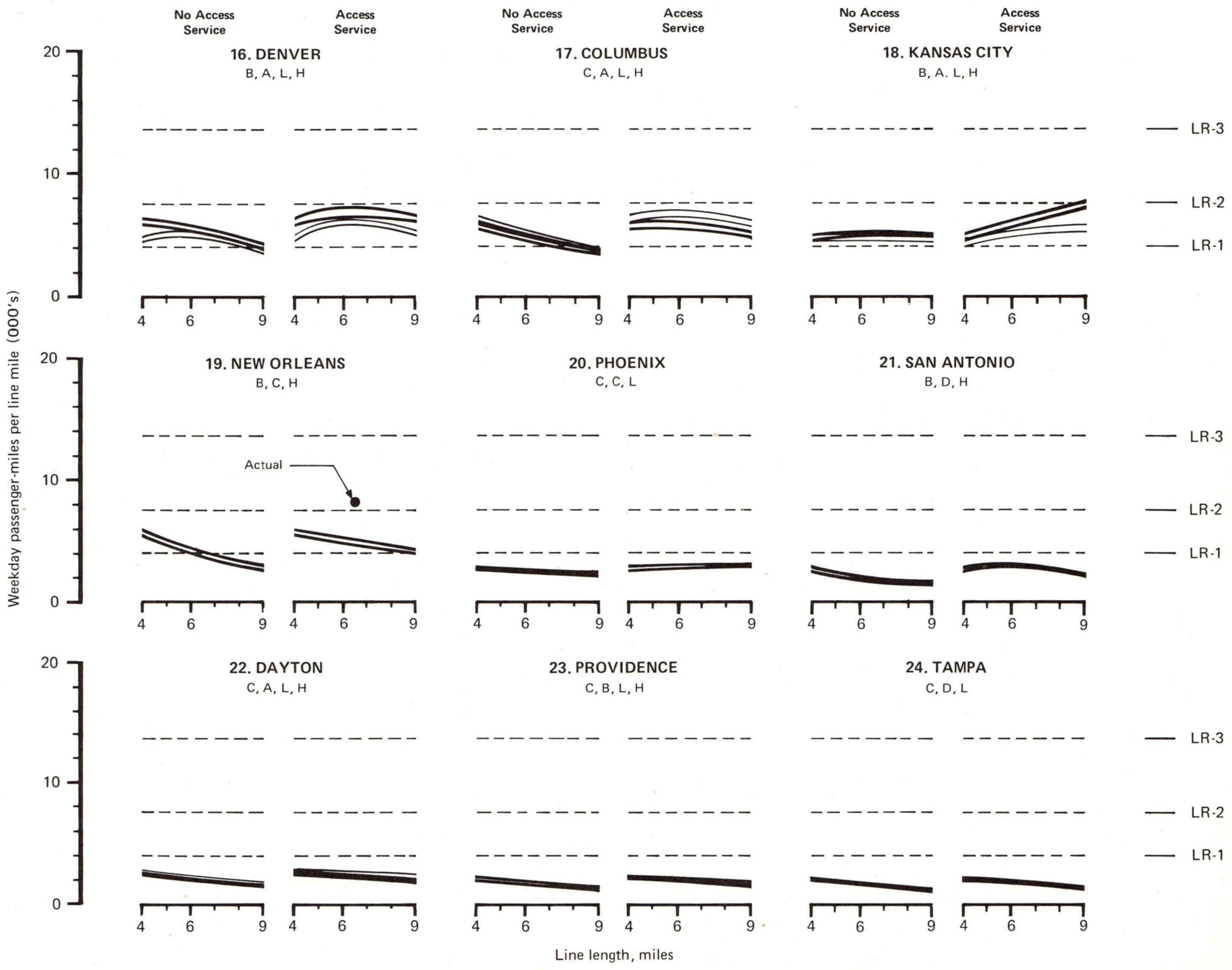

Cincinnati, and possibly *Denver* exceed the middle threshold volume necessary to support light rail lines with considerable grade-separation, but no tunnels. Except for Minneapolis–St. Paul and perhaps Buffalo, such lines cannot be supported with walk-in traffic and must assume a larger integration with feeder services.

Among these cities, Buffalo, Portland, and San Diego had light rail systems under construction or committed in 1980. The Buffalo system includes 6.4 miles (10.3 km) of tunnel, which is certainly much more than its anticipated travel volume can support, given the criteria advanced here. The tunnel option was chosen in Buffalo in preference to an elevated structure as a result of strong community pressure. Politically, the choice was an expensive line—or no line at all, because the densest corridor lacked other suitable right-of-way.

Portland's Banfield Corridor project does not include any underground construction, and is in scale with the criteria. The slope of the travel volume curve with feeder services indicates that to attain maximum travel volume a light rail line in Portland would have to be more than 9 miles (14.5 km) long; in fact, a 14.4-mile (23 km) line is under design. Because of the difference in length, travel estimates presented here for Portland are not directly comparable to those developed locally; still, the local projection is 1.9 times greater than that shown here. As in Atlanta, extensive bus diversion and the inclusion of non-CBD oriented trips account for much of the difference. The San Diego project—fully funded from local sources—is more modest than would be allowed by the criteria here. Strict comparability, again, is difficult, because Exhibit 4.6 merely suggests a line more than 9 miles (14.5 km) long; the actual line is 15.9 miles (25.6 km), with a somewhat shorter second leg envisaged. Lastly, Denver is planning a 15.8-mile (25.4 km) light rail line on an existing right-of-way. This would be in scale with the criteria advanced, while Denver's earlier proposal for full-scale rapid transit, rejected by UMTA, would definitely not.

Columbus, Kansas City, and *New Orleans* have estimated travel volumes which exceed the lowest light rail threshold but do not quite—except for Kansas City under the assumption of high transit use—reach the middle threshold. The lowest threshold does not provide a strong justification for building light rail unless exceptional local right-of-way opportunities for high-speed service or other special circumstances exist. Among these cities, New Orleans has a surviving streetcar line in a landscaped median on St. Charles Avenue; its passenger volume per line-mile is 1.8 times greater than that estimated here for a comparable length of the line and of the average trip, mostly because of non-CBD oriented trips and of the very high transit riding habit in New Orleans.

Lastly, *Phoenix, San Antonio, Dayton, Providence,* and *Tampa–St. Petersburg* have estimated travel volumes which fall below the lowest light rail threshold. Even doubling these volumes provides little justification for light rail.

The possibility of more than one line is not evaluated for light rail by city. Generally speaking, if travel through the CBD adds 10 to 20 percent to the CBD-oriented travel alone (which is the only travel shown for the different cities) and if the first leg just meets a threshold volume, then a second leg on the opposite side of the CBD needs only 82 to 67 percent of the first leg's traffic for both legs combined to meet the threshold volume. Origin-destination data for transit trips in 15 urban areas indicate that the higher percentage, which assumes 10 percent of through traffic, is exceeded by the second corridor in 60 percent of the cases; the lower percentage, which assumes extensive through traffic (20 percent), is exceeded in 80 percent of the cases. On the average, adding through traffic, the second corridor is likely to meet the criteria in about 70 percent of the cases, the third, in 30 percent of the cases, and the fourth, in 15 percent of the cases, *if* the first corridor just meets the criteria. If it exceeds the criteria, the probability of more than one line becomes accordingly greater. Of course, especially in the case of *light rail*, the probability of several lines is conjectural in the absence of site-specific data because it depends so much on the location of existing rights-of-way.

The possibility of branches feeding one entry point into the CBD is another issue worth mentioning in the context of light rail. In the analytical framework used here, a branch adds to the tributary area within "rail territory," where mode choice relationships different from those in the "nonrail territory" apply. Thus, a corridor ring with two branches will appear to have roughly twice the passenger volume of that with one branch, if a similar residential area is traversed. In real life, this effect will be moderated because the undefined outer tributary areas of the two lines—those beyond the median access distance—will tend to overlap, even if the diamonds shown in Exhibit 4.2 do not. Therefore, the actual travel produced by two lines will be less than twice that produced by one line, especially if feeder modes are heavily relied upon. Generally, the attractiveness of a branch increases the less its tributary area is competitive with that of the other branch for topographic reasons or otherwise.

All of these issues are a proper subject for site-specific alternatives analysis. For the purposes here, Exhibits 4.5 and 4.6 have singled out the most likely candidate cities for rapid transit and light rail, worthy of such an analysis, and indicated the approximate extent of possible "starter lines."

The findings are limited to the 29 urban areas studied. Based purely on population (the more relevant downtown floorspace data are not systematically available) there are at least 20 urban areas in the United States that are smaller than most considered so far, but larger than Honolulu, Edmonton, and Fort Worth, the first of which is deemed here capable of supporting rapid transit, the second of which is developing a light rail network with a 2-mile (3.2 km) tunnel downtown, and the third of which has a one-mile streetcar subway that acts as a downtown peoplemover. These 20 "in-between" cities range from San Juan, Norfolk, Memphis, Sacramento, and Rochester through Hartford and Albany to Richmond and Nashville. Insofar as they have large Central Business Districts and conveniently located rights-of-way, it is possible that additional candidates for light rail among them could be found.

PEOPLEMOVERS IN DOWNTOWNS

To examine whether a peoplemover is a reasonable means to meet the circulation needs in a downtown, assumed travel volumes by downtown size developed in a companion study[4] are compared to the threshold criteria defined in Chapter 2. The comparisons are shown in Exhibit 4.7.

Three illustrative sets of assumptions about the travel markets served by the peoplemover are pursued here. Option A assumes that only internal CBD trips are diverted. Option B includes the internal trips and adds some diversion from about one-quarter of all auto users and one-quarter of all transit users assumed to arrive at the downtown fringe. Option C includes the internal trips, adds some diversion from among one-quarter of all auto users assumed to arrive at the downtown fringe, and some from among all the transit users who are assumed to arrive at the downtown center. In essence, option A describes a minimum condition; option B describes close to the maximum condition for a downtown typically served by buses; option C describes close to the maximum condition for a downtown with rapid transit, or with buses that are not short-turned to feed the DPM.

As indicated in Chapter 3, potential DPM travel is influenced by the areal extent of a downtown and by the distribution of activities within it. To illustrate this, two CBD land areas are chosen: 1 square mile (2.59 km^2) and 1.5 square miles (3.89 km^2). Within each of these areas, two distributions of floorspace are assumed: a spread one, following the lower curve in Exhibit 3.14, and a concentrated one, following the upper curve. Total nonresidential floorspace in the CBD is taken to range from 10 to 100 million square feet (0.929 to 9.29 million m^2). It should be noted that downtowns with more than 50 million square feet (4.65 million m^2) are generally not confined to a square mile; however, over 160 million square feet of nonresidential floorspace can be found in one square mile in Midtown Manhattan, and about four-fifths of that amount in a half square mile in lower Manhattan.

Travel estimates by CBD size for each of these four CBD types are shown for downtown peoplemovers assumed to serve the travel markets defined as options A, B, and C. These travel estimates vary depending on the peoplemover configuration, such as line length and the number of stations. For each combination of CBD land area and floorspace distribution, only the option which produced the highest travel volume of the configuration tested is shown. This is indicated at the bottom of each graph in Exhibit 4.7 for each of the three travel market assumptions.

Drawn horizontally across the graphs in Exhibit 4.7 are dashed lines representing the downtown peoplemover threshold volumes defined here, following the discussion in Chapter 2, as follows:

DPM 1: *A low-capital peoplemover guideway** with about 5,000 weekday passenger-miles, or 6 million annual place-miles per line-mile, allows a construction expenditure of roughly $6 million a mile in 1977 prices using the "median" investment level; its passenger volume is comparable to that of existing systems such as Morgantown and Airtrans; it can begin to attain labor savings compared to downtown buses operating at 6 mph (9.6 km/h) if it is about 3 miles (4.8 km) long or longer; it can begin to use land during peak periods more efficiently than a local arterial; it will not save any energy directly in a downtown setting.

DPM 2: *A peoplemover guideway for the currently prevalent rubber-tired vehicles* with about 12,000 weekday passenger-miles, or 14 million annual place-miles per line-mile, allows a construction expenditure of $15 million a mile in 1977 prices using the "median" investment level; it begins to attain labor savings compared to local buses operating at the same speed if it is about 3 miles (4.8 km) long or longer, or compared to downtown buses at 6 mph (9.6 km/h) if it is shorter; it uses land

*Such guideways were not in operation in the United States as of 1980; examples of relevant technologies are the German Cabintaxi system and the "Project 21" two-in-one guideway, using steel-wheeled vehicles moving in two directions on one steel beam with a triangular cross-section. The latter guideway is designed for a manned rather than an automated system, but is adaptable to automation, if needed.

Exhibit 4.7
Peoplemover Travel and Threshold Levels as a Function of CBD Characteristics and System Configuration

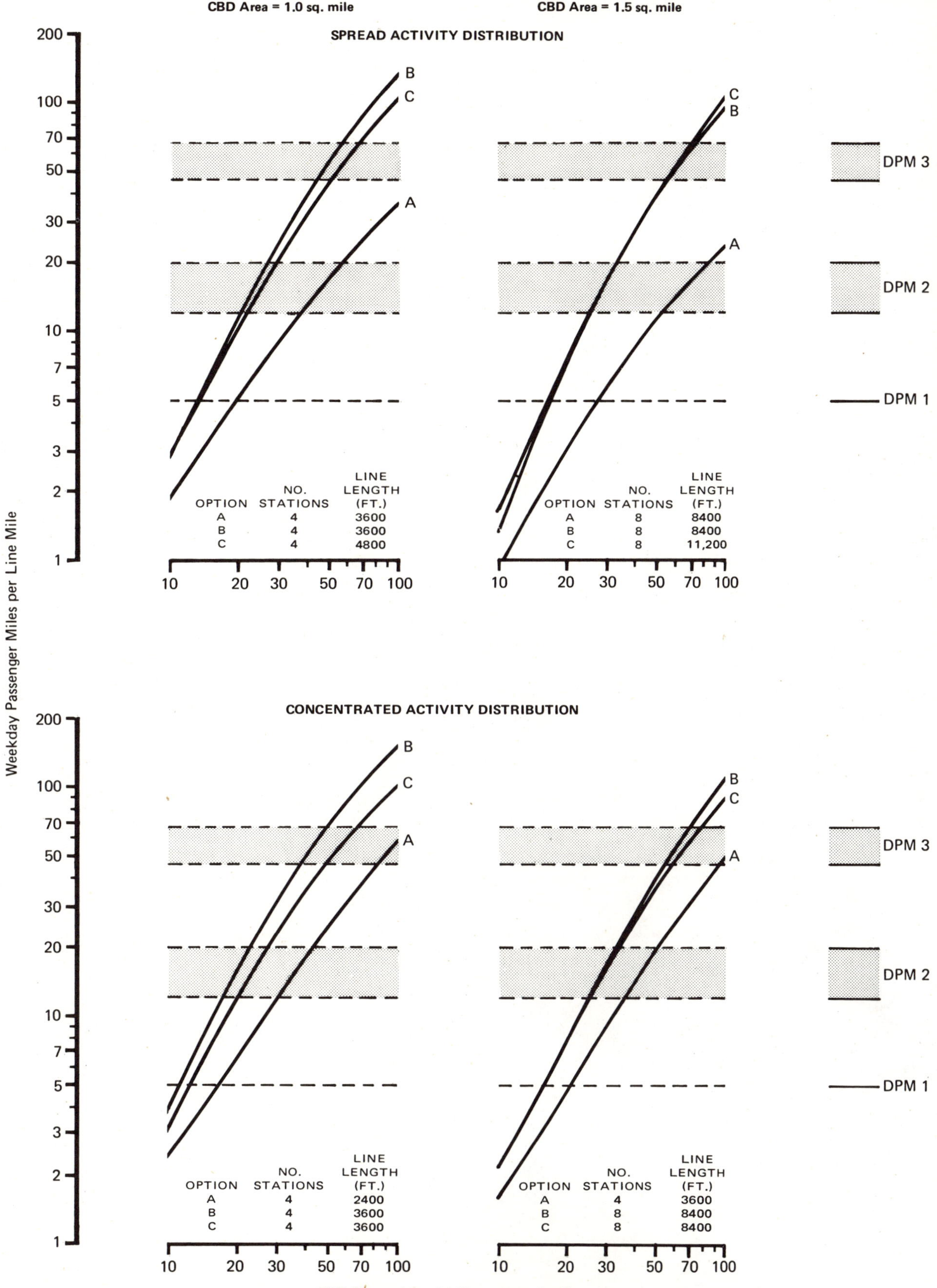

The German Cabintaxi—the first bona-fide "personal rapid transit" (PRT) system, operating automobile-sized vehicles on a single beam automatically. Note that vehicles in the configuration shown can only operate in discrete loops. *(Cabintaxi)*

during the peak period more efficiently than a local arterial; it will not save any energy directly in a downtown setting. The $15 million a mile in 1977 dollars price tag used in Chapter 2 to calculate construction energy is optimistic, assuming as it does that one-quarter of the DPM is at grade and ignoring expenditures for utility relocation and the adaptation of existing buildings which are likely in a downtown. The cost per mile could easily be some 60 percent greater. The passenger volume shown for the middle criterion is therefore indicated as a range between 12,000 and 20,000 weekday passenger-miles per mile of line.

DPM 3: *A peoplemover guideway described under DPM 2 generally above ground in a downtown setting will begin to offer direct energy savings* at volumes in excess of 46,000 weekday passenger-miles or 55 million annual place-miles per line-mile, if no snowmelting is required. *If the guideway is in tunnel* the energy saving threshold rises to 67,000 weekday passenger-miles or 80 million annual place-miles per line-mile; it rises *above that level,* if the guideway is in the open air and requires *snowmelting.* The range of these volumes is indicated in Exhibit 4.7.

It is clear from this array of threshold volumes that those required to attain energy savings are virtually an order of magnitude above the others. At such high volumes, peoplemovers of current design may encounter capacity constraints. For example, if one assumes that a 15-second headway can be sustained for an entire hour, that peak hour one-directional load for internal downtown travel is one-fifth of the daily load, and that spatially the load distribution is even, then the maximum daily capacity of a Morgantown-type system is about 46,000 passenger-miles per line-mile, the same as the minimum threshold required for energy savings in a downtown setting. For higher volumes, shorter headways or systems with entraining capability are needed.

Recognizing the limited scale of DPM energy consumption compared to all urban travel and the indirect savings in energy inherent in downtown development compared to "spread city" locations, the energy-saving requirement for downtown peoplemovers can reasonably be waived.

Based on the estimates in Exhibit 4.7, the *middle threshold* volume of 12,000 *daily passenger-miles per line-mile can only be reached in downtowns with more than about 30 to 50 million square feet of nonresidential floorspace, (2.8 to 4.6 million m²) if the DPM market is limited to internal trips.* The threshold volume of 20,000 passenger-miles per line-mile, which assumes higher construction costs, can only be reached in downtowns with more than 40 to 80 million square feet (3.7 to 7.4 million m²). This limits peoplemovers relying on internal travel to the largest downtowns.

If maximum practical diversion from autos and buses intercepted at the downtown fringe is included, the feasibility threshold drops at the lowest to between *18 and 30 million square feet* (1.7 to 2.8 million m²) *in concentrated downtowns,* and about *25 to 35 million square feet* (2.3 to 3.2 million m²) *in downtowns with a spread activity distribution.* The inclusion of a portion of regional trips expands the DPM market to cover a number of middle-sized downtowns.

Lastly, if the cost of building automated guideways were brought down sharply by the use of *lightweight single-beam guideways* exemplified by the German Cabintaxi system or the "Project 21" two-in-one guideway, the market for peoplemovers would expand to cover a *large number of downtowns that have between 10 and 15 million square feet* (0.93 to 1.4 million m²) of nonresidential floorspace.

At the volumes attainable in such downtowns automated systems can produce labor savings compared to local buses if the line is relatively long, suggesting some line-haul functions, and not just internal distribution functions, for this technology.

In 1977, as many as 19 cities were giving some consideration to downtown peoplemovers.[5] Of these, only Lower Manhattan and Los Angeles meet all the criteria, including energy savings. Houston, Dallas, Detroit, Cleveland, Atlanta, Seattle, and Baltimore stay above the middle criteria related to construction cost only if substantial numbers of regional travelers are directed to the DPM. For Miami, St. Louis, and Indianapolis, downtown peoplemovers may be problematic even with the diversion of regional trips. Miami, one might note, designed its DPM as the main feeder to regional rapid transit, which has only one station near downtown. The other downtowns, namely St. Paul, Jacksonville, Sacramento, Memphis, and Norfolk, not to speak of Anaheim, California and Bellevue, Washington, fall below the middle criteria under any conditions. A number of them, however, could reasonably be served by lightweight single-beam guideways.

By 1981 the Miami DPM went ahead but most other plans were shelved for a variety of reasons, the cost of building heavy guideways for the present generation of hardware and the visual bulk of the structures being not least. It should be recalled from Chapter 2 that the median capital expenditure to which the middle criteria in Exhibit 4.7 are scaled translates into 18¢ per passenger-mile in constant dollars if a 45-year amortization period and a 3 percent interest rate are used. While most of this cost on a line-haul rail line can be covered by savings of energy, labor, and parking charges, not even including savings in time, on a DPM system there are no savings in energy, savings in parking costs are reduced because of the smaller proportion of former auto users, and savings in time cannot be overwhelming at an operating speed of 10 mph (16 km/h). Therefore, it can be legitimately argued that levels of investment appropriate for line-haul systems are too high for a DPM. This reinforces the case for low-cost, single-beam guideway technologies and for expanding the function of the systems to include line-haul travel.

THE PROSPECT FOR URBAN RAIL

In view of the long chains of assumptions needed to produce the travel estimates and the threshold volumes shown here, the figures presented are conditional, and the exact values should not be taken too literally. What is important is the *relative scale* of the estimates, and the *general ranking* of the urban areas with respect to their prospect for fixed guideway transit.

The estimates of rapid transit and light rail travel clearly are very conservative. On the other hand, the labor and the energy savings estimates may be liberal, approaching as they do the best existing, rather than average, practice. While no other assumption would be proper for planning new systems, to ensure against any slippage in labor and energy efficiency the patronage estimates are deliberately left low.

It is also clear that site-specific conditions are a matter for local alternatives analysis and cannot be given justice in a macro-study at the national scale. Locally available alignments for light rail may not, in fact, reach the highest density corridor; local travel estimates, local types of construction, and local costs will always be different from the average values shown here. The importance of the data presented is that they are prepared in a *standardized and consistent manner,* enabling *comparisons between cities* that hold as many variables as possible constant.

The results indicate that, given extant commitments, there are only four urban areas left in the United States that are *strong candidates for rapid transit:* these are *Los Angeles, Seattle, Honolulu,* and *Houston.* A more tentative case can be made for Dallas. (The potential for rapid transit in San Juan was not evaluated.) We need not fear that there will be a "bottomless pit" of rapid transit construction or "little BART's" proliferating all over the country.

The results also indicate that *serious candidates for light rail construction are more numerous.* To begin with, they include the potential rapid transit cities of Seattle, Honolulu, and Houston. Whether rapid transit or light rail is more appropriate in these cities is for local analyses to determine.

Given extant commitments to light rail, *Dallas, St. Louis,* and *Milwaukee* appear to be *candidates for light rail lines built to high standards, with some mileage in tunnel.*

Minneapolis, Indianapolis, Louisville, and *Cincinnati, with the possible addition of Denver, Columbus,* and *Kansas City,* appear to be *candidates for light rail lines without any tunneling,* but with considerable grade-separation near the surface. This adds 10 potential light rail cities to the four potential rapid transit cities. It is possible that in the next tier of 20 cities below the 29 evaluated here, additional candidates for light rail can be found. The 20 include Sacramento, Rochester, and Hartford, which have been considering light rail; their prospects are not evaluated here.

The results can also be compared to recent decisions about rail transit made on the basis of local analyses in a number of cities. In Washington, the full 101-mile system under construction appears to conform to the criteria advanced, though a somewhat shorter system would attain higher passenger use per mile of line. Atlanta and Baltimore, while generally conforming to the criteria advanced, are flagged as relatively high-capital-cost systems, while Miami's low-cost above-ground construction is in scale with the criteria.

With respect to recent light rail decisions, Detroit and Pittsburgh are found to warrant some tunnel construction on which they in fact are embarking, while Buffalo's extensive tunneling is not in scale with the travel volume anticipated. The proposed above-ground system in Portland is found to be in scale with the criteria advanced, while San Diego built a line more frugal than the criteria would require.

The decision to forego a high-capital system in Denver is supported by the analysis, as is the decision not to proceed with light rail in Dayton. Still, Denver is found to be a possible candidate for low-capital light rail transit, and a more substantial light rail system is found to be possible in St. Louis, even though a local alternatives analysis decided against it for the near future.

Another possible comparison is, if city A were found to warrant rail transit, what about cities B, C, and D, which have the same or higher potential passenger volumes per mile of line? Viewed this way, the data suggest that if Atlanta, Miami, and Baltimore can support rapid transit, then so could Pittsburgh (which opted for light rail), possibly Dallas, Detroit (which opted for light rail), Houston, Honolulu, Seattle, and Los Angeles, in ascending order.

Similarly, if Portland can support light rail, then so should Louisville, Indianapolis, San Diego (which in fact built a line), Buffalo (with a line under construction), Minneapolis, Pittsburgh (with downtown tunnel extensions to existing lines under construction), Milwaukee, St. Louis, and Dallas, in ascending order.

The precise ranking of the various cities is subject to error, in view of the varying quality of the underlying data noted in Exhibits 4.5 and 4.6. However, the major weaknesses of the data are in the smaller urban areas, which do not appear as candidates for either rapid transit or light rail. The real differences between actual and estimated prospect for rail transit will arise from right-of-way availability, which can only be determined by site-specific local studies.

Given the prospects for rapid transit and light rail in cities presently without them, the next question is: how do these needs compare with the additional needs of the *existing rail cities*?

The prospect for extensions to existing systems is very site-specific and would require much more detailed calculations than those performed here for new systems. For a *short-cut assessment,* one can look at the number of daily passengers boarding at terminal stations, listed in Table A-8 in the Appendix. To the extent that number (doubled to include returning passengers) exceeds the threshold criteria for rapid transit, extension would seem indicated. Of course, this method cannot estimate the length of the extension, or the prospect for lines originating other than at outer terminals. Also, the assessment differs from that for new systems because station passenger counts include all trips, and not just those to the Central Business District.

In *Cleveland* existing rapid transit volumes at terminal stations are low and do not indicate any need for extensions; however, a separate calculation suggests that the northeasterly corridor from downtown Cleveland could have enough volume to support a tunnel for a distance of nearly 5 miles (8 km), which conforms to past local proposals; with the resulting realignment of the existing system, which lacks adequate downtown access, an additional 7-mile (11 km) northeasterly extension would appear to meet the threshold volume for an above-ground rapid transit line.

In the *San Francisco Bay Area,* existing volumes at the Concord, Fremont, and Richmond terminals are low, and do not indicate the need for extensions in the near future; however, the volume at the southern Daly City terminus exceeds the criteria for an above-ground rapid transit line, indicating that an extension into San Mateo County, part of the original BART design, should receive priority consideration.

In *Boston,* the volume at the Harvard Square station exceeds the criteria for a rapid transit line in tunnel and in fact a tunnel extension from Harvard Square to Alewife is under construction. Its further extension above ground would also seem warranted. The volume on the new South Braintree line is in scale with the criteria for an above ground line but indicates no further extensions, nor do the volumes at the northern ends of the Blue and the Orange lines. The volume at the Ashmont terminal, which connects to a light rail line, exceeds only slightly the threshold for above-ground rapid transit. However, that at the southern end of the Orange line at Forest Hills exceeds this threshold by a wide margin, suggesting that after relocation of the line is completed, further extension would deserve priority consideration.

In *Philadelphia,* the high volume at the 69th Street terminal reflects extensive light rail feeder services, while that at the recently completed southerly extension of the Broad Street line is low. However, the volumes at the northern ends of the Broad Street, and especially the Frankford Street line, are very high, substantially exceeding the criteria for underground rapid transit. A new subway in this general area (planned for many years under Roosevelt Boulevard to North Philadelphia) would appear to be well within the criteria advanced. The volumes at the various stations of the Lindenwold line cannot give any clue to the feasibility of the two proposed branches; each of these would have to attain two-thirds the present volume on the main line to meet the lowest, above-ground rapid transit threshold. At Lindenwold itself, the present station volume is not high enough to indicate further extension.

In *Chicago*, station volumes at most line terminals are low and only two of them indicate that extensions are justified. One is the Jefferson Park terminal, which exceeds the middle criterion for a rapid transit line predominantly above ground. The O'Hare Airport extension—with only a short section in tunnel—is in fact being built there. The other is the southern terminal of the Dan Ryan line at 95th Street, which exceeds the criteria for a rapid transit line in tunnel, having a large bus-oriented tributary area to the south and southwest. Apart from a southward extension, this indicates the general need for rapid transit in the Southwest corridor in Chicago, the only one lacking such service. Beyond service extensions, the dominant need in Chicago—rehabilitation of existing lines and stations aside—is the replacement of elevated lines. Two major steps toward that goal, the Franklin and Monroe Street subways in the downtown area, totalling about 6 miles (10 km), have been deferred.

In *New York*, the highest terminal station volumes are found in *Queens*, at the ends of the Flushing and Hillside Avenue lines; they exceed the minimum criteria for rapid transit in tunnel by two to three times. They are indicative of the general need for a large-scale Queens transit expansion program, under study since the 1960s, parts of which include the 63rd Street tunnel and Archer Avenue subway, under construction for a decade. The remaining parts, however, have been deferred. In *Brooklyn*, heavy station volumes at the Utica, Flatbush, and Kings Highway stations indicate continued need for a Southeast Brooklyn line in the direction of the Gateway National Recreation area. In *The Bronx*, terminal station volumes are below any criteria for rapid transit, reflecting excessively long travel times and the need for a basic restructuring of the Bronx system, which requires completing the Second Avenue subway and removing several elevated lines. Aside from being a tool for restructuring the Bronx system, the Second Avenue subway itself serves the purposes of relieving overcrowding, referred to earlier in Chapter 2, and providing improved access to the East Side of Manhattan.

Large needs for the rehabilitation of existing lines and stations aside, a pending need in New York, just as in Chicago, continues to be the removal of elevated lines. The detrimental effect of their noise, among others, is increasingly being recognized. An exploratory investigation, which did not rank the various projects by potential passenger volume,[6] indicated the need for 74.2 miles (119.4 km) of new line in New York City, which would be partly balanced by the removal of nearly half of the remaining elevated lines, or 30.4 miles (49 km) for a net addition of 19 percent to the existing system.

In *New Jersey*, the PATH station volumes at Newark and Journal Square exceed the middle criterion for rapid transit partially in tunnel, suggesting the continued reasonableness of at least two rapid transit extensions in Essex, Hudson, and neighboring counties.

The set of maps of urban rail networks presented after the end of this chapter shows the inventory of existing lines, lines under construction, and proposed lines as of the end of 1980 in twelve urban areas in North America. The proposals reflect local plans: not all of them meet the criteria advanced here, as can be seen by referring from the maps to the discussion above. The maps, drawn at an identical scale, also make it possible to compare the size of other proposals—not shown here in map form—to that of existing networks.

It is difficult to give a close estimate of the *total national rapid transit and light rail mileage that could be built to meet the criteria advanced here.* Analysis in this book is focused on one corridor per city; the number of corridors that could warrant rail is less firm. In the "old" rail cities, only the number of potential extensions that can be deduced from terminal station volumes is a hard figure. The length of these lines and possible other routes are less firm.

Beginning with the hard figures, the four rapid transit starter lines in Los Angeles, Seattle, Honolulu, and Houston, assuming one corridor per city, would total 50 miles (80 km). The 10 light rail starter lines, assuming one corridor per city, would total 90 miles (145 km). This would add only 7 percent to the national rapid transit mileage, but 42 percent to the national streetcar and light rail mileage.

In the five "old" rail regions outside New York, the 7 readily discernible extensions would total about 50 miles (80 km). For New York, an analogous goal might be completion of the Second Avenue subway (realigned to serve the central Bronx), construction of three lines in Queens and one in southeast Brooklyn, for a total length of 37 miles (60 km), or a net addition of 16 percent to the existing system. This is less than was envisaged in the "Grand Design" of the late 1960s, nor does it address the issue of elevated replacement. It would, however, provide relief to overcrowding, serve most of the presently unserved areas, and provide trunkline capacity for future realignments of the system within the cost-per-passenger-mile criteria advanced here.

Added to this must be prospective mileage conforming to the criteria in Washington, Atlanta, and Baltimore on which construction has not yet started, and which may total 55 miles (88 km) in 10 corridors. As for the prospective mileage in the "future" rail cities, beyond the four starter lines enumerated above, it will primarily depend on the ultimate size of the Los Angeles system. If one assumes that it may reach about 70 miles (113 km), the additional mileage in the cities with future rapid transit may be some 120 miles (193 km). These figures are summarized in the second and third columns of Exhibit 4.8. The fourth column adds possible mileage in northern and southern New Jersey, for which even a rough estimate is difficult without site-specific studies.

Altogether, one can estimate that there are about 40 urban corridors in the United States with sufficient volume to support new rapid transit lines of varying capital-intensity, and that these lines might total about 350 miles (560 km), representing roughly a 50 percent increment to the existing national system. Two-thirds of the corridors and about half the mileage are in cities with rapid transit in existence or under construction. For a clearer sense of priorities among the corridors, site-specific construction costs would be necessary, to array the corridors by cost per passenger-mile. Basically, rapid transit expansion can be seen as a program of

Exhibit 4.8

Approximate Estimate of Total Potential Rapid Transit and Light Rail Mileage in the United States Meeting Threshold Criteria

	Existing miles completed and under construction, 1980, from Exhibit 1.5 (rounded)	Potential miles meeting threshold criteria (Number of corridors shown in parentheses): Estimated for "starter lines" directly from Exhibits 4.5 and 4.6	Estimated indirectly based on number of potential corridors	Possible additional mileage, conjectural estimate	Total potential miles	Order of magnitude construction cost in 1977 $$ billions
RAPID TRANSIT	(1)	(2)	(3)	(4)	(5)	(6)
New York - Northern New Jersey Region	264	--	37 (5)	25 (2)*	62 (7)**	5.0**
Other "old" rail regions (Chicago, Philadelphia, Boston, San Francisco, Cleveland)	266	--	50 (7)	15 (2)*	65 (9)**	1.7**
"New" rail regions (Washington, Atlanta, Baltimore, Miami)	117	--	55 (10)	--	55 (10)	1.5
Future rail regions (Los Angeles, Seattle, Houston, Honolulu)	--	50 (4)	118 (10)	--	168 (14)	5.1
Total, Rapid Transit	**647**	**50 (4)**	**260 (32)**	**40 (4)**	**350 (40)**	**13.3**
LIGHT RAIL						
"Old" rail regions (mostly Philadelphia, Boston, San Francisco, Pittsburgh, Cleveland, Newark)	193	--	--	25	25	0.3
"New" rail regions (Buffalo, San Diego, Portland, Detroit)	22	--	--	50	50	0.6
Future rail regions (mostly Dallas, Milwaukee, St. Louis, Minneapolis, Indianapolis, Louisville, Cincinnati, Denver, Columbus, Kansas City)	--	90 (10)	--	155	245	3.0
Total, Light Rail	**215**	**90 (10)**	**--**	**230**	**320**	**3.9**
					Total, new lines (or $22 billion in 1980 dollars)	**$17.2 billion**

* In New Jersey

** Excludes replacement of elevated lines

Exhibit 4.9
Daily Rapid Transit Travel to the Central Business District Representative of First Corridor
Sixteen Urban Areas

Urban Area	CBD Floor Space (msf)	Transit Orientation (Bold-More Probable)	Auto Speed	5.5 MILE ROUTE One-way Trips 000's	5.5 MILE ROUTE Trip Length Miles	5.5 MILE ROUTE Passenger-Miles per Line-Mile 000's	9 MILE ROUTE One-way Trips 000's	9 MILE ROUTE Trip Length Miles	9 MILE ROUTE Passenger-Miles per Line-Mile 000's	15 MILE ROUTE One-way Trips 000's	15 MILE ROUTE Trip Length Miles	15 MILE ROUTE Passenger-Miles per Line-Mile 000's	SPECIFIC ROUTES	Line Length Miles	One-way Trips 000's	Trip Length Miles	Passenger-Miles per Line Mile 000's
1. Washington	100	**High**	Slow	24.2	3.48	30.6	31.6	4.58	32.2	37.2	5.78	28.7					
			Fast	23.0	3.41	28.5	29.6	4.45	29.3	34.5	5.61	25.8					
2. Los Angeles	80	**High**	Slow	15.4	3.90	21.8	24.1	5.58	29.9	32.5	7.44	32.2	Wilshire Corridor only	17	29	8.8	31
			Fast	14.6	3.83	20.3	22.3	5.31	26.3	29.8	7.31	29.0					
													Wilshire extended to Westwood & Van Nuys	28	39	10.5	30
													Harbor Freeway to Long Beach	27	25	10.7	20
													San Bernardino Freeway to El Monte	13	11	7.0	12
3. Seattle	40	**High**	Slow	19.4	3.67	25.9	23.3	4.64	24.0	27.9	5.78	21.5					
			Fast	18.2	3.58	23.7	22.1	4.37	21.5	25.6	5.56	19.0					
4. Honolulu	25	**High**	Slow	19.6	3.36	23.9	22.2	3.80	18.7	22.2	3.80	n/a					
			Fast	19.2	3.33	23.2	20.7	3.66	16.8	20.7	3.66	n/a					
5. Houston	70	**Low**	Slow	11.8	3.50	15.1	16.9	5.05	19.0	22.2	6.69	19.8					
			Fast	11.0	3.38	13.6	15.1	4.83	16.2	19.6	6.44	16.8					
		High	Slow	14.1	3.66	18.8	21.0	5.28	24.6	27.9	6.92	25.7					
			Fast	13.2	3.57	17.1	19.2	5.13	21.9	25.3	6.76	22.8					
6. Detroit	50	**Low**	Slow	15.8	3.31	19.0	20.4	4.41	20.0	24.0	5.72	18.3					
			Fast	14.9	3.21	17.4	18.7	4.23	17.6	21.7	5.47	15.8					
		High	Slow	16.9	3.62	22.2	22.9	4.81	24.5	27.9	6.13	22.8					
			Fast	16.0	3.57	20.8	21.2	4.67	22.0	25.6	6.09	20.8					
7. Dallas	70	**Low**	Slow	11.6	3.73	15.7	16.6	5.02	18.5	20.9	6.59	18.4					
			Fast	10.7	3.62	14.1	14.7	4.82	15.7	18.4	6.36	15.6					
		High	Slow	14.2	3.86	19.9	21.0	5.22	24.4	25.6	6.60	22.5					
			Fast	13.3	3.78	18.3	19.2	5.09	21.7	23.0	6.36	19.5					
8. Baltimore	40	**High**	Slow	17.1	3.38	21.0	20.1	4.04	18.0	21.1	4.44	12.5					
			Fast	16.3	3.30	19.6	19.2	3.96	16.9	19.8	4.27	11.3					
9. Miami	30	**High**	Slow	11.0	3.33	13.3	15.3	4.69	15.9	18.7	6.22	15.5					
			Fast	10.4	3.24	12.3	14.0	4.50	14.0	16.6	6.14	13.6					
10. St. Louis	40	**Low**	Slow	10.5	3.58	13.7	12.7	5.07	14.3	14.7	6.10	12.0					
			Fast	9.8	3.47	12.4	11.2	4.95	12.3	12.8	5.91	10.1					
		High	Slow	12.0	3.72	16.2	16.3	4.87	17.6	20.4	6.40	17.4					
			Fast	11.3	3.64	15.0	14.8	4.76	15.7	18.5	6.20	15.3					

11. Pittsburgh	40	**High**	Slow	9.2	3.98	13.3	12.0	5.13	13.7	15.3	6.24	12.7
			Fast	8.5	3.89	12.0	11.7	5.00	13.0	13.7	6.12	11.2
12. Atlanta	50	**High**	Slow	10.0	3.58	13.0	12.5	4.66	12.9	15.3	6.17	12.6
			Fast	9.5	3.47	12.0	11.3	4.42	11.1	13.7	5.89	10.8
13. Milwaukee	35	**High**	Slow	10.8	3.48	13.7	13.2	4.32	12.7	14.4	5.01	9.6
			Fast	10.1	3.38	12.4	12.2	4.16	11.3	13.2	4.81	8.5
14. Minneapolis-St. Paul	30	**High**	Slow	8.5	3.61	11.2	11.5	4.70	12.0	12.5	6.20	10.3
			Fast	7.9	3.37	9.7	10.6	4.46	10.5	12.1	5.57	9.0
15. Buffalo	27	**High**	Slow	7.7	3.26	9.1	9.9	4.26	9.4	10.8	5.02	7.2
			Fast	7.3	3.15	8.4	9.1	4.08	8.3	9.9	4.79	6.3
16. Denver	35	Low	Slow	5.4	3.43	6.7	6.4	4.10	5.8	6.7	4.40	3.9
			Fast	4.6	3.31	5.5	5.8	3.89	5.0	6.0	4.18	3.3
		High	Slow	6.0	3.66	8.0	7.4	4.25	7.0	7.7	4.54	4.7
			Fast	5.6	3.56	7.2	6.8	4.09	6.2	7.1	4.37	4.1

Exhibit 4.10
Daily Light Rail Travel to the Central Business District Representative of First Corridor
Twenty-four Urban Areas

				4 MILE ROUTE						6 MILE ROUTE						9 MILE ROUTE					
				Without Access			With Access			Without Access			With Access			Without Access			With Access		
Urban Area	CBD Floor Space (msf)	Transit Orientation (Bold-More Probable)	Auto Speed	One-way Trips 000's	Trip Length Miles	Passenger-Miles per Line-Mile 000's	One-way Trips 000's	Trip Length Miles	Passenger-Miles per Line-Mile 000's	One-way Trips 000's	Trip Length Miles	Passenger-Miles per Line-Mile 000's	One-way Trips 000's	Trip Length Miles	Passenger-Miles per Line-Mile 000's	One-way Trips 000's	Trip Length Miles	Passenger-Miles per Line-Mile 000's	One-way Trips 000's	Trip Length Miles	Passenger-Miles per Line-Mile 000's
1. Seattle	40	**High**	Slow	15.3	2.62	20.0	15.3	2.62	20.0	16.9	3.30	18.6	21.2	3.43	24.2	16.9	3.81	14.3	24.6	4.11	22.5
			Fast	14.3		18.7	14.3		18.7	15.8		17.4	19.7		22.5	15.7		13.3	22.8		20.8
2. Detroit	50	**Low**	Slow	12.2	2.50	15.3	12.2	2.50	15.3	13.8	3.17	14.6	16.2	3.27	17.7	15.0	3.89	13.0	11.6	4.16	18.1
			Fast	11.4		14.3	11.4		14.3	12.9		13.6	15.0		16.4	14.0		12.1	18.1		16.9
		High	Slow	13.4	2.59	17.4	13.4	2.59	17.4	15.0	3.33	16.7	18.5	3.43	21.2	16.1	4.16	14.9	23.0	4.43	22.6
			Fast	12.7		16.4	12.7		16.4	14.1		15.7	17.3		19.8	15.1		14.0	21.6		21.3
3. Honolulu	25	**High**	Slow	14.8	2.58	19.1	14.8	2.58	19.1	14.4	2.98	14.3	17.6	3.17	18.6	13.5	2.91	8.7	18.9	3.30	13.9
			Fast	13.8		17.8	13.8		17.8	13.3		13.2	16.3		17.2	12.5		8.1	17.4		12.8
4. Houston	70	**Low**	Slow	9.8	2.45	12.0	9.8	2.45	12.0	11.3	3.12	11.8	13.0	3.22	14.0	13.5	4.34	13.0	15.3	4.03	13.7
			Fast	9.0		11.0	9.0		11.0	10.5		10.9	12.0		12.9	12.6		12.2	14.0		12.5
		High	Slow	10.9	2.57	14.0	10.9	2.57	14.0	12.3	3.29	13.5	15.1	3.43	17.3	15.2	4.76	16.1	20.7	4.87	22.4
			Fast	10.1		13.0	10.1		13.0	11.6		12.7	14.0		16.0	14.2		15.0	19.3		20.9
5. Dallas	70	**Low**	Slow	8.7	2.73	11.9	8.7	2.73	11.9	10.6	2.99	10.6	12.5	3.64	15.2	12.2	4.53	12.3	16.3	4.66	16.9
			Fast	8.1		11.1	8.1		11.1	9.7		9.7	11.4		13.8	11.2		11.3	14.8		15.3
		High	Slow	9.5	2.77	13.2	9.5	2.77	13.2	12.0	3.79	15.2	15.1	3.80	19.1	13.4	4.84	14.4	20.2	4.96	22.3
			Fast	8.9		12.3	8.9		12.3	11.1		14.0	14.1		17.9	12.4		13.3	18.7		20.6
6. St. Louis	40	**Low**	Slow	8.7	2.62	11.4	8.7	2.62	11.4	9.9	3.22	10.6	11.7	3.40	13.3	11.7	3.65	9.5	14.1	4.24	13.3
			Fast	8.0		10.5	8.0		10.5	9.2		9.9	11.0		12.5	10.9		8.8	13.0		12.2
		High	Slow	9.6	2.71	13.0	9.6	2.71	13.0	10.7	3.48	12.4	14.3	3.54	16.9	12.5	4.30	11.9	17.5	4.40	17.1
			Fast	9.0		12.2	9.0		12.2	10.0		11.6	13.4		15.8	11.6		11.1	16.3		15.9
7. Pittsburgh	40	**High**	Slow	7.2	2.87	10.3	7.2	2.87	10.3	7.6	3.67	9.3	10.0	3.74	12.5	8.0	4.53	8.1	12.6	4.72	13.2
			Fast	6.7		9.6	6.7		9.6	7.0		8.6	9.2		11.5	7.4		7.4	11.2		11.7
8. Milwaukee	35	**High**	Slow	9.1	2.47	11.2	9.1	2.47	11.2	10.0	3.09	10.3	12.0	3.22	12.9	9.8	3.41	7.4	13.6	3.81	11.5
			Fast	8.5		10.5	8.5		10.5	9.3		9.6	11.2		12.0	9.2		7.0	12.6		10.7
9. Minneapolis-St. Paul	30	**High**	Slow	7.0	2.41	8.4	7.0	2.41	8.4	7.9	3.13	8.2	10.2	3.39	11.5	8.5	3.90	7.4	11.7	4.02	10.5
			Fast	6.5		7.8	6.5		7.8	7.3		7.6	9.5		10.7	7.9		6.8	10.8		9.6
10. Buffalo	27	**High**	Slow	7.0	2.26	7.9	7.0	2.26	7.9	7.8	2.90	7.5	9.0	3.03	9.1	7.9	3.25	5.7	10.5	3.74	8.7
			Fast	6.5		7.3	6.5		7.3	7.3		7.1	8.4		8.5	7.3		5.3	9.7		8.1
11. San Diego	25	**High**	Slow	5.3	2.64	7.0	5.3	2.64	7.0	5.9	3.40	6.7	7.2	3.50	8.4	6.4	4.20	6.0	9.2	4.46	9.1
			Fast	4.9		6.5	4.9		6.5	5.5		6.2	6.6		7.7	5.9		5.5	8.3		8.2
12. Indianapolis	31	**Low**	Slow	5.4	2.36	6.4	5.4	2.36	6.4	6.0	2.92	5.8	6.8	3.04	6.9	6.3	3.37	4.7	8.0	3.75	6.7
			Fast	5.0		5.9	5.0		5.9	5.5		5.4	6.2		6.3	5.9		4.4	7.2		6.0
		High	Slow	5.8	2.42	7.0	5.8	2.42	7.0	6.4	3.08	6.6	7.6	3.18	8.1	6.6	3.54	5.2	8.9	3.95	7.8
			Fast	5.3		6.4	5.3		6.4	5.9		6.1	7.1		7.5	6.0		4.7	8.1		7.1

13. Portland	30	**High**	Slow	4.7	2.73	6.4	4.7	2.73	6.4	5.0	3.41	5.7	5.7	3.44	6.5	5.3	4.04	4.8	7.6	4.31	7.3
			Fast	4.3		5.9	4.3		5.9	4.6		5.2	5.2		6.0	4.9		4.4	7.0		6.7
14. Louisville	26	Low	Slow	5.7	2.27	6.5	5.7	2.27	6.5	6.0	2.69	5.4	6.8	2.81	6.4	6.2	3.07	4.2	7.6	3.37	5.7
			Fast	5.3		6.0	5.3		6.0	5.6		5.0	6.3		5.9	5.8		4.0	6.9		5.2
		High	Slow	6.1	2.33	7.1	6.1	2.33	7.1	6.3	2.75	5.3	7.4	2.93	7.2	6.5	3.21	4.6	8.4	3.56	6.6
			Fast	5.6		6.5	5.6		6.5	5.8		5.8	6.8		6.6	6.0		4.3	7.7		6.1
15. Cincinnati	30	**Low**	Slow	5.4	2.08	5.6	5.4	2.08	5.6	6.2	2.70	5.6	6.7	2.82	6.3	6.6	3.29	4.8	8.0	3.43	6.1
			Fast	5.0		5.2	5.0		5.2	5.7		5.1	6.2		5.8	6.1		4.5	7.2		5.5
		High	Slow	5.6	2.14	6.0	5.6	2.14	6.0	6.5	2.83	6.1	7.3	2.97	7.2	6.9	3.48	5.3	9.0	3.94	7.9
			Fast	5.3		5.7	5.3		5.7	6.1		5.8	6.7		6.6	6.5		5.0	8.3		7.2
16. Denver	35	Low	Slow	4.2	2.33	4.9	4.2	2.33	4.9	5.2	3.06	5.3	6.0	3.17	6.3	5.2	3.36	3.9	6.7	3.69	5.5
			Fast	3.9		4.6	3.9		4.6	4.7		4.8	5.5		5.8	4.8		3.6	6.1		5.0
		High	Slow	5.0	2.51	6.3	5.0	2.51	6.3	5.5	3.24	5.9	6.6	3.36	7.4	5.4	3.46	4.2	7.6	3.88	6.6
			Fast	4.6		5.8	4.6		5.8	5.0		5.4	5.8		6.5	5.0		3.8	7.1		6.1
17. Columbus	26	**Low**	Slow	4.7	2.53	6.0	4.7	2.53	6.0	4.9	3.03	4.9	5.8	3.14	6.1	5.0	3.36	3.7	6.4	3.64	5.2
			Fast	4.3		5.5	4.3		5.5	4.5		4.5	5.3		5.5	4.6		3.4	5.9		4.8
		High	Slow	5.1	2.60	6.6	5.1	2.60	6.6	5.2	3.16	5.5	6.5	3.25	7.0	5.2	3.49	4.0	7.3	3.81	6.2
			Fast	4.7		6.1	4.7		6.1	4.8		5.1	6.0		6.5	4.8		3.7	6.7		5.7
18. Kansas City	30	Low	Slow	3.3	2.71	4.5	3.3	2.71	4.5	3.8	3.45	4.4	4.5	3.50	5.3	4.4	4.48	4.4	5.8	4.61	5.9
			Fast	3.0		4.1	3.0		4.1	3.5		4.0	4.0		4.7	4.1		4.1	5.3		5.4
		High	Slow	3.6	2.77	5.0	3.6	2.77	5.0	4.1	3.79	5.2	5.1	3.62	6.2	4.7	4.88	5.1	6.9	5.03	7.7
			Fast	3.3		4.6	3.3		4.6	3.8		4.8	4.7		5.7	4.3		4.7	6.4		7.2
19. New Orleans	26	**High**	Slow	5.4	2.19	5.9	5.4	2.19	5.9	5.3	2.44	4.3	6.1	2.59	5.3	5.2	2.48	2.9	6.5	2.97	4.3
			Fast	5.0		5.5	5.0		5.5	4.9		4.0	5.7		4.9	4.8		2.6	6.0		4.0
20. Phoenix	20	**Low**	Slow	2.5	2.30	2.9	2.5	2.30	2.9	2.8	2.88	2.7	3.1	2.99	3.1	3.0	3.53	2.4	3.7	3.83	3.1
			Fast	2.2		2.6	2.2		2.6	2.5		2.4	2.8		2.8	2.7		2.1	3.3		2.8
21. San Antonio	15	**High**	Slow	2.2	2.52	2.8	2.2	2.52	2.8	2.1	2.83	2.0	2.9	3.20	3.1	2.2	3.11	1.5	3.0	3.51	2.3
			Fast	2.0		2.5	2.0		2.5	1.9		1.8	2.6		2.8	2.0		1.4	2.8		2.2
22. Dayton	16	**Low**	Slow	2.4	2.18	2.6	2.4	2.18	2.6	2.5	2.53	2.1	2.8	2.65	2.5	2.5	2.75	1.5	2.9	3.02	1.9
			Fast	2.2		2.4	2.2		2.4	2.2		1.9	2.4		2.1	2.3		1.4	2.7		1.8
		High	Slow	2.5	2.24	2.8	2.5	2.24	2.8	2.6	2.64	2.3	3.0	2.79	2.8	2.6	2.89	1.7	3.2	3.23	2.3
			Fast	2.3		2.6	2.3		2.6	2.3		2.0	2.7		2.5	2.4		1.5	2.9		2.1
23. Providence	12	**Low**	Slow	2.3	1.91	2.2	2.3	1.91	2.2	2.4	2.19	1.8	2.6	2.33	2.0	2.4	2.43	1.3	2.7	2.69	1.6
			Fast	2.1		2.0	2.1		2.0	2.2		1.6	2.3		1.8	2.2		1.2	2.4		1.4
		High	Slow	2.3	1.95	2.2	2.3	1.95	2.2	2.4	2.27	1.8	2.7	2.43	2.2	2.5	2.52	1.4	2.9	2.87	1.8
			Fast	2.1		2.0	2.1		2.0	2.2		1.7	2.6		1.9	2.2		1.2	2.6		1.7
24. Tampa-St. Petersburg	10	**Low**	Slow	2.1	2.10	2.2	2.1	2.10	2.2	2.2	2.41	1.8	2.4	2.50	2.0	2.2	2.53	1.2	2.5	2.78	1.5
			Fast	1.9		2.0	1.9		2.0	2.0		1.6	2.2		1.8	2.0		1.1	2.3		1.4

Note: Average trip length assumed identical for all auto speeds.

finite magnitude, even though it would take some 30 years to implement at the current rate of construction.

With respect to light rail, any estimates beyond the 10 corridors identified in Exhibit 4.6 must remain conjectural, in part because additional corridors will depend so strongly on available rights-of-way. Assuming that each of the 10 potential cities named can develop between two and three corridors with sufficient volume, making some allowance for smaller cities not considered here, and for additional mileage in cities with light rail in existence such as Pittsburgh and San Francisco, or committed, such as Buffalo, San Diego, Portland, and Detroit, potential lines might total some 230 miles (370 km) in addition to the 90 miles identified earlier. This would more than double the existing light rail system.

Looking beyond the period immediately ahead, opportunities for new light rail lines may move into the foreground, as rapid transit emphasis shifts from new lines toward replacement of elevated structures in New York and Chicago. If public transit ridership continues to grow at its current pace, more urban corridors, which now fail to meet the test of rail transit feasibility, will meet it. More of these are likely to be at the light rail end of the spectrum, for the simple reason that it is easier to reach a threshold of 7,000 passenger-miles per line-mile, supportive of light rail, than it is to reach one of 24,000 passenger-miles per line-mile, supportive of "real" rapid transit with some tunneling. In a muted replay of the early years of the century, portrayed in Exhibit 1.1, light rail growth may again outpace the growth of rapid transit, with an added wave of trolleybuses superimposed. Trolleybus installations are likely to outpace light rail, as the cost differential between electricity and liquid fuels increases.

The role of automated peoplemovers in this scenario is much more difficult to foretell. Judging by the threshold criteria established here—which obviously are more tentative for a nascent technology than for a mature one—automated or semiautomated systems, if they adopt low-capital, single-beam guideways, and if they break out of the downtown-only environment, will be in direct competition with conventional light rail as well as with buses. If their automatic controls become reliable and routine, they can capture a significant market in middle-sized urban areas and an additional market in some major cities as feeders to rapid transit. Alternatively, the low-capital, single-beam guideway concept may make manned grade-separated transit so successful that the need for reliable automation would be deferred.

This concept, known as Project 21, opens a dramatically new perspective for urban rail. The keys to it are an ingenious car suspension and a patented switch that let trains run in opposite directions on two sides of one hollow, triangular steel beam, less than 5 × 6 feet (1.5 × 1.8m) in cross-section. These slim dimensions offer several advantages: visual obstruction, the nemesis of traditional elevated structures (including so-called monorails), is dramatically reduced; construction cost is cut to about one-fifth that of traditional rail or peoplemover elevated structures; quick erection and reuse of the simple, prefabricated elements are possible; should the system be placed underground, the tunnel dimensions and cost are about half those of conventional subways, because the small cars, which do not ride on trucks, require a cross-section which is that much smaller; lastly, fixed maintenance costs are low, because the usual maintenance concerns of drainage, ballast and ties, or guideway heating in the case of rubber-tired systems, are eliminated.

The price paid for these advantages is that the cars are small and storage yards require more than the usual construction. Nevertheless the trains, consisting typically of four to eight cars, have a passenger capacity equivalent to 2½ to 5 standard buses, or 1¼ to 2½ articulated light rail cars. They are run manually by one operator per train at speeds in excess of those of light rail, because the guideway is fully grade-separated.

The combination of modest manning requirements and high speed begins to attain labor economies compared to conventional buses (assuming a typical bus operating speed of 11 mph or 18 km/h) at volumes as low as 13 buses per direction per hour; at volumes in the 30 to 40 buses per hour range, these savings become sufficiently large to fully amortize the low construction cost. At higher volumes, construction yields a clear profit for the transit agency, compared to conventional bus service.[7] This condition is unique, for, as was shown earlier in Chapter 2, labor savings can rarely amortize more than *one-third* of traditional rail transit construction. The rest is split among passenger time, parking cost, and energy savings. In the case of Project 21 at moderate volume of service, all of these other savings are a net profit.

Based on material presented in this chapter, the cities where labor savings compared to bus operations would fully pay for the cost of Project 21 guideways are Los Angeles, Seattle, Honolulu, Houston, Detroit, Dallas, St. Louis, Milwaukee, Minneapolis, and Denver. The former seven are likely to realize substantial cost savings for the operting agency, while the latter three would about break even, limiting their "profit" mostly to passenger time, parking cost, and energy savings.

This excludes cities with rail transit in being or under construction, where feeder lines based on this new technology are possible. A large additional market exists in smaller cities, where some construction subsidy, based on the nonlabor benefits, would be necessary. The remarkable thing is that for a broad range of medium passenger volumes—from about 1,000 to 12,500 passengers per direction per hour at the maximum load point—this new "appropriate technology" offers a promise of high-quality rail transit sufficiently low in cost that it can be funded mostly from local sources, and even involve significant private sector participation through lease-back and similar arrangements. In an era of fiscal restraint, this could produce hundreds of miles of flourishing rail systems in a much shorter time and at a fraction of the cost estimated earlier in this chapter for conventional rail technology.

The "Project 21" overhead streetcar—designed for manual operation in trains along a slender, single-beam guideway. *(Lawrence K. Edwards)*

MAPS OF NORTH AMERICAN URBAN RAIL NETWORKS

	1980 Urbanized area population, 000's*	Downtown Nonres. floorspace m.s.f.	Downtown Land area sq. mi.	1980 Passenger miles of RT and LR travel (millions)	1980 Line miles Rapid Transit	1980 Line miles Light Rail
NEW YORK	15,589	590	9.0	7,466	258.0	4.3
CHICAGO	6,711	278	13.6	1,130	89.4	--
PHILADELPHIA	4,114	125	2.5	661	38.6	99.7
SAN FRANCISCO	3,192	88	2.2	668	71.0	24.2
MONTREAL	2,743*	91	2.7	692	25.4	--
TORONTO	2,628*	120	1.7	1,326	33.8	45.6
WASHINGTON	2,762	106	1.7	382	37.2	--
BOSTON	2,678	100	2.3	456	36.7	28.9
PITTSBURGH	1,810	32	0.9	35	--	24.1
CLEVELAND	1,752	45	1.0	127	19.3	10.5
ATLANTA	1,613	50	2.2	76	11.8	--
EDMONTON	495*	21	1.0	23	4.5	--

* 1971 population for Canadian urbanized areas.

NEW YORK N

Note: In the absence of a currently valid New Routes Program, Regional Plan proposals for new lines are shown; 2nd Ave. construction is currently discontinued.

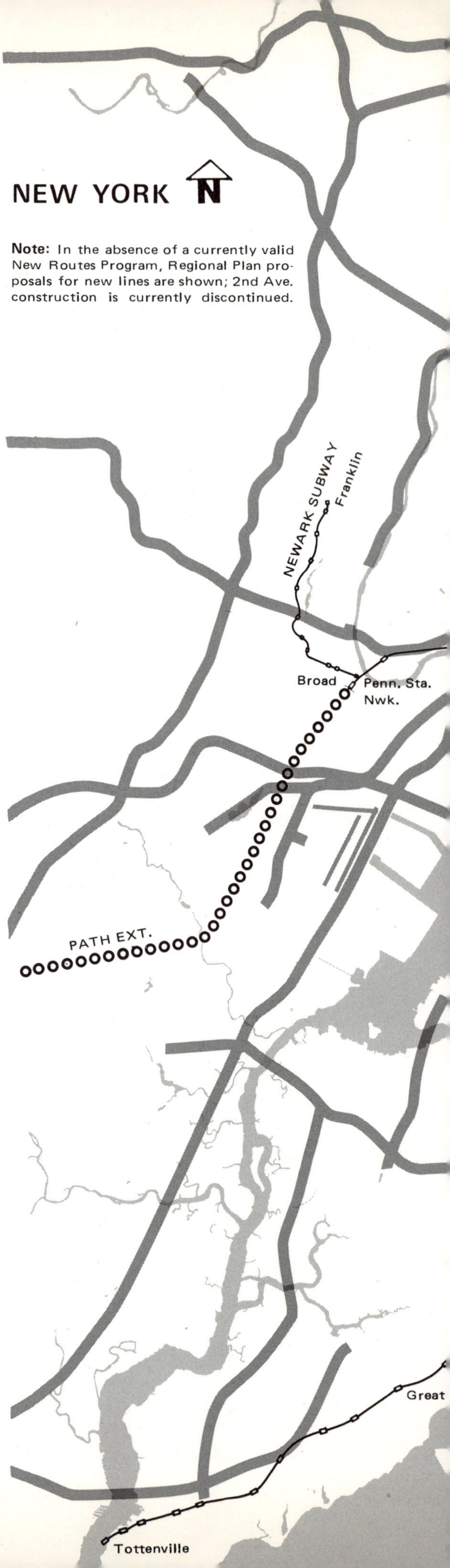

NEWARK SUBWAY
Franklin
Broad
Penn. Sta. Nwk.
PATH EXT.
Great
Tottenville

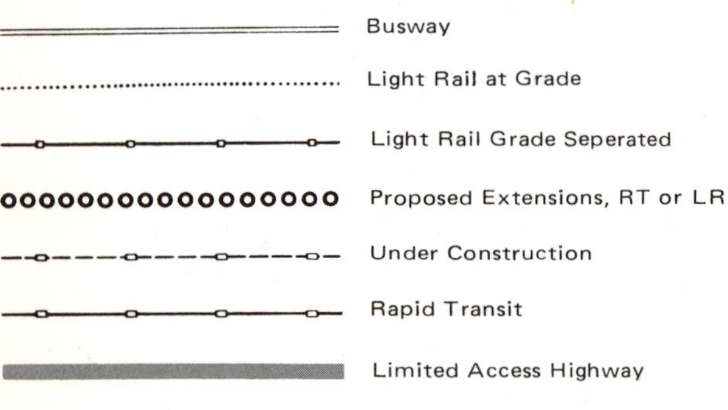

Legend and scale apply to this and the following maps.

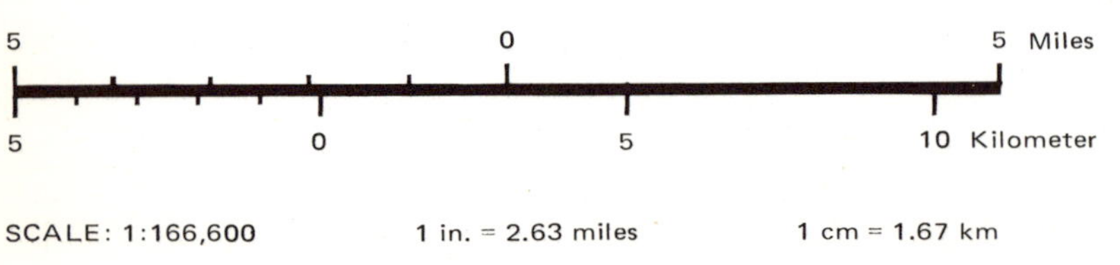

E. 241 St.
242 St.
Woodlawn
Dyre Ave.
205 St.
207 St.
WHITE PLAINS
JEROME
CONCOURSE
GRAND
Pelham Bay
E. 180 St.
148
B'WAY.
LENOX
LEXINGTON
2 AVE.
Ditmars
CONTRAFLOW
BUS LANE
8 AV
63 ST.
53 ST.
42 ST.
ASTORIA
Flushing
Roosevelt
TH
Hoboken
Journal Square
6 AV
HOUST.
14 ST.
QUEENS BLVD.
JEWEL AVE.
MONTAUK
Metropolitan Ave.
BYPASS
HILLSIDE AVE.
179 St.
ARCHER AV
WTC
CROSS TOWN
B'WAY.
MYRTLE
E.N.Y.
JAMAICA AVE.
S.E. QUEENS
Hoyt
FULTON
Lefferts Blvd.
Franklin
Utica Ave.
E. PKWY
New Lots
NOSTRAND
JFK Airpt. (Howard B.)
St. George
WEST END
Rockaway Pkwy.
Flatbush
4 AVE.
SEA BEACH
McDONALD
BRIGHTON
S.E. BROOKLYN
95 St.
Far Rockaway
Stilwell Ave.
Rockaway Park

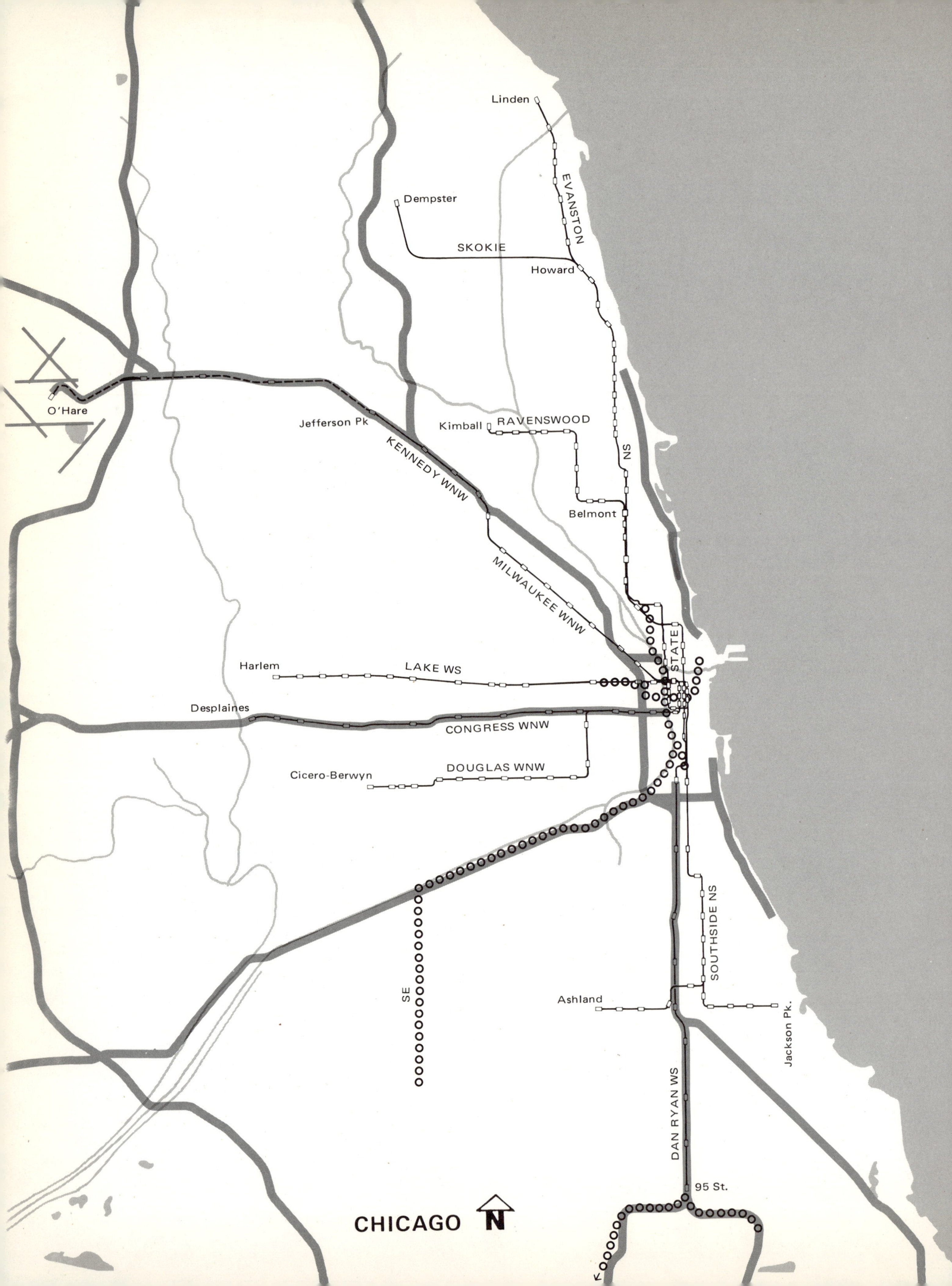
Linden
EVANSTON
Dempster
SKOKIE
Howard
O'Hare
Jefferson Pk
Kimball
RAVENSWOOD
KENNEDY WNW
NS
Belmont
MILWAUKEE WNW
STATE
Harlem
LAKE WS
Desplaines
CONGRESS WNW
Cicero-Berwyn
DOUGLAS WNW
SOUTHSIDE NS
SE
Ashland
Jackson Pk.
DAN RYAN WS
95 St.
CHICAGO
N

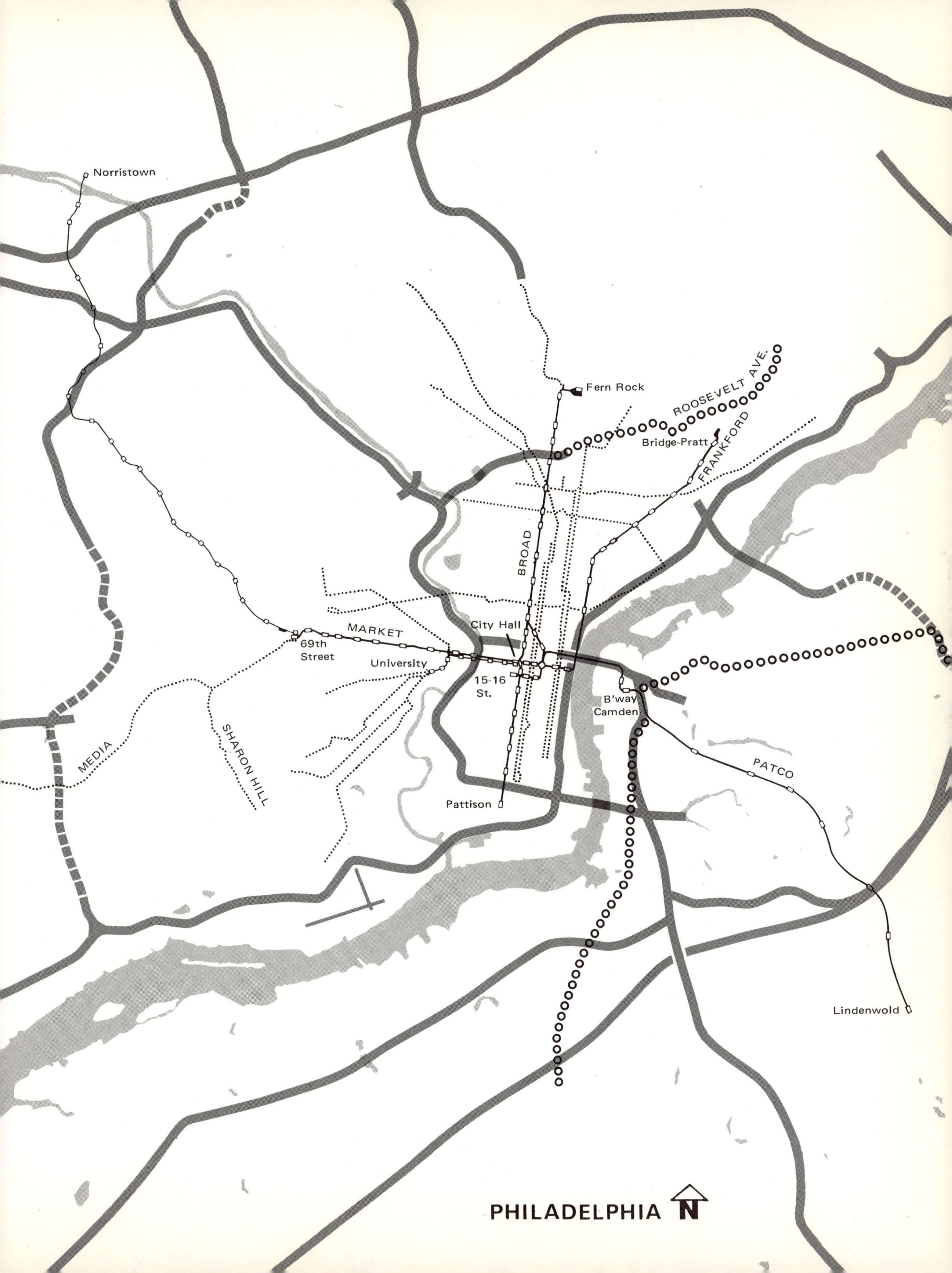

Norristown
Fern Rock
ROOSEVELT AVE.
Bridge-Pratt
FRANKFORD
BROAD
MARKET
City Hall
69th
Street
University
15-16
St.
B'way
Camden
PATCO
MEDIA
SHARON HILL
Pattison
Lindenwold
PHILADELPHIA
N

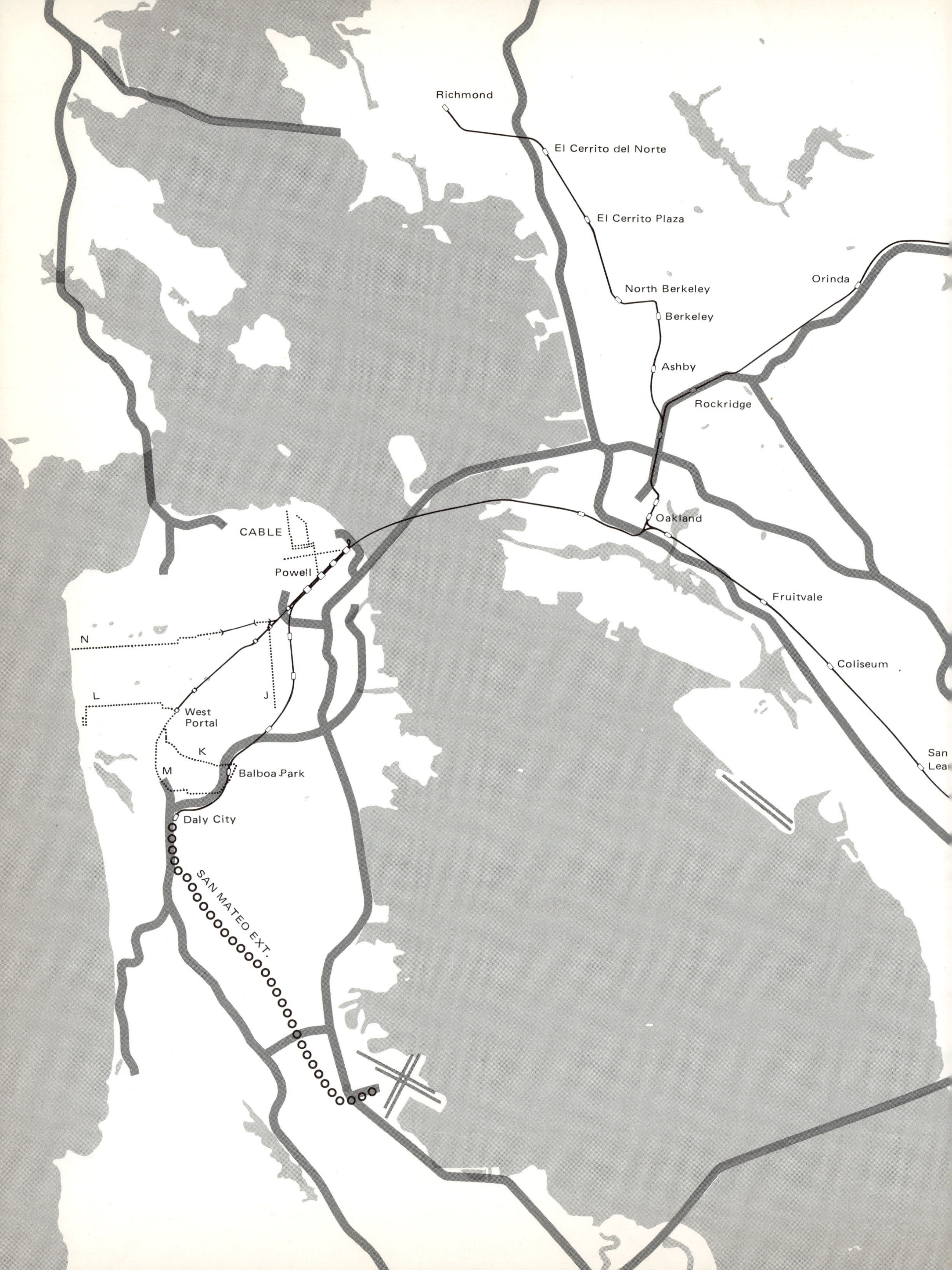
Richmond
El Cerrito del Norte
El Cerrito Plaza
North Berkeley
Berkeley
Ashby
Orinda
Rockridge
Oakland
Fruitvale
Coliseum
San
Lea
CABLE
Powell
N
L
J
West
Portal
K
M
Balboa Park
Daly City
SAN MATEO EXT.

SAN FRANCISCO N

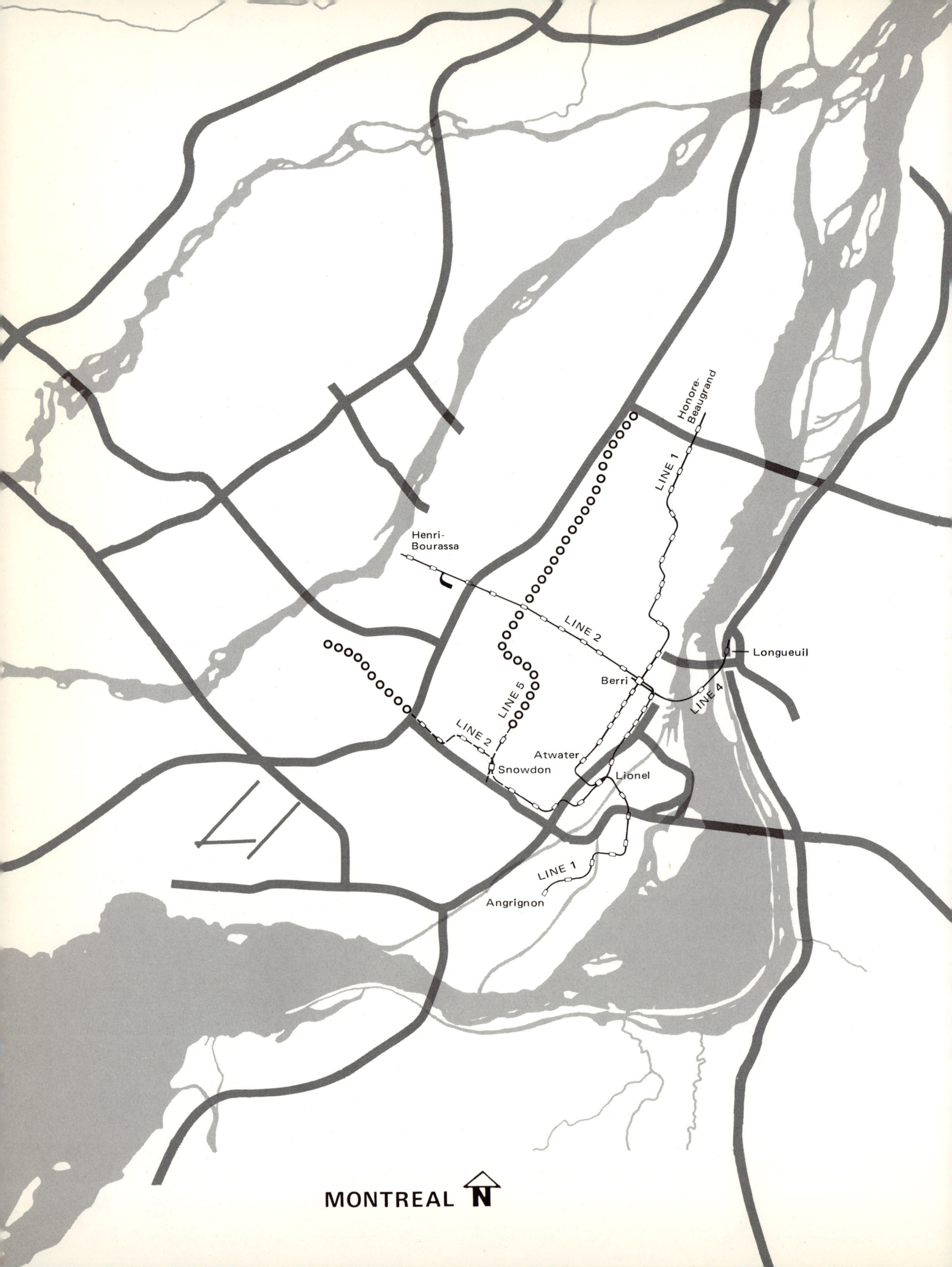

Honore-Beaugrand
LINE 1
Henri-Bourassa
LINE 2
Longueuil
Berri
LINE 4
LINE 5
LINE 2
Atwater
Snowdon
Lionel
LINE 1
Angrignon
MONTREAL
N

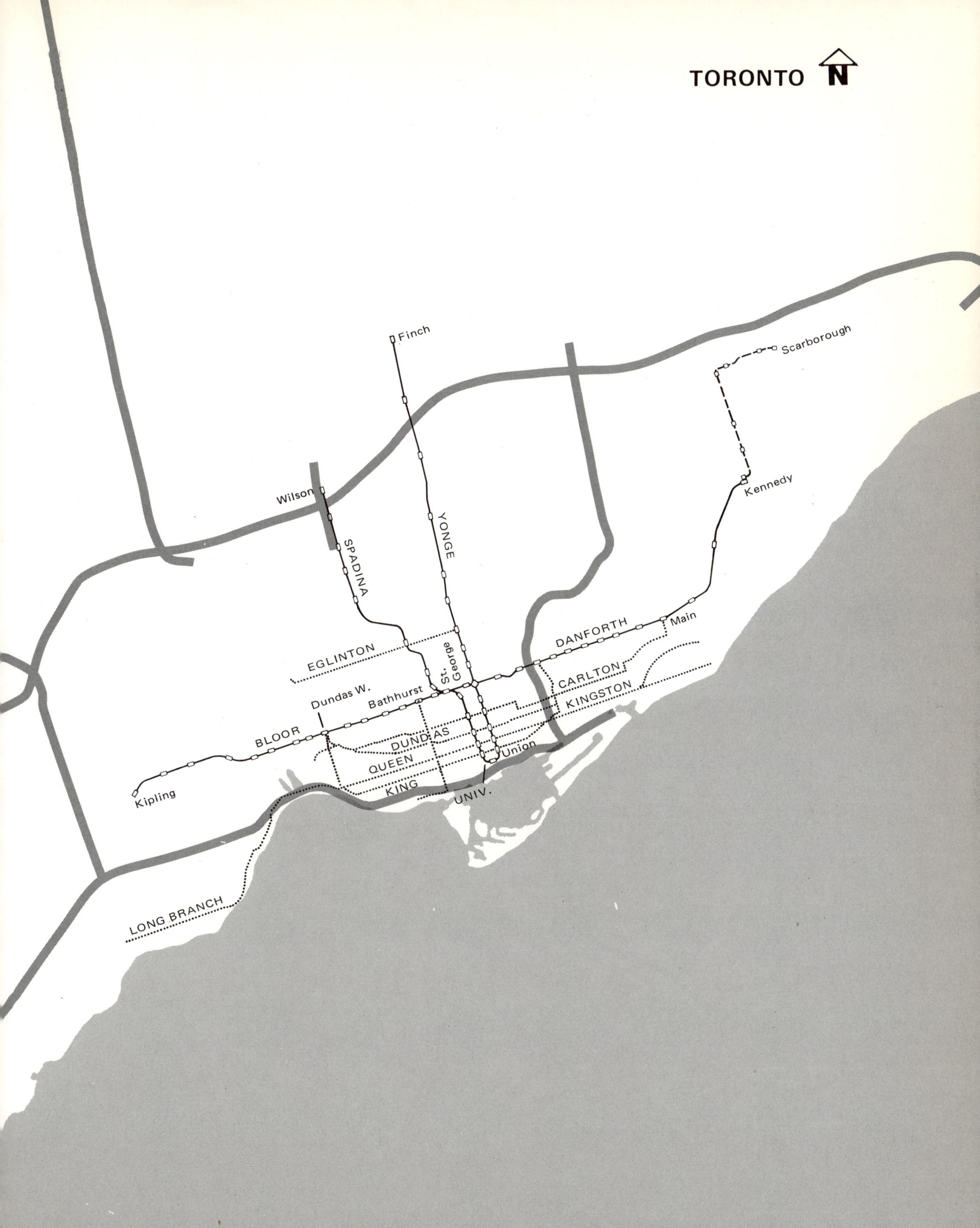
TORONTO
N
Finch
Scarborough
Wilson
YONGE
SPADINA
Kennedy
Main
DANFORTH
EGLINTON
St. George
CARLTON
Bathhurst
Dundas W.
KINGSTON
BLOOR
DUNDAS
Union
QUEEN
Kipling
KING
UNIV.
LONG BRANCH

Shady Grove
Glenmont
Silver Spring
RED LINE
Bethesda
RED LINE
New Carrolton
YELLOW
GREEN
ORANGE LINE
Dupont Circle
ORANGE LINE
Union Sta.
Metro Center
Rosslyn
Stadium Armory
BLUE LINE
← Vienna
Addison Rd.
Ballston
Pentagon
National Airport
GREEN
SHIRLEY BUSWAY
YELLOW
King St.
BLUE
WASHINGTON
N

Oak Grove
ORANGE LINE
Wonderland
BLUE LINE
Alewife
Harvard
Square
Lechmere
RED LINE
COMMONWEALTH
BEACON
Riverside
GREEN LINE
HUNTINGTON
Relocation
ORANGE
To be removed
Forest Hills
RED
Ashmont
RED LINE
Quincy
Center
South
Braintree
BOSTON
N

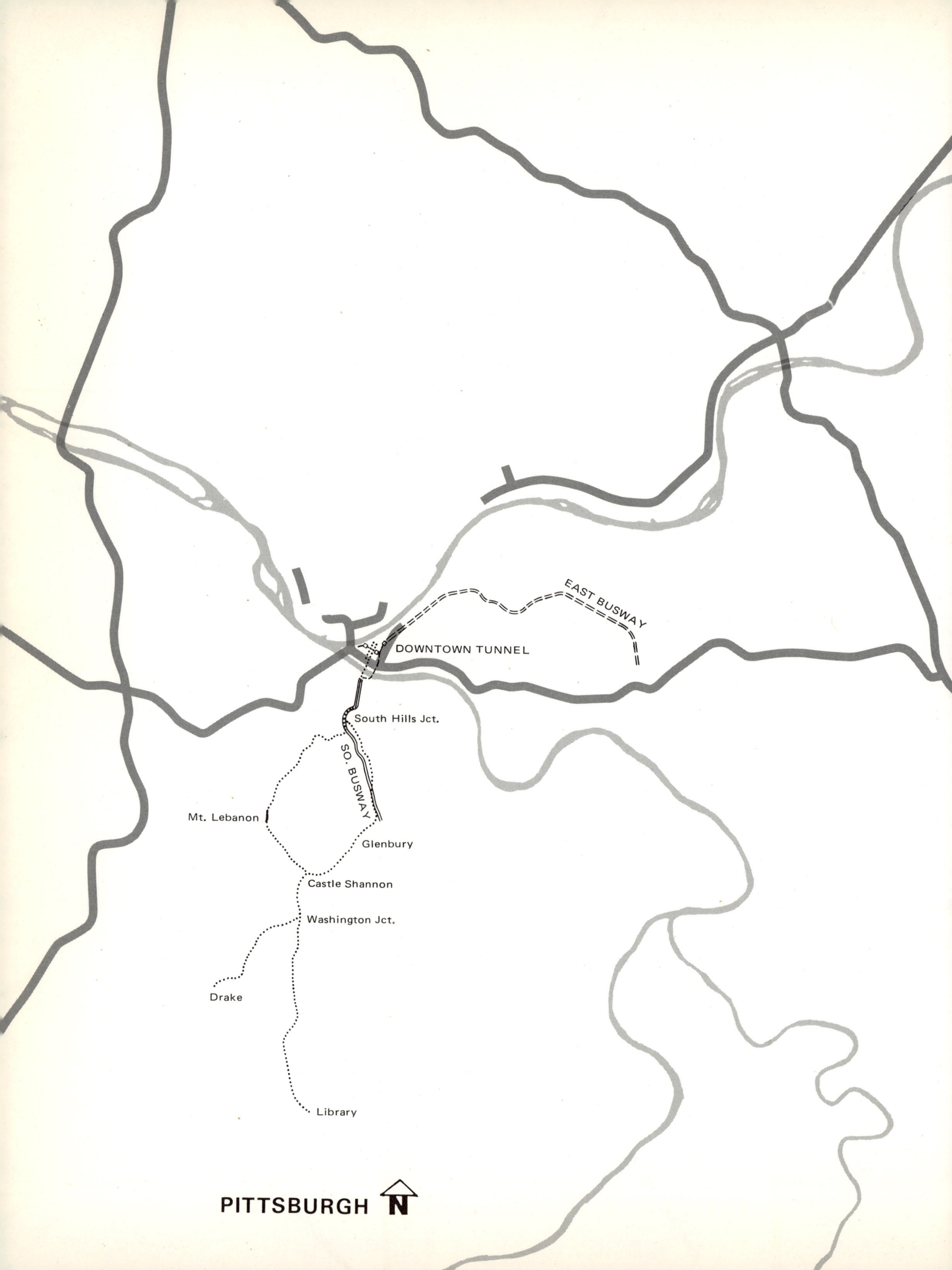
EAST BUSWAY
DOWNTOWN TUNNEL
South Hills Jct.
SO. BUSWAY
Mt. Lebanon
Glenbury
Castle Shannon
Washington Jct.
Drake
Library
PITTSBURGH
N

Windermere
EUCLID
Shaker Square
SHAKER
VAN AKEN
Public
Square
Airport
CLEVELAND
N

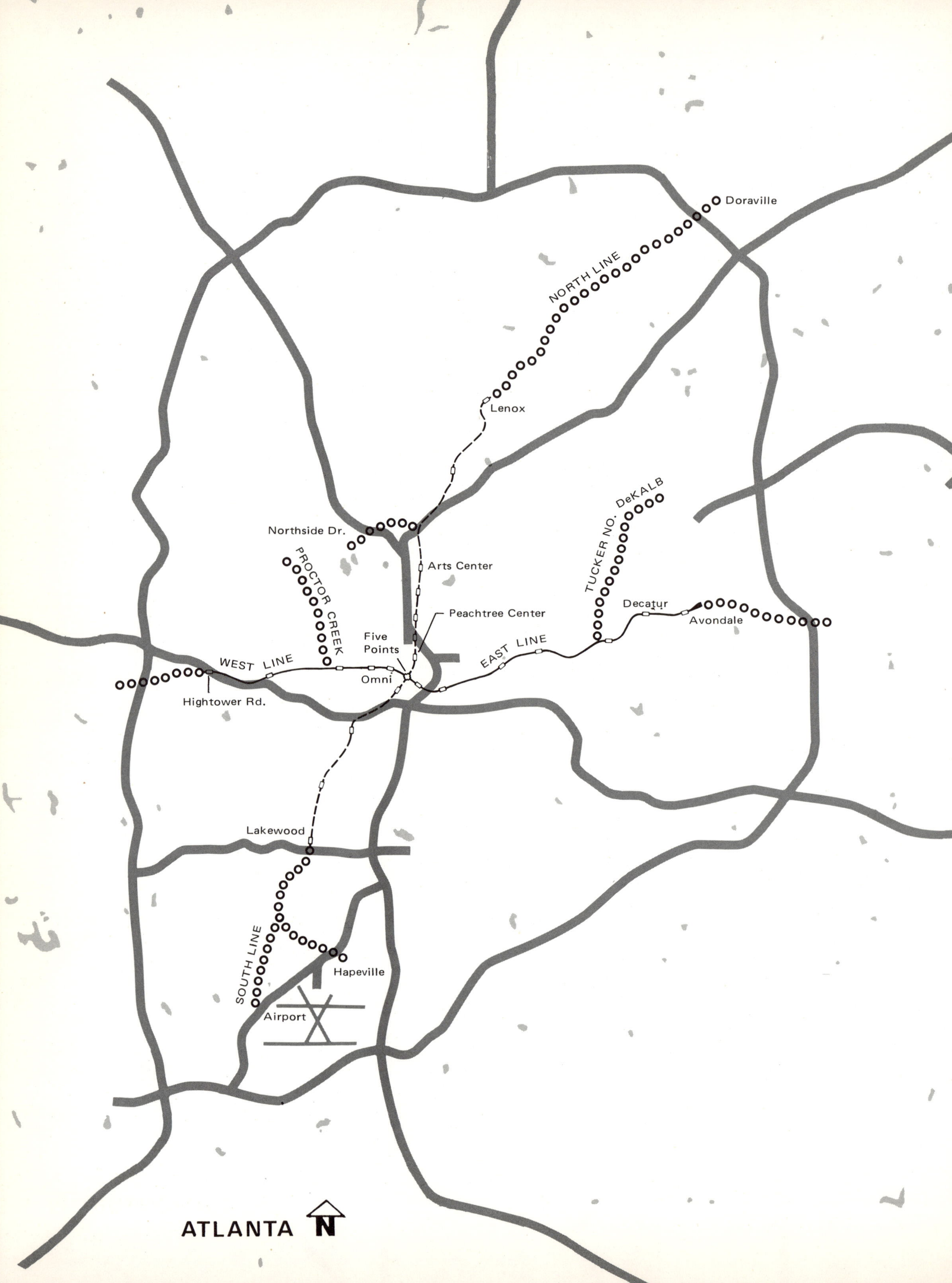

Doraville
NORTH LINE
Lenox
Northside Dr.
PROCTOR CREEK
Arts Center
Peachtree Center
DeKALB
TUCKER NO.
Decatur
Avondale
EAST LINE
Five Points
Omni
WEST LINE
Hightower Rd.
Lakewood
SOUTH LINE
Hapeville
Airport
ATLANTA
N

Castle
Downs
Clearview
Belvedere
Coliseum
Stadium
Govt.
Centre
Central
Campus
Mill Woods

EDMONTON N

(Metropolitan Atlanta Rapid Transit Authority)

APPENDIX

HISTORICAL TABLES

ANALYTICAL TABLES

Table H-1
Total Miles of Single Track by Transit Mode in the United States, 1860-1980

Year	Rapid Transit	Surface Rail Transit: Electric	Cable	Other	Animal	Total Surface Rail	Total Rail Transit	Dual Trolleybus Wire	Automated Peoplemover*
1860	none			none	150e	150	150		
1870	5e		none	. . .	650e	650	655		
1880	90e	none	30e	. . .	2,250e	2,280	2,370		
1890	160e	1,262	488	551	5,662	7,963	8,123		
1902	313e	21,712	240	53	259	22,264	22,577		
1907	437e	33,601	62	146	136	33,945	34,382	none	
1912	530e	40,278	56	143	58	40,535	41,065	. . .	
1917	716e	43,961	45	102	11	44,119	44,835	. . .	
1922	927n	42,862	46	93	4	43,005	43,932	. . .	
1923	990n	. . .	. . .	. . .	none		. . .	. . .	
1924	1,007	. . .	. . .	. . .			. . .	. . .	
1925	1,078	. . .	. . .	. . .			. . .	. . .	
1926	1,099	. . .	. . .	. . .		40,570	41,669	. . .	
1927	1,109 (977n)	39,609	43	94		39,746	40,855	. . .	
1928	1,134	. . .	. . .	. . .		38,235	39,369	39	
1929	1,149	. . .	. . .	. . .		36,520	37,699	59	
1930	1,149	. . .	. . .	. . .		34,320	35,469	146	
1931	1,149	. . .	. . .	. . .		32,120	33,269	194	
1932	1,199(1,148n)	30,283	39	77		30,418	31,617	251	
1933	1,239	. . .	. . .	. . .		28,730	29,969	281	
1934	1,299	. . .	. . .	. . .		27,270	28,569	423	
1935	1,299	. . .	. . .	. . .		25,470	26,769	548	
1936	1,329	. . .	. . .	. . .		24,040	25,369	859	
1937	1,379	. . .	. . .	. . .		22,460	23,839	1,166	
1938	1,369	. . .	. . .			20,500	21,869	1,398	
1939	1,369	. . .	. . .			19,300	20,669	1,543	
1940	1,311	. . .	. . .			18,360	19,671	1,925	
1941	1,311	. . .	. . .			17,100	18,411	2,098	
1942	1,290	. . .	. . .			16,950	18,240	2,330	
1943	1,300	. . .	. . .			16,950	18,250	2,305	
1944	1,291	. . .	. . .			16,860	18,151	2,302	
1945	1,291	. . .	. . .			16,480	17,771	2,370	
1946	1,295	. . .	. . .			15,490	16,785	2,441	
1947	1,295	. . .	. . .			13,750	15,045	2,797	
1948	1,293	. . .	. . .			. . .	. . .	. . .	
1949	1,300	. . .	. . .			. . .	. . .	. . .	

1950	1,292	. . .	. . .	9,590	10,882	3,513	
1951	1,286	. . .	. . .	8,240	9,526	3,678	
1952	1,292	. . .	. . .	7,309	8,601	3,736	
1953	1,280	. . .	. . .	6,126	7,406	3,663	
1954	1,272	. . .	. . .	5,547	6,819	3,630	
1955	1,275	. . .	. . .	4,976	6,251	3,428	
1956	1,305	. . .	. . .	4,495	5,800	3,293	
1957	1,299	. . .	. . .	3,774	5,073	3,007	
1958	1,298	. . .	. . .	2,600	3,898	2,723	
1959	1,299	. . .	. . .	2,200	3,499	2,491	
1960	1,297	. . .	. . .	1,900	3,197	2,196	
1961	1,300	. . .	. . .	1,355	2,655	2,017	
1962	1,299	. . .	. . .	1,312	2,611	1,849	
1963	1,297	. . .	. . .	990	2,287	1,119	
1964	1,306	. . .	. . .	918	2,224	986	
1965	1,306	. . .	. . .	918	2,224	766	
1966	1,306	. . .	. . .	898	2,204	676	
1967	1,311	. . .	. . .	790	2,101	616	
1968	1,319	. . .	. . .	775	2,094	616	
1969	1,360	. . .	. . .	762	2,122	563	
1970	1,370	479	11**	490n	1,860	563	none
1971	1,383	479	11	490	1,873	. . .	1.4
1972	1,444	479	11	490	1,934	. . .	1.4
1973	1,523	473	11	490	2,007	. . .	3.1
1974	1,539	473	11	484	2,023	. . .	15.9
1975	1,543	473	11	484	2,027	. . .	21.2
1976	1,559	475	11	486	2,045	. . .	21.8
1977	1,585	475	11	486	2,071	. . .	21.8
1978	1,612	475	11	486	2,098	. . .	21.8
1979	1,652	475	11	486	2,138	. . .	24.7
1980	1,665	484	11	495	2,160	. . .	25.8

e - estimated; n - new series, figure not strictly comparable to preceding one; . . . - data not readily available.
* Airport and urban systems only; excludes amusement parks and intramural systems.
** San Francisco cable car only; excludes inclined planes.

Sources: 1890-1922 and surface rail detail for 1927 and 1932: *U.S. Census of Electric Railways.*
1923-1969 Rapid transit: American Public Transit Association (APTA) adjusted to include unreported Staten Island Rapid Transit and Hudson & Manhattan, later Port Authority Trans-Hudson trackage as follows: 1923-24, + 17 mi.; 1925-52, + 69 mi.; 1953-62, + 54 mi.; 1963-69, + 51 mi.
1926-1969 Surface rail: APTA data, unadjusted; apparently overstated by about 270 mi. in the 1960s.
1970-1980 Rapid transit and surface rail: Table H-3, based on correspondence with operating agencies and published agency reports.
Beginning with 1940, rapid transit excludes grade-separated portions of streetcar lines, which are included in surface rail. This definition may not always be consistent for prior years.

Table H-2
Annual "Total" Passenger Trips by Transit Mode in the United States, 1860-1980
(in millions, including transfer & non-revenue passenger trips)

Year	Rapid Transit	Surface Rail Transit: Electric	Cable	Other	Animal	Total Surface Rail	Total Rail	Total Trolleybus	Total Motorbus	Total Transit
1860	none			none	40e	40e	40e			40
1870	. . .		none	. . .	140e	140	140e			140
1880	80e	none	5e	. . .	570e	575	655			655
1890	250	410e	65e	3e	1,295e	1,773	2,023*			2,023
1902	363	5,403.5	24.4	0.2	45.5	5,473.6	5,836.6		none	5,837
1907	675	8,842.6	13.8	0.5	1.2	8,858.1	9,533.1	none	. . .	9,533
1912	1,041	11,091	18e	. . .	. . .	11,109	12,150	. . .	. . .	12,150
1917	1,332	13,176	17e	. . .	. . .	13,193	14,525	. . .	. . .	14,525
1918	1,385	. . .	. . .	. . .	. . .	12,876	14,261	. . .	. . .	14,261
1919	1,505	. . .	. . .	. . .	. . .	13,430	14,935	. . .	. . .	14,935
1920	1,792	. . .	. . .	. . .	. . .	13,770	15,562	. . .	. . .	15,562
1921	1,909	. . .	. . .	. . .	. . .	12,688	14,597	. . .	. . .	14,597
1922	1,942	. . .	. . .	. . .	. . .	13,413	15,355	. . .	404	15,759
1923	2,081	. . .	. . .	. . .		13,593	15,674	. . .	661	16,335
1924	2,207	. . .	. . .	. . .		13,130	15,337	. . .	989	16,326
1925	2,264	. . .	. . .	. . .		12,924	15,188	. . .	1,484	16,672
1926	2,350	. . .	. . .	. . .		12,895	15,245	. . .	2,009	17,254
1927	2,451	. . .	. . .	. . .		12,469	14,920	. . .	2,301	17,221
1928	2,492	. . .	. . .	. . .		12,044	14,536	3	2,470	17,009
1929	2,571	. . .	. . .	. . .		11,804	14,375	5	2,623	17,003
1930	2,559	. . .	. . .	. . .		10,530	13,089	16	2,481	15,586
1931	2,408	. . .	. . .	. . .		9,191	11,599	28	2,315	13,942
1932	2,204	. . .	. . .	. . .		7,662	9,866	37	2,138	12,041
1933	2,133	. . .	. . .	. . .		7,086	9,219	45	2,077	11,341
1934	2,206	. . .	. . .	. . .		7,404	9,610	68	2,376	12,054
1935	2,236	. . .	. . .	. . .		7,286	9,522	96	2,625	12,243
1936	2,323	. . .	. . .	. . .		7,512	9,835	143	3,188	13,166
1937	2,307	. . .	. . .	. . .		7,174	9,481	289	3,500	13,270
1938	2,236	. . .	. . .			6,552	8,788	395	3,488	12,671
1939	2,368	. . .	. . .			6,178	8,546	452	3,866	12,864
1940	2,382	. . .	. . .			5,951	8,333	542	4,255	13,130
1941	2,421	. . .	. . .			6,085	8,506	669	4,948	14,123
1942	2,566	. . .	. . .			7,290	9,856	918	7,264	18,038
1943	2,656	. . .	. . .			9,150	11,806	1,220	9,070	22,096
1944	2,621	. . .	. . .			9,516	12,137	1,292	9,713	23,142
1945	2,698	. . .	. . .			9,426	12,124	1,298	9,946	23,368
1946	2,835	. . .	. . .			9,027	11,862	1,354	10,247	23,463
1947	2,756	. . .	. . .			8,096	10,852	1,398	10,374	22,624
1948	2,606	. . .	. . .			6,506	9,112	1,558	10,759	21,429
1949	2,346	. . .	. . .			4,839	7,185	1,691	10,193	19,069

1950	2,264	...	...	3,904	6,168	1,686	9,447	17,301
1951	2,189	...	...	3,101	5,290	1,658	9,227	16,175
1952	2,124	...	...	2,477	4,601	1,666	8,901	15,168
1953	2,040	...	...	2,036	4,076	1,587	8,280	13,943
1954	1,912	...	...	1.489	3,401	1,387	7,643	12,431
1955	1,870	...	...	1,207	3,077	1,223	7,269	11,569
1956	1,880	...	...	876	2,756	1,163	7,062	10,981
1957	1,843	...	...	679	2,522	1,003	6,903	10,428
1958	1,815	...	...	572	2,387	843	6,540	9,770
1959	1,828	...	...	521	2,349	749	6,498	9,596
1960	1,850	...	...	463	2,313	657	6,425	9,395
1961	1,855	...	...	434	2,289	601	5,993	8,883
1962	1,890	...	...	393	2,283	547	5,865	8,695
1963	1,836	...	...	329	2,165	413	5,822	8,400
1964	1,877	...	...	289	2,166	349	5,813	8,328
1965	1,858	...	...	276	2,134	305	5,814	8,253
1966	1,753	...	...	282	2,035	284	5,764	8,083
1967	1,938	...	...	263	2,201	248	5,723	8,172
1968	1,928	...	...	253	2,181	228	5,610	8,019
1969	1,980	...	...	249	2,229	199	5,375	7,803
1970	1,881	...	...	235	2,116	182	5,034	7,332
1971	1,778	...	...	222	2,000	148	4,699	6,847
1972	1,731	...	...	211	1,942	130	4,495	6,567
1973	1,714	...	...	207	1,921	97	4,642	6,660
1974	1,726	...	...	150	1,876	83	4,976	6,935
1975	1,673	124	13**	137	1,810	78	5,084	6,972
1976	1,632	112	15**	127	1,759	75	5,247	7,081
1977	1,611e	103e	15**	118e	1,729e	70e	5,345e	7,144e
1978	1,707e	104e	16**	120e	1,833e	70e	5,443e	7,466e
1979	1,779e	107e	15**	122e	1,909e	75e	5,864e	7,970e
1980	1,750e	105e	15**	120e	1,869e	85e	5,992e	8,066e
(1980	1,548	152	see Table H-4)					

* Distribution within Census total estimated.

** Includes Inclined Plane.

Sources: 1890-1917: *U.S. Census of Electric Railways,* with some adjustment in internal allocation by mode for 1890, 1912 and 1917.
1918-1976: APTA, unadjusted.

In 1977, APTA discontinued the "Total" trips series; to maintain comparability with earlier data, the 1977-1980 data are expanded from "linked trips" or "revenue rides" to fit the old definition, and are marked "e."

The APTA "total" trip estimates for Rapid Transit and Electric Surface Rail Transit for 1969-76 do not agree with the data reported by individual properties, as listed in Table H-4. While the latter appear more accurate, the full series is listed here for historical continuity.

Table H-3
Miles of Single Track and Miles of Line of Urban Rail Transit in the United States by Property, 1968-1980

1. RAPID TRANSIT

	New York Region				Chicago	Philadelphia Region			Boston	Clevl.	S. F.	Wash.	Atlanta	U.S.
	NYCTA	PATH	SIRT	Total	CTA	SEPTA	PATCO	Total	MBTA	GCRTA	BART	WMATA	MARTA	Total
1968 Track	847	35	37	919	209	86		86	62	43				1,319
Line	239.9	13.9	14.3	268.1	72.3	26.5		26.5	24.3	19.3				410.1
1969 Track	842	35	37	914	228	79	34	113	62	43				1,360
Line	237.2	13.9	14.3	265.4	84.4	22.9	14.5	37.4	24.3	19.3				430.4
1970 Track	842	35	37	914	238	79	34	113	62	43				1,370
Line	237.2	13.9	14.3	265.4	89.4	22.9	14.5	37.4	24.3	19.3				435.8
1971 Track	842	35	37	914	238	79	34	113	75	43				1,383
Line	237.2	13.9	14.3	265.4	89.4	22.9	14.5	37.4	30.8	19.3				442.3
1972 Track	842	35	37	914	238	79	34	113	75	43	61			1,444
Line	237.2	13.9	14.3	265.4	89.4	22.9	14.5	37.4	30.8	19.3	25.7			468.0
1973 Track	830	35	37	902	238.	81	34	115	75	43	150			1,523
Line	231.7	13.9	14.3	259.9	89.4	24.1	14.5	38.6	30.8	19.3	63.0			501.0
1974 Track	830	35	37	902	238	81	34	115	75	43	166			1,539
Line	231.7	13.9	14.3	259.9	89.4	24.1	14.5	38.6	30.8	19.3	71.0			509.0
1975 Track	829	35	37	901	238	81	34	115	80	43	166			1,543
Line	230.7	13.9	14.3	258.9	89.4	24.1	14.5	38.6	32.9	19.3	71.0			510.1
1976 Track	829	35	37	901	238	81	34	115	80	43	166	16		1,559
Line	230.7	13.9	14.3	258.9	89.4	24.1	14.5	38.6	32.9	19.3	71.0	4.6		514.7
1977 Track	827	35	37	899	238	81	34	115	82	43	166	42		1,585
Line	229.8	13.9	14.3	258.0	89.4	24.1	14.5	38.6	33.7	19.3	71.0	17.6		527.6
1978 Track	827	35	37	899	238	81	34	115	82	43	166	69		1,612
Line	229.8	13.9	14.3	258.0	89.4	24.1	14.5	38.6	33.7	19.3	71.0	30.8		540.8
1979 Track	827	35	37	899	238	81	34	115	82.	43	166	78	31	1,652
Line	229.8	13.9	14.3	258.0	89.4	24.1	14.5	38.6	33.7	19.3	71.0	33.7	11.8	555.5
1980 Track	827	35	37	899	238	81	34	115	88	43	166	85	31	1,665
Line	229.8	13.9	14.3	258.0	89.4	24.1	14.5	38.6	36.7	19.3	71.0	37.2	11.8	562.0

2. STREETCARS AND LIGHT RAIL (includes grade-separated sections as shown below)

	Philadelphia Region					Boston	S.F.	Pittsbg.		Clevl.	Newark	Ft. W.		U.S.
	Str.	S-Surf.	Media	P.&W.	Total	MBTA	MUNI	PAT	N. Orl.	GCRTA	NJT	Tandy	Detroit[4]	Total
1975 Track	136[2]	58	24	28	246	89	42	44	15	25[3]	9	3	0	473
Line	53.4	20.8	11.9	13.6	99.7	28.9	19.4	24.1	6.5	10.5	4.3	1.2	0	194.6
of which: in street	53.4	17.3	1.6	0	72.3	2.5	14.5	6.0	0.9	0	0	0	0	98.2
reserved[1]	0	1.0	10.3	0	11.3	9.7	1.9	17.5	5.6	7.1	0	0	0	53.1
grade-separated	0	2.5	0	13.6	16.1	14.7	3.0	0.6	0	3.4	4.3	1.2	0	43.3
1980 Track	136	58	24	28	246	89[5]	51[6]	44[7]	15	25	9	3	2	484
Line	53.4	20.8	11.9	13.6	99.7	28.9	24.2	24.1	6.5	10.5	4.3	1.2	0.8	200.2
of which: in street	53.4	17.3	1.6	0	72.3	4.5	16.0	6.0	0.9	0	0	0	0.8	100.5
reserved	0	1.0	10.3	0	11.3	9.7	1.9	17.5	5.6	7.1	0	0	0	53.1
grade-separated	0	2.5	0	13.6	16.1	14.7	6.3	0.6	0	3.4	4.3	1.2	0	46.6

3. COMMUTER RAIL

	N. Y. Region	Chicago	Phila.	Boston	S. F.	Detroit	Wash.	Pittsb.	U. S. Total
1976 Line	1,042	429	365	228	49	36[8]	110[8]	18.2	2,267

(1) Reserved means a private right-of-way or a street median with intersections at grade. Grade-separated may be in tunnel, elevated or near grade, but as a rule without grade intersections.
(2) After the 1975 Woodland depot fire, various Philadelphia surface routes were temporarily taken out of service, but their physical extent has not changed.
(3) The Shaker Heights lines operate over 30 miles of track or 13.1 miles of line, but about 5 track-miles or 2.6 line-miles are shared with Rapid Transit and are not included to avoid duplication.
(4) Downtown Detroit line introduced in 1976; El Paso line with 6 miles of track discontinued in 1973; there were no other changes in 1970-79.
(5) Includes 2 miles of street line not in operation; line-miles operated 26.9 per Table A-6.
(6) Includes surface track on Market Street temporarily maintained after commencement of tunnel operations; this is also included in line-miles.
(7) Includes tunnel bypass not in regular service; line-miles operated 22.3 per Table A-6.
(8) Excludes Amtrak 36 and 40 miles, respectively.

Note: Miles of single track include yards, sidings, and non-revenue spurs and correspond to data in Table H-1; miles of line correspond to data in Table H-5. Mileages are as of December 31 of each year.

Table H-4
Annual Passengers and Passenger Miles of Urban Rail Transit in the United States by Property, 1969-1980 (000's)

1. RAPID TRANSIT

	New York Region				Chicago	Philadelphia Region			S.F.	Boston	Wash.	Clevl.	Atlanta	U.S.
	NYCTA	SIRT	PATH	Total	CTA	SEPTA	PATCO	Total	BART	MBTA	WMATA	GCRTA	MARTA	Total
1969 Pass.	1,343,270	5,244	37,751	1,386,265	148,600	92,422	6,116	98,538		92,400		16,490		1,742,293
Pass. mi.	9,671,544	34,086	169,880	9,875,510	1,084,780	452,868	54,738	507,606		332,640		126,973		11,917,509
1970 Pass.	1,257,569	4,756	38,954	1,301,279	157,300	87,769	8,607	96,376		86,900		14,100		1,655,955
Pass. mi.	9,054,497	30,914	175,293	9,260,704	1,148,290	430,068	77,033	507,101		312,840		108,570		11,337,505
1971 Pass.	1,196,876	4,722	38,877	1,240,475	153,900	77,641	9,563	87,204		82,000		13,288		1,576,867
Pass. mi.	8,617,507	30,693	174,947	8,823,147	1,123,470	380,441	85,589	466,030		295,200		102,318		10,810,165
1972 Pass.	1,145,129	4,100	40,282	1,189,511	150,900	79,649	10,950	90,599	1,182	82,500		12,702		1,527,394
Pass. mi.	8,244,929	26,650	181,269	8,456,848	1,101,570	390,280	98,003	488,283	15,366	297,000		97,805		10,452,872
1973 Pass.	1,101,414	3,950	30,040	1,135,404	140,600	79,418	10,127	89,545	8,414	80,300		11,810		1,466,073
Pass. mi.	7,930,181	25,675	135,180	8,091,036	1,026,380	389,148	90,637	479,785	109,382	289,080		90,937		10,086,600
1974 Pass.	1,099,970	4,556	37,774	1,142,300	151,300	71,557	11,110	82,667	21,926	79,500		11,348		1,489,041
Pass. mi.	7,919,784	29,614	169,983	8,119,381	1,104,490	350,629	99,435	450,064	285,038	286,200		87,380		10,332,553
1975 Pass.	1,053,931	4,371	38,339	1,096,641	149,000	81,059	11,120	92,179	31,089	78,900		10,885		1,458,694
Pass. mi.	7,588,303	28,412	172,526	7,789,241	1,087,700	397,189	99,524	496,713	467,284	284,040		83,815		10,208,793
1976 Pass.	1,010,497	2,827	40,688	1,054,012	149,200	84,629	11,523	96,152	34,024	80,200	4,279	11,757		1,429,624
Pass. mi.	7,275,578	18,376	183,096	7,477,050	1,089,160	414,682	103,131	517,813	449,558	288,720	8,558	90,529		9,921,388
1977 Pass.	998,455	4,399	40,667	1,043,521	148,900	70,370	10,984	81,354	35,715	80,700	19,010	10,643		1,419,843
Pass. mi.	7,188,876	28,594	183,002	7,400,472	1,086,970	344,813	98,307	443,120	458,443	290,520	58,931	81,951		9,820,407
1978 Pass.	1,042,730	4,687	41,750	1,089,167	150,382	86,920	10,924	97,844	41,666	83,300	48,043	10,791		1,521,193
Pass. mi.	7,507,656	30,466	187,875	7,725,997	1,097,789	425,908	97,770	523,678	528,589	299,880	194,574	83,091		10,453,598
1979 Pass.	1,076,535	5,381	44,273	1,126,189	150,710	83,040	11,043	94,083	31,720	88,962	69,195	10,819	2,655	1,574,333
Pass. mi.	7,751,052	34,977	199,229	7,985,258	1,100,183	406,896	98,835	505,731	381,466	320,263	338,364	83,306	11,151	10,725,722
1980 Pass.	1,008,120	6,019	35,865	1,050,004	154,700	89,839	11,900	101,739	45,300	90,501	76,776	11,027	18,000	1,548,047
Pass. mi.	7,258,464	39,124	160,458	7,458,046	1,130,000	485,130	106,505	571,635	544,500	325,803	382,463	87,258	75,600	10,595,305

2. STREETCARS AND LIGHT RAIL

	Newark NJT	Philadelphia Region - SEPTA				S. F. MUNI	Boston MBTA	Clevl. GCRTA	Pittsbg. PAT	New Orleans	Ft. W. Tandy	U. S. Total
		City Transit	P.&W.	Media-Sharon Hill	Total							
1969 Pass.	4,201	63,001	2,515	3,317	68,833		52,900	4,970	10,510	9,583	1,200	
Pass. mi.	10,503	164,739	16,851	11,143	192,733	. . .	132,250	37,772	58,331	24,916	960	
1970 Pass.	4,272	54,314	2,498	3,319	60,131	FY 56,672	49,800	4,834	10,428	8,878	1,200	196,215
Pass mi.	10,680	140,442	16,737	11,185	168,364	154,148	124,500	36,738	57,875	23,083	960	576,348
1971 Pass.	3,475	47,112	2,332	3,124	52,568	FY 52,131	46,900	4,413	9,267	8,716	1,200	178,670
Pass mi.	8,688	121,002	15,624	10,564	147,190	141,797	117,250	33,538	51,432	22,662	960	523,517
1972 Pass.	2,020	51,881	2,470	3,177	57,528	FY 50,142	47,250	3,894	6,703	8,452	1,200	177,189
Pass mi.	5,050	133,972	16,549	10,557	161,078	136,387	118,125	29,594	37,202	21,975	960	510,371
1973 Pass.	2,355	51,774	2,826	3,276	57,876	FY 50,187	46,000	3,668	6,650	8,146	1,200	176,082
Pass. mi.	5,888	132,764	18,934	10,355	162,053	136,510	115,000	27,877	36,908	21,180	960	506,376
1974 Pass.	2,443	50,976	2,425	3,736	57,133	FY 47,939	45,500	3,727	6,662	7,828	1,200	172,432
Pass. mi.	6,108	130,418	16,248	13,306	159,972	130,393	113,750	28,325	36,974	20,353	960	496,835
1975 Pass.	2,409	41,427	2,161	3,559	47,147	FY 48,704	45,200	3,612	7,303	5,687	1,200	161,262
Pass. mi.	6,023	104,556	14,479	12,977	132,012	132,474	113,000	27,451	40,532	14,786	960	467,238
1976 Pass.	2,249	38,794	2,218	3,511	44,523	FY 41,422	46,000	4,717	6,455	6,789	1,200	153,355
Pass. mi.	5,623	97,145	14,861	12,638	124,644	112,667	115,000	35,849	35,825	17,651	960	448,219
1977 Pass.	2,519	29,318	1,688	2,993	33,999	FY 44,477	46,200	4,863	6,191	6,527	1,300	146,076
Pass. mi.	6,298	72,688	11,310	11,159	95,197	120,978	115,500	36,959	34,360	16,970	1,040	427,302
1978 Pass.	3,445	29,980	1,992	3,327	35,299	FY 41,772	47,700	4,972	6,185	6,690	1,400	147,463
Pass. mi.	8,613	73,306	13,346	12,185	98,837	113,621	119,250	37,787	34,327	17,394	1,120	430,949
1979 Pass.	3,450	30,227	2,395	3,567	36,189	FY 44,977	51,229	5,298	6,393	6,958	1,500	155,994
Pass. mi.	8,625	72,711	16,047	12,571	101,329	122,296	128,073	40,265	35,481	20,052	1,200	457,321
1980 Pass.	3,413	27,478	2,468	3,400	33,346	FY 43,018	52,105	5,049	6,307	6,637	1,675	151,550
Pass. mi.	8,533	60,451	16,784	11,901	89,136	123,053	130,263	39,770	35,004	19,069	1,340	446,168

Note: San Francisco MUNI passenger data for 1970-78 adjusted to reflect 1979-80 counts; do not agree with unadjusted 1976 figures reported in Table A series.

Table H-4 (cont'd.)
Annual Passengers and Passenger Miles of Urban Rail Transit in the United States by Property, 1969-1980 (000's)

3. COMMUTER RAIL

	New York Region	Chicago RTA	Phila. SEPTA	S. F. S. Pacific	Detroit SEMTA	Boston MBTA	Wash.	Pittsbg. PAT	U. S. Total
1969 Pass.	147,912	. . .	33,598	6,108	410	8,063	. . .	. . .	. . .
Pass. mi.	3,638,635		430,054	151,220	5,945	130,621			
1970 Pass.	148,609	. . .	32,210	5,826	323	8,017	. . .	. . .	. . .
Pass mi.	3,442,725		412,288	144,429	4,684	129,875			
1971 Pass.	145,036	66,500	32,046	5,484	342	8,149	1,105	383	259,045
Pass. mi.	3,359,601	1,359,000	410,189	134,130	4,959	132,014	25,084	5,750	5,430,727
1972 Pass.	133,863	. . .	30,748	5,439	365	7,659	. . .	. . .	. . .
Pass. mi.	3,129,408		393,574	130,672	5,293	124,076			
1973 Pass.	128,325	. . .	29,635	5,386	389	7,558	. . .	. . .	. . .
Pass. mi.	3,006,744		379,328	132,625	5,641	122,440			
1974 Pass.	141,845	. . .	30,812	5,523	432	8,145	1,105	. . .	. . .
Pass. mi.	3,327,579		394,394	135,655	6,480	131,999	25,084		
1975 Pass.	143,406	69,316	30,535	4,720	369	7,945	1,237	357	257,885
Pass. mi.	3,356,775	1,404,342	390,848	116,499	5,535	131,093	28,080	5,355	5,438,527
1976 Pass.	145,361	70,262	31,205	4,366	331	7,562	1,403	360	260,850
Pass. mi.	3,396,594	1,423,508	399,424	107,268	5,131	128,554	31,848	5,400	5,497,727
1977 Pass.	148,735	68,500	34,368	4,320	323	7,842	1,599	347	266,034
Pass. mi.	3,475,522	1,387,810	439,910	106,070	5,168	137,235	36,297	5,205	5,593,217
1978 Pass.	152,137	FY 72,388	31,460	4,341	412	7,831	1,680	383	270,632
Pass. mi.	3,551,699	1,466,581	402,688	107,021	6,798	140,958	38,136	5,745	5,719,626
1979 Pass.	160,203	79,130	32,221	5,699	477	8,700	1,763	377	288,570
Pass. mi.	3,744,780	1,636,102	412,429	134,823	8,109	159,900	40,020	5,655	6,141,818
1980 Pass.	166,315	80,914	31,566	6,113	515	9,339	(1,908)	353	297,023
Pass. mi.	3,887,556	1,683,226	401,823	142,181	8,748	171,644	43,312	5,295	6,343,785

FY - Fiscal year; all other data for calendar years.

Addendum to Tables H-3 and H-4: Canadian Systems 1976 and 1980

	Miles of Track and Line					Passengers and Passenger-Miles, 000's			
	Toronto	Montreal	Edmonton	Total		Toronto	Montreal	Edmonton	Total
1. RAPID TRANSIT									
1976 Track	n.a.	n.a.	––	n.a.	1976 Pass.	198,200	148,023	––	346,223
Line	26.6	18.5	––	45.1	Pass. mi.	824,512	503,280	––	1,327,779
1980 Track	99.9	63.4	10.0	173.3	1980 Pass.	231,120	172,975	6,500	410,595
Line	33.8	25.4	4.5*	63.7	Pass. mi.	1,040,040	691,901	22,750	1,754,691
2. STREETCARS									
1976 Track	n.a.	––	––	n.a.	1976 Pass.	100,917	––	––	100,917
Line	46.3	––	––	46.3	Pass. mi.	292,659	––	––	292,659
1980 Track	125.0	––	––	125.0	1980 Pass.	97,175	––	––	97,175
Line	45.6**	––	––	45.6****	Pass. mi.	285,810	––	––	285,810
3. COMMUTER RAIL									
1976 Track	n.a.	n.a.	––	n.a.	1976 Pass.	9,158	9,100	––	18,258
Line	90.0	149.0	––	239.0	Pass. mi.	192,318	109,357	––	301,675
1980 Track	n.a.	n.a.	––	n.a.	1980 Pass.	12,540	4,121	––	16,661
Line	111.2***	159.8	––	271.0	Pass. mi.	225,720	52,244	––	277,964

* Includes 1 mile of tunnel, the rest on exclusive right-of-way with some grade crossings; due to high-quality right-of-way all is listed under rapid transit.
** In addition, 4.4 miles of Light Rail were under construction, to be opened in 1983.
*** An additional 31.3 miles added 10/6/81.
**** In addition, 7.8 miles of Light Rail were opened in Calgary in 1981.

Table H-5

Miles of Line of Grade-Separated Rail Transit in the United States by Urban Area, by Type, Section, and Year Opened or Closed, 1870-1980

Line-miles (also known as miles of first track, or route-miles without duplication) measure the length of a transit line irrespective of the number of tracks it has; they tend to be measured center-to-center of stations and to the outer limit of turnback points at terminals, but exclude non-revenue spurs. The type **E** (Elevated), **O** (Open ballasted track) and **T** (Tunnel) refers to the predominant character of a section, not to individual structures. **RT** means Rapid Transit, **LRg-s** Light Rail or streetcar-type lines which are fully grade-separated. Partially grade-separated mileage is not included, except to a minor extent in Chicago. Mileages for each year are as of December 31.

1. NEW YORK REGION

(Place designations: M—Manhattan, Bn—Brooklyn, Bx—Bronx, Q—Queens, H—Hudson County, SI—Staten Island, E—Essex County)

						Cumulative miles of line in operation			
Year	Line-miles	Type	Place	Line (present name)	Section	E	O	T	Sum
1870	+ 3.3	E	M	9th Av. El	Battery Pl. to 30 St.	3.3			3.3
1873	+ 0.3	E	M	9th Av. El	B'way to Cortlandt	3.6			3.6
1875	+ 0.4	E	M	9th Av. El	30 St. to 42 St.	4.0			4.0
1876	+ 0.9	E	M	9th Av. El	42 St. to 61 St.	4.9			4.9
1877	+ 0.2	E	M	9th Av. El	B'way to So. Ferry	5.1			5.1
1878	+ 5.1	E	M	6th Av. El	Morris St. to 59 St.				
1878	+ 8.7	E	M	3d Av. El	So. Ferry to 129 St. & 2d Av. + GCT link	18.9			18.9
1879	+ 0.3	E	M	6th Av. El	53 St. link to 8th Av.				
1879	+ 0.4	E	M	3d Av. El	City Hall-Chatham Sq. link				
1879	+ 5.1	E	M	9th Av. El	61 St. to 155 St. & 53 St. link to 8th Av.	24.7			24.7
1880	+ 7.2	E	M	2d Av. El	Chatham Sq. to 127 St.				
1880	+ 0.3	E	M	3d Av. El	34 St. Ferry link	32.2			32.2
1883	+ 1.2	E	M+Bn	Myrtle Av. El	Brooklyn Bridge Railroad	33.4			33.4
1885	+ 6.8	E	Bn	Lex. Av. El	Fulton Ferry to Van Sicklen	40.2			40.2
1886	+ 0.9	E	Bx	3d Av. El	129 St. to 143 St. + Willis Av. link	41.1			41.1
1888	+ 2.7	E	Bn	BMT Jamaica	B'way Ferry to Gates Av. (Lex. junction)				
1888	+ 1.8	E	Bn	Myrtle Av. El	Sands to Grand				
1888	+ 4.5	E	Bn	Fulton St. El	Fulton Ferry to Rockaway Av.				
1888	+ 1.4	E	Bx	3d Av. El	143 St. to 169 St.				
1888	+ 0.9	E	Bn	5th Av. El	Park-Hudson to Atlantic	52.4			52.4
1889	+ 0.4	E	Bn	Fulton St. El	Rockaway to East N.Y. junction				
1889	+ 2.0	E	Bn	5th Av. El	Atlantic Av. to 25 St.				
1889	+ 2.8	E	Bn	Myrtle Av. El	Grand to Wyckoff (incl. 1.3 BMT Myrtle)	57.6			57.6
1890	+ 1.0	E	Bn	Fulton St. El	East N.Y. junction to Pitkin + Van Sicklen				
1890	+ 0.6	E	Bn	5th Av. El	25 St. to 36 St.	59.2			59.2
1891	+ 1.1	E	Bx	3d Av. El	169 St. to 177 St.				
1891	– 1.0	E	Bn	Lex. Av. El	Park-Hudson to Grand—Myrtle closed	59.3			59.3
1892	+ 0.6	E	Bn	Fulton St. El	Van Sicklen to Montauk Av.	59.9			59.9
1893	+ 1.5	E	Bn	BMT Jamaica	Van Sicklen to Cypress Hills				
1893	+ 2.5	E	Bn	5th Av. El	36 St. to 65 St. + 3d Ave.	63.9			63.9
1894	+ 0.7	E	Bn	Fulton St. El	Montauk Av. to Queens border	64.6			64.6

1901	+ 1.2	E	Bx	3d Av. El	177 St. to Fordham Rd.	65.8			65.8
1902	+ 0.3	E	Bx	3d Av. El	Fordham Rd. to Bx. Pk.	66.1			66.1
1904	– 1.3	E	Bn	Lex. Av. El	Fulton Ferry to Myrtle closed				
1904	+12.8	T	M	IRT Lex.-B'way	City Hall via Lafayette & Park Av. to 42 St., B'way to 157 St. & Lenox to 145 St.				
1904	+ 2.5	E	Bx	IRT White Plains	3d Av. to 177 St.	67.3		12.8	80.1
1905	+ 1.1	T	M	IRT Lex.	City Hall to So. Ferry				
1905	+ 1.5	T	M-Bx	IRT Lenox	145 St. to 3d Av.				
1905	+ 2.5	O	Bn	BMT Brighton	Fulton–Franklin to Church	67.3	2.5	15.4	85.2
1906	+ 2.3	T	M	IRT B'way	157 to Dyckman St.				
1906	+ 1.0	E	M	IRT B'way	Dyckman to 221 St.				
1906	+ 0.8	O	Bn	BMT Canarsie	B'way junction to Rock. Pk. (excluding trolley)				
1906	+ 1.5	E	Bn			69.8	3.3	17.7	90.8
1907	+ 0.5	E	Bx	IRT B'way	221 St. to 230 St.				
1907	+ 4.7	O	Bn	BMT Brighton	Church Av. to Sheepshead	70.3	8.0	17.7	96.0
1908	+ 2.7	T	M-Bn	IRT Joralemon	Bowling Green to Atl. Av.				
1908	+ 2.8	T	H-M	PATH uptown	Hoboken to 23 St. & 6th Av.				
1908	+ 0.8	E	Bx	IRT B'way	230 St. to 242 St.				
1908	+ 1.2	E	M-Bn	BMT Jamaica	Williamsburg Bridge to Delancey	72.3	8.0	23.2	103.5
1909	+ 2.4	T	H-M	PATH downtown	Hudson term. via Ex. Pl. to Hoboken	72.3	8.0	25.6	105.9
1910	+ 0.9	T	H-M	PATH uptown	23 St. to 33 St. + Ex. Pl. to Grove	72.3	8.0	26.5	106.8
1911	+ 0.7	T	H	PATH					
1911	+ 7.1	O	H-E	PATH	Grove St. to Newark	72.3	15.1	27.2	114.6
1913	+ 1.2	T	M	BMT-Delancey	Centre St. tunnel to Chambers	72.3	15.1	28.4	115.8
1915	+ 1.5	E	Q	BMT Myrtle	Wyckoff to Metropolitan				
1915	+ 5.1	O	Bn	BMT Sea Beach	4th Av. to Stillwell (Coney Is.)				
1915	+ 7.3	T	M-Bn	BMT 4th Av.	Chambers via Bridge to 65 St. + Sea B. conn.				
1915	+ 1.3	T	M-Q	IRT Flushing	Steinway tunnel GCT to Jackson				
1915	+ 2.2	E	Q	Fulton St. El	Hudson to Lefferts (IND since 1956)	76.0	20.2	37.0	133.2
1916	+ 1.0	T	Bn	BMT 4th Av.	65 St. to 86 St.				
1916	+ 0.2	T	Q	IRT Flushing	Jackson Av. to Hunterspoint Av.				
1916	+ 4.9	E	Bn	BMT-West End	36 St. to 25th Av.				
1916	+ 0.9	E	Q	IRT Flushing	Hunterspoint Av. to Queensboro Plaza				
1916	– 0.4	E	Bn	BMT Jamaica	B'way Ferry to Marcy St. closed	81.4	20.2	38.2	139.8
1917	+ 2.8	E	Q	BMT Astoria	Queens Plaza to Ditmars Blvd.				
1917	+ 5.2	E	Bx	IRT White Plains	177 St. to 238 St. + Bx. Pk.				
1917	+ 4.0	E	Q	IRT Flushing	Queens Plaza to Junction Blvd.				
1917	+ 2.3	E	B-Q	BMT Jamaica	Cypress Hills to 111 St.				
1917	+ 3.5	E	Bx	IRT Jerome	149 St. to Kingsbridge Rd.				
1917	+ 0.3	T	Bx						
1917	+ 0.4	T	M	IRT 7th Av.	Times Sq. to Penn. Sta.				
1917	+ 0.1	E	Bx	3d Av.	Bergen cutoff				
1917	+ 1.6	E	Bn	BMT West End	25th Av. to Stillwell (Coney Is.)				
1917	+ 1.5	E	M-Q	2d Av. El	Queensboro Bridge to Queens Plaza				
1917	+ 1.3	T	M	BMT B'way	Canal to 14 St.	102.4	20.2	40.2	162.8
1918	+ 2.0	E	Bx	IRT Jerome	Kingsbridge to Woodlawn				
1918	+ 0.7	E	M-Bx	9th Av. El	155 St. to 167 St. Polo Grounds				
1918	+ 2.4	T	M	BMT B'way	Rector to Canal & 14 St. to 42 St.				
1918	+ 3.8	T	M	IRT 7th Av.	So. Ferry to Penn. Sta.				
1918	+ 2.8	E	Q	BMT Jamaica	111 St. to 168 St. Jamaica				
1918	+ 6.1	T	M-Bx	IRT Lex.	42 St. to 149 St.				
1918	+ 0.3	T	M	BMT B'way	Rector to Whitehall	107.9	20.2	52.8	180.9
1919	+ 3.4	T	Bx	IRT Pelham	125 St. to Hunts Point				
1919	+ 4.6	E	Bn	BMT Culver	9th Av. to Av. X (3.5 IND since 1954)				
1919	+ 1.9	T	M-Bn	IRT 7th Av.	Wall to Boro Hall (Clark St. tunnel)				
1919	+ 1.6	T	M	BMT B'way	42 St. to Lex.	112.5	20.2	59.7	192.4

Year	Line-miles	Type	Place	Line (present name)	Section	Cumulative miles of line in operation: E	O	T	Sum	RT only	LRg-s
1920	+ 3.0	E	Bn	BMT Culver	Av. X to Stillwell (& Brighton link?)						
1920	+ 4.3	E	Bx	IRT Pelham Bay	Hunts Point to Pelham Bay Park						
1920	+ 2.2	E	Bx	3d Av. El	Fordham to Gun Hill Rd.						
1920	+ 0.4	E	Bx	IRT White Plains	238 St. to 241 St.						
1920	+ 4.3	T	M-Bn	BMT Montague	Whitehall to DeKalb to Prospect Pk.						
1920	+ 1.7	T	M-Q	BMT 60 St.	Lex. to Queens Plaza						
1920	+ 3.3	T	Bn	IRT Eastern Pkwy	Atlantic to Sutter						
1920	+ 2.0	E	Bn	IRT Livonia Av.	Sutter to Pennsylvania Av.						
1920	+ 2.5	T	Bn	IRT Nostrand	President to Flatbush	124.4	20.2	71.5	216.1		
1922	+ 0.6	E	Bn	IRT Livonia Av.	Pennsylvania to New Lots	125.0	20.2	71.5	216.7		
1923	– 0.2	E	M	3d Av. El	42 St. Spur closed	124.8	20.2	71.5	216.5		
1924	– 0.3	E	M	6th Av. El	53 St. to 57 St. closed						
1924	+ 4.3	T	M-Bn	BMT 14 St.	6th Av. to Montrose	124.5	20.2	75.8	220.5		
1925	+ 0.8	E	Q	IRT Flushing	Junction (Alburties) to 111 St.						
1925	+ 0.4	T	Bn	BMT 4th Av.	86 St. to 95 St.						
1925	+21.7	O	S	SIRT modernization & electrification		125.3	41.9	76.2	243.4		
1926	+ 0.4	T	M	IRT Flushing	GCT–5th Av.	125.3	41.9	76.6	243.8		
1927	+ 0.3	T	M	IRT Flushing	5th Av. to Times Square						
1927	+ 0.5	E	Q	IRT Flushing	111 St. to Willets Pt.	125.8	41.9	76.9	244.6		
1928	+ 0.5	E	Q	IRT Flushing	Willets Pt. to Flushing						
1928	+ 0.3	T	Q	IRT Flushing	Willets Pt. to Flushing						
1928	+ 3.3	T	Bn	BMT 14 St.	Montrose to B'way Junction	126.3	41.9	80.5	248.7		
						126.3	41.9	80.5	248.7		
1930	– 0.3	E	M	3d Av. El	34 St. spur to East River closed	126.0	41.9	80.5	248.4		
1931	+ 0.3	T	M	BMT 14 St.	6th Av. to 8th Av.						
1931	+ 0.8	T	M	BMT Nassau Loop	Chambers St. to Montague tunnel	126.0	41.9	81.6	249.5		
1932	+12.7	T	M	IND 8th Av.	Chambers St. to 207 St.	126.0	41.9	94.3	262.2		
1933	+ 0.9	E	Bn	IND 8th Av.	Chambers St. to Chambers-Smith St						
1933	+ 6.9	T	M-Bn	IND 8th Av.	Chambers St. to Church Av. (Fulton St. tunnel)						
1933	+ 5.7	T	Bx	IND Concourse	145 St. to 205 St.						
1933	+ 7.1	T	M-Q	IND Queens	8th Av. M. to Roosevelt						
1933	+ 2.4	T	Q-B	IND Crosstown	Queens Plaza to Nassau St.	126.9	41.9	116.4	285.2	285.2	
1935	+ 2.8	O	E	Newark Subway	Warren to Heller Pky						
1935	+ 0.8	T	E	––	Warren to Broad	126.9	44.7	117.2	288.8	285.2	3.6
1936	+ 3.4	T	M-Bn	IND Rutgers St.	West 4 St. to Jay–Boro Hall						
1936	+ 4.4	T	Bn	IND Fulton	Jay–Boro-to Rockaway Av.						
1936	+ 4.1	T	Q	IND Queens	Roosevelt to Union Turnpike						
1936	+ 0.5	T	E	Newark Subway	Broad St. to Penn Station	126.9	44.7	129.6	301.2	297.1	4.1
1937	+ 2.4	T	Q	IND Queens	Union Tpke to 169 St.						
1937	+ 4.6	T	Bn	IND Crosstown	Nassau to Hoyt-Schermerhorn					MAX	
1937		O	E	PATH Park Pl.	closed, changed to Penn. Sta.	126.9	44.7	136.6	308.2	304.1	4.1
1938	– 5.1	E	M	6th Av. El	Morris St. to 53 St. + 9th Av. closed	121.8	44.7	136.6	303.1	299.0	4.1

1940	+ 2.4	T	M	IND 6th Av.	West 4 St. to 53 St.						
1940	– 3.5	E	M	2d Av. El	57 St. to 129 St. closed						
1940	–10.2	E	M	9th Av. El	South Ferry to 155 St. closed						
1940	– 6.0	E	Bn	5th Av. El	Navy St. to 65 St. closed						
1940	– 4.5	E	Bn	Fulton St. El	Fulton Ferry to Rockaway Av. closed						
1940	+ 0.2	O	E	Newark Subway	Heller Pky to Franklin Av.	97.6	44.7	139.0	281.3	277.0	4.3
1941	+ 3.2	O									
1941	+ 0.3	E	Bx	IRT Dyre Av.	233 St. to E. 180 St.	97.9	47.9	139.0	284.8	280.5	4.3
1942	– 5.2	E	M-Q	2d Av. El	Chatham Sq. to Queens Plaza	92.7	47.9	139.0	279.6	275.3	4.3
1944	– 1.8	E	M-Bn	Myrtle Av. El	Park Row to Jay (Bn. Br.) closed	90.9	47.9	139.0	277.8	273.5	4.3
1946	– 0.1	E	Bx	3d Av. El	Bergen Av. cutoff closed						
1946	+ 0.4	T	Bn	IND Fulton St.	Rockaway Av. to East N.Y.	90.8	47.9	139.4	278.1	273.8	4.3
1948	+ 2.0	T	Bn	IND Fulton St.	East N.Y. to Euclid Av.	90.8	47.9	141.4	280.1	275.8	4.3
1950	– 2.6	E	Bn	Lex. Av. El	Grand Av. to Broadway closed						4.3
1950	– 1.2	E	M	3d Av. El	South Ferry to Chatham Sq. closed						4.3
1950	+ 0.5	T	Q	IND Queens	169 St. to 179 St.	87.0	47.9	141.9	276.8	272.5	4.3
1951	– 0.3	E	Bx	3d Av. El	Fordham Rd. to Bx Pk Spur closed	86.7	47.9	141.9	276.5	272.2	4.3
1952	– 0.2	E	Bx	IRT White Plains	177 St. to Bx Pk Spur closed	86.5	47.9	141.9	276.2	271.9	4.3
1953	– 0.4	E	M	3d Av. El	City Hall–Chatham Sq. Spur closed						
1953	– 2.3	O	S	SIRT	South Beach Branch closed						
1953	– 5.1	O	S	SIRT	Arlington Branch closed	86.1	40.5	141.9	268.5	264.2	4.3
1954	+ 0.5	T	Bn	IND Culver	Church Av. to Ditmas	86.1	40.5	142.4	269.0	684.7	4.3
1955	– 8.6	E	M	3d Av. El	Chatham Sq. to 149 St. closed						
1955	+ 0.5	T	Q	BMT 60 St.	BMT–IND connection	77.5	40.5	142.9	260.9	256.6	4.3
1956	– 2.7	E	Q	Fulton St. El	Rockaway Av. to Hudson St. closed						
1956	+ 6.8	O	Q	IND Rockaway	Liberty Av. to Beach Channel Dr.						
1956	+ 4.8	E	Q	IND Rockaway	Rockaway Pk. to Wavecrest						
1956	+ 0.5	E	Q	IND Rockaway	Wavecrest to Far Rockaway	80.1	47.3	142.9	270.3	266.0	4.3
1957	– 0.3	E	Bx	IRT Dyre Av.	linked to Wh. Pl. Rd. line	79.8	47.3	142.9	270.0	265.7	4.3
1958	– 0.7	E	M-Bx	9th Av. El	155 St. to 167 St. closed	79.1	47.3	142.9	269.3	265.0	4.3
1967	+ 1.5	T									
1967	+ 0.9	E	M-Bn	IND Chrystie	DeKalb to Houston	80.0	47.3	144.4	271.7	276.4	4.3
1968	+ 0.4	T	M	IND 6th Av.	53 St. to 58 St.						
1968	+ 0.3	T	M	IRT Lenox	148 St. extension	80.0	47.3	145.1	272.4	268.1	4.3
1969	– 2.7	E	Bn	Myrtle Av. El	Bridge-Jay to B'way closed	77.3	47.3	145.1	269.7	265.4	4.3
1973	– 5.5	E	Bx	3d Av. El	149 St. to Gunhill closed	71.8	47.3	145.1	264.2	259.9	4.3
1975	– 1.0	E	Bn	Culver Shuttle	9th Av. to Ditmas closed	70.8	47.3	145.1	263.2	258.9	4.3
1977	– 0.9	E	Q	BMT Jamaica El	168 St. to Queens Blvd. closed	69.9	47.3	145.1	262.3	258.0	4.3
1980						69.9	47.3	145.1	262.3	258.0	4.3

Sources:

New York Region:

Robert A. Hall, *New York City Rapid Transit Chronology*. Ann Arbor, Mich.: 1945. (A comprehensive listing of opening and closing dates, but without mileages).
New York City Transit Authority, *Demolished Elevated Structures.* (A press release with mileages and dates).
New York City Transit Authority, *Budget Data and Transit Facts.* (Annual, with line-miles by division by type of construction for recent years and a brief chronology of events).
New York City Transit Authority, *Distance and Running Time Between Stations.*
Tri-State Regional Planning Commission, *The Region's Unique Rapid Transit System in Newark*. New York: 1968.

Chicago:

Chicago Transit Authority Memorandum dated May 30, 1980, prepared by Robert D. Heinlein, Assistant Superintendent, Control Center.

Cleveland:

Cleveland Transit System, *Highlights of Rapid Transit Operations,* 1976; also Robert J. Landgraf, "Pre Metro Conversion Now or Never," in *Transportation Research Board Special Report 182,* 1978.

San Francisco:

Primarily R. Ellis and A. Sherret, *Transportation and Travel Impacts of BART.* Burlingame, Calif.: Peat, Marwick, Mitchell & Co., 1976.

Other Cities:

Primarily correspondence with operating agencies and agency leaflets; selected issues of *Headlights,* published by the Electric Railroaders' Association. Other than in Chicago, the data should largely be viewed as estimates, based on secondary sources.

Due to differences in definition and in reporting times, line-mile data in Table H-5 **prior to 1968** do not necessarily match track-mile data in Table H-1. For 1968-1980, both track-mile and line-mile data are consistently reported in Table H-3.

2. CHICAGO REGION

Year	Line-miles	Type	Line (present name)	Section	Cumulative miles of line in operation: E	O	T	Sum
1892	+ 6.0	E	NS South Side	Congress to 55 St.	6.0			6.0
1893	+ 2.6	E	NS South Side	55 St. to Jackson Pk.				
1893	+ 3.3	E	WS Lake	Wacker to California	11.9			11.9
1894	+ 3.0	E	WS Lake	California to Laramie				
1894	+ 0.2	E	WS Lake	Wacker to Tower 18				
1894	+ 0.3	E	Loop	Tower 18 to State/Lake	15.4			15.4
1895	+ 4.5	E	WNW Garfield	Franklin/Jackson to Damen				
1895	+ 1.8	E	WNW Milwaukee	Damen to Logan Sq.				
1895	+ 4.0	E	WNW Garfield	Marshfield Jct. to Cicero				
1895	+ 2.1	E	Humboldt Pk.	Damen Jct. to Lawndale				
1895	+ 1.3	E	WNW Douglas	Marshfield Jct. to 18 St.	29.1			29.1
1896	+ 1.1	E	WNW Douglas	18 St. to Western	30.2			30.2
1897	+ 1.7	E	Loop	State/Lake to Tower 18				
1897	+ 0.2	E	WNW Garfield	Wacker to Tower 8				
1897	−0.1	E	WNW Garfield	Wacker to Franklin/Jackson				
1897	+ 0.2	E	NS South Side	Harrison to Tower 12	32.2			32.2
1899	+ 0.2	E	WS Lake	Laramie to Randolph/Wisconsin				
1899	+ 2.4	O			32.4	2.4		34.8

1900	+ 2.9	E	Ravenswood	Tower 18 to Armitage				
1900	+ 3.7	E	NS North Side	Armitage to Wilson	39.0	2.4		41.4
1901	+ 1.3	O	WS Lake	Lombard Jct. to Harlem	39.0	3.7		42.7
1902	+ 2.1	E	WNW Douglas	Western to Pulaski				
1902	+ 0.2	E	WNW Garfield	Cicero to Laramie (closed)				
1902	+ 0.3	O						
1902	−1.4	O	WS Lake	Lobard Jct. to Randolph/Wisc.	41.3	2.6		43.9
1904	+ 0.2	E	WNW Garfield	Wacker to Wells	41.5	2.6		44.1
1905	+ 3.5	O	WNW Garfield	Laramie to Desplaines Loop				
1905	+ 0.6	E	NS South Side	59 St. to Wentworth	42.1	6.1		48.2
1906	+ 1.2	E	NS South Side	Wentworth to Halsted	43.3	6.1		49.4
1907	+ 0.6	E	NS South Side	Halsted to Racine				
1907	+ 3.5	E	Ravenswood	Clark Jct. to Western				
1907	+ 0.1	E	WNW Douglas	Pulaski to Kenton				
1907	+ 0.6	O						
1907	+ 0.8	E	Normal Pk.	Stewart Jct. to 69 St.				
1907	+ 0.2	E	NS South Side	Racine to Loomis				
1907	+ 0.2	E	Kenwood	Indiana Jct. to 42 Pl.				
1907	+ 1.0	O						
1907	+ 1.2	O	Ravenswood	Western to Kimball				
1907	+ 0.3	O	WNW Douglas	Kenton to Cicero	48.7	9.2		57.9
1908	+ 2.9	E	Stock Yards	Indiana Jct. to Stock Yard Loop				
1908	+ 0.1	E						
1908	+ 3.9	O	NS North Side	Wilson to Howard Jct.				
1908	+ 3.2	O	Evanston	Howard Jct. to Central				
1908	+ 0.2	E	Ravenswood	Wells to N. Water Term.	51.9	16.3		68.2
1910	+ 0.2	O	WS Lake	Harlem to Marengo				
1910	+ 0.5	O	WNW Douglas	Cicero to Laramie	51.9	17.0		68.9
1912	+ 0.7	O	Evanston	Central to Linden				
1912	+ 0.5	O	WNW Douglas	Laramie to Central	51.9	18.2		70.1
1913	+ 0.2	E	NS North Side	Montrose to Lower Wilson	52.1	18.2		70.3
1915	+ 0.8	O	WNW Douglas	Central to Lombard	52.1	19.0		71.1
1921	−0.2	E	NS North Side	Leland to Howard reloc.	51.9	19.2		71.1
1921	+ 0.2	O						
1924	+ 0.8	O	WNW Douglas	Lombard to Oak Pk.	51.9	20.0		71.9
1925	+ 4.9	O	Niles Center	Howard Jct. to Dempster	51.9	24.9		76.8
1926	+ 4.6	O	Westchester	Desplaines to Roosevelt	51.9	29.5		81.4
1930	+ 1.0	O	Westchester	Roosevelt to Mannheim	51.9	30.5		82.4
1943	+ 4.6	T	NS State St. subway	Armitage to 15 St.	51.9	30.5	4.6	87.0
1948	−4.9	O	Niles Center	Howard Jct. to Dempster (closed)				
1948	−0.2	E	WS Lake	Wacker terminal (closed)	51.7	25.6	4.6	81.9
1949	−0.2	E	Ravenswood	Wells to N. Water Term. (closed)				
1949	−1.1	E	NS South Side	Tower 12 to 15 St. (closed)				
1949	−0.1	E	NS South Side	Harrison to Congress Term. (closed)				
1949	−0.2	E	NS North Side	Montrose to Lower Wilson (closed)	50.1	25.6	4.6	80.3

Year	Line-miles	Type	Line (present name)	Section	Cumulative miles of line in operation: E	O	T	Sum
1950	+ 0.1	O	NS North Side	Howard to Howard loop	50.1	25.7	4.6	80.4
1951	+ 3.6	T	WNW Milwaukee subway	Evergreen to LaSalle				
1951	−2.2	E	WNW Milwaukee	Evergreen to Marshfield Jct. (closed)				
1951	−5.6	O	Westchester	Desplaines to Mannheim (closed)				
1951	−0.2	E	WNW Garfield	Wacker to Wells (closed)	47.7	20.1	8.2	76.0
1952	−1.7	O	WNW Douglas	54 St. to Oak Park (closed)				
1952	−2.1	E	Humboldt Pk.	Damen Jct. to Lawndale (closed)	45.6	18.4	8.2	72.2
1953	+ 0.4	E	WNW Garfield	Aberdeen to Sacramento & Desplaines loop				
1953	+ 2.2	O						
1953	−1.7	E	WNW Garfield	Marshfield Jct. to Sacramento (closed)	44.3	20.6	8.2	73.1
1954	−0.8	E	Normal Pk.	Stewart Jct. to 69 St. (closed)				
1954	+ 0.8	E	WNW Douglas	Congress Jct. to Lake/Paulina				
1954	−0.8	E	WNW Garfield	Marshfield Jct. to Aberdeen (closed)				
1954	−0.1	E	WNW Douglas	Congress Jct. (closed)	43.4	20.6	8.2	72.2
1955	+ 0.2	E	WNW Garfield	Wacker to Tower 22				
1955	−0.2	E	WNW Garfield	Wacker to Tower 8 (closed)	43.4	20.6	8.2	72.2
1957	−2.9	E	Stock Yards	Indiana Jct. to Stock Yds. loop (closed)				
1957	−0.2	E						
1957	−1.0	O	Kenwood	Indiana Jct. to 42 Place (closed)	40.3	19.6	8.2	68.1
1958	−0.1	E	WNW Garfield	Desplaines loop (closed)				
1958	+ 6.0	O						
1958	0.7	T	WNW Congress	LaSalle to Lotus (Expwy.)				
1958	−3.9	E						
1958	−3.0	O	WNW Garfield	Tower 22 to Lotus (closed)				
1958	+ 0.5	E	WNW Douglas	Loomis Jct. to Congress Jct.				
1958	−0.8	E	WNW Douglas	Congress Jct. to Lake/Paulina (closed)	36.0	22.6	8.9	67.5
1959	+ 0.3	O	WNW Congress	Lotus to Waller				
1959	−0.3	O	WNW Garfield	Lotus to Waller (closed)	36.0	22.6	8.9	67.5
1960	+ 2.4	O	WNW Congress	Waller to Lathrop				
1960	−2.4	O	WNW Garfield	Waller to Lathrop (closed)	36.0	22.6	8.9	67.5
1962	−0.2	E						
1962	+ 0.2	O	WS Lake	Laramie to Harlem (closed)				
1962	−0.1	O	WS Lake	Harlem to Marengo (closed)	35.8	22.7	8.9	67.4
1964	+ 4.9	O	Skokie Swift	Howard Jct. to Dempster	35.8	27.6	8.9	72.3
1969	+ 0.6	E	NS South Side	Loomis to Ashland				
1969	+ 9.4	O						
1969	+ 2.1	E	WS Dan Ryan	Tower 12 to 95 St.	38.5	37.0	8.9	84.4
1970	+ 3.9	O	WNW Milwaukee	Linden Pl. to Jefferson Pk.				
1970	+ 1.2	T						
1970	−0.1	E	WNW Milwaukee	Linden Pl. to Logan Sq. (closed)	38.4	40.9	10.1	89.4
1980					38.4	40.9	10.1	89.4

3. BOSTON REGION

Year	Line-miles	Type	Line (present name)	Section	E	O	T	Sum	RT only	LRg-s
					Cumulative miles of line in operation					
1897	+ 0.7	T	LR Green	Tremont, Publ. Gdn. to Park & B'way portal			0.7	0.7		0.7
1898	+ 0.8	T	LR Green	Tremont ext. Park St. to North Station			1.5	1.5		1.5
1901	+ 5.8	E	Orange	Dudley to Sullivan Sq. via Atlantic El	5.8		1.5	7.3	5.8	1.5
1904	+ 1.7	T	Blue (LR)	East Boston tunnel Court to Maverick	5.8		3.2	9.0	5.8	3.2
1908	+ 1.1	T	Orange	Washington St. tube	5.8		4.3	10.1	6.9	3.2
1909	+ 2.4	E	Orange	Dudley to Forest Hills	8.2		4.3	12.5	9.3	3.2
1912	+ 1.1	E	LR Green	Lechmere viaduct from North Station						
1912	+ 2.9	T	Red	Park St. to Harvard Sq.	3.3	0.3	7.2	16.8	12.5	4.3
1912	+ 0.3	O	Red							
1914	+ 1.1	T	LR Green	Boylston, Publ. Garden to Auditorium	9.3	0.3	8.3	17.9	12.5	5.4
1915	+ 0.2	T	Red	Beacon Hill tunnel. Park St. to Washington	9.3	0.3	8.5	18.1	12.7	5.4
1916	+ 0.3	T	Red	Washington St. to South Station						
1916	+ 0.3	T	Blue (LR)	Extension to Bowdoin from Court	9.3	0.3	9.1	18.7	13.0	5.7
1917	+ 0.9	T	Red	Dorchester tunnel South Sta. to B'way	9.3	0.3	10.0	19.6	13.9	5.7
1918	+ 1.2	T	Red	Dorchester tunnel B'way to Andrew	9.3	0.3	11.2	20.8	15.1	5.7
1919	+ 1.0	E	Orange	Sullivan Sq. to Everett extension	10.3	0.3	11.2	21.8	16.1	5.7
1926	–	–	Blue	LR operation converted to RT	10.3	0.3	11.2	21.8	18.1	3.7
1927	+ 2.5	E	Red	Andrew to Fields Corner	12.8	0.3	11.2	24.3	20.6	3.7
1928	+ 1.2	E	Red	Fields Corner to Ashmont	14.0	0.3	11.2	25.5	21.8	3.7
1932	+ 0.8	T	LR Green	Auditorium to Kenmore	14.0	0.3	12.0	26.3	21.8	4.5
1938	– 2.3	E	Orange	Atlantic Av. El closed	11.7	0.3	12.0	24.0	19.5	4.5
1941	+ 0.8	T	LR Green	Huntington Av. Copley to Symphony	11.7	0.3	12.8	24.8	19.5	5.3
1952	+ 4.8	O	Blue	Maverick to Orient Hghts and Revere	11.7	5.1	12.8	29.6	24.3	5.3
1959	+ 9.4	O	LR Green	Highland Branch or Riverside line	11.7	14.5	12.8	39.0	24.3	14.7
1971	+ 6.5	O	Red	South Shore to Quincy	11.7	21.0	12.8	45.5	30.8	14.7
1975	+ 1.0	T	Orange	Haymarket north tunnel						
1975	+ 3.6	O	Orange	Community College to Malden						
1975	– 2.5	E	Orange	Everett El closed	9.2	24.6	13.8	47.6	32.9	14.7
1977	+ 0.8	O	Orange	Malden to Oak Grove	9.2	25.4	13.8	48.4	33.7	14.7
1980	+ 3.0	O	Red	Quincy Center to Braintree	9.2	28.4	13.8	51.4	36.7	14.7

4. PHILADELPHIA REGION

Year	Line-miles	Type	Line (present name)	Section	E	Cumulative line-miles O	T	Sum	RT only	LR g-s
1905	+ 0.6	T	Market LR	22 St. to 15 St.			0.6	0.6		0.6
1907	+ 4.3	E	Market	Schuylkill river to 69 St. terminal						
1907	+ 7.8	O	P & W LR	69 St. to Villanova	4.3	7.8	0.6	12.7	4.3	8.4
1908	+ 2.0	T	Market	Schuylkill river to Front St.						
1908	+ 0.7	E	Market spur	2 St. and Market to South St.						
1908	+ 0.4	T	Market LR	15 St. to City Hall	5.0	7.8	3.0	15.8	7.0	8.8
1912	+ 3.3	O	P & W LR	Villanova to Strafford						
1912	+ 5.9	O	P & W LR	Villanova to Morristown	5.0	17.0	3.0	25.0	7.0	18.0
1922	+ 6.5	E	Frankford	Broad to Bridge St.	11.5	17.0	3.0	31.5	13.5	18.0
1928	+ 6.0	T	Broad	City Hall to Olney	11.5	17.0	9.0	37.5	19.5	18.0
1930	+ 0.6	T	Broad	City Hall to South St.	11.5	17.0	9.6	38.1	20.1	18.0
1932	+ 1.5	T	Ridge spur	Girard to Market & 8 St.	11.5	17.0	11.1	39.6	21.6	18.0
1933	+ 0.4	T	Market LR	22 St. to 30 St.	11.5	17.0	11.5	40.0	21.6	18.4
1936	+ 1.5	O	PATCO	Benjamin Franklin Bridge section						
1936	+ 1.1	T	PATCO	To 8 & Market and B'way Camden	11.5	18.5	12.6	42.6	24.2	18.4
1938	+ 1.4	T	Broad	South St. to Snyder	11.5	18.5	14.0	44.0	25.6	18.4
1939	– 0.7	E	Market spur	2 St. and Market to South closed	10.8	18.5	14.0	43.3	24.9	18.4
1953	+ 1.0	T	PATCO	8 St. and Market to 16 and Locust	10.8	18.5	15.0	44.3	25.9	18.4
1955	– 1.7	E	Market	23 St. to 44 St. closed and						
1955	+ 1.7	T	Market	replaced by subway						
1955	+ 1.1	T	Market LR	Market St.–University tunnel to 40 St.	9.1	18.5	17.8	45.4	25.9	19.5
1956	– 3.4	O	P & W LR	Villanova to Strafford closed						
1956	+ 0.4	T								
1956	+ 0.2	O	Broad	Olney to Fern Rock	9.1	15.3	18.2	42.6	26.5	16.1
1959	–	T	Broad	Express tracks Erie to Locust 4.5 mi.	9.1	15.3	18.2	42.6	26.5	16.1
1969	+10.9	O	PATCO	B'way Camden to Lindenwold	9.1	26.2	18.2	53.5	37.4	16.1
1973	+ 1.2	T	Broad	Snyder to Pattison	9.1	26.2	19.4	54.7	38.6	16.1
1977	– 1.2	E	Frankford	Broad to south of Girard St.						
1977	+ 1.2	O	Frankford	Relocation in Delaware freeway median	7.9	27.4	19.4	54.7	38.6	16.1
1980	–		–	–	7.9	27.4	19.4	54.7	38.6	16.1

5. CLEVELAND REGION

Year	Line-miles	Type	Line (present name)	Section	E	O	T	Sum	RT only	LRg-s
					Cumulative miles of line in operation					
1920	+ 4.5	O	Shaker Hgts. LR	E. 34 St. to Shaker Sq.		4.5		4.5		4.5
1930	+ 1.5	O	Shaker Hgts. LR	E. 34 St. to Union Terminal		6.0		6.0		6.0
1955	+ 5.4	O	Cleveland RT	Union Terminal to Windermere						
1955	+ 5.3	O	Cleveland RT	Union Terminal to W. 117 St.		16.7		16.7	13.3	3.4*
1958	+ 1.8	O	Cleveland RT	W. 117 St. to Lorain		18.5		18.5	15.1	3.4
1968	+ 4.2	O	Cleveland RT	Lorain to Hopkins Int. Airport		22.7		22.7	19.3	3.4
1980	–		–	–		22.7		22.7	19.3	3.4

* 2.6 miles of the Shaker Heights LR line shared with Rapid Transit

6. SAN FRANCISCO REGION

Year	Line-miles	Type	Line (present name)	Section	E	O	T	Sum	RT only	LRg-s
1917	+ 2.2	T	Muni Metro LR	Twin Peaks tunnel (surf. service)						
1927	+ 0.8	T	Muni Metro LR	Sunset tunnel (surf. service)						
1972	+25.7	–	BART Fremont	Fremont to MacArthur						
1973	+10.3	–	BART Richmond	Richmond to MacArthur						
1973	+19.1	–	BART Concord	Concord to MacArthur						
1973	+ 7.9	–	BART Daly City	Daly City to Montgomery						
1974	+ 8.0	–	BART Transbay	Montgomery to Oakland	24.0	27.0	20.0	71.0	71.0	
1980	+ 3.2	T	Muni Metro LR	Market St. Embarcadero to Twin Peaks	24.0	27.0	26.2	77.2	71.0	6.2

7. WASHINGTON METROPOLITAN AREA

Year	Line-miles	Type	Line (present name)	Section	E	O	T	Sum	RT only	LRg-s
1976	+ 4.6	–	Red Line	Rhode Island to Farragut North	0.5	0.3	3.8	4.6	4.6	
1977	+13.0	–	Red, Blue	To Dupont; Stadium Armory to Airport	0.9	0.7	16.0	17.6	17.6	
1978	+13.2	–	Red, Orange	To Silver Spring; to New Carrolton	11.3	3.5	16.0	30.8	30.8	
1979	+ 2.9	–	Orange	Courthouse to Ballston	11.3	3.5	18.9	33.7	33.7	
1980	+ 3.5	–	Blue	Benning Rd. to Addison Rd.	11.3	3.5	22.4	37.2	37.2	

8. ATLANTA REGION

Year	Line-miles	Type	Line (present name)	Section	E	O	T	Sum	RT only	LRg-s
1979	+11.8	–	East-West	Avondale to Hightower Rd.	3.6	5.6	2.6	11.8	11.8	

Belvedere
1005

Table A-1
Definition of Terms in Appendix Tables

PASSENGER USE

Annual passengers (or passenger trips) — all passengers entering a system (rail or bus) in the course of a year, including fare-paying (revenue) passengers, non fare-paying passengers, and those transferring from a different system. Transfers within a system are **not** counted as separate trips. In this respect, the definition differs from the APTA Unlinked Trip definition, where an estimate of internal transfers is included to reflect vehicle boardings rather than system boardings. The definition applies to all tables except H-2, which contains estimates of intra-system transfers.

Weekday passengers (or passenger trips) — include all passengers entering a system in the course of an average weekday, using the same definition as above.

Trip length — the distance travelled by a passenger, as defined above, within a system (rail or bus). Distance travelled outside a system (on foot, by auto, etc.) is **not** included as a part of the transit trip. In this respect, the definition differs from that of many Area Transportation Studies, which usually refer to the combined length of a linked trip.

Passenger-miles — the number of passengers multiplied by the average trip length in miles, as defined above.

SYSTEM EXTENT

Line-miles (also known as first-track-miles or route miles without duplication) — the total length of the right-of-way in regular use by transit vehicles.

Track-miles — the total length of all tracks, including non-revenue spurs, yards and sidings. One line-mile usually has two or more track-miles.

Route-miles — the total length of all routes along which services are scheduled. A line may represent only one or any number of routes. In contrast to a line and a track, a route is a scheduling, rather than a physical concept.

SERVICE

Vehicles in service — the active fleet of vehicles, both those available for operation and those in routine maintenance.

Vehicle-miles — the sum of the number of miles each vehicle travelled during a day, a year, etc.

Place-miles — the number of vehicle-miles operated multiplied by the average number of passenger places per vehicle. A passenger place is assumed at 5.38 square feet ($0.5m^2$) of gross vehicle floorspace.

Vehicle-hours — the sum of the number of hours each vehicle was in service during a day, a year, etc.

Operating speed including layover — total vehicle-miles divided by total vehicle-hours.

Operating speed excluding layover — the distance traversed by a vehicle along a route divided by the scheduled time required to do so.

Load factor — the ratio of passenger-miles to place-miles.

Traffic density — the ratio of passenger-miles to line-miles.

Service density — the ratio of place-miles operated to line-miles.

EMPLOYEE CATEGORIES

Vehicle operation — motormen, drivers and all other employees either on vehicles or directly concerned with moving vehicles, such as dispatchers and central control personnel. Excludes conductors only **if** their primary function is fare collection.

Vehicle maintenance — mechanics, car cleaners, and all other personnel directly concerned with servicing and repairing rolling stock.

Maintenance of way, power and signals — mechanics, electricians and other personnel concerned with servicing and repairing the fixed plant, except stations.

Station and fare collection — station cleaners, information clerks and all personnel concerned with fare collection, including servicing automated fare equipment.

Administrative — top managers of each of the above departments, secretarial and related jobs in these departments; central administrative personnel, including legal, financial, purchasing, planning and data processing.

Excluded are in all cases police and employees carried by the capital budget. The allocation of administrative workers shared by several modes within one agency is in proportion to the remaining non-administrative workers.

ENERGY USE

Vehicle operation — electricity drawn **from** rectifier substations through third rail or overhead wires or liquid fuel used by buses.

Total purchased — electricity purchased from utility **prior to** delivery to rectifier substations, all other electricity purchased (lighting, ventilating, escalators, yards, etc.) as well as all other fuel and lubricating materials purchased (incl. garage heating, etc.) if available.

Table A-2
Extent and Use of Rail Rapid Transit in the World

Includes standard Rapid Transit (RT) and extent of fully grade-separated portions of Light Rail (LR); excludes commuter rail
Length of lines in kilometers (1 Km. = 0.62 miles)

	Year open	1880 total	1900 total	1920 total	1940 total	1960 total	1970 total	1975 RT	1975 LR	1975 tunnel	1980 total	Under const. '80	Annual RT rides (millions) (6)	Trip length Km.	1975 Passenger Km. by RT	P Km. line km. (million)	Approximate population in area served (million)	Trips person RT	Line Km. million pop.
1. London (1)	1863	56.3	177.0	252.6	321.8	392.6	400.0	408.9	--	156.0	414.6	3.2	546	8.0	4,354	10.6	7.0	78	58.4
2. New York Region	1867	51.8	103.9	347.7	452.9	433.3	433.9	416.4	6.9	233.5	422.0	10.3	1,097	11.3	12,461	30.0	8.3	132	50.2
3. Chicago	1892		66.6	114.4	132.6	108.6	143.8	143.8	--	16.2	143.8	12.2	149	11.9	1,778	12.4	3.4	44	42.3
4. Budapest	1896		3.9	3.9	3.9	3.9	10.1	14.0	--	11.9	18.7	16.8	53	3.6	190	13.6	1.9	28	7.4
5. Glasgow	1897		10.5	10.5	10.5	10.5	10.5	10.5	--	10.5	10.5	--	15	3.5e	53	5.0	0.9	17	11.7
6. Boston	1897		2.4	35.9	38.8	62.7	62.7	52.9	23.6	23.0	82.7	5.1	80	8.0	452	8.5	2.6	31	29.4
7. Vienna	1898		26.7	26.7	26.7	26.7	26.7	26.7	5.9	12.2	33.1	19.9	75	5.4	405	15.1	1.9	39	17.1
8. Paris	1900		10.3	95.9	172.8	188.4	230.4	252.9	--	183.2	280.8	19.8	1,248	5.8	7,244	28.6	7.3	171	34.6
9. Berlin (2)	1902			35.6	75.9	82.6	99.1	110.8	--	88.5	118.7	16.1	331	6.0	1,986	17.9	3.2	103	34.6
10. Philadelphia	1905			40.2	69.8	68.5	86.0	62.1	25.9	31.2	88.0	--	92	8.7	800	12.9	2.4	38	35.3
11. Hamburg	1912			32.7	64.5	71.4	88.5	90.7	--	32.0	90.7	--	187	5.6	1,048	11.5	1.8	104	50.4
12. Buenos Aires	1913			8.0	22.5	28.0	31.6	31.6	--	31.6	34.7	10.2	242	5.0e	1,210	38.3	3.0	81	10.5
13. Madrid	1919			2.5	29.0	29.0	45.5	60.4	--	54.9	74.0	30.0	547	5.2	2,844	47.0	3.1	176	19.5
14. Barcelona	1924				16.0	18.8	30.2	41.7	--	37.4	55.4	27.2	268	4.5	1,204	28.9	1.7	158	24.5
15. Athens	1925				13.2	25.7	25.7	25.7	--	2.9	25.7	--	92	7.6	701	27.3	0.9	102	28.5
16. Tokyo	1927				14.3	40.2	137.2	163.2	–	138.0	186.7	26.6	1,758	7.0	12,306	75.4	9.0	195	18.1
17. Osaka	1933				7.6	16.7	64.3	70.2	--	56.7	75.6	17.0	759	4.1	3,112	44.3	3.0	253	23.4
18. Moscow	1935				26.3	81.1	139.0	164.5	--	146.0	196.3	9.8	2,083	8.8	18,334	111.5	7.6	274	21.6
19. Stockholm	1950					40.0	65.5	89.8	--	47.7	103.1	6.2	185	6.0	1,110	12.3	1.5	123	60.0
20. Toronto	1954					7.4	34.1	42.8	–	32.0	54.4	--	201	6.7	1,347	31.5	2.2	91	19.5
21. Cleveland	1955					24.5	31.1	31.1	--	0.5	31.1	--	11	12.4	135	4.3	2.0	6	15.5
22. Leningrad	1955					14.2	40.0	52.5	--	51.0	62.0	10.0	613	6.8	4,167	79.3	4.3	143	12.2
23. Rome	1955					11.0	11.0	11.0	--	5.9	25.5	--	22	6.3	137	12.5	2.7	8	4.0
24. Nagoya	1957					6.4	32.4	38.1	--	30.0	51.5	6.0	319	4.2	1,340	35.2	2.0	160	19.0
25. Lisbon	1959					7.2	8.5	12.0	--	12.0	12.0	5.0	70	3.9	275	22.9	1.6	44	7.5
26. Kiev	1960					5.0	14.0	18.2	--	14.0	28.2	8.2	211	5.6	1,180	64.8	1.9	111	9.6
27. Milan	1964						21.0	34.2	--	20.7	40.3	8.3	127	3.5	443	12.9	1.7	75	20.1
28. Oslo	1966						29.1	29.2	--	7.4	33.4	1.5	32	6.3	201	6.9	0.5	64	58.4
29. Montreal	1966						22.0	22.0	--	22.0	41.3	13.1	122	5.5	670	30.5	1.9	64	11.6
30. Tbilisi	1966						10.0	13.0	--	11.4	15.0	6.0	115	3.7	425	32.7	1.0	115	13.0
31. Stuttgart LR	1966						1.3	--	5.2	5.2	7.0	--	n.a.	n.a.	n.a.	n.a.	0.6	n.a.	8.7
32. Baku	1967						11.0	18.0	--	18.0	24.9	--	110	4.9	537	29.8	1.4	79	12.9
33. Cologne LR	1968						4.5	--	12.1	12.1	12.1	8.3	n.a.	n.a.	n.a.	n.a.	0.9	n.a.	13.3
34. Frankfurt LR (3)	1968						4.1	--	7.1	7.1	9.4	--	n.a.	4.8	n.a.	n.a.	0.7	n.a.	10.1
35. Rotterdam	1968						7.5	17.0	--	12.7	17.0	13.5	30	4.1	123	7.2	1.1	27	15.5
36. Brussels (4)	1969						3.5	--	8.0	8.0	17.2	11.5	n.a.	n.a.	n.a.	n.a.	1.2	n.a.	6.7
37. Mexico	1969						42.0	42.0	--	30.9	50.6	32.6	560	7.6	4,256	101.3	7.3	77	5.8
38. Peking	1971							23.0	--	23.0	23.0	16.0	204	6.0e	1,224	53.2	7.6	27	3.0
39. Munich	1971							16.0	--	13.5	36.0	20.0	73	3.9	250	15.6	1.3	53	14.4
40. Sapporo	1971							12.6	--	8.0	24.2	7.0	108	3.7	400	31.7	1.0	108	12.6
41. Yokohama	1972							5.2	--	5.2	11.5	10.7	11	3.2	35	6.8	2.2	50	2.4
42. San Francisco	1972							114.3	--	32.2	114.3	--	33	21.7	713	6.3	2.4	14	47.6
43. Nuremberg	1972							8.5	--	6.2	9.3	12.5	10	4.0e	40	4.7	0.6	17	14.2
44. Sao Paulo	1974							17.2	--	14.0	21.4	21.1	168	7.0	1,176	68.3	7.0	24	2.5
45. Kharkov	1974							9.8	--	9.8	9.8	7.6	98	4.0e	390	36.8	1.4	70	7.6
46. Seoul	1974							10.3	--	8.6	10.3	29.8	180	4.0e	720	70.0	5.5	33	1.9
47. Prague	1974							6.7	--	6.7	16.4	5.3	50e	3.5e	175e	26e	1.1	45e	6.1
48. Bonn LR	1975							--	3.2	3.2	3.2	--	n.a.	n.a.	n.a.	n.a.	0.3	n.a.	10.7
49. Hannover LR	1975							--	3.9	3.9	4.9	10.0	n.a.	n.a.	n.a.	n.a.	0.5	n.a.	14.0
50. Dortmund LR	1975							--	6.8	6.8	6.8	--	n.a.	n.a.	n.a.	n.a.	0.6	n.a.	11.3
51. Antwerp LR	1975							--	1.6	1.6	2.8	6.3	n.a.	n.a.	n.a.	n.a.	0.3	n.a.	5.3
52. Santiago	1975							15.1	-	12.0	20.4	4.6	34	5.0	170	113	2.7	13	5.6

53. Pyongyang	1976										8.0	--							
54. Washington	1976										59.9	43.4							
55. Amsterdam	1977										17.2	--							
56. Marseille	1977										9.6	8.2							
57. Tashkent	1977										11.3	4.1							
58. Essen LR	1977										5.0	10.0							
59. Kobe	1977										5.8	8.0							
60. Lyons	1978										11.1	3.2							
61. Bochum LR	1978										2.1	2.4							
62. Edmonton LR	1978										1.6	1.6							
63. Rio de Janeiro	1979										21.7	8.0							
64. Atlanta	1979										19.0	18.7							
65. Hong Kong	1979										15.6	10.7							
66. Duesseldorf LR	1980										1.7	4.3							
67. Bucharest	1980										8.0	--							
68. Newcastle LR	1980										18.8	35.0							
69. Yerevan	1980										11.4	--							
70. Tianjen	1980										5.0	--							
71. Fukuoka	1980										14.8	--							
72. Kyoto	1981										6.9	5.1							
73. Caracas	1982e										--	20.0							
74. Helsinki	1983e										--	11.5							
75. Lille	1983e										--	12.7							
76. Bilbao	1983e										--	18.0							
77. Seville	1983e										--	10.5							
78. Minsk	1983e										--	13.5							
79. Baltimore	1983e										--	13.7							
80. Miami	1984e										--	33.0							
81. Buffalo	1984e										--	8.4							
82. Gorki	1984e										--	10.0							
83. Calcutta	1985e										--	16.5							
84. Novosibirsk	1985e										--	13.0							
85. Sofia	1986e										--	7.5							
86. Naples	1986e										--	11.0							
87. Baghdad	1986e										--	12.0							
Subtotals:																			
U.S.S.R.		--	--	--	26.3	100.3	214.0	276.0	--	250.2	358.9	82.2	3,230	7.75	25,033	90.4	17.6	183	15.7
ASIA		--	--	--	21.9	63.3	233.9	322.6	--	269.5	438.9	165.4	3,339	5.7	19,137	59.3	30.3	110	10.6
LATIN AMERICA		--	--	8.0	22.5	28.0	71.6	105.9	--	88.5	148.8	96.5	1,004	6.78	6,812	48.0	20.0	50	5.2
NORTH AMERICA		51.8	172.9	538.2	694.1	705.0	813.6		56.4	390.6	1,058.1	159.5	n.a.	n.a.	n.a.	n.a.	25.2	n.a.	37.2
Without LR		51.8	170.5	502.9	651.1	648.7	757.3	885.4			1,000.1	157.9	1,785	10.3	18,356	21.0	25.2	71	35.0
EUROPE		56.3	228.4	460.4	743.3	907.8	1,122.7		53.8	776.5	1,552.1	375.7	n.a.	n.a.	n.a.	n.a.	46.9	n.a.	28.3
Without LR		56.3	228.4	460.4	734.3	907.8	1,109.3	1,266.7			1,478.3	299.4	3,961	5.8	22,783	18.0	41.8	95	30.9
TOTAL—WORLD		108.1	401.3	1,006.6	1,499.1	1,804.4	2,455.8	2,966.8		1,775.3	3,556.8	879.3	n.a.	n.a.	n.a.	n.a.	140.0	n.a.	21.2
Without LR		108.1	398.9	971.3	1,456.1	1,748.1	2,386.1	2,856.6		1,708.9	3,425.0	801.4	13,319	6.9	92,121	32.3	134.9	99	21.2

Notes: (1) Includes 22.5 km. operated jointly with British Rail.
(2) Includes 5 km. inoperable due to partition of the city in 1961.
(3) Total "U-Bahn" length in 1975 36.2 km.; of this 29.1 km. represents surface trackage with grade crossings.
(4) LR only until 1976, when full metro operations were added.
(5) Passenger and passenger-km. data for 1975 when available (as for the U.S., Japan and Canada); some patronage figures represent 1973, 1974 or 1976 (the latter for London and the U.S.S.R.).
Tokyo excludes 109 km. of joint operation on commuter rail line.
Data for New York, Paris, Berlin, Philadelphia and Tokyo include more than one operating system.
n.a. = not applicable; Light Rail patronage figures not shown due to difficulty of separating grade-separated portions from rest of the system.
e. = estimated.

Sources: International Union of Public Transport, *UITP Handbook of Urban Transport*, Brussels, 1975; Paul J. Goldsack, ed.: *Jane's World Railways*, London, 1979 (21st edition); correspondence with selected operating agencies and reports in the periodical press.

Table A-3

Annual and Peak Hour Travel in U.S. Urban Areas by Mode, 1971-72

	A 6 urban areas over 2 million with rail	B 4 urban areas over 2 mill. without rail	C 42 urban areas 0.5 to 2 million	D 189 urban areas 0.05 to 0.5 mill.	Sources in 1974 U.S. DOT National Transportation Report Urban Data Supplement:
1. Total population (000's)	40,717	18,592	38,138	30,744	Table G-1
2. Annual PMT bus (000,000)	7,801	2,180	5,385	1,492	Table D-30
3. Annual PMT rail (000,000)	17,237	19	59	13	Table D-30; 17,557 million for the 6 rail cities reduced by 320 million to correct for apparent overestimates of trip length in Chicago, Philadelphia and Boston.
4. Annual per capita bus PMT	191.6	117.3	141.2	48.5	line 2: line 1 (see also Table D-31)
5. Annual per capita rail PMT	423.3	1.0	1.5	0.4	line 3: line 1 (see also Table D-31)
6. Annual Highway VMT (000,000)	154,543.8	102,503.4	181,657.9	150,112.1	Table D-1, part 1
7. Per capita Highway VMT (000)	3,795.5	5,513.3	4,763.2	4,882.6	line 6: line 1
8. PMT by auto per capita	4,782	6,947	6,002	6,152	line 7 X 0.84 (to exclude truck VMT) X 1.5 occupancy (Table E-3)
9. VMT on freeways (000,000)	48,492.4	32,442.5	47,234.0	27,371.3	Table D-1, part 2
10. % on Freeways	31.3	31.6	26.0	18.2	line 9: line 6
11. Peak hr. PMT bus (000's)	3,422	1,348	3,149	865	Table D-27
12. Peak hr. PMT rail (000's)	11,356	42	52	3	Tables D-28 and D-29 (both rail modes)
13. Per capita peak bus PMT	0.0840	0.0725	0.0826	0.0281	line 11: line 1
14. Per capita peak rail PMT	0.2789	0.0023	0.0014	0.0001	line 12: line 1
15. Per capita peak auto PMT	0.9084	1.3196	1.1400	1,1686	line 7 X 0.84 X 1.3 occupancy (Table E-3): 365 X 0.08 (peaking factor assumed to be the same on freeways and non-freeways)
16. Total peak hr. PMT/Capita	**1.2713**	**1.3944**	**1.2240**	**1.1968**	**Sum of lines 13, 14 and 15**
17. Total annual PMT/Capita	**5,396.9**	**7,065.3**	**6,144.7**	**6,200.9**	**Sum of lines 4, 5 and 8**

PMT = Person-miles travelled

VMT = Vehicle-miles travelled

Note: A includes N.Y.-N.J. area, Chicago, Philadelphia, San Francisco, Boston and Cleveland
B includes Los Angeles, Detroit, Washington and St. Louis

Source: 1974 National Transportation Report Urban Data Supplement (U.S. DOT, Washington, D.C. May, 1976).

Table A-4
Rapid Transit Trains, Cars and Passengers Entering Downtowns

FROM (DIRECTION) VIA (LINE)	PEAK HOUR INBOUND (8-9 A.M.)				Gross Floorspace		ALL DAY INBOUND (24 hours)				8–9 A.M. as % of all day	
I. MANHATTAN CBD (October, 1976)	Trains	Cars	Passengers	Cars/train	m^2/car	m^2/pass.	Trains	Cars	Passengers	Cars/train	Cars	Passengers
1. N IRT Lexington Avenue express	23	230	35,710	10.0	41.7	0.27**	255	2,320	125,120	9.1	9.9	28.5
2. local	18	180	26,450	10.0	41.7	0.28**	227	2,104	113,540	9.3	8.5	23.3
3. E IND Queens (53d St. tun.)	28	266	53,330	9.5	58.7	0.29**	310	2,542	157,450	8.2	10.5	33.9
4. N IND Eighth Avenue express	23	224	32,660	9.7	55.9	0.38*	283	2,396	133,820	8.5	9.3	24.4
5. local	19	152	13,770	8.0	55.9	0.62	178	1,136	42,000	6.4	13.4	32.8
6. N IRT Broadway express	19	181	27,290	9.5	41.7	0.28**	243	2,117	110,780	8.7	8.5	24.6
7. local	14	140	14,590	10.0	41.7	0.40*	230	1,730	78,410	7.5	8.1	18.6
8. E BMT Manhattan Bridge north	20	176	24,010	8.8	57.0	0.42*	426	3,095	121,850	7.3	9.8	31.9
9. south	16	128	14,860	8.0	56.6	0.49						
10. E IRT Flushing (Steinway tun.)	29	319	37,060	11.0	41.7	0.36**	258	2,447	96,620	9.5	13.0	38.4
11. E BMT Astoria (60th St. tun.)	25	200	31,720	8.0	59.2	0.37*	237	1,756	94,140	7.4	11.4	33.7
12. E IND Eighth Avenue (Cranberry tun.)	21	190	28,110	9.0	55.9	0.38*	192	1,657	88,220	8.6	11.5	31.9
13. E IRT Lexington (Joralemon tun.)	17	170	22,460	10.0	41.7	0.32*	198	1,830	72,440	9.2	9.3	31.0
14. W PATH World Trade Center	38	266	20,960	7.0	43.8	0.56	306	1,725	44,105	5.6	15.4	47.5
15. E BMT Fourth Ave. (Montague tun.)	23	184	19,470	8.0	55.9	0.53	231	1,628	54,900	7.0	11.3	35.4
16. E IRT Broadway (Clark tun.)	17	162	15,870	9.5	41.7	0.43*	225	1,957	54,160	8.7	8.3	29.3
17. E BMT Jamaica (Williamsburg Br.)	18	144	14,820	8.0	55.9	0.54	211	1,408	44,930	6.7	10.2	33.0
18. E BMT Canarsie (14th St. tun.)	10	80	11,020	8.0	55.9	0.41*	136	859	38,970	6.3	9.3	28.3
19. W PATH Hoboken	20	110	9,979	5.5	43.8	0.48	244	1,282	27,670	5.3	8.6	36.1
20. E IND Sixth Ave. (Rutgers tun.)	12	108	9,840	9.0	55.9	0.61	152	1,200	40,610	7.9	9.0	24.2
E IND 63d Street tun. (under constr.)	--	--	--	--	--	--	--	--	--	--	--	--
Subtotal, NYCTA	**352**	**3,234**	**433,040**	**9.2**	**50.4**	**0.38**	**3,992**	**32,182**	**1,467,960**	**8.1**	**10.0**	**29.5**
Subtotal, PATH	**58**	**376**	**30,939**	**6.5**	**43.8**	**0.53**	**550**	**3,007**	**71,775**	**5.5**	**12.5**	**43.1**
21. **S Staten Island Rapid Transit (to ferry)**	**8**	**26**	**3,600**	**3.2**	**69.7**	**0.50**	**65**	**202**	**6,800**	**3.1**	**12.9**	**52.9**
TOTAL, MANHATTAN CBD	**418**	**3,636**	**467,579**		**49.8**	**0.39**	**4,607**	**35,391**	**1,546,535**		**10.3**	**30.2**
II. **TORONTO (October, 1976)**		**(8-9 A.M.)**						**(19:10 hours)**				
1. N Yonge-University line	30	210	22,871e	7.0	61.6	0.57	363	2,338	101,233	6.4	9.0	22.6e
2. E Danforth Avenue line	22	132	22,739e	6.0	71.5	0.42*	298	1,788	90,289	6.0	7.4	25.2e
3. W Bloor Street line	22	132	21,481e	6.0	71.5	0.44*	292	1,752	95,572	6.0	7.5	22.4e
											--	
TOTAL, TORONTO DOWNTOWN	**74**	**474**	**67,091**	**6.4**	**67.1**	**0.47**	**953**	**5,878**	**287,094**	**6.2**	**8.0**	**23.4e**
4. N Spadina line (February, 1980)	25	162	10,427				346	2,082	37,099			
III. **MONTREAL (1976)**		**(8-9 A.M.)**						**(20 hours)**				
1. N Line 2 Rue Berri	23	207	28,230	9.0	42.5	0.31**	251	2,259	98,000e	9.0	9.2	
2. E Line 1 Bl. de Maisonneuve	17	153	19,110	9.0	42.5	0.34*	231	2,079	70,000e	9.0	7.3	27.3e
3. S Line 4 St. Lawrence River tunnel	16	96	13,913	6.0	42.5	0.29*	211	720	30,900e	3.4	13.3	45.0e
4. W Line 1 from Atwater (ext. under constr.)	14	126	4,333	9.0	42.5	1.24	231	2,079	42,100e	9.0	6.0	10.3e
5. W Line 2 (extension under constr. 1976)	--	--	--	--	--	--	--	--	--	--	--	--
TOTAL, MONTREAL CENTER	**70**	**582**	**65,586**	**8.3**	**42.5**	**0.38**	**924**	**7,137**	**241,000e**	**7.7**	**8.2**	**27.2e**

IV. CHICAGO (May, 1976)		(8-9 A.M.)						(24 hours)				
1. S W-S Dan Ryan (Wabash Ave. el.)	17	136	12,498	8.0	41.5	0.45*	243	1,156	51,000	4.8	11.8	24.5
2. NW W-NW (Milwaukee Ave. subway)	22	132	10,213	6.0	41.5	0.54	308	1,084	40,000	3.5	12.2	25.5
3. N N-S Howard (State St. subway)	17	132	8,038	7.8	41.5	0.68	256	1,268	51,000	5.0	10.4	15.8
4. N Ravenswood & Evanston (Wells Street el.)	28	140	7,329	5.0	41.5	0.79	221	780	21,600	3.5	17.9	33.9
5. W W-S Lake (Lake Street el.)	12	96	5,015	8.0	41.5	0.79	243	1,156	26,000	4.8	8.3	19.3
6. W W-NW Congress & Douglas (subway)	17	102	4,921	6.0	41.5	0.86	308	1,084	38,000	3.5	9.4	13.0
7. S N-S Jackson Park & Englewood (State St subway)	11	86	4,802	7.8	41.5	0.74	256	1,268	30,000	4.9	6.8	16.0
TOTAL, CHICAGO DOWNTOWN	**121**	**828**	**52,816**	**6.8**	**41.5**	**0.65**	**1,835**	**7,796**	**257,600**	**4.25**	**10.6**	**20.5**
V. PHILADELPHIA (1976)		(8-9 A.M.)						(24 hours)				
1. N SEPTA Broad Street (2 tracks)	23	126	10,600	5.5	64.0	0.76	247	999	61,300	4.0	12.6	17.3
2. W SEPTA Market Street	22	132	9,200	6.0	46.5	0.67	212	1,057	48,000	5.0	12.5	19.2
3. E SEPTA Frankford Street	22	132	9,800	6.0	46.5	0.63	212	1,057	50,900	5.0	12.5	19.3
4. E **PATCO Ben Franklin Br. to Locust**	**13**	**69**	**7,500**	**5.3**	**62.7**	**0.58**	**150**	**450**	**19,500**	**3.0**	**15.3**	**38.5**
5. W **SEPTA Market Street LR tunnel**	**73**	**73**	**3,700**	**1.0**	**33.9**	**0.67**	**676**	**676**	**14,900**	**1.0**	**10.8**	**24.8**
6. S SEPTA Broad Street	16	96	3,100	6.0	64.5	2.00	165	755	19,500	4.6	12.7	15.9
Subtotal, SEPTA RT (4 entries)	**83**	**486**	**32,700**	**5.8**	**54.6**	**0.81**	**836**	**3,868**	**179,700**	**4.6**	**12.6**	**18.2**
TOTAL, PHILADELPHIA DOWNTOWN	**169**	**628**	**43,900**		**53.1**	**0.76**	**1,662**	**4,994**	**214,100**		**12.6**	**20.5**
VI. BOSTON (LR Sping, 1976, RT June, 1977)		(8-9 A.M.)						(19:10 hrs. RT; 19:50 hrs. LR)				
1. S Red line (Dorchester Ave. subw.)	22	88	8,651	4.0	58.9	0.60	260	860	37,762e	3.3	10.2	22.9e
2. S Orange line (Washington St. el.)	13	52	8,350	4.0	42.6	0.27*	174	616	23,929e	3.5	8.4	34.9e
3. W Green line (Boylston St. tun.) LR	36	88	6,897	2.4	33.8	0.43*	592	1,097	36,204e	1.9	8.0	19.1e
4. NW Red line (Longfellow Bridge)	22	88	6,526	4.0	58.9	0.79	260	860	28,651e	3.3	10.2	22.8e
5. N Orange line (Haymarket N)	13	52	6,050	4.0	42.6	0.37*	174	616	14,780e	3.5	8.4	40.9e
6. E Blue line (East Boston tunnel)	15	60	5,088	4.0	36.6	0.43*	165	602	15,762e	3.6	10.0	32.3e
7. N Green line (Lechmere elevated) LR	16	48	1,499	3.0	33.8	1.08	267	592	6,000e	2.2	8.1	24.2e
Subtotal, MBTA LR (2 entries)	**52**	**136**	**8,396**	**2.6**	**33.8**	**0.55**	**859**	**1,689**	**42,204e**	**2.0**	**8.0**	**19.9e**
Subtotal, MBTA RT (5 entries)	**85**	**340**	**34,665**	**4.0**	**50.0**	**0.49**	**1,033**	**3,554**	**120,884e**	**3.4**	**9.6**	**28.7e**
TOTAL, BOSTON DOWNTOWN	**137**	**476**	**43,061**		**45.4**	**0.50**	**1,892**	**5,243**	**163,088e**		**9.0**	**26.4e**
VII. SAN FRANCISCO (June 1977)		(8-9 A.M.)						(18 hrs. RT; 24 hrs. LR)				
1. E BART Transbay tube	11	98	8,016	8.9	70.2	0.86	129	836	28,869	6.5	11.7	27.8
2. W BART Mission St. subway	10	85	6,510	8.5	70.2	0.92	130	844	18,843	6.5	10.1	34.5
Subtotal, BART (2 entries)	**21**	**183**	**14,526**	**8.7**	**70.2**	**0.89**	**259**	**1,680**	**47,712**	**6.5**	**10.9**	**30.4**
3. W **MUNI Market St. LR***	**68**	**68**	**4,914**	**1.0**	**37.7**	**0.52**	**730**	**730**	**40,000**	**1.0**	**9.3**	**12.3**
TOTAL, SAN FRANCISCO DOWNTOWN	**84**	**246**	**19,440**		**61.4**	**0.78**	**922**	**2,343**	**87,712**		**10.5**	**22.2**

*Street operation pending relocation in subway

VIII. CLEVELAND (December, 1976)		**(8-9 A.M.)**						**(24 hours)**				
1. E Joint track from Windermere	9	31	4,100	3.4	51.9	0.39*	157	282	17,084	1.8	11.0	24.0
from Shaker Hgts. LR	**20**	**40**	**4,390**	**2.0**	**41.0**	**0.37***	**181**	**252**	**14,300**	**1.4**	**15.9**	**30.7**
2. W From Airport	14	52	5,413	3.7	51.9	0.50	171	362	22,553	2.1	14.4	24.0
Subtotal, RT	**23**	**83**	**9,513**	**3.6**	**51.9**	**0.45***	**328**	**644**	**39,637**	**2.0**	**12.9**	**24.0**
TOTAL, CLEVELAND DOWNTOWN	**43**	**123**	**13,903**		**48.4**	**0.43***	**509**	**896**	**53,937**		**13.7**	**25.8**
IX. PITTSBURGH (1976)		**(8-9 A.M.)**						**(20 hours)**				
1. S **South Hills LR Smithfield St. Br.***	**51**	**51**	**3,819**	**1.0**	**32.8**	**0.44***	**316**	**316**	**12,421**	**1.0**	**16.1**	**30.7**
*Street operation pending relocation in exclusive R.O.W.												
X. NEWARK (1976)		**(8-9 A.M.)**					**(21 hrs. LR; RT 24 hrs., data for 18 hrs.)**					
1. N **Newark Subway LR**	**30**	**30**	**1,512**	**1.0**	**36.8**	**0.73**	**235**	**235**	**5,877**	**1.0**	**12.8**	**25.7**
2. E PATH (in reverse direction)	15	105	1,150	7.0	43.8	4.00	141	807	20,303	5.7	13.0	5.7
TOTAL, NEWARK DOWNTOWN	**45**	**135**	**2,662**		**42.2**	**2.14**	**376**	**1,042**	**26,180**		**12.9**	**10.2**
XI. WASHINGTON (1980)		**(8-9 A.M.)**						**(18 hours)**				
1. W Blue line Potomac Tunnel	20	120	13,000e	6	71	0.65	238	1,428	52,000	6.0	8.4	25.0
2. N Red line from Union Sta.	12	82	12,000e	6.8	71	0.49	137	924	47,600	6.7	8.8	25.2
3. E Blue line from Eastern Market	20	120	8,000e	6	71	1.07	238	1,428	29,600	6.0	8.4	27.0
NW Red line under constr.												
S Yellow line under constr.												
TOTAL, WASHINGTON DOWNTOWN	**52**	**322**	**33,000e**	**6.2**	**71**	**0.69**	**613**	**3,780**	**129,200**	**6.2**	**8.5**	**25.5**
XII. ATLANTA (June 1980)		**(8-9 A.M.)**						**(19:45 hours)**				
1. East line	6	36	4,250	6	73	0.62	104	468	20,065	4.5	7.7	21.2
2. West line	6	36	3,725	6	73	0.71	104	468	16,963	4.5	7.7	21.9
TOTAL, ATLANTA DOWNTOWN	**12**	**72**	**7,975**	**6**	**73**	**0.65**	**208**	**936**	**37,028**	**4.5**	**7.7**	**21.5**
XII. EDMONTON (Fall 1978)		**(8-9 A.M.)**						**(20 hours)**				
1. NE line	12	24	2,085	2	61.0	0.70	130	260	9,000	2	9.2	23.2

Indicators of crowding: *Less than 0.5 m^2 per passenger provided under current operating conditions

**Less than 0.5 m^2 per passenger would be provided even with operation at maximum capacity

Gross floorspace per car shown as an average of cars operating on a given line; see Table A-5 for detail.

RT – Rapid Transit; **LR** – Light Rail e – estimated

Source: Correspondence with operating agencies; Tri-State Regional Planning Commission (for New York data).

Table A-5
Rolling Stock Dimensions, 1975

(Basis for capacity calculations in Table A-4 and subsequent tables) 1 m = 3.281 feet 1 m^2 = 10.764 square feet 1 ton = 1,000 kg = 2,204.6 lbs.

Agency and Vehicle	Number of units	length m	width m	Gross area m^2	Net area m^2	Net as % of gross	Seats	Places @ 0.5 gross m^2	Seats as % of places	Maximum train consist	Weight, metric tons	tons/m^2	Motors @ hp	hp/ton
NYCTA														
IRT car RT	2,784	15.55	2.68	41.7			44	83.4	(52.8)	10 (11 Flushing)	35.7–31.5	0.86–0.75	4@ 100	11.2–12.7
IND car RT	3,590	18.35	3.05	55.9	49.7	(88.9)	50	111.8	(44.7)	10	38.6–31.7	0.69–0.57	4@ 100	10.4–12.6
R-44 car RT	300	22.86	3.05	69.7			73	139.4	(52.4)	8	39.7	0.57	4@ 115	11.6
All RT	**6,674***			**50.6**			**48.5**	**101.2**	**(47.9)**	**8-11**				
	*During 1976-78, 745 R-46 cars were being delivered, to replace 842 IND cars; their dimensions are the same as R-44													
Buses	4,096	varies		32.2			44.4	64.3	(69.0)	1				
CTA														
All RT	**1,094**	**14.63**	**2.84**	**41.5**			**49**	**83.1**	**(59.0)**	**8**	**19.6–23.1**	**0.47–0.56**	**4@ 100**	**20.4–17.3**
Buses	2,376	varies		31.4			49.5	62.7	(78.9)	1	9.1	0.29		
TTC														
1962-75 car RT	342	22.71	3.15	71.5	69.0	(96.5)	82	143.0	(57.3)	6	27.0–25.2	0.38–0.35	4@ 100	14.8–15.8
1953-58 car RT	134	17.37	3.12	54.2	51.0	(94.0)	62	108.4	(57.2)	8	38.3	0.71	4@ 68	7.1
All RT cars	**476**			**66.6**			**76.3**	**133.2**	**(57.3)**	**6-8**				
PCC LR*	386	14.15	2.54	33.9			50	67.8	(73.7)	1				
	*Being replaced in part by 200 Canadian LRV's													
Buses	1,198	varies		31.0			41.3	62.0	(66.6)	1				
Trolleybuses	151	12.57	2.59	32.5			40.0	65.0	(61.5)	1				
BART														
A-car RT	176	22.86	3.20	73.2			72	146.4	(49.2)	--	26.8	0.37	4@ 150	22.4
B-car RT	274	21.34	3.20	68.3			72	136.6	(52.7)	--	25.4	0.37	4@ 150	23.6
All RT	**450**						**72**	**140.4**	**(51.4)**	**10**				
MUCTC														
RT powered	238	17.20	2.51	43.2			40	86.4	(46.3)	--	26.1	0.60	4@ 155	17.2
RT trailer	119	16.40	2.51	41.2			40	82.4	(48.5)	--	20.0	0.49	0@ 0	
All RT	**357**			**42.6**			**40**	**85.2**	**(47.0)**	**9**				
Buses	2,004	varies		30.6			42.7	61.3	(69.7)	1				
SEPTA														
Market RT	267	16.86	2.76	46.5	43.5	(93.5)	55	93.0	(59.1)	6	22.3	0.48	4@ 100	17.9
Broad RT	223	20.52	3.12	64.0	62.4	(97.5)	67	128.0	(52.3)	6				
All RT	**490**			**54.5**			**60.5**	**108.9**	**(55.5)**	**6**				
PCC LR	156	14.02	2.54	33.6			53	67.2	(78.9)	1	16.3	0.48	4@ 100	24.5
PCC LR	197	14.23	2.54	34.1			46	68.2	(67.4)	1	17.3	0.51	4@ 100	23.1
PCC LR	29	14.15	2.54	33.9			51	67.8	(75.2)	1	17.1	0.50	4@ 100	23.4
All PCC LR	**382**			**33.9**			**49.2**	**67.8**	**(72.6)**	**1**	**16.9**	**0.50**		**23.7**

MBTA													
Red RT	76	21.18	2.77	58.7	47.3 (80.6)	63	117.3	(53.7)	4	28.3	0.48	4@ 102	14.4
Red RT	89	21.18	2.79	59.1	55.2 (93.4)	54	118.2	(45.7)	4	32.0	0.54	4@ 102	12.8
Orange RT	100	16.76	2.54	42,6	38.6 (90.6)	46	85.1	(54.0)	4	26.3	0.62	4@ 102	15.5
Blue RT	37	14.78	2.51	37.1	34.4 (92.7)	46	74.2	(62.0)	4				
Blue RT	38	14.40	2.51	36.1	34.4 (95.3)	44	72.3	(60.9)	4				
All RT	**340**			**49.2**		**51.7**	**98.4**	**(52.5)**	**4**				
PCC LR	24	14.33	2.54	34.4		49	68.8	(71.2)	3				
PCC LR	85	14.15	2.54	33.9		42	67.8	(61.9)	3				
PCC LR	170	14.02	2.54	33.6		42	67.2	(62.5)	3				
PCC LR	6	14.17	2.54	34.0		42	68.0	(61.8)	3				
All LR	**285**			**33.8**		**42.6**	**67.6**	**(63.0)**	**3**	15.0–19.0			
Standard LRV*	**175**	**21.60**	**2.70**	**56.6**		**52**	**113.2**	**(45.9)**	**2+**	30.8	0.54	2@ 210	13.6
	*Being delivered 1976-78 to replace most of existing fleet												
PATH													
All RT	**298**	15.54	2.82	**43.8**		**41**	**87.6**	**(46.8)**	**7**	26.8	0.61	4@ 150	22.3
PATCO													
All RT	75	20.57	3.05	**62.7**	61.2 (97.6)	**80**	**125.5**	**(63.7)**	**8**	34.6	0.55	4@ 160	18.5
GCRTA													
RT "Airporter"	29	21.40	3.18	68.0		80	136.0	(58.8)	4	29.1	0.43	4@ 100	13.7
RT 1955	87	14.86	3.15	46.8		53	93.6	(56.6)	6	24.5	0.52	4@ 55	9.0
All RT	**116**			**52.1**		**59.8**	**104.2**	**(57.4)**	**4-6**				
All LR	57*	15.24	2.82	41.0		62	82.0	(75.6)	2				
	*Being replaced with 48 articulated cars of 23.5 x 2.82m or 66.2m²												
SIRT													
R-44 RT	**52**	**22.86**	**3.05**	**69.7**		**74**	**139.4**	**(53.0)**	**4**	39.7	0.57	4@ 115	11.6
WMATA													
All RT	**300**	**22.78**	**3.09**	**70.4**		**81**	**140.8**	**(58.3)**	**8**	**32.9**	**0.47**	**4@ 175**	**21.3**
Buses	2,035	varies		30.2		49.9	60.4	(82.6)	1				
MUNI													
PCC LR	25	14.17	2.72	36.5		59			1				
PCC LR	10	15.37	2.74	40.2		60			1				
PCC LR	11	14.15	2.54	33.9		50			1				
PCC LR	69	14.02	2.74	36.5		53			1				
All PCC	**115**			**37.75**		**54.6**	**75.5**	**(72.3)**	1	15.0–19.0			
Standard LRV*	**100**	**21.60**	**2.70**	**56.6**		**68**	**113.2**	**(60.0)**	2+	**30.8**	**0.54**	**2@ 210**	**13.6**
	*Being delivered 1978-79 to replace PCC cars												
Buses	600	varies		30.6		44	62.1	(71.9)	1				
Trolleybuses	333	varies		29.9		45.8	59.8	(76.6)	1				
Cable cars	12	9.27	2.43	22.5		34	45.0	(75.5)	1				
	27	8.23	2.39	19.7		29	39.4	(73.6)	1				
PAT													
PCC	69	13.72	2.54	32.8		50	65.6	(76.2)	1				
PCC	26	13.72	2.54	32.8		54	65.6	(82.3)	1				
All PCC	**95**			**32.8**		**51**	**65.6**	**(77.7)**	1				
Buses	1,006	varies		27.9		44.6	55.8	(79.9)	1				

Agency and Vehicle	Number of units	length m	width m	Gross area m^2	Net area m^2	Net as % of gross	Seats	Places @ 0.5 gross m^2	Seats as % of places	Maximum train consist	Weight, metric tons	tons/m^2	Motors @ hp	hp/ton
NJT														
PCC	26	14.15	2.74	**36.8**			**55**	**73.5**	**(74.8)**	1				
Buses	**1,847**	varies		**29.6**			**49.8**	**59.2**	**(84.1)**	1				
Edmonton														
DuWag LR car	**14**	23.0	2.65	**60.0**			**64**	**120**	**(53.3)**	2+	**30.0**	**0.50**	**2@ 218**	**14.5**
Buses	590	12.2	2.59	31.5			n.a.	63	n.a.					
PEOPLEMOVER VEHICLES														
Airtrans Dallas	51	6.77	2.19	14.85			16	29.7	(53.8)	2	6.44	0.43	1@ 60	9.3
Morgantown	29	4.72	2.03	9.58			8	19.2	(41.7)	1	3.90	0.41	1@ 70	7.3
Sea-Tac Airport	12	11.28	2.84	32.04				64.0		2	11.57	0.36	2@ 100	17.2
Tampa Airport	8	11.05	2.84	31.38				62.8		1	9.75	0.31	1@ 100	10.3
Fairlane (ACT)	2	7.53	2.03	15.29			10	30.6	(32.7)	1	6.89	0.45	2@ 60	17.4
SCRTD														
Buses	2,173	varies		30.5			48.4	61.0	(79.3)					
Maryland														
Buses	1,043	varies		30.1			50.7	60.2	(84.2)					
AC Transit														
Buses	878	varies		29.2			47.6	58.4	(81.5)					
St. Louis														
Buses	925	varies		29.8			49.3	59.5	(82.9)					
MARTA														
Buses	785	varies		31.3			48.5	62.5	(77.6)					
Seattle														
Buses (incl. trolleybuses)	617	varies		28.0			47.0	56.0	(83.9)					
Buffalo														
Buses	556	varies		28.8			47.6	57.6	(82.6)					
Milwaukee														
Buses	523	varies		32.5			52.5	64.9	(80.9)					
Denver														
Buses	480	varies		29.6			46.7	59.2	(78.9)					
Dallas														
Buses	449	varies		31.6			51.0	63.2	(80.7)					
Cincinnati														
Buses	419	varies		31.5			49.0	63.0	(77.7)					
Portland														
Buses	422	varies		28.8			44.4	57.7	(76.9)					
Houston														
Buses	421	varies		31.3			52.4	62.6	(83.7)					
Dayton														
Buses (incl. trolleybuses)	125	varies		29.6			44.4	59.2	(75.0)					
San Diego														
Buses	351	varies		27.8			45.1	55.5	(81.3)					

Sources: *APTA Transit Passenger Vehicle Fleet Inventory* (February, 1976); *UITP International Statistical Handbook of Urban Transport* (1975 edition); *Lea Transit Compendium*, 1975 and Supplement 1976-77.

M
Bowling Green Station
4 5
M
Bowling Green Station
4 5
New York Shipping Association
MEDICAL CENTER
JEWELRY EXCHANGE
MARTINS

Table A-6 Part I:
Rapid Transit Operating Data
(ranked by annual place-miles operated)

	NYCTA	TTC	CTA	BART	WMATA	MUCTC
1. Year ending	12-31-76	12-31-76	12-31-76	6-30-77	3-80 annualized	12-31-76
PASSENGER USE						
2. Annual passengers (000)	1,010,497	198,200	149,200	34,599	80,450	148,023
3. Trip length (miles)	7.2	4.16	7.3	13.0	4.9	3.4
4. Annual passenger-miles (000)	7,275,578	824,512	1,087,700	449,696	394,200	503,280
SERVICE						
5. Annual vehicle-miles (000)	281,206.6	34,575.8	49,682.0	22,862.9	18,329.2	21,922.6
6. Places per vehicle (@ 5.38 sq. ft. or $0.5m^2$)	101.2	133.2	83.1	140.4	142.0	85.2
7. Annual place-miles (000)	28,458,107	4,605,497	4,128,574	3,209,961	2,602,746	1,867,806
8. Passenger-miles per place mile: load factor	**25.6%**	**17.9%**	**26.3%**	**14.0%**	**15.1%**	**26.9%**
Vehicle-miles per vehicle-hour:						
9. speed incl. layover	**18.3mph**	**20.4mph**	**19.9mph**	**33.6mph**	**20.7mph**	**17.4mph**
10. (excluding layover)			**(24.6)**	**(40.0)**	**(30.0)**	**(22.3)**
11. Weekday cars/train (c=cordon, s=system wide, a=annual	**8.1c**	**6.3c**	**4.25c**	**6.5c**	**5.9a**	**8.35s**
12. Vehicles in service	6,674	476	1,094	425	290	357
13. Annual vehicle-miles per vehicle	42,135	72,638	45,413	53,795	63,204	61,408
14. Number of stations	439	49	142	34	37	35
15. Distance between stops* (mi.)	n.a	0.54	0.81	2.30	0.94	0.54
TRAFFIC DENSITY						
16. Line-miles (first track)	230.6	26.6	89.4	71.5	33.7	18.5
17. Place-miles/mile (000)	**123,409**	**173,139**	**46,180**	**44,895**	**77,233**	**100,962**
18. Passenger-miles/mile (000).	**31,551**	**30,997**	**12,167**	**6,289**	**11,697**	**27,204**
NUMBER OF EMPLOYEES						
19. Vehicle operation	7,225	328	1,370	272	192	345
20. Vehicle maintenance	4,895	953e	570	357	327	360
21. Way Power & Signals	6,974	131	1,196	562	349	418
22. Station	4,917	446	789	165	317	342
23. Administrative**	1,672	283	467	461	250	323
24. TOTAL	25,683	2,141	4,392	1,817	1,435	1,788
EMPLOYEE RATIOS						
25. Operating employees/train in use during peak hour***	13.04	5.20	10.00	8.24	4.8	10.8
26. Maint. employees/vehicle	0.73	2.00	0.43	0.84	1.13	1.00
27. W & P employees/line mile	30.24	4.92	13.38	7.86	10.35	22.6
27a. (Equalized for tracks/line)	(19.38)	––	(11.60)	––	––	––
28. Station employees/station	11.20	9.10	5.56	4.85	8.56	9.8
29. TOTAL employees/vehicle	3.85	4.50	4.01	4.28	4.95	5.0
EMPLOYEE OUTPUT						
30. Place-miles/employees (000)	**1,108**	**2,151**	**940**	**1,767**	**1,814**	**1,045**
31. Passenger-miles/employee (000)	**283**	**385**	**248**	**247**	**275**	**281**
EMPLOYEES NEEDED per million place-miles of service:						
32. Vehicle operation	0.254	0.071	0.332	0.085	0.074	0.185
33. Vehicle maintenance	0.172	0.207	0.138	0.111	0.126	0.193
34. Way, Power & Signals	0.245	0.028	0.290	0.175	0.134	0.223
35. Station	0.173	0.037	0.191	0.051	0.121	0.183
36. Administrative	0.059	0.062	0.113	0.114	0.096	0.173
37. TOTAL **employees/million place-miles**	**0.902**	**0.465**	**1.064**	**0.566**	**0.551**	**0.957**
per million place-hours of service:						
38. Vehicle operation	4.65	1.45	6.27	2.86	1.53	3.22
39. Vehicle maintenance	3.14	4.24	2.61	3.73	2.61	3.36
40. Way, Power & Signals	4.48	0.57	5.48	5.88	2.77	3.88
41. Station	3.16	1.98	3.61	1.71	2.50	3.18
42. Administrative	1.08	1.26	2.14	4.84	1.99	3.01
43. TOTAL employees/million place-hours	**16.51**	**9.50**	**20.11**	**19.02**	**11.40**	**16.65**
ENERGY USE Kwh/place-mile						
44. Vehicle operation	0.0544	0.0535	0.0554	0.0509	.0831e	0.0590
45. TOTAL purchased	0.0667	n.a.	0.0630	0.0726	n.a.	0.0967

* Distance at which average car stops, not line distance.
** For multi-modal agencies, administrative employees are those assigned directly to a given mode plus a share of central administrative employees allocated in proportion to all other employees. Definitions of administrative employees and other categories vary somewhat from system to system.
*** See Table A-7, line 3.

SEPTA	MBTA	PATH	MARTA	PATCO	GCRTA	SIRT
12-31-76	12-31-76	12-31-76	3-80 annualized	12-31-76	12-31-76	12-31-77
84,629	80,200	40,688	21,372	11,523	11,757	5,002
4.9	3.6	4.5	4.2	8.95	7.7	6.5
448,533	288,720	183,096	89,762	103,131	90,530	32,513
14,942	10,523.4	9,969.1	3,997.8	4,069.5	3,611.2	1,802.8
108.9	98.4	87.6	146.0	125.5	104.2	139.4
1,627,184	1,035,503	873,293	583,673	510,722	376,288	251,310
27.5%	**27.9%**	**21.0%**	**15.4%**	**20.2%**	**24.0%**	**12.9%**
17.5mph	**15.6mph**	**18.6mph**	**24.5mph**	**28.0mph**	**22.8mph**	**17.5mph**
(n.a.)		**(22.7)**	**(33.7)**	**(34.8)**	**(29.0)**	**(22.0)**
4.7s	**3.1s**	**5.5c**	**4.4s**	**3.0s**	**2.0s**	**3.0s**
467	340	298	40	75	116	52
31,995	30,951	33,453	99,945	54,260	31,131	34,669
53	43	14	13	13	18	22
n.a.	0.78	1.07	0.98	1.18	1.13	0.65
24.1	32.9	13.9	11.8	14.5	19.3	14.3
67,518	**31,474**	**62,827**	**49,463**	**35,222**	**19,497**	**17,574**
18,611	**8,776**	**13,172**	**7,606**	**6,678**	**4,691**	**2,274**
246	500	338	61	58	84	107
254	339	211	80	69	85e	52
609	693e	231	56	48	68e	65
153	310	33	51	26	45	14
80	186	183	60	62	51	28
1,342	2.028	996	308	263	333	266
4.7	8.8	9.1	10.16	4.46	3.65	10.7
0.52	1.00	0.71	2.00	0.92	0.73	1.00
27.56	21.06	16.62	4.75	3.31	3.52	4.54
(18.87)	(20.25)	(15.3)	——	——	——	——
2.89	7.21	2.36	3.92	2.00	2.50	0.64
2.74	5.96	3.34	7.70	3.51	2.87	5.11
1,213	**510**	**877**	**1,895**	**1,942**	**1,130**	**944**
334	**142**	**184**	**291**	**392**	**272**	**122**
0.151	0.483	0.387	0.105	0.114	0.223	0.425
0.156	0.327	0.242	0.137	0.135	0.226	0.207
0.374	0.669	0.264	0.096	0.094	0.181	0.258
0.094	0.299	0.038	0.087	0.051	0.120	0.056
0.149	0.180	0.209	0.103	0.121	0.135	0.111
0.824	**1.958**	**1.140**	**0.528**	**0.515**	**0.885**	**1.058**
2.64	7.53	7.20	2.57	3.19	5.08	7.45
2.73	5.10	4.50	3.36	3.78	5.15	3.62
6.54	10.44	4.91	2.35	2.63	4.13	4.52
1.65	4.66	0.70	2.13	1.43	2.73	0.98
0.86	2.81	3.89	2.52	3.39	3.08	1.94
14.42	**30.54**	**21.20**	**12.93**	**14.42**	**20.17**	**18.51**
n.a.	n.a.	0.0650	n.a.	0.0653	n.a.	0.0531
n.a.	n.a.	0.0730	n.a.	0.0770	0.0834	0.0561

Table A-6 Part II:
Selected Light Rail Annual Operating Data
(ranked by annual place-miles operated)

	TTC	MBTA	MUNI	SEPTA	PAT	GCRTA	ETS	SEPTA	NJT
1. Year ending	12-31-76	12-31-76	12-31-76	12-31-76 subw.-surf.	12-31-76	12-31-76	12-31-79	12-31-76 P.&W.	12-31-76
PASSENGER USE									
2. Annual passengers (000)	112,628	46,000e	19,266	14,836.5	6,455	4,717	6,256	2,218	2,249
3. Trip length (miles)	2.0e	2.5	3.4	3.5	5.55	7.7	3.5	6.7	2.5
4. Annual passenger-miles (000)	225,256e	117,000e	65,504	51,928	35,824	36,324	21,896	14,860	5,623
SERVICE									
5. Annual vehicle-miles (000)	10,103.6	5,671.0	3,073.0	2,849.7e	1,940.0	1,249.8	758.0	690.0	545.0
6. Places per vehicle (@5.38 sq. ft. or $0.5m^2$)	67.8	67.6	75.5	67.8	65.6	82.0	122	85e	73.5
7. Annual place-miles (000)	685,024	383,360	232,012	193,210	127,261	102,484	92,476	58,650	40,057
8. Passenger-miles per place mile: load factor	**32.9%**	**30.5%e**	**28.2%**	**26.9%**	**28.2%**	**35.4%**	**23.6%**	**22.7%**	**14.0%**
Vehicle-miles per vehicle hour:									
9. Speed incl. layover	**9.0mph**	**10.05mph**	**9.38mph**	**9.0mph**	**11.8mph**	**16.8mph**	**18.0mph**	**22.0mph**	**15.0mph**
10. (excluding layover)	**(9.7)**	**(12.3)**		**(11.2)**	**(13.6)**	**(23.0)**	**(22.5)**	**(30.0)**	**(21.5)**
11. Weekday cars/train	**1.0**	**2.0**	**1.0**	**1.0**	**1.0**	**1.4**	**2.0**	**1.0**	**1.0**
12. Vehicles in service	386	285	115	137	95	57	14	21	24
13. Annual vehicle-miles per vehicle	26,175	19,898	26,722	20,800	20,421	21,926	54,142	32,857	20,961
TRAFFIC DENSITY									
16. Line-miles, total	46.3	26.9	19.4	20.8	22.3	13.1	4.5	13.6	4.3
17. Place-miles/mile (000)	**14,795**	**14,251**	**11,959**	**9,289**	**5,707**	**7,823**	**20,550**	**4,313**	**9,316**
18. Passenger-miles/mile (000)	**4,865**	**4,349**	**3,376**	**2,497**	**1,606**	**2,772**	**4,866**	**979**	**1,308**
NUMBER OF EMPLOYEES									
19. Vehicle operation	525	435	210	166	138	65	28	26	21
20. Vehicle maintenance	300e	341	20	62	92	33	15	18	8
21. Way, Power & Signals	86	389e	45e	107	140	27	20	23e	7
22. Station	--	98	--	32	--	--	37	1	6
23. Administrative	137	128	54	40	33	22	13	5	2
24. TOTAL	1,048	1,391	329	407	403	147	113	73e	44
EMPLOYEES RATIOS									
25. Operating employees/train in use during peak hour	1.96	6.30	2.19	1.56	1.89	2.95	4.66	2.16	1.31
26. Maint. employees/vehicle	0.77	1.20	0.17	0.45	0.97	0.58	1.07	0.86	0.33
27. W & P employees/line mile	1.86	14.46	2.27	5.14	6.28	2.55	4.44	1.70e	1.63
28. Sta. empl./manned station	---	(11) 8.91	--	(7) 4.57	--	--	(5) 7.40	(1) 1.00	(1) 2.00
29. TOTAL employees/vehicle	2.72	4.88	2.86	2.97	4.24	2.58	8.00	3.48	1.83
EMPLOYEE OUTPUT									
30. Place-miles/employees (000)	**654**	**276**	**707**	**475**	**316**	**697**	**818**	**805**	**910**
31. Passenger-mile/employee (000)	**215**	**84**	**199**	**128**	**89**	**247**	**194**	**182**	**128**
EMPLOYEES NEEDED per million place-miles of service									
32. Vehicle operation	0.766	1.135	0.905	0.859	1.084	0.634	0.303	0.442	0.524
33. Vehicle maintenance	0.438	0.889	0.086	0.320	0.723	0.322	0.162	0.306	0.200
34. Way, Power & Signals	0.126	1.015	0.194	0.554	1.100	0.263	0.216	0.391	0.174
35. Station	--	0.255	--	0.166	--	--	0.400	0.017	0.150
36. Administrative	0.200	0.334	0.233	0.207	0.259	0.215	0.141	0.086	0.050
37. TOTAL **employees/million place-miles**	**1.530**	**3.628**	**1.418**	**2.106**	**3.167**	**1.434**	**1.222**	**1.242**	**1.098**
per million place-hours of service:									
38. Vehicle operation	6.90	11.41	8.49	7.73	12.79	10.65	5.45	9.72	7.86
39. Vehicle maintenance	3.94	8.93	0.81	2.88	8.53	5.41	2.92	6.73	3.00
40. Way, Power & Signals	1.13	10.20	1.82	4.99	12.98	4.42	3.89	8.60	2.61
41. Station	--	2.56	--	1.49	--	--	7.20	0.37	2.25
42. Administrative	1.80	3.36	2.18	1.86	3.06	3.61	2.54	1.90	0.75
43. TOTAL **employees/million place-hours**	**13.77**	**36.46**	**13.30**	**18.95**	**37.36**	**24.09**	**22.00**	**27.32**	**16.47**
ENERGY USE, kwh/place-mile									
44. Vehicle operation	n.a.	n.a.	n.a.	n.a.	n.a.	n.a.	0.0313	n.a.	0.0575
45. TOTAL purchased	n.a.	n.a.	0.0732	0.1128	0.0962	0.0794	0.0865	0.1098**	n.a.

*Includes 2.6 mi. joint trackage with RT.

**Rate includes the Media-Sharon Hill line.

Table A-6 Part III:
Selected Bus Annual Operating Data
Systems in cities with rail operations*

	NYCTA	MABSTOA	CTA	NJT	WMATA	TTC	MUCTC	PAT
1. Year ending	12-31-76	6-30-76	12-27-75	12-31-75	6-30-75	12-31-76	12-31-76	12-31-75
PASSENGER USE								
2. Annual passengers (000)	339,927.7	310,434.9	n.a.	116,690	122,842	290,500	156,371	103,743
3. Trip length (miles)	2.0	1.5	n.a.	5.0	4.5	n.a.	n.a.	4.6
4. Annual passenger-miles (000)	679,855	465,652	n.a.	583,450	552,789	n.a.	n.a.	477,218
SERVICE								
5. Annual vehicle-miles (000)	666,527.2	41,868.0	88,484	62,544	56,855	50,701	51,082	38,128
6. Places per vehicle (@53.8 sq. ft. or $0.5m^2$)	64.3	64.3	62.7	59.2	60.4	62.3	61.3	55.8
7. Annual place-miles(000)	4,277,699	2,692,112	5,547,947	3,702,605	3,434,042	3,158,672	3,131,357	2,127,542
8. Passenger-miles per place mile: load factor	**15.9%**		**n.a.**	**15.8%**	**20.0%**	**n.a.**	**n.a.**	**22.4%**
9. Vehicle-miles per vehicle-hour: speed incl. layover	**8.08 mph**	**5.55mph**	**12mph**	**14.18mph**	**11.96mph**	**12.00mph**	**9.73mph**	**13.84mph**
12. Vehicles in service	2,786	2,050	2,444	1,670	2,120	1,349	2,004	978
13. Annual vehicle-miles per vehicle	23,879	20,423	36,205	37,451	26,818	37.584	25,490	38,985
TRAFFIC DENSITY								
16. Line-miles, one way	628.8	319	n.a.	3,086	n.a.	n.a.	570	n.a.
17. Place-miles/line mile (000)	**6,803**	**8,439**	**n.a.**	**1,199**	**n.a.**	**n.a.**	**5,494**	**n.a.**
18. Passenger-miles/line mile (000)	**1,081**	**1,460**	**n.a.**	**189**	**n.a.**	**n.a.**	**n.a.**	**n.a.**
NUMBER OF EMPLOYEES								
19. Vehicle Operation	5,536	4,661	6,098	2,346	3,151	2,411	4,191	1,755
20. Vehicle maintenance	1,858	1,318	1,500	n.a.	n.a.	810e		519
23. Administration	531	472	906	n.a.	n.a.	493	778	200
24. TOTAL	7,925	6,451	8,495	3,935	4,891	3,714	4,969	2,474
EMPLOYEE RATIOS								
29. Employees/vehicle	2.8	3.1	3.5	2.4	2.3	2.8	2.5	2.5
EMPLOYEE OUTPUT								
30. Place-mles/employee (000)	**540**	**417**	**653**	**941**	**702**	**850**	**630**	**860**
31. Passenger-miles/employee (000)	**86**	**72**	**n.a.**	**148**	**113**	**n.a.**	**n.a.**	**193**
EMPLOYEES NEEDED per million place-miles of service								
32. Vehicle operation	1.294	1.731	1.099	0.634	0.917	0.763	1.338	0.825
33. Vehicle maintenance	0.434	0.490	0.270	n.a.	n.a.	0.256		0.244
36. Administration	0.124	0.175	0.163	n.a.	n.a.	0.156	0.248	0.094
37. TOTAL	**1.852**	**2.396**	**1.531**	**1.063**	**1.424**	**1.175**	**1.586**	**1.163**
per million place-hrs of service:								
43. TOTAL	**15.0**	**13.3**	**18.4**	**15.1**	**17.0**	**14.1**	**15.4**	**16.1**
ENERGY USE								
44. Kwh/place mile (trolle. buses)	--	--	--	--	--	--	--	--
46. Gallons of diesel oil/vehicle-mile	0.278	0.314	0.296	0.191	0.270	n.a.	0.243	0.245
47. Ditto per place-mile	0.00432	0.00488	0.00472	0.00323	0.00447	n.a.	0.00396	0.00439

* MBTA and SEPTA bus operations not shown due to incomplete data.

AC Transit	GCRTA	MUNI		SCRTD	Baltimore	MARTA	St. Louis	Seattle	Milwaukee
				Systems in cities without rail operations in 1976					
6-30-75	12-31-75	12-31-76	1.	6-30-76	6-30-75	6-30-75	12-31-75	12-31-75	12-31-75
57,528	67,552	87,837	2.	309,800	126,656	74,935	60,455	38,001	66,468
5.0	3.9	2.5	3.	3.8	2.7	5.2	5.4	6.5	3.4
287,640	263,452	219,593	4.	1,177,240	341,971	389,665	326,457	247,007	225,991
24,363	18,886	14,155	5.	103,000	27,666	26,985	24,125	23,337	17,338
58.4	61e	62.1	6.	61.0	60.2	62.5	59.5	56.0	64.9
1,422,787	1,152,046	879,026	7.	6,283,000	1,665,493	1,686,563	1,435,438	1,306,872	1,125,236
20.2%	**22.9%**	**n.a.**	8.	**18.7**	**20.5%**	**23.1%**	**22 7%**	**18.9%**	**20.0%**
14.46mph	**11.80mph**	**10.04 mph**	9.	**14.32 mph**	**12mph**	**13.95mph**	**12.72mph**	**13.78mph**	**11.77mph**
803	785	532	12.	2,394	1,043	819	925	608	501
30,340	24,058	26,607	13.	43,024	26,525	32,948	26,081	38,383	34,606
926	520	n.a.	16.	n.a.	771	899	1,093	970	486
1,536	**2,215**	**n.a.**	17.	**n.a.**	**2,160**	**1,876**	**1,313**	**1,347**	**2,135**
310	**507**	**n.a.**	18.	**n.a.**	**444**	**433**	**299**	**255**	**465**
1,315	1,084	880	19.	5,041	1,487	1,066	1,208	1,069	878
n.a.	351	230	20.	n.a.	n.a.	n.a.	n.a.	n.a.	n.a.
n.a.	315	217	23.	n.a.	n.a.	n.a.	n.a.	n.a.	n.a.
1,798	1,750	1,327	24.	7,498	2,091	1,967	1,891	1,603	1,337
2.2	2.2	2.5	29	3.1	2.0	2.4	2.0	2.6	2.7
791	**658**	**662**	30.	**838**	**797**	**857**	**759**	**815**	**841**
160	**150**	**n.a.**	31.	**157**	**164**	**198**	**173**	**154**	**169**
0.924	0.941	1.001	32.	0.802	0.893	0.632	0.843	0.818	0.780
n.a.	0.305	0.262	33.	n.a.	n.a.	n.a.	n.a.	n.a.	n.a.
n.a.	0.273	0.247	36.	n.a.	n.a.	n.a.	n.a.	n.a.	n.a.
1.263	**1.519**	**1.510**	37.	**1.193**	**1.255**	**1.166**	**1.317**	**1.227**	**1.188**
18.3	**17.9**	**15.2**		**17.1**	**15.1**	**16.3**	**16.8**	**16.9**	**14.0**
--	--	--			--	--	--	0.1273	--
0.202	0.258	n.a.		0.227	0.283	0.250	0.249	0.214	0.212
0.00346	0.00423	n.a.		0.00371	0.00470	0.00400	0.00418	0.00382	0.00327

Note: Some of the apparently low bus employee requirements result from subcontracted services not translated into staff equivalents.

Portland	Houston	Denver	Dallas	ETS	San Diego	Cincinnati	Buffalo	GG Transit	Lousiville
6-30-75	12-31-75	12-31-75	9-30-75	12-31-76	6-30-75	12-31-75	3-31-75	6-30-75	6-30-75
27,698	36,961	28,105	16,284	56,477	33,526	34,181	40,253	8,851	13,986
6.3	n.a.	n.a.	5.0	n.a.	n.a.	n.a.	2.8	n.a.	4.1
174,497	n.a.	n.a.	131,420	n.a.	n.a.	n.a.	112,708	n.a.	57,343
16,599	16,173	15,370	14,181	14,142	12,687	11,735	9,386	8,226	4,942
57.7	62.6	59.2	63.2	63.0	55.5	63.0	57.6	62.9	61.8
957,762	1,012,430	909,904	896,239	891,034	704,129	739,305	540,634	517,415	305,416
18.2%	**n.a.**	**n.a.**	**14.7%**	**n.a.**	**n.a.**	**n.a.**	**20.8%**		**18.8%**
14.59mph	**13.40mph**	**13.21mph**	**13.98mph**	**9.0mph**	**14.48mph**	**12.69mph**	**10.80mph**	**17.13mph**	**12.42mph**
422	438	530	450	590	300	419	483	250	186
39,334	36,924	29,000	31,513	23,972	42,290	28,000	19,433	32,905	26,570
689	n.a.	1,248	n.a.	n.a.	469	502	630	202	306
1,390	**n.a.**	**729**	**n.a.**	**n.a.**	**1,501**	**1,473**	**858**	**2,561**	**998**
253	**n.a.**	**n.a.**	**n.a.**	**n.a.**	**n.a.**	**n.a.**		**n.a.**	**187**
693	694	951	589	1,261	534	525	547	305	264
n.a.	n.a.	n.a.	n.a.		n.a.	n.a.	n.a.	n.a.	n.a.
n.a.	n.a.	n.a.	n.a.	**152**	n.a.	n.a.	n.a.	n.a.	n.a.
992	980	1,048	905	1,413	751	860	888	412	423
2.4	2.2	1.8	2.0	2.4	2.5	2.0	1.8	1.6	2.3
965	**1,033**	**868**	**990**	**631**	**938**	**860**	**609**	**1,256**	**722**
176	**n.a.**	**n.a.**	**145**	**n.a.**	**n.a.**	**n.a.**	**127**	**n.a.**	**135**
0.724	0.685	1.045	0.657	1.415	0.758	0.710	1.012	0.589	0.864
n.a.	n.a.	n.a.	n.a.		n.a.	n.a.		n.a.	n.a.
n.a.	n.a.	n.a.	n.a.	0.170	n.a.	n.a.		n.a.	n.a.
1.035	**0.968**	**1.152**	**1.010**	**1.586**	**1.066**	**1.163**	**1.643**	**0.796**	**1.385**
15.1	**13.0**	**15.2**	**14.1**	**14.3**	**15.4**	**14.8**	**17.7**	**13.6**	**17.2**
..	..	..	..	..	..	..	..		..
0.223	0.251d	0.220	0.257	n.a.	0.204	0.272	0.228	0.1928	0.226
0.00386	0.0040	0.0037	0.00407	n.a.	0.00367	0.00432	0.00396	0.0031	0.00366

Table A-6 Part IV:
Selected Peoplemover Annual Operating Data

	Dallas (Airtrans)	Sea-Tac (Westinghouse)	Tampa (Westinghouse)	Morgantown (Boeing)	Fairlane (Ford ACT)
1. Year ending	3-77	12-76	12-76	9-77	2-77
PASSENGER USE					
2. Annual passengers (000)	6,126	10,100	14,500	1,909	250
3. Trip length (miles)	1.4e	0.36	0.17	1.62	0.47
4. Annual passenger-miles (000)	8,576	3,636	2,465	3,092	118
SERVICE					
5. Annual vehicle-miles (000)	3,745.4	410.6	405.0	579.5	60.3
6. Places per vehicle (@ 5.38 sq. ft. or $0.5m^2$)	29.7	64.0	62.8	19.2	30.6
7. Annual place-miles (000)	111,238	26,278	25,434	11,126	1,845
8. Passenger-miles per place mile: load factor	7.7%	13.8%	9.7%	27.8%	6.4%
Vehicle-miles per vehicle-hour:					
9. Speed including layover	**10.0mph**	**8.2mph**	**6.8mph**	**9.65mph**	**9.7mph**
10. (excluding layover)		**(9.2)**	**(8.8)**	**(16.5)**	**(17.8)**
11. Weekday cars/train	**1-2**	**1-2**	**1**	**1**	**1**
12. Vehicles in service	51	12	8	29	2
13. Annual vehicle-miles per vehicle	73,439	34,217	50,625	19,983	30,150
14. Number of stations (passenger)	28	6	8	3	2
15. Distance between stops (mi.)	n.a.	(one-way) 0.24	0.17	1.1	0.47
TRAFFIC DENSITY					
16. Line-miles (equivalent)	6.4	0.85	0.7	2.1	0.5
16a. Track miles	12.8	1.7	1.4	5.3	0.6
17. Place-miles/line mile (000)	**17,381**	**30,915**	**36,334**	**5,298**	**3,690**
18. Passenger-miles/line mile (000)	**1,340**	**4,278**	**3,521**	**1,472**	**236**
NUMBER OF EMPLOYEES (incl. contract services)					
19. Vehicle operation	10	7.5	2	12	n.a.
20. Vehicle maintenance	75	13.5	6 + 5e	} 29	n.a.
21. Way & Power	23	--	--		n.a.
22. Station	35* + 4e**	2e**	2e**	1e**	n.a.
23. Administrative	13	1	1	9	n.a.
24. TOTAL	160	24	16	51	10
EMPLOYEE RATIOS					
29. TOTAL employees/vehicle	3.1	2.0	2.0	1.8	5.0
EMPLOYEE OUTPUT					
30. Place-miles/employee (000)	**695**	**1,095**	**1,590**	**218**	**184**
31. Passenger-miles/employee (000)	**54**	**152**	**154**	**61**	**12**
EMPLOYEES NEEDED Per million place-miles of service:					
32. Vehicle operation	0.090			1.079	
33. Vehicle maintenance	0.674			} 2.606	
34. Way & Power	0.207				
35. Station	0.350			0.090	
36. Administration	0.117			0.809	
37. TOTAL	1.438	0.913	0.629	4.584	5.420
per million place-hrs. of service:					
38. Vehicle operation	0.90			10.41	
39. Vehicle maintenance	6.74			} 25.99	
40. Way & Power	2.07				
41. Station	3.50				
42. Administrative	1.17			7.80	
43. TOTAL	**14.38**	**7.49**	**4.28**	**44.20**	**52.6**
ENERGY USE kwh/place-mile					
44. Vehicle operation only	0.0529	0.0457	n.a.	n.a.	n.a.
45. Vehicle and wayside	0.0945	0.0818	0.1014	0.2606	0.1951
46. Snowmelting				4,952 Btu gas	0.4336 kwh electric
TOTAL O + M cost in 1976 $	2,957.6	751.2	478.5	1,365.9	395.0
O + M/place-mile	0.0265	0.0285	0.0188	0.1228	0.214

Note: * Station personnel on Airtrans consists of passenger service agents; these may be subtracted as belonging on the airport public relations account.
** Janitorial services at stations performed by the university and the airports, respectively; their estimated requirements were added based on floor area of stations.

New subway entrance from pedestrian plaza at Bowling Green station in Manhattan.

TABLE A-7

Rapid Transit and Light Rail Weekday Operating Characteristics (as of the periods shown in Table A-6)

SYSTEM WIDE	NYCTA	TTC	CTA	BART	WMATA	MUCTC	SEPTA	MBTA	PATH
1. Weekday AM peak vehicles in use	4,965	410	916	264	238	282	285	226	239
2. Ditto as % of vehicles in service	74.4	86.1	83.7	62.1	82.0	79.0	58.2	67.0	80.0
3. Weekday AM peak trains in use	554	63	137	33	40	32	52	57	37
4. Vehicles per peak hr. train	9.0	6.5	6.7	8.0	6	8.8	5.5	4.0	6.5
5. Vehicles per average train	8.0	6.2	4.2	6.5	6	8.35	4.7	3.1	5.5
6. Weekday vehicle - miles	890,740	104,304	162,800	88,274	60,895	78,591	46,395	34,281	33,000
7. Weekday vehicle - hours	48,674	5,116	8,524e	2,626	2,942	4,521	2,651	2,197	1,774
8. Weekday train - hours	6,084	825	2,030	404	480	541	564	708	323
9. Train hours per peak-hr. train	**11.0**	**13.1**	**14.8**	**12.2**	**12.0**	**16.9**	**10.8**	**12.4**	**8.7**
10. Service span, hours	24	19.2	24	18	18.0	20	24	19.2	24
CBD CORDON-RELATED									
11. AM peak hr. vehicle entries, CBD	3,234	474	828	183	322	582	486	340	376
12. Weekday vehicle entries, CBD	32,182	5,878	7,796	1,680	3,780	7,137	3,868	3,554	3,007
13. Average round trip run per entry, miles (line 6 / line 12)	27.7	17.7	20.9	52.5	16.1	11.0	12.0	9.6	11.0
14. Average time per entry, hrs.* (line 7/ line 12)	1.51	0.87	1.10	1.56	0.78	0.63	0.69	0.62	0.60
ANNUAL-TO-WEEKDAY RATIOS									
15. Annual VMT/ weekday VMT	315.7	331	305	259	301	333	322	307	302
16. Annual passengers/weekday passengers	297.1	286	294	270	277	(**)	278	n.a.	278
PEAKING INDICATORS									
17. CBD 8-9 passgr. entries as % of day	29.5	23.4	20.5	30.4	25.5	22.5	18.2	28.7	43.1
18. CBD 8-9 place entries as % of day	10.0	8.0	10.6	10.9	8.5	8.2	12.6	9.6	12.5
LOAD FACTORS (% places @ 5.4 sq. ft. occupied):									
19. Weekday 8-9 AM inbound CBD cordon	132.8	105.5	76.8	56.1	72.2	132.5	61.6	102.0	93.9
20. Weekday all day inbound CBD cordon	45.0	36.7	39.8	20.2	24.0	39.6	42.7	34.4	27.3
21. Weekday all day inbound outlying terminals	5.7	10.1	10.5	7.6	6.6	20.2	15.6	15.7	17.9
22. Annual systemwide average	25.6	17.9	26.3	14.0	15.1	26.9	28.3	27.9	21.0
TRAIN CREW & SIZE									
23. Employees/ train, typical	2	2	2	1	1	2	2	2-3	2
24. Nighttime & other exceptions	2	2	1	1	1	2		2	2
25. Places per average train	**810**	**826**	**349**	**912**	**880**	**711**	**512**	**305**	**482**

* Theoretically, Hours per entry (round trip) x Vehicles crossing cordon during peak hr. = Vehicles needed for peak hr. operation; hence, line 1: line 11 = line 14; deviations from this rule in the table are due to various operating details, e.g., differences between peak hour and average daily operations.

** Reflects operation of the eastern extension of Line 1 for half the year only.

MARTA	PATCO	GCRTA	SIRT	TTCLR	MBTALR	MUNI	SEPTALR 5 routes	PAT	GCRTALR	ETS	SEPTA P&W	NJT
36	69	81	34	268	173	96	83e	73	43	12	12	16
90.2	92.0	69.8	65.4	69.4	60.7	83.5	60.0	76.8	75.4	85.7	66.6	66.6
6	13	23	10	268	69	96	83e	73	22	6	12	16
6	5.3	3.6	3.4	1.0	2.5	1.0	1.0	1.0	2.0	2.0	1	1.0
4.4	3.0	2.0	3.06	1.0	1.9	1.0	1.0	1.0	1.4	2.0	1	1.0
11,900	12,744	12,620	5,317	31,332	18,425	10,783	8,850	6,179	4,793	2,340	2,160	1,960
485	455	554	264	3,049	1,834	1,149	986	523	285	130	98	131
109	152	277	86	3,049	957	1,149	986	523	203	65	98	131
18.2	**11.7**	**12.0**	**8.6**	**11.4**	**13.9**	**12.0**	**11.8e**	**7.2**	**9.3**	**10.8**	**8.1**	**8.2**
19.7	24	24	23	19	19.8	24	24	20	24	20	20.5	21
72	69	83	26	n.a.	136	63	73	51	40	24	14	30
936	450	644	202	n.a.	859	663	676	316	252	260	104	235
12.7	28.3	19.6	26.3	n.a.	21.4	16.2	13.1	19.5	19.0	9.0	20.8	8.3
0.52	1.01	0.86	1.31	n.a.	2.1	1.52	1.45	1.65	1.08	0.5	0.82	0.56
(335e)	319	286	339	322	308	285	(322e)	314	261	319	319	278
n.a.	270	270	275								n.a.	
21.3	38.5	24.0	52.9	n.a.	19.9	9.5	24.8	30.7	30.7	23.2	n.a.	25.7
7.7	15.3	12.9	12.9	n.a.	8.0	9.5	10.8	16.1	15.9	9.2	13.5	12.8
	86.6	110.0	99.3	n.a.	91.3	66.2	74.8	114.1	133.8	71.2	n.a.	68.6
	34.5	59.0	24.1	n.a.	36.9	65.9	32.5	59.9	69.2	23.2	n.a.	34.0
	9.6	9.7	0.7	n.a.	n.a.	n.a.	n.a.	n.a.	n.a.	15.6	n.a.	n.a.
	20.2	24.0	12.9	32.9	30.5	26.6	26.9	28.2	35.4	21.7	22.7	14.0
1	1	2	3-4	1	2-3	1	1	1	1-2	1	1	1
1	1	1	2-3	1	1	1	1	1	1	1	1	1
642	**377**	**208**	**426**	**67.8**	**135**	**75.5**	**67.8**	**65.6**	**98.4**	**240**	**85e**	**73.5**

Table A-8
Weekday Passengers Entering Rapid Transit Stations by System

1. NEW YORK, NYCTA
Weekday average*, calendar year 1976

Station	Line	Passengers
1. Grand Central	IRT Lex/Flushing	108,810C
2. 34th-Herald Sq.	IND 6th Ave/BMT	85,110C
3. Times Square	IRT 7th Ave/Flush./BMT	78,944C
4. Penn Station	IRT 7th Ave	60,517C
5. 47-50th St.	IND 6th Ave	53,929C
6. Fulton St.	IRT 7th Ave/Lex/IND/BMT	53,846C
7. Union Sq.	BMT B'way/Canarsie/IRT	52,704C
8. 59th St.	IRT Lex/BMT	49,685C
9. 34th St.(Penn S)	IND 8th Ave	46,482C
10. Main St.	IRT Flushing	45,759T
11. 42nd St. PABT	IND 8th Ave.	44,598C
12. Columbus Circle	IRT B'way/IND	36,991C
13. Chambers-WTC	IND 8th Ave	36,329C
14. 86th St.	IRT Lex	35,311
15. 42nd St.	IND 6th Ave	34,485C
16. Lexington Ave	IND Queens	33,094C
17. 179th St.	IND Queens	31,896T
18. Fifth Ave	IND Queens	26,420C
19. W 4th St.	IND 6th/8th Ave	26,285C
20. Bklyn Bridge	IRT Lex/BMT Nassau	26,191C
21. 74th-Roosevelt	IND Queens/IRT Flushing	24,312C
22. 23d St.	IRT Lex	23,533C
23. Wall-William St.	IRT 7th Ave	23,505
24. 68th St.	IRT Lex	23,026C
25. Borough Hall	IRT Lex/7th Ave/BMT	23,025
26. Wall-B'way	IRT Lex	22,953C
27. 96th St.	IRT B'way	22,849
28. 51st St.	IRT Lex	22,602
29. 77th St.	IRT Lex	21,091
30. 72nd St.	IRT B'way	20,953
31. Bowling Green	IRT Lex	20,580C
32. 71st-Continental	IND Queens	20,072
33. Utica Ave	IRT Bklyn	19,944
34. Broad St.	BMT Nassau	19,920C
35. 14th St.	IRT B'way	19,517C
36. Kew Gdn's - Un.	IND Queens	19,482
37. 50th St.	IRT B'way	18,604C
38. 169th St.	IND Queens	18,410
39. 57th St.	BMT B'way	18,155C
40. 33d St.	IRT Lex	17,308C
41. 28th St.	IRT Lex	17,166C
42.Atlantic Ave	IRT Bklyn/BMT Brighton	16,443
43. 23d St.	IND 6th Ave	16,053C
44. Jay Boro' Hall	IND 8th Ave	15,921
45. Canal—Lafayet.	BMT B'way	15,700C
46. 14th St.	IND 6th Ave/BMT Canarsie	15,682C
47. Parsons Blv.	IND Queens	15,548
48. 14th St.	IND 8th Ave/BMT Canarsie	15,524C
49. 175th St. GWB	IND 8th Ave	15,398
50. Whitehall	BMT B'way	15,221C
51. 125th St.	IND 8th Ave	15,120
52. King's Hwy	BMT Brighton	15,098
53. Flatbush Ave	IRT Nostrand	15,086
54. Woodhaven Blv	IND Queens	14,669
55. Fifth Ave	BMT B'way	13,754C
56. 145th St.	IND 8th Ave	13,485
57. Delancey St.	IND Houston/BMT Jamaica	13,258C
58. 63d Drive	IND Queens	12,898
59. 86th St.	IRT B'way	12,699
60. 168th St.	IRT B'way/IND 8th Ave	12,694
61. 149th St./3d Av	IRT Lenox Wh. Pl.	12,616
62. 49th St.	BMT B'way	12,346C
63. 23d St.	BMT B'way	11,970C
64. 7th Ave	IND Queens	11,942C
65. Ditmars Blv	BMT Astoria	11,820T
66. 161st St.	IND Concourse	11,790
67.Church Ave	BMT Brighton	11,640
68. 125th St.	IRT Lex	11,387
69. 96th St.	IRT Lex	11,218
70. Sheepshead Bay	BMT Brighton	11,184
71. Dekalb Ave	BMT 4th Ave	11,018
72. Junction Blv	IRT Flushing	10,712
73. 5th Ave	IRT Flushing	10,660C
74. 66th St.	IRT B'way	10,656
75. 137th St.	IRT B'way	10,634
76. 82nd St. J. Hts.	IRT Flushing	10,596
77. Cortlandt-WTC	BMT B'way	10,528C
78. 110th St.	IRT B'way	10,436
79. 103rd St.	IRT B'way	10,433
80. Canal St.	IND 8th Ave.	10,416C
81. 79th St.	IRT B'way	10,345
82. South Ferry	IRT B'way	10,208C
83. 116th St.	IRT B'way	10,189
84. 23rd St.	IRT B'way	10,138C
85. 23rd St.	IND 8th Ave	10,045C
86. 8th St.	BMT B'way	10,041C
87. Astor Pl.	IRT Lex	9,974C
88. 90th St. Elmh't.	IRT Flushing	9.898
89. 61st St. Wdside	IRT Flushing	9,845
90. 103rd St.	IRT Lex	9,805
91. E. 177th St.	IRT Pelham	9,774
92. Church Ave	IRT Bklyn	9,767
93. Sutphin Blv	IND Queens	9,703
94. 135th St.	IRT Lenox WhPl.	9,567
95. 205St.	IND Concourse	9,474T
96. Fordham Rd.	IND Concourse	9,366
97. B'way—Lafay	IND Houston	9,354C
98. Queens Plaza	IND Queens	9,169
99. 116th St.	IRT Lex	9,105
100. Nostrand Ave	IND 8th Ave	9,045
101. Burnside Ave	IRT Lex	9,005
102. Stilwell Ave	IND & BMT	8,933T
103. Christopher	IRT B'way	8,619C
104. Franklin Ave	IRT Bklyn	8,582
105. 67th Ave	IND Queens	8,512
106. 1st. Ave	BMT Canarsie	8,482C
107. Hoyt St.	IND 8th Ave	8,441
108. 50th St.	IND 8th Ave	8,427C
109. 49th St.	IRT Flushing	8,324
110. Grand Ave	IND Queens	8,139

*Weekday average calculated as annual turnstile passengers x 1.09169 (for non-turnstile revenue passengers) divided by 297.12 (weekday equivalents in a year). Both factors vary by station from these systemwide averages; actual counts may for instance, be higher due to low weekend use, or due to more non-token passengers, such as school children.

T = terminal station
C = CBD station

Rank/Station	Line	Count
111. 167th St.	IND Concourse	8,066
112. B'way	BMT Astoria	8,057
113. 110th St.	IRT Lex	8,036
114. Grand Ave.	BMT Astoria	8,009
115. E. B'way	IND Houston	8,005**C**
116. Tremont Ave	IND Concourse	7,987
117. 28th St.	IRT B'way	7,852**C**
118. Grand St.	IND Houston	7,811**C**
119. Newkirk	IRT Bklyn	7,802
120. 46th St.	IRT Flushing	7,792
121. 170th St.	IRT Lex	7,761
122. Hoyt St.	IRT Bklyn	7,759
123. Queensboro Pl	IRT Flushing/BMT	7,727
124. Brighton Beach	IND Brighton	7,723
125. Nevins St.	IRT Bklyn	7,555
126. 181st St.	IND 8th Ave	7,534
127. Chambers St.	IRT B'way	7,299**C**
128. Newkirk	BMT Brighton	7,283
129. Prospect Ave.	IRT Lenox WhPl.	7,117
130. 207th St.	IND 8th Ave	7,103**T**
131. Rector St.	BMT B'way	7,070**C**
132. 28th St.	BMT B'way	7,042**C**
133. 125th St.	IRT Lenox WhPl.	7,015
134. City Hall	BMT B'way	7,013**C**
135. Houston St.	IRT B'way	7,011**C**
136. Elmhurst	IND Queens	6,440
137. Utica Ave	IND 8th Ave	6,914
138. 104 St. Corona	IRT Flushing	6,913
139. Soundview	IRT Pelham	6,874
140. Steinway St.	IND Queens	6,815
141. Myrtle Ave	BMT Canarsie	6,787
142. 170th St.	IND Concourse	6,764
143. 177th St.	IRT Lenox WhPl.	6,505
144. Euclid Ave	IND 8th Ave	6,488
145. 167th St.	IRT Lex	6,478
146. 2nd Ave	IND Houston	6,404**C**
147. 36th St.	BMT 4th Ave	6,366
148. Rockaway Pk.	BMT Canarsie	6,317**T**
149. Fordham Rd.	IRT Lex	6,301
150. 181st St.	IRT B'way	6,289
151. Bedford Ave.	IND Concourse	6,270
152. Kingsbridge Rd.	IND Concourse	6,269
153. Church Ave	IND Coney Island	6,211
154. Prospect Pk	BMT Brighton	6,199
(155. 168th St.	BMT Jamaica	6,185**T**)
156. Pelham Bay Pk.	IRT Pelham	6,184**T**
157. Sutter Ave	IRT Bklyn	6,144
158. 49th St. Lowry.	IRT Flushing	6,118
159. Marcy Ave	BMT Jamaica	6,100
160. Ave U	BMT Brighton	6,090
161. Simpson St.	IRT Lenox WhPl.	6,052
162. 157th St.	IRT B'way	5,989
163. Hunts Pt.	IRT Pelham	5,956
164. 46th St.	IND Queens	5,919
165. Grand Army Pl.	IRT Bklyn	5,877
166. Hoyt Ave	BMT Astoria	5,788
167. 86th St.	IND 8th Ave	5,720
168. 200th St.	IND 8th Ave	5,716
169. 57th St.	IND 6th Ave	5,708**C**
170. 95th–Ft. Ham.	BMT 4th Ave	5,703**T**
171. Canal St.	BMT B'way	5,664**C**
172. Kingston–Thrp	IND 8th Ave	5,652
173. Winthrop St.	IRT Bklyn	5,632
174. Lawrence St.	BMT 4th Ave	5,624
175. 59th St.	BMT 4th Ave	5,612
176. Greenpoint Ave	IND Bklyn crosst.	5,599
177. Bay Ridge Ave	BMT 4th Ave	5,564
178. 161st St.	IRT Lex	5,534
179. 33rd St./Rawsn.	IRT Flushing	5,500
180. 4th Ave/9th St.	IND Coney Isl./BMT	5,416
181. 81st St.	IND 8th Ave	5,393
182. 174th St.	IRT Lenox WhPl	5,353
183. 125th St.	IRT B'way	5,350
184. Sterling Pl.	IRT Bklyn	5,317
185. Kingsbridge Rd	IRT Lex	5,296
186. Van Wyck	IND Queens	5,283
187. Lefferts Bl.	IND 8th Ave	5,205**T**
188. 96th St.	IND 8th Ave	5,187
189. 7th Ave	IND Coney Isl.	5,164
190. 149th St.	IRT Lex	5,090
191. Jackson St.	IRT Lenox WhPl.	5,062
192. Elder Ave	IRT Pelham	4,964
193. Ave J	BMT Brighton	4,950
194. 176th St.	IRT Lex	4,916
195. Nassau Ave	IND Bklyn crosst.	4,906
196. 86th St.	BMT 4th Ave	4,906
197. Saratoga Ave	IRT Bklyn	4,904
198. Pacific St.	BMT 4th Ave	4,887
199. 174th St.	IND Concourse	4,883
200. Vernon/Jksn.	IRT Flushing	4,849
201. 111th St. Crna.	IRT Flushing	4,830
202. 191st St.	IRT B'way	4,830
203. Gun Hill Rd.	IRT Dyre	4,810
204. Carroll St.	IND Coney Isl.	4,753
205. 183d St.	IND Concourse	4,101
206. Washington Av	BMT Astoria	4,688
207. 138th St.	IRT Pelham	4,681
208. Kingston Ave	IRT Bklyn	4,674
209. 145th St.	IRT B'way	4,612
210. 7th Ave	BMT Brighton	4,643
211. 18th St.	IRT 7th Ave	4,639**C**
212. Cortlandt-WTC	IRT 7th Ave	4,634**C**
213. 116th St.	IRT Lenox Wh. Pl.	4,627
214. Brook Ave	IRT Pelham	4,591
215. Bedford Ave	BMT Canarsie	4,590
216. Bleeker St.	IRT Lex	4,580**C**
217. 231st St.	IRT B'way	4,474
218. Rockaway Blv	IND 8th Ave	4,473
219. Mt. Eden	IRT Lex	4,460
220. 52nd St./Linc.	IRT Flushing	4,429
221. Dyckman St.	IRT B'way	4,425
222. Northern Blv	IND Queens	4,424
223. Ave M	BMT Brighton	4,423
224. Bergen St.	IND Coney Isl.	4,422
225. Bay Parkway	BMT West End	4,402
226. Spring St.	IND 8th Ave	4,400**C**
227. Pelham P'way	IRT Lenox WhPl.	4,393
228. Rector St.	IRT 7th Ave	4,389**C**
229. Mosholu P'way	IRT Lex	4,371
230. 22nd Ave	BMT Sea Beach	4,323

231. Penn Ave	IRT Bklyn	4,302	291. 110th St.	IND 8th Ave	3,237
232. Beverly Rd.	IRT Bklyn	4,290	292. 36th St.	IND Queens	3,208
233. Ely Ave	IND Queens	4,287	293. Fresh Pond	BMT Myrtle	3,204
234. Clark St.	IRT Bklyn	4,280	294. Prospect Park	IND Coney Isl.	3,195
235. 77th St.	BMT 4th Ave	4,274	295. Union St.	BMT 4th Ave	3,184
236. Parkside Ave	BMT Brighton	4,212	296. 18th Ave	BMT West End	3,177
237. Prince St.	BMT B'way	4,208**C**	297. Metropolitan Ave	BMT Myrtle	3,173
238. Myrtle Ave	BMT Jamaica	4,160	298. E. 180th St.	IRT Lenox WhPl.	3,105**T**
239. 183d St.	IRT Lex	4,154	299. Neck Rd.	BMT Brighton	3,051
240. 72nd St.	IND 8th Ave	4,128	300. Canal St.	IRT 7th Ave	3,027**C**
241. Flushing Ave	BMT Jamaica	4,119	301. 55th St.	BMT West End	3,014
242. Castle Hill	IRT Pelham	4,112	302. B'way East NY	IND 8th Ave/BMT	3,006
243. Metro./Lorimer	IND crosst./BMT	4,061	303. Halsey St.	BMT Canarsie	2,987
244. 242d St.	IRT B'way	4,059	304. 135th St.	IND 8th Ave	2,971
245. Gates Ave	BMT Jamaica	4,049	305. Mott Ave	IND Rockaway	2,925**T**
246. Grant Ave	IND 8th Ave	4,041	306. Freeman Ave	IRT Lenox WhPl.	2,894
247. 45th St.	BMT 4th Ave	3,987	307. Jefferson St.	BMT Canarsie	2,834
248. Ralph Ave	IND 8th Ave	3,985	308. Ocean P'way	BMT Brighton	2,833
249. Eastern Pk'way	IRT Bklyn	3,981	309. 225th St.	IRT B'way	2,824
250. 18th Ave	IND Coney Isl.	3,981	310. President St.	IRT Bklyn	2,820
251. 110th St.	IRT Lenox WhPl.	3,926	311. E. 149th St.	IRT Pelham	2,801
252. Rockaway Ave	IRT Bklyn	3,904	312. Prospect Ave	BMT 4th Ave	2,763
253. Ft. Hamiltion P'way	BMT Sea Beach	3,897	313. Dyre Ave/233 St.	IRT Dyre	2,699**T**
254. 18th Ave	BMT Sea Beach	3,884	314. Kings Highway	IND Coney Isl.	2,692
255. 50th St.	BMT West End	3,874	315. Franklin Ave	IRT B'way	2,684
256. Westchester Ave	IRT Pelham	3,871	316. 103d St.	IND 8th Ave	2,682
257. High St.	IND 8th Ave	3,846	317. Cypress Ave	IRT Pelham	2,664
258. 163d St.	IND 8th Ave	3,840	318. Smith/9th St.	IND Coney Isl.	2,645
259. Nostrd. Ave/E P'way	IRT Bklyn	3,811	319. 45th Road	IRT Flushing	2,625
260. Park Pl.	IRT 7th Ave	3,763**C**	320. 9th Ave	BMT West End	2,617
261. Cortelyou Rd.	BMT Brighton	3,737	321. Burke Ave	IRT Lenox WhPl.	2,614
262. Woodlawn	IRT Lex	3,727**T**	322. Van Siclen	IRT Bklyn	2,614
263. E. 241st St.	IRT Lenox WhPl.	3,724**T**	323. Shepherd Ave	IND 8th Ave	2,598
264. 53d St.	BMT 4th Ave	3,724	324. 69th/Fisk Ave	IRT Flushing	2,588
265. DeKalb Ave	BMT Canarsie	3,706	325. Franklin Ave	IND 8th Ave	2,581
266. E. 233d St.	IRT Lenox WhPl.	3,706	326. 238th St.	IRT B'way	2,581
267. Fort Hamilton P'way	BMT West End	3,666	327. 145th/Lenox	IRT Lenox WhPl.	2,574
268. New Lots Ave	IRT Bklyn	3,603**T**	328. Canal St.	IRT Lex	2,574**C**
269. Spring St.	IRT Lex	3,579**C**	329. Lorimer	BMT Jamaica	2,554
270. Willets Pt.	IRT Flushing	3,542	330. Grand St.	BMT Canarsie	2,521
271. Halsey St.	BMT Jamaica	3,542	331. Canal St.	BMT Nassau Loop	2,475**C**
272. Ditmas Ave	IND Coney Isl.	3,536	332. Myrtle/Willoughby	IND B'way crosst.	2,517
273. Bedford/Nostrand	IND Bklyn Crosst.	3,512	333.71st St.	BMT West End	2,460
274. Clinton/Wash.	IND 8th Ave	3,495	334. 155th St.	IND 8th Ave	2,459
275. St. Lawrence	IRT Pelham	3,482	335. Ave X	IND Coney Isl.	2,441
276. Allerton Ave	IRT Lenox WhPl.	3,470	336. Ave H	BMT Brighton	2,414
277. Clinton/Wash.	IND Bklyn crosst.	3,450	337. Morgan Ave	BMT Canarsie	2,397
278. 155th St.	IND Concourse	3,382	338. E. 219th St.	IRT Lenox WhPl.	2,394
279. 8th Ave	BMT Sea Beach	3,381	339. Baychester Ave	IRT Dyre Ave	2,376
280. Kings H'way	BMT Sea Beach	3,365	340. 75th Ave	IND Queens	2,369
281. Rockaway Blv	IND 8th Ave	3,323	341. Ave N	IND Coney Isl.	2,362
282. 79th St.	BMT West End	3,321	342. Kosciusko St.	BMT Jamaica	2.357
283. Gun Hill Rd.	IRT Lenox WhPl.	3,314	343. Bergen St.	IRT Bklyn	2,335
284. Graham Ave	BMT Canarsie	3,302	344. E. 105th St.	BMT Canarsie	2,329
285. Liberty Ave	IND 8th Ave	3,293	345. 25th Ave	BMT West End	2,318
286. 190th St.	IND 8th Ave	3,288	346. New Utrecht Ave	BMT Sea Beach	2,310
287. 20th Ave	BMT West End	3,283	347. Ft. Hamilton Pk'way	IND Coney Isl.	2,307
288. Buhre Ave	IRT Pelham	3,243	348. Hewes Ave	BMT Jamaica	2,292
289. 116th St.	IND 8th Ave	3,242	(349. Sutphin Blvd.	BMT Jamaica	2,280)
290. E. 225th St.	IRT Lenox WhPl.	3,241	350. Lafayette Ave	IND 8th Ave	2,261

351. Classon Ave	IND Bklyn crosst.	2,242
352. 20th Ave	BMT Sea Beach	2,221
353. 207th St.	IRT B'way	2,182
354. 3d Ave	BMT Canarsie	2,176
355. B'way	IND Bklyn crosst.	2,176**C**
356. Van Siclen Ave.	IND Coney Isl.	2,164
357. Montrose Ave	BMT Canarsie	2,134
358. W. 8th St.	BMT/IND Coney Isl.	2,092
359. Sutter Ave	BMT Canarsie	2,069
360. Van Siclen Ave	IND 8th Ave	2,065
361. 65th St.	IND Queens	2,048
362. Ave U	BMT Sea Beach	2,037
363. Chauncey St.	BMT Jamaica	2,015
364. 148th/Lenox	IRT Lenox Wh. Pl.	2,010**T**
365. Crescent St.	BMT Jamaica	1,994
366. Intervale Ave	IRT Lenox WhPl	1,984
367. Knickerbocker Ave	BMT Myrtle Ave	1,973
368. Wilson Ave	BMT Canarsie	1,947
369. Longwood Ave	IRT Pelham	1,946
370. Pelham Pk'way	IRT Dyre	1,945
371. Forest Ave	BMT Myrtle	1,917
372. 86th St.	BMT Sea Beach	1,911
373. Bay 50th St.	BMT West End	1,883
374. Beebe Ave	BMT Astoria	1,870
375. Ave P	IND Coney Isl.	1,857
376. Hudson St.	IND 8th Ave	1,854
377. Beverly Rd.	BMT Brighton	1,840
378. 25th St.	BMT 4th Ave	1,839
379. Van Siclen	BMT Jamaica	1,814
380. Cleveland	BMT Jamaica	1,810
381. York St.	IND Houston	1,777
382. Norwood	BMT Jamaica	1,731
383. New Lots Ave	BMT Canarsie	1,720
384. Bedford Ave	IRT Lex	1,700
385. Ave I	IND Coney Isl.	1,684
386. E. 238th St.	IRT Lenox WhPl.	1,670
387. Boyd Ave	IND 8th Ave	1,667
388. 138th St.	IRT Lex	1,656
389. Woodhaven Blv	BMT Jamaica	1,640
390. Forest Ave	BMT Jamaica	1,630
391. Flushing Ave	IND Bklyn crosst	1,584
392. Ave U	IND Coney Isl.	1,563
(393. 160th St.	BMT Jamaica	1,504)
394. Straiton Ave	IND Rockaway	1,483
395. Middletown Rd.	IRT Pelham	1,479
396. Junius St.	IRT Bklyn	1,432
397. Morris Rd.	IRT Dyre	1,381
398. Zerega Ave	IRT Pelham	1,358
399. Bronx Pk. E.	IRT Lenox WhPl.	1,350
400. Greenwood Ave	IND 8th Ave	1,304
401. Wavecrest Ave	IND Rockaway	1,302
402. E. 143d St.	IRT Pelham	1,297
403. Elderts La.	BMT Jamaica	1,280
404. Livonia Ave	BMT Canarsie	1,203
405. Seneca Ave	BMT Myrtle	1,137
406. Central Ave	BMT Myrtle	1,131
407. 102d St.	BMT Jamaica	1,111
408. 121st St.	BMT Jamaica	1,106
409. Gaston Ave	IND Rockaway	1,061
410. Oxford Ave	IND 8th Ave	1,034
411. 111th St.	BMT Jamaica	999
412. Park Pl.	BMT Brighton	995
413. Holland	IND Rockaway	955
414. Atlantic Ave	BMT Canarsie	915
415. Rockaway Park	IND Rockaway	872**T**
416. Van Alst Ave	IND Bklyn crosst.	871
417. Fulton	IND Bklyn crosst.	834
418. Wyckoff Ave	BMT Myrtle Ave	810
419. Whitlock Ave	IRT Pelham	758
420. Alabama Ave	BMT Jamaica	754
421. Howard Beach	IND Rockaway	743
422. Metropolitan Ave	BMT Jamaica	690
423. Botanical Garden	BMT Brighton	684
424. Bowery	BMT Nassau Loop	590**C**
425. 215th St.	IRT B'way	564
426. Court Sq.	IND Bklyn crosst.	545
427. Aqueduct	IND Rockaway	540
428. Bushwick	BMT Canarsie	539
429. Frank Ave	IND Rockaway	537
430. Queens Blv	BMT Jamaica	492
431. Cypress Ave	BMT Jamaica	482
432. Playland	IND Rockaway	441
433. Seaside Blv	IND Rockaway	413
434. 22d Ave	IND Coney Isl.	362
435. Franklin Ave	BMT Brighton	362
436. Broad Channel	IND Rockaway	301
437. Edgemere	IND Rockaway	272
438. 62d St.	BMT West End	259
439. Dean St.	BMT Brighton	179
TOTAL		**3,400,973**
CBD		1,459,475
Terminals		163,641

( ) Stations in parentheses closed.

2. NEW YORK, SIRT

Typical Weekday, November 1977

1. St. George	6,800**C**
2. Great Kills	1,639
3 Oakwood Heights	1,505
4. Eltingville	1,130
5. Huguenot	1,122
6. New Dorp	816
7. Grant City	671
8. Grasmere	665
9. Dongan Hills	644
10. Bay Terrace	532
11. Annandale	507
12. Old Town	348
13. Jefferson Ave	304
14. Princess Bay	269
15. Pleasant Plains	209
16. Tottenville	200**T**
17. Tomkinsville	191
18. Clifton	188
19. Atlantic	167
20. Nassau	113
21. Stapleton	93
22. Richmond Valley	77
TOTAL	**18,190***

***Note:** Expanded from 12-hour count of 16,551.

3. NEW YORK, PATH
Typical Weekday, Spring 1977

1. World Trade Center	Dt.	41,250**C**
2. Hoboken	Upt.	28,589**T**
3. 30–33d St.	Upt.	18,370**C**
4. Newark	Dt.	18,329**T**
5. Journal Square	Dt.	18,015
6. Grove St.	Dt.	6,284
7. Exchange Place	Dt.	3,887
8. 14th St.	Upt.	3,029**C**
9. 23d St.	Upt.	2,896**C**
10. Harrison	Dt.	2,472
11. 9th St.	Upt.	1,942**C**
12. Christopher St.	Upt.	1,041**C**
13. Pavonia	Upt.	380
TOTAL		**146,484**
CBD		68,528
Terminals		46,918

4. TORONTO, TTC
Typical Weekday

		Feb. 1980	Feb. 1977
1. Bloor-Yonge	Bloor-Yonge	34,198**C**	34,483
2. Islington	Bloor	30,439**T**	31,643
3. Eglinton	Yonge	29,936	33,263
4. Queen	Yonge	29,299**C**	40,424
5. Dundas	Yonge	27,620**C**	19,324
6. Finch	Yonge	27,172**T**	25,059
7. Warden	Danforth	26,213**T**	22,539
8. King	Yonge	25,556**C**	24,263
9. Union	University	23,955**C**	21,915
10. St. Clair	Yonge	18,615	25,607
11. Sheppard	Yonge	18,552	16,639
12. College	Yonge	17,722**C**	24,804
13. Bay	Bloor	17,400**C**	16,632
14. Bathurst	Bloor	16,527	23,730
15. Pape	Danforth	16,156	18,028
16. Queen's Park	University	14,139**C**	14,033
17. Victoria Park	Danforth	14,010	15,788
18. Broadview	Danforth	13,768	15,320
19. Spadina	Bloor-Spadina	13,768	12,747
20. Wellesley	Yonge	13,377**C**	12,213
21. St. Andrew	University	13,048**C**	10,747
22. Dundas West	Bloor	12,616	9,592
23. St. Patrick	University	11,926**C**	11,130
24. St. Clair West	Spadina	11,234	
25. York Mills	Yonge	11,179	13,497
26. Ossington	Bloor	10,924	14,889
27. Main	Danforth	10,793	10,180
28. Wilson	Spadina	10,419**T**	
29. St. George	Bloor-Univ.	10,395**C**	14,735
30. Royal York	Bloor	10,376	9,218
31. Sherbourne	Danforth	10,361	9,553
32. Davisville	Yonge	10,285	12,668
33. Lawrence	Yonge	10,237	14,364
34. Jane	Bloor	9,434	11,265
35. Osgoode	University	9,285**C**	8,528
36. Lansdowne	Bloor	8,885	10,635
37. Dufferin	Bloor	8,836	11,469
38. Runnymede	Bloor	7,693	8,528
39. Woodbine	Danforth	7,184	8,846
40. Eglinton West	Spadina	6,873	
41. Coxwell	Danforth	6,625	7,677
42. Keele	Bloor	6,200	6,231
43. Lawrence West	Spadina	5,126	
44. Greenwood	Danforth	5,111	4,973
45. Donlands	Danforth	5,030	4,701
46. High Park	Bloor	4,938	5,328
47. Yorkdale	Spadina	4,783	
48. Christie	Bloor	4,525	4,924
49. Museum	University	4,196**C**	3,635
50. Dupont	Spadina	3,963	
51. Castle Frank	Danforth	3,559	4,014
52. Rosedale	Yonge	3,425	4,380
53. Old Mill	Bloor	2,845	2,805
54. Summerhill	Yonge	2,621	3,224
55. Chester	Danforth	2,488	2,887
56. Glencairn	Spadina	2,149	
57. Kennedy	Danforth	u.c.**T**	
58. Kipling	Bloor	u.c.**T**	
TOTAL		**697,989**	**692,827**
CBD		252,116	256,866
Terminals		94,243	79,241

5. MONTREAL, MUCTC
Typical Weekday

		Sept. 1980	Fall 1976
1. McGill	Line 1	36,820**C**	31,846
2. Berri	1+2+4	36,758**C**	27,536
3. Henri-Bourassa	Line 2	33,999**T**	32,882
4. Longueuil	Line 4	31,875**T**	30,605
5. Atwater	Line 1	29,323**C**	42,118
6. Guy	Line 1	25,046**C**	21,932
7. Jean-Talon	Line 2	24,833	22,626
8. Pie IX	Line 1	24,467	10,987
9. Peel	Line 1	23,859**C**	22,756
10. Place-des-Arts	Line 1	22,950**C**	21,087
11. Honore-Beaugrand	Line 1	20,187**T**	17,607
12. Sauve	Line 2	20,150	21,928
13. Cremazie	Line 2	18,935	18,257
14. Laurier	Line 2	18,336	21,214
15. Sherbrooke	Line 2	15,069	16,254
16. Square Victoria	Line 2	14,747**C**	14,101
17. Bonaventure	Line 2	13,389**C**	17,281
18. Beaubien	Line 2	13,271	16,236
19. Rosemont	Line 2	12,211	13,410
20. Jarry	Line 2	11,868	13,828
21. Angrignon	Line 1	10,801**T**	
22. Mont-Royal	Line 2	10,468	11,853
23. Place-d'Armes	Line 2	10,402**C**	10,318
24. Papineau	Line 1	9,751	10,440
25. Radisson	Line 1	9,110	7,411
26. Viau	Line 1	8,745	7,736
27. Cadillac	Line 1	8,635	7,526
28. Lionel-Groulx	Line 1+2	8,367	
29. Langelier	Line 1	8,352	7,163
30. Jolicoeur	Line 1	7,765	
31. Frontenac	Line 1	7,641	9,835
32. Champ-de-Mars	Line 2	7,534**C**	6,419
33. Joliette	Line 1	6,374	3,941
34. De l'Eglise	Line 1	5,665	
35. LaSalle	Line 1	5,420	
36. Place Saint Henri	Line 2	4,750**T**	
37. Verdun	Line 1	4,339	
38. St-Laurent	Line 1	4,302**C**	4,454

39. L'Assomption	Line 1	3,941	3,105
40. Beaudry	Line 1	3,364C	3,484
41. Monk	Line 1	3,170	
42. Prefontaine	Line 1	2,913	2,639
43. Charlevoix	Line 1	2,857	
44. Georges-Vanier	Line 2	643	
45. Lucien-l'Allier	Line 2	597	
46. Ste-Helene	Line 4	534	366
TOTAL		**604,533**	**531,181**
CBD		228,494	223,332
Terminals		101,612	81,094

6. CHICAGO, CTA
Weekday, November 1976

1. 95th St.	WS	23,700 **T**
2. Washington	NS	20,550 **C**
3. Washington	WNW	14,400 **C**
4. Jefferson Park	WNW	13,500 **T**
5. Adams/Wabash	Loop	11,850 **C**
6. Jackson	NS	11,650 **C**
7. Clark/Lake	Loop	10,500 **C**
8. Chicago	NS	10,300 **C**
9. Lake Transfer	WNW	10,200 **C**
10. 79th St.	WS	10,050
11. Randolph/Wabash	Loop	9,950 **C**
12. Monroe	WNW	9,650 **C**
13. Howard	NS	9,600
14. 69th St.	WS	9,400
15. Monroe	NS	9,300 **C**
16. Jackson	WNW	9,100 **C**
17. State/Lake	Loop	9,000 **C**
18. 87th St.	WS	8,350
19. U of I/Halsted	WNW	7,850
20. Madison/Wabash	Loop	7,500 **C**
21. Logan Square	WNW	7,350
22. Fullerton	NS	6,450
23. Loyola	NS	5,950
24. Ashland	NS	5,600 **T**
25. Morse	NS	5,300
26. Wilson	NS	5,150
27. Bryn Mawr	NS	4,950
28. Grand	NS	4,950
29. Harlem	WS	4,800 **T**
30. Belmont	NS	4,700
31. Division	WNW	4,600
32. Jackson Park	NS	4,350 **T**
33. Austin	WS	4,200
34. Quincy/Wells	Loop	4,200
35. Kimball	Ravenswood	4,150 **T**
36. Belmont	WNW	4,050
37. Desplaines	WNW	3,950 **T**
38. Irving Park	WNW	3,800
39. 63rd St.	WS	3,800
40. Sox/35	WS	3,750
41. Tech/35	NS	3,700
42. 47th St.	NS	3,700
43. Addison	WNW	3,500
44. Central	WS	3,500
45. Clinton	WNW	3,450
46. Polk	WNW	3,450
47. Clark/Division	NS	3,400
48. Merchandise Mart	Ravenswood	3,350 **C**
49. Garfield	WS	3,300
50. Roosevelt	NS	3,300
51. Cicero/Berwyn	WNW	3,200 **T**
52. Damen	WNW	3,150
53. Clinton/NW Passage	WS	3,000 **C**
54. Dempster	Skokie	3,000 **T**
55. Pulaski	WS	2,950
56. 51st St.	NS	2,900
57. Davis	Evanston	2,850
58. Medical Center	WNW	2,800
59. Madison/Wells	Loop	2,750
60. Cicero (Douglas)	WNW	2,700
61. Granville	NS	2,700
62. Western	Ravenswood	2,650
63. Sheridan	NS	2,550
64. Cicero	WS	2,500
65. Berwyn	NS	2,450
66. Cottage Grove	NS	2,450
67. Oak Park	WS	2,400
68. Addison	NS	2,350
69. LaSalle	WNW	2,350
70. 43rd St.	NS	2,350
71. Halsted	NS	2,250
72. Austin	WNW	2,200
73. Cermak/Chinatown	WS	2,200
74. LaSalle/Van Buren	Loop	2,200
75. California (Douglas)	WNW	2,150
76. Harrison	NS	2,150
77. Linden	Evanston	2,150 **T**
78. Montrose	WNW	2,150
79. Thorndale	NS	2,150
80. Kedzie (Congress)	WNW	2,050
81. 47th St.	WS	2,000
82. California (Milwaukee)	WNW	1,950
83. Laramie	WS	1,950
84. Western (Milwaukee)	WNW	1,950
85. Racine	WNW	1,900
86. Chicago	WNW	1,800
87. Irving Park	Ravenswood	1,800
88. Oak Park	WNW	1,800
89. Kedzie	Ravenswood	1,700
90. Garfield	NS	1,650
91. Homan	WS	1,650
92. North/Clybourn	NS	1,650
93. Ridgeland	WS	1,600
94. Ashland	WS	1,550
95. Cicero (Congress)	WNW	1,550
96. Argyle	NS	1,500
97. King Drive	NS	1,500
98. Pulaski (Congress)	WNW	1,500
99. Racine	NS	1,500
100. Jarvis	NS	1,450
101. Lawrence	NS	1,450
102. 18th St.	WNW	1,450
103. Addison	Ravenswood	1,350
104. Diversey	Ravenswood	1,350
105. Indiana	NS	1,350
106. Main	Evanston	1,350
107. Damen	Ravenswood	1,300
108. Cermak	NS	1,250
109. Harlem	WNW	1,250
110. Kedzie (Douglas)	WNW	1,250

111. Pulaski (Douglas)	WNW	1,250
112. Montrose	Ravenswood	1,200
113. Halsted	WS	1,150
114. Randolph/Wells	Loop	1,150
115. Central Park	WNW	1,100
116. Grand	WNW	1,100
117. 61st St.	NS	1,100
118. 58th St.	NS	1,050
119. Armitage	Ravenswood	1,000
120. Western (Douglas)	WNW	1,000
121. Chicago	Ravenswood	950
122. Hoyne	WNW	950
123. Central	Evanston	900
124. Rockwell	Ravenswood	900
125. Southport	Ravenswood	900
126. University	NS	900
127. Wellington	Ravenswood	850
128. Harvard	NS	800
129. Wentworth	NS	800
130. Western (Congress)	WNW	800
131. Kedzie	WS	700
132. Laramie	WNW	700
133. Noyes	Evanston	700
134. South Boulevard	Evanston	700
135. Dempster	Evanston	650
136. Francisco	Ravenswood	650
137. California	WS	600
138. Kildare	WNW	600
139. Sedgwick	Ravenswood	600
140. Foster	Evanston	550
141. 50th St.	WNW	500
142. Paulina	Ravenswood	450
TOTAL		**507,350**
CBD		150,300
Terminals		68,400

7. PHILADELPHIA, SEPTA
Average Weekday, 1975

1. 15th Street	Market	32,517**C**
2. City Hall	Broad	23,473**C**
3. Bridge-Pratt	Frankford	23,067**T**
4. Olney	Broad	18,581
5. 8th Street	Market	17,256**C**
6. 69th Street	Market	17,041**T**
7. 13th Street	Market	13,706**C**
8. 30-31st Streets	Market	13,108
9. Erie	Broad	8,690
10. 11th Street	Market	8,524**C**
11. 52nd Street	Market	8,134
12. Allegheny	Frankford	7,812
13. Columbia	Broad	7,280
14. Margaret	Frankford	7,122**C**
15. 5th Street	Market	6,341**C**
16. Walnut-Locust	Broad	6,299
17. 60th Street	Market	6,274
18. Erie-Torresdale	Frankford	6,202
19. Snyder	Broad	5,888
20. No. Philadelphia	Broad	5,872
21. 56th Street	Market	5,557
22. Spring Garden	Broad	5,169
23. Fern Rock	Broad	4,881**T**
24. 40th Street	Market	4,302
25. Oregon	Broad	4,120
26. 34th Street	Market	4,111
27. Girard	Broad	4,078
28. Girard	Market	4,013
29. 46th Street	Market	3,839
30. Tasker-Morris	Broad	3,747
31. Wyoming	Broad	3,602
32. Logan	Broad	3,596
33. Allegheny	Broad	3,535
34. Hunting Park	Broad	3,343
35. Race-Vine	Broad	3,274**C**
36. 8th & Market	Ridge	3,235**C**
37. Ellsworth	Broad	3,140
38. Susquehanna	Broad	3,139
39. 2nd Street	Market	2,626**C**
40. Somerset	Frankford	2,765
41. Lombard-South	Broad	2,624**C**
42. Pattison	Broad	2,508**T**
43. 63rd Street	Market	2,202
44. Huntingdon	Frankford	2,033
45. Tioga	Frankford	1,892
46. Berks	Frankford	1,663
47. York-Dauphin	Frankford	1,567
48. Fair Mount	Broad	1,026
49. Fair Mount	Frankford	941
50. Church	Frankford	736
51. Millbourne	Market	689
52. Vine	Ridge	104**C**
53. Spring Garden	Ridge	54
TOTAL		**337,298**
CBD		117,248
Terminals		47,497

8. PHILADELPHIA, PATCO
Average Weekday, Fall 1976

1. 8th St. & Market	7,656**C**
2. 15-16th St. & Locust	6,696**C**
3. Lindenwold	5,449**T**
4. Ferry Avenue	3,594
5. Haddonfield	3,445
6. 12-13th St. & Locust	3,050**C**
7. Ashland	2,919
8. City Hall Camden	2,434
9. Westmont	2,125
10. Collingswood	1,977
11. Broadway	1,825
12. 9-10th St. & Locust	666**C**
13. Franklin Square	314**C**
14. Woodcrest	u.c.
TOTAL	**42,150**
CBD	18,382
Terminal	5,449

9. WASHINGTON, WMATA

February 1980

	Station	Line	Passengers
1.	Farragut West	Blue	25,785**C**
2.	Pentagon	Blue	18,156
3.	Metro Center	Red + Blue	16,831**C**
4.	Silver Spring	Red	15,484**T**
5.	Dupont Circle	Red	13,964**C**
6.	Rosslyn	Blue	12,950
7.	Farragut North	Red	12,895**C**
8.	Foggy Bottom	Blue	12,607**C**
9.	McPherson Square	Blue	12,085**C**
10.	L'Enfant Plaza	Blue	11,736**C**
11.	Union Station	Red	10,939
12.	Ballston	Orange	8,632**T**
13.	Judiciary Square	Red	8,447**C**
14.	Crystal City	Blue	7,725
15.	Smithsonian	Blue	6,483**C**
16.	New Carrollton	Orange	6,449**T**
17.	Brookland	Red	5,834
18.	Capitol South	Blue	5,762**C**
19.	Federal Triangle	Blue	5,610**C**
20.	Potomac Ave.	Blue	5,456
21.	Fort Totten	Red	4,931
22.	Eastern Market	Blue	4,776
23.	Federal Center SW	Blue	4,736**C**
24.	Takoma	Red	4,688
25.	National Airport	Blue	4,654**T**
26.	Rhode Island Ave.	Red	3,951
27.	Gallery Place	Red	3,882**C**
28.	Stadium-Armory	Blue	3,861
29.	Minnesota Ave.	Orange	3,529
30.	Pentagon City	Blue	3,213
31.	Landover	Orange	2,885
32.	Deanwood	Orange	2,587
33.	Court House	Orange	2,503
34.	Clarendon	Orange	1,762
35.	Virginia Square	Orange	1,603
36.	Cheverly	Orange	1,447
37.	Arlington Cemetery	Blue	85
	TOTAL		**278,923**
	CBD		140,823
	Terminals		35,219

10. BOSTON, MBTA

December 8, 1976

	Station	Line	Passengers
1.	Washington	Red + Orange	33,854**C**
2.	Park	Red + LR	23,595**C**
3.	Harvard	Red	21,576**T**
4.	State	Blue + Orange	13,091**C**
5.	Forest Hills	Orange	10,760**T**
6.	Ashmont	Red	8,836**T**
7.	South Station	Red	8,679**C**
8.	Central	Red	8,587
9.	Government Center	Blue + LR	8,561**C**
10.	Quincy Center	Red	7,937**T**
11.	North Station	Orange	7,513**C**
12.	Sullivan Square	Orange	7,327
13.	Haymarket	Orange + LR	6,377**C**
14.	Charles	Red	6,140**C**
15.	Dudley	Orange	5,560
16.	Maverick	Blue	5,402
17.	Columbia	Red	4,473
18.	Fields Corner	Red	4,371
19.	Essex	Orange	4,330**C**
20.	Wellington	Orange	4,277
21.	Andrew	Red	4,061
22.	Broadway	Red	4,046
23.	North Quincy	Red	3,652
24.	Malden Center	Orange	3,542**T**
25.	Orient Heights	Blue	3,490
26.	Egleston	Orange	3,450
27.	Northampton	Orange	3,404
28.	Dover	Orange	3,155
29.	Kendall Square	Red	3,152
30.	Wollaston	Red	3,092
31.	Wonderland	Blue	2,807**T**
32.	Bowdoin	Blue	2,171**C**
33.	Community College	Orange	2,041
34.	Savin Hill	Red	1,765
35.	Shawmut	Red	1,676
36.	Beachmont	Blue	1,520
37.	Green St.	Orange	1,495
38.	Revere Beach	Blue	1,432
39.	Suffolk Downs	Blue	1,383
40.	Aquarium	Blue	1,294
41.	Airport	Blue	1,253
42.	Wood Island Park	Blue	1,041
43.	Oak Grove	Orange	n.d.
	TOTAL		**256,168**
	CBD		114,311
	Terminals		55,458

(Excludes holders of free passes and transfers from LR at joint stations; includes LR passengers at joint stations)

11. SAN FRANCISCO, BART
Typical Weekday

	Station	Line	Sept. 1980	May 1977
1.	Montgomery St.	Westbay	16,795	16,837C
2.	Embarcadero	Westbay	15,661	10,417C
3.	Powell St.	Westbay	11,043	10,415C
4.	Daly City	Westbay	9,152	8,420T
5.	Civic Center	Westbay	7,469	7,188C
6.	19th St. Oakland	Rich.+Con.	6,403	5,686
7.	Berkeley	Richmond	6,283	5,405
8.	12th St. Oakland	Rich.+Con.	5,731	4,750
9.	Concord	Concord	5,673	4,578T
10.	Fremont	Fremont	4,521	3,658T
11.	Walnut Creek	Concord	4,476	3,772
12.	Balboa Park	Westbay	4,120	4,117
13.	Pleasant Hill	Concord	3,996	3,432
14.	Hayward	Fremont	3,954	3,476
15.	Glen Park	Westbay	3,807	3,575
16.	Fruitvale	Fremont	3,691	2,915
17.	Bay Fair	Fremont	3,567	2,767
18.	24th St. Mission	Westbay	3,478	3,207
19.	Union City	Fremont	2,954	2,287
20.	San Leandro	Fremont	2,918	2,174
21.	El Cerrito Del N.	Richmond	2,886	1,931
22.	Lake Merritt	Fremont	2,724	2,723
23.	Rockridge	Concord	2,545	2,067
24.	Lafayette	Concord	2,509	2,156
25.	MacArthur	Rich.+Con.	2,437	1,956
26.	16th St. Mission	Westbay	2,427	2,183
27.	Coliseum	Fremont	2,392	2,450
28.	Oakland West	Westbay	2,309	1,745
29.	South Hayward	Fremont	2,131	1,656
30.	Orinda	Concord	2,112	1,882
31.	Richmond	Richmond	1,822	1,416T
32.	El Cerrito Plaza	Richmond	1,714	1,448
33.	North Berkeley	Richmond	1,381	1,262
34.	Ashby	Richmond	1,280	1,013
	TOTAL		**156,361**	**135,274**
	CBD		50,968	44,857
	Terminals		21,168	18,072

12. ATLANTA, MARTA
Typical Weekday, June 1980

1.	Five Points	21,386C
2.	Hightower	13,884T
3.	Avondale	9,265T
4.	Georgia State	4,490C
5.	West Lake	4,357
6.	Decatur	4,336
7.	Omni	4,083C
8.	Ashby	3,827
9.	East Lake	3,132
10.	Edgewood	2,945
11.	Vine City	1,719
12.	Inman Park	1,578
13.	King Memorial	1,325
	TOTAL	**76,330**
	CBD	29,959
	Terminals	23,149

13. CLEVELAND, GCRTA
Estimated average weekday, 1976 based on 1975 annual entries by station.

	Station	Line	
1.	Union Terminal	East + West	15,151C
2.	Windermere	East	5,024T
3.	University Circle	East	2,826
4.	Brookpark	West	2,659
5.	Puritas	West	2,520
6.	W 117th-Madison	West	2,295
7.	Triskett	West	2,126
8.	West Park	West	2,040
9.	W 68th-Detroit	West	1,609
10.	Airport	West	1,455T
11.	Superior	East	1,452
12.	W 25th Street	West	945
13.	E 105th Street	East	936
14.	W 65th Street	West	734
15.	E 55th Street	East	528
16.	E 79th Street	East	498
17.	Campus	East	428
18.	E 120th-Euclid	East	319
	TOTAL		**43,545**
	CBD		15,151
	Terminals		6,479

14. EDMONTON
Typical Weekday, Fall 1978

1.	Central	6,370C
2.	Belvedere	4,980T
3.	Coliseum	3,320
4.	Churchill	2,190C
5.	Stadium	1,140
	TOTAL	**18,000**
	CBD	8,560
	Terminal	4,980

Notes

1. Extent and Use of Rail Transit

1. The basic data source for the early history of urban rail in the United States is the Bureau of the Census *Special Reports* series entitled "Street and Electric Railways," with statistics for 1890, 1902, 1907, 1912, 1917, 1922, 1927, 1932, and 1937; beginning with 1917, the series appears in the *Census of Electrical Industries*.

2. Sam B. Warner, *Streetcar Suburbs: The Process of Growth in Boston 1870–1900* (Cambridge, Mass: Harvard University Press and MIT Press, 1962).

3. American Transit Association, *Transit Fact Book* (New York, N.Y.: 1948), p. 45.

4. Stephen P. Carlson and Fred W. Schneider, III, *PCC: The Car That Fought Back* (Glendale, Calif.: Interurban Press, 1980). See also the forthcoming study of the PCC car by Seymour Kashin and Harre W. Demoro.

5. Richard J. Solomon and Arthur Saltzman, *History of Transit and Innovative Systems* (Cambridge, Mass.: MIT Urban Systems Laboratory, 1971). See also: B. Snell, "American Ground Transport," in *Hearings Before the Subcommittee on Antitrust and Monoply of the Committee on the Judiciary, U.S. Senate on S. 1116, 93rd Congress, 2nd Session* (Washington, D.C.: Government Printing Office, 1974).

6. Boris Pushkarev, "The Future of Manhattan" in *New York City's Changing Economic Base* (New York, N.Y.: Pica Press, 1981). For an analysis of ridership response to changes in CBD employment, fares, auto ownership, and subway service in New York, see "Power for the MTA," *RPA Bulletin 126* (June 1977), pp. 34–39.

7. Herbert S. Levinson and F. Houston Wynn, *Future Highways and Urban Growth* (New Haven, Conn.: Wilbur Smith & Associates, 1961), pp. 153–154.

8. U.S. Department of Transportation, *1974 National Transportation Report Urban Data Supplement* (Washington, D.C.: 1976).

9. Literature questioning new rapid transit construction dates back to the June 1962 report *Technology and Urban Transportation*, prepared by John R. Meyer, John F. Kain, and Martin Wohl for the Office of Science and Technology, where the authors state: "Most importantly, it would seem best to *define* the public transit problem as that of finding ways to meet the transit rider's different needs . . . with reasonable economy and to reject those approaches . . . that place the emphasis on reshaping the city and its growth pattern" (p. 40). This theme was further developed in idem, *The Urban Transportation Problem* (Cambridge, Mass.: Harvard University Press, 1966). A less serious study in the same vein was H. Boyd, N.J. Asher, and E.S. Wetzler, *Evaluation of Rail Rapid Transit and Express Bus Service in the Urban Commuter Market* (Arlington, Va.: Institute for Defense Analyses, 1973). It is discussed in "Transit Planning," *Transportation Research Record* 559 (Washington, D.C.: Transportation Research Board, 1976), pp. 44–62. More informative, but no less negative, was Andrew M. Hamer, *The Selling of Rail Rapid Transit* (Lexington, Mass.: D.C. Heath & Company, 1976). Critical literature also followed the BART Impact Program, summarized in: Melvin Webber, *The BART Experience—What Have We Learned?* (Berkeley, Calif.: University of California, 1976). Responses to this paper were prepared by BART management and by

Vukan R. Vuchic. The energy conservation by new rail systems was questioned in *Urban Transportation and Energy: The Potential Savings of Different Modes* (prepared by the Congressional Budget Office for the U.S. Senate Committee on Environment and Public Works, September 1977). This report was strongly contested at a hearing before the Senate Subcommittee on Transportation on October 5, 1977.

10. "Major Urban Mass Transportation Investments; Statement of Policy," *Federal Register* (September 27, 1976); also "Policy toward Rail Transit," *Federal Register* (February 28, 1978).

11. Of the total federal operating assistance of some $462 million in 1976, approximately $50 million went to commuter rail, about $94 million to rapid transit, and about $318 million to buses. These figures are based on actual outlays by region and agency, where known; in the case of multimodal agencies, the subsidy is apportioned in relation to operating deficits or, if not known, in relation to passenger-miles.

12. U.S. Department of Transportation, *1974 National Transportation Report Urban Data Supplement* (Washington, D.C.: 1976), Tables SD–17, SD–23, D–23, and D–30. The rail data are for calendar year 1971. The rail transit total of 11,861 million PMT is adjusted downward by 190 million in Chicago, 80 million in Boston, and 50 million in Philadelphia to correct for an apparent overstatement of the rapid transit trip length in these cities. Exhibit 1.7 shows this adjusted total of 11,541 million rail transit PMT, plus 5,787 million commuter rail PMT for 1971, as shown also in Table A-2. The 1976 bus estimate in Exhibit 1.7 is based on the 1971 NTR total of 16,858 million PMT expanded by 1.097 which is the increase in revenue bus ridership over the period according to the American Public Transit Association *Transit Fact Book* ('76–77 edition), Table 8. The bus PMT data may likewise be overstated (alternative estimates suggest about 15 billion PMT in the early 1970s) but there is no basis for correcting them.

13. Raymond Ellis and Allistair Sherret, *Transportation and Travel Impacts of BART: Interim Service Findings* (Burlingame, Calif.: Peat, Marwick, Mitchell & Co., 1976), pp. 73–75. All non-BART weekday transit trips totaled some 596,000 in May 1972 and some 610,000 in May 1975; BART trips increased from zero to 121,000 over the period.

14. Jeffrey M. Zupan and Robert Cumella, "The Use of Automobiles," *RPA News 108* (August 1981).

15. Thomas F. Golob and Lawrence D. Burns, "Effects of Transportation Service on Automobile Ownership in an Urban Area," *Transportation Research Record 673* (Washington, D.C.: Transportation Research Board, 1978).

16. Morton Schneider, "Access and Land Development," *Highway Research Board Special Report* 97 (Washington, D.C.: 1968), pp. 164–177.

17. John R. Hamburg, Geoffrey J.H. Brown, Morton Schneider, *Impact of Transportation Facilities on Land Development* (n.p.: Creighton, Hamburg, Inc., 1970). See also: Creighton, Hamburg, Inc., *Final Report, Transportation and Land Development; A Unified Theory and Prototype Model*, prepared for the U.S. Department of Transportation, Federal Highway Administration, Bureau of Public Roads, under contract FH-11-6792. (Bethesda, Md.: 1969).

18. Herbert S. Levinson and F. Houston Wynn, "Effects of Density on Urban Transportation Requirements," *Highway Research Record* 2 (Washington, D.C.: 1963).

19. David Harrison, *The Impact of Transit Systems on Land Use Patterns in the Pre-Automobile Era* (Cambridge, Mass.: Harvard University Department of City and Regional Planning, 1978).

20. David Harrison, *Transportation and the Dynamics of Urban Land Use* (Cambridge, Mass.: Harvard University Department of City and Regional Planning, 1978), pp. 21–24.

21. Morton Schneider, op. cit., p. 170.

22. Thomas Muller, Kevin Neels, John Tilney, Grade Dawson, *The Impact of Beltways on Central Business Districts* (Washington, D.C.: The Urban Institute, 1978), pp. 13–14.

23. Steven R. Lerman, David Damm,

Eva Lerner-Lamm, Jeffrey Young, *The Effect of the Washington Metro on Urban Property Values,* Massachusetts Institute of Technology Center for Transportation Studies (Washington, D.C.: U.S. Department of Transportation, 1978).

24. D.E. Boyce, W.B. Allen, and F. Tang, "Impact of Rapid Transit on Residential Property Values," in *Space, Location and Regional Development*, M. Chatterji, ed. (London: Pion Ltd., 1976), pp. 145–153.

25. Paul J. Ossenbruggen and Michael Fishman, *The Impact of Transit Line Extension on Residential Land Use* (New York: J.C. Penney Co., n.d. [1976?]).

26. Kenneth A. Small, *Land Use Goals and Transportation Policy: The Case of Central City Decline* (Washington, D.C.: The Brookings Institution, 1979).

27. Federal City Council, *Staff Report on Metro-Related Private Investment in the Washington Metropolitan Area* (Washington, D.C.: July 1979).

28. This finding does not contradict the data presented by Melvin M. Webber, op.cit. Among the eight cities he lists, those two with rapid transit averaged an increment of 4.4 square feet of center city "high-rise office buildings" per metropolitan resident, while those without rapid transit averaged only 2.7 square feet for the 1964–75 period. The data shown in Exhibit 1.13 are based on Regina B. Armstrong, "National Trends in Office Construction, Employment and Headquarter Location," in *Spatial Patterns of Office Growth and Location*, P.W. Daniels, ed., (Chichester, England: John Wiley & Sons, 1979), p. 89.

29. Robert L. Knight and Lisa L. Trygg, *Land Use Impacts of Rapid Transit: Implications of Recent Experience.* De Leuw, Cather & Company (Washington, D.C.: U.S. Department of Transportation, 1977). See also: *New Urban Rail Transit: How Can Its Development and Growth-Shaping Potential Be Realized?* U.S. House of Representatives Committee on Banking, Finance and Urban Affairs (Washington, D.C., 1979).

30. Urban Land Institute with Gladstone Associates, *Joint Development: Making the Real Estate-Transit Connection* (Washington, D.C.: Urban Land Institute, 1979). See also Robert Witherspoon, "Transit and Urban Economic Development," *Transit Journal* (Spring 1979), p. 63.

31. Boris S. Pushkarev with Jeffrey M. Zupan, *Urban Space for Pedestrians.* (Cambridge, Mass.: MIT Press, 1975), p. 124.

32. Boris S. Pushkarev and Jeffrey M. Zupan, *Public Transportation and Land Use Policy* (Bloomington, Ind.: Indiana University Press, 1977), p. 174.

33. An Urban Land Institute questionnaire in 1978 revealed that 28 percent of the developers surveyed expected "more in-fill development," 16.4 percent expected "less sprawl in fringe areas," and 11.7 percent "shifts to sites with public transportation." Only 4 percent expected more decentralization of commercial and office space.

34. Glenn D. Westley, *Planning the Location of Urban-Suburban Rail Lines: An Application of Cost-Benefit and Optimal Path Analysis* (Cambridge, Mass.: Ballinger Publishing Company, 1978), p. 11.

35. Louis J. Gambaccini, "The Need to Look Ahead; Remarks at the Seminar on Urban Mass Transit" (Honolulu, Hawaii: January 1978), p. 12. For the underlying data, see Eugene J. Lessieu, "A Computer Aided Traffic Forecasting Technique—the Trans-Hudson Model," paper presented at Spring Joint Computer Conference, Atlantic City, 1971.

36. Thomas B. Deen, Walter M. Kulash, Stephen E. Baker: "Critical Decisions in the Rapid Transit Planning Process," *Transportation Research Record 599* (Washington, D.C.: Transportation Research Board, 1976), p. 40. See also: Thomas B. Deen, "Relative Costs of Bus and Rail Transit Systems," *Highway Research Record 293* (Washington, D.C.: Highway Research Board, 1969).

37. These rates are adapted, with some corrections and adjustments for vehicle occupancy, from Alan Altschuler, *The Urban Transportation System: Politics and Policy Innovation* (Cambridge, Mass.: MIT Press, 1979), pp. 218–23; also from Tri-State Regional Planning Commission, "Safety Characteristics of Passenger Rail Service in the Tri-State Region," *Interim Technical Report 2126* (New York, 1979).

38. Alan Altschuler, op.cit., p. 224.

39. Thomas B. Deen, Robert E. Skinner, "Responses to Alternatives Analysis Requirements," *Transit Journal* (November 1976).

40. Herbert S. Levinson and William F. Hoey, "Optimizing Bus Use of Urban Highways," *Transportation Engineering Journal* (May 1974), p. 443.

2. Operating Performance

1. Boris S. Pushkarev and Jeffrey M. Zupan, *Urban Space for Pedestrians* (Cambridge, Mass: MIT Press), 1975, pp. 12–13 and 77–79.

2. Institute of Traffic Engineers, *Capacities and Limitations of Urban Transportation Modes* (Washington, D.C.: Institute of Traffic Engineers, 1965), p. 16.

3. New York City Transportation Administration, et al., *Standards for Rapid Transit Expansion: A Report to the Mayor and the Board of Estimate.* (New York, N.Y.: August 14, 1968), p. 15; R.F. Corley, *Calculation of Capacities & Loading of Transit Vehicles* (Toronto Transit Commission, 1975). Also, see reported capacities for peoplemover vehicles, which are in the 0.31 to 0.37 m^2 per passenger range: *Lea Transit Compendium: Light Guideway Transit,* vol. II, No. 3, 1975 and vol. III, No. 3, 1976–77.

4. Tri-State Regional Planning Commission, "Subway Overcrowding, 1956–1976," *Interim Technical Report 2121* (New York, N.Y.: November, 1977), p. 10.

5. Hermann Botzow, "Level-of-Service Concept for Evaluating Public Transport," *Transportation Research Record 519* (Washington, D.C.: 1974), p. 77.

6. Tri-State Regional Planning Commission, op. cit., pp. A1–A19.

7. The cost-of-time value of 5¢ a minute, or $3 and hour in 1977 prices, is derived from the average of 4.4¢ a minute in 1975 prices, which the value at which Tri-State Regional Planning Commission's transit trip assignment model, which simulates the largest transit market in the nation, reaches an equilibrium.

8. A waiting time of about 12 minutes has been found by one study to be the borderline between "walk-in" use, where passengers come to the station at random, and their aiming for a specific, scheduled vehicle; see P.A. Seddon and M.P. Day, "Bus Passenger Waiting Times in Greater Manchester," *Traffic Engineering and Control* (January 1974).

9. The relationship between development density in dwellings per acre and bus speed is shown in Pushkarev and Zupan, *Public Transportation and Land Use Policy* (Bloomington, Ind.: Indiana University Press, 1977), Exhibit 4.1 on p. 106.

10. For more bus speed data by system, see the annual American Public Transit Association, *Transit Operating Report.* Derived Statistics Item 4, bus miles per bus hour. Not all systems report this item.

11. For a detailed discussion, see John W. Schumann, "Evaluations of Operating Light Rail Transit and Streetcar Systems in the United States" in *Light Rail Transit Planning and Technology,* Transportation Research Board Special Report 182 (Washington, D.C.: 1978), p. 94.

12. American Public Transit Association, *Transit Fact Book* (Washington, D.C.: annual), Table 13.

13. Vehicle operation and maintenance tend to be above the average, maintenance-of-way about average, and stations and administration below average; the latter is so because numerous low-paid clerical employees far outweigh the few high-priced lawyers in this category. See New York City Transit Authority, *Budget Data and Transit Facts* (New York, N.Y.: 1976), p. 26–27.

14. Louis J. Gambaccini, "*Evaluating Transit Performance: Purposes and Pitfalls,*" remarks delivered at National Conference on Transit Performance, Norfolk, Va., September 1977.

15. Massachusetts Bay Transportation Authority, *Central Area Systems Study Summary* (Boston, Mass.: June 1971), p. 5.

16. N.D. Lea & Associates, *Summary of Capital and Operations & Maintenance Cost Experience of Automated Guideway Transit Systems.* Report No. UMTA IT 06-0157–78–2 (Washington, D.C.: 1978).

17. This is the average of the systems shown in Table A-6, part III. It matches the nationwide figure of 11.5 passenger-miles

per bus-mile reported by the 1974 *National Transportation Report* (op. cit.), if one assumes that the average bus contains 61 places at 5.4 square feet (0.5 m²).

18. Louis T. Klauder & Associates, *O&M Costs for Articulated Bus Alternative.* File No. 1450, Dec. 21, 1978.

19. The estimate is based on data provided in De Leuw, Cather & Company, *Characteristics of Urban Transportation Systems* (prepared for the U.S. Department of Transportation, May 1975), Table 2–16ff. For related data, see also: U.S. Department of Transportation, *National Transportation Study Manual II: Procedures and Data Forms* (Washington, D.C.: October 1972). A comparative overview is contained in: American Public Transit Association, *Transit Fact Book 1976–77* (Washington, D.C.: 1978), p. 39.

20. The 1.5 percent loss in delivery is based on the Brookhaven National Laboratory Reference Energy System; the 32.9 percent power plant efficiency reflects the 1976 national average fossil fuel heat rate of 10,369 Btu needed to generate 1 kwh (3,413 Btu); this and the transmission loss from Edison Electric Institute; the conversion loss of 2.5 percent assumes modern silicon rectifiers; on transit systems with obsolete rectifier substations this item is higher. *Not included* is the nonelectrical energy consumption of the electric utilities.

21. Refining and distribution loss for transport fuels from: Transportation Research Board, *Energy Effects, Efficiencies and Prospects for Various Modes of Transportation.* National Cooperative Highway Research Program, Synthesis of Highway Practice No. 43, Washington, D.C.: 1977. This 17.3 percent loss is calculated by input-output methods and presents an inclusive picture of the energy consumption by the transport fuel refining and distribution industry. Refining losses alone are estimated at 15 percent: W.A. Reardon, *An Input-Output Analysis of Energy Use Changes from 1947 to 1963* (Richland, Wn.: Battelle Northwest Laboratories, 1971). Energy conversion efficiency of petroleum refining, if defined as a ratio of the energy contained in the finished product to the energy in the primary resource, is about 90 percent: J.M. Colucci and N.E. Gallopoulos, *Future Automobile Fuels* (New York, N.Y.: Plenum Press, 1977).

22. Energy consumption data from operating agencies in Table A-6, lines 44 and 45, are supplemented by data from: Clark Henderson, Hazel Ellis, and James Wilhelm, *Energy Study of Rail Passenger Transportation,* vol. 2 (Menlo Park, Calif.: Stanford Research Institute), 1977.

23. John Baerwald, ed., *Transportation and Traffic Engineering Handbook,* Institute of Traffic Engineers. (Englewood Cliffs, N.J.: Prentice-Hall, 1976), p. 219.

24. De Leuw, Cather & Company, *Light Rail Transit. A State of the Art Review* (Washington, D.C.: U.S. Department of Transportation, 1976), p. 184.

25. Auto data based on Transportation Research Board, *Energy Effects, Efficiencies and Prospects,* Table 16, p. 21.

26. Kenneth M. Chomitz, *A Survey and Analysis of Energy Intensity Estimates for Urban Transportation Modes*. (Berkeley and Irvine, Calif.: Institute of Transportation Studies, University of California, 1978), p. 15. Overall average auto occupancy, including rural and weekend driving, has been estimated by the Nationwide Personal Transportation Study of 1969–1970 at 2.2, a figure that is skewed upwards by the high occupancy of long trips.

27. Regional Plan Association, "Power for the MTA." Prepared for the Power Authority of the State of New York, *RPA Bulletin 126* (New York, N.Y.: 1977), p. 56; see also R. Ellis and A. Sherret, *BART's Energy Consumption and Costs* (Washington, D.C.: Peat, Marwick, Mitchell & Co., 1977), concerning the regenerative potential of BART with increased traffic density.

28. William Hamilton, *Electric Car Technology for Demonstration and Development* (General Research Corporation, mimeographed, n.d.).

29. This is based mostly on Transporation Research Board, *Energy Effects, Efficiencies and Prospects.* The increment to gross fuel used for operating the private auto from this source, however, is only 30 percent, whereas it is between 55 and 62 per-

cent according to Eric Hirst, *Energy Consumption for Transportation in the U.S.*, Oak Ridge, Tenn.: Oak Ridge National Laboratories, 1972. While the latter definition is definitely too broad, the former definition was expanded here by assigning a greater weight to the sales, service, and repair component, following some of the Hirst data. The resulting total gross energy consumption of the auto at 13.5 mpg, namely 2,620 Btu per place-mile for an auto assumed to have six places, is about 15 percent below the Hirst value. It is about 10 percent above the "middle estimate" in: Congressional Budget Office, *Urban Transportation and Energy: The Potential Savings of Different Modes* (Washington, D.C.: Government Printing Office, 1977), pp. 33, 35.

30. The lower value, or 860 Btu per bus-mile, is used in: Congressional Budget Office, *Urban Transportation and Energy*, pp. 33, 63. This is barely more than the lubricating oil requirement, which adds about 1.5 percent to diesel fuel use, and hence averages over 610 Btu per bus-mile at 12 mph. The upper value of 8,000 per bus-mile is suggested by E.L. Tennyson in: U.S. Congress, *Hearing . . . on the Congressional Budget Office Report "Urban Transportation and Energy . . ."* (Washington, D.C.: Government Printing Office, 1977), p. 156. On a per place-mile basis, the lower figure is about one-half, the upper four times the requirement for rail cars; twice the rail car requirement per place-mile is assumed as the most probable value for buses in Exhibit 2.13 because, among other things, they incur bus garage heating costs in winter, which electric cars usually do not.

31. Margaret F. Fels, *Breakdown of Energy Costs for Rapid Rail Systems* (Princeton, N.J.: Princeton University Center for Environmental Studies, 1977).

32. Annual electrical power consumption (kwh) by station which includes lighting, ventilating, and escalators, as well as signaling and tunnel lighting in its vicinity in Edmonton is as follows:

Central	2,820,280	underground station
Churchill	2,184,600	underground station
Stadium	36,425	large surface station
Coliseum	44,530	large surface station
Belevedere	13,026	genuine L.R.T. station

33. DeLeuw, Cather & Co. and ABAM Engineers, Inc., *AGT Guideway and Station Technology*, vol. 2, *Weather Protection Review* (Washington, D.C.: U.S. Department of Transportation, 1978), pp. 38, 49, 54.

34. *Lea Transit Compendium*: Group Rapid Transit, vol. III (1977): "Project 21," pp. 47–50. See also: John Armstrong, "Project 21: Double Track and Six Feet Wide," *Railway Age*, February 9, 1981.

35. Eric Hirst, *Energy Consumption for Transportation;* Margaret Fels, "Comparative Energy Costs of Urban Transportation Systems," *Transportation Research*, vol. 9 (1975):197–308; DeLeuw, Cather & Co., "Indirect Energy Consumption for Transportation Projects," prepared for California Department of Transportation (October 1975); Bjorn N.A. Lamborn, "Energy Consumption in Vehicle Manufacture," *Transportation Engineering Journal of ASCE*, vol. 101, No. TE2 (May 1975).

36. Congressional Budget Office, *Urban Transportation and Energy*, p. 65, Table A-4.

37. Bruce Hannon et al., *Energy Use for Building Construction*, Document 228 (Center for Advanced Computation, Urbana-Champaign, Ill.: 1976), found local transit construction to cost 62,447 Btu per 1967 dollar, when GNP cost 74,000 Btu per dollar. Gwynne Pierce Williams, *Energy Costs of Heavy Rail Transit Construction* (Princeton University Transportation Program, June 1978), in analyzing the construction cost of BART by several methods, found the "middle-of-the-road estimate" to be around 71,000 Btu per 1967 dollar. Inflation in the construction industry between 1967 and 1977 raised prices by a factor of 2.1 to 2.4 depending on the cost index.

38. *The AASHO Road Test: Report 5, Pavement Research*. Highway Research Board Special Report 61E (Washington, D.C.: 1962).

39. "Environmental and Conservation Concerns in Transportation: Energy, Noise

and Air Quality." *Transportation Research Record 648* (Washington, D.C.: 1977), p. 19.

40. V.R. Vuchic and G.F. List, "Discussion of the Paper Energy Consumption and Cost of the Journey-to-Work with and without a Suburban Rapid Transit Line by D.C. Boyce and K. Nguyen." p. 5. See also: David E. Boyce, Mark E. Ferris, and Khanh Nguyen, "Energy Consumption of the Journey-to-Work with and without a Suburban Rapid Transit Line," in: "Energy Efficiency of Various Transportation Modes," *Transportation Research Record* 689 (Washington, D.C.: 1978), p. 38.

41. David E. Boyce, et al., *Personal Travel Energy Consumption* (Chicago, Ill.: Chicago Area Transportation Study, 1980), pp. 57–58, 70.

42. Most notably, the 1977 Congressional Budget Office study by Damian J. Kulash and Richard R. Mudge; and Charles A. Lave, "Rail Rapid Transit: The Modern Way to Waste Energy" in "Environmental and Conservation Concerns," *TRB Record 648*; also some interpretative aspects of the Stanford Research Institute's *Energy Study of Rail Passenger Transportation.*

43. De Leuw, Cather & Co., *Light Rail Transit*, p. 219; also, New York City Transit Authority, *Structural Design Standards*, 1955, pp. 5–9, and similar geometric design references.

44. Herbert S. Levinson and William F. Hoey, "Optimizing Bus Use of Urban Highways," *Transportation Engineering Journal ASCE*, vol. 100, No. TE 2 (May 1975), pp. 443–59.

45. Wilbur Smith & Associates, *Parking in the City Center* (New Haven, Conn.: 1965). Also: Wilbur Smith & Associates, *Transportation and Parking for Tomorrow's Cities* (New Haven, Conn.: 1966).

46. U.S. Department of Transportation-Transportation Systems Center, Cambridge Systematics, Inc. and Regional Plan Association, *DPM: Planning for Downtown Peoplemovers* (Cambridge, Mass.: Transportation Systems Center, 1979), volume I, p. 195.

47. M.G. Myers, et al., *Analysis of Nationwide Demand for Urban Transportation Tunnels* (Cambridge, Mass.: U.S. Department of Transportation-Transportation Systems Center, n.d.).

48. Thomas K. Dyer, Inc., *Rail Transit Systems Cost Study* (Washington, D.C.: USDOT Urban Mass Transportation Administration, 1975).

49. Matt S. Walton and Richard J. Proctor, "Urban Tunnels—An Option in the Transit Crisis," *Transportation Engineering Journal ASCE* vol. 102, No. TE 4 (November 1976). See also *Proceedings* of the March 1978 symposium on urban tunnel construction at California Institute of Technology.

50. Glenn D. Westley, *Planning the Location of Urban-Suburban Rail Lines: An Application of Cost-Benefit and Optimal Path Analysis* (Cambridge, Mass.: Ballinger Publishing Company, 1978), p. 29.

51. Robert Stobaugh and Daniel Yergin, eds., *Energy Future: Report of the Energy Project at the Harvard Business School* (New York, N.Y.: Random House, 1979).

3. Travel Demand

1. Boris S. Pushkarev and Jeffrey M. Zupan, *Public Transportation and Land Use Policy.* Bloomington, Ind.: Indiana University Press, 1977, pp. 37–63.

2. L. Bronitsky, M. Costello, C. Haaland, and S. Schiff, *Urban Data Book.* Report No. DOT-TSC-OST-75-45.1 (Washington, D.C.: U.S. Department of Transportation, November 1975).

3. Area transportation studies and other local sources consulted for this chapter are listed below, alphabetically by metropolitan area.

State Highway Department of Georgia, Division of Highway Planning, *Atlanta Area Transportation Study, Existing Conditions Report,* 1967.

Atlanta Regional Commission, *1976 Population and Housing*, 1976.

———, *Systems Report ARC 1970–1971 Inventories,* 1972.

Baltimore Metropolitan Area Transportation Study, *Volumes I and II*, 1962.

Alan M. Voorhees & Associates, Inc., *Baltimore Regional Environmental Impact Study Technical Memorandum No. 1*,

Socio-Economic and Land Use Analysis, 1974.

Boston Redevelopment Authority, *Transportation Facts for the Boston Region*, 1967, 1968, 1969.

Wilbur Smith & Associates, *Comprehensive Traffic and Transportation Inventory* prepared for the Boston Regional Planning Project, 1965.

Chicago Area Transportation Study, *Volumes One, Two, Three*, 1959–62.

———, *1956 Origin–Destination Data*, unpublished.

Chicago Area Transportation Study and Northwestern Indiana Regional Planning Commission, *A Summary of Travel Characteristics*, 1977.

Dallas–Ft. Worth Regional Transportation Study, *Volumes 1-A, 2*, 1964/67.

City and County of Denver, Public Works Department, *Central Area Transportation Study*, 1963.

Colorado Department of Highways, Planning and Research Division, *Denver Metropolitan Area Transportation Study*, Origin and Destination Report, 1962.

Detroit Metropolitan Area Traffic Study, *Report on the Detroit Metropolitan Area Traffic Study, Parts 1, 2*, 1955.

Houston Metropolitan Area Transportation Study, *Origin-Destination Survey*, 1960.

Wilbur Smith & Associates, *Houston Transit Study*, 1960.

Metropolitan Planning Department, Marion County, Indiana, *Indianapolis Regional Transportation and Development Study*, 1968.

Wilbur Smith & Associates, *Kansas City Metropolitan Area Origin and Destination Survey*, 1959.

Montreal Urban Community Transit Commission Service and System Planning Department, *Origin-Destination Survey*, 1975.

———, *Autumn 1970 O-D Survey*, 1972.

Traffic and Planning Section, Louisiana Department of Highways, *New Orleans Metropolitan Area Transportation Study 1959–1960, Volumes 1 and 2.*

Wilbur Smith & Associates, *Planning Analysis and Projections Oklahoma City Area Regional Transportation Study*, 1966.

———, *Vol. IV. Oklahoma City Area Regional Transportation Study*, Origin-Destination and Statistical Data, 1968.

Pennsylvania Highway Department, New Jersey State Highway Department, *Penn Jersey Transportation Study, Volumes 1 and 2*, 1964.

Wilbur Smith & Associates, *Technical Report on Transportation and Parking, Market Street East General Renewal Plan*, Philadelphia, Pa., 1966.

Pittsburgh Area Transportation Study, *Volumes 1 and 2*, 1963.

Arthur D. Little, Inc., *Center City Transportation Project—Pittsburgh*, September 1970.

San Antonio-Bexar County Urban Transportation Study, *Reports No. 6A and 6B Origin-Destination Survey*, 1969.

Wilbur Smith & Associates, *Salt Lake Area Transportation Study, Volumes I and III*, 1963, 1964.

———, *Seattle Center City Transportation Study*.

DeLeuw, Cather & Company et al. *Report on a Comprehensive Public Transportation Plan for the Seattle Metropolitan Area*, October 1967.

Arthur D. Little, Inc., *Center City Transportation Project—Seattle,* September 1970.

Wilbur Smith & Associates, *Springfield Urbanized Area Comprehensive Transportation Study Volume 1, Land Use, Transportation and Travel Inventories*, 1969.

4. Pushkarev and Zupan, op. cit. pp. 56–63.

5. Ibid, pp. 37–55.

6. Ibid., pp. 126–128, 213, 221–32.

7. For a more complete summary see "Design Considerations for Downtown People Mover Systems," Jeffrey M. Zupan, Donald E. Ward, and Granville E. Paules, *Transportation Research Record*, 1979.

8. U.S. Department of Transportation-Transportation Systems Center, Cambridge Systematics, Inc., and Regional Plan Association, *DPM: Planning for Downtown Peoplemovers* (Cambridge, Mass.: Transportation Systems Center, 1979), vol. I, ch. VI: "Aggregate Analysis of System Feasibility" (by J.M. Zupan), pp. 187–280.

9. Municipality of Metropolitan Seattle, *Magic Carpet Evaluation Report*. Seattle, 1977. Cambridge Systematics, "Albany Free-Fare Zone Demonstration," Memorandum, June 29, 1979.

4. Fixed Guideway Potential

1. J. J. Bakker, "LRT-Bus Integration in Edmonton," paper prepared for the 58th Annual Meeting, Transportation Research Board, January 1979.

2. Washington Metropolitan Area Transit Authority, *Quarterly Report on Metrobus-Metrorail Ridership*, January 1980; March 1980; includes origin-destination data. Metropolitan Atlanta Rapid Transit Authority. *Daily Rail Utilization Report* and summaries, various dates, January–June 1980.

3. Daniel Mann, Johnson and Mendenhall, *Mass Transit Program for the St. Louis Metropolitan Area* (Los Angeles, Calif.: 1978), report no. UMTA IT–09–0067.

4. U.S. Department of Transportation-Transportation Systems Center, Cambridge Systematics, Inc., and Regional Plan Association, *DPM: Planning for Downtown Peoplemovers* (Cambridge, Mass.: Transportation Systems Center, 1979), vol. I, ch. 6: "Aggregate Analysis of System Feasibility" by J.M. Zupan, pp. 187–280.

5. Mitre Corporation, *Review of Downtown People Mover Proposals: Preliminary Market Implications for Downtown Application of Automated Guideway* Transit (Cambridge, Mass.: 1977), report no. UMTA IT–06–0176–77–1.

6. Regional Plan Association, *Power for the MTA: An Examination of Future Ridership, Service, and Electric Power Requirements* (New York: 1977).

7. Boris Pushkarev, "Why Would Anyone Want to Buy an Overhead Streetcar Named Project 21?" (unpublished); paper based on adjusted specifications from: L.K. Edwards, "Project 21: A Practical New Intermediate Capacity Rapid Transit System," paper presented at Transportation Research Board, Jan. 14, 1981, Washington, D.C.

Index of Cities and Agencies

Subject Index